# Business Marketing

# McGraw-Hill/Irwin Series in Marketing

# Business Marketing

**Third Edition**

**Frank G. Bingham, Jr.**
*Bryant College*

**Roger Gomes**
*Clemson University*

**Patricia A. Knowles**
*Clemson University*

Boston    Burr Ridge, IL    Dubuque, IA    Madison, WI    New York    San Francisco    St. Louis
Bangkok    Bogotá    Caracas    Kuala Lumpur    Lisbon    London    Madrid    Mexico City
Milan    Montreal    New Delhi    Santiago    Seoul    Singapore    Sydney    Taipei    Toronto

**Irwin**

Source information for exhibits can be found on the exhibits themselves or on pages 456 and 457, which should be considered an extension of this copyright page.

BUSINESS MARKETING

Published by McGraw-Hill/Irwin, a business unit of The McGraw-Hill Companies, Inc., 1221 Avenue of the Americas, New York, NY, 10020. Copyright © 2005, 2001 by The McGraw-Hill Companies, Inc. All rights reserved. No part of this publication may be reproduced or distributed in any form or by any means, or stored in a database or retrieval system, without the prior written consent of The McGraw-Hill Companies, Inc., including, but not limited to, in any network or other electronic storage or transmission, or broadcast for distance learning. Some ancillaries, including electronic and print components, may not be available to customers outside the United States.

This book is printed on acid-free paper.

2 3 4 5 6 7 8 9 0 DOW/DOW 0 9 8 7 6 5 4

ISBN 0-07-285911-3

Editorial director: *John E. Biernat*
Sponsoring editor: *Barrett Koger*
Editorial assistant: *Jill O'Malley*
Director of marketing: *Jim Kourmades*
Marketing manager: *Ellen Cleary*
Media producer: *Craig Atkins*
Senior project manager: *Lori Koetters*
Senior production supervisor: *Rose Hepburn*
Designer: *Kami Carter*
Lead supplement producer: *Cathy L. Tepper*
Senior digital content specialist: *Brian Nacik*
Cover design: *Ryan Brown*
Cover Image: *© Getty*
Typeface: *10/12 Times New Roman*
Compositor: *GAC Indianapolis*
Printer: *R. R. Donnelley*

**Library of Congress Cataloging-in-Publication Data**

Bingham, Frank G.
    Business marketing / Frank G. Bingham, Jr., Roger Gomes, Patricia A. Knowles. — 3rd ed.
        p. cm.
    Includes bibliographical references and index.
    ISBN 0-07-285911-3 (alk. paper)
    1. Industrial marketing. 2. Industrial marketing—Management. 3. Industrial
procurement—Management. 4. Industrial marketing—United States—Case studies. I.
Gomes, Roger. II. Knowles, Patricia A. III. Title.
HF5415.1263.B56 2005
658.8—dc22
                                                                                    2003058597

www.mhhe.com

# About the Authors

**Frank G. Bingham, Jr.** is an award-winning professor and researcher in the Department of Marketing at Bryant College. He is the author or co-author of three previous editions of *Business Marketing*. He has published more than 85 research articles in journals and conference proceedings, and is a frequent speaker at industry, academic, and executive education programs. Before entering academe, Dr. Bingham spent more than 20 years as a business marketing executive and as a self-employed entrepreneur.

**Roger Gomes** is a professor and researcher in the Department of Marketing at Clemson University. His academic publications span business marketing, logistics, leadership, and e-commerce. In addition to being on the editorial review boards of leading journals, Dr. Gomes has twice been an elected officer and board member of the Academy of Marketing Science, President of the regional Council of Logistics Management, and member of the Board of the Institute for Supply Management. Dr. Gomes spent 15 years in the automotive, copier, and computer industries prior to entering academe.

**Patricia A. Knowles** is a professor and researcher in the Department of Marketing at Clemson University. Her academic publications span business marketing, leadership, and e-commerce. She teaches professional selling, sales management, and research courses at both the undergraduate and graduate level. Dr. Knowles has spent 10 years consulting in strategic planning with major organizations.

# Brief Contents

# Contents

# Preface

We are experiencing a tremendous expansion in the teaching of business marketing. Trade magazines and scholarly journals are giving ever more space to the special issues and concerns of business marketers and students of business marketing. The recent focus on these markets reflects the recognition that the largest part of American business is not driven by consumer business methods but by its own practices and complexities. Students are also realizing that a variety of career opportunities exists in business marketing and are eager to prepare themselves with the practical information and theoretical principles of business marketing practice.

Business marketing is also in a period of transformation, reflecting the changing face of American business in general: less growth in heavy industry and more in service, the evolution of information as a product, and the increasing prominence of international opportunities. A few years ago this text would have been called *Industrial Marketing,* but smokestack industries are on the decline, and course and text titles are changing to reflect the broader range of enterprises that rightfully fall under the umbrella of business marketing. Almost every available product or service either is aimed at business users or has a business marketing facet. Financial services, company car fleets, construction cranes, trade magazines, industrial lubricants, corporate jets, convention services—the list is vast.

The business-to-business information boom has led to a parallel rise in the number of textbooks devoted to business marketing. But quantity has not always proven to be quality. *Business Marketing* offers a practical grounding in the real-world activities of the business marketer along with a full integration of the newest developments and insights into the study of this evolving discipline. *Business Marketing* has been enthusiastically praised by corporate recruiters and addresses accreditation priorities as set forth by the American Assembly of Collegiate Schools of Business (AACSB).

## The Intended Audience for the Book

The business marketing course, often called Business Marketing, Business-to-Business Marketing, or Industrial Marketing, is taught at both the junior or senior level at two- and four-year colleges, as an MBA level course, and at trade schools. The necessary background for *Business Marketing* would require a basic marketing principles course, or relevant managerial experience.

## Features of the Text

While the business market has rapidly changed, business marketing textbooks have been slow to do the same. In addition to a comprehensive updating of numbers and figures where needed, this third edition of *Business Marketing* includes several completely rewritten and restructured chapters—specifically those concerning ethics, selling and sales management, research and supply chain management, and logistics—therefore, instructors can be sure that they will be presenting timely and pertinent information. Because of the changes to the text, generally, it is easier for instructors to lecture from and easier for students to read and understand, thus making the learning process smoother and more effective. Further, *Business*

*Marketing* is the only current text on the market that features a full chapter devoted strictly to ethical considerations (Chapter 2). This addition was strongly urged by reviewers, so we consider it a real strength of the book.

In addition, this text includes a number of special features and pedagogical aids, many of which will be new to this market (e.g., website cases, quizzes, PowerPoint slide shows, and an extensive Test Bank), to add structure and depth to the learning process. There is also a set of videos to accompany the text. Professional Selling Skills III has been provided by AchieveGlobal, Inc. The text has been designed to allow instructors to use it in an e-commerce orientation through the inclusion of e-commerce/Internet assignments and cases in each chapter. The text also has real-world ethics assignments ("What would you do?" boxes), "Business Marketing in Action" boxes and "Strategy at Work" boxes in each chapter. As such, *Business Marketing* allows the class to be taught with three orientations (or a combination of the three): general business marketing, e-commerce/Internet marketing, and business ethics.

## Chapter Outlines

The chapter outlines at the beginning of each chapter are simply a supplement to the table of contents, enabling you to see at a glance the chapter structure and content without having to turn to the front of the book. They also reflect the way in which various topics are related, serving as a sort of road map to the chapter.

## Learning Objectives

Each chapter begins with a listing of the major topics of the chapter and some indication of what you should be able to glean from the text. These are perhaps the primary points of interest in the chapter road map.

## Concept Questions

Concept questions occur two or three times within each chapter and are designed to test recall of the preceding material. They are a simple and effective way to check retention of concepts before the end of the chapter.

## Business Marketing in Action Boxes

Each Business Marketing in Action box contains a brief story of real business dilemmas or tactics and illustrates a major concept in the chapter.

## Strategy at Work Boxes

We feel that the formulation of effective marketing strategy is critical to the achievement of an organization's goals. As such, each Strategy at Work box illustrates a key strategy concept or concepts. All are new, and all illustrate real-life marketing strategy at work. Most can be used for lively classroom interaction and/or team presentations.

## What Would You Do? Boxes

Each What Would You Do? box presents an ethical issue or issues for discussion and/or team presentations. The insertion of these boxes into this edition of the textbook reflects our beliefs that ethical considerations are integral to marketing decision making. All What Would You Do? boxes present challenging situations that call into question some of the most fundamental concepts of marketing.

## Enumerated Summaries

The end-of-chapter summary recaps the chapter contents point by point, rather than in a cluttered paragraph format, and is numbered for easy reference.

## Chapter Cases

*Business Marketing* provides two case studies at the end of each chapter, a minimum of two longer cases at the end of each part. In addition, cases that are longer and still more comprehensive will be posted on the website, in response to reviewers who request more detailed cases for class study. The chapter-ending cases are generally short and give a more focused examination of the chapter's topics and issues than do the cases provided at the end of each part or those posted on the Web. Most cases are followed by assignments that help to probe the case scenario for causes, solutions, and lessons, while others are left to the individual instructor's input.

## Unique Content

This new edition of *Business Marketing* makes it easy for instructors to meet the growing demand of marketing students to receive significant Internet exposure and Web experience in the classroom. The text allows the business marketing course to serve as a major e-commerce offering, has been classroom tested and received enthusiastic student reviews, and provides an excellent platform whereby a segment of classroom time can be allotted to student presentation and discussion of the Internet cases and assignments.

*Business Marketing*, again relying on an expert review panel, presents in 12 (twelve) chapters, what other texts take 15 to 18 chapters to present. In our opinion, and that of our reviewers, our presentation fits perfectly into a typical semester, allowing instructors to complete the text within a limited time frame. In addition, we have been creative in our presentation, while at the same time covering all relevant aspects of business-to-business marketing, to be able to present to our colleagues and their students a quality book at a substantial price discount from that of our competitors. This was a major goal of our latest edition.

# Business Marketing

# The Business Marketing Environment

## CHAPTER ONE

# Introduction to the Business Marketing Environment

**Learning Objectives**

After reading this chapter, you should be able to:

- Explain why we study business marketing.
- Discuss the differences between business and consumer marketing.
- Describe the characteristics of business demand.
- Understand the nature of business buying behavior.
- Distinguish among the basic types of business goods and services.
- Differentiate among the various kinds of business customers.
- Explain the pivotal importance of planning and strategy formulation to the business marketing effort.

**Chapter Outline**

Business Marketing: An Overview
Why Study Business Marketing?
How the Business Market Differs from the Consumer Market
Characteristics of Business Demand
The Nature of Business Buying Behavior
A Classification of Business Goods and Services
Business Customers
Business Marketing Planning and Strategy Formulation
Format of this Text

## Business Marketing: An Overview

The business market is *huge,* with over 13 million business-to-business organizations such as DuPont, Xerox, Boeing, and International Paper buying more than $3 trillion worth of goods and services. When measured in dollars, the market for organizational goods and services is four times larger than the consumer market.[1] This market will continue to grow. Companies that sell to other organizations must do their best to understand organizational buying behavior and the needs, resources, motivations, and buying processes that shape such behavior. Business marketing must be tailored to meet diverse needs that can vary enormously from one market segment to another. In addition to understanding the business buyer and the related buying process, the marketer must have a firm grasp of how some of the traditional marketing tools and techniques used for years present both major opportunities and challenges in today's business marketing environment.

**Business marketing** involves those activities that facilitate exchanges involving products and customers in business markets. It includes all organizations that buy goods and services for use in the production of other products and services that are sold, rented, or supplied to others. Business-to-business customers include manufacturers, wholesalers, retailers, and other types of organizations such as hospitals, universities, and government units (including about 88,000 federal, state, and local governmental agencies).

A **business marketing transaction** takes place whenever a good or service is sold for any use other than personal consumption. This market includes buyers from many types of industries: manufacturing; construction; transportation; communication; banking, finance, and insurance; agriculture, forestry, and fisheries; mining; and public utilities. The growing importance of highly technical business products, the significant changes in the pattern of final demand, the rapid pace of technological change, the increasing size and complexity of the business firm and its customers, the growing impact of e-commerce and management services, and the increase in world trade (the largest exporting industries in the United States focus on organizational customers, not ultimate consumers), have all highlighted the need for innovative business marketing strategies. All formal organizations, public or private, profit or not-for-profit, participate in the buying and selling of business products and services. This buying and selling process is the focus of this book.

## Why Study Business Marketing?

Although business marketing (often called industrial marketing) drives a domestic market much larger than its consumer counterpart, business marketing is not what most people think of when marketing is mentioned. Traditionally, business marketing has been a distant cousin to the mainstream of marketing thought. However, employment opportunities, the growing importance of high-technology business products, and the success of foreign competition have highlighted the need for increased emphasis on business marketing study. In fact, the majority of students graduating with bachelors' and masters' degrees begin their careers with business-to-business firms rather than with consumer goods companies. Business marketing is where the jobs are!

There are other reasons, as well, for the increased importance of business marketing. Among them are the significance of international interdependence for many firms, along with the importance of the service sector, which is more than twice as large as the manufacturing sector in the U.S. economy. Deregulation, changes in professional buyer associations' standards, and the application of computer technology have combined to produce dramatic changes in the environment of most business-to-business firms.

The business marketer must be capable of formulating and implementing policies that call not only for economic reasoning but for ethical awareness as well. Students and practitioners must realize that standards and beliefs about what is right and proper change over time. Further, the realization that buyers, influencers, and end users can be researched just as consumers can, has given an edge to those with both a working knowledge of sales and sales management, along with the organizational buying process. Segmentation, demand analysis, and product development have taken on increased importance in response to advancing technology and increasingly sophisticated business market buyers. Price planning and decision making remain a challenge for business marketers, as they must determine what they want pricing to do for their business. Indeed, pricing decision strategy, along with business promotional strategy and the understanding of all elements of the promotional mix as they relate to business customers must be understood.

Finally, channel selection, physical distribution strategy, supply chain management and logistics, along with an understanding of international marketing, have the potential to enhance the production, marketing, and profit potential of the business firm. Students studying this text will develop a strong foundation in all of these functional areas of the business-to-business organization.

## How the Business Market Differs from the Consumer Market

Identical products manufactured by the same firm may be purchased in both the consumer and business market; products such as office supplies, furniture, and computers. However, the marketing of business goods will usually differ significantly from the marketing of consumer goods. What distinguishes one market from the other is the *intended buyer* and the buyer's *intended use* of the product. It is essentially the differences in the kinds of products and the nature of the customer that give rise to the different problems and marketing approaches one encounters in the two domains.

Business customers buy *materials,* such as steel, plastics, copper, and *component parts* such as motors, stampings, and packaging. They also buy *capital equipment,* such as machine tools, forklift trucks, and measuring equipment, and *construction,* such as manufacturing plants, grain elevators, and warehouses. They are consumers of *services,* such as consulting, food service, and industrial cleansing. They buy *supplies,* such as preprinted paper forms, heat, light, and power; cutting tools, and lubricants.[2] In short, they buy what they need to produce other products and services that are sold, rented, or supplied to others. Although some of the distinctions between business and consumer goods marketing may be matters of degree, business marketing is, indeed, *different.* Some specific ways in which business markets differ significantly from consumer markets are listed in Exhibit 1-1 and discussed briefly in the text that follows.

### Greater Total Sales Volume

Total dollar sales in the business market are greater than total dollar sales in the consumer market, even though there are far fewer business buyers than final consumers. An automobile bought by a final consumer is viewed as one sale in the consumer market. However, numerous sales transactions occurred in the business market in the process of manufacturing that automobile. For example, iron ore was mined and sold to a steel producer which, in turn, sold steel to the automobile manufacturer. Similarly, items such as tires and radios are produced elsewhere, then sold to the automobile manufacturer for final assembly.

### Larger-Volume Purchases

Business marketers also sell to customers who buy in larger quantities than do final consumers. While consumers may buy new automobile tires in sets of four, Ford Motor Company buys several hundred thousand tires from a few major tire manufacturers.

**EXHIBIT 1-1**
**Characteristics of Business Markets as Compared with Consumer Markets**

| Characteristic | Business Market | Consumer Market |
|---|---|---|
| Sales volume | Greater | Smaller |
| Purchase volume | Larger | Smaller |
| Number of buyers | Fewer | Many |
| Size of individual buyers | Larger | Smaller |
| Location of buyers | Geographically concentrated | Diffuse |
| Buyer-seller relationship | Closer | More impersonal |
| Nature of channel | More direct | Less direct |
| Nature of buying | More professional | More personal |
| Nature of buying influence | Multiple | Single |
| Type of negotiations | More complex | Simpler |
| Use of reciprocity | Yes | No |
| Use of leasing | Greater | Smaller |
| Primary promotional method | Personal selling | Advertising |

Additionally, while consumers buy home heating oil by the gallon, the electric company buys thousands of barrels (approximately 42 gallons per barrel) of oil under a long-term contract with the distributor. Also, a consumer may buy a single unit of laundry detergent every few weeks, whereas a company that rents uniforms to other businesses would buy hundreds of drums of laundry detergent each year to clean the uniforms.

## Fewer Buyers

A business marketer generally deals with far fewer buyers than does the consumer marketer. He or she manages a clearly structured network of suppliers and subcontractors, with an emphasis on trust and cooperation. Firms that sell to manufacturers usually have less difficulty identifying prospective customers than do firms that sell to final consumers. For example, General Electric sells its jet engines to a very few airplane manufacturers, while its major appliance division sells appliances for the consumer market through a network of distributors and retail stores.

## Larger Buyers

Unlike final consumer markets, a few large buyers account for most of the purchasing in many business markets. In the telephone, aircraft engine and engine parts, motor vehicle, and organic fiber industries, the top four manufacturers account for over 70 percent of total production.

## Geographically Concentrated Buyers

Business buyers are geographically concentrated, whereas final consumers are found virtually everywhere. As shown in Exhibit 1-2, over two-thirds of the business firms in the United States are located in the Middle Atlantic, East North Central, South Atlantic, and Pacific states. Over half of U.S. business buyers are located in just seven states: New York, Pennsylvania, New Jersey, Ohio, Michigan, Illinois, and California. The aircraft and microelectronics industries are concentrated on the West Coast, and many of the firms that supply the automobile manufacturing industry are located in and around Detroit. Most agricultural output also comes from relatively few states. The downside to this type of concentration was illustrated by the plight of the nation's financial services industry following the terrorist attacks in September 2001. It was estimated that approximately 20 percent of the city's office space was destroyed and an additional 30 percent was made temporarily noninhabitable by dust and debris. In a single blow many of the country's leading banks and brokerages had to relocate to other parts of the city or elsewhere while Wall Street struggled to rebound.[3]

**EXHIBIT 1-2**
Geographic
Distribution of U.S.
Manufacturing
Plants Based on
Selected Criteria

| Region | Number of Plants | Thousands of Manufacturing Employees | Value Added by Manufacturing* | Value of Manufacturers' Shipments* |
|---|---|---|---|---|
| Northeast | 26,393 | 1,350 | $ 78,908 | $ 136,989 |
| Middle Atlantic | 61,894 | 3,007 | 180,165 | 346,759 |
| East North Central | 69,756 | 4,186 | 266,248 | 590,487 |
| West North Central | 24,513 | 1,322 | 84,891 | 196,637 |
| South Atlantic | 53,476 | 3,104 | 179,075 | 373,181 |
| East South Central | 19,718 | 1,303 | 74,296 | 164,862 |
| West South Central | 31,304 | 1,432 | 101,009 | 262,832 |
| Mountain | 16,479 | 596 | 35,822 | 73,554 |
| Pacific | 65,362 | 2,650 | 165,503 | 330,371 |
| TOTAL | 368,895 | 18,950 | $1,165,917 | $2,475,672 |

*In millions of dollars.

## Close Supplier-Customer Relationship

There is a close relationship between sellers and customers in business markets because of the smaller customer base, the greater volume and cost of the average sale, and the importance and power the larger customers wield over their suppliers. **Relationship marketing**—establishing, developing, and maintaining successful relational exchanges—constitutes a major shift in marketing theory and practice. Typically, the suppliers who closely cooperate with the buyer on technical specifications and delivery requirements are those who make the sales. The early integration of suppliers into all decisions affecting them is critical to effective business marketing.[4]

Businesses have never operated in isolation. Even the firms most committed to vertical integration (e.g., the big oil companies) still have had to establish, manage, and maintain relationships with important suppliers.[5] An increasing number of U.S. manufacturers and suppliers are moving from adversarial to cooperative exchange attitudes that focus on long-term relationships. As world markets become increasingly competitive, firms have discovered that close partnership relationships with important suppliers can produce managerial, technological, and financial benefits. The nature of the buying firm's relationship with its suppliers can help lower a customer firm's costs.[6] Relationship marketing will be discussed in detail in Chapter 4.

## More Direct Channels of Distribution

In consumer markets, the majority of goods are sold through a complex structure of wholesalers and retailers who serve as intermediaries between the producer and the consumer. Frozen foods, for example, are sold to several types of wholesalers or food brokers. In turn, these distributors sell to supermarkets and institutional users. In the majority of business markets, however, sellers and buyers are more directly linked. Industrial distribution strategy is time-consuming to set up and is difficult to change. Business-to-business distribution systems take a long time to build and involve complex relationships with an important group of end customers. When dealing with very large purchasers, marketers can make direct sales rather than go through industrial distributors or other intermediaries. However, some products sold to business buyers are commonly sold through one or two levels of wholesalers. A detailed examination of channel structures and strategy is presented in Chapters 10 and 11.

## Professional Buying

Business buyers normally take a more formalized approach to buying than do final consumers. Contrast the approach of a salesperson who sells laptop computers in a Sears store and generally handles only one prospect at a time with that of an IBM computer salesperson who may give product demonstrations not only to a firm's purchasing manager but to the office manager and secretaries as well. The professional training of purchasing personnel has resulted in a professional certification program whereby the individual earns the designation of **Certified Purchasing Manager (C.P.M.).** This designation is awarded after several years in the discipline, a degree from a recognized college or university, several years of training, and passing grades on a series of examinations. Business buyer behavior will be discussed at length in Chapter 4.

## Multiple Buying Influences

Typically, more people influence business buying decisions than consumer buying decisions. The people who participate in the business buying decision, often including technical experts and senior management, comprise the buying committee (referred to as the **buying center**). An average business buying center will have three members and will change from one buying situation to another. For example, a decision concerning a routine purchase of a standard off-the-shelf product, such as office supplies, would be made by only one or two members of a buying team; the purchase of a complex, expensive product assembly platform might involve eight or more members. With the growing importance of relationship marketing, business marketers are recognizing that the creation, structure, and composition of the buying center are becoming increasingly important,[7] complicating the marketing communications process. Therefore, business marketers must employ sales representatives and sales teams equipped to deal with highly skilled, highly trained, professional buyers. Buying centers will be discussed in more detail in Chapter 4.

## Complex Negotiations

In the consumer goods marketplace, negotiation commonly takes place only in the sale of automobiles or real estate. In the business marketplace, in contrast, considerable professional buyer-seller negotiation occurs, particularly in the purchase and sale of more expensive business products. In fact, in many cases buyer representatives will meet with seller representatives several times to negotiate sales contracts, with the process continuing over several months. At these meetings, buyers and sellers will negotiate not only price, but also terms, delivery, quality, and transportation costs, among other things. Negotiating successfully is an art, but few things are sweeter than when both parties leave with a winning solution.[8] More on buyer-seller negotiations will be presented in Chapter 4.

## Reciprocity

Business buyers often choose suppliers who also purchase from them. **Reciprocity** is one of the toughest roadblocks to overcome in business selling, and it is more common among larger companies. For instance, a paper manufacturer may buy the chemicals for its production process from a chemical company that buys large amounts of its paper. General Motors buys engines for use in its automobiles and trucks from Borg Warner, which, in turn, buys many of the automobiles and trucks it needs from GM. Reciprocity is considered to be illegal only if one of the parties uses coercive pressure that results in reduced competition. Otherwise, reciprocity in the business marketplace is an accepted practice that makes good common sense!

## Leasing

Many business buyers lease rather than buy their equipment. Businesses may find that leasing offers several advantages over purchasing. For example, leasing allows for greater use of capital. Lease payments are entered on the books as current operating expenses, rather than as liabilities; as such, they do not reduce a company's credit line or ability to borrow. The major advantages of leasing are decreased capital outflow, easier cost forecasting, and protection against equipment obsolescence. Computers, packaging equipment, heavy-construction equipment, machine tools, and sales-force automobiles are examples of equipment that often is leased. As a general rule, most equipment that can be purchased can also be leased. Leasing will be covered in detail in Chapter 8.

## Emphasis on Personal Selling

Because of each of the characteristics discussed above, business marketers emphasize *professional selling* more than advertising in designing and implementing their marketing mixes. A good salesperson can tailor presentations and highlight different features for those individuals involved in the business product or service purchase. The cost of a business sales call can be justified for most business products and services because of the size, complexity, and sales volume per account, as compared to a typical consumer product or service. Professional selling and sales management will be covered in detail in Chapter 3.

| Concept Review | |
|---|---|
| 1. Why study business marketing? | 4. Why is personal selling, rather than advertising, more commonly used in business marketing? |
| 2. What are the major differences between the business market and the consumer market? | |
| 3. The business market utilizes the direct channel of distribution more than the consumer market. Why? | |

## Characteristics of Business Demand

Business demand differs from consumer product demand in a number of significant aspects. Further, there is joint demand for some business goods. The following discussion briefly examines some characteristics of business demand.

### Derived Demand

All demand for business goods is derived from the demand for consumer goods and services. **Derived demand** can be defined as the demand for a business product that is linked to demand for a consumer good. Thus, the demand for plastic bottles to be sold to Coca-Cola would be directly related to the demand by consumers for the soft drink. When consumers purchase more automobiles, the need for materials, components, and subassemblies goes up. The original demand occurs among consumers and is reflected in the business-to-business market. This ripple effect is felt all along the supply chain, and it drives economic growth. In the long run, no business demand is totally unrelated to consumer demand.

### Inelastic Demand

Because of the derived demand for business products, there is less opportunity for business marketers to stimulate primary demand (demand for a particular product category) through price cuts than there is for consumer goods marketers to do so. Therefore, the primary demand for business products is more price inelastic than that for consumer products. **Inelastic demand** takes place if price changes have little impact on the quantity of goods or services demanded. For example, automobile manufacturers purchase headlights as component parts for automobiles. If the price of headlights goes down, the automobile manufacturers are not very likely to greatly increase their purchase of headlights. Likewise, the price of headlights would have to increase significantly before prices would have to be raised enough to have much effect on the sale of automobiles.

## BUSINESS MARKETING IN ACTION

### DAMAGE RESISTANT PLASTIC BUMPERS

In 5 mph crash tests, most small cars sustain damage in excess of $1000, with the worst incurring $3000 worth of damage. Solvay Engineered Polymers has developed thermoplastic front and rear bumpers for the new Volkswagen Beetle that help limit damage to the Beetle to $134. The material requires less energy to produce than thermoset urethane foam bumpers, yet has good low temperature impact resistance, low coefficient of linear expansion, and durability when painted.

### Action Assignment

Research the bumper designs on small cars and compare them with the Beetle's bumpers. Research Solvay Engineered Polymers and their competitors.

http://www.soplachim.com/english/ automotive.htm
http://www.solvay.com/index.htm

Report your findings to the class, and identify additional potential applications and customer segments for the materials. As a Solvay representative, outline your sales presentation for a first visit to a new buyer.

See *Machine Design,* April 22, 1999, p. 39.

### Fluctuating Demand

The demand for business goods and services tends to be more volatile than the demand for consumer goods and services. This **fluctuating demand** is especially true of the demand for new products and equipment. A given percentage increase in consumer demand can lead to a much larger percentage increase in the demand for plant and equipment necessary to produce the additional output. This phenomenon often is referred to as the *acceleration principle* (also called the *multiplier effect*). An example would be air travel. Even a small percentage increase in demand for air travel can cause airlines to order new equipment, creating a dramatic increase in the demand for airplanes. This demand volatility has caused many business marketers to diversify their product lines and markets to achieve more balanced sales over the business cycle.

### Joint Demand

The demand for a number of business products, such as raw materials and component parts, is affected by joint demand. **Joint demand** occurs when two or more items are used in combination to produce a product. For instance, a firm that manufactures hammers needs the same number of handles as it does hammer heads; these two products are demanded jointly. If the supplier of handles cannot furnish the required number, and the hammer producer cannot obtain them elsewhere, the producer will stop buying hammer heads.

## The Nature of Business Buying Behavior

Much research has been devoted to organizational buying. As shown in Exhibit 1-3, businesses tend typically to be more cautious in their buying than are final consumers. Generally, business buyers make a conscious and deliberate effort to act rationally and to do what is best for the company. Business marketers should recognize, however, that business buyers are not totally rational in their buying behavior. In fact, according to many marketing practitioners, selling to business buyers is very frequently a personality-oriented sales situation, as is often the case in final consumer transactions. Though it is true that the demand or need for business products usually is economically motivated and rational, the actions taken to satisfy that need or the behavior of the business purchaser may not be so. This issue will be explored in depth in Chapter 4.

**EXHIBIT 1-3**  **Evaluating Products: Business Users' and Final Consumers' Approaches**

| Product | Questions Asked by Typical Business Users | Questions Asked by Typical Ultimate Consumers |
| --- | --- | --- |
| Personal computers | Will it increase office efficiency? What is its capital investment value? Does it have special features that will help improve our company image? | Will it help my child learn? Will it improve my correspondence? Is a laptop worth the extra cost? |
| Automobiles | How efficient is the vehicle to operate? Would it be more economical to lease it or purchase it? What is the expected working life span of the car? | How does it enhance my status? What is its potential trade-in value? Will I get reasonable gas mileage? |
| Telephones | Will expanded service lower the cost of communicating with our customers? Should our intercom system be separate from or connected to the telephone system? | How long will it take to have one installed? Can I get three jacks and two telephones? |

In order to succeed in business-to-business markets then, selling firms must possess an understanding of customer firms' buying behavior. However, such an understanding may be difficult to achieve because organizational buying behavior often is a multiphase, multiperson, multidepartmental, and multiobjective process. Management practices that have emerged over the past several years (just-in-time, concurrent engineering, lean production) require closer relationships with an organization's suppliers. This dynamic and intricate process frequently presents sellers with a set of complex issues and situational factors that directly or indirectly influence buying firm behavior.[9]

Most business marketers and sales managers go to great lengths to differentiate their products or services. Yet no matter how favorably the seller presents an offering, unless the buyer is convinced of the seller's integrity and of the adequacy of postsale support, it is unlikely that the purchase will be made from that seller. To be successful, companies will not seek to achieve cost reductions or profit improvement at the expense of their supply chain partners, but rather seek to make the supply chain as a whole more competitive.[10] This convincing is largely subjective in nature, and subjective judgments seldom are entirely rational in an economic sense.

**Concept Review**

1. How is the demand for business goods based on the demand for consumer goods?
2. Why is the demand for business goods said to be inelastic?
3. When does joint demand occur in business markets?
4. How does organizational buying differ from consumer buying?

## A Classification of Business Goods and Services

Although business goods and services can be classified in a variety of ways, they are grouped according to tax treatment and end user. A useful scheme for classifying business products might include at least the following categories: major equipment; accessory equipment; process materials; maintenance, repair, and operating (MRO) supplies; business services; fabricated and component parts; and raw materials. Each of these categories is presented in Exhibit 1-4.

Having classified business goods and services, the marketer must also consider how each is marketed. Indeed, a *marketing strategy* used for one type of business good or service might be totally inappropriate for another. For example, distribution, promotional, and

**EXHIBIT 1-4   A Classification of Business Goods and Services**

| Type | Characteristics | Examples |
|---|---|---|
| Major Equipment | Often referred to as "installations" <br> Exhibits inelastic demand curve <br> Usually involves direct distribution <br> Requires close cooperation between buyers and sellers | Machinery, machine tools, stamping machines, robots |
| Accessory Equipment | Used to facilitate production, administrative, clerical, or marketing activities <br> Exhibits elastic demand curve <br> Distribution channels often longer <br> Standardized and less costly than major equipment | Office equipment, personal computers, desktop printers, hand tools, fire extinguishers |
| Process Materials | Generally bought per specifications prepared by the customer (user) <br> Cannot be identified or regrouped in the finished product <br> Most marketed to original equipment manufacturers (OEMs), or to distributors who sell to the OEM market <br> Considerable emphasis on price and service in the sales process | Chemicals, plastics, cement, asphalt |
| Maintenance, Repair, and Operating (MRO) Supplies | Facilitate the production operation <br> Short life and less expensive <br> Usually standardized specifications <br> Longer channels of distribution | Brooms, paint, cleaning supplies, bearings, gears, filters, pens, greases, lubricating oils |
| Business Services | Support organizational operations <br> Spectacular growth <br> Specialized providers <br> Cost effective | Banking, insurance, financial, advertising, marketing research, employment services, consulting |
| Fabricated and Component Parts | Become part of other product <br> Identified and distinguished easily <br> Consistent quality required <br> Delivery schedules critical | Spark plugs, timing devices, switches |
| Raw Materials | Basic lifeblood of industry <br> Become part of manufactured product <br> Exhibit inelastic demand curve <br> Usually bought in large quantities <br> Long or short channels of distribution | Farm products, lumber, iron ore, resins |

pricing strategies required for the marketing of major equipment such as heavy machinery would be unsuited to the marketing of maintenance, repair, and operating (MRO) supplies.

## Business Customers

A study of business marketing would not be complete without an attempt to examine customer types within this broad category. Business customers are classified into three types: commercial enterprises, governmental organizations, and institutions. Each buys goods and services differently, thus requiring a thorough understanding of how marketing strategy differs with the customer type being pursued.

### Commercial Enterprises

*Commercial enterprises* include (1) indirect channel members; (2) **original equipment manufacturers (OEMs)**; and (3) user-customers.

### *Indirect Channel Members*

The indirect channel category consists of firms that are engaged in reselling business goods to commercial, governmental, or institutional markets. Some, most notably business distributors and dealers, take title to—that is, own—the goods. The functions, scope, and limitations of the channel intermediary will be discussed in detail in Chapter 10.

### *Original Equipment Manufacturers (OEMs)*

OEMs typically buy business goods to incorporate into the products they produce for eventual sale to either the business or consumer market. Thus, a tire producer such as Firestone, Goodyear, or Michelin that sells tires to Ford Motor Company would consider Ford an OEM.

### *User-Customers*

The user-customer generally buys products to support a manufacturing facility. For example, Ford Motor Company would buy stamping equipment to form auto parts made from metal, plastic-injection molding machines to produce parts made from plastic, and milling machines to produce precision tooling for use in conjunction with the metal-stamping operation. These purchases do not become part of the finished product; they only help to produce it.

### *Overlap of Categories*

The preceding classification of business customers centers on how those customers use products. Note that a manufacturer can be a user, purchasing goods to support a manufacturing process, or an OEM, purchasing goods for inclusion into a manufactured product. Likewise, a manufacturer of machinery can be a user, purchasing raw material to support a production process, or an OEM, purchasing gear assemblies to incorporate into the machinery being manufactured. Again, the business customer classification depends on product use.

## Governmental Organizations

*Governmental organizations* comprise a classification of business customers (approximately 88,000 federal, state, and local governmental agencies as noted earlier in the chapter), that accounts for about 20 percent of our gross national product (GNP). In 2003, the U.S. government spent over $2.1 trillion, with the military being by far the largest purchaser of goods and service ($368 billion of U.S. spending). In 2005, the projected U.S. government budget will pass $2.3 trillion with $412 billion earmarked for defense spending.[11] Companies such as General Dynamics Corporation, TRW Inc., Boeing Corporation, and thousands of others, both large and small, participate in this market. All levels of government in the United States make up what is considered to be the largest single market for goods and services in the world.

Much government procurement is done on a bid basis, with the government advertising for bids, stating product specifications, and accepting the lowest bid that meets these specifications. Such a procedure sometimes results in the rejection of the lowest bids, however. For example, the board of New York City's Metropolitan Transportation Authority must provide toilet paper in more than 1,000 restrooms included in the services of the system. When deciding whether to accept a toilet paper purchase in the amount of $168,840, which was higher than three other bids, the board asked why the Authority had rejected the lower bids. The president responded that one supplier was rejected because there was insufficient tissue on the roll, while two other suppliers were ruled out because their tissues were somewhat like sandpaper and obviously not soft enough. In light of this explanation, the board approved accepting the higher bid!

## BUSINESS MARKETING IN ACTION

### AUTOMOTIVE MEGAMERGERS MEAN CHANGES FOR SUPPLIERS

The merger of Mercedes and Chrysler means increased purchasing power with suppliers. Gary C. Verlade, Daimler-Chrysler AG's executive vice president of global procurement and supply, expects total savings of $1.4 billion by the second year and $ 3.5 billion by 2001, with the largest share coming from procurement and supply. According to Verlade, "If we were to jointly buy commodities like steel for 900,000 Mercedes vehicles and three million Chrysler vehicles each year, the savings would be considerable." Consolidating purchasing will take three to five years but will go much more quickly than would consolidating manufacturing operations.

Realizing that the world is now a single market means reorganizing traditional supply chain patterns dictated by national boundaries. "We are expecting our tier one suppliers to take active roles in managing their own supply chains, fostering better communications, better products, and cost savings," Verlade emphasizes. "We will continue to count on our suppliers to take the lead in programs ranging from engineering research and development to designing and producing complete vehicle systems better and faster than we could ourselves."

### Action Assignment

As the vice president of marketing for a tier one (direct) steel supplier to Chrysler, develop a presentation to Mr. Verlade that supports your effort to retain the current Chrysler business. Next, add the Mercedes requirements to your projection. As you present this to the class, another team will have the assignment to act as Mr. Verlade's staff and ask appropriate questions concerning your company's capabilities. Be sure to review the websites of competitive steel suppliers for pertinent information.

See *Manufacturing Engineering,* March 1999, Volume 122, No. 1, pp. 20–22.

Although the governmental market could be a lucrative market for some astute business marketers, many sellers make no real effort to sell to the government, not wanting to negotiate through the red tape involved. Business marketers must recognize that dealing with the government to any significant extent usually requires specialized marketing techniques and information.

### Institutions

Some long overdue attention now is being paid to the third category of business customer to be discussed here—the multibillion dollar market consisting of nonbusiness or not-for-profit institutions. This potentially lucrative market includes such diverse institutions as colleges and universities, museums, hospitals, labor unions, charitable organizations, and churches. These organizations experience real marketing problems and spend billions of dollars buying products and services to run their organizations.

Business marketers who desire to sell to the institutional market must be aware of the diversity of this market and tailor their marketing programs to meet the particular needs and wants of prospective customers. For instance, suppose that Acme Foods, a small food products marketer, wanted to market its products to hospitals and nursing homes in smaller communities. Most likely, Acme's primary focus would be on the chief dietitian, who must approve food products before the hospital or nursing home's purchasing director can contract for their purchase. However, if Acme also intended to sell its products to larger health care institutions in metropolitan areas, it would need to target its marketing program to a diverse group of individuals (the institution's administrator, business manager, purchasing director, and chief dietitian), each of whom influences the buying decision.

## Business Marketing Planning and Strategy Formulation

*Marketing planning and strategy formulation* begins with an analysis of changing environments, including both the internal and the external macro and micro environments. The environments in which the business marketer works represent a "dynamic" rather than a "static" model. As a business marketer, the one constant you can depend on is continuous change!

Central to the analysis of a constantly changing environment is an assessment of the organization's strengths and weaknesses in relation to the competition, along with a matching of the strengths with unsatisfied customer needs in the marketplace. Effective business marketing strategy must continually monitor product, price, promotion, and distribution, making sure that each is consistent with the others and that there is synergy, wherein the impact of the whole is greater than the sum of the parts. For example, if the marketing manager decides to lower price, increase a particular promotional outlay, or both, it is essential that he or she advise the sales department of these plans. Likewise, if members of the sales department learn of minor product faults, they should bring this information to management's attention. If all members of the marketing team "sing off the same sheet of music," then there will indeed by synergy.

The aforementioned business goods and services classification system (major equipment, accessory equipment, and so forth) serves to illustrate how planning and strategy differ by category of goods. A marketing strategy deemed appropriate for one category of goods or services may be entirely unsuitable for another. Unique promotion, pricing, and distribution strategies might be required for each, along with more or less attention to other internal activities, such as manufacturing, technical service, and engineering. For example, producers of sophisticated aerospace and defense equipment place more emphasis on the product and pricing facets of the marketing mix and less emphasis on the sales and distribution effort than other types of business goods producers. A manufacturer of a standard industrial widget, on the other hand, might emphasize sales and distribution, giving less emphasis to product and price.

In summary, marketing planning takes the best information about customers and competitors, analyzes that information, generates alternatives (taking into account the organizational issues), and, finally, proposes a plan that best suits the organization at a specific moment. Following these steps ensures that the myriad issues concerning customers, competitors, and organizational issues are considered.

---

| **Concept Review** | 1. How can the three major categories of commercial enterprises overlap? | 2. What is meant by "achieving synergy" in the business marketing mix? |

## Format of this Text

The material covered in this text is organized and presented quite differently from all other business marketing textbooks. Early in the book the authors highlight the differences between consumer and business markets—dissimilarities so significant that they can spell the difference between success and failure in the business marketing environment. The text emphasizes the important topic of ethical considerations in business-to-business marketing, along with an examination of professional selling and sales management. The special relationship between buyers and sellers within the entire supply chain arena, as well as the general management of the business buying center (purchasing procedures, organizational considerations, purchasing systems, source selection, and quality determination and control) are presented. Marketing research and information systems are also examined, in addition to market segmentation, positioning, and demand projection. The remainder of the text addresses the traditional tools and techniques employed in the marketing of goods and services to the business sector. Product development and management strategy, price

## WHAT WOULD YOU DO?

### BASIC ETHICAL CONSIDERATIONS FOR BUSINESS MARKETING PROFESSIONALS

"What I did violated not just the law but all of my principles and values. I deeply regret it, and will for the rest of my life. I am truly sorry."

For every high profile person who has found himself or herself making such a statement (from Michael Milken to President Clinton), undoubtedly there are tens of thousands of average business people who find themselves in the same situation. Although some may be cynical about the sincerity of the individuals expressing apologies, there is little question that their poor decisions harmed themselves as individuals, their organizations, and those in their personal lives.

By integrating ethical issues into each chapter of this text, our objective is to help prevent a future business decision maker from having to make a similar declaration someday. Real world examples, it is hoped, will help readers recognize integrity when they see it and prevent their falling into the trap of rationalization to somehow try to justify actions that professionals would consider unethical.

The following section headed "Personal Characteristics Expected" was drawn from a recent business marketing employment ad. It demonstrates that companies have clear ethical expectations.

### Marketing Director

**Salary**
$115,000 base (negotiable), plus 20–30% incentive bonus, automobile, and executive benefits.

**Personal Characteristics Expected**
Must have a balanced, healthy lifestyle and be a person of high integrity and impeccable character whom people will trust and respect. Must have emotional maturity, be even tempered and growing as a person, with a sense of purpose. Must be poised and have executive presence. This person will bring immediate credibility by his or her demeanor, professional knowledge, and approach. Must have high energy and a motivation and drive to achieve the goals of a demanding business. Must be decisive and able to make "tough" decisions.

### Assignment
Survey actual business-to-business executives from a cross section of functional areas and determine their agreement or disagreement with the content of the above ad. Prepare a report of the results to present to the class.

planning and promotional strategy, and business channel and supply chain management and logistics are covered in as much detail as is allowed within the confines of a textbook. Finally, international business marketing is not only examined in chapter format, but is also interworked throughout the text (as are ethical considerations).

## Summary

- Business marketing can be defined as those activities that facilitate exchanges of products and services between organizations. A business marketing transaction occurs whenever a good or service is sold for any use other than personal consumption.

- Differences between business and consumer marketing are many and varied. In contrast to consumer marketing, business marketing is characterized by a greater total sales volume, larger volume purchases, fewer buyers, larger buyers, geographically concentrated buyers, a close supplier/customer relationship, more direct channels of distribution, professional buying, multiple buying influences, complex negotiation, reciprocity, leasing, and an emphasis on personal selling.

- The demand for business goods is derived from the demand for consumer goods and services. Business demand is relatively inelastic because demand is not likely to change significantly in the short run and tends to be less volatile than demand for consumer goods and services. There is a joint demand for some business products when two or more items are used in combination to produce a product.

- It is generally thought that business buyers tend to be more cautious than final consumers; however, they are not totally rational in their buying behavior. Frequently, selling to business buyers is a personality-oriented sales situation, as is true of many consumer transactions.

- Business goods can he classified in a number of ways. One major classification system uses the categories of major equipment, accessory equipment, fabricated and component parts, process materials, MRO supplies, raw materials, and business services.

- Business customers usually are classified into three broad categories: commercial enterprises, which include indirect channel members, original equipment manufacturers, and user-customers; governmental organizations; and nonbusiness and not-for-profit institutions.

- Marketing planning and strategy formulation begin with an analysis of a firm's environment. Central to this analysis is an assessment of the organization's strengths and weaknesses in relation to the competition, along with a matching of its strengths with unsatisfied customer needs in the marketplace.

## Key Terms

| | | |
|---|---|---|
| business marketing | derived demand | reciprocity |
| business marketing transaction | fluctuating demand | relationship marketing |
| buying center | inelastic demand | |
| Certified Purchasing Manager (C.P.M.) | joint demand | |
| | original equipment manufacturer (OEM) | |

## Review Questions

1. How is business marketing defined? What constitutes a business marketing transaction?

2. What are the reasons for studying business marketing?

3. Detail the major differences between business and consumer marketing. Create examples to show your understanding of derived demand, fluctuating demand, inelastic demand, and joint demand.

4. Why is business buying behavior not purely rational in nature? Give an example of a situation in which a business buyer might be influenced by a marketer's use of emotional appeals.

5. Identify and define five major categories of business goods and services. Is there a different classification system that can he used? If so, what are the major categories included in such a classification system?

6. What are the three fundamental types of business customers? Identify three types of commercial enterprises. How can these categories overlap?

7. Why is it important for the business marketer to know and utilize an organization's strengths and weaknesses in marketing planning and strategy formulation?

## Case 1-1

# The Relationship of Mission and Marketing

### Introduction

A case usually involves looking at a real company situation, imagining you are an involved employee (or a consultant), and applying business theory to resolve the problem or to act on the opportunity. In this text, the cases all will involve business-to-business marketing, and the objective will be to better understand the material covered in the chapters by applying it to a situation as a professional might.

This first case, instead of looking deeply into one company, looks at an important factor across a number of companies. This factor is "mission," which we will interpret as the company's statement of its purpose and an expression of its values.

Perhaps you are wondering what mission might have to do with business marketing. To find the answer, consider what a company is likely to expect of its marketing function given its mission or central philosophy of operation. Published mission statements (values, vision, etc.) are part of the basis for company culture and provide employees with guidance for decision making. They tell employees: "This is who we are; This is why we are here; This is what we believe is important; This is how we conduct our business."

Companies, like individuals, can make a conscious decision about what they stand for and how they will function in the business world. In competitive business markets, some companies decide that their central operating philosophy will be "the marketing concept." These companies view their purpose as finding, satisfying, and keeping customers. To them, that philosophy is the key to reaching other organizational goals. You will find many companies that have this customer orientation, and their mission will be evident in everything they do. Some people misunderstand the marketing concept, however, thinking that it means that the marketing department is dominant. In reality, it is a philosophy of running a company oriented around satisfying customers needs. It is about everyone within the company thinking like a marketer.

As marketers, we recognize that there are market situations in which companies can function and be successful utilizing other guiding philosophies. For example, the culture in some companies directs everyone to think like engineers, production managers, or accountants. Marketers in these companies may be uncomfortable with decisions to maximize technology, productivity, or shareholders' wealth at the expense of meeting customer needs. It would be helpful at this point to review the chapter of your Principles of Marketing text where the implications of the product, selling, production, or technology concepts, orientations, or philosophies are discussed.

In the case that follows, the objective is to help you recognize a particular philosophy when you see evidence of it. You will also need to think about what that philosophy means for the company's marketing department and for its customers. Other stakeholders (suppliers, community leaders, etc.) also have access to these published mission statements. Think about what is being communicated to them through the mission statement. This case uses actual published company mission statements. You may be surprised at how clearly they express company values.

This case involves three people who happen to be looking at the same information about a list of companies. Jesse Moore is a purchasing agent at Mega Telecom Systems, Inc., and he is scanning a list of potential suppliers. Jesse needs to pick the most promising candidates to invite to make a presentation concerning why Mega should do business with them. Rita Jackson is a direct sales person for R-Systems (the world's largest producer of copier products) and is looking at a list of potential customers. Rita needs to decide how to approach each customer. Tom Lee is a student graduating with a degree in marketing. Tom is looking at the list trying to decide where to send a job application.

## The List

Note: Many well-known companies have statements of mission (values, guiding principles, vision) that cover several pages. Within the size limits of this case, we have extracted only a few sentences of each company's statements that seem to represent their main message. Since this paraphrasing may not completely express the company's intent, we have not identified the companies involved. Our intention is not to point out good statements or bad statements, but to foster academic discussion.*

1. "We truly care for each customer. We build enduring relationships by understanding and anticipating each customer's needs and by serving them better each time than the time before. Our customers can count on us to consistently deliver superior products and services that help them achieve their business objectives."

2. "We are dedicated to maintaining our position as a profitable organization and a leader in our industry. In this way, we provide our shareholders a solid return on their

investment, our employees with the benefits of gainful employment, and the surrounding community with a share in our prosperity."

3. "To be the number one _____ company in the world and among the premier industrial concerns in terms of quality, profitability, and growth."

4. "We are dedicated to the creation and demonstration of a new corporate concept of linked prosperity. Our mission consists of three interrelated parts: (a) to make and distribute the finest quality innovative products, (b) to operate the company in such a way that actively recognizes the central role that business plays in the structure of society . . . by improving the quality of life of the broad local, national, and international community."

5. "We believe that our past, current, and future successes come from a total dedication to excellent service to those who buy our products. Satisfying our customers and consumer needs in a superior way is the only reason we are in business."

6. "We are in business to please our customers . . . to provide greater value than our competitors."

7. "BOUNDARYLESS in all our behavior. SPEED in everything we do. STRETCH in every target we set. Our mission statement is just these three words."

8. "Being the best at everything we do."

9. "Our mission is to achieve or enhance clear leadership, worldwide, in the existing or new core product categories in which we choose to compete."

10. "We believe that our first responsibility is to those who use our products and services. In meeting their needs everything must be of high quality. We must constantly strive to reduce our costs in order to maintain reasonable prices. Customer orders must be serviced promptly and accurately. Our suppliers and distributors must have an opportunity to make a fair profit."

11. "_____ is a global company committed to building long-term growth in volume and profit and to enhancing its worldwide leadership position by providing products of superior value."

12. "We are committed to achieving outstanding value for our clients, rewarding careers for our staff, and excellent performance for our owners."

13. "OUR FUNDAMENTAL OBJECTIVE (Everyone's Overriding Responsibility) is one phrase: 'Total Customer Satisfaction.'"

14. "To market products developed and manufactured in the United States that are world leaders in quality, cost, and customer satisfaction through the integration of people, technology, and business systems and to transfer knowledge, technology, and experience throughout our parent company."

15. "Our mission is dedication to the highest quality of Customer Service delivered with a sense of warmth, friendliness, individual pride, and company spirit."

16. "Our mission is to provide the world's best products, services, and intelligence . . . designed to help people work more effectively."

17. "The first corporate goal is to earn money for our shareholders and increase the value of their investment. We believe that the best measure of the accomplishment of our goal is consistent growth in earnings per share."

18. "We will be the global leader in our industry."

19. "The University of _____ exists so that human knowledge be treasured, preserved, expanded, and disseminated and that the human mind, body and spirit be nurtured and strengthened through learning. The University is committed to meet these great obligations: That its students learn well, guided, stimulated, and helped by scholarly, dedicated teachers so that each may grow according to his or her own talents; That its

students broaden and deepen their knowledge of life and thought and values, encouraged to understand what has gone before, to wonder what may yet come, and to dream; That its undergraduate study include rigorous, disciplined exploration of the accumulated core of human knowledge, and that graduate and professional study include mastery of that mix of knowledge, expertise and skills that provides the foundation for effective, ethical service to others; That there be fostered respect for the differences among people, the nurturing of curiosity, the insistence upon high standards of thought, study, communication and the skills that should characterize the educated person; That its graduates be broadly educated men and women, prepared to bear that special responsibility in a free, pluralistic society of those privileged to have a higher education; That the University firmly maintain its independence; That there be and be defended an atmosphere of tolerance and the freedom to explore, to question, to argue, to create, to accept or reject; . . .

20. Put your college or university's mission statement here.

## Assignment

**Team One:** analyze the company information from Jesse's perspective.

**Team Two:** analyze the company information from Rita's perspective.

**Team Three:** analyze the company information from Tom's perspective.

Each team will present its analysis to the class. Although each team is responsible for its own presentation, it would be logical for the teams to collaborate their presentations to best utilize the time allowed.

*The company mission statements are an adapted and paraphrased selection from those in P. Jones and L. Kahaner, *Say It and Live It* (New York: Doubleday, 1995).

---

## Case 1-2

# Researching the Duties of Actual Marketing Professionals

### Introduction

Lisa Martin and Brian Robello are senior marketing majors at a mid-sized university. It is their first day in their business marketing class, and they have just received the class syllabus. To Lisa's surprise, Brian starts coughing and she whispers, "What in the world is the matter?" Brian (looking as if he has seen a ghost) replies, "This class has a project and we even have to make a presentation." Lisa whispers back, "That's not unusual for senior classes. Let's see what this one requires."

Professor Jones wanted to get the students started on their projects as soon as possible. After introducing the concept of business-to-business marketing and assigning the first two chapters to be discussed in the next class meeting, he spent the remaining thirty minutes going over the details of the project. At the end of the class Lisa looked over her notes. She read:

### Business Marketing Project

**I.  Objectives**

1. To increase student's knowledge of the functional roles of business-to-business marketers.

2. To share the information with the rest of the class in a way that captures interest and imagination.

3. To increase student's network of professional contacts.
4. Where possible, to invite marketing professionals to speak to the class regarding their specific job duties.

**II.  Method**

1. Interview local business-to-business marketing professionals in roles such as inside strategic marketing (marketing managers, product managers, customer service managers) and outside field sales (sales representative, sales manager, manufacturer's representative). In addition (but not in place of), students may also interview professionals in logistics and purchasing.
2. Determine each person's title, job responsibilities, and relationships with other functional areas.
3. Provide a written report, including project diary and interview results. For each person interviewed, provide a complete address and telephone number (attaching a copy of his or her business card will be acceptable). Be sure to send a thank you note to each person you interview.
4. Present a professional quality PowerPoint or traditional transparency overhead class presentation of your findings. Discuss marketing job duties across different types of companies.
5. Teams of up to three are allowed, but the number interviewed should increase with team size.
6. Begin by handing in a detailed project plan with dates indicated for each step's completion. The professor's feedback will indicate whether the plan is reasonable for this particular area. The plan should include handing in periodic status reports.

**III.  Evaluation**

1. Effort, professional quality, and contribution to the class
2. Extra credit will be allowed for teams that arrange for a business-to-business marketing professional to speak to the class (in addition to their own presentation of their research results).

Lisa was an excellent note taker, and she knew that she had captured what Professor Jones had said about the project. Brian was looking unhappy. Lisa said "Cheer up! The professor isn't even going to hand out the formal assignment instructions until next week. By that time we should be able to have made appointments with the marketers at the best companies. We will have a huge head start on the other teams. Besides, these will be great contacts for us—people we should get to know." Brian said, "Fine, since you are all excited about the project, you make the calls and I'll drive you to the meetings." Lisa smiled and replied, "No, I have a better idea. We'll write a team contract splitting up all the work, with clear statements of what happens when the contract is violated."

## Assignment

Your team also is in Professor Jones's class. Plan and execute the project. Keep in mind that certain other teams probably will be proactive and begin the project early. In the research plan you hand in for the professor's approval, suggest a means to ensure that only one team contacts each department at each company. Be sure your class presentation captures some of the excitement and enthusiasm marketing professionals have for their jobs.

**References**

1. U.S. Statistical Abstract (1997): 330.
2. These examples appear in E. Raymond Corey, *Industrial Marketing,* 8th ed. (Englewood Cliffs, New Jersey: Prentice Hall, 1991): Chapter 1.
3. Donna Clapp, "After September 11, 2001: The Impact of Terrorism on Corporate America," *Business Facilities* (October 2001), accessed at www.facility.com/busfac/bf_01_10_cover.asp.

4. Ram Narasimhan and Joseph R. Carter, "Environmental Supply Chain Management," Center for Advanced Purchasing Studies, National Association of Purchasing Management, 1998.

5. Pratibha A. Dabholkar and Sabrina M. Neeley, "Managing Interdependency: A Taxonomy for Business-To-Business Relationships," *The Journal of Business and Industrial Marketing* 13 (6) (1998): 439–60.

6. Joseph P. Cannon and Christian Homburg, "Buyer-Supplier Relationships and Customer Firm Costs," *Journal of Marketing* 65 (January 2001): 29–43.

7. John F. Tanner Jr., "Users' Role in the Purchase: Their Influence, Satisfaction and Desire to Participate in the Next Purchase," *The Journal of Business and Industrial Marketing* 13 (6) (1998): 479–91.

8. Dianna Wike, "Revisting Negotiation Fundamentals," *Inside Supply Management* 13, no. 5, (May 2002): 16–17.

9. Wesley J. Johnston and Jeffrey E. Lewin, "Organizational Buying Behavior: Toward an Integrative Framework," *Journal of Business Research* 35 (1) (January 1996): 1–15.

10. S. Li and F. Chen, "Measuring the Performance of Integrated Supply Chain Management," *Proceedings,* Midwest Business Administration Association, P & O Track, Chicago, IL, (March 9, 2001): 9–14.

11. www.whitehouse.gov/usbudget/fr2003/maindown.html.

## CHAPTER TWO

# Ethical Considerations in Business-to-Business Marketing

**Learning Objectives**

After reading this chapter, you should be able to:

- Identify the major changes that impact business-to-business marketing strategy in the future.
- Better understand corporate social responsibility.
- Understand ethical issues faced in buyer-seller relationships.
- Explain the role of ethics in business-to-business marketing research.
- Differentiate among various types of ethical issues in business pricing.
- Distinguish among ethical issues faced by business salespeople in dealing both with their customers and their employers.
- Speak about the ethical problems that can arise in implementing business-to-business marketing strategy.

**Chapter Outline**

Marketing Ethics: An Overview
Marketing Strategy and Ethics
An Ethical Issue: The Organizational Buying Function and Buyer-Seller Relationships
Ethical Issues in Marketing Research
Ethics and the Management of the Pricing Function
Ethics and Sales Force Management
Ethics and Advertising Strategy

## Marketing Ethics: An Overview

From Watergate through Irangate to Whitewater in government, and from Enron, World-Com, Aurora Foods, National Century Financial Enterprises Inc., Ernst & Young, and Arthur Anderson in private industry, unethical behavior is a perennial topic of media coverage. Given the excesses of Enron and Anderson (and the others noted), it is tempting to attribute the recent scandals to a few bad eggs. But consider the accounting scandals that preceded the above. We can point to Waste Management, Sunbeam, Cendant, Rite-Aid, Phar-Mor, Adelphia, Global Crossing, Halliburton, Tyco, and Xerox. All have been in the regulatory woodshed in the past, but to attribute all of these scandals to deliberate corruption would be to believe that the accounting profession is rife with crooks, a point which anyone who has worked with accountants knows is untrue.[1] The costs associated with unethical activity include fines, liability, negative publicity, and in some cases, bankruptcy. Consider the following:

Former Enron chief financial officer, Andrew Fastow, pleaded not guilty to dozens of federal fraud, money-laundering and conspiracy charges stemming from the Houston energy trader's collapse.[2]

Bernard J. Ebbers, the former chairman and chief executive of WorldCom, used millions of dollars in loans from the company for purposes that were never properly disclosed to shareholders. Mr. Ebbers used $27 million of the loans for personal and private business expenses, including $1.8 million to build a new house and $3 million in gifts and loans to family and friends.[3]

The former chairman and chief executive of Aurora Foods Inc. was sentenced to two years and nine months in prison for his role in a conspiracy to fix the company books. Ian R. Wilson, 73 years old, is one of four former Aurora executives who pleaded guilty last year to securities fraud and related charges. The St. Louis company, which makes Duncan Hines cake mix, Mrs. Butterworth's syrup and Lender's bagels, was forced to restate results for five quarters after it uncovered evidence of improper accounting practices.[4]

Health-care-industry financier, National Century Enterprises Inc., filed for Chapter 11 bankruptcy court protection as federal agents continued their search of the company's Dublin, Ohio headquarters office. National Century's finances were in chaos for weeks after it revealed that reserves that were supposed to underpin a $2.1 billion bond offering had been depleted almost to zero. It was revealed that some affiliates of National Century or its chairman, Lance Poulsen, held significant ownership stakes in a majority of the health-care providers that received funds from the firm. Bank One Corp., which administers payments, alleged that "the evidence of trickery continues to mount." "The recently discovered financial irregularities and manipulation of books and records of the company are pervasive."[5]

The government has filed a $548 million fraud and negligence lawsuit against accounting giant Ernst & Young in connection with the failure of a savings and loan in 2001. The lawsuit, brought by the Federal Deposit Insurance Corp., accused Ernst & Young of misstating Superior Bank's assets and deliberately delaying reporting of the error for fear it would hurt an $11 billion sale of the accounting firm's consulting arm.[6]

The prosecution and defense in the criminal trial of Arthur Anderson, the once mighty accounting firm, have had their say. The jury has found the firm guilty of obstruction of justice. The 5th Circuit will review the conviction, but Anderson is already finished as a firm, with its 28,000 employees out of work, and its overseas network sold to rivals.[7]

**Ethics** are a standard of behavior by which conduct is judged; however, standards that may be legal may not always be ethical. Standards or beliefs about what is right and proper change over time, evolving as our economy becomes more competitive and global and our technology more complex. Ethical reasoning is no more reducible to a mechanical decision procedure than is economic or administrative reasoning. Indeed, the factors that affect people's propensity to make ethical or unethical decisions are not fully understood. There is speculation that three general sets of factors influence the ethics of one's decisions:

- *Individual factors* such as values, knowledge, attitudes, and intentions are believed to influence personal decisions.
- *Opportunity* resulting from the absence of professional codes or policies of ethics or of punishment may encourage unethical decision making.
- The *values, attitudes, and behavior* of peers, supervisors, and top management affect the ethics of one's business decisions.

Marketing is the functional area most closely related to ethical abuse. The marketing manager must be capable of formulating and implementing policies that call for economic reasoning as well as ethical awareness. In the competitive business world there are many practices that raise ethical questions, with the current public perception of marketplace behaviors being less than flattering. Virtually all marketing managers will face an ethical dilemma at some point in their careers.

**Marketing ethics** are moral judgments, standards, and rules of conduct relating to marketing decisions and situations. By studying business ethics, marketers gain a solid foundation from which to operate, better equipping them to function in a fast-paced marketplace in which the stakes are high. Yet a study of ethics is not a straightforward examination of facts. With it come issues of interpretation and conflicting philosophies.

## What Does Ethics Involve?

Ethics involves perceptions regarding right or wrong. An ethical individual feels compelled to behave according to the rules of moral philosophy. What should be the guiding philosophy with regard to ethical considerations in the twenty-first century? Ironically, the driving force of business today is the marketing concept—that business succeeds by giving customers what they truly want. The social discontents and ethical issues associated with the marketing concept stem not necessarily from greed and deception, but from functional limitations on its implementation. For many years there has been uncertainty within some industries regarding the position that corporate management should take. Corporate responsibility has been defined according to three different views:[8]

- *The Invisible Hand.* Under this philosophy, the true and only social responsibilities of business organizations are to make profits and obey the laws . . . the common good is best served when each of us and our economic institutions pursue not the common good or moral purpose . . . but competitive advantage. Morality, responsibility, and conscience reside in the invisible hand of the free market system, not in the hands of the organizations within the system—much less in the hands of managers within the system.
- *The Hand of Government.* Under this philosophy, the corporation [has] no moral responsibility beyond legal obedience . . . corporations are to seek objectives, which are rational and purely economic. The regulatory hand of the law and the political process, rather than the invisible hand of the marketplace, turn these objectives to the common good.

- *The Hand of Management.* This philosophy "encourages corporations to exercise independent, noneconomic judgment over matters of morals and ethics which face them in their short- and long-term plans and operations." It seeks "moral reasoning and intent" from the corporation, and for managers to "apply . . . individual morality to corporate decisions."

## Examples of Corporate Social Responsibility

In companies today, one can find examples of all three of the ethical philosophies presented above. Some firms are totally profit oriented and leave social results to the marketplace. Others operate within the letter of the law, but provide no moral or ethical leadership. Some managers, however, are looking beyond the narrow goal of profit to act as social citizens and ethical leaders, following today's societal trend that expects moral and ethical leadership from business managers. Many think that the culture of their organization is pretty much the way they want it to be. They conduct workshops to define values; they display mission statements and corporate goals on posters, e-mail, and in manuals; they conduct orientation sessions for new employees that describe what the firm stands for. However, in reality, a firm's culture is defined by what the top executives actually do.

As we enter this new century, it appears that the new generation of marketing executives is indeed more cognizant of both present and potential ethical and social issues and has a tendency to just "do the right thing." Consider: A CEO at a major international plastics manufacturer recently told us the firm's rationale for the accelerated promotion of women: "It may have a social orientation, but it is also crass economics." A similar comment came from a chemical industry senior vice president for environment: "Our proactive policies have reduced emissions well below standards, cut our liabilities, and all but eliminated accidents—all with a positive impact on the bottom line." A corporation can and should have a conscience. Corporations should be no more and no less morally responsible than ordinary persons.

Business has moved beyond its traditional, limited role of improving the standard of living by generating jobs, offering products and services, and paying taxes to federal and local governments. Today an overlay of sensitivity supports employees, empowers customers and investors, and relates to the needs of local, national, and international communities. This "increase of business" in society has been countered by society's involvement in business as never before. On a micro level, there are many customers who will boycott, not invest in, or not buy the products of "socially irresponsible companies", participating in loud public criticism of such companies. As Exhibit 2-1 shows, the American Marketing Association published a code of ethics as far back as 1988. This is an example of many similar codes being proposed by business organizations. The growth of formal codes of ethics in U.S.-based firms has been well documented, especially since the defense industry scandals of the mid-1980's and the implementation of the federal sentencing guidelines in the early 1990s.[9] Cultural values also are likely to influence whether companies adopt formal ethics codes.[10] Indeed, codes of ethics and rules of conduct that are specific enough to provide guidelines for common marketing dilemmas and are enforceable would be useful. Many large corporations—such as Caterpillar Tractor, IBM, Johnson Wax, ITT, Security Pacific Corporation, Primerica Corporation, Chemical Banking Corporation, and Champion International Corporation—have adopted formal codes of ethics. More are sure to follow.[11]

**McDonnell-Douglas Code of Ethics (Reprinted by permission of Boeing Company)**

Integrity and ethics exist in the individual or they do not exist at all. They must be upheld by the individual or they are not upheld at all. In order for integrity and ethics to be characteristics of McDonnell-Douglas, we who make up the corporation must strive to be:

Honest and trustworthy in all our relationships. . . .

## EXHIBIT 2-1  The American Marketing Association Code of Ethics

Members of the American Marketing Association (AMA) are committed to ethical professional conduct. They have joined together in subscribing to this Code of Ethics embracing the following topics:

**Responsibilities of the marketer**

Marketers must accept responsibility for the consequence of their activities and make every effort to ensure that their decisions, recommendations, and actions function to identify, serve, and satisfy all relevant publics: customers, organizations, and society. Marketers' professional conduct must be guided by:

1. The basic rule of professional ethics: not knowingly to do harm.
2. The adherence to all applicable laws and regulations.
3. The accurate representation of their education, training, and experience.
4. The active support, practice, and promotion of this Code of Ethics.

**Honesty and fairness**

Marketers shall uphold and advance the integrity, honor, and dignity of the marketing profession by:

1. Being honest in serving consumers, clients, employees, suppliers, distributors, and the public.
2. Not knowingly participating in conflict of interest without prior notice to all parties involved.
3. Establishing equitable fee schedules, including the payment or receipt of usual, customary, and/or legal compensation for marketing exchanges.

**Rights and duties of parties in the marketing exchange process**

Participants in the marketing exchange process should be able to expect that:

1. Products and services offered are safe and fit for their intended uses.
2. Communications about offered products and services are not deceptive.
3. All parties intend to discharge their obligations, financial and otherwise, in good faith.
4. Appropriate internal methods exist for equitable adjustment and/or redress of grievances concerning purchases.

It is understood that the above would include, but is not limited to, the following responsibilities of the marketer:

**In the area of product development and management:**

- Disclosure of all substantial risks associated with product or service usage.

- Identification of any product component substitution that might materially change the product or impact on the buyer's purchase decision.
- Identification of extra-cost added features.

**In the area of promotions:**

- Avoidance of false and misleading advertising.
- Rejection of high-pressure manipulations or misleading sales tactics.
- Avoidance of sales promotions that use deception or manipulation.

**In the area of distribution:**

- Not manipulating the availability of a product for purpose of exploitation.
- Not using coercion in the marketing channel.
- Not exerting undue influence over the reseller's choice to handle a product.

**In the area of pricing:**

- Not engaging in price fixing.
- Not practicing predatory pricing.
- Disclosing the full price associated with any purchase.

**In the area of marketing research:**

- Prohibiting selling or fund raising under the guise of conducting research.
- Maintaining research integrity by avoiding misrepresentation and omission of pertinent research data.
- Treating outside clients and suppliers fairly.

**Organizational relationships:**

Marketers should be aware of how their behavior may influence or impact on the behavior of others in organizational relationships. They should not demand, encourage, or apply coercion to obtain unethical behavior in their relationships with others, such as employees, suppliers, or customers.

1. Apply confidentiality and anonymity in professional relationships with regard to privileged information.
2. Meet their obligations and responsibilities in contracts and mutual agreements in a timely manner.
3. Avoid taking the work of others, in whole or in part, and representing this work as their own or directly benefiting from it without compensation or consent of the originator or owner.
4. Avoid manipulation to take advantage of situations to maximize personal welfare in a way that unfairly deprives or damages the organization or others.

Reprinted by permission of the American Marketing Association.

### Johnson & Johnson Credo (Reprinted courtesy of Johnson & Johnson)

We believe our first responsibility is to the doctors, nurses and patients, to mothers and all others who use our products and services. In meeting their needs, everything we do must be of high quality. We must constantly strive to reduce our costs in order to maintain reasonable prices. Customers' orders must be serviced promptly and accurately. Our suppliers and distributors must have an opportunity to make a fair profit.

Today, many firms are recognizing that ethical issues and **social responsibility** find their expression in the daily decisions of marketers rather than in abstract ideals. Consider the following:

- DuPont Company, which was the world's leading producer of chlorofluorocarbons (CFCs), called for a total phaseout of the chemicals to prevent destruction of the earth's protective ozone layer. The company was convinced that an international treaty calling for 50 percent cuts in CFC production was not stringent enough to prevent serious damage to the ozone layer. DuPont invented CFCs and sold $600 million worth of them annually, about one-fourth of the world's supply. DuPont no longer produces chlorofluorocarbons.

- Two-thirds of upper-level executives think people are "occasionally" unethical in their business dealings, while another 15 percent believe people are "often" unethical; 16 percent consider people "seldom" without ethics. These are among the findings of a survey of 1,000 corporate executives on ethical behavior commissioned by McFeely-Wacherle Jett, a Chicago-based executive-recruiting firm. Nearly one in four executives believes that ethical standards can impede successful careers, while 68 percent agree that younger executives are driven to compromise their ethics "by the desire for wealth and material things." Still, 54 percent think that business executives and managers have higher ethical standards and behavior than the general population.[12]

- When fire destroyed Malden Mills Industries ($400 million annual sales), Aaron Feuerstein, the 70-year-old owner could have taken the $300 million in insurance money and retired, but instead he felt he owed something more to the community. He vowed to rebuild and did so, while continuing the 3,000 employees' salaries and benefits.[13]

## The Individuality of Ethical Standards

Every marketing manager must work out his or her own philosophy of socially responsible and ethical behavior, looking beyond what is legal and allowed and developing standards based on personal integrity and corporate conscience. Business-to-business marketing executives will continue to face many challenges, not the least of which will be ethical considerations in decision making. Those marketers who are able to practice socially responsible behavior in carrying out the day-to-day decision-making process should be in a position to promote legality, fairness, and decency in organizations in the years ahead, as they realize that responsive corporate policy within this area makes good business sense.

## Marketing Strategy and Ethics

Ethical concerns in business have become very important both to practitioners and academicians in the last decade. Comparing the marketing strategies and tactics of business-to-business firms today versus 10 or so years ago, the most striking impression is one of general marketing strategy obsolescence. Just a few years ago, computer companies were introducing ever more powerful hardware for more sophisticated uses. Today, these same companies emphasize mini- and microcomputers and software; competitors launch new products and customers switch their allegiance; distributors lose their appeal; promotion costs skyrocket; new government regulations are announced and old ones are enforced; and consumer groups attack. At a time when more than half of the American public believes that the level of business ethics has declined significantly in the past decade, it might be time for academics and marketers to become involved in emphasizing ethics in marketing strategy. While we cannot slight education in training, research and development, market development, and other disciplines that are central to our business system, we must nonetheless start sensitizing managers to the interface of ethical values and the implementation of business-to-business marketing strategy.

# STRATEGY AT WORK

## TAKING THE HIGH ROAD WITH A SUPER ETHICAL BUSINESS STRATEGY

An organization that strives to give its employees a coherent sense of purpose and meaning creates a tightly knit community of people with aligned values. An aligned business unit generates a powerful sense of pride and commitment associated with contributing something good to the larger group (and through them to society).* Few schools teach this organizational approach as a business strategy and differential market advantage, but there does seem to be an increasing number of CEOs who are incorporating the tenets of the "Golden Rule" in their business plans.

The founder of Huntsman Corp, the largest privately held chemical company in the United States ($4.8 billion annual sales), emphasizes family values and spirituality across the organization in a way that is not specific to any religion. He says, "I think it is important that they hear they're good people, and that their most important assignment in life will be building loving relationships with family and neighbors."

The CEO of Silicon Valley's BioGenex Laboratories ($12 million annual sales) chaired an international conference at Stanford University to discuss how spirituality and technology can serve society (1,200 business leaders attended).

The founder of the ten-year-old Worldwide Technology Inc. ($200 million annual sales) believes that his privately held company has flourished because of business practices based on care, support, love, integrity, loyalty, commitment, and trust. "These," he explains, "help create a sense of energy, pride, excitement, security, and fun, working for one another and serving and supporting one another, and interjecting this back into the community."

It is important for graduating marketing students to realize that there are companies whose purpose is not just "maximizing shareholder's wealth." They are founded on the belief that you should do what's right, value your employees, cherish your customers, and contribute to the community. This approach is consistent with the needs-serving basis for the marketing concept. It is also worth applying on a personal level. Another way to express this philosophy is "work at what you love and success will follow."

One of the most important decisions you will ever make will be choosing the kind of company for which you will work. You spend a lot of time and energy at work, and if the company's values are not in alignment with your own, it can be very difficult (particularly for a marketing manager implementing company policy). The following highly successful (yet lesser-known) global business-to-business companies have been selected by *Industry Week* as three-time winners for "best managed," based on market performance and commitment to employees and society. The complete current list of all categories of winning companies can be viewed at (www.industryweek.com). The list includes: Abbott Laboratories, AMP Inc., Bayerische Motoren Werke AG, Cemex SA de CV, Cisco Systems Inc., DuPont & Co., Eastman Chemical Co., Emerson Electric Co., L. M. Ericsson Telephone AB, Illinois Tool Works, Johnson Controls Inc., Kyocera Corp., Matsushita Electric Industrial Co. Ltd., Novo Nordisk A/S, Nucor Corp., Smiths Industries PLC, Solectron Corp., Tenneco Inc., and Williams PLO. There are many more on the list, underscoring the point that there are companies that take ethics seriously.

*Reprinted from *Leading with Soul* by L. G. Bolman and T. E. Deal, © 1995 by Jossey-Bass Publishing Co. Adapted by permission of Jossey-Bass, Inc., a subsidiary of John Wiley & Sons, Inc. Many of the examples are drawn from J. Braham, "The Spiritual Side," *Industry Week*, February 1, 1999, pp. 49–57.

Questions should be asked: What laws are being proposed that might affect future marketing strategy? Which government agencies should we be working within our quest for improved social and ethical behavior? What can the marketer expect in pollution control, product safety, advertising, price controls, and other areas relevant to present and future marketing strategy development? What is the attitude of the business customer (and ultimately the public) toward the firm and the firm's products? In short, what major changes are occurring that will impact the implementation of future marketing strategies in the short, the intermediate, and the long term? Effective management of ethical behavior requires that organizations espouse ethics, expect ethical behavior from all employees, and establish implementation and enforcement structures.

## An Ethical Issue: The Organizational Buying Function and Buyer-Seller Relationships

As discussed previously, decisions made by the typical buying organization involve personal judgment. The purchasing manager, through contacts and dealings with business salespeople, is the custodian of the firm's reputation for courtesy and fair dealing. Likewise, the business salesperson also is expected to retain his or her firm's reputation for courtesy and fair dealing. A high ethical standard of conduct is essential for both business buyers and sellers. Courtesy and fair dealing beget confidence and cooperation—intangibles that, in the end, contribute to efficiency and profitability.

## Business Ethics Is Not a One-Sided Proposition

The subject of business ethics certainly is not one-sided, as noted above. Members of a buying center are faced from time-to-time with unethical temptations. These might include some of the following:

- participating in collusive bidding
- placing restrictive conditions when defining specifications
- overestimating demand to secure a price advantage
- purchasing "sample orders" that are magnified to excessive quantities
- burying obscure contract clauses in small type
- accepting bribes or gifts

Salespeople are not under direct continuous supervision; rather, they are under constant pressure to produce sales and are faced with additional temptations offered by the myriad opportunities for unethical behavior that the position invites. Some of the more common areas of misconduct are as follows:

- overselling
- promising more than can be delivered
- lying or making exaggerated claims
- failing to keep customer confidences by divulging information to competitors
- offering inappropriate or illegal entertainment

Salesperson deception may be more common than we think. In a recent *SMM* survey, 36 percent of respondents said salespeople now conduct business in a less ethical manner than they did five years ago, while 36 percent believe there has been no change at all. The survey also shows that 45 percent of managers have heard their reps lying about promised delivery times; 20 percent have overheard their team members give false information about the company's service; and, nearly 78 percent of managers have caught a competitor lying about their company's products or services. In the short term, unethical sales tactics may prove lucrative, but in the long term, every executive should worry about resorting to such strategies.[14]

In the buyer-seller relationship, the best opportunity to maintain ethical standards is through competent buying and selling supported by training; insistence on purchase contract performance; acceptance testing; and the like. Most sellers respect the buyer who is thorough and honest in the conduct of the buying office or buying center, and they usually will respond in kind.

| **Concept Review** | 1. Ethics implies a standard of behavior. How can a standard be legal but not ethical? Provide an example. How can an action be illegal but the law not enforceable? Provide an example. | 2. Why are more business firms implementing a code of ethics? <br><br> 3. How are business buyers the custodians of their firm's reputations for courtesy and fair dealing? |
| --- | --- | --- |

## Ethical Issues in Marketing Research

Business-to-business marketing research poses significant potential ethical problems. It is important that not only marketing research students but also practitioners and professors of marketing research develop an awareness and concern for the ethical issues of the profession. Ethics in this context concern the proper conduct of the marketing research process. Indeed, deceptive marketing research practices completely undermine the whole enterprise. Specific manifestations of such deceptive practices include incomplete reporting, misleading reporting, and nonobjective research. As business-to-business marketing research grows as a form of marketing intelligence, researchers will be forced to examine the ethical aspects of their activities. People engaged in business marketing research may unknowingly use techniques and practices that the general public might consider unethical. Because of this, researchers should examine the profession for activities that may be questionable, ensuring that practices used are appropriate to the general ethical expectations of society in general. This approach is not only "good" in an absolute sense, but it is also self-serving. Self-regulation that is guided by a vision of advertising and business in the service of society, as well as the marketer's sense of integrity, addresses problems better than external regulation does. Most marketing researchers would prefer to maintain high standards of conduct voluntarily, rather than have standards set and enforced by governmental action.

### Society's Rights

Business is a social phenomenon that coexists with many other organizations and entities in society. Like these other organizations, business has responsibilities to society to honor certain rights, including the right to be informed of research results that may impact society as a whole and the right to expect objective research results. The right to be informed of research results is a very basic right and expresses the fundamental belief that if business discovers something, accidentally or otherwise, that may affect the general health and well-being of society, then the public deserves to be informed.

The chemical industry, in general, had a long history of indifference toward the health and safety of citizens in surrounding communities. Hazardous air emissions were considered to be acceptable as long as they did not exceed federal guidelines. This has changed, as industry leaders, through the exercise of solid marketing research, have realized the importance of social responsibility and the importance of being good corporate citizens. Consider the following:

- Chemical industry research has clearly connected hazardous air emissions to the health and safety of surrounding populations. Being a good corporate citizen, Monsanto Company reduced all its hazardous air emissions by 90 percent, though the company previously met federal guidelines.
- Dow Chemical Company and the Sierra Club have jointly endorsed a proposed federal law that would sharply reduce hazardous waste production. Dow itself has adopted an aggressive waste-reduction program.
- The Chemical Manufacturers Association has proposed for the first time to set operating and safety standards that its 170 members would have to meet to retain membership.

The right to expect objective research results implies that if research results are made public, then the general public has a right to expect that the research was objective, complete, unbiased, and scientifically sound. If the results are used to deny a claim, then this behavior is unethical and violates a basic right of society.

## BUSINESS MARKETING IN ACTION

### FIRST WOMAN NAMED TO LEAD HIGH-TECH BLUE-CHIP FIRM

*July 20, 1999:* "Today Silicon Valley pioneer Hewlett-Packard Co. named Carly (Carleton) Fiorina as Chief Executive. She replaces Lew Platt, who oversaw the company as it nearly tripled in revenue to $47 billion in 1998. The move makes Fiorina the first female leader of a high-technology blue-chip company, an industry dominated by men. She is also the first chief executive hired from outside the company. The 44-year-old Fiorina is moving over from a group president position at Lucent Technologies where she had earned a reputation as a fearless, high energy corporate leader."

While HP's printer business dominates that market, the number two computer company badly missed out on the development of the Internet. Earlier this year, Platt admitted the misstep and announced his impending retirement. Recently, the company has begun repositioning itself under the rubric of "e-services" and has been buying or teaming with smaller, nimbler firms to help sell its hardware, software, and consulting to corporate customers that provide business applications online. Fiorina is widely seen as a good bet to push the slow-moving HP ahead in the fast-moving Internet-centric economy. The announcement of Fiorina's move drove HP shares to a record high, and dropped the share price of Lucent.

Fiorina received her MBA from MIT and initially worked as a business sales representative for AT&T. John Jones, computer sector analyst for Salomon Smith Barney, expressed the investment community's confidence in Fiorina: "Her kind of marketing savvy could be a big boost for HP as it pushes to distinguish itself. She's been a practicing sales and marketing person. HP hasn't had someone like that (as chief executive)."

### Action Assignment

Senior business marketing executives often have access to the highest corporate positions. Since an increasing number of women hold the title of vice president of marketing, does it follow that an increasing number of women will advance to chief executive officer? If every employment (and promotion) decision in the United States was 100 percent fair and based on equal opportunity, would the gender, race, ethnic background, and age representation at every organizational level be equal to their proportions in the general population? To research these questions, schedule appointments to interview: (1) the highest-ranking women in administration at your college or university and (2) high-ranking women in local industrial positions. In your discussions, attempt to identify lesser-recognized factors that have traditionally made it difficult for women to advance to high-ranking positions in organizations. What is their advice for today's students? Present your findings to the class.

Adapted from Joseph Menn, "First Woman Named to Lead Blue-Chip Firm." Copyright 1999 *Los Angeles Times.* Reprinted by permission.

## Clients' Rights

For the sake of simplicity, the word *client* will be used to denote either a client of a professional research firm or the researcher's employer within the business sector. Clients' rights include both the right of confidentiality of the working relationship and the right to expect quality research. The right of confidentiality is basic, as it may benefit competitors to know that a study is being done. The anonymity of the client must be preserved, whether the study performed is internal or is commissioned by an outside research firm. The right to expect quality research also is fundamental. Overly technical jargon, numbers rounded incorrectly, unnecessary use of complex analytical procedures, or incomplete reporting can make good research difficult to understand and can cloud faulty research. Several years ago, as reported in *The Wall Street Journal,* two groups of graduate students polled competitors of H. O. Penn Machinery Company in Armonk, New York, and Yancy Brothers in Atlanta, Georgia— both Caterpillar dealers. These dealerships wanted the students to conduct competitive analyses on actual competitors, with the dealers providing names of competitors and even suggesting questions to include. The students were able to obtain and analyze information on competitors' inventory levels, sales volume, advertising expenditures, and even potential new product introductions. The students identified themselves only as university students working on a class project, and when corresponding with the dealers, used university marketing department stationery. Said one of H. O. Penn's competitors: "I wouldn't give out that type of stuff if I knew it was going to someone other than students."[15] Even as "future executives in training," the students should have sensed that they were involved in misrepresentation by omission. Such practice is improper for those providing the research service as well as for those requesting it. Can such practices be eliminated? Probably not. Can they be reduced? We think so.

### Researchers' Rights

Several issues can arise in which the researcher, department, or firm needs protection. Researchers have the right for protection against improper solicitation of proposals. For example, proposals should not be solicited for the specific purpose of driving down prices, nor should a proposal from an outside research firm be given to an in-house research department for implementation. Actions such as these are referred to as "**sharp practices**." Researchers have the right to expect accurate presentation of findings. Distorted findings can not only mislead the client, they can also be potentially damaging to other involved parties as well. Researchers have the right to expect confidentiality of proprietary information on techniques; this is included to help researchers who develop special methods such as proprietary modeling and simulation techniques for dealing with certain types of problems encountered.

## Ethics and the Management of the Pricing Function

Pricing is perhaps the most difficult of all the areas of marketing to examine from an ethical viewpoint because of the complexity of the price variable. There is an expansive realm of ethical issues in pricing—issues that may be raised at all levels of the distribution chain, across different market structures and competitive situations, and across industry types. The following is an overview of some of the more important areas of ethical issues in pricing.

### Setting a Fair Price

Generally speaking, new products should be priced to gain experience and market share, which, if done correctly, should meet stated company objectives in terms of profit and return on investment. As market share increases, lower costs should result. If a **skimming price strategy** is used initially, is the business firm under any moral obligation to lower prices later without a clear market-oriented reason for doing so (such as competitive entry, competitive price move, etc.)? None of us is in a position to make a judgment on this question, and the question is raised only to point out that if profit goals are overemphasized, line management may perceive that profit should be placed above ethical considerations. It is hoped that competitive forces will keep prices and demand for the company products or product lines on an even keel.

### Altering Product Quality Without Changing Price

Product quality usually will determine price, as business buyers are reluctant to pay for unnecessary product quality. An overanxious line manager may be tempted to reduce quality standards as part of a value-analysis effort (see Chapter 4). Assume that a large equipment manufacturer initiates a major cost reduction effort, substituting plastic for steel in several subassemblies. Though realizing that the life of the equipment may drop slightly, the manufacturer does not point this out to prospective customers and does not reduce the price of the finished product to reflect the cost savings. (It must also be assumed that price exhibits an inelastic demand curve in this situation.) Is this ethical? Should the possibility of a shortened useful product life be brought to the attention of prospective business buyers? Will this decision depend on competitive forces, the stage in the product life cycle, profitability of the product line, or pressure exerted by top management for increased profitability? Glib answers might be easy to generate here; however, in reality, ready answers to such questions are not easy to produce.

## Practicing Price Discrimination with Smaller Accounts

Although the **Robinson-Patman Act** makes it unlawful to discriminate in price between commodities of like grade and quality and prohibits unfair competition (as discussed in Chapter 8), would someone be naive enough to think that **price discrimination** against smaller accounts does not happen occasionally with some business-to-business companies? In an effort to please, or because of a long-standing business (or even personal) relationship, in addition to both internal and external pressures, it is very probable that the business marketer will at least be tempted to treat some customers better than others when price is an issue. In most cases, this marketer would be shocked to learn of a potential violation of the law here, and in all probability is doing what he or she thinks is best for the company given the realities of the situation. Even so, serious ethical and legal questions and issues can be raised here.

## Price Fixing

One way of controlling competition is for a small group of producers to collude for their common good, agreeing on the price to charge (see Chapter 8). This practice, known as **price fixing**, is illegal because it undermines the competitive system to the detriment of the buyer; it also is immoral. If firms use their combined power to fix prices, drive out competitors, or earn excessive profits at the expense of not only the business buyer but also the ultimate consumer, the market ceases to be competitive; the result is a decline in, or restriction of, a buyer's freedom to make economic choices. The revelation of alleged price fixing at the Archer Daniels Midland (ADM) Company may be the most bizarre case in recent years, but it's certainly not the only one. The $12.6 billion ADM, the organization that brings us National Public Radio, pled guilty and paid a $100 million criminal fine (at the time, the largest criminal antitrust fine ever) for its role in conspiracies to fix prices to eliminate competition and allocate sales in the lysine and citric acid markets worldwide.[16] The ADM case followed another major price-fixing case involving General Electric and De-Beers Cantenary AG. The Justice Department alleged that General Electric and DeBeers Cantenary were guilty of price fixing in the industrial diamond industry. Although this particular case was thrown out because of a lack of evidence, it shows that no firm is immune to antitrust action.

The purpose behind federal and state antitrust law is to keep markets competitive so that businesses and ultimately consumers can purchase the best possible goods and services at the lowest competitive prices. The antitrust laws apply to virtually all industries and to every level of business, including manufacturing, transportation, distribution, and marketing. They prohibit a variety of practices that restrain trade. The **Sherman Act**, enacted in 1890, prohibits all agreements and conspiracies in restraint of interstate trade and commerce. What companies and executives need to know is that violations of the Sherman Act are punished as criminal felonies. Individuals can be fined up to $350,000 and sentenced up to three years in federal prison for each offense. Corporations can be fined up to ten million dollars for each offense. In addition to federal prosecution, private parties can sue for damages if they have overpaid.

Unlike the Sherman Act, both the **Clayton Act** and the **Federal Trade Commission** Act do not carry criminal penalties. The Clayton Act prohibits mergers and acquisitions that could weaken the competition. The Federal Trade Commission Act forbids unfair methods of competition in interstate commerce, and serves as the source that created the Federal Trade Commission (FTC) to police such violations.

## Typical Examples of Antitrust Violations

The following examples illustrate some common ways in which businesses or individuals may commit serious violations of the antitrust laws. There are many others, too numerous to explore here. These examples are hypothetical and do not refer to actual cases or investigations.[17]

### *Bid Rigging*

**Bid rigging** is an agreement among potential bidders about which companies will bid for certain contracts, or in which areas and at what prices. It can also be unlawful to tailor contract specifications to the product of a particular company or otherwise attempt to predetermine which company will win a bid.

Example: A member of a buying center, in collusion with a favored supplier, develops a set of restrictive specifications for the purchase of all the janitorial supplies needed by a school district. The specifications exclude all but the current supplier. The RFQ (Request for Quotation) is sent out and the district receives only one bid. The primary reason many competitors did not bid is that the bid specifications were so restrictive as to discourage participation. The supplier who wrote the specifications submits an apparent low bid for most of the products, and of course meets all specifications. This subversion of the bidding process is an unreasonable restraint of trade.

### *Price Fixing*

Any agreement between competitors regarding price is considered price fixing and is illegal. Agreements to adhere to a book price; agreements to engage in cooperative price advertising; agreements to standardize credit terms offered to purchasers; agreements to use uniform trade-in allowances; agreements to discontinue free service or to fix any other element of price; agreements to use a specific method of quoting prices; agreements to use a multiple-basing point-pricing system; agreements establishing uniform costs and markups; agreements to impose mandatory surcharges; and, agreements specifying price differentials between grades of a product and adopting common classifications of customers entitled to discounts, are all considered price fixing and are therefore illegal.

Example: A group of competing engineers, acting through their trade association, agrees to not supply lump sum bids. Because the effect of the agreement is to stabilize price, such an agreement is actionable as price fixing.

### *Tying*

**Tying arrangements** are agreements by a party to sell one product but only on condition that the buyer also purchase a different (or tied) product, or at least agrees that they will not purchase that product from any other supplier. A tying arrangement is one in which the availability of one item (the tying item) is conditioned upon purchase or rental of another item (the tied item), or agreeing to not purchase the tied item from the seller's competitors.

Example: A manufacturer of high-end copy machines would only sell replacement parts to third parties if they agreed not to buy their service from independent service organizations. The firm sought to justify this conduct on the rationale that if customers did not like the parts policy they would just not buy the firm's copiers.

### *Market Allocations*

**Market allocations** include agreements between competitors that they will not compete with respect to specified customers, geographical territories, or products. These agreements are illegal at all levels of distribution, whether among manufacturers, wholesalers, or retailers.

## BUSINESS MARKETING IN ACTION

### SUPPLY ALLIANCES POSE ETHICAL QUESTIONS

According to a survey of buyers, new policies involving closer alliances with suppliers (e.g., single-source relationships) are creating ethical concerns. The changed policies include:

1. A switch from frequent buyer rotation to buyers specializing in one commodity area (Traditionally, buyer rotation acted as a check on preferential supplier treatment. If a buyer provided a particular supplier an unfair advantage, the next buyer assigned to the area would likely uncover it.)

2. Allowing exceptions to conventional competitive bid approaches to supplier selection (Traditionally, competitive bidding was used to establish fair market pricing levels. Without competitive bidding, buyers must make an extra effort in researching supplier costs and profitability levels, e.g., zero-based pricing.)

3. The greater tendency to share confidential insider information between customer personnel and "preferred" supplier personnel (Insider information can be an unfair competitive advantage to the suppliers who can gain access to it, plus there have been cases of individuals making personal investment decisions based on insider information.)

4. An alliance with one supplier can create the impression that the supplier is somehow improperly influencing the buyer's sourcing decisions (This perception can negatively impact a buyer's professional reputation.)

The survey also uncovered evidence that buyers want their companies to establish clear and strict ethical standards concerning their dealings with suppliers. Buyers who rated their company's ethical policies most favorably tended to be those from companies that prohibited all forms of gifts, favors, and entertainment. With single-source and other supplier alliances becoming commonplace, companies are having to find new ways to deal with the ethical problems and concerns that these relationships produce.

**Action Assignment**

Research how companies have dealt with the ethical concerns described above, as they reduce the numbers of suppliers with which they deal. Interview purchasing agents or buyers at local companies. Most will meet with a student, but you will need to make an appointment and dress professionally. To start, set up your first appointment with a buyer in the purchasing department at your own college or university. You can develop a list of buyers to contact by visiting the website of the Institute for Supply Management (www.ism.ws). Click on "ISM Membership" to find the closest affiliate chapter of ISM. At a chapter website you will often find telephone numbers and e-mail addresses for buyers in your area. If your buyer interviews uncover no ethical concerns, consider why an anonymous pencil and paper survey might have brought them out. Present your findings to the class.

**Source:** "Purchasing Survey Supplier Alliances Pose New Ethical Threats," *Purchasing*, May 20, 1999, pp. 20–22. © 1999.

Example: Company X and Y manufacture industrial valves. The companies agree informally that in the state of California, Company X will distribute its valves only through industrial distributors in San Francisco, while Company Y agrees to distribute its valves only to industrial distributors in Los Angeles. Company X will stay out of Los Angeles and Company Y will stay out of San Francisco. This agreement is illegal!

### *Using a Competitor's Quote to Requote or Rebid*

When competitive bidding is used, requests for bids are usually sent to several potential vendors, depending on the dollar size of the purchase. If the bidding process is to be fair, then a violation of secrecy by any of the parties in the process violates the fairness condition of the bidding process. The leaking of competitor bid information to other potential suppliers is unfair, immoral, and unethical and could be the result of bribery, or offers of a cash kickback. The bidding process is open to abuses and must be controlled.

Example: Company A receives an RFQ for 10,000 steel gear casings. The company may seek to win the bid by conducting research and development (at considerable cost to them) to show that a less expensive reinforced plastic would perform better, and at less cost per unit, than the steel material specified. Company A's bid is the lowest due to the plastic material suggested. But, rather than awarding the contract to Company A, the buyer might repeat the entire bidding process, this time specifying the plastic material engineered by Company A.

### *Reciprocity*

Many business buyers often select suppliers who also buy from them. **Reciprocity**, by itself, is not illegal. However, the Justice Department and the Federal Trade Commission monitor reciprocity because it may substantially lessen competition. Reciprocity is forbidden if it eliminates competition in an unfair manner. As long as the buyer can show that competitive prices, quality, and service is being supplied, then reciprocity just makes good business sense. However, if these conditions are not being met, then the question of ethical standards should be addressed.

Example: A packaging manufacturer buys needed chemicals from a particular chemical company or industrial distributor that is buying a considerable amount of its packaging products.

---

**Concept Review**

1. How can the practice of marketing research pose significant ethical problems?
2. Why is pricing such a difficult area to examine from an ethical viewpoint?
3. Is the use of reciprocity a legal practice?

---

## Ethics and Sales Force Management

As key links between their organizations and the business buyer, business salespeople encounter situations that, on occasion, lead to ethical conflict. For this discussion, ethical issues confronting sales personnel will be categorized into two broad areas: ethics in dealing with customers and ethics in dealing with employers. First, consider the following vignettes:

*Scenario 1:* A business machinery salesperson faced the following problem. When a newly installed milling machine continued to malfunction, the customer demanded that the piece of equipment be immediately replaced with a new machine. Management within the selling firm decided to replace the machine with a slightly used demo that looked new. The salesperson did not know whether to inform the customer of the replacement, with the obvious risk of losing the sale, or to defer to management's action, thus not only salvaging the sale but perhaps even his or her job.

*Scenario 2:* A business real estate salesperson was attempting to sell a building to a client who finally had decided to make an offer on the building. The offer was several thousand dollars below not only the asking price but also the appraised value of the property. Knowing that the seller would decline such an offer, the salesperson considered telling the potential buyer that the seller was considering a higher offer extended by another potential buyer, even though no such offer existed.

*Scenario 3:* A business salesperson was attempting to sell cleaning supplies to a large, multiplant manufacturer of business widgets. The business buyer bluntly told the salesperson that for a private "fee" of $500, the contract could be signed very quickly. The salesperson, being fairly new in the position, told the sales manager what had happened. The sales manager, in turn, told the salesperson to do whatever was necessary to get the order, even if that included the payment of a $500 "fee."

These situations are commonplace for many people in the business sales force. Now we turn to the two broad areas of ethical considerations confronting sales personnel.

## Ethics in Dealing with Customers

Occasionally, business salespeople will find themselves in the position of being tempted to compromise their ethical standards when dealing with some customers because the customer or a competitor is engaged in an unethical strategy. A half-truth or misrepresentation, a subtle demand for a gift or extraordinary entertainment, or some other unethical trick might tempt the salesperson to relax standards, especially when a large order is at stake.

The key driver of a sound sales strategy in this and other like scenarios is leadership. The leaders of the organization exhibit the values that they want employees to follow, says Steve Walker, President of Walker Communications, a stakeholder research and measurement firm in Indianapolis. "Most people want to do the right thing, but when bad situations arise it is usually when the leadership has created an environment that tolerates it," he says. "Until boards of directors want to sniff it out, the scheming will stay in the hallways."[18] The major problem areas involved here include bribes, gifts, entertainment, and reciprocity.

### *Bribes*

The use of bribes, although widespread and considered very acceptable behavior within some cultures, should be refused tactfully, allowing salespeople to act in the best interests of their employers and in fairness to all customers. Bribery not only is unethical, it also can be illegal. For example, a few years ago a large American steel company was fined $325,000 for paying $400,000 in bribes to obtain ship repair business for its domestic shipyards. Often it is difficult to distinguish between a bribe, a gift to show appreciation, and a reasonable commission for services rendered. Bribery distorts the operation of fair bargaining, and salespeople should resist efforts for bribes from the occasional member of the business buying center who might want to engage in such activity.

### *Gifts*

Accepting or giving gifts may or may not be ethical, but the practice of gift giving is under careful scrutiny within many business-to-business firms. If the giving of a gift is done as a condition of doing business (subtle or otherwise), then clearly the act is immoral and unethical. Further, it causes prejudice against those who fail to give a gift. Many firms have stopped the practice of giving holiday gifts to customers, offering instead to contribute to a customer's favorite charity. The problem with this approach, however, is that even those gratuities given to create legitimate goodwill may influence the purchasing decision in some way. Some common sense and social intelligence should be good guides in keeping the business selling firm within ethical boundaries. Maureen Scully, Assistant Professor of Management and Business Ethics at Massachusetts Institute of Technology's Sloan School of Management, agrees that most firms should strictly enforce their ethical policies. If in doubt, Scully advises first asking a client whether his or her company publishes an ethics handbook. If the message is a clear "Thanks, but no thanks," salespeople should respect the organization's rules and refrain from giving anything that could be considered a gift.[19]

### *Entertainment*

Although the entertainment of customers and potential customers is quite common and may even be expected, it too can pose ethical questions. Is taking a customer to lunch or to a ball game fair, reasonable, and expected? If that is deemed to be acceptable, then how about a few days at the company resort or fishing lodge, or a trip with the buyer's spouse to view an equipment installation near Disneyland? Many times, members of the buying center resent attempts to influence them unduly and find efforts to obligate them to buy from a particular seller quite offensive. As a general rule, lavish entertainment can become unethical if the attempt is to substitute it for good selling techniques. "If you can't sell your product based on the product attributes, you have no business being in sales," says Ron Black, one-time Southern regional manager for Welch Foods, Inc.[20]

### *Reciprocity*

As referred to earlier in this chapter, this phenomenon occurs when a buyer gives preference to a supplier who also is a customer; usually it is found in industries in which products are homogeneous and/or there is not a high degree of price sensitivity. The buyer of business goods thus has the opportunity to use purchases to generate sales by a threat, overt or implied, to withdraw patronage unless it is reciprocated. Forced reciprocity obviously has ethical and perhaps legal implications. Chemical Bank, the New York-based financial institution with some 270 branches in the United States and 55 offices abroad, has long been noted for its innovative approach both to business ethics and to corporate responsibility. Its purchasing department has procedures to ensure fair and equitable treatment of the bank's suppliers; in order to avoid even the appearance of reciprocity, there is no review to determine which suppliers are Chemical customers before the bank awards contracts. Further, Chemical's own printing subsidiary is expected to compete against other companies for most of the bank's printing orders.[21]

An underlying principle of purchasing practice, advocated by the Institute for Supply Management (ISM), is the avoidance of situations that might influence, or even appear to influence, purchasing decisions. In the future, there will be increasing pressure for firms to demonstrate a sense of social responsibility and an awareness of ethical problems. Clearly, this suggests a need to review sales techniques including gift giving, business lunches, and entertainment.

## Ethics in Dealing with Employers

In dealing with their own employers, business salespeople encounter situations that may lead to unethical conduct. The major problem areas involved include moonlighting, changing jobs, expense accounts, and contests.

### *Moonlighting*

Salespeople who waste or misuse time (especially those who work on a straight salary compensation plan) are in a sense stealing profits from the employing company. *Moonlighting,* or holding more than one job, may be construed as a misuse of company time and therefore raises potential ethical and moral questions. Employers have a right to expect full-time work from salespeople employed to sell their products, and those who work another job in the evening or have a side business of their own may violate the principle of time accountability. A salesperson who handles another product line (even if it is noncompetitive) is engaged in the unethical practice of *kiting.* The key here is disclosure; informing the employer that extra hours are being spent doing something else.

### *Changing Jobs*

Another area in which salespeople face ethical responsibility is in changing jobs. An active effort by sales managers to "pirate" salespeople away from competitors is likely to be seen as unethical. Companies invest considerable money in training salespeople, in addition to the fact that, over a period of time, they build up customer knowledge and goodwill, of which they may take advantage if they change jobs and accept a position with a competitor. Job switchers generally have had access to confidential information, and perhaps competitive secrets which, if used as a ploy to gain new employment, would be considered unethical of both the prospective employee and the recruiting sales manager.

### *Expense Accounts*

Most companies provide the sales force with sufficient travel and entertainment expense money to cover all justified expenses of doing business, and it is the responsibility of the salespeople and the sales managers to allocate expense dollars effectively. *Expense accounts* present special temptations and represent the area where ethical abuses may occur most frequently within a sales organization. The fine line that the sales manager must walk when controlling expense accounts can be trying: a tight control might cause the salesperson to curtail travel and necessary entertainment to the detriment of the company; loose control may result in selling expense ratios that are higher than they should be. Allowing salespeople to overspend is dangerous because it is a behavior that can quickly get out of control. "We tell salespeople to think of the company budget as their own," says Carolyn White, a New York-based software sales manager for IBM. White instructs her staff of six to make strategic purchasing decisions—taking the decision makers to dinner, for example, not just any client. More important, warns John Reddish, President of Advent Management International Ltd., a management consulting firm in Chadds Ford, Pennsylvania, is the fact that generous expense accounts can set salespeople up to make destructive assumptions. They think, "If I keep spending money on my client, they will eventually buy from me." Reddish says that in today's market, that simply will not happen.[22]

### *Contests*

Contests are designed to motivate sales representatives to make more sales of all products or to make more sales of specific products within a product line. The pressure to win can result in the "stockpiling" of orders until the contest begins, the selling of unneeded product to "friends" for later return for credit, or the overselling of unneeded products to good customers. All of these practices are easy to rationalize, and all are unethical.

## Ethics and Advertising Strategy

When, in 1880, Winston Churchill took his entrance examination for admission to Sandhurst, he was given a choice of three essay questions to answer: Riding versus Rowing; Advertisements, Their Use and Abuse; and The American Civil War. (He chose the essay question on the American Civil War.) That the use and abuse of advertising tools and techniques were up for discussion well over a century ago reveals that today's criticisms of advertising are not new. Advertising techniques often have been criticized by those outside the field as a dubious practice involving the use of questionable methods to accomplish nefarious ends. The consumers of advertising and the industry's other publics demand a sensitivity to ethical issues. No business discussion of ethics would be complete without a section of study devoted to ethics and advertising strategy.

### Truth in Advertising

**Truth in advertising** is a complex issue. Advertisements make statements with the purpose of trying to persuade buyers to purchase the product advertised. But statements supported solely by a reference to a scientific study would probably be very dull and may or may not be effective. Persuasion may take place by making statements or by simply creating associations in the mind of the buyer. Some business advertisements simply show a picture of the product, with the belief being that when the buyer sees the name, it has an effect on purchasing. A statement made about a product may be true, may not mislead, and may not deceive, but it may nevertheless be morally and ethically objectionable. Sometimes what the advertisement does not say is as important as what it does say. It is wrong to advertise and to sell a hazardous product without indicating its dangers. General rules concerning truth in advertising can be summarized in the following way: It is immoral to lie, mislead, or deceive in advertising. It is immoral to fail to indicate dangers that are not normally expected. It is not immoral to use a metaphor or other figure of speech if these will be normally understood as the figurative use of language; nor is it immoral to persuade as well as to inform.

## WHAT WOULD YOU DO?

### LOOSE CANNONS IN MARKETING: ETHICS IN DEALING WITH OTHER FUNCTIONAL AREAS

Tom Griffith, director of quality control (QC) for GCY Manufacturing, was in a foul mood. He had just returned from a meeting with marketing, and they wanted him to revise his entire division quality control program so that they could meet the requirements of a new customer. Tom had refused, telling them that the present quality program was certified by some of the largest high-tech companies in the world (who were already their customers). There was no way he was going to allow marketing to bully QC into changing their huge manual of procedures and retrain the entire corporation just to meet some new standard. "And get all that done in two weeks. Ridiculous!"

Pete Martin, GCY marketing VP, also was in a foul mood. He knew that sales had been working on getting a chance with this new customer for over two years. Now the customer was going to spend a good deal of its own money to fly out and evaluate GCY's plants, procedures, and equipment. This was a super accomplishment by the salespeople, and he would be darned if he would let GCY be rejected. Pete believed strongly that it was the marketing department who decided what products would be sold to what customers, at what price, with what promotion, and using what distribution. Pete agreed that the upgraded QC program exceeded the requirements of the current customers, but he was sure that it would not be long before it became a standard requirement. It was in GCY's best interest to make the change as soon as possible.

Pete thought about going to the president and having him order Tom to cooperate, but he discarded that idea. First, he might not agree, since Tom had considerable political clout (due to his 35 years with the company). Moreover, the biggest problem was that the president was not in the best position to make the decision. No one else in top management had a technical background; Pete did. That's why they put him in charge of making marketing mix decisions. Prior to becoming head of marketing, Pete had been head of engineering, and before that, he headed up QC for a large competitor. Pete figured, "Well, if you don't get yelled at occasionally, probably you are not making the tough decisions the job requires."

Pete arranged with field sales to have Tom called out of town on a customer problem. While he was in the field, it seemed only logical that Tom might as well spend another week and accompany the salesperson on some goodwill customer visits. With Tom out of the way, Pete called in Tom's assistant, Mary; explained the situation; and asked her if she would present a new tentative QC program for the potential customer's visit. Under Pete's direction, marketing would redo the entire Quality Control Manual and all systems paperwork. If Mary approved it, it would be presented to the customer as the program that would be used, in place, and approved before any orders were shipped. The customer visit was successful, and GCY received tentative approval, based on implementation of the proposed QC system. The customer made it quite clear that without the new QC system proposal, the result would have been a flat rejection (plus they would not have appreciated GCY wasting their time). The new customer would represent many millions of dollars of new sales.

As soon as Tom returned, he stormed into the president's office.

### Assignment

Define the ethical issues for all concerned (Pete, Tom, Mary, the president, the field salesperson who asked for Tom to help with the customer problem, and the customer). Develop a plan of action for the president.

## Comparative Advertising

**Comparative advertising** is an advertisement or sales promotional piece that actually names the competitors and proceeds to compare one product with another. It has the potential to present both ethical and legal problems. Because of this, some business-to-business marketing managers prohibit, or at least discourage, comparative advertising practices within their own firms, feeling that such practices serve no real purpose. If comparisons are made, then clearly the standard should insist on accurate comparisons, as there might be a temptation to imply that a product that is superior to the competition in one characteristic is therefore superior overall. It might be recommended that a more ethical and responsible course of action would be to point out competitive differences, leaving the business customer to judge the superiority of the product offering (or its lack thereof).

Inherent in the semantics of advertising and promotion in general are the notions of lying, misrepresentation, deception, manipulation, and other questionable practices. Those that are unethical, immoral, or illegal should be labeled as such. Peers or members of top management influence most ethical decisions related to advertising in particular and promotion in general. Ethical decision making within this area is conceptually complex, and a multiplicity of factors can influence the final outcome. To implement and monitor ethical decision making in advertising in particular, and in other promotional activities in general, both philosophical and organizational dimensions of ethics should be examined.

## Concept Review

1. Why have many firms stopped the practice of gift giving?

2. When might entertainment border on bribery?

3. Why is truth in advertising a complex issue?

## Summary

- Ethics means the standards by which behavior is judged. Standards that may be legal may not be ethical. Standards and beliefs about what is right and proper change over time. This question is becoming more important as our economy becomes more competitive and global and our technology more complex. Marketing ethics involve moral judgments, standards, and rules of conduct relating to marketing decisions and situations.

- Comparing the marketing strategies and tactics of business firms today versus those of a decade ago, the most striking impression is one of general marketing strategy obsolescence. Business marketers must become sensitized to the interface of ethical values and the implementation of business marketing strategy; they must learn to recognize the major changes that will impact the implementation of future marketing strategies.

- Through contacts and dealings with business salespeople, the purchasing manager is the custodian of his or her firm's reputation for courtesy and fair dealing. The subject of business ethics applies equally both to the business buyer and seller. In the buyer-seller relationship, the best opportunity for maintaining ethical behavior is competent buying supported by training, insistence of purchase contract performance, and acceptance testing. Most business salespeople respect the buyer who is thorough and honest in his or her purchase transactions.

- People engaged in business marketing research may unknowingly use techniques and practices that the general public might consider unethical. Because of this, researchers should examine their profession for

activities that may be questionable, in order to avoid such practices. Business marketing researchers should be aware of society's rights, clients' rights, and researchers' rights in discharging their professional duties.

- Business pricing is perhaps the most difficult of all the areas of marketing to examine from an ethical perspective because of the complexity of the price variable. Common areas of ethical concern in business pricing include setting a price that meets company objectives while not taking advantage of the customer, altering product quality without changing price, practicing price discrimination with smaller accounts, price fixing, obtaining information on a competitive price quotation in order to requote or rebid, and reciprocity.

- As key links between their organizations and the business buyer, business salespeople encounter situations that, on occasion, lead to ethical conflict. Business salespeople may be tempted to lower their ethical standards in dealing with their customers in such areas as bribes, gifts, entertainment, and reciprocity. They may be likewise tempted in their dealings with employers in such areas as moonlighting, changing jobs, expense accounts, and contests.

- A statement made about a product may be true, may not mislead, may not deceive, but may nevertheless be morally and ethically objectionable. What the advertisement does not say may be more important than what it does say. In comparative advertising, the business marketer should carefully point out competitive differences, leaving the customers to judge the superiority of the product offering.

## Key Terms

bid rigging
Clayton Act
comparative advertising
ethics
Federal Trade Commission
market allocations

marketing ethics
price discrimination
price fixing
reciprocity
Robinson-Patman Act
sharp practices

Sherman Act
skimming price strategy
social responsibility
truth in advertising
tying arrangements

## Review Questions

1. Identify and describe three different views of corporate social responsibility. Provide a business example for each one.

2. What kinds of questions should business marketers ask in order to sensitize themselves to the interface of ethical values and the implementation of business marketing strategy?

3. How can the purchasing manager be the custodian of his or her firm's reputation for courtesy and fair dealing? What types of unethical sales practices are business buyers likely to face from time to time? What types of ethical misconduct are more associated with the business salesperson?

4. Of what three sets of rights should all professional marketing researchers be aware in the discharge of their activities? How can ethics be applied to the business-to-business marketing research function?

5. Why is pricing perhaps the most difficult of all the marketing areas to examine from an ethical perspective? Discuss six types of potential unethical conduct in business pricing.

6. What are four types of ethical problems that business salespeople might encounter in dealing with their customers? What are four types of ethical problems that business salespeople might encounter in dealing with their employers?

7. What are two ways in which persuasion may take place in business promotion? How can comparative advertising be used in an unethical manner?

---

### Case 2-1

## McDonell Corporation: *What Is Unethical Competitive Research?*

This case was written by Dr. Roger Gomes and Dr. Patricia Knowles, Clemson University © 1999

Hank Jones, corporate director of marketing, was looking over requests by the divisions for marketing research on competitors' activities. Since the divisions overlapped on many competitors' industries, there was some potential for ethical problems. The customer contracts that the divisions were bidding on were worth several million dollars, and Hank worried that the stakes were high enough (not to mention commissions and bonuses) that the competitors might not be as ethical as his company policy forced him to be. Some individuals or companies might use some underhanded and unethical tactics to gain an edge. Further, if the competitor had no differential advantage in its product offering, it might try to make it up with insider information. Hank suspected that some competitors might even resort to eavesdropping devices, such as tapped phones, monitored e-mail, diverted faxes, chemicals that allow snoops to read mail right through the envelope, and electronic bugs in offices. These were all things that had to be checked for, but not tactics that Hank planned to employ.

Hank proceeded to make a list of potential tactics that he might use to gather competitive research. His plan was to list as many as he could think of, then go back and eliminate those that might be considered unethical. Hank's list was as follows:

1. Check competitors' annual reports, 10K, and other filings with the SEC, and get copies of competitors' officer's public speeches.

2. Consider asking competitors for information. Hank had read about one company that would send out a team to a competitor's sales office and honestly identify itself. Invariably, the competitor's sales managers were so proud of their accomplishments, they would give information freely.

3. To get inside information on competitor costs, buy some of the competitors' products and take them apart. Analyze them for component material and processing methods, and then ask the suppliers of those component materials to submit bids for the components.

4. Hire a headhunting firm to interview key managers from competitor firms (for a fabricated higher-paying job at an unidentified company in the industry). The headhunter can report on pay levels, training, competitors' values, projects they have worked on, and standard service behavior. Hank thought that he might someday hire one or two, but he would have to be very careful since one might be a spy.

5. Hire a management consulting firm to gather information. The firm would interview the competitor(s) under the guise of doing an industry study in which the individual company's information would be kept confidential, with the aggregate information to be shared with all participants. Actually, the consultant's client (Hank) will get the competitor's confidential information. Hank made a note to remind himself to warn all his managers not to participate in any outside research, especially if the researcher identifies himself or herself as a consultant, professor, or student.

6. Ask his salespeople to indirectly encourage their customer buying center contacts to talk about their competitors. Hank recalled a story in which a company told its distributor the date they were launching a new product nationwide. The distributor promptly told the firm's competitor, with whom it also did business. The advance notice allowed the competitor to be ready with its own new product.

7. Get a customer's buyer (or other member of the buying center) to request a phony bid from a competitor and forward it to one of his people. The competitor's bid proposal would probably contain some valuable information.

8. Analyze competitor's help wanted ads, among others. Annual reports and 10K reports, help wanted ads, and others often originate from a nonmarketing department that is not aware of what would be useful information to competitors. If the competitor is hiring 10 infrared engineers, then probably it is going to use that technology.

9. Analyze reports on competitors' labor contracts. It can help with backing into the labor part of their costs.

10. Study aerial and satellite photographs of competitors' facilities (if available).

11. Obtain Freedom of Information Act information on anything the competitor files with the government (this can be handled confidentially by a "friend" that will act for the company).

12. Consider having someone measure the frequency of trailer load shipments from the competitors' plants and warehouses. If a competitor is using a public warehouse, store some material there to gain access. Make note of what the competitor has there, where it is going, and/or where it came from.

13. Take a plant tour of the competitor's plant during an open-house. Plants often allow tours for employees' families and friends and for groups such as the Boy Scouts. Once inside, note all equipment and processes.

14. Buy competitor's garbage. Once dumped or assigned to a trash company, the competitor gives up ownership. Most companies do not realize that their office shreds little,

and production specifics often go into the trash, even with identifying customer part numbers.

15. Infiltrate a competitor's business operations. No . . . Hank found that he was getting tired and probably going too far. He crossed out 15 but wrote himself a note to try to find out how he might check out whether the night cleaning crew might have spies. Hank thought to himself, "I wonder if our accounting and marketing files are locked up at night?"

16. Hank also remembered that his firm often had engineers and others working inside a customer's operations (early supplier involvement in new designs). Perhaps they could get access to some of this competitor information. After several seconds, he thought that this might interfere with future customer relationships. After careful consideration, he crossed this off the list.

17. Hank also imagined hiring some computer science students from the local university to hack through a competitor's extranet. It wouldn't be difficult to find out how its salespeople are externally accessing the company computer system, or perhaps they have their Web pages on their main server. It might be possible to access their entire internal computer system. If hackers can get into the Pentagon's defense programs, it should not be difficult to find out things about competitors' bids. After careful consideration, Hank crossed that one off the list also. He thought, "The more you think about this competitive intelligence stuff, the more it tempts you to cross the line."

18. Perhaps this would be best handled by a professional information broker. He could simply look at (www.burwellinc.com) to get a copy of the *Burwell World Directory of Information Brokers.*

Hank decided to consider later which tactics to pursue. At first it seemed exciting, but after creating the list, he felt a little tired and somewhat dirty. All in all, there were other parts of marketing that Hank liked a lot better than gathering competitive intelligence.

## Assignment

Define the ethical issues for all methods mentioned. Create a policy memo from Hank concerning warnings about protecting the company's confidential information from competitors' ethical and unethical (specific) competitive intelligence-gathering efforts. In the memo, provide a checklist for department heads.

---

**Case 2-2**

# Diameter Products Corporation: *Is Diversity An Ethical Issue?*

Nate Christian, newly hired sales representative, was excited to be attending his first national sales meeting with the Diameter Products Corporation. Nate was proud to be hired, since he knew that DPC had the most rigorous test program in the industry. In the interviewing process, he had spent three days just on written tests, and that was followed by several levels of interviews on location across several weeks. No one else from his school had made it even halfway through the process.

While listening to the uplifting, energetic presentations from the top marketing staff, Nate was really starting to feel that he was part of something special. Nate listened as the corporate vice president used a stirring multimedia presentation to show that the sales force was the best, and that many people depended on them to continue being the best. The energy in the room was strong and getting stronger. The culture here was very powerful.

Nate had been wondering about the source of the strong team feelings and how everyone could all have such similar values and motivation. At one point Nate began looking around, and it struck him how much they were all alike. Indeed, the more he looked, the more alike they seemed. All male, 20 to 35 years old, no minorities, clearly they all dressed alike, and he bet that they even all talked alike.

While he knew that the company did not discriminate, he wondered if something in the testing was responsible. He also knew that sometimes people and systems discriminated unconsciously, and he began thinking how that could happen. He thought, "Maybe they unconsciously value certain schools or majors where the student body is more like them. Perhaps the recruiters are unconsciously presenting the company in a way that repels other types of people."

Nate may have been new, but he knew better than to bring up the question with anyone from the Human Resources Department. He would ask his district manager, who, as far as Nate could tell, knew everything about everything.

## Assignment

**Team One:** Pick a random sample of 10 companies from the list in Case 5-2. Using the Internet resources described in that case, collect a list of the senior management group (company officers) for each company (10K SEC filings and annual reports will have the information) (www.freeedgar.com). Alternatively, collect library hard copy annual reports from major companies involved in business marketing, and make a list of the senior management group (company officers) for each company. The objective is to measure diversity by collecting data on gender, age, ethnicity, etc. Use your own judgment on how best to infer gender, etc., from the names. Age is often listed in company literature as well as in SEC filings. Does this rough approximation of the actual diversity present in major company management teams suggest any further research? Why would it be a concern to Nate if he fit the profile the company apparently preferred? How does it impact a company's marketing strategy when all the decision-makers have the same perspectives? Will this be an issue you might consider in evaluating job offers? Present your results to the class.

**Team Two:** Same as above, but use a different sample of companies.

## References

1. Don A. Moore, "An Honest Account," *The Wall Street Journal*, (November 13, 2002): A24.
2. Paul Tiffany, "Fastow Pleads Not Guilty to 78 Enron Charges," *The Washington Post*, (November 11, 2002): E06.
3. Kurt Eichenwald, "Corporate Loans Used Personally, Report Discloses," *The New York Times*, (November 5, 2002): C1.
4. Dow Jones Newswires, "Ex-CEO of Aurora Gets Prison Term For Role in Fraud," *The Wall Street Journal*, (November 11, 2002): A9.
5. Paul Beckett, "National Century Files Chapter 11," *The Wall Street Journal*, (November 19, 2002): C5.
6. Mike Robinson, Associated Press writer, "FDIC Sues Ernst & Young Over Bank Failure," *The Washington Post*, (November 11, 2002): E05.
7. Stephen Presser, "The Arthur Anderson Verdict," *Northwestern University Newsfeed,* (April 21, 2003): 1.
8. Kenneth E. Goodpaster and John B. Matthews, Jr., "Can a Corporation Have a Conscience?" *Harvard Business Review* (January–February 1982): 132–41.
9. G. R. Weaver, L. K. Trevino, and P. L. Cochran, "Corporate Ethics Practices in the Mid-1990's: An Empirical Study of the Fortune 1000," *Journal of Business Ethics* 18 (1999): 283–294.

10. Jacqueline N. Hood and Jeanne M. Logsdon, "Business Ethics in the NAFTA Countries: A Cross-Cultural Comparison," *Journal of Business Research* 55 (November, 2002): 883–90.

11. Kumar C. Rallapalli, Scott J. Vitell, and James H. Barnes, "The Influence of Norms on Ethical Judgments and Intentions: An Empirical Study of Marketing Professionals," *Journal of Business Research* 43 (November 1998): 157–68.

12. Timothy D. Schellhardt, "What Bosses Think About Corporate Ethics" *The Wall Street Journal* (April 6, 1988): 27.

13. Kenneth D. Campbell, "Malden Mills Owner Applies Religious Ethics to Business," *MIT Tech Talk* 41, no. 27, MIT News Office, Massachusetts Institute of Technology, Cambridge, Mass, (April 16, 1997): 7

14. Erin Strout, "To Tell The Truth," *Sales & Marketing Management* (July 2002): 40–47.

15. Clare Ansberry, "For These M.B.A.s, Class Became Exercise in Corporate Espionage," *The Wall Street Journal* (March 22, 1998): 37.

16. Russell Mokhiber and Robert Weissman, "The Corporate Century," *The MOJO Wire,* (November 18, 2002): 6.

17. Information and examples furnished by the Office of the Attorney General of the State of New York, The Capitol, Albany, New York 12224. November 18, 2002. Also, the Office of the Attorney General, Antitrust Division, 900 Fourth Avenue, Suite 2000, Seattle, WA 98164-1012. November 18, 2002.

18. Erin Strout, "To Tell The Truth," *Sales & Marketing Management,* (July 2002): 40–47.

19. Anne M. Phaneuf, "Is It Really Better to Give?" *Sales & Marketing Management* (September 1995): 95–101.

20. Geoffrey Brewer, "Making a Federal Case Out of Topless-Bar Entertaining," *Sales & Marketing Management* (September 1995): 17.

21. "Chemical Bank Programs in Business Ethics and Corporate Responsibility," Ethics Resource Center, Inc., in *Corporate Ethics: A Prime Business Asset,* the Business Roundtable (February 1998): 31–40.

22. Betsy Cummings, "Living Large on the Company's Dime," *Sales & Marketing Management* (July 2002): 13.

## CHAPTER THREE

# Professional Selling and Sales Management

## Learning Objectives

After reading this chapter, you should be able to:

- Understand the difference between business selling and selling to consumers.
- Appreciate the nature of the business salesperson's daily activities.
- Understand the cost of professional selling.
- Understand buyer needs and how to uncover them.
- Understand the professional selling process including preliminary, face-to-face, and follow-up activities.
- Be aware of current trends in professional selling.
- Grasp the important functions required in sales management.
- Explain the common forms of sales force organization.
- Understand the critical roles of recruitment, selection, and training of a business sales force.
- Realize the importance of effective direction and motivation of the business sales force.
- Appreciate the role of continuous monitoring and evaluation of sales performance.

## Chapter Outline

How Professional Business Selling Differs from Selling to Consumers
Profile of a Professional Salesperson
The Cost of Professional Selling
Understanding Buyer Behavior: A Seller's Perspective
The Professional Selling Process
Contemporary Trends in Business Selling
Sales Management
Planning the Sales Organization
Staffing a Business Sales Force
Training a Business Sales Force
Directing and Motivating a Sales Force
Analyzing and Evaluating a Sales Force

## How Professional Business Selling Differs from Selling to Consumers

**Personal selling** involves persuasive, deliberate contact between a buyer and a seller for the specific purpose of creating an exchange between them. In consumer marketing, personal selling is used to complement other elements in the promotional mix, which also includes advertising, publicity, public relations, and sales promotion. In business marketing, on the other hand, **professional selling generally is the primary means of selling business goods and services.** The other elements of the promotional mix frequently are employed to support or augment the persuasive nature of the personal selling function.

To gain and maintain a competitive edge, industrial or business-to-business salespeople must focus on serving their customers' needs. To meet these needs, salespeople must have knowledge extending beyond product specifics to aspects of the customer's business that add, or potentially add, value. In turn, business buyers typically view business salespeople not only as experts from whom they can seek information and advice about product applications, purchasing, and inventory, but also as partners in the process of business.

Many students of professional selling are turned off by the myth that good salespeople have to be aggressive and adversarial. Exhibit 3-1 clarifies the difference in mind-set and skills required in professional business selling versus those found in one-time market transactions and/or the functional relationships often evident in consumer selling. Worst-case examples of such one-time market transactions and functional relationships (where market exchanges are usually win-lose relationships) are found in movies like *Used Cars* (which depicts high-pressure used car sales) and *Tin Men* (which depicts manipulative door-to-door aluminum home siding sales) which have reinforced the public's negative perception of selling.

## Profile of a Professional Salesperson

The professionalization of the business sales force has come about as greater numbers of college-educated individuals (often with technical or business backgrounds) have moved into sales, as training programs have expanded (both sales and product or technical training), as training technology has improved, and in response to the increasing professionalization of the purchasing function (see Chapter 4). With technologies such as the Internet, Intranets, Extranets, and databases becoming as important as the telephone in most offices today, there is a tremendous amount of information for marketers to process. "It's amazing how our jobs have changed," says Karyn Erickson, senior market research analyst for Hiram Walker, a distributor of wine and spirits based in Southfield, Michigan. "I sit in my office with more data than I could ever deal with and the sales force expects reports quicker than they've ever wanted them."[1]

**EXHIBIT 3-1**
**Differences in Consumer "Hard Sell" Versus Business Goods and Services Sales**

| Traditional "Hard Sell" Still Used in Some Personal Selling to Consumers | Modern Professional Selling to Businesses (Relationship Marketing) |
|---|---|
| Selling requires a "killer instinct." | Selling requires a problem-solving instinct. |
| Selling involves a one-sided "pitch." | Selling involves two-way communication. |
| Selling is adversarial, with a winner. | Selling involves win-win for both sides. |
| Selling is based on manipulation. | Selling is based on listening, sensitivity, and follow-through. |
| Salespeople are on their own. | Salespeople are part of a customer value creation team. |
| Salespeople are employees. | Salespeople are professionals. |
| The most important thing is getting the sale. | The most important thing is customer satisfaction (which is the basis for future sales). |

Sales professionals have made a strong effort to improve their image. They have become more sensitive to their buyers' needs and have developed more honest relationships with their customers. For most business sellers, success involves several factors, including looking at marketing and selling as an integrated process. The following tips covering various aspects of the marketing process can help salespeople improve their sales skills:

- Understand how customers run their businesses.
- Show how the good or service fits into the customer's business (i.e., specifically show the benefit, and, wherever possible, the quantitative added value the good or service provides).
- Segment the business market in order to tailor the marketing mix to each group of customers.
- Be certain the benefits being emphasized remain clear, current, and important to the customer.
- Find ways to value-price to suit each segment.
- Understand the policies and procedures involved in customer buying, and fit the promotional strategy to them.
- Talk with everyone (if possible) who has a role in the buying process.
- Communicate to each member of the buying center the message that will address that person's chief concerns.
- Be sure all actions and communications are consistent with the predetermined level of quality, service, price, and performance required.
- Understand the competition's strengths and weaknesses.

How do salespeople spend a workday? Of course it depends on what their job requires. Selling jobs have been classified several ways. In the classic article by H. Robert Dodge, one way to classify sales jobs is to subdivide them into those that are *development*-oriented, *missionary*-oriented, *maintenance*-oriented, and *support*-oriented.[2] Exhibit 3-2 arranges these tasks in a continuum from service selling to creative selling, with examples of the type of sales tasks that might be associated with each. *Sales development,* also known as *order-getting,* refers to the creation of customers through methods such as motivating customers to change suppliers. According to the exhibit, development requires the highest level of creativity. *Missionary salespeople* provide necessary professional selling assistance but do not intend to sell anything. They may simply provide information or may work to instill goodwill with buyers and/or influencers in the decision-making process. *Maintenance selling* involves the continuation of present sales volume from existing customers. Examples in the exhibit include the driver salesperson that continues to supply products as needed for the buyer. *Support sales* involve the least amount of creativity in selling but provide continuing service to the buyer. They may, occasionally, engage in direct sales by suggesting a replacement item rather than the repair of an older product. All of these tasks are important, and each makes a significant contribution to the total marketing effort, however the bulk of the information in this chapter is concerned with sales development and, to a lesser extent, missionary sales.

The day of a business salesperson involved in sales development generally averages over nine and one-half hours. Less than 30 percent of that time is spent in actual face-to-face selling, while approximately one-third is spent in travel and in waiting for interviews. These statistics paint a picture of a busy professional who must make every minute count when engaged in face-to-face selling with a buyer.

The business salespersons' need for techniques for coping with stressful aspects of their jobs says much about the nature of their work. Indeed, the business salesperson faces more

**EXHIBIT 3-2** **Continuum of Business Sales Tasks**

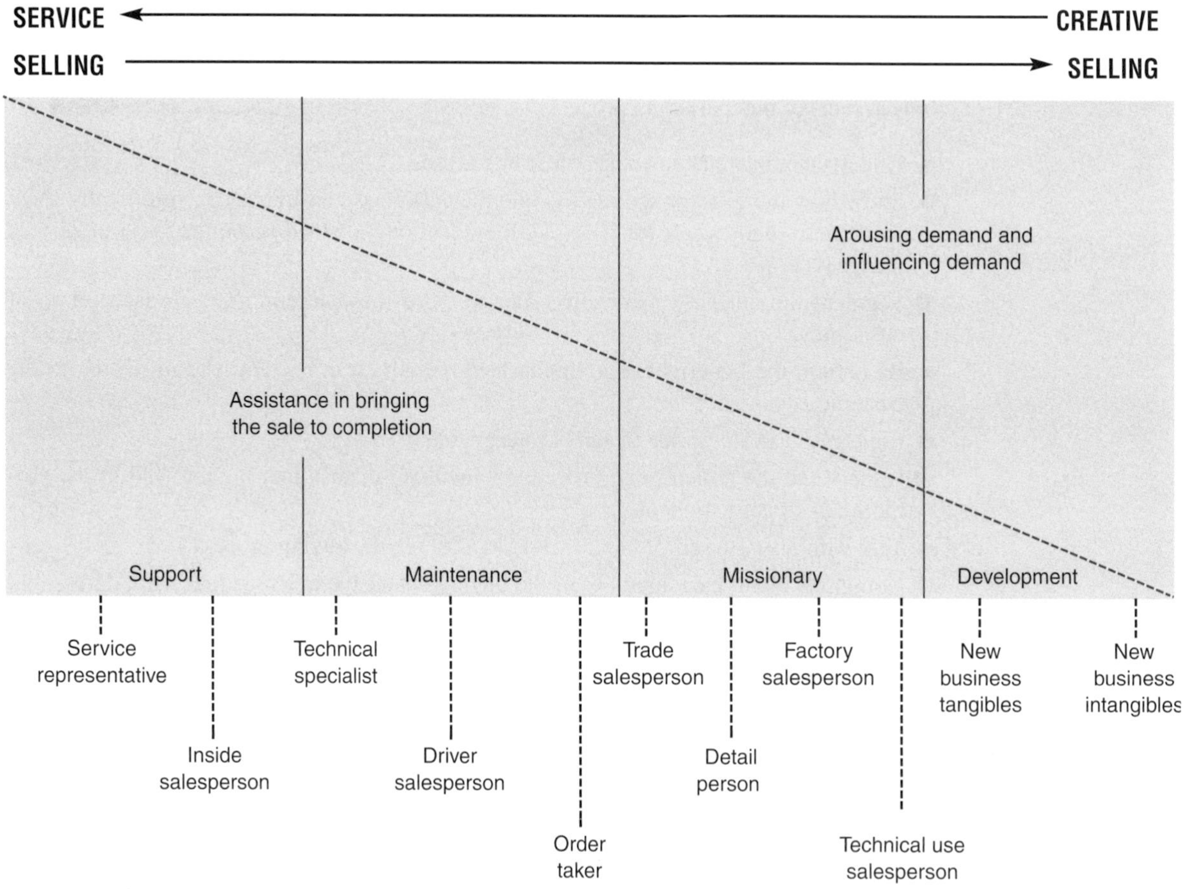

SERVICE ← ─────────────────────────────────────────────────── CREATIVE

SELLING ─────────────────────────────────────────────────── → SELLING

Arousing demand and
influencing demand

Assistance in bringing
the sale to completion

| Support | Maintenance | Missionary | Development |
|---|---|---|---|

Service
representative

Technical
specialist

Trade
salesperson

Factory
salesperson

New
business
tangibles

New
business
intangibles

Inside
salesperson

Driver
salesperson

Detail
person

Order
taker

Technical use
salesperson

intense competition and a more well-informed and sophisticated buyer than ever before. Salespeople work in emotionally charged environments in which disappointment and frustration alternate with excitement and elation. Successful salespeople generally have an optimistic "can do" attitude and are energized when challenged to solve a problem.

The salesperson performs many types of activities, including *selling, servicing customers, time management,* and *communication.* These activities are examined below.

## Selling

Selling involves prospecting for new accounts and making presentations to new prospects and existing customers. In short, the business salesperson describes the product and offers reasons to buy it. Additionally, the salesperson frequently is called upon to provide consulting services. For example, salespeople often are asked to demonstrate how their products mesh with the product design and operational aspects of the customer's firm, as the products being sold will either become part of the customer's products or be used in producing them.

## Servicing Customers

Salespeople also have to engage in after-sale activities such as following-up with customers, contacting and working with other company employees to ensure that deliveries are made, equipment is properly installed, and customers are trained in how to use the equipment. They must also maintain cooperative relationships with various members of the distribution channels with whom they are involved or face the consequences of channel conflict. Finally, salespeople need to ensure that any customer questions or complaints are handled quickly and professionally.

## Time Management

Salespeople learn to be efficient and effective in their time management. They must plan the scheduling and routing of sales calls, the frequency of contact with established accounts, and the proper amount of time to allocate to prospecting for new accounts. They also must allocate time for servicing customers, assisting the sales manager in budgeting and sales forecasting and completing required paperwork. In addition, time management involves analysis of sales potential within the total sales territory. A company does not enjoy the same rate of net profit on every sale. In most firms, a large proportion of the orders, customers, territories, or products account for only a small share of the profits. This relationship between selling units and profits has been referred to as the 80/20 axiom, in that 80 percent of a firm's profits are accounted for by 20 percent of its selling units. When this axiom is applicable, salespeople should devote the lion's share of their time to the most profitable 20 percent of the selling units.

## Communication

Salespeople must communicate as a part of their job. They must, of course, communicate with their established and potential customers and members of the distribution channel. They also must communicate with their sales managers about sales potential within the total sales territory, provide information about their sales expenses, calls made, competitive activities, general business conditions, and the like. Research indicates that salespeople typically spend more than 70 percent of their working hours in communication.

## The Cost of Professional Selling

The cost of professional selling can vary significantly, depending on the type of product and industry, the size of the firm, and the degree of personal contact with the customer necessary to close a sale. Overall, though, the cost of a typical business sales call is about $350. U.S. firms spend over $140 billion annually on professional selling.[3] The approximate $350 cost to a firm of a business sales call applies regardless of whether a sale is made. And that is not the whole story. Only about 6 percent of business sales are made following one sales call, 9 percent following a second call, and 33.5 percent following a third call. Overall, an average of 4.3 calls are needed to close a business sale. Thus, the average cost per sale ranges from a low of $350 to more than $1505. It is apparent that professional selling carries a high cost to the firm.

The cost of professional selling has risen substantially over the past decade and likely will continue to grow. Given this, business-to-business companies must constantly monitor and assess the methods they use to distribute and sell their products.

---

**Concept Review**

1. What major types of activities do salespeople perform?

2. Why is the 80/20 axiom important to salespeople?

3. What factors contribute to the cost of closing a business sale?

## BUSINESS MARKETING IN ACTION

### CORPORATE WEB PAGES AS INTERNET SUPPORT TO FIELD SALES

**Action Assignment**

Your team is the marketing manager of Premix, Inc. Complete the assignment detailed in the memo below from the vice president and present the result to the class.

The websites can be found at the following addresses:

Premix Inc.
www.premix.com

Andover Plastics
www.andoverplastics.com

Media Genesis
www.mediag.com

For additional information, see: *Automotive Engineering International,* "Internet Marketing Strategies Demonstrated," February 1999, p. 76.

---

722 West Chase Avenue
North Kingsville, Ohio 45044
(513) 555-1234 Phone
(513) 555-1235 Fax

**Premix, Inc.**

# Memo

**To:**      Izabella Gorecki, Marketing Manager

**From:**   Jerry Galazka, VP Sales

**Date:**   1/7/00

**Re:**      Web Site

---

Several of our salespeople have reported that their key accounts have commented on the high quality and usefulness of our competitor's (Andover Plastics) new website. Through research, we discovered the company that developed the competitor's website. The company is Media Genesis, which develops interactive solutions for the Internet.

I feel strongly that our customers develop an image of our corporation based on all of our sales support materials (including our Web pages). Our Web pages have been considered the most impressive in our industry, and I believe that they still are. To be sure, however, I would like you to look into Media Genesis' capabilities and compare our website to that of Andover Plastics. Also compare our site to any other major competitors listed in the *Thomas Register*. If you would recommend changing the Premix website, prepare a detailed recommendation (with storyboard sequential sketches of your proposal).

## Understanding Buyer Behavior: A Seller's Perspective

Business buyers use a decision-making process very similar to that used by final consumers. Both are interested in products that provide benefits. Benefit selling appeals to the buyers' professional and personal motives by answering the questions, What's in it for my company? and What's in it for me?

Benefit selling is facilitated by the use of benefit segmentation, which divides the total business target market into groups according to the particular utilities or benefits expected from a specific product. For example, in the case of an industrial janitorial service, one group of companies may look for dependability and reliability, while another may require specific cleaning procedures. The business marketer who uses benefit selling to reach prospective customers demonstrates an understanding and a willingness to meet the buying needs and objectives of those prospects. Generally speaking, business buyers value quality and dependability over price. After all, a good price is of little value if costs are driven up by poor quality or late delivery. In most technical markets, certainly, extremely high quality and dependability are a fundamental requirement for all suppliers.

### Understanding Buyer Needs

Specific buying needs include satisfying the requirements of internal user departments, increasing profits, increasing sales, producing a quality product, and improving the operation's efficiency to create cost reductions (value analysis). Buying motives, or reasons to buy, include service, time payments, trade-in allowances, efficient delivery, and low price. If salespeople are to be successful, they must determine each prospect's unique and important buying needs and motives. That is, they must understand the information business buyers use in making a purchase decision. The principal way for a seller to influence a purchase decision is to provide pertinent information to the decision makers.[4]

Buyer needs can be broadly classified into needs that are more and less important. A salesperson's task upon meeting the buyer is to distinguish between the two and emphasize product benefits that meet the important needs of the buyer. If, for example, the buyer says that price is important but the salesperson determines that the firm can afford the product and that the firm also is primarily interested in quality, then the salesperson must emphasize the quality of the product.

### Methods Used to Uncover Important Buyer Needs

It is easy enough to say that a salesperson must differentiate between more important and less important needs, but how does one do that? There are several methods:

- *Ask questions.* Questions often can bring out needs that the prospect would not reveal or does not know exist. However, this method must be used moderately: salespeople should not play "20 questions" with their prospects.
- *Observe.* Look at the prospects and study their surroundings. Experienced salespeople can determine a great deal about people by observing them. Successful salespeople also are particularly sensitive to customer expressions and body language.
- *Listen.* Salespeople must remember that telling is *not* selling. The average person speaks at 125 to 150 words per minute, but the average person thinks at 500 to 600 words per minute. When a salesperson is talking, a prospect can listen and think of several other things simultaneously. The more a salesperson talks, the more time the prospect has to think of objections, criticisms, doubts, fears, and so forth. However, the instant a salesperson asks a question and waits quietly for an answer, the prospect's entire attention is focused on the salesperson. Thus, a basic rule of selling is never to say something if you can ask it.

- *Talk to others.* Ask others about a prospect's needs. For example, ask an office manager's secretary about the manager's level of satisfaction with a personal computer.
- *Combination.* A skillful salesperson may talk to others, listen to a prospect, probe with questions, and make careful observations—all in an effort to uncover the prospect's needs.

Once salespeople ascertain a prospect's major buying need(s), they can then relate the customer's needs to product benefits. Business salespeople can effectively sell to the business buyer only after they have determined the prospect's buying needs and motivations and have identified the problems the buyer is attempting to solve by purchasing a particular product.

Rarely is it easy for salespeople to learn a customer's needs and to demonstrate how their product directly meets those needs. Business buyers and other members of the buying center typically have a multitude of needs, including some not clearly understood or even recognized. The salesperson's challenge is to "read" the behavior of a prospective buyer and convert that customer's apparently unconscious needs into needs he or she recognizes and understands. Exhibit 3-3 lists several behavioral styles that prospective buyers typically exhibit when interacting with business salespeople.

A beneficial exchange relationship results when the salesperson uses adaptive selling techniques (*adaptive selling*) and tailors selling strategy to a buyer's behavioral style.

## The Professional Selling Process

To get a real sense of the *professional selling process* in business markets, one must simplify the description and focus on the important elements. From the perspective of the business salesperson, a sequential listing of the fundamental steps in professional selling can be organized into three categories of activities: *preliminary, face-to-face,* and *follow-up.* Of course, in different business selling situations each firm would have its own set of steps, but these three categories reflect the fundamental steps in the professional selling process. So, for our purposes, the term "buyer" refers to a business customer or prospective customer.

### Preliminary Activities

*Preliminary or presale activities* arm the business salesperson with the tools necessary to close a sale effectively, as well as with the ability to create the type of sales situation most favorable to meeting actual buyer needs and wants. The most successful professional salespeople plan their sales calls. Planning serves to focus thinking and prepare the salesperson

**EXHIBIT 3-3**
**Uncovering the Behavioral Styles of Buyers**

---

What behavioral styles do buyers exhibit when interacting with salespeople? Buyers can be classified into the following categories:

- The *hard bargainer* obtains several price quotations or uses several sources of supply for the same item; salespeople may find it difficult to make a sale.
- The *sales job facilitator* is amenable to a salesperson's solicitations and even attempts to make the transaction go smoother.
- The *straight shooter* behaves with integrity and propriety; this buyer rarely uses his or her buying power to obtain concessions.
- The *socializer* enjoys the personal interaction of the buyer-seller relationship.
- The *persuader* will attempt to market his or her own company to a salesperson to stimulate a favorable impression of the buying firm.
- The *considerate buyer* displays compassion and concern for the salesperson; this buyer may be willing to accept substitute products.

for what is expected to be relevant. Although planning can necessitate extensive research, the following is typical:

- Set *objectives* for the sales call.
- Prepare an attention-getting *opener* that demonstrates value for the buyer.
- Choose and prepare an *appropriate sales presentation* approach for the buyer.
- List expected buyer *objections* and prepare to handle them.
- Plan how to *close* on the objective of the sales call.

### Setting Objectives

When it comes to setting objectives for a sales call, the first task is to review buyer accounts to ascertain which buyers should be serviced next, as well as which buyer could be placing larger orders or procuring additional product items and lines of the seller's firm. Many firms keep "Major (Potential) Account Data Files (MADF)," computer files that contain all-important information about an account. Among examples of information that should be in an account file are current new releases, information gleaned from previous contacts with the account, identification of important contacts within the account firm, buyer needs, wants, financial information, and the like. Such files should be available to anyone in the company that needs the information such as salespeople who call on the account. Business salespeople must try to regularly monitor and update their profile on each account. At the same time, salespeople should make sure they are thoroughly familiar with their own respective product mixes as well as with competitors' product offerings. With all of this information, the salesperson would then be ready to set objectives for a sales call with a particular buyer. Since business selling usually requires a series of relationship-building buyer visits, objectives will range from "selling x units of Product A" to simply securing a second meeting with important members of the buying center for this decision. Usually salespeople plan a sales call to achieve more than one objective per sales call so objectives should be prioritized into primary and secondary call objectives. Call objectives, like any other sort of objectives, should be specific, measurable, reasonable, and include a time frame.

### Preparing the Opener

Once the objectives have been set, the salesperson next must make an appointment to make a sales call. The appointment is usually made over the telephone. When making an appointment, it is important to make the appointment with the right person at the right time and in the right place. Information that will help here may be found in the MADFs described earlier. If such information is not available, then it is up to the salesperson to use his/her skills and abilities to ascertain the information (i.e., through talking with other company salespeople who have previously called at the firm, observations, etc.).

### Choosing and Preparing the Sales Presentation

Several general approaches to the business sales presentation should be considered. Although there are many approaches, three sales presentation approach models often used are: (1) the formularized model (AIDA), (2) the buying-decisions model, and (3) the problem-solving model. Exhibit 3-4 reveals the processes used in the three models. Each furnishes an insight into the buying-selling process but from differing points of view. Which approach is the right approach in any given situation depends on the situation and the buyer. It's important to keep in mind that successful salespeople tend to practice adaptive selling. Adaptive selling refers to using different sales presentations for each buyer and changing a sales presentation during a sales call if it seems warranted. Part of adaptive selling, therefore, may involve choosing different selling models for different buyers.

**EXHIBIT 3–4** **Three Approaches to the Buying-Selling Process**

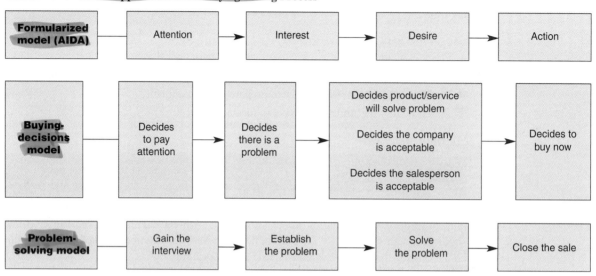

**Formularized Model (AIDA)** AIDA is an acronym for *attention, interest, desire,* and *action.* In the **formularized model (AIDA)**, often referred to as the persuasive selling presentation, the salesperson takes the buyer through the first three stages in order to evoke an action (purchase). However, an inherent danger in this type of sales presentation is that it is very difficult for a salesperson to know where the buyer is in terms of the stages; whether the buyer is only interested in a product or has moved to desire for it. Salespeople can learn to be sensitive to buyer expressions and body language and from those predict where the buyer is in AIDA, but there is no foolproof way to know. The AIDA model is akin to the old-fashioned "canned presentation" but seems to be well suited for use by a relatively new salesperson who is inexperienced at recognizing buying motives of individual buyers. Preparation for the formularized model (AIDA) involves putting together a somewhat structured, general outline for making the presentation based on what has been learned about the buyer. After a very brief rapport-building opener, perhaps referring to the weather or sports, the salesperson likely would plan an attention-getting opener that demonstrates value for the buyer. The opener may be (1) a statement, such as "Ms. Bowen, I want to talk with you today about our newest bonding substance, which can reduce your costs by 20 percent," (2) a demonstration wherein, for example, the salesperson may repeat the lines from an ad for a bonding product and then show the buyer how strong the product is by having the buyer examine a cup where a broken handle has been bonded with the product, or (3) a question, such as "Would you be interested in a bonding product that reduces your costs by 20 percent." Following the opener would be a discussion of features, advantages, and benefits of the product. Then, the salesperson would plan to involve the buyer by stimulating questions through trial closes. The salesperson would anticipate objections, plan how to handle them and plan a final close.

**Buying-Decisions Model** The **buying-decisions model**, a form of "outlined presentation," assumes that buyers make a series of smaller, individual decisions before making a final decision either to accept or reject a product. Therefore, after an attention-getting opener, the salesperson will tailor the presentation to achieve a number of smaller decisions aimed at an ultimate decision to purchase the product in question. For instance, a photo-copier salesperson might lead an office manager toward the final decision of investing in a new copying machine by having the manager decide such issues as the size of copier that is needed, the features the copier must have, the usage the copier is likely to receive, the degree of copy clarity that is necessary, and so on. Through application of this model, buyer needs are revealed, such as what size of copier is needed, what features are important, and so on. Once the buyer reveals his/her needs via answers to the various questions, it is much easier for the salesperson to promote the features and benefits of the product in such a way as will lead the potential buyer to a positive purchasing decision. As with the formulized model, however, a possible weakness in the buying-decision model is that, at any given moment, it is very difficult for a salesperson to know if the buyer is ready to make a positive purchase decision. However, this model can be very effective if it is well organized and is flexible.

*Problem-Solving Model*   The problem-solving model centers on the specific needs, motives, and objectives of the buyer and requires that there be mutual trust and respect between the salesperson and the prospective buyer. Given this foundation, the problem-solving model functions like the need-satisfaction theory of personal selling. The salesperson must skillfully integrate product knowledge into the solution to the buyer's problem so as to exert *expert power* (the degree of perceived knowledge, information, and skill possessed by the power holder) over the prospect. Expert power exists when the power vested in a person by qualification or experience is acknowledged. Expert power of the salesperson has been found to be a stronger determinant of perceived trust by the buyer than *referent power* (the degree of perceived attraction between the salesperson and the buyer). A salesperson who holds expert power is much more likely to close a sale because the buyer generally feels more comfortable in accepting the judgment of the salesperson that the product will solve the buyer's purchasing need or problem. In this case, "what you know" seems to be, for once, more important than "who you know." The problem-solving model is particularly useful when the situation calls for *creative selling* (arousing and influencing demand for a product). Preparing for a sales presentation based on the problem-solving model, then, requires salespeople to carefully assess needs and wants of buyers and their companies and then developing a presentation that will uncover those needs and wants and that matches the benefits of the salesperson's product to the buyer's needs and wants. Salespeople may use the SPIN method (ask questions about the general **S**ituation and **P**roblems of the buyer as they concern their current product followed by questions about the **I**mplication of problems that are uncovered and **N**eed-payoff questions where buyers are asked if they have explicit needs). Another way to prepare for this sort of presentation is to think of it as progressing through need-development, need awareness, and need-fulfillment phases and determine how to proceed through the phases. During need-development, the salesperson should work to uncover buyer needs, restate those needs during need-awareness, and show how the product would meet those needs during need-fulfillment.

### List Possible Objections

As part of the sales presentation preparation process, salespeople should prepare a list of expected buyer *objections* and ways to handle them. Although technically a part of sales presentation preparation, anticipating possible objections is so important that it is addressed here separately. During a sales presentation buyers may object for many different reasons. Objections may be related to buyer's needs, to the product itself, to the salesperson, to the price, and to time. Also, buyers may object to some aspect of the presentation such as the opener or a closing technique. It would be impossible for anyone to anticipate every possible objection during a sales presentation, but there are some objections that are more likely than others for any given product. Salespeople may be able to locate such objections from the Major Account Data Files discussed earlier, if those files are complete, or they may be able to logically predict possible objections.

Salespeople should also prepare ways to handle objections. First and foremost, salespeople should plan to remain positive in the face of objections and to listen to the entire objection. Following that, salespeople should evaluate objections and handle them appropriately, not over- or under-reacting to the concern. There are several effective response methods salespeople can use to handle objections (e.g., anticipate the objection, dodge the objection, directly deny the objection, indirectly deny the objection, compensate for the objection, use the feel-felt-found method, boomerang the objection, rephrase the objection, pass-up the objection and postpone the objection). Before applying any response method, salespeople should begin handling each objection by asking questions to clarify the objection. Once salespeople are content that the real objection has been stated, then they can plan to use one or another of the possible response methods to handle that objection.

### Plan the Closing

Finally, salespeople have to plan how to *close* on the objective of the sales call. If the presentation has been well planned and objections have been anticipated and ways to handle them planned, then the close should be relatively easy. The purpose of any close is to ask the prospect for a formal commitment to purchase (or agree to the objective of the sales call, which could be a trial order or other step in the process of building the relationship and gaining the trust to finally win the purchase commitment). Since business buyers are trained professionals, and would quickly spot a tricky close, most business closes are quite direct. Hence, salespeople should simply plan on some sort of nonmanipulative and honest way to close a sales call. Still, if used properly, any number of closing techniques may be used in an effort to finalize the sale, including a restatement or summary of product benefits, repeating successful responses to buyers' objections, closing on minor points and better arranging the terms of sale to suit the needs of the buyer.

## Face-to-Face Activities

Although presale planning and buyer follow-up activities are important, the real moment of truth occurs when the salesperson is face-to-face with the buyer.[5] *Face-to-face activities* consist of three primary stages: introduction, presentation, and closing.

The *introduction stage* attempts to capture the attention of the buyer; to create a positive selling atmosphere; and to build a comfortable professional, and perhaps personal, rapport with the buyer. Additionally the salesperson must ask appropriate questions to glean information about the buyer's specific needs and wants in order to "set the stage" for the upcoming sales presentation.

The *presentation stage* focuses on the business of selling. The salesperson tries to present the product in the most favorable light. Alert salespeople constantly study their buyers, looking for verbal and nonverbal cues as to how the presentation is progressing and how the buyers are receiving the information. Salespeople should also engage in signal detection in order to potentially enhance their face-to-face selling effectiveness. Yawns, frequent checking of watches, frowns, wrinkled foreheads, or raised eyebrows may be indicators that the buyer is bored, confused, or uninterested in some aspect of the presentation and should never go unnoticed or ignored. One may think of these cues as nonverbal objections that need to be handled.

Inevitably, the buyer will raise one or more verbal objections during the sales presentation. As already discussed, these are normal. Objections can indicate that the product features, advantages, and/or benefits outlined by the salesperson might be unclear to, or even disbelieved by, the buyer. Exhibit 3-5 outlines a four-step method by which the business salesperson can handle sales objections (resistance). These four steps include establishing readiness, clarifying the objection, mentally formulating the order, and using questioning to have the prospect answer the objection.

**EXHIBIT 3-5** **The Four-Step Method of Handling Sales Resistance**

### Step 1—Establishing Readiness

| | |
|---|---|
| *Prospect* | That price is far too high. |
| *Salesperson* | Everything seems to cost more today, doesn't it? |
| *Prospect* | You're sure right about that. |
| *Salesperson* | Your firm expects you to make profitable purchases? |
| *Prospect* | Yes, I do my best. |
| *Salesperson* | This means you have to analyze carefully the full value in any proposition, doesn't it? |
| *Prospect* | Yes, but I still say that your price is out of line. |

### Step 2—Clarifying the Objection

| | |
|---|---|
| *Salesperson* | Might I ask what you consider a fair price based on your value analysis? |
| *Prospect* | Well, I don't have exact figures, but I'd say about 30 cents less a unit. |
| *Salesperson* | What unit value would you place on our guarantee of uniform quality from batch to batch? |
| *Prospect* | I don't know, but that doesn't amount to much. We test a sample out of each delivery ourselves. |
| *Salesperson* | That sounds like a good precaution if you are not certain of quality. What does that cost? |
| *Prospect* | I'd say about 5 cents prorated over the normal order. |
| *Salesperson* | From a cost standpoint, what is your optimum order quantity? |
| *Prospect* | About 1,000 units. |
| *Salesperson* | Would it increase your unit cost to order 4,000 at a time? |
| *Prospect* | There would be more dollars tied up in inventory. |

### Step 3—Mentally Formulating the Order

| | |
|---|---|
| *Salesperson* | (Our price breaks 30 cents a unit at 4,000 quantity. The buyer's estimate of testing cost is 5 cents. I can meet the price if I can get an order for 4,000 with delivery in modules of 1,000 as needed.) |

### Step 4—Questioning to Have the Prospect Answer the Objection

| | |
|---|---|
| *Salesperson* | If you could eliminate the testing of incoming purchases, it would save you at least 5 cents a unit, wouldn't it? |
| *Prospect* | That is right, but we would need to be certain of quality if we did. |
| *Salesperson* | Would a guarantee covering replacement of goods plus any and all costs or damages through faulty quality be attractive? |
| *Prospect* | Yes. |
| *Salesperson* | Would you place an order if you could save 5 cents under your own unit value estimate? |
| *Prospect* | I sure would. |
| *Salesperson* | By ordering 4,000 units, you gain the advantage of our volume price, which is 30 cents less per unit than when purchases are in smaller quantities. We will guarantee quality as I have outlined above so you can save the 5-cent unit cost of testing. |

During the entire sales presentation, and particularly during the time that objections to selling points are being raised, the salesperson must work diligently to get the buyer actively involved in the presentation and genuinely interested in learning more about the product the salesperson is attempting to sell.

Some methods the salesperson can use to involve and interest buyers include:

- Stopping the presentation for a moment to inquire whether buyers have understood a particular product feature and the resulting benefit.
- Probing for likes and dislikes and for general customer preferences regarding the product being sold.
- Giving buyers an opportunity to handle the product or to explain any questions or problems that they might be having with the selling points being offered by the salesperson.

The *closing stage* is the ultimate and most critical step in the face-to-face interaction and involves getting the buyer to make a commitment to your product at some level. Remember that a close may not result in an order for a product but, instead, may simply involve making a second appointment. It helps if the salesperson maintains a positive attitude and waits until the buyer is ready to make a commitment. Again the salesperson should engage in signal detection. Buyers that ask questions, lean forward, pull out a pen and purchase

**EXHIBIT 3-6** Closing Techniques Used in Business Selling

*Closing* is simply asking for an order. There are many ways to do this. The professional industrial salesperson knows several closing techniques and which to select, according to the specific prospect and selling situation. Some effective closing techniques are described below:

- *Alternate proposal close* This technique offers the prospect a choice: "Do you prefer a truck or rail shipment?" "Will the standard drill suit your needs, or would you prefer the superior model you have been examining?" The philosophy of this close is to ask for a relatively minor decision.
- *Assumptive close* With this technique, the salesperson assumes that the prospect will make a commitment. After receiving a positive buying signal and verifying this with a trial close, the salesperson proceeds to write up the order or complete a shipping form. Then he or she asks the prospect to "sign here, please, so I can process the shipment."
- *Gift close* The prospect has an added inducement for taking immediate action. "If you sign the purchase order today, I'm sure we can have the order delivered to you next week."
- *Action close* This technique suggests that the sales representative take an action that will consummate the sale. "Let me arrange an appointment with your attorney to work out the details of the transaction."
- *One-more-yes close* Based on the principle that saying yes can become a habit with this technique, the salesperson restates the benefits of the product in a series of questions that will result in positive responses. The final question asks the prospect to complete the sale.
- *Balance-sheet close* An effective technique to use with procrastinators, the salesperson and the prospect list the reasons for acting now on one side of a sheet of paper and the reasons for delaying action on the other. If the salesperson has built a persuasive case, the reasons for immediate action will outweigh the reasons for delay.
- *Direct close* This technique is clear and simple: the salesperson asks the prospect for a decision. Many salespeople feel this is the best closing approach, especially if there are strong positive buying signals. Frequently, the salesperson briefly summarizes major points made during the presentation prior to asking for the close.

order form, and the like may be signaling that they are ready to buy. Successful salespeople act on such signals and attempt to close the sales call.[6] Exhibit 3-6 describes some additional closing techniques commonly used in business selling. If the sales call is successfully closed then the salesperson is not finished. Details need to be reviewed, choices confirmed, and signatures obtained. The salesperson should remember to show appreciation and, if appropriate, set up future appointments to meet with the buyer and other members of the buying center. If the sales call is not successfully closed, then the salesperson should express appreciation to the buyer for the appointment and keep the interaction with the buyer positive.

## Follow-Up Activities

The business selling process does not end with the close. Earlier in this chapter we indicated that salespeople must attend to a wide variety of *follow-up activities* once the sale is complete. Following up after the sale is really customer service, and good customer service is a powerful sales tool. Moreover, the follow-up activity should be carefully planned.

A timed follow-up program may lead to large secondary orders. A truly successful sale requires that an order be completed and that all support arrangements (product design, order processing, credit approval, shipping, delivery, and the like) be completed in a timely manner. After the sale, if the selling company is actively following the tenets of the marketing concept, customer satisfaction with both the product sold and the entire selling process must be evaluated.

Salespeople should reflect upon the reasons their sales presentations resulted in an exchange or in failure. If salespeople are unable to close the sale, they should carefully and thoughtfully examine individual and collective factors that likely accounted for the no-sale situation. Exhibit 3-7 lists some common reasons for failure to close a sale. It is not unusual for salespeople to benefit from conducting this review with their sales or marketing manager. Selling, like a golf swing, is a highly personal activity and can benefit from an outside expert's suggestions and insights.

**EXHIBIT 3-7**
**Why Customers
Leave**

Source: Michaelson &
Associates

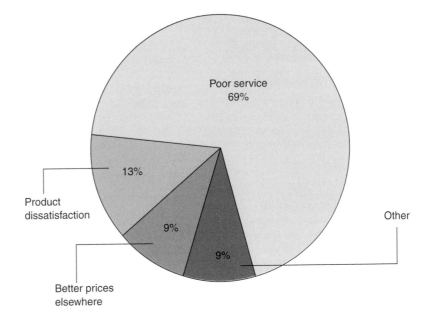

---

**Concept
Review**

1. What are the major differences between the formularized model (AIDA), the buying-decisions model, and the problem-solving model?

2. Why is it necessary to understand the three primary steps in the face-to-face sales activity?

3. What are some of the methods used to involve and interest prospects during the sales presentation?

## Contemporary Trends in Business Selling

### The Increase in Use of Customer Relationship Management and Data Mining

Among technologies that have been touted as especially helping businesses is **customer-relationship management** (CRM). CRM plans are a form of proactive customer service. They may be prepared by a firm itself or outsourced. Using CRM, a firm may segment customers according to products purchased or length of time as a customer. Salespeople may contact customers on a schedule suggested by the CRM program and, depending on the customer, simply check in, suggest a re-supply of a particular product, cross-promote a new product, or any of a host of possibilities depending on the information available to the CRM program software. CRM software is now widely available so even small businesses can take advantage of this important tool. Also, software is available so that some customers may be able to engage in "self care"—go online to ask and get answers to questions.

One can expect to see integration of CRM systems with other computer data software such that so-called "outbound marketing activity," which includes sales, is integrated into major accounts data files (MADF). That way everyone in the organization can access information that they need when they need it.

A technique that can be integrated with CRM and that has been used a great deal in business-to-consumer (B2C) companies is data mining. Data mining, also known as knowledge

# BUSINESS MARKETING IN ACTION

## SELLING AN INNOVATIVE AUTOMOTIVE BUMPER DESIGN

An innovative polyurethane bumper concept developed by Bayer will give pedestrians greater protection in an accident. Thanks to a combination of Bayflex® 180 and Bayfill® EA, injuries to pedestrians who are struck by a car can be significantly reduced.

Road safety is a topic that concerns not only car drivers, but also all road users. The automotive industry currently is discussing and testing new vehicle front ends to comply with a planned European Union regulation on pedestrian safety that aims to significantly reduce the injuries sustained when a person is struck by a car. Against this background, Bayer is working on an innovative concept in the form of bumpers made of polyurethane that will give pedestrians greater protection in an accident.

The bumpers designed by Bayer combine good dimensional stability with surface elasticity. This is achieved through a polyurethane skin just 1.5 mm thick made of fiber-reinforced Bayflex® 180, backed with energy-absorbing Bayfill® EA semirigid foam. The polyurethane flexible skin of the bumper is manufactured by the RRIM thin-wall technique developed by Bayer. The impact energy is absorbed by the polyurethane foam inside the bumper. The elasticity of the complete system keeps the impact on a pedestrian's lower leg to within the required limits. This novel combination of materials enables the elasticity and strength of the skin, the energy absorber, and the support to be adapted to the new requirements of pedestrian protection without impairing the inherent stability of the bumper module. It also prevents the slight damage to the bumper that often occurs in minor accidents.

Initial crash tests show that the new front end module already substantially complies with the EU pedestrian safety regulation planned for 2004. Apart from being safer, the new bumpers also are lighter than conventional ones, and thus contribute to further fuel savings.

http://www.bayer.com/bayer/ueberblick/arbeits gebiete/polymere/polyurethane/e_cont4.htm

### Action Assignment

**Team 1:** Using the sales call planning process, the objection handling, and closing techniques presented in this chapter, plan and execute a sales call as a representative of the Bayer polyurethane bumper. **Team 2:** You will be the buying center at BMW. Assign buying center roles as presented in this chapter and Chapter 4 and evaluate Team 1 as to evidence of their sales presentation being consistent with the chapter material. **Team 3:** You will be the sales representative for the company that makes the thermoplastic automotive bumpers discussed in the Business Marketing in Action box in Chapter 1. You will not be present when Team 1 calls on Team 2, but will make your own sales call, and be judged by the same criteria. After both presentations are complete, Team 2 (the buying center) will present its analysis. Then the class will judge the performance of each team, based on chapter material.

For additional information, see *Automotive Engineering,* January 1999, "Bumper Provides Greater Crash Protection," p. 135, and http://www.bayer.com

discovery in databases, has been defined as the nontrivial extraction of implicit, previously unknown, and potentially useful information from data. For example, a catalog company might keep track of the kinds of clothing items their consumers have purchased from them in the past. Data mining would be used to extract that information such that the company might be able to make suggestions about future purchases that would fit with previous ones. Data mining is not appropriate only for B2C firms but can help business-to-business (B2B) firms engage their customers as well. It can be used to perform customer-segmentation studies, learn about emerging sales-channel problems, and find unmet customer needs. Appropriate application of that information can be translated into increased sales and revenue.

## The Increasing Use of Handheld Devices and Other Communication Technology

Handheld technology such as the Palm, Handspring Visor and the BlackBerry will be a boon to salespeople. Not only are communication tools getting smaller and faster, they are also getting cheaper. A business salesperson might use a powerful handheld device to access a corporate database and then update information stored there using a mini-spreadsheet.

## STRATEGY AT WORK

**IN RELATIONSHIP MARKETING, SOMETIMES IT IS THE SMALL THINGS THAT COUNT**

Royal Packaging Industries Van Leer, NV (a Dutch company) is one of the world's leading producers of drum containers, with a 25 percent share of the world market (147 plants in 47 countries). As with many global companies, Van Leer found entry into the Japanese market particularly challenging. Still, their new Nippon–Van Leer Ltd. plant near the petrochemical and shipping center of Yokkaichi City has received substantial positive publicity. It was not Van Leer's unmatched quality, service, and environmental performance that attracted attention (all of which are expected), but their sensitivity toward relationship building. For example, following a courtesy call to Van Leer's Headquarters by Municipal Assembly representatives from the Japanese plant's new home, the company responded by having 5,000 Dutch tulip bulbs sent as a gift to the town's elementary and middle schools. As the bulbs grow and proliferate, they will symbolize the growth and beauty of the relationship between the town and the company. In international marketing, relationship building with clients (missionary selling actions) includes goodwill building in ways appropriate to the specific culture and country.

**Source:** "Tulips Blossom from Drums," *Focus Japan,* June 1999, pp. 12–13.

On those handheld tools, next generation instant messaging (IM) is likely to become more important for salespeople. Newer, more powerful IM programs allow files to be transmitted, conferences to be held, and even collaboration on documents over the Internet. A salesperson that is online might "see" a colleague is also online and be able to set up a conference or work session instantly, significantly reducing telephone or e-mail tag. In the near future, we may find standards in place that will allow different IM products to communicate with each other.

Other cutting-edge technology includes computers that can fit on a pane of glass, which can result in portable computers that are not much larger than their displays. Thus, we are likely to see even smaller handhelds, tablet PCs, and notebooks than are presently available.

### The Increasing Presence of Diversity in the Sales Force

Business sales were once considered to be exclusively the domain of the white male. In 1972, women comprised only 4.7 percent of the nonretail sales force. By 1989, the percentage of women in sales reached 20.4 percent; and by 2000 it had increased to about 40 percent. In a recent study, women were found to have a clear advantage over men in complex, business-to-business selling because women had an edge in five of nine sales competencies, namely, aligning customer/supplier strategic objectives, listening beyond product needs, orchestrating organizational resources, consultative problem solving, and engaging in self-appraisal and continuous learning.[7]

Minorities, including Hispanics, African-Americans and Asians, are also moving into business sales forces in increasing numbers. Because of the need to become more competitive globally, downsizing, and demographics, many firms have found that a multicultural sales force can provide them a competitive advantage, especially if those salespeople can speak languages other than English.

### Mass Customization of Business Markets

Mass customization is a concept that has been a part of the B2C marketplace for a number of years now. As for B2B situations, however, the concept was not too appropriate since businesses rarely engage in "mass" selling of any sort. B2B marketing is characterized by personal selling and sales promotions aimed at distinct sorts of distribution channel members. If a major account asked for a special consideration, the salesperson would know what to do and how to handle the request. However, as in the consumer situation where

## WHAT WOULD YOU DO?

### EXPENSE REPORT ITEM ADJUSTMENTS

George Steinfield, a new sales representative, was concerned about this week's expense account. He knew that when entertaining customers, dinners were not to exceed a cost of $35.00 per person. However, the client VP considered himself something of a gourmet, particularly with wine, and that meant a dinner at an expensive restaurant plus a huge wine bill. George thought, "That's the last time I let the client choose the wine. I thought I was being polite, but maybe I was just showing that I was naive." It had been a particularly frustrating week for George. Besides the irritation of the excessive restaurant bill, he had also ruined a tie and soiled his best suit, all in the line of duty.

Since George had been assigned to an experienced salesperson to use as a resource, he e-mailed a request for advice on handling the entertainment expense, which had exceeded the allowable amount by about $125.00. "Surely the company doesn't expect me to pick up the extra?" he queried. The experienced salesperson quickly responded: "No, George. This type of thing happens all the time. Just spread out the amount of the excess over the other days when you didn't go over the entertainment expense limit. If you spread it over a few weeks, it won't even be noticeable, but if you have to do it in larger amounts, just cover it by filling in the new amounts on blank restaurant receipts that you collect. If you need some extra, a good tip to a few waiters will get you all the blanks you need. Everyone does it. It's just a way to get the paperwork through accounting. After all, you did spend the money in the company's name."

George sent back a thanks with a :-). As he decided how to allocate the excessive amount over the month's expenses, he thought, "Heck, I might as well include the cost of replacing my tie and cleaning my suit. They wouldn't have been ruined or soiled if I hadn't been out with customers."

### Assignment

On an average day, using his company car and direct-billed gas card, George calls on four customers. Last week he took buying center members to lunch three times and to dinner twice. The first lunch included George and the customer's purchasing agent. The other lunches and dinners included two others. At George's company, lunch was not expected to exceed a cost of $15.00 per person; it had run about $10.00 each this week. While George's expenses had exceeded the allowable amount on the first dinner, the cost for the second dinner was only about $20.00 per person.

Prepare George's expense account voucher for the week, based upon the information given in the case. List the ethical issues for everyone involved.

individual consumers of Levi's wanted to special order jeans for a low price, in B2B firms, increasingly, small customer firms began to ask for special considerations just like major accounts. B2B firms that have hundreds of small firms as customers now consider these individual requests as legitimate and can purchase software applications that build customer profiles and allow the selling firm to set guidelines for dealing with potential special requests. Salespeople, then, can access the software and find the answers immediately, markedly increasing buyer satisfaction.

## Sales Management

Who is responsible for the success of the sales force? The sales manager is. Effective management of the sales force is fundamental to the firm's success. As Exhibit 3-8 indicates, the sales manager must not only organize resources efficiently, but also allocate, maintain, direct, and control the sales efforts of a large group of people who tend to be rather independent and who are not in daily contact with management. Management of the sales function, incorporating a multitude of challenges, has been described as both an art and a science, requiring the sales manager to walk a tightrope between subjective creativity and objective detachment.

Managing the activities of salespeople is important because they are **boundary spanners** (i.e., they work at the boundaries of the organization, and oversight and supervision are difficult). Because the fate of an organization depends upon sales force performance, controlling salespeople's activities to improve their performance is crucial.[8]

**EXHIBIT 3-8    The Functions of Sales Managers**

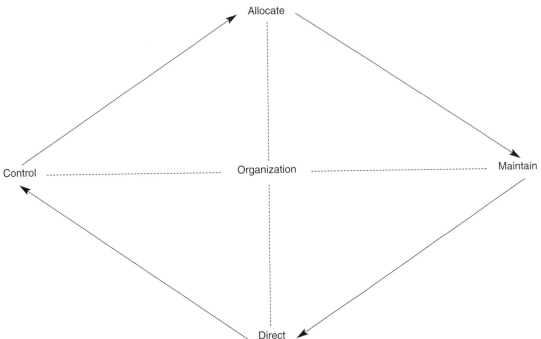

Sales managers, who are often promoted from the ranks of the sales force, have different perspectives, goals, responsibilities, sources of satisfaction, job skill requirements, and relationships than salespeople. They must adopt a "big picture" approach toward their job taking into account the needs of the firm as well as the needs of the sales force when making decisions. *Sales management* is simply the planning, organizing, leading, and controlling of the sales force. As such, sales managers may be responsible for the sales force organization and specialization, staffing the sales force including recruiting and selecting, training the sales force, directing and motivating the sales force, and finally, analyzing and evaluating the sales force.

## Planning the Sales Organization

Just as important as selecting the right type of sales manager is choosing the most appropriate type of sales organization. The business sales force can be organized in several ways, with the key to organizational design being logical consistency. Developing the structure is not easy; the final decision depends on the needs and objectives of the firm. Although there are many variations, the line organization, the line and staff organization, and the functional organization are the most common in the business sector. Each will be considered, followed by a discussion of modifications to these basic types—modifications based on the need to centralize or decentralize, or to organize by activity, product, customer, geographic territory, or some combination of these.

### Line Organization

The line organization is the simplest sales organization design. As shown in Exhibit 3-9, it has a clear line of authority from the highest level of sales management down to the salesperson. Small business-to-business firms frequently use line organizations.

In its simplest form, a line organization prescribes that the sales manager recruits, hires, trains, and supervises the salespeople, in addition to designing sales territories, forecasting

**EXHIBIT 3-9**   Line Organization

sales levels, and carrying out other functions or special projects as assigned by top management. When the firm is small, this organizational structure is efficient, effective, and very flexible. However, as the firm grows, and as problems become more complex, the line organization may tend to overburden the managers.

## Line and Staff Organization

When highly specialized skills are needed (advertising, marketing research, and the like) and when the volume of work becomes too much for one person, a **line and staff organization** emerges. The line function is primary, and the staff function is supportive. That is, staff people provide the manager with specialized skills and report to the line position that they support. As Exhibit 3-10 demonstrates, market forecasters, sales analysts, and training directors are directly supportive of field sales, so these people generally report directly to the national sales manager.

## Functional Organization

With **functional organization**, the staff specialist has line authority to control a function. As Exhibit 3-11 illustrates, the training director would have authority over the business sales-

**EXHIBIT 3-10**   Line and Staff Organization

**EXHIBIT 3-11**  **Functional Organization**

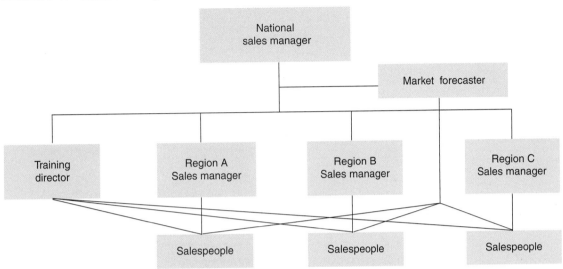

people for all training. Ideally each specialist is highly qualified, so this structure should yield improved performance in each functional area.

## Centralized Versus Decentralized Organization

A **centralized sales organization** is structured so that major decisions, such as recruitment, training, forecasting, and short- and long-term planning are carried out by upper management personnel at a centralized headquarters location. Conversely, a **decentralized sales organization** is designed to allow these types of decisions to be made at the local or regional level by branch sales managers. The *centralized versus decentralized organization* decision concerns the organizational location of the responsibility and authority for specific sales management tasks, such as planning, forecasting, budgeting, and recruiting. Generally, some functions are centralized at company headquarters, while others are spread among branch or field offices. For example, RIBCO Industries, a business-to-business supply firm located in Providence, Rhode Island, allows the individual, company-owned sales branches to do most of the planning and recruitment at the local level, while sales forecasting and financial budgeting are performed at headquarters. Some factors that influence the decision include the following: cost, size of the sales force, geographic size of the market, the role of personal selling in the promotional mix, the need for decentralized inventories, and the need for service.

## Organizing by Specialization

In addition to the various types of sales-force organizations discussed previously, some firms find that additional efficiencies and economies may accrue through organization by: (1) geographical specialization, (2) sales activities, (3) product-line specialization, (4) customer specialization, or (5) combination organizations. This organizational approach commonly is referred to as **organization by specialization**.

### Geographic Specialization

*Geographic specialization* is the most common way to organize a business field sales force, with each region treated virtually as a separate company or profit center. Note that three separate and distinct divisions (Dallas, Omaha, and Chicago) have been established in the

**EXHIBIT 3-12**
**A Sales Force**
**Organized on a**
**Geographic Basis**

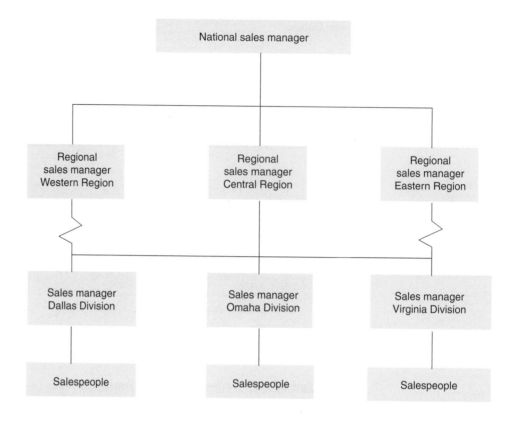

example of geographic organization shown in Exhibit 3-12. Some firms may have further breakdowns between the national sales manager and the salespeople by having branch, district, or field sales manager units. Advantages of the geographic specialization form of organization include smaller territories, allowing salespeople better understanding of their customers' needs; better cultivation of local markets; faster reaction time to external environmental changes; and, usually, better service at less expense. Some disadvantages might include lack of the salesperson's knowledge of all business products within a line; excessive time spent on business products and customers who are easier to sell; and, with the creation of multiple offices, a duplication of services and administrators.

### Sales Activities

A company can grow by selling additional products to present customers, by selling present products to new customers, or by selling new products to new customers. Many business-to-business companies have found it useful to organize the selling function into separate, specialized sales groups, thus allowing the firm to emphasize searching out and selling new accounts. The company may choose to subdivide the sales function when: (1) there is significant difference in the skills needed; or (2) fast growth through acquiring new accounts is considered necessary.

### Product-Line Specialization

Organization by business product, known as *product-line specialization,* often is reserved for large and diverse product lines for which technical knowledge is important to maintain efficiency. General Electric and Westinghouse have used this organizational structure effectively, as have IBM and Xerox. A company may have regional, district, and even area

**EXHIBIT 3-13**
**A Sales Force Organized on a Product-Line Basis**

managers within each product-line sales force. Exhibit 3-13 illustrates a typical sales force organized according to product-line specialization. Note that there is a product manager and salespeople for Product A and for Product B, but that the advertising department and the marketing services department handle these needs for both products. With product-line specialization salespeople and sales managers concentrate their efforts on particular product lines or individual items, allowing a high degree of specialized attention, that should substantially increase the efficiency of each product-line sales force. It also allows for decentralization, whereby those closest to the problem can make decisions to resolve them. On the downside, however, two or more salespeople may be calling on the same customer, which may not only upset the customer but also cause expensive duplication of sales effort, resulting from having more than one representative in a geographic locality.

### Customer Specialization

With *customer specialization,* a salesperson sells an entire product line to selected buyers. This approach is consistent with the marketing concept's emphasis on customer satisfaction, as the salesperson is knowledgeable about the unique problems and needs of each customer. In addition, major accounts receive special attention. Greater feedback of new product ideas and new marketing methods may also accrue through the customer-oriented sales force organization. The biggest disadvantage is the potential for overlapping territories, along with a concomitant increase in costs.

### Combination Specialization

Combinations of types of business sales organizations allow a company to choose the structure that best serves its immediate objectives. Exhibit 3-14 illustrates a sales force organized by territories, products, and customers. In fact, as they grow in size, most firms find it necessary to develop some type of combination organization. General Foods, DuPont, and National Cash Register all use the combination sales organization.

**Concept Review**

1. What are a sales manager's leadership functions?

2. How do selling skills and management skills differ?

3. What are some of the differences between line, line and staff, and functional sales organizations?

**EXHIBIT 3-14**    **A Sales Force Organized by Territory, Product, and Customer**

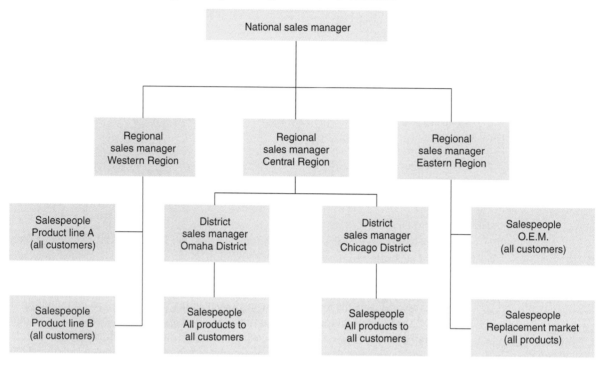

## Staffing a Business Sales Force

After a company decides upon the most appropriate manner in which to organize its sales function, it must turn its attention to determining sales force size, and then to recruiting and selecting competent sales representatives. The sales manager may be very efficient and capable, but he or she is doomed to failure if poorly qualified salespeople on whom training, compensation, and motivation techniques will have a negligible impact comprise the sales force. Indeed, hiring talented salespeople may be a manager's most important responsibility. If sales managers were given a choice of skills at which to become proficient, recruitment and selection certainly would be popular choices. Hiring is among the most rewarding and most difficult parts of the job, according to a national survey of 260 executives conducted by Caliper, a Princeton, N.J.–based human resources consulting firm. When sales executives were asked to rank the best and worst aspects of leadership, more than 35 percent ranked hiring among the most problematic aspects of the job.[9]

### Determining Sales Force Size

A business-to-business firm must be as careful in buying the services of salespeople as it is in making the products that these people sell. The number of salespeople to hire depends primarily on two things: growth and sales force turnover. Growth dictates the need for additional sales volume, while *sales force turnover* creates the need for replacements. Turnover rates vary among industries. Companies in the United States report an average annual salesperson turnover rate of 9.6 percent.[10] As noted earlier, management of the sales force is both an art and a science: Excessive turnover could be a symptom of problems in hiring, training, compensating, and motivating the sales force.

### SECURITY AT NATIONAL SALES MEETINGS

A recent study of Fortune 1000 companies suggested that losses from illicit competitive intelligence-gathering could soon reach the level of $300 billion. The chief targets are in high-tech, high-value-added industries such as the semiconductor, computer software, and pharmaceutical industries, but others also are at risk. With global markets becoming increasingly competitive, all sales meeting planners should become more aware of information security issues. Information regarding strategic direction, product development, pricing, and budgets, in particular, should be protected. American companies tend to be quite naïve about corporate espionage, and are especially unaware of recent technological improvements in electronic eavesdropping.

If you are planning a sales meeting for a large number of attendees and a site under your complete control is not big enough, consider only an upscale hotel where background checks have been run on employees. Rent all the meeting areas, and do not allow hotel staffers access during meetings. Be sure not to use wireless microphones or speakers that can be intercepted. Require identification for all attendees and account for all copies of handouts. While it would be wise to consider the possibility of electronic listening devices or even listening via vibrations in the meeting room window glass (an infrared beam can be directed at the window from the parking lot or an adjacent building), usually corporate spies do not even have to try that hard. With badges usually arranged on the reception table, the spy can just take one and walk in. How does the spy know where to go? Most hotels put up signs and even list events on their inside-the-hotel television system. How would the spy know of the meeting itself? With all those salespeople, it would take only one to mention that he would miss his usual sales calls "because I'll be away at an important sales meeting." Or, if the company has used this site before, all that would be required is access to the hotel's meeting schedule.

#### Action Assignment

Each major hotel in your area will have special marketers on staff for working with corporate meeting planners. Have your team visit several hotels to discuss these issues with their meeting marketers. These employees are accustomed to dealing with a variety of business people and their unique needs, and most will be happy to describe their meeting security services, discuss the types of companies that use their facilities, and let you see typical corporate meeting rooms. Report what you find to the class.

Adapted from "Defense Against Corporate Espionage," *Successful Meetings,* May 1999, pp. 70–71.

### Turnover Expected

For many business-to-business firms, turnover is a persistent problem. The formula for *sales force turnover expected* is as follows:

$$\text{Turnover} = \frac{\text{Number of salespeople hired during the period}}{\text{Average size of sales force during the period}}$$

Thus, a 50 percent turnover (which would be totally unacceptable in most business sales departments) would result if 100 people were hired in a year, assuming the average size of the sales force was 200. A 50 percent turnover rate does not necessarily mean that half of the sales force was replaced during a particular period of time; perhaps 50 to 75 positions had to be filled, but some of these had to be filled twice. Generally speaking, a firm can reduce the turnover rate by upgrading the job, screening more carefully, and tailoring supervision more closely to the requirements of the job.

### Three Methods

Still, Cundiff, and Govoni identify three rational methods of approaching the problem of determining the optimal size of the sales force: the *workload method,* the *sales-potential method,* and the *incremental method.*[11] The *workload method,* sometimes called the *buildup method,* categorizes accounts based on their sales and potential importance. The frequency and length of sales calls are determined for each category, with larger accounts (or those with large-volume potential) being called on often (every two weeks, or perhaps once per month). Small accounts (or those with low-volume potential) may be called on every three months or even less frequently. This method incorporates several factors in determining the number of sales personnel needed, including:

- Number of sales calls to be made
- Number of accounts in the territory
- Frequency of sales calls on given customers
- Time intervals between sales calls
- Travel time around the territory
- Nonselling time

The number of accounts multiplied by the call frequency equals the total number of sales calls per year that the sales force must make. The available interview time is estimated by subtracting time devoted to nonselling activities (such as travel time) from total work time available. In the final step, the yearly interview time available to a sales representative is divided into the total number of hours of customer interview time the firm needs. The result is a fairly accurate estimate of the number of salespeople needed. This method, although simple and easy to use, does not recognize the fact that all customers do not have similar characteristics and requirements.

In the *sales-potential method,* the yearly sales volume is divided by the volume each salesperson can be expected to sell. The resulting number is adjusted for turnover among sales force personnel and territorial differences in travel time. A major drawback of this method is that sales volume depends on the number of salespeople selling for the firm.

The *incremental method* of determining a sales force size is based on the assumption that an additional salesperson may be hired if profit contributions from sales made by that person exceed the cost of hiring that person. The major element to consider is total incremental or marginal cost relative to the incremental or marginal revenue of the territory. This method is theoretically attractive, but often it is impractical to apply because of the difficulty of estimating marginal sales directly due to the added salesperson, in addition to the difficulty of estimating marginal costs and costs of production and distribution.

Finally, other factors (including instinct) must also be considered when estimating the number of salespeople needed in the next year or two. Other internal and external conditions, including the level of economic activity and labor relations in general, may override numerical methods such as those discussed here.

## Recruitment

Once business sales managers have determined the size of the sales force, they must concern themselves with the *recruitment and selection process. Recruiting,* the task of finding and attracting qualified applicants for sales positions, is difficult and time-consuming. The cost of inefficient sales recruiting not only wastes company resources but requires the manager to spend an inordinate amount of time on the recruiting process.

> Hiring the wrong person is a drain on sales resources, and on the sales manager's time. It doesn't matter how much motivation and training or coaching and counseling is provided, dealing with the wrong hire will be an uphill struggle, and will continue until the person leaves the sales organization. Scouting for sales talent should be a top priority for every sales manager, but too often the job is neglected until an emergency arises.
>
> Hiring mistakes take an emotional toll on any sales team. But they take an even larger financial toll. It can cost anywhere from $10,000 to $100,000 a year, in terms of training, salary and benefits, and lost productivity, when a manager hires the wrong person. A wrong hire can also damage a company's reputation, ruin established relationships with customers,

and undermine the sales force's morale. The manager who understands those costs will realize why it's so critical to make good hiring choices.[12]

Referrals for sales recruits come from outside the company, from friends, customers, and suppliers, and from internal sources. The most frequently used sources are: (1) company sources, (2) company salespeople, (3) educational institutions, (4) professional associations, (5) suppliers and customers, (6) employment agencies, and (7) advertisements. These sources can be compared at some point to determine which method yields the best recruit for the money spent.

An important first step in the recruitment process is to analyze the job thoroughly and to prepare a list of qualifications needed for successful performance. This preparation helps to ensure that new recruits have a reasonably good chance of being successful in a particular sales situation. Three specific procedures should be followed: (1) conduct a job analysis; (2) prepare a written job description; and (3) develop sales job qualifications for selectees (job specification).

### Conduct a Job Analysis

A job analysis is a careful and objective study and written summary of the job in question. It includes a definition of roles or activities to be performed and the personal qualifications determined necessary for the position. A job analysis commonly is used in preparing job descriptions, writing job specifications, recruiting and selecting, evaluating performance, training and developing, and determining compensation.

### Prepare a Written Job Description

As noted above, the job analysis is used, among other things, in preparing a job description. A job description details the components of the job and the functions or activities the employee must perform, such as prospecting, traveling, selling, and providing service assistance. The job description should be written, should be acceptable to employees and management, and should be specific, inclusive, brief, and easy to read.

### Develop Sales Job Qualifications

The job specification is a list of the duties and responsibilities outlined in the job description that spells out the critical characteristics (e.g., decisiveness, maturity, openness) needed to perform the job satisfactorily.

## Selection

Once the firm accumulates a pool of candidates, the next step is to select and attract the best business salespeople for the job at hand. Exhibit 3-15 shows how hiring criteria for sales jobs are used to guide the process of selecting salespeople from a pool of available applicants. Too often, sales managers think of the managerial function of hiring as a one-way decision, when really it is effective only when it involves decision making on the part of the applicant as well as management. Both parties have a financial stake in making the right decision. Applicants want compensation commensurate with their skills and ability. The company wants to hire a salesperson who will succeed and will remain with the organization, thereby minimizing the considerable cost of training replacement personnel.

While firms might vary in the time sequence of the steps used in the hiring process, the selection interview inevitably becomes the final step in the employment decision. The sales manager must now resolve moot points, make judgments on the capabilities and overall talents of the candidates, and decide whether a candidate will fit as a member of the sales team.

**EXHIBIT 3-15**
**A Model for Selecting
Salespeople**

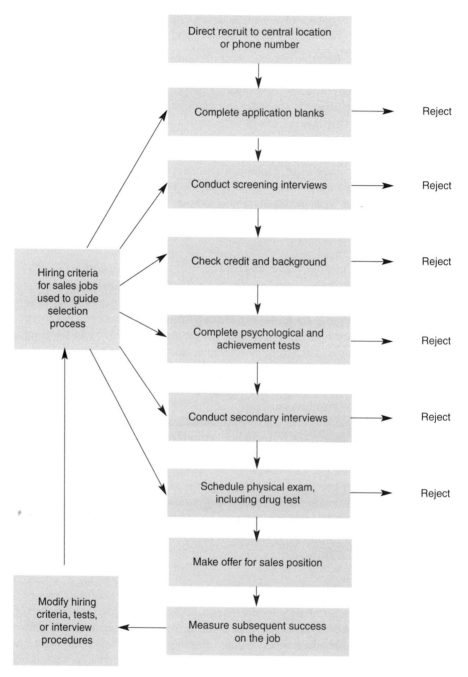

## Training a Business Sales Force

Now that sales representatives have been properly recruited and carefully selected, the sales manager (either directly or indirectly) has the responsibility of training and developing the sales force. Sales training is an important consideration, as evidenced by the significant amounts of money industrial companies invest in training their salespeople. Top-level salespeople spend an average of 29.6 days each year honing sales skills and product knowledge, with entry-level reps spending an average of 73.4 days in training each year.[13]

Successful sales managers use training methods that enhance the productivity of the salespeople under their supervision. Willie Loman, the tragic 1940s hero of Arthur Miller's *Death of a Salesman,* worked for a small, family-owned business. In preparation for his selling position, he received only a calling card and a sample case; the rest was up to him. Willie represented the end of a somewhat romanticized era for salespeople. Today, the business salesperson needs more than friends, a good shoe shine, and a pleasant smile to obtain orders. *Sales training* is imperative and must be ongoing. A good training program can boost a sales force's productivity if it includes considerable planning, commitment, and reinforcement.

In addition to increased sales volume, training can help to accomplish the following:

- Improve morale, thereby reducing absenteeism and turnover
- Create and foster an information flow from headquarters or the field-sales office to the salesperson and encourage feedback from the salesperson
- Improve knowledge of the product, the competition, and the customer; improve time and territory management; and improve selling techniques
- Increase sales of a particular product, product line, or customer category
- Encourage and develop future sales managers

## What a Training Program Should Cover

The basic principle in sales training has been to focus on those areas the business salesperson needs to know in order to do an adequate selling job. However, as sales organizations have become more complex and more international, the role of the sales manager in training salespeople is compounded, and new priorities for deciding what to include may have to be set. The sales manager must choose and rank priorities in deciding what information to impart, what skills to teach, and when to teach them. Although specific content will vary, an analysis of training needs usually reveals the necessity of training in a combination of the following general areas: (1) company knowledge, (2) product knowledge, (3) selling techniques, (4) customer knowledge, (5) competitive knowledge, and (6) time and territory management. Generally speaking, while firms continue to cover the traditional topics, they also are beginning to add less-traditional topics such as regulations regarding the issue of sexual harassment as well as computer and technical applications.

### Company Knowledge

Facts about the firm's history, size, and reputation provide needed assurances, especially to the customer contemplating the purchase of expensive equipment that will require costly installation and servicing. Also, knowledge of the firm's history and capabilities can increase morale, confidence, and efficiency among the firm's sales representatives. Company policy on allowable returns, advertising allowances, freight costs, payment terms, cancellation penalties, and minimum orders should be known and understood by the salesperson.

### Product Knowledge

Because of the importance of product knowledge in addition to the accelerating nature of technological change, most business sales managers provide ongoing or continuous product training to their respective sales forces. Product features must be turned into customer benefits, which means that the salesperson must have enough product knowledge to feel confident in presenting the goods or services.

### Selling Techniques

To be successful, selling techniques must be based on how people buy; most sales managers believe that a logical, sequential series of steps exists that, if followed, will convert a prospect into a customer. As discussed earlier in this chapter, the *selling process* is an adaptation by a salesperson to the decision-making process of business buyers; it is a starting point in understanding the use of numerous persuasive communications techniques. Salespeople, both beginners and old pros alike, must be reminded that selling is a process that starts with prospecting, moves forward through several steps to the sale, and ends with follow-up and service.

### Customer Knowledge

Sales trainees are taught who the customers are, where they are, and how important they are. Experienced business salespeople need additional essential knowledge concerning changes in the segments in which they are selling, along with trends that might be noted over time. Sales by product or product line should be reviewed for each customer or customer class, noting trends that are up or down and the reason for the change.

### Competitive Knowledge

Sales management must provide information on competitors' products, policies, services, competitive advantages and disadvantages, warranties, and credit policies, among other things. "Know thy competition" is wise counsel both to recruits and to seasoned sales professionals. Knowledge increases the probability of success, while ignorance increases the probability of failure.

### Time and Territory Management

A *sales territory* represents a group of current and potential customers. In order to achieve optimum efficiency and effectiveness in servicing accounts within a specific territory, salespeople must plan and control their activities carefully. As noted earlier in this chapter, salespeople face considerable demands on their time. Given that and the fact that the average cost of a sales call is $350, effective *time and territory management* is particularly important for salespeople.

## Who Should Do the Training?

Business sales training programs normally are conducted at a central, companywide site by professional trainers, in the field by branch managers and sales personnel, and/or by private consulting organizations and professional trainers. In general, the training site, the relative sophistication of the facilities, and the professionalism of the trainers are determined by the particular training needs involved and by the size of the firm's sales training budget. When it comes to sales training, most managers don't find themselves at multibillion-dollar corporations with huge sales forces and budgets to match. In fact, only 16 percent of industrial companies develop and deliver all training in-house, with the balance either being outsourced or using both in-house and outside training personnel.[14] The following sections examine the three methods of sales training most widely used: home office, field or local, and private consulting organizations and professional trainers.

### Home Office Sales Training

Many large firms have a *sales training department* that acts as a sort of nerve center for all sales training activities undertaken by the company. Most of these centralized training facilities are designed to supplement the basic sales training done in the field by a field sales manager or branch manager. These centralized training units concentrate on professionalizing the selling skills of sales representatives who have several months or even many years of experience, in addition to training field sales managers needing to update their training skills. These facilities have classrooms, closed-circuit television and videotapes, projection equipment, and nearby facilities for housing trainees during the course of the training period.

## STRATEGY AT WORK

### SALES TRAINING AT ARMSTRONG WORLD INDUSTRIES

Sales organizations across the world have seriously begun exploring a host of new Web-based products for training, communication, virtual sales meetings, and even virtual sales calls. Armstrong World Industries, Inc., (www.armstrong. com) is a manufacturer and marketer of interior furnishings, including vinyl and hardwood floor coverings, acoustical ceilings, and insulation materials for heating and cooling systems. With sales in excess of $3.5 billion and over 20,000 employees, Armstrong is a recognized industry leader and is very involved in utilizing the Web to increase sales service and efficiency.

Recently, Armstrong World Industries was planning to adopt a new customer contact management software product, "SalesTrak," (www.aurum.com), across its entire sales staff. The problem the company faced was that it did not have any regional or national sales meetings planned that would allow it to train its employees on the new software package. Alternatives included calling a special training sales meeting, videoconferencing, sending a videotape, or developing Web-based training.

Armstrong's marketing executives decided to conduct online training via Symposium, a Web-based training solution developed by Centra Software (www.centra.com). Typical cost to implement is about $100,000 for 200 users. Armstrong conducted seven different training sessions in which reps simply dialed up a website via their laptop modems and viewed a live PowerPoint presentation. Participants could ask questions whenever they needed to (the software has audio capabilities). They could share typed comments and information and actually try out the new software for themselves while participating in the session. Both the company and its salespeople were pleased with the results.

#### Assignment

Estimate the costs of the above alternatives, and evaluate the Web-based solutions at the following sites:

www.centra.com

www.contigo.com

www.placeware.com

www.vuepoint.com

Present your analysis and recommendation to the class.

See also M. Ligos, "Point, Click, Sell," from *Sales & Marketing Management,* May 1999, pp. 51–56.

### Field or Local Sales Training

*Field or local sales training* exposes the trainee to the real-world business sales environment, where the techniques learned in formal training can be tried, with additional training being provided as needed. A note of caution is in order here: Too many companies put new salespeople in out-of-the-way corners of field sales offices, providing them with little attention, supervision, or instruction, and expect sales orientation and training to occur by experiencing the sales office atmosphere. Clearly, this mentality should be avoided, as it can cause trainees to feel disillusioned and even to question their choice of employment. A positive aspect of field or local sales training, however, is that it moves the learning process closer to the customers. It introduces a measure of realism as well, as the recruits will observe top salespeople selling to customers similar to those they will encounter in their own, yet-to-be-determined territories.

### Private Consulting Organizations and Professional Trainers

Many private consulting firms provide sales training services that are sold to business and industry and are conducted by professional trainers—most of whom have extensive experience within the areas they teach. Most private consultants who provide sales training services develop programs tailored to the client's products, personnel, and sales policies. For many companies, outsourcing both training development and delivery makes sense. Rainier Industries' Scott Campbell chose outsourcing, he said, because, "I realized I wasn't very good at sales training." Campbell, the president of Seattle-based Rainier Industries, a 102-year-old manufacturer of custom fabric products, also recognized the company's weakness when it came to in-house training programs.[15] Many outside suppliers exist, but

**EXHIBIT 3-16** Specific Criteria to Measure When Determining the Effectiveness of Sales Training

| | |
|---|---|
| Absenteeism | Number of calls |
| Average commission per sale | Number of lost customers |
| Average size of the sale | Percentage of objectives overcome |
| Average time to "break even" | Product mix sold |
| Bad-debt ratio | Qualitative call improvement |
| Competitive investigations | Ratio of carload sales to total sales |
| Complaint letters | Reduced cost of training |
| Compliment letters | Reduced training time |
| Developing new product demand | Reduction in legal actions |
| Earnings of salespeople | Referral rate |
| Implementation of promotional programs | Sales forecasting accuracy |
| Improvement in sales-rank position | Sales-force turnover |
| Improvement of call quality | Sales/phone call ratio |
| Increased active selling time | Sales/travel ratio |
| Items per order | Sales volume |
| New customers per week/month | Volume increase for existing accounts |
| New/old customer ratio | Volume of returned merchandise |

perhaps the most popular are Learning International, Wilson Learning Corporation, Forum Company, and Dale Carnegie. Learning International, for example, has worked with 80 percent of the Fortune 500 business-to-business corporations.

### How Sales Training Should Be Evaluated

The cost of sales training is substantial, with sales training budgets of many large business-to-business companies exceeding hundreds of thousands of dollars. Determining whether this investment is paying off requires, where possible, determining and measuring the contributions sales training made. A three-step evaluation process is suggested:

1. Set objectives (both overall and specific) for the company sales training program.
2. Determine whether the objectives as set are being met or already have been met.
3. Try to measure the effect of training on profitability.

Some objectives cannot be measured, or are difficult to measure, while other performance criteria can be measured rather simply. Exhibit 3-16 lists some criteria that a firm might measure in order to demonstrate the effectiveness of a sales training program. Although a company will not necessarily use all of these, many of the criteria listed will be helpful in evaluating the effectiveness of a sales training program.

---

**Concept Review**

1. What is the difference between a job analysis and a job description?
2. In professional sales training, why is there such a focus on time and territory management?
3. Why is sales training evaluation important?

---

## Directing and Motivating a Sales Force

Assume that the business sales manager has effectively organized the sales force, hired capable salespeople, assigned them to territories that will optimize sales, and has trained them well. Now the sales manager must effectively direct and motivate each salesperson to capitalize fully on his or her potential. Is the sales quota system fair? Is the compensation system important? Is it fair? This section addresses many interrelated factors such as these that motivate the sales force, as well as techniques for optimizing business sales force members' performance.

## Providing Leadership

Leadership is the first qualification for a good sales manager. It is not just good management; it also is a matter of establishing values, sharing visions, creating enthusiasm, maintaining focus on a few clear objectives, and building a sales force that works as a team. Successful business sales managers vary greatly in style, from an autocratic to a laissez-faire leadership style. Exhibit 3-17 lists some actions of both strong and weak leaders. It should be noted that any one particular sales manager may use a variety of leadership styles, depending on the situation. That is, a particular sales manager may be autocratic but friendly with a new sales trainee; democratic with an experienced employee who has many good ideas; and laissez-faire with a trusted, long-term employee.

Much research has been conducted in an ongoing effort to find out what makes a person an effective leader. There is no such thing as leadership traits that are effective in all situations, nor are there leadership styles that always work best. The style that should be used at a particular time depends on the sales manager, the salespeople, and the internal and external macro and micro environments.

---

**EXHIBIT 3-17** **The Twelve Golden Rules and the Seven Deadly Sins of Leadership**

**The Twelve Golden Rules**

1. *Set a good example.* Your subordinates will take their cue from you. If your work habits are good, theirs are likely to be too.
2. *Give your people a set of objectives and a sense of direction.* Good people seldom like to work aimlessly from day to day. They want to know not only what they're doing but why.
3. *Keep your people informed.* Discuss new developments at the company and how they'll affect them. Let your close assistants in on your plans at an early stage. Let people know as early as possible of any changes that will affect them. Let them know of changes that won't affect them but about which they may be worrying.
4. *Ask your people for advice.* Let them know that they have a say in your decisions whenever possible. Make them feel a problem is their problem too. Encourage individual thinking.
5. *Let your people know that you support them.* There's no greater morale killer than a boss who resents a subordinate's ambitions.
6. *Don't give orders.* Suggest, direct, and request.
7. *Emphasize skills, not rules.* Judge results, not methods. Give a person a job to do and let him or her do it. Let an employee improve his or her own job methods.
8. *Give credit where credit is due.* Appreciation for a job well done is the more appreciated of "fringe benefits."
9. *Praise in public.* This is where it'll do the most good.
10. *Criticize in private.*
11. *Criticize constructively.* Concentrate on correction, not blame. Allow a person to retain his or her dignity. Suggest specific steps to prevent recurrence of the mistake. Forgive and encourage desired results.
12. *Make it known that you welcome new ideas.* No idea is too small for a hearing or too wild for consideration. Make it easy for them to communicate their ideas to you. Follow through on their ideas.

**The Seven Deadly Sins**

These items can cancel any constructive image you might try to establish.

1. *Trying to be liked rather than respected.* Don't accept favors from your subordinates. Don't do special favors trying to be liked. Don't try for popular decisions. Don't be soft about discipline. Have a sense of humor. Don't give up.
2. *Failing to ask subordinates for their advice and help.*
3. *Failing to develop a sense of responsibility in subordinates.* Allow freedom of expression. Give each person a chance to learn his or her superior's job. When you give responsibility, give authority too. Hold subordinates accountable for results.
4. *Emphasizing rules rather than skills.*
5. *Failing to keep criticism constructive.* When something goes wrong, do you do your best to get all the facts first? Do you control your temper? Do you praise before you criticize? Do you listen to the other side of the story?
6. *Not paying attention to employee gripes and complaints.* Make it easy for them to come to you. Get rid of red tape. Explain the grievance machinery. Help a person voice his or her complaint. Always grant a hearing. Practice patience. Ask a complainant what he or she wants you to do. Don't render a hasty or biased judgment. Get all the facts. Let the complainant know what your decision is. Double-check your results. Be concerned.
7. *Failing to keep people informed.*

## Sales Quotas

Quotas are based on company and sales objectives established during a planning process. There are several different uses for quotas, including: (1) to provide incentive, (2) to provide a basis for compensation, and (3) to evaluate a salesperson's performance. They can be expressed as *sales quotas, expense quotas, profit quotas,* or *activity quotas.* To be effective, quotas must be established fairly, be within the reach of salespeople, be easy to understand and control, and be consistent with company revenue goals. A **sales quota** is simply a goal set for a particular product line, division, or sales representative. It is a powerful management tool that, if correctly used, should stimulate the sales effort. Sales quotas are useful for directing, motivating, and evaluating sales activities and salespeople: Their use should uncover strengths and weaknesses in the selling structure, improve the compensation plan's effectiveness, control selling expenses, and enhance sales contents.

## Compensation Plans

Employees listen closely when the president of Electro-Scientific Industries in Portland, Oregon, reports sales and profits, with few in the audience failing to grasp the subtleties of before-tax and after-tax profits. This intense interest is not surprising: the employees are paid 25 percent of the before-tax profits each quarter, with one-fourth of that going straight into their pockets and the rest into retirement or stock ownership accounts. Raychem, Tektronix, Johnson Wax, Lowe's Companies, Hewlett-Packard, Goldman-Sachs, Marion Labs, Readers' Digest, and Quad/Graphics are among other companies that pay out some portion of before-tax profits to all employees, either outright or into trusts.

A sound, solid, equitable **compensation plan**—financial and nonfinancial methods of rewards—is essential to successful management of the business sales force. Whenever selling effort has a major impact on creating a sale, an incentive compensation system generally is advocated. However, there is some confusion and disagreement about the role of financial incentives as motivators. Some sales managers feel that salespeople are motivated strictly by financial rewards, while others believe financial compensation is relatively unimportant as a true behavior motivator. An accurate analysis probably lies somewhere in between these two extremes. In terms of payment plans, the relative advantages of salary-based and commission-based compensation plans for salespeople have been important concerns in the literature. While past research has provided many insights, there remains some uncertainty about the circumstances under which one compensation mode is preferable to the other.[16] Today, most company sales compensation plans feature salary plus incentive in the form of a commission or a bonus.

Most discussions with sales executives reveal a consensus that: (1) compensation is the most important element in motivating a sales force; and (2) a properly designed and applied compensation package must be geared both to the needs of the company and the products the firm sells. The compensation package should allow the company to attract good business salespeople and to keep them motivated to produce. Although compensation clearly is fundamental to motivating salespeople, the issue is far more complicated than simple payment rewards. The amount of satisfaction and the sense of personal achievement that individuals feel from performing tasks are also important motivators.

## Analyzing and Evaluating a Sales Force

All firms evaluate their salespeople—whether the firm is large or small, is in consumer or business-to-business sales, sells goods or services, or employs a few or several thousand. The evaluation itself may be formal or informal, and its conclusions may be based on objective criteria or on executive opinion. Whatever its scope, sales force analysis and evaluation make supervision of salespeople possible.

## BUSINESS MARKETING IN ACTION

### SPRITE BUSINESS SOFTWARE, INC.

Charlie Dobbs, sales manager for Sprite Business Software, recently hired Jeremy Hudson to fill a sales slot. Dobbs and Hudson, both 36, have been good friends since their days as undergrads at Penn State. Hudson is a seasoned seller and has been hitting quota or above since he has been with Sprite—but not without stepping on some toes. Hudson is exceptionally demanding of the support staff, and he often speaks to them in a brusque, demotivating manner. All of the Sprite salespeople have distinct territories, divided by industries. Where there is any crossover (for example, a client that serves more than one industry), Hudson competes with his peers for accounts, rather than collaborating with them.

After several people spoke with Dobbs regarding Hudson's approach, Dobbs took him to lunch to discuss the matter. Dobbs casually mentioned the problem, almost in passing, not wanting to insult his long-time friend. Hudson's reply was terse: "So not everyone likes me. I generate revenue, and lots of it." Three months and no changes later, a number of sales and support staffers again reported the problem to Dobbs. People were unhappy—very unhappy.

Dobbs knows he has to have another meeting with Hudson, but he worries that Hudson, annoyed with the whole matter, will quit. Then Dobbs would lose both a top salesperson and a good friend. Dobbs would not even think of firing Hudson, but if Hudson doesn't change his attitude Dobbs could lose other top-performing sales and support people.

### Action Assignment

Develop and present a detailed plan for dealing with difficult salespeople such as Hudson, and make suggestions for Dobbs in handling this situation. Base your answer on library research. Include citations and references concerning how to deal with "problem" or difficult salespeople (employees). A considerable amount has been published on this topic, so your presentation to the class should be very informative.

See also, "What Would You Do," from *Sales & Marketing Management,* May 1999, p. 104.

---

What does a sales manager expect to accomplish through sales force analyses and evaluations? The following list suggests desired outcomes:

1. To determine areas in which each salesperson needs improvement.
2. To assess the validity of the standards used.
3. To spot people who are ready for promotion, salary raises, or assignment to new territories and responsibilities.
4. To supply evidence on salespeople who should be disciplined or terminated.
5. To check the effectiveness of the sales compensation plan, training, supervision, recruitment, territory assignments, and operating procedures.

An evaluation plan should be tailored to the specific company for which it is being used. For example, in one company, sales calls made per day may be an important criterion of performance, while in another the number of new accounts opened may be more significant. Regardless of the specific tasks, the overall evaluation program should be realistic, motivational, participatory, flexible, and specific. It is better to have no formal analysis and evaluation program than to have a poorly designed and administered one.

Most business sales managers would agree that the salesperson's immediate superior should be the primary evaluator. Most evaluations include constructive criticism from the immediate supervisor, as well as recommendations for raises and promotions. Some companies use an entire regional management group and a home office personnel specialist to evaluate salespeople. The specialist ensures that approved evaluation procedures are followed and that each person being evaluated is treated fairly.

Informal evaluation should be almost a daily occurrence, as it is best to bring mistakes to the salesperson's attention as soon as possible. Likewise, a formal evaluation program should be conducted on a regular basis. The frequency of this formal evaluation, however, should be determined by the time required to evaluate and the activities involved in the

# WHAT WOULD YOU DO?

## ENTERTAINMENT FOR CUSTOMERS: HOW MUCH IS TOO MUCH?

James Gifford was head of marketing for MMM Industries, a major producer of components that go into electronic printing devices. James was considering a creative way to bring together the buying center members from his biggest customers and the key staff members at MMM. He knew that his two main competitors each threw a big annual party, with plenty of food and drink. At one competitor's party, reliable rumor reported that customers who wished it were slipped keys to rooms at an upscale hotel across the street, where the competitor had arranged additional free entertainment (which would be illegal in most of the United States). It was said that similar arrangements could be made by this competitor's salespeople at other times during the year. James didn't know if that approach increased sales, but he did note that many industry customers seemed to have nothing but good things to say about both the competitor and its products.

The second competitor took a completely different approach. It maintained a house in a private upscale neighborhood on a canal (which led to the ocean) in the Florida Keys. The house came with the use of a boat and could easily handle two or three families. While the competitor's top management occasionally vacationed there, the house was mostly made available for important customer buying center members and their families (as recommended and scheduled through the sales department). James was concerned that MMM's share of the business was third after these two competitors, and he knew that their products and service were all about equal.

MMM, being a relatively conservative company, had a strict rule that no gift to a buyer (or other customer employee) could exceed $25 dollars per year. MMM's general guideline for its employees was that "nothing could be given that could not be consumed in one sitting." Thus, a bottle of champagne might be acceptable as a wedding gift for a buyer, but not a case. Tickets to a sporting event might be approved, but certainly not season tickets.

James knew that his options were limited but was considering an option being pushed strongly by an MMM salesperson who enjoyed fishing on the North Carolina shore. The proposal was that MMM would rent a house on the beach, and selected MMM staff and key customer staff would spend a few days surf fishing. MMM would pick up the tab only for the house rental, beverages, and food. James agreed that this was much more ethical than what the competitors were offering, but he wasn't sure if it would be useful. The idea of being cooped up with people smelling of fish, drinking beer, and probably telling fish stories far into the night was not very appealing to James. The president of MMM was more of a country club/golf type, and James was sure he would not want to attend. "Still," James thought, "I suppose our entertainment should match the customer's interests rather than our own. . . . "

### Assignment

Define the ethical issues for all concerned. What would you do?

See also "What Would You Do," from *Sales & Marketing Management,* May 1999, p. 104.

---

evaluation cycle. Generally, each salesperson should receive a minimum of one formal evaluation yearly.

## Concept Review

1. What is leadership?
2. Why is a sound, solid, equitable compensation plan essential to successful management of the business sales force?
3. What does a sales manager expect to accomplish through sales force analysis and evaluations?

## Summary

- Professional selling involves persuasive and deliberate contact between a buyer and a seller for the specific purpose of creating an exchange between them. Business buyers typically view business salespeople not as adversaries but as experts and partners in the process of business. Unlike selling to consumers, professional selling is the primary promotional tool utilized in business selling and generally is supported by other elements of the promotional mix. For these reasons professional business selling is different from selling to consumers.

- Professional business selling can be truly appreciated only when both the scope and nature of salespeople's daily activities are understood. Sales jobs range from those that are development-oriented to those that are support-oriented. Salesperson activities typically include selling, servicing customers, time management and communication.

- The cost of a business sales call has been rising rapidly over the last decade, as has the cost of professional selling in general. Because the cost of professional selling can vary significantly depending on the type of product and industry, the size of the firm, and the degree of personal contact with prospects necessary to close a sale, business-to-business companies must constantly monitor and assess the best methods by which to sell and support the selling of their products.

- Buyers in the business sector seek to buy for many reasons, including increasing profits and sales, producing a quality product, obtaining helpful service from a manufacturer, and receiving trade-in allowances. Once salespeople have identified the buyer's important buying needs, they can specifically tailor a sales presentation for that buyer that relates buyer needs to product benefits.

- The professional selling process includes preliminary, face-to-face, and follow-up activities. Among preliminary activities are setting objectives for the sales call, preparing an attention-getting opener, choosing and preparing an appropriate sales presentation approach, listening and preparing to handle buyer objections, and planning how to close the sales call. Face-to-face activities involve introductory, presentation, and closing stages. Finally, once the presentation is over, the salesperson still has work to do, for example, ensuring that orders are sent. If a sale is not made, the salesperson should still work to keep lines of communication open with the buyer.

- Professional selling is always changing due to ever changing technology and social factors. Among current trends in professional business selling are: use of customer relationship management; data mining; handheld devices and other communication technology, diversity in the sales force, and mass customization of business markets.

- Sales managers must allocate financial resources and allocate, maintain, direct, and control the sales efforts of a sales force that tends to be independent and not in daily contact with management.

- When it comes to planning the sales force, sales managers may choose between line, line and staff, functional, and/or centralized or decentralized type organizations. They may further decide to specialize the sales force according to geography, type of sales activities needed, product-line, and/or types of customers. Sales managers should evaluate their specific situations and choose the type of organization and/or specialization that best meets buyer needs.

- Staffing a business sales force is a very important task for sales managers. First, the size of the business sales force needs to be determined. Once that has been accomplished, recruitment may begin, aided by a job analysis, written job descriptions, and developing job qualifications as well as tapping various internal and external sources of sales recruits. Once an adequate number of qualified people have been recruited, the sales manager can select the right salespeople.

- Sales training must be ongoing and should include instruction in product knowledge, competitive knowledge, new selling techniques, development of sales skills, and knowledge of time and territory management. Companies are interested in providing sales training for a variety of reasons, but primarily to increase sales volume, productivity, and profits. Home office sales trainers, field or local sales training, and/or private consulting organizations and professional trainers generally provide sales training.

- The sales manager must effectively direct and motivate salespeople to capitalize on their potential. Sales managers must provide proper leadership, personal and professional support, and attractive compensation. Appropriate sales quotas should be set for each salesperson.

- An evaluation program for salespeople should be tailored to the company for which it is being used. The overall evaluation program should be realistic, motivational, participatory, flexible, and specific. Both formal and informal evaluations should be completed regularly.

## Key Terms

benefit segmentation
benefit selling
boundary spanners
buying-decisions model
centralized sales
   organization
compensation plan
customer-relationship
   management

decentralized sales
   organization
formularized model
   (AIDA)
functional organization
job analysis
job description
job specification
leadership

line and staff organization
line organization
organization by
   specialization
personal selling
problem-solving model
professional selling
sales quota

## Review Questions

1. How does the use of professional selling differ in business markets versus consumer markets? What is the primary promotional element utilized in selling to each of these markets?

2. Discuss the four primary activities that professional business salespeople typically perform on a daily basis.

3. What factors contribute to the cost of professional business selling?

4. Explain the importance of using benefit selling in reaching business buyers. Discuss five methods by which a business salesperson can identify the important buying needs of prospects.

5. Describe the professional selling process. What are the three major activities and what is involved in each?

6. Describe three major models commonly used in making business sales presentations. Under what circumstances would the use of each model be most appropriate?

7. Be able to define and describe CRM, data mining, and mass customization.

8. Describe the expected functions of sales managers.

9. Differentiate among the five major types of sales force organization. Identify five means by which a sales force can be organized by specialization.

10. Explain how the size of a sales force can be determined by the workload method, the sales-potential method, and the incremental method. How is sales force turnover determined?

11. What are the roles of a job analysis, a job description, and a job specification in recruiting business salespeople?

12. Identify the reasons for sales training. Discuss areas of instruction that should be included in any business sales training program.

13. Describe three types of sales training methods. What are the steps involved in the sales training evaluation process?

14. How does a sales manager utilize leadership skills in directing and motivating the sales force? What are sales quotas, and how do business sales managers establish them? How is compensation related to the successful management of the business sales force? How often should a sales manager evaluate the sales performance of the individual members of the sales force?

---

**Case 3-1**

# Transit Systems Contractors Inc. (A) and (B)

This case was written by Dr. Roger Gomes and Dr. Patricia Knowles, Clemson University © 1999

NOTE: In Part A of this case you will follow and analyze the efforts of a field salesperson attempting to close on a major order involving high-technology component assemblies. Part B of the case will allow you to follow and analyze the competitor's actions over the same time period.

# Part A

June 30, 1999, 8:45 A.M.—Ray Mentzer, field salesperson for MPF Polymers, is making his first sales call of the day. He is in the reception area at TSC (Transit Systems Contractors Inc.) and is 15 minutes early for his appointment with Karen Ozanne, Purchasing Agent. Ray is hoping to get a chance to bid on some components for TSC which, by the looks of the construction site photographs on the wall, has continued to be successful, with hundreds of millions of dollars worth of transit construction contracts each year. Ray makes a mental note to ask Karen about which parts of the systems shown (Baltimore, Washington, D.C., and Atlanta) were handled by her company.

While waiting, Ray reviews his TSC account file and notes that it has been six weeks since his last visit, and that this is his eighth visit since first discovering the company last year. Ray has been attempting to be added to the TSC "bid list" of supplier companies who will be allowed to bid on new requirements. Although most of the previous sales calls had been routine relationship development for a new account, Karen's e-mail last week promised that this visit would include his picking up part prints and a request to bid on an upcoming contract.

Right at 9:00, Karen's administrative assistant (Brian) entered the reception area and greeted Ray. "Hi Ray, How's that BMW of yours running?" Ray made it a point to be friendly and respectful with all his buyers' administrative assistants. Many of them were not only important gatekeepers, but he suspected that they also had some undefined input into purchasing decisions. "Karen is going to meet with you in conference room B so that she and Jessica from engineering can go over some part drawings with you." Even though the prints that covered the entire table were stamped "preliminary," Ray was excited to see that they represented some type of assembly that would probably sell between $20 to $50 each. Ray could hardly contain himself when Karen stated the volume would be 10,000 units in this first contract, and probably 50,000 in total. By the time Ray left at 10:00, he had collected all the information his engineers and cost estimators would need to put together a bid. Karen left no question in Ray's mind that regardless of all the other strengths of MPF, price would be the determining factor in choosing the new part's supplier.

June 30, 1999, 12:30 P.M.—Before his next sales call, Ray mailed by overnight courier the TSC part prints and request for quotation to the home office and personally called the vice president of marketing to lobby for a quick turnaround and a bid at the lowest price possible. As expected, the July 4th holiday was going to slow things down, but Ray was promised that he could take in a bid by the end of July. Ray assures the marketing department that a good bid will get the contract.

July 15, 1999, 9:00 A.M.—Ray calls in to the cost estimating department to make sure the bid will be ready on time. Hearing no problems, Ray makes an appointment with Karen to present the bid.

July 27, 1999, 2:00 P.M.—Ray presents Karen with a bid of $32.14 each for 10,000 vibration isolators. Ray tries to uncover how the price looks compared to competitive quotes, but Karen just replies that she has a "somewhat lower" price target. She does note that Ray's is the first bid in, and that the design is yet to be finalized. Ray asks if it is OK to telephone next week. Based on Karen's compliments on being the first bid in, Ray calls in to his marketing department to express his confidence of getting the contract.

August 4, 1999, 9:30 A.M.—After several tries, Ray gets through to Karen, and she tells him that it will be a while before she has any information. After talking with Karen, Ray has a long talk with his sales manager, who reminds Ray that business selling takes time and patience. Ray assures his sales manager that he will do whatever it takes to get the order, and that he is sure that there is only one other company being asked to bid. Ray expresses some frustration, but expresses a 95 percent confidence level that the contract will be awarded within the next quarter, and a 70–80 percent chance that MPF will be awarded the contract.

October 15, 1999, 11:30 A.M.—Ray receives new print revisions from Karen and mails them overnight express to his home office. Ray arranges to have them hand carried through the estimating process and has a two-hour telephone discussion with the director of marketing concerning reducing the margin. At MPF, meetings are held, and every effort is made to support Ray's request.

October 30, 1999, 10:30 A.M.—Ray calls in (and faxes) his bid to Karen at $28.73 each, and stresses how each MPF department has contributed to making the cost savings possible.

November 7, 1999, 9:30 A.M.—At Ray's next sales call, Karen tells him that his price was "in the ballpark," but the contract was awarded to the competitor. Karen thanked him for his efforts and assured him that MPF would be in the running for the next bid.

November 7, 1999, 9:00 P.M.—Ray explains to his sales manager that although MPF didn't get the contract, the buyer was sincere that the firm is well positioned for the next bid. "I suspect that we were close in price, but we need a bigger difference in the price next time. It isn't enough to be in the 'ballpark.' We need pricing that will make the buyer stand up and take notice." The sales manager passes this information along to the vice president.

## Assignment

Analyze Ray's and MPF's strategy and performance and develop some new strategies for Ray to use on the next bid. Do not read Part B of the case until you have finished this assignment.

## Part B

June 30, 1999, 1:00 P.M.—Matt Campbell, field salesperson for Chicago Polymers, is making his first sales call on TSC (Transit Systems Contractors) and quickly goes over his company's successful contracts with leaders in the transit and rail industries for Karen Ozanne, a TSC purchasing agent. Karen asks Matt to look over some engineering drawings of a new part, to see what he thinks. Matt replies, "Karen, I'm happy to do that, but I need to involve my engineers. Give me about 30 minutes in your conference room and I'll scan them into my laptop, discuss them with my engineers (who have worked on similar projects), and we will undoubtedly need to discuss a few details with your engineers around 2:00 P.M." Karen replies that she will be in another meeting, but that Brian (her assistant) will arrange to have the product engineer come by at 2:00.

July 1, 1999, 8:00 A.M.—Having learned from the TSC product engineer that the final configuration of the assembly would be determined by test specifications that were under development at the Regional Transit Authority Headquarters (RTAH), Matt has flown with his engineer to meet with the appropriate RTAH engineer. Clearly the RTAH engineer is an expert in vibration isolation, but she is challenged to specify the response characteristics of a yet-to-be built assembly needed to properly isolate a yet-to-be built concrete foundation from a yet-to-be built set of transit cars. Matt's engineer suggests that they build prototypes with successive thickness and material hardness and measure their response under static load, followed by measuring their response between the track ties on part of an existing transit system.

July 2–12, 1999—Matt spends each day at the local university looking for books on vibration. He returns several times and eventually uncovers the names and addresses of professors working in mechanical engineering, polymer science, materials engineering, and packaging science. Their expertise will be useful to the project.

July 4–12, 1999—Matt's R & D department works over the holiday and creates a series of prototypes that are tested over the weekend and sent to RTAH.

July 15, 1999—Matt arranges a meeting with Karen to go over what they learned at RTAH and at the university. Matt reviews proposed changes to the preliminary part prints with Karen and her product engineer. After incorporating TSC's requirements concerning the changes, Matt has the TSC engineer initial and date the changes and scans them into his computer. Matt's estimators agree to bid based on the marked-up print. Matt returns to RTAH with his company's projections of the performance of the assembly. Over the next week the RTAH engineer finalizes the specification requirements based on Matt's data. TSC's engineers receive the new specification and are glad that Matt's company has made prototypes that—through custom design, formulations, and hardness of materials—exactly meet the response requirements needed.

July 27, 1999, 11:00 A.M.—Matt presents Karen with a set of samples that completely meet the response requirements of the RTAH specification. Karen has her development department place them under a variety of accelerated life tests such as fuel resistance, UV, and salt spray. Matt assures Karen that between his own R & D and the university experts, that all the tests will be successful. Matt promises a bid on the final configuration by the end of the week.

August 5, 1999—Matt presents Karen with a bid of $34.77 each, based on the marked-up drawing.

October 14 1999—Following successful accelerated life test results, TSC engineering issues final prints to purchasing, which Karen forwards to Matt.

October 15, 1999, 8:00 A.M.—Matt receives the new print revisions from Karen, confirms that they agree with the marked-up print (previously quoted) and advises Karen that there will be no change in the price of $34.77 each. Since Karen already is late in placing the order, she awards the contract to Matt's company, and he scans it into his order-processing department. Fortunately, Chicago Polymers has already made tentative arrangements with suppliers and scheduled production. Although the product development process has delayed Karen's releasing the order, Chicago Polymers' actions will allow products to be shipped on time.

## Assignment

You probably will agree that Ray and Matt have very different approaches to selling. Ray thinks that after he and his company made a good effort, he lost the bid because his price was too high. Note that he will pass this message on to his management and they will use the information as a basis for future strategic decisions. When did Ray actually start losing this bid? Develop some strategies for Ray to use on the next bid. How could Ray's management assure that they will have more insight into reality from the customer's point of view?

---

**Case 3-2**

# American Excelsior

Melissa Waters, CEO of Waters Manufacturers' Representatives Inc., had called Brian Washington, a sales trainee and recent graduate of the state university, into her office. Waters started by asking Brian how his initial sales calls were going, and if he felt that he had a clear understanding of the principals' products. (In manufacturers representative talk, a principal is one of the manufacturers that contract with the rep company to sell its products.) Brian replied, "I could repeat the specifications and customer benefits of every product of every principal backward." Waters liked that Brian had taken business marketing and selling classes at the university. It was very rare that she did not have to start from scratch with new college graduates. Brian had arrived ready to start selling, and ready to make a contribution to the success of the organization. He had the right attitude, saw every potential problem as a challenge, and took every opportunity to exceed performance expectations.

Waters continued, "Brian I've got some good news! How would you like to spend a couple of days at one of the nicest resorts in the country? I've watched you one-on-one with buyers and you are great at that skill set; your training really shows. Of course, now and then, sales reps also have to speak to larger groups. Sometimes the purchasing agent will call in buying center members from all over the corporation to hear your sales presentation." Brian thought, "Uh-oh, this doesn't sound good!"

Waters was full of smiles (as always) and said, "I'm scheduled to give a 15- or 20-minute speech at the National Conference of Shipping Executives and now it looks like I'll need to be in London closing a sale for one of our other principals. I would like you to represent us and make the speech." Brian felt like she had just asked him to skydive onto a shark-infested reef. He had never spoken to any group other than his college classes. But Brian was smart enough to know that he was being tested, so he swallowed and asked nonchalantly, "About how many will be there?" Waters replied, "Oh, only about 200." Brian thought, "AGHHH!," but asked calmly, "What is the topic?" Waters said, "That's why I know that you will have no problem with it. The topic is the new starch-based packaging products, you know, the foam 'peanuts' from American Excelsior. They're better than polystyrene peanuts sold by AE's competitors and also have advantages over treated popcorn as packaging material. You have already been selling some of their other products to our customers. Here is a copy of the presentation body. I was just planning to add some company introduction and ask for questions at the end." Brian knew that the only answer at this point was, "OK, I'll do my best."

Brian went back to his desk and read through the material that she had given him. It read:

> Imagine sending customers a package of Eco-Foam peanuts with nothing but a postcard inside. That's exactly what American Excelsior did. The catch? The peanuts used to pack the postcard were biodegradable. Customers were invited to test the biodegradability by putting a few pieces in a glass of water. Many customers had a good time performing this chemistry experiment as they watched the new material dissolve.
>
> American Excelsior is not a stranger to natural packaging. The company is the largest producer of excelsior, a cushioning medium composed of thin wood strips. Other companies have tried using popcorn and craft paper for packaging material. The problem is that these materials do not meet the industrial-type requirements met by peanuts.
>
> Popcorn breaks into small pieces and clogs standard peanut dispensers. To switch to paper, companies must make a capital investment. Eco-Foam can be used in the normal peanut dispensers and does not suffer from the static cling that annoys users of the polystyrene peanut product.
>
> Eco-Foam costs less than popcorn and paper, but it is more expensive than polystyrene. Polystyrene peanuts cost $.30 to $.60 per cubic foot. Eco-Foam costs $1 to $1.50 per cubic foot. American Excelsior is the exclusive licensee for the manufacturing and distribution of Eco-Foam peanuts in the United States. The current market for packing peanuts in the United States is 50 million to 60 million pounds per year. American Excelsior has about a 10-percent share of the market.
>
> Moreover, Eco-Foam seems to address environmentalists' concerns by solving two complaints about the standard polystyrene loose-fill product. The traditional peanuts are manufactured with a chemical blowing agent, chlorofluorocarbon, which has been shown to be harmful to Earth's ozone layer. Eco-Foam does not use chlorofluorocarbon. Eco-Foam is composed of 95 percent cornstarch and 5 percent polyvinyl alcohol. The manufacturing

process is similar to that of many breakfast cereals—a process using heat and steam to form the pieces. This also makes the product biodegradable. In addition, the company recommends reusing the product. If that's not practical, Eco-Foam can be spread on the lawn and watered into the soil, since it's completely nontoxic. Customers have suggested that Eco-Foam could be used as a gravy thickener. However, the company does not recommend eating the product, although most of the employees of American Excelsior have tried it."*

"This is just great," Brian thought. "If I present this it will last about five minutes, and I'll have to stand there looking dumb for the remaining 15 minutes. I'll have to collect much more information and add some interest and punch to the talk. I suppose public speaking is just one of those things that you can get used to only by practice. Waters probably wants me to try this at a conference rather than in front of customers (in case I mess up)."

That night Brian pulled out his class notes from his public speaking class. He read: Task one—Capture the listener's attention; Task two—Take control of the meeting and the room; Task three—Build a feeling of rapport; Task four—Help the audience understand something of value; Task five—Present a list of points to remember; Task six—Have a good close.† Flipping through the rest of the notebook, Brian reviewed a list of common mistakes: (1) poor preparation, (2) poor first impression, (3) no objectives, (4) dry and boring, (5) weak eye contact, (6) no humor, (7) no audience involvement, (8) no enthusiasm, (9) poor visual aids and overheads, and (10) weak close.‡

Brian thought, "OK, here's my plan. I'll read some books about presentations and collect more information about American Excelsior's products. Finally, I will come up with some creative ways to make the presentation unique and memorable. It must be hard for the audience to sit through several days of product and service presentations. I need to make my presentation different, hut in a way that will make Waters and American Excelsior proud. As usual, I'll exceed their expectations, and not do just a good job, but a great job."

## Assignment

You are Brian and you will need to prepare his presentation and deliver it at the conference (class). Start with some research on the principal (www.amerexcel.com) and particularly read about Eco-Foam starch-based packaging. As Brian found, speech class was OK, but now it is time to learn more about making professional presentations. Your library's business librarian can direct you to appropriate reference materials. Practice and more practice is the best way to become more comfortable with public speaking often required of marketers. We don't speak in front of groups because it's easy for us; we do it because it must be done and we are in the best position to do it well.

*From *Principles of Marketing,* 1st edition, by C. Lamb, J. Hair, and C. McDaniel. © 1992. Reprinted with permission of South-Western College Publishing, a division of Thompson: 277-78. FAX 800-730-2215

†D. J. Whalen, *I See What You Mean: Persuasive Business Communication* (Thousand Oaks, CA: Sage Publications, 1996): 159.

‡D. A. Peoples, *Presentations Plus,* 2nd edition (New York: John Wiley & Sons, 1992): 23.

---

## Case 3-3

# Clarkton Laboratories

## Part A

Jason and Jessica Bowen were twins, and both were senior marketing majors. Although they didn't often agree on many things, they were both considering careers in business-to-business professional selling. This morning they were particularly excited to be spending the day shadowing Mike Jenson, New England district sales manager for Clarkton Laboratories. Clarkton was a major producer of medications prescribed by doctors and purchased in volume by pharmacies.

Their day began at 8:00 A.M., when the twins met Mike at the Hampton Inn just off US Rt. 95 in North Providence, R.I. Mike also was meeting Bob Johnson, Clarkton's Providence region sales representative. Mike invited everyone to have some coffee or breakfast at the hotel's complimentary breakfast bar for guests. Mike began by describing the responsibilities of a sales manager and a sales representative for the visiting students. He explained that as a sales manager, he typically spent four days a week in the field with the sales representatives and spent the fifth day at home catching up on paperwork. Today was his day to spend with Bob, and the day would include several routine customer sales calls on hospitals, starting with a particularly important opportunity to close on becoming a preferred (almost sole) supplier.

Mike explained that the important opportunity was at the University Hospital, where the medical staff was considering a changeover from the medical products supplied by Clarkton's competitors. The change would be a significant increase in territory sales, and potentially it could be used to influence other customers. Before they started, Mike also explained that pharmaceutical sales are highly technical and that the technical details are constantly changing. He explained that it is a major challenge to keep the main decision-makers and the buying center influencers current on product information.

At 10:00 A.M. the group arrived at University Hospital and proceeded to the office of Debbie Jones, chief pharmacist. The meeting began with an informal discussion of the opportunities for trained pharmacists in the manufacturing side of the industry. Apparently Debbie was considering a career change, and Mike wanted to be sure that she would be considering options at Clarkton. The students were glad to hear Bob eventually get down to business, but were surprised to hear the chief pharmacist report that there were still several new drug committee doctors who were reluctant to switch. Bob provided some data sheets showing that his company's product worked as well as the competitors' and was considerably cheaper. Bob thought Debbie could use the information to help change the minds of the reluctant doctors.

Throughout the meeting Mike watched how Bob handled the situation but did not say much. That is, until Debbie asked Bob about the details of some new research findings on the side effects of the main drug in question. Bob fumbled with a nonanswer, and Mike responded promptly with the necessary information. Bob wrapped up the sales call by thanking Debbie for her efforts and interest and promised to call again next week. Outside in the car, Mike and Bob went over what they had learned, and both concluded that the sale would eventually be made.

At 11:00 A.M. the group made their next call, Union Hospital. Their first stop was the hospital pharmacy, where they chatted with two pharmacists and checked the inventory of Clarkton products. In a semiserious voice, Bob scolded one of them for not pushing enough of a certain drug. As he went on, it was clear to the students that he was probing for a reason for the lack of inventory turnover. They could clearly see the part of Bob's job that involved being both politician and detective.

From there they went to see a doctor who, it turned out, was busy with an operation. When it became apparent they would have to wait, Bob brought the group into the nurses' lounge where they could relax. Normally, the nurses' lounge would have been strictly off limits to visitors, but Bob was on very good terms with the nurses, and they turned out to be a useful information source concerning which doctors were using which products. They finally caught the doctor coming out of surgery, but he rushed away, asking Bob to come back another time. From there, Bob took the group to see another doctor but managed to speak to him only briefly. The doctor was about to leave for a luncheon appointment, and

Bob was able only to run through a quick presentation on a new Clarkton drug. On the way out Mike stressed that business-to-business sales took time to develop, and persistence would be a determining factor.

It was after 1:30 P.M. when the group was through at Union. Bob went on to some additional sales calls, while Mike offered to buy the twins lunch at a nearby upscale seafood restaurant. The twins were wise enough to order conservative lunches with soft drinks. During lunch, Mike shared some of his views of sales management. He told the twins, "The biggest problem that every sales manager faces is motivation. The toughest part of a sales rep's job is just getting out of bed in the morning." In addition, he stated that he believed it was important to manage by support and positive reinforcement, rather than by conflict. He said that he did not believe in simply telling his people to meet their quotas—or else. On the subject of high turnover of salespeople, Mike stated, "New people are too sensitive and take rejections and failures too personally. Such a person simply cannot survive in the long run." In summing up his feelings, Mike made a comment on the lifestyle that goes along with a career in selling. He pointed out that although the work is hard, the rewards are great. "We work hard and we play hard. It's not for everyone."

As the twins were driving home, Jessica was quiet, but Jason could not stop chatting about how great it must be to sell for a company like Clarkton. "The sales representatives are paid more than the other positions we have looked at, and the territories are much smaller, meaning less overnight trips. Clarkton products are recognized as high-quality, and you don't even have to close on orders. Most of the job is just keeping the doctors and pharmacists up-to-date on product developments." Jason was confident as he declared, "I don't know about you, but I am definitely going to apply to Clarkton and put them on the top of my list. I know that the competition is going to be tough, so what I am going to do is pick a couple of hot Clarkton drugs, learn all about them, and plan a sample sales call on both a single practitioner, a doctor on staff at a hospital, and a pharmacist. That will show them that I know how to differentiate myself by exceeding expectations, and that I know how the buyer needs vary by situation."

## Assignment

Sales manager responsibilities include training. Help Jason to plan his sales calls in such a way that you can present the information about making sales calls to all the sales representatives (class). If you use a particular drug as an example, be sure that you pick a noncontroversial one. Your presentation to the class should be as professional as one would expect from a sales manager addressing a sales meeting. You will not need to read part B to complete this assignment.

## Part B

Jessica had heard enough. It had been a difficult morning, and listening to Jason go on and on was getting on her nerves. "Jason," she said firmly, "remember the business-to-business selling class you didn't want to take because we had to practice selling in front of the camera? I think you decided to take Consumer Behavior III, while I was taking selling." Jason just grunted. He knew his sister well enough to realize that she was just getting started. Jessica continued, "I'm no expert, but lots of what we saw today went against what I learned in that selling class. Customer relationships hadn't been built. Those doctors didn't even want to see Bob. Bob was wasting their time and his. He didn't even know that new drug's major side effects. What could be more important than that? At the end, when Mike was telling us about it being hard for sales reps to get up in the morning, what he really was saying was how he feels. The scary part is that a sales manager's lack of enthusiasm will be reflected in those reporting to him." Jessica continued, "Mike's a burned-out, sorry excuse for a sales manager, and Bob doesn't really know how to sell. And, most telling of all is that

Clarkton Laboratories isn't doing anything about it. First of all, a good salesperson would love helping customers. I'll bet that Clarkton's competitors had their representatives out building relationships while we were all having breakfast this morning. I'll bet that they would all have appointments, plan sales call content, and be welcomed by their customers as valued problem solvers and information providers—someone who helps them serve their patients better. Also, I don't think that Hampton Inn would have been thrilled for us to be eating their complimentary breakfast, and, further, we didn't belong in that hospital's nurses' lounge. I wonder how much time Bob spends there? I wonder if on the fifth day, Bob does paperwork like Mike? I never heard of sales managers or representatives at home doing paperwork while the customers were available." Jessica finished with, "I am definitely not going to apply to Clarkton, and after today, I'm not sure I want any part of this whole industry." Before Jason could even reply, Jessica added, "And what was that stuff about hinting that there might be a job at Clarkton Labs for that chief pharmacist whom they want to help persuade that hospital to change to their products? That couldn't have been ethical!"

## Assignment

Review the day (Part A) from the perspective of the national sales manager (Mike reports to you). Present your analysis to the class, along with your action plan to support, facilitate, or change current procedures and personnel. Keep in mind that any drastic action could have a major negative impact throughout the sales force. Consider how other individuals like Mike and Bob would react to your presentation. It is your decision.

Clarkton Laboratories, Part A, is adapted from a case by Eugene M. Johnson, David L. Kurtz, and Eberhard Scheuing titled "Barton Laboratories," which was featured in an earlier edition of this text.

**References**

1. Andy Cohen, "Faster, Faster, Faster!" *Sales & Marketing Management* (July 1998): 13.
2. H. Robert Dodge, "The Role of the Industrial Salesman," *Mid-South Quarterly Review* (January 1972): 11–15.
3. Philip Kotler, *Marketing Management* (Upper Saddle River, NJ: Prentice-Hall, 2000): 620.
4. Charles J. Quigley, Jr., Frank G. Bingham, Jr., and Michael B. Patterson, "The Information Flow for a Business-to-Business Buying Decision Process: A Modeling Approach," *The Journal of Marketing Theory and Practice* 2 (Fall 1993): 103–21.
5. John J. Withy and Eric Panitz, "Face-to-Face Selling: Making It More Effective," *Industrial Marketing Management* 24 (August 1995): 239–46.
6. Patricia A. Knowles, Stephen J. Grove, and Kay Keck, "Signal Detection Theory and Sales Effectiveness." *Journal of Personal Selling and Sales Management* 14 (Spring 1994): 1–14.
7. Bernard L. Rosenbaum, "Seven Emerging Sales Competencies." *Business Horizons* 44 (January 2001): 33.
8. Ibid, #4.
9. "Hiring: Love It or Hate It?" *Sales & Marketing Management* (January 1999): 14.
10. *Sales & Marketing Management*'s 1998 Productivity Study.
11. Ronald R. Still, Edward W. Cundiff, and Norman A. Govoni, *Sales Management: Decisions, Strategies, and Cases,* 9th ed. (Englewood Cliffs, N.J.: Prentice-Hall, 1981): 63–68. Also see Richard F. Wendel and Walter Gorman, *Selling*, 5th ed. (New York: Random House Business Division, 1988): 576–77.
12. Barry J. Farber, "On the Lookout," *Sales & Marketing Management* (October 1995): 34–35.
13. Chad Kaydo, "Give Us 2 Weeks and We'll Give You a New Sales Force," *Sales & Marketing Management* (December 1998): 33.
14. Training magazine survey. Repeated in *Sales & Marketing Management* (January 1999): 49.

15.  Erika Rasmusson, "Getting Schooled in Outsourcing," *Sales & Marketing Management* (January 1999): 49–53.

16.  Jhinuk Chowdhury and Victor J. Massad, "An Electric Paradigm of Salesperson Compensation: Toward a Comprehensive Framework of the Determinants of Sales Compensation Modes," *The Journal of Marketing Management* 6 (Spring/Summer 1997): 61–80.

## CHAPTER FOUR

# The Organizational Buying Process

## Learning Objectives

After reading this chapter, you should be able to:

- Articulate the objectives of efficient business buying.
- Appreciate the changing role of the business buyer.
- Discuss the steps involved in the business buying process.
- Describe the process by which potential vendors are evaluated.
- Differentiate between types of business buying situations.
- Realize the role and significance of the buying center.
- Understand the materials management concept.
- Discuss the impact of the Internet on buyers and sellers.
- Understand the environmental forces that influence business buying decisions.

## Chapter Outline

Objectives of Business Buyers

Profile of a Professional Buyer

The Changing Role of the Buyer

The Business Buying Process

Business Buying Situations

The Buying Center

The Materials Management Concept

Purchasing and the Internet

Environmental Forces and Buying Decisions

Purchasing's Impact Upon Company Profit

## Objectives of Business Buyers

Every transaction involving the transfer of a property between a buyer and seller is a *contract*. While some contracts are simple, others in the business sector are lengthy written agreements defining in technical terms the nature of the material or service, the method of payment, and other contractual conditions. The authority and responsibility of buying business materials and services and ensuring that the obligations of the buyer/seller contract are met rest with the purchasing department of the buying firm.

Business buyers have several distinct objectives in purchasing goods and services. In general, business-buying objectives such as product and service availability, reliability of sellers, and consistency of quality, delivery, and price, are important for all types of firms. However, different types of organizational buyers, such as manufacturers, wholesalers, government customers, and not-for-profit institutions, emphasize one or more of these objectives.

Managing the cost of purchased goods and services continues to be one of the hottest issues in supply chain management today. Indeed, purchasing costs are the largest single component in the operation of many organizations. The magnitude of the purchasing task becomes apparent as managers learn the importance of the relationship between the cost of purchased goods and materials and the sales dollar. In general, the ratio ranges between 40 percent and 60 percent of sales revenue—typically the largest single component of expenditures in industry. Thus, the decisions made by business buyers directly impact the costs and thus the profitability of the firm. In the future, the purchasing function will be expected to play a greater role in cost reduction projects of all types.

Throughout the years, American business organizations have focused on finding better ways to perform the tasks and develop the relationships that are essential to a dynamic, industrial world civilization. The materials acquisition-retention cycle in the overall purchasing process is undergoing rapid change as the business buying process has become not only time consuming but also highly involved. Any strategy for decreasing the overall costs of buying materials and equipment requires the application of modern methods of procurement. Business buying has evolved into a complex process of decision making and communication that takes place over time, can involve several organizational members, and includes relationships with other firms and institutions. Clearly, the task of business buying encompasses far more than the simple act of placing an order with a vendor or a selling organization.

## Profile of a Professional Buyer

The Institute for Supply Management (ISM) has issued a report detailing a profile of purchasing and supply chain management professionals. This survey not only profiles the purchasing executive but also provides an indication of developing trends as both buyers and sellers prepare to face marketplace challenges in the twenty-first century. The survey results indicate that a typical ISM member is 36 to 55 years old, is a male caucasian (89.9 percent) who holds a bachelor's degree (59 percent). Twenty-one percent hold a graduate degree, with 54 percent majoring in business. Thirty-seven percent are women. Most ISM members have worked in purchasing 16 years or longer, earn at least $45,000 per year, and purchase more than $10 million of goods and services each year.[1]

One of the most notable aspects of the data retrieved is the continued rapid rise in ISM female membership. As a percentage of total membership, female membership rose from 16 percent in 1986 to 29 percent in the mid-1990s to 37 percent today. The rate of new female memberships outpaces that of males by five to one, and it appears that this trend will continue.

The marketing implications of these findings are enormous. The organizational status of purchasing individuals seems to be rising, which is reflected not only in the title of chief purchasing officer, but also in the functions that typically report to the purchasing executive. Business sellers cannot avoid interaction with the purchasing person on most buying decisions, so a clear understanding and appreciation of his or her duties and responsibilities is imperative. Additionally, purchasing executives are opting for more long-term buying contracts, and they will continue to buy from fewer sources. This will force many vendors (or potential vendors) to assume more responsibility for the inventory burden, which coincides with the continued trend toward just-in-time (JIT) buying in many industries. Thus, make-and-hold arrangements via long-term buying contracts, strong negotiation skills, an increased awareness of such factors as the small-order problem, and the continued growth of *electronic commerce (EC)* can put the astute seller or potential seller in a commanding position. These buying strengths, accompanied by buyers' trend toward *single sourcing* (buying a particular product or service from one versus several vendors), puts additional pressure on the sales executive.

| **Concept Review** | 1. What are some of the recent changes that have occurred in the materials acquisition-retention cycle in the overall purchasing process? | 2. How are purchasing personnel different from their counterparts of only a few years ago? |
|---|---|---|

## The Changing Role of the Buyer

The role of the business buyer is constantly changing. The historical trend toward profit planning results in the buying organization placing a great amount of pressure on the purchasing executive. Effective business marketing depends upon an understanding of market behaviors, particularly organizational buying behavior. Most U.S. industries spend resources for materials, services, direct production labor, and energy. Purchasing is directly involved in the decision to acquire materials, services, and energy. This involvement is a key reason business sellers and buyers must work together and must establish and maintain an enduring relationship if both buyer and seller are to survive. Earning the buyer's trust is thus a prerequisite for success in selling business goods and services.

### Relationship Marketing

*Relationship marketing* (often called *alliances* or *strategic partnerships*) is the process whereby a firm builds long-term alliances with prospective as well as current customers so that both seller and buyer work toward a common set of specified goals. These goals are met by: (1) understanding customer needs, (2) treating customers as partners, (3) ensuring that employees satisfy customer needs, and (4) providing customers with the best possible quality, relative to individual needs.

When a supplier and buyer develop a working partnership over a period of time, the supplier practically becomes a part of the buyer's organization. Smart suppliers adjust their thinking, management styles, and methods of responding to a purchaser's standards and operational requirements. The relationship a supplier builds with a buyer is not driven by a faddish trend but by a combination of four strong business forces: quality, speed, cost-effectiveness, and new design techniques. The combination of these four forces has fostered closer working relationships between purchasers and suppliers. In today's environment, businesses increasingly depend on the relationships they have with their suppliers and are demanding that they adhere to high standards. It is increasingly important that buyers have strong relationships with their suppliers to stay ahead of competition. In competitive business situations, there is always a chance that a seller can be replaced by a competitor. Therefore, it is useful to understand the seller characteristics that buyers think influence quality buyer-seller relationships.[2] Consider:

> At Disneyland, the true innovation is the relationships we are building with key suppliers of goods and services. I need to understand my supplier's business as much as he or she needs to understand mine.
>
>    *Leslie R. Monroe, Contract Coordinator, Disneyland, Anaheim, California*

> To consistently improve the entire MRO (maintenance, repair, and operating) supply order chain, reduce costs to our customers, and increase service levels we must tap into our supplier's expertise on a daily basis. To achieve this, we find it necessary to be innovative in our communications with suppliers. As an example we use the Internet to source and exchange information with suppliers. Also, to reduce the number of calls, our accounts payable department provides an automated information phone line that allows suppliers to receive automated responses and payment information.
>
>    *Edward Kallaway, C.P.M., Buyer, Eddie Bauer, Inc. Redmond, Washington*

> Alberto Culver negotiates multiyear contracts with key suppliers, which includes a performance-based incentive rebate. We hold quarterly meetings to review the supplier's performance. For each successive year of the contract, the supplier and Alberto Culver agree to higher performance targets as we work toward continuous improvement. The goal is to have on-time delivery and quality exceed 99 percent by the end of the contract period.
>
>    *Judy K. Spencer, C.P.M., Senior Buyer, Alberto Culver, Melrose Park, Illinois.*

*Purchasing Today,* February 1999, p. 68. National Association of Purchasing Management, Tempe, Arizona.

This trend is accelerating rapidly, particularly among high-tech manufacturers. These companies have learned that strategic partnerships are more than just desirable—they are critical. Currently, suppliers are cutting their vendor lists and treating the remaining vendors as allies, sharing strategic information freely and drawing upon supplier expertise in developing new products that meet the quality, cost, and delivery standards of the marketplace. Across industries, firms increasingly assign greater responsibility to suppliers in order to produce innovative, high-quality products at a competitive cost and in a timely fashion. To ensure that suppliers are capable and continuously improving, buying firms may engage in supplier development.[3] In today's business climate adversarial and exploitative buyer-seller relationships are the exception rather than the rule. Partnerships and strategic alliances link firms, promoting joint cost savings, product enhancements, and competitive services. Busy buyers who become accustomed to regular and timely assistance from creative sellers will not change sources of supply very readily.

Finally, it should be noted that partnerships and alliances can develop intra- or interindustry. The major U.S. automakers have formed an alliance to develop an efficient battery for an electric car. This is an example of *intraindustry alliance.* The Dupont-Merck alliance is an example of an *interindustry alliance* between chemical and pharmaceutical giants. Dupont brings its productive discovery capabilities, while Merck contributes its development expertise, market rights to several brands, and established skills in bringing products to commercial fruition. Strategic alliances can be as simple as two companies sharing their technological and/or marketing resources. Likewise, alliances can be highly complex, involving several companies located in different countries.[4]

## Value Analysis

**Value analysis (VA)** is the task of studying a product and all of its components in order to determine ways to produce it at a lower cost, to improve its quality, or to make it with a material in greater or more stable supply. Value analysis is a creative task, thought of as a scientifically organized method for reducing costs of manufactured items and for encouraging

**EXHIBIT 4-1**
**The Value-Analysis Approach: Comparison of Function with Cost**

1. Select a relatively high-cost or high-volume purchased item to value analyze. This can be a part, material, or service. Select an item you suspect is costing more than it should.
2. Find out how the item is used and what is expected of it, i.e. its function, in detail.
3. Ask the following questions:
   a. Does its use contribute value?
   b. Is it cost-proportionate to usefulness?
   c. Does it need all its features?
   d. Is there anything better, at a more favorable purchase price, for the intended use?
   e. Can the item be eliminated?
   f. If the item is not standard, can a standard item be used?
   g. If it is a standard item, does it completely fit the proposed application, or is it a misfit?
   h. Does the item have greater capacity than required?
   i. Is there a similar item in inventory that could be used instead?
   j. Can the weight be reduced?
   k. Are closer tolerances specified than are necessary?
   l. Is needless machining performed on the item?
   m. Are unnecessarily fine finishes specified?
   n. Is commercial quality specified?
   o. Can you make the item now? Can you buy it for less?
   p. If you are making it now, can you buy it for less?
   q. Is the item properly classified for shipping purposes to obtain the lowest transportation rates?
   r. Can cost of packaging be reduced?
   s. Are you asking your suppliers for suggestions to reduce costs?
   t. Do material, reasonable labor, overhead, and profit total the item's cost?
   u. Will another dependable supplier provide it for less?
   v. Is anyone buying it for less?
4. Now:
   a. Pursue those suggestions that appear practical.
   b. Get samples of the proposed item(s).
   c. Select the best possibilities and propose changes.

a seller's (vendor's) cooperation in lowering costs of purchased items. Professional buyers usually are responsible for the value analysis (VA) effort in the buying firm. Exhibit 4-1 details the *value-analysis approach* in a comparison of function to cost.

Let's examine a brief example of value analysis in action. Assume that a seller of industrial gears has always supplied a particular buyer with the gears made from steel. In an effort to reduce the cost of the gears to the customer, the seller experiments with other materials, concluding, after research, development, and testing, that a gear made out of cast metal will do the job just fine. The delivered price of the gear can now be delivered at a 20 percent cost saving to the buyer. The buyer is happy; the seller looks good. If the seller had not initiated such action, perhaps a more aggressive competitor would have offered the "new" gear to the buyer first. The old supplier would become the "out" supplier, and the new, innovative supplier would become the "in" supplier.

Value analysis is not cost or price oriented. Rather, it is function oriented, with people involved in trying to determine the best way to do a job at the lowest possible cost. Due to their exposure to other applications of their products (parts, materials, or services), sellers are in a unique position to help the members of the business buying center obtain maximum value for each dollar spent. The business seller's knowledge encompasses materials, services, fabrication methods, and equipment. He or she should advise buyers on tolerances, finishes, or anything else that might affect the cost, as well as the feasibility, of the design. In short, the trained marketer should be an important part of the customer's value analysis team, understanding the objectives of the customer's programs and earning the customer's continued confidence. The seller's role in value analysis cannot be overemphasized; if the current seller cannot or will not get involved in a customer's value analysis program, a more astute seller eventually will!

## Make-or-Buy Analysis

To make or to buy is a question frequently asked by supply managers who want to reveal and exploit every competency within the links of the supply chain. The decision of whether to manufacture a product in-house or to purchase it from an outside source (outsourcing) can have a significant impact on the long-term, as well as the day-to-day operation of the firm. The one indisputable fact is that the use of outsourcing for acquiring products and services is growing rapidly in both the manufacturing and service sectors. Deciding what should be made and what should be bought constitutes what is commonly referred to as the **make or buy analysis.** This analysis is typically part of the business buyer's job and presents another opportunity for the astute business marketer to extend the idea of relationship marketing. Salespeople, along with buying firm personnel, such as engineering and production supervisors, should supply the buyer with pertinent data that will contribute to a thorough analysis. Aggressive sellers should be especially aware of the value of their expertise in this area. Exhibit 4-2 illustrates the decision-making process and the various functional groups involved in a make or buy analysis.

A company may decide to manufacture rather than purchase for the following reasons: the item is required in large volume, can be adapted to the existing production facilities, can be produced by the company at a cost low enough to allow a savings over a supplier's price, and is not protected by patents that would necessitate payment of sizable royalties. A company may also choose to manufacture rather than purchase an item when faced with the existence of one or more unreliable suppliers.

**EXHIBIT 4-2   Participants in the Make-or-Buy Decision**

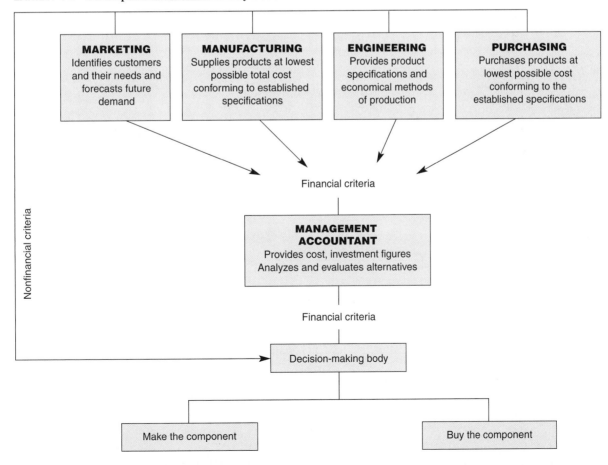

## Negotiation

Most business buyers are trained negotiators; those engaged in the organizational or business buying and selling process practice negotiation almost daily. **Negotiation** is a technique for communicating ideas in which both buyers and sellers attempt to convince the other party to yield to their demands, with the ultimate objective being a mutually beneficial agreement.

The ideal negotiator, whether buyer or seller, should possess the complementary traits of courage, confidence (high self-esteem and self-acceptance), flexibility, humility, patience, charm (or likeability), and an understanding of human nature and need satisfaction. In addition, he or she should possess the logical traits of high tolerance for ambiguity, strong cognitive complexity (abstract thinking), high intelligence, and realistic decision-making ability. Both sides must win something in the negotiation process, and both sides must leave the session feeling some satisfaction; otherwise, the process was not productive. Exhibit 4-3 outlines the fundamentals of successful negotiation. It is interesting to note that communication is key to successful negotiation.

Negotiation is not about price alone. Negotiating the terms and conditions for a good or service requires buyers and sellers to understand the total cost concept. Even among

**EXHIBIT 4-3   Fundamentals of Successful Negotiation**

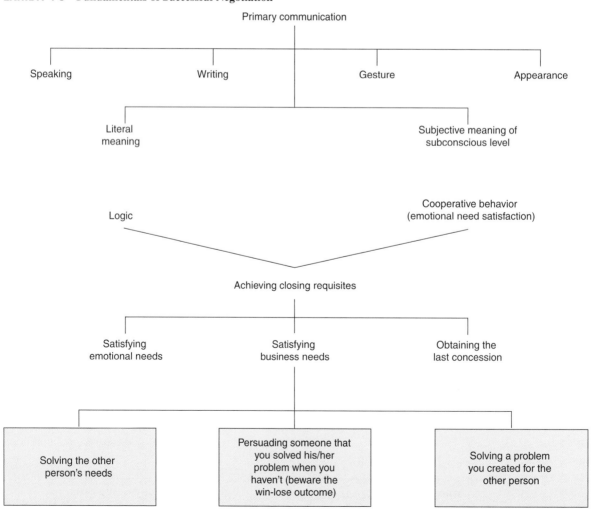

**EXHIBIT 4-4** **A Buyer's Viewpoint of Both a Buyer's and a Seller's Negotiating Position**

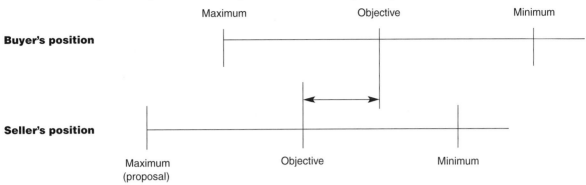

noncritical, high-volume items, when price may be a primary goal of the negotiation, its often not prudent to negotiate the lowest price if the materials can't be delivered on time or to a user's specifications.[5] Also, prior to the negotiation session, both the buyer and the seller should learn as much as possible about the other's position. For example, the economic trade-offs that underlie a company's make-or-buy decision almost always are an important influence on negotiation strategy. Understanding the economic influences and their potential outcomes may allow both sides more flexibility in negotiating. Both buyer and seller must attempt to analyze the other's primary negotiating objectives and minimum and maximum positions on those objectives. Exhibit 4-4 presents a visualization of the position of the two parties from the buyer's standpoint. Note that both the buyer and the seller have maximum and minimum positions, indicating a willingness to give up certain things and an unwillingness to give up others. Note also that each has an objective and that the difference (distance) between the buyer's objective and the seller's is not very substantial. The objective for both buyer and seller, then, is to identify this area of difference and to work to reduce it to the point where both parties can agree to a contract.

## Centralization Versus Decentralization of the Buying Function

Some business-to-business companies centralize purchasing activity completely, doing the buying for all plants from a central headquarters office. Others decentralize the function entirely, giving each plant full authority to conduct all of its purchasing activities. Still other firms—in fact, the majority—develop an organizational buying structure somewhere between the extremes of centralization and decentralization. Because both approaches offer significant benefits, the marketer should understand the philosophy of each.

In **centralized purchasing**, an individual or department is given authority to make all purchases (except the very unusual buy, such as a new company aircraft). The advantages to be gained from centralized purchasing are as follows: (1) The standardization of purchased parts is easier as all decisions go through a central control point. (2) Administrative duplication is eliminated or reduced because only one order is sent for the firm's total requirement for a particular product or service. (3) By combining requirements from several locations, order quantities can be increased. Buyers and sellers can then negotiate for faster delivery, quantity discounts, and freight savings for carload quantities. (4) Sellers need not call on several people within the buying firm, providing the buyer with better control over purchase commitments. (5) The development of specialization and expertise in purchasing decisions is fostered.

Indeed, the advantages of centralization are so great in comparison to decentralized purchasing that almost all firms are moving in that direction. For example, prior to centralizing its purchasing function and realizing substantial savings, General Motors spent millions of dollars each year, with more than 100 buying locations purchasing 24 million pairs of work gloves in 225 styles from nearly 100 different vendors.

In **decentralized purchasing**, the buying function is done at the local or regional level with division buyers buying all products and services needed to support a production operation. The advantages to be gained from decentralized purchasing include: (1) Less inventory is required, as the source of supply is nearby. (2) Cost may be lower due to local economic conditions. (3) Local buyers and sellers become well acquainted with each other, thus facilitating the movement of products and service through the local supply chain. (4) Buyers reap the advantages (real or imagined) by buying "locally," thereby creating the impression of being a good corporate customer and "neighbor."

## The Business Buying Process

A **buying situation** is created when some member of the organization perceives a problem that can be solved through the purchase of a product or service. Since there are wide variations among industries, companies, products, and personnel, it would not be feasible to establish a single set of buying procedures that apply to all cases. In one way or another, however, essential steps must be taken to complete a buying transaction. These steps are shown in Exhibit 4-5. We will track each of the stages in this purchasing process, using General Electric (GE) as a hypothetical example.[6] Assume that GE decides to design and build a new line of industrial clothes dryers and needs an electric motor as a key component in the dryer.

### Recognizing the Need

Following the decision of GE appliance division top management to introduce a new line of clothes dryers, engineering and research and development (R & D) personnel create a

**EXHIBIT 4-5   Steps in the Business Buying Process**

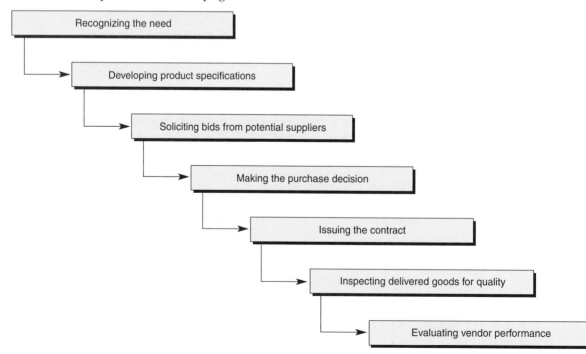

- Recognizing the need
- Developing product specifications
- Soliciting bids from potential suppliers
- Making the purchase decision
- Issuing the contract
- Inspecting delivered goods for quality
- Evaluating vendor performance

workable design that is tested and approved. They then confer with the purchasing executive to determine whether the electric motor needed for the clothes dryer should be purchased from an outside supplier or be manufactured by the firm itself. The make-or-buy decision the group reaches is that the electric motor used in the dryer should be bought from an outside supplier rather than manufactured by GE.

## Developing Product Specifications

Engineering and R & D personnel develop product specifications for the electric motor that include detailed technical requirements regarding horsepower, life in hours, and ability to operate at a stated temperature and humidity level. In determining the exact production specifications needed, often the purchasing department calls upon the technical expertise of vendors in developing appropriate design specifications. Members of the buying team (buying center) must develop the necessary buying criteria for the electric motor, which, in this example, are: (1) quality requirements, (2) on-time delivery, and (3) price, in that order. The purchasing manager is then given the responsibility of selecting the supplier and negotiating a contract for the motors.

## Soliciting Bids from Potential Suppliers

Buying personnel select the names of potential vendors believed to be qualified to supply the item and send each a **request for quotation (RFQ)** form describing the quantity needed, the delivery date required, and the product specifications. Typically, they also perform a *vendor analysis* to evaluate all potential suppliers objectively according to the criteria or standards determined as important. Exhibit 4-6 presents a typical vendor rating sheet. Bidder lists are updated continuously by adding the names of potential new vendors and deleting the names of unsatisfactory vendors. Many buying firms require that as many as three bids be solicited for purchases exceeding a specified dollar amount.

## Making the Purchase Decision

Unlike the short purchase stage in a consumer buying decision, such as buying a six-pack of soft drinks, the purchase stage in organizations covers the period from selecting the vendor and placing the purchase order through product delivery. This period may take weeks, or even months. During this time, the GE purchasing manager follows up with the vendor, expedites the order, and renegotiates the contract terms if specification changes are made after the initial contract is awarded.

## Issuing the Contract

The contract stage, in which GE and the seller enter into an agreement that is legally binding on both sides, is a crucial part of the purchasing process. Sometimes contracts are awarded directly to vendors based on the data they provide in RFQ forms. At other times, the purchasing manager selects the vendor and awards a contract in the form of a purchase order, which is an authorization for the vendor to provide the items under the agreed-upon terms and to bill the purchasing firm upon completion of the order.

## Inspecting Delivered Goods for Quality

When the electric motors are delivered, the quality control department tests them to ensure that they meet specifications. If the motors are unsatisfactory, the purchasing manager will negotiate with the supplier to rework the items according to specifications or will arrange for a new shipment.

**EXHIBIT 4-6** **Vendor Rating Sheet**

Beach Valve, Inc.
San Francisco, California

Supplier:                          Bay Valve, Inc.

Location:                          Los Gatos, California

Product(s) purchased:              Industrial Valves

Locations served:                  San Francisco Bay Area

|                                        | Excellent | Good | Fair | Poor |
|----------------------------------------|-----------|------|------|------|
| Overall quality of merchandise         | X         |      |      |      |
| Variety of models available            | X         |      |      |      |
| Speed of routine shipments             |           |      | X    |      |
| Speed of back orders                   |           |      | X    |      |
| Service provided after the sale        |           | X    |      |      |
| Amount of defective merchandise shipped| X         |      |      |      |
| Handling of defective merchandise      | X         |      |      |      |
| Conditions of sale                     |           | X    |      |      |
| Wholesaler profitability               |           | X    |      |      |
| Overall customer satisfaction          | X         |      |      |      |

Comments:     Very pleased with this supplier, particularly in terms of quality and variety of items kept in stock and overall customer satisfaction. Supplier needs to improve upon speed of routine and back-order shipments, and wholesale profitability could be slightly better.

|  |  |
|---|---|
| December 2, 2003 | Sara McMahon, Director of Purchasing |
| (Date) | (Signed) |

## Evaluating Vendor Performance

As the final step in the business buying process, GE's purchasing manager evaluates the vendor's performance after final delivery of the purchased items. Often, this information is noted on the vendor-rating sheet discussed previously and is used to update the bidder list. Performance on past contracts determines a vendor's chances of being asked to bid on future purchases; poor performance might result in a vendor's name being dropped from the bidder list.

**Concept Review**

1. Why is earning the buyer's trust a prerequisite for success in selling business goods and services?

2. It is said that strategic partnerships are more than just desirable—they are critical. Why?

3. Why is a vendor analysis performed as part of the business buying process?

# BUSINESS MARKETING IN ACTION

## SINGLE SOURCING

In the pursuit of a highly integrated supply chain, many companies have reduced their supplier base to a minimum. Particularly for JIT relationships, the model of one supplier per commodity group has proven itself in a variety of industries across the globe. A reader survey by *Purchasing Magazine* found 81 percent of companies operating with at least one voluntary single source supply relationship. The relationship requires new levels of trust and involvement. Maytag, for example, is developing long-term 3- to 10-year agreements with suppliers, such as Emerson, as its sole source for motors, Exxon Chemical for polypropylene resins, Inland Steel for steel sheets, and Ferro Corp. for paints and coatings. In some cases "partnership" becomes so close that supplier personnel become residents at the customer's plants (becoming part of the customer's technical or management team, while actually employed by the supplier). At the Bose audio systems plant, "in-plant" supplier personnel make up entire departments (e.g., Ryder has an in-plant office handling all of the traffic management function).

Although it seems clear single sourcing will expand in the future (particularly among high-tech firms), there have been problems. In the *Purchasing Magazine* survey mentioned above, 60 percent responded yes to the question, "Have you ever been disappointed with the performance of a single-source supplier?" Additionally, 43 percent responded yes to the question, "Have you ever needed to switch back from single to multiple sources for any reason?" As a result, many companies who use single sourcing leave themselves leeway for backing out of contract commitments.

**Sample Single-Source Contract for Action Assignment**
(Preliminary)        XYZ CORP. PURCHASE AGREEMENT

Between XYZ Corp., the buyer, and _____
_____, the seller.

Term of contract: January 1, 2000, through December 31, 2002.

1. Seller shall furnish all goods and services listed as scheduled and released F.O.B. destination without additional charges.

   XYZ Part #426F37 Revision A,
      125,000,000 units @ $55.00 per thousand units

   XYZ Part #426588 Revision D,
      5,000,000 units @ $15.78 per thousand units

   XYZ Part #426C56 Revision E,
      450,000 units @ $525.00 per thousand units

   XYZ Part #426333 Revision O,
      125,000 units @ $1,250.00 per thousand units

   XYZ Part #426452 Revision B,
      40,000 units @ $2500.00 per thousand units

2. Above quantities may be adjusted as necessary by XYZ Corp. over the term of the agreement.

3. Seller will provide technical support as required by XYZ Corp. at no additional cost.

4. Goods will meet all XYZ Corp. product and quality specifications.

5. If delivery is not completed within time specified, XYZ Corp. reserves the right to any or all of the following:

   1. Terminate the agreement.

   2. Purchase replacement goods at seller's expense.

   3. Bill seller for all downtime costs.

6. Seller will, at no cost to XYZ Corp., have its materials certified by an independent laboratory as meeting XYZ Corp. specifications.

7. Seller is restricted from making any changes in the product after sample approval is granted, including, but not limited to, materials, production operations, and packaging.

8. Sellers will allow XYZ Corp. personnel access to all areas and records necessary to verify compliance.

9. Seller shall assume all responsibility in connection with liability based on seller's performance and for the performance of its goods, including, but not limited to, patent infringement, civil liability, and criminal liability.

10. Seller shall treat as confidential all information, data, specifications, and processes involved in this agreement.

11. XYZ Corp. may terminate this agreement by way of written notice with liability limited to products actually produced to a scheduled delivery date 10 days in the future.

12. Part price is fixed for the term of the agreement; 24 months from the agreement date.

13. Seller agrees that all terms expressed here are in addition to the terms of the Uniform Commercial Code, laws of the State, and laws of the United States.

**Action Assignment**
Team 1, representing the customer's purchasing function, is to consider the above contract clause by clause and decide where changes will better serve its company's interests. Likewise, Team 2, representing the supplier's marketing function, will consider the above contract clause by clause and decide where changes will better serve its company's interests. Team 1 and Team 2 will then meet in the classroom to work out the final details of the contract. Unless the teams are quite advanced, some private direction from the instructor should be scheduled prior to the classroom negotiation.

**Source:** *Purchasing* "Single Sourcing—Some Love It—Most Fear It," June 5,1999, pp. 22–24; and "How Purchasing Handles Intense Cost Pressure," April 8, 1999, pp. 61–66. © Cahners Business Information Group.

## Business Buying Situations

Understanding organizational buyer behavior becomes easier if the task is divided and analyzed under different buying situations. This enables the marketer to identify critical decision points, the information needs of the buying organization, and various criteria that buyers consider when making a buying decision. Three types of buying situations have been delineated: (1) new task buying, (2) straight rebuy buying, and (3) modified rebuy buying. Characteristics of these buying situations are presented in Exhibit 4-7.

Each type of buying situation is related to the business buying process presented earlier. The process of making a purchase may change significantly when changing buying situations—even if the purchases made are identical. Therefore, marketing strategy must begin by identifying the type of buying situation that the selling firm is facing.

### New-Task Buying

When confronting a **new-task buy** situation, organizational buyers are in a stage of decision making that might be referred to as an extensive problem- solving stage, in which the buyer faces a buying situation that is different from any previous buying experiences. For example, a new type of machine, part, material, or service is needed, and the purchaser is in an unfamiliar buying situation. These circumstances offer the marketer a chance to participate in the early stages of the procurement process (thus increasing his or her probability of making the sale). In fact, an astute marketer prepared to respond to a buyer's new task needs often can anticipate a problem even before the present or potential customer recognizes it.

As an example of new-task buying, consider a hospital's purchase of a computer-aided tomography (CAT) scanner—a device that x-rays tiny slices of body structures and then

**EXHIBIT 4-7   Characteristics of Three Types of Buying Situations**

| New Task | Straight Rebuy | Modified Rebuy |
|---|---|---|
| A requirement or problem that has not arisen before. | Continuing or recurring requirement, handled on a routine basis. | May develop from either new task or straight rebuy situation. |
| Little or no relevant past buying experience to draw upon. | Usually the decision on each separate transaction is made in the purchasing department. | The requirement is continuing or recurring, or it may be expanded to a significantly larger level of operations. |
| A great deal of information is needed. | Formally or informally, a list of acceptable suppliers exists. | The buying alternatives are known, but they are changed. |
| Must seek out alternative ways of solving the problem and alternative suppliers. | No unlisted supplier is considered. | Some additional information is needed before the decisions are made. |
| Occurs infrequently, but very important to marketers because it sets the pattern for the more routine purchases that will follow. | Buyers have much relevant buying experience; hence, little new information is needed. | May arise because of outside events, such as an emergency or the actions of a marketer (value analysis, make or buy, etc.) |
| May be anticipated and developed by creative marketing. | Appears to represent the bulk of the individual purchases within companies. | May arise internally because of new buying influences or for potential cost reductions, potential quality improvements, or potential service benefits. |
| | Item purchases, price paid, delivery time, etc., may vary from transaction to transaction, so long as these variations do not cause new sources of supply to be considered. | Marketers who are not active suppliers try to convert customers' straight rebuys into modified rebuys. |

combines the thousands of shots into a composite picture. The customer recognizes the need—the hospital can vastly improve its diagnostic work and make the equipment available to the entire community—and identifies how to meet it—a scanner with high resolution and thin-sectioning capabilities. The buying center for this purchase probably includes the hospital chief of staff, the senior radiologist, the purchasing director, and other influencers such as representatives from neurosurgery, cardiology, orthopedics, neurology, ophthalmology, oncology, and so on. They identify the CAT units available, set up interviews with potential vendors, and check out the reputation of each manufacturer with present users of the specific equipment. After a few weeks, several units are rejected for various reasons, with three remaining in contention. Marketing representatives and technical specialists from those three contenders are invited to make formal presentations to the buying committee. Following these, negotiations are conducted and a unit is selected. In a new task buy situation such as this, the better informed the sellers are about the customer's buying procedures and decision makers, the better the seller's chances for success.

## Straight Rebuy

A **straight rebuy** situation is the most common purchasing situation in business buying. The buyer purchases a part, material, or service routinely, with little thought going into the buying process. The marketing goal of the business seller is to become a supplier for such relatively routine types of purchases. This can be a difficult challenge, however, because of buyer time constraints and previously established relationships. Present suppliers strive to maintain product and service quality, while potential suppliers attempt to establish their worth by promising better quality products, more reliable and efficient service, and lower prices. Exhibit 4-8 shows the strategies of present "in" suppliers versus potential "out" suppliers in responding to different business buying situations.

As an example of a straight rebuy, assume that the hospital purchasing director in the new task scenario buys several hundred routine items every month. Articles such as surgical gloves, thermometers, and cleansing supplies are routinely reordered without the involvement of other hospital employees in the buying center.

## Modified Rebuy

In **modified rebuy**, the distinctive element is the reevaluation of alternatives. The buying requirements have changed so that the relatively routine buy or purchase is no longer

**EXHIBIT 4-8**   **Reacting to Various Buying Situations: Profiling Essential Marketing Strategies**

| Buying Situation | The Supplier Who Is "In" | The Supplier Who Is "Out" |
|---|---|---|
| New Task | • Keeps track of evolving purchasing needs in the organization.<br>• Recognizes specific needs.<br>• Engages actively in early phases of buying process by supplying information and technical advice. | • Recognizes specific needs.<br>• Engages actively in early phases of buying process by supplying information and technical advice. |
| Straight Rebuy | • Strengthens the buyer-seller relationship by achieving organization's expectations.<br>• Adapts to evolving needs of the customer. | • Shows organization that the potential benefits of reexamining requirements and suppliers exceed the costs.<br>• Seeks to be positioned on an organization's preferred list of suppliers even as a second or third choice. |
| Modified Rebuy | • Corrects problems with customer.<br>• Analyzes and meets customer needs. | • Determines and reacts to the organization's problem with an existing supplier.<br>• Persuades organization or try alternative offerings. |

routine. Because the customer's needs have changed, the business marketing effort must change in response. Assume that the hospital in the previous buying scenarios is opening a new emergency room care facility. At about the same time, the chief of staff has complained about poor hygiene in other wards of the hospital. The hospital's contract for janitorial services comes up for renewal, possibly transforming this situation from a straight rebuy into a modified rebuy. A *request for quotation (RFQ)* is issued to the present supplier, along with potential new suppliers, with the present supplier being urged to upgrade performance if it is to be considered for the new contract.

## The Buying Center

Recall from Chapter 1 that people within the business buying organization who participate in the buying process, often including technical experts and senior management, are members of what is called a *buying center.* A key to success in business marketing is understanding customer *buying behavior.* Achieving an understanding is difficult, however, because the organizational buying process often is dynamic and complicated. It is rare for one person in any particular organization to be solely responsible for the buying decision. Thus, understanding the dynamics of interpersonal influence that drive the buying process may play a key role in formulating successful business marketing strategies. If a seller does not identify and communicate with key **influencers**, he or she might lose the sale, despite technical superiority and competitive pricing. Yet, the identity of influencers and the activities through which they exert influence may not be readily obvious.

The size of a buying center varies with the complexity and importance of a purchase decision. Business sellers must determine who participates in an organizational purchase decision and the nature and extent of their influence. Usually, several people comprise the buying center, or the decision-making unit, and the composition of the buying group often will change from one purchase to another. The astute business marketer must determine the appropriate influencers for a particular situation—a task that may not be simple. The situation is further complicated by the fact that several people may play the same role (several influencers in a purchase decision, for example), and one particular person may play two or more roles (**decider** and **buyer**, or **user**, for example). In addition, identifying influences is only part of the business marketer's challenge: the debate continues among business-to-business marketers on how to get a message past a secretary (**gatekeeper**) to the people in the inner office. Exhibit 4-9 defines roles of various members in the business buying process.

**EXHIBIT 4-9    Roles of Buying Center Members in the Business Purchasing Process**

| Role | Description |
| --- | --- |
| Users | Those who will use the product in question. Their influence on the purchasing decision can range from minimal to major. In some cases users begin the purchase process and even develop product specifications. |
| Gatekeepers | Those who keep a tight control on the flow of information to other members of the buying center. They can open the gate to members of the buying center for some salespeople, yet close it for others. |
| Influencers | Those who provide information to buying center members for evaluating alternative products or who set purchasing specifications. Normally, influencers operate within the buying center, such as quality control or research and development personnel. Yet, at other times influencers operate outside the buying center, such as architects who create very specific building requirements. |
| Deciders | Those who, in reality, make the buying decision, regardless of whether they hold the formal authority. A decider often is quite difficult to identify since a decider can be a company president, a purchasing director, or a research and development analyst. |
| Buyers | Those who are assigned the formal authority to select vendors and complete the purchasing transaction. Sometimes other more powerful members of the buying center take the prerogative of the buyer. A purchasing manager who carries out the clerical duties of the purchase order often acts in the role of the buyer. |

Business marketers have the critical task of determining who is involved and the specific role in which each buying center participant is cast. Upon identifying the players, the marketer can tailor the language, tone, and timing of a sales presentation in a manner appropriate to the role of the buying center participant. Marketers usually find that, while most contacts are with purchasing department personnel, the buying center participants having the greatest influence often are not employed in the purchasing department at all. Exhibit 4-10 illustrates some examples of typical buying influencers and shows how these individuals may affect buying decisions and marketing strategy. Note the implied influence of the production manager, the comptroller, the engineer, and the plant manager. At the least, these individuals are regarded as influencers certain to affect the buying decision. They may have the final say as to what is bought, especially if they are the *user*. Also, the impact of one buying decision on subsequent decisions often is underemphasized; sellers should not overlook the importance of outcomes on the buying decision process.

The buying center membership and the relative importance of different members vary from company to company. In engineering-dominated firms like Texas Instruments or General Dynamics, where ever-present technical innovation typically shortens the product life cycle, the buying center may consist almost entirely of engineers. In more market-oriented firms such as General Foods or IBM, marketing and engineering have almost equal authority. In a small manufacturing company, the buying center may consist of several individuals with very different backgrounds and demands. Members may consist of everyone from the CEO to a particular production worker, each having a say as to what is purchased in a particular situation. This complicates the task for business marketers because many varied personalities and interests may have to be dealt with in a particular selling situation. Business sellers also have to be concerned with so-called "hidden agendas" that might come into play in a particular purchase decision. Exhibit 4-11 lists a number of different

**EXHIBIT 4-10**   **Effects of Buying Influences on Purchasing Decisions and Marketing Strategy**

| Buying Influence | Effects on Buying | Appropriate Marketing Strategy |
|---|---|---|
| Purchasing agent, buyer | Handles requisitions from the plant. Maintains personal library of suppliers' catalogs. Does some discretionary purchasing—especially when delivery is critical. Usually honors sources recommended by key plant personnel. | See regularly. Keep informed if you see others in the plant. Keep supplied with new product and price information. Offer a benefit on every call. Allow to pave the way to other buying influences in the plant. |
| Production manager, general foreman | Usually confined to specific production operations such as assembly, finishing. Can describe specific problems in detail. | Sell brand superiority, depth of inventory, delivery, and potential for contributing to productivity of production people and equipment. Leave catalog, put on general mailing list. Call only with constructive offering. |
| Plant comptroller, head bookkeeper | With purchasing department, interested in terms of sale or systems contract. | Be fully prepared with terms stated simply. Come armed with benefits over and above those offered by others. |
| Director, vice president of engineering | Concerned with product or process improvements. Generally involved with future changes; seldom with immediate needs. Searches continually for new, improved products. Relies heavily on library of suppliers. Also relies heavily on technical aid from vendors. Strong influence on OEM and MRO product type and brand selection. | Responds favorably to outside help in the form of new, potentially useful data and technical counsel. Offer complete catalog. Offer technical capabilities via experts. Personally introduce new improved products regularly. Put on your general mailing list and keep supplied with your latest complete catalog. |
| Plant manager, general manager, vice president of operations, vice president of manufacturing | Key buying influence on larger plant expenditures. May direct vendors to key personnel and problem areas in the plants. | Receptive to constructive information. Often easier to reach than floor personnel. Contact periodically with your management, to demonstrate interest in serving, to sell firm's capabilities, and to probe for prospect's problems and plans. Keep informed on important product breakthroughs. |

**EXHIBIT 4-11**   **Decision Makers in Selected Buying Centers**

| Company | Capital Equipment | Decision Maker | Business Services | Decision Maker |
|---|---|---|---|---|
| Chemical manufacturer | Heat exchanger | Purchasing manager | Construction contract labor | Purchasing manager |
| Business safety product manufacturer | Automatic drilling machine | Engineer vice president of manufacturing | Plant janitorial service | Purchasing manager |
| Steel manufacturer | Coke oven | Purchasing manager | Maintenance repair contract | Buyer |
| Machine tooling company | Vertical boring mill | Vice president of operations | Fabricating work | Purchasing manager |
| Metal and wire manufacturer | Wrapping machine | Division manager | Machinery rigging for shipping | Traffic manager |
| Aerospace and automotive products manufacturer | Metalworking machine tool | Divisional purchasing manager | Technical consultant | Director of purchasing |
| Paper products manufacturer | Banding system | General manager | Vending machine service | Personnel manager |
| Petroleum products manufacturer | Gasoline storage tank | Buyer | Printing of advertising materials | Vice president of marketing |
| Mining equipment manufacturer | Executive office desk | Purchasing agent | Training for first-line supervisors | General manager |
| Engineering and construction company | Cooling vessel | Jobs supervisor | Tar sludge removal | Buyer; Purchasing manager; Divisional vice president |
| Home products manufacturer | Mixing machines | Buyer engineer | Drapery cleaning | Service manager |
| Building materials manufacturer | Pump | Engineer | Engineering services | Executive vice president |

manufacturers involved in a variety of purchase situations and reveals who the true decision makers are.

---

**Concept Review**

1. Why is the straight rebuy the most common purchasing situation in business buying?

2. Why is it important for business sellers to determine who is involved in the buying center?

3. What causes the size of the buying center to change?

---

## The Materials Management Concept

**Materials management** is the grouping of functions involved in obtaining and bringing materials into a production operation. Often, this concept is referred to as logistics, which would incorporate materials management and physical distribution. An organization that has adopted the materials management organizational concept usually will have a single manager responsible for planning, organizing, and controlling all the activities principally concerned with the flow of materials into an organization. Material management views material flow as a system.

The specific functions that might be included under the materials manager (who usually comes from the ranks of purchasing) are material planning and control, production scheduling, material and purchasing research, purchasing, incoming traffic, inventory control, receiving, incoming quality control, stores, in-plant materials movement, and scrap and surplus disposal. The continued adoption of the materials management concept will force many business marketing managers to coordinate activities that affect the materials management function of their customers. Marketers who can coordinate their own production, inventory, distribution, credit, traffic, and warehousing, so as to match their customer's requirements, have the best chance to establish long-range business relationships. The materials management approach to business buying and selling will continue to expand into the areas of raw materials, component parts, and inventory control, along with being an important tool in planning and forecasting future supply needs. Both buyers and sellers must be directly involved in this continuing trend toward integrated supply chain management (covered in detail in Chapter 11).

## Alternative Approaches to Materials Management

Critics of the materials management form of organization emphasize that it is difficult, if not impossible, for one person to coordinate and control the many variables involved in materials operations and that effective coordination is too difficult to achieve merely by establishing a new organizational structure. Some alternative approaches have been suggested.

### *Traditional Approach*

Traditionally, inventory has been used to buffer transportation, production, distribution, and sales imbalances when availability and demand occur at different rates. This situation is intensified with the great product variety that has been created and, therefore, is expected in our economy. Consequently, U.S. firms have emphasized materials delivery systems, and business marketers have reacted accordingly. Also, traditionally, inventory has been built into an operation to cover problems. Despite advanced control systems and the realization that inventory tied up capital, the relationship between inventory and its effects on manufacturing methods or measurement systems was seldom analyzed.

### *Just-in-Time (JIT) Approach*

Another form of business exchange, commonly referred to as the **just-in-time (JIT) exchange relationship**, has been adopted and implemented by many original equipment manufacturers (OEMs) and suppliers of component parts and materials. The JIT concept, an inventory supply system that requires low inventory and fast delivery, is an operational philosophy thought to epitomize the relationship marketing model. The JIT purchasing relationship can be described as a marriage between the manufacturer and the supplier. The commitment to implement a JIT system involves compromise and hard work for long-term benefits to accrue for both partners. Because JIT systems require such activities as more frequent deliveries of smaller lot sizes, reductions in the supplier base, and greater interaction among various departments, buyers and sellers are strengthening their relational bonds. In terms of practice, descriptive expressions such as "stockless production" or "zero inventories" are often used.

### *Integrated Supply Strategies*

Many organizations are now taking things one step further and improving on models such as JIT. For some, it means a supplier is actually on-site. For others, a supplier is close by and inventory is handled fewer times, stored more efficiently, and transported in strategic amounts. Whatever the specifics, these organizations are all involved in integrated supply strategies. NAPM's *Glossary of Key Purchasing Terms* (second edition) defines **integrated supply** as: "A special type of partnering arrangement usually developed between a purchaser and a distributor on an intermediate to long-term basis. The objective of an integrated supply relationship is to minimize, for both the buyer and seller, the labor and expense involved in the acquisition and possession of items that are repetitive, generic, high transaction, and have a low unit cost." Consider:

> At PPG Industries' chemical complex near Lake Charles, Louisiana, customer shipments of more than 7,000 tons a day of basic chemicals makes the 1600-employee plant the largest of nearly 100 PPG plants worldwide. "We have taken a 10-year-old JIT concept and improved it. Vendor City consists of 11 maintenance, repair, and operating (MRO) suppliers located less than a half mile from our complex. These suppliers supply a variety of MRO items such as gaskets, safety equipment, pipe, valves, and fittings. Our facility spends in excess of $12 million annually with these 11 suppliers. Using one common carrier, Vendor City suppliers provide PPG with MRO supplies, just in time. This 10-year-old program includes four scheduled daily deliveries plus emergency service. The system has allowed PPG to reduce our inventory of MRO parts by more than $5 million, or in excess of 30 percent."
>
>   James V. Veronesi, Manager of Procurement at the Lake Charles Complex, PPG Industries, in Lake Charles, Louisiana[7]

### Reasons for Adopting the Materials Management Concept

There are many reasons for the adoption of the materials management type of organization, with the greatest advantage being the improved communication and coordination between departments that such an organizational structure permits. Materials management provides a central administration where conflicting functional or departmental interests can be balanced out in the overall interests of the company. Centralized responsibility and control also make for a smoother, faster flow of materials from the time they are requisitioned by various departments to the time they are shipped out to customers as finished products.

## Purchasing and the Internet

The Internet has reinvented the role of traditional buying and selling. *Web-based* purchasing continues to win business-to-business converts. E-commerce and e-procurement are here to stay. Regardless of the dot-com meltdowns and the implications that e-procurement has for organizational change, the technology is here, it is being used, and it is gaining wider acceptance. In the May 2002 update to the CAPS Research (Center for Advanced Purchasing Studies), *Cross-industry Benchmarking Report*, participants reported that their business-to-business e-commerce activities continue to increase since CAPS Research started measuring B2B spending in October 2001. (To see the report online, go to *www.capsresearch.org* and select Research Reports. Then select the Benchmarking section for the most current data.) With increased use of B2B technology, it has become more important to measure the efficiency of these tools and to find ways to make them even more effective.

Western Geophysical, a $1.4 billion seismic exploration services unit of Baker Hughes, Inc., has moved most of its several hundred million dollars in annual purchasing to the Web. Phillips Electronics has announced that it will move all of its purchasing of nonproduction goods and services to the Web.[8] Online procurement has been embraced by several companies, including Bristol-Myers Squibb, Chevron, Ford, General Electric, Pacific Gas and Electric, and United Technologies. National Semiconductor is using its national supply catalog to obtain more than $1 million worth of materials monthly for all their MRO products. They have reduced their purchasing staff by half, slashed inventory by $1 million, and trimmed inventory holding costs by $300,000.

In July 2002, a Forrester Report on eBusiness,[9] reported:

> The organizations surveyed made significant strides in using the Internet for purchasing over the past three months. For the quarter ending in June 2002, the percentage of organizations

purchasing both direct and indirect materials jumped substantially from the previous quarter. Among the more significant increases were: More than 90 percent of large-buying organizations reported purchasing some indirect materials online, and nearly three-fourths of these organizations purchased some direct materials online. Also, a larger fraction of companies reported collaborating with suppliers online and also reported higher levels of satisfaction with their suppliers' online capabilities.

Having reported the above, Forrester also noted that only 17.1 percent of all respondents reported being about halfway or further along the way toward fully adopting the Net, while 18.9 percent report no progress at all toward adopting the Net. When asked about obstacles to their Internet activities, organizations most often mentioned a lack of budget or resources and the difficulty justifying the investment. Looking ahead to the next twelve months, 83.1 percent said that the Internet would be important. Finally, 11.1 percent of organizations reported that the Internet has introduced major changes to their procurement processes over the past three months; 84.2 percent bought some indirect material online during the same time period. It is safe to say that Internet purchasing will continue to grow and flourish.

## Environmental Forces and Buying Decisions

Marketing success depends upon developing a sound marketing mix (the controllable variables) adapted to the trends and developments in the marketing environment (the uncontrollable variables). The marketing environment presents a set of largely uncontrollable forces to which the company must adapt it's marketing mix. Buyers and sellers must understand the environment within which they operate and must communicate with each other so that they can monitor, adapt to, and develop strategies to meet environmental changes that impact either one or both of the buying and selling organizations. Marketers must monitor changes in the economic environment, the physical environment, the competitive environment, the technological environment, the legal-political environment, and the ethical environment.

### The Economic Environment

The economic environment includes factors both at home and abroad, along with variables that determine the income and wealth-generating ability of the economy. Because of the derived nature of business demand (see Chapter 1), few business buyers and sellers are immune to its effects. The dangers of derived demand for business suppliers, when final consumers' demand for a product produced by these suppliers' customers begins to decline, must be understood and monitored.

### The Physical Environment

Contained in the physical environment are not only the geographic characteristics or region of the country where the firm operates but also the political stability of the country within the international environment and its location and transportation infrastructure. As transportation costs increase (see Chapter 11), business buyers will generally prefer suppliers whose mining, manufacturing, and storage facilities are nearby. When compared with domestic supplier selection, international supplier selection decisions are fraught with countless risks and complexities.

### The Competitive Environment

All other sellers who are competing for the patronage of the same business buyer are included in this environment. Many industrial firms find themselves in intensely competitive industries, where astute responses to competitive pressures are critical for such firms to maintain and/or improve their market positions.

# BUSINESS MARKETING IN ACTION

## MRO PRICE TRACKING

Although inflation has declined to record levels, buyers of many maintenance, repair, and operating (MRO) supplies are still seeing price increases. To some degree, MRO manufacturers are often sheltered from the ultimate user by middlemen distributors. A manufacturer may raise the price and the distributor just passes the increase along. Lower volume purchases may mean that the user lacks leverage to resist the increase. This is producing the unusual situation where manufacturer's direct costs (particularly for materials) are known to be decreasing, yet selling prices to users are going up. For example, manufacturers of SIC code 2891 Adhesives & Sealants (NAICS U.S. description code is 32552) in 1999 raised prices 1.8 percent despite realizing significant cost savings of 4.2 percent.

In most of this text and your other marketing courses you have been trained to think from the perspective of a manufac-

turer's marketer. From that perspective you would be pretty happy to have such a nice increase in your profit margin. However, in this chapter you are learning to think like a buyer. If you have been doing your job as a buyer, you have been tracking these price indexes, and you are very aware of what the manufacturer is doing. Feel the rage! Well, maybe not rage, but at least feel the challenge. That increase in supplier profitability is coming off your bottom line, and you need to be doing something about it. Letting the sales representative know that you track such things and are not happy would be a first step.

Buyers have access to a number of sources for producer price index data (e.g., The Bureau of Labor Statistics), and you should be familiar with the process. MRO purchasing is a typical entry-level assignment, and in this assignment you are responsible for the following product categories:

| BLS Code | Product | Price to buyer % change 3/98-3/99 | Producer Cost % change 3/98-3/99 |
|---|---|---|---|
| PCU2992#12113 | Industrial Metalworking Fluids | +0.3 | −4.7 |
| PCU3612#1 | Distribution Transformers | +0.4 | −3.9 |
| PCU2851#115 | Enamels & Tinting Bases—Paint | +1.6 | −4.2 |
| PCU3491#4 | Butterfly Valves—Metal | +3.3 | −1.8 |
| PCU3621#184 | Perm. Split Capacitor Motors | +0.7 | −2.7 |
| PCU3563#12 | Gas Compressors | +2.0 | −1.1 |
| PCU3585#2 | Unitary Air Conditioners | +1.8 | −0.9 |
| PCU3535#319 | Unit Handling Conveyors | +2.0 | −0.9 |
| PCU3536#460 | Parts for Cranes & Monorails | +2.4 | −0.6 |

**Source:** Thinking Cap Solutions Inc.

## Action Assignment

You are the MRO buyer for a large company. Each year you purchase many millions of dollars of MRO products. Even a 1 percent improvement in prices would add a significant amount to your company's bottom line. To prepare for your meeting with a supplier's sales representatives, update the price column in the above table using the Producer Price Index available at the Bureau of Labor Statistics (website: www.bls.gov). From the BLS home page, click on "DATA," then click on "SERIES REPORT." Then, list all the BLS codes from the above table, leave the default format details, and go down and click on "RETRIEVE DATA." The data will be referenced to some base date as 100 (e.g., March 1999 = 120.1, March 2000 = 125.4, with a base date of 8012, which would indicate that

December 1980 was the series base date of 100). You will probably be more concerned with the yearly increase, rather than the base date.

Prepare for your meeting with the supplier sales representatives, and present your approach to the class as if they were the sales representatives. You may want to look back to the selling chapter and consider how sales representatives "plan" their meetings (sales calls) with you. Perhaps you will want to follow a similar procedure. Also be sure to consider the information on "Zero Based Pricing" in this chapter. Remember, you are the buyer.

**Source:** *Purchasing,* "MRO Report," June 3, 1999, pp. 42–47. © 1999 Cahners Business Information Group.

## STRATEGY AT WORK

### EXPANDING ROLES IN PURCHASING

The procurement profession's single-minded goal of adding value through cost efficient purchasing may soon be looked upon as limiting and old fashioned. For several years, leading OEMs have been revolutionizing purchasing's strategic role. Companies like Pratt & Whitney and Maytag now expect buyers to go beyond their traditional duties, to become an "innovation development arm" of the business. They are involving buyers deep in the strategic process including design, production, and the search for additional customer value creation. These new expectations are requiring purchasing professionals to increase their technical competence, team skills, and project management skills. The buyers of the future will also be broadly multifunctional.

In a turn of events that few would have predicted, some purchasing professionals are being required to develop sales and marketing skills. In the search for customer value creation, the purchasing departments at some high-tech companies have noted that they have developed systems and skills that exceed those available to the average firm. At some point, someone with an innovative spirit suggested: "Why not sell our purchasing services to other companies?"

IBM, for example, has established a new unit that, for a fee, will take over the purchasing function for clients. They call it "Business Process Management for Procurement and Sourcing (www.ibm.com/services/bpm). American Express offers a new "Partner Supply Program," which includes charging for purchasing consulting and services. At Delta Airlines, a subsidiary called Epsilon shares Delta's fuel purchasing staff and performs the function for other companies.

An even more challenging role for purchasing is developing as companies "outsource" entire production processes to "contract manufacturers." For these reasons and more, the purchasing manager's function is expanding from simple parts buyer to business manager, supply chain manager and corporate alliance and partnership manager.

### Assignment

Research the terms *outsourcing* and *contract manufacturing* as they relate to "virtual" companies. Also, review the information from The Outsourcing Institute at (www.outsourcing.com) and from the Contract Manufacturers Association at (www.outsource1.com). Make a class presentation that considers the issues presented in this box; and 1) how they will impact purchasing career development, 2) marketing career development, and 3) your career development.

**Source:** *Purchasing,* "Purchasing for Profit," January 14, 1999, pp. 71–73; "Purchasing Unlocks Supply Treasures," March 11, 1999, pp. 50–57; and "Rapid Growth Changes Rules for Purchasing," June 17, 1999, pp. 33–39. © 1999 Cahners Business Information Group.

### The Technological Environment

The technological environment consists of the application of science to develop new ways of doing various tasks. High technology, with the resulting knowledge explosion, has presented buyers and sellers with different sets of marketing problems, and it deserves special attention. Significant new developments in manufacturing technology have the potential for altering buyer-seller relationships. The increase in the number of high-tech marketing articles and entire issues offered by the more traditional business press, such as *Business Marketing, The Wall Street Journal,* and the *New York Times,* to name but a few, serve to illustrate this point.

High technology represents a whole new arena for marketing theories, practices, and research. The requirement of a technical background for business sales and buying personnel has been especially noted in such areas as biotechnology, electronics, medical instrumentation, ceramics, and robotics.

### The Legal-Political Environment

Included in the legal-political environment are the rules and regulations that society has imposed on business firms and the political interest groups that affect the environment. Additionally, this environment would include international trade restrictions, government attitudes toward business and social activities, and government funding of selected programs. The dictates of agencies, such as the Food and Drug Administration, the Federal

# WHAT WOULD YOU DO?

## PREFERENTIAL TREATMENT ON BID

Kelly Clausen, a buyer with Superior Innovative Equipment Company, was reviewing six bids she had requested from suppliers. She knew that SIE's volumes were so attractive to the potential suppliers that even the ones who were unlikely to be successful were happy to be given the chance to compete. She didn't doubt for a minute that preparing this type of bid (for several millions of dollars of components per year) required a significant supplier investment. She noticed that the bids ranged from $217.00 per thousand to $89.00 per thousand. The required SIE investment in tooling, dies, and equipment ranged from $126,500 to $6,500. Kelly's cost estimators had determined a target price to purchase the product at about $190.00 per thousand.

Kelly preferred to purchase this type of product from Juarez Fabricators. She and the firm's sales representative had a good relationship, and she knew she could trust their performance. Juarez Fabricators, however, did not have the lowest price on this bid, and in fact they were only third lowest (with a bid of $167.00 and $50,000 of tooling). Kelly's company specifically did not require her to buy from the lowest bidder; SIE expected her to purchase from the supplier who offered the highest life cycle value (a combination of price, capability, dependability, and contribution to the goals and success of SIE).

Kelly wanted to see what Juarez Fabricators would be willing to do about the lower bids. While she didn't expect Juarez Fabricators to match them, she hoped they would reduce their bid price. She knew that the marketing manager at Juarez Fabricators would want his salesperson to provide him with the results of the bidding process, in order to decide if they should adjust their price. Kelly also knew that it was not professional to specifically discuss the competitor's bid numbers with a Juarez Fabricators' sales representative. As expected, Bob (the sales rep and a good friend), called that afternoon to schedule a meeting to go over the bid with Kelly.

As Bob arrived for the meeting, he was dreaming about closing on the order. Wow, the commission on even one million dollars of sales at 4 percent was, . . . let's see . . . Entering Kelly's office, Bob started with some small talk, and Kelly invited him to take a seat in one of the chairs in front of her desk. From Bob's perspective, Kelly started right in by refreshing her mind about all the bids by looking over each bid folder and making some general comments about the importance of the program to SIE. Bob could see that Kelly put three folders aside and was concentrating on the three remaining. Kelly went on to explain that the Juarez Fabricators' bid was too high, but she was not open to discuss specifics. Bob was thinking that at least one and possibly both of the lower bidders did not really have the capability to produce the products (or more correctly, they could probably produce the products, but they would introduce some amount of risk). Bob was considering what he would tell his marketing manager (about how much to factor in the value of the relationship he had built at SIE, how much risk was Kelly willing to deal with, and, of course, what did Bob find out about who the other bids were from and what prices they had bid).

As Bob went over the benefits of purchasing from his company, he noticed that Kelly had the competitors' bids open flat on her desk in front of her. Bob thought, "now if only I could read upside down at three feet, like most every other salesperson I know." Bob was still struggling with what type of questions to ask Kelly to try to uncover the information he needed, yet not cross the line she had drawn. Then Kelly surprised him by saying, "I know that we have more to go over, but I'm going to have to excuse myself for about ten minutes. I was supposed to get some information to personnel an hour ago, and I need to take a short restroom break." Bob, assured her that he appreciated the fact that she was willing to continue the meeting after her errands, and that he had several cell phone calls to make himself. As Kelly left, Bob noticed that she had left the competitors' bids closed on her desk, but within his easy reach.

### Assignment

Define the ethical issues for everyone concerned. Develop an action plan for Kelly and one for Bob. If you were Bob, what would you do?

---

Trade Commission, the Environmental Protection Agency, and the Federal Communications Commission, must be adhered to by both buyers and sellers in the development of their products and overall marketing strategies.

## The Ethical Environment

The norms, or moral behavior, that society imposes on business and marketers comprise the ethical environment (revisit Chapter 2). Ethics serve as part of a system for social control, a system that is important to buyers and salespeople, as well as to their respective firms. As key links between their organizations and their customers, business salespeople encounter situations that might lead to ethical conflict.

## Purchasing's Impact Upon Company Profit

Purchasing plays an important role with regard to the impacts that occur from price increases or decreases for the goods and services procured. All other things being equal, a $1 savings in the purchase price results in a $1 profit increase. A cost increase by the same amount, on the other hand, harms the firm by $1 of decreased profits.

The term *profit* applies to three key measures used to describe the periodic financial performance of a firm. The first is profit as a percentage of sales. This figure is a rough measure of how much is left over from sales revenue after all costs of the firm have been paid. It is the general measure of the profit-generating potential of sales and operating activities. The second measure is asset turnover. This is a measure of how effectively the assets in the firm are being utilized. It is found by dividing total assets into the sales revenue for the year. A high asset turnover is generally considered preferable to a low asset turnover. The third key measure is return on assets. This indicator is a measure of the profit-generating power of a firm based upon the assets necessary to produce the desired profit. This figure is related to the interest that people associate with savings account or money-market-fund earnings. Of course, a higher return figure is far more desirable than a lower one.

The interaction of all key company financial components to the overall profit is seen in Exhibit 4-12. A hypothetical company is shown with a revenue of $1.00 for the year. Purchases cost $.55; depreciation $.15; and other costs of operation, $.25; for a total cost of $.95 for the year. Profit is $1.00 less the $.95, or $.05. Use of assets, cash, inventories, and other assets totals $.40. Sales are $1.00, which sets asset turnover rate at 2.5 times. Profit as a percentage of sales is .05 (or 5 percent), and the asset turnover rate of 2.5 times causes company return on assets to be 12.5 percent. This shows how a firm could have a low return on sales but a high turnover, resulting in a good overall return on assets. Another firm

**EXHIBIT 4-12   Interaction of All Key Company Financial Components on Overall Profits**

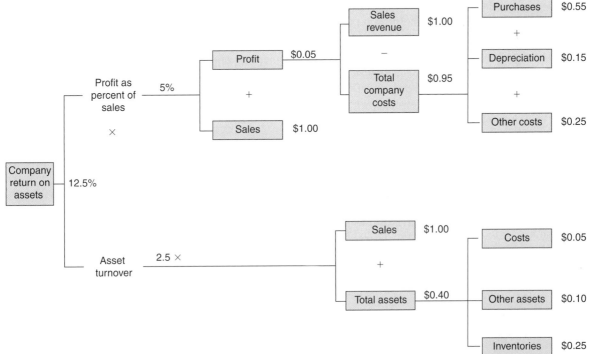

will have a very high return on sales but a low asset turnover, resulting in a low return on assets. All three indicators are viewed separately, as well as in a combined manner.

As can be easily calculated, a reduction in the purchase price by $.01 reduces the cost of purchases from $.55 to $.54 and total company costs to $.94. Profit is now $.06, and profit as a percentage of sales has increased from 5 to 6 percent. Return on assets is now 15 percent (.06 × 2.5).

Therefore, a reduction in purchase price has a direct positive impact upon profit and return on assets.

## Concept Review

1. What is the greatest advantage in a firm's adopting the materials management concept?
2. How has the Internet reinvented the role of traditional buying and selling? Why must both buyers and sellers be concerned with the relationship between the economic environment and derived demand?

## Summary

- A well-educated purchasing executive increasingly confronts marketers. Relationship marketing may well be the way of future relationships between buyers and suppliers. Four forces drive relationship marketing: quality, speed, cost-effectiveness, and new design techniques. The combination of these has fostered closer working relationships between purchasers and suppliers. In light of the strong competition present within the business sector, marketers need to make every effort to learn as much about their customers as possible. Buyer profiles are very useful in this endeavor.

- Business buying has evolved into a complex process of decision making and communication that takes place over time, involves several organizational members, and includes relationships with other firms and institutions. The primary objective of business buyers is to purchase the right materials in the right quantity, for delivery at the right time and in the right place, from the right source with the right service, and at the right price.

- In developing marketing strategy, both existing and potential suppliers should be aware of buyers' decision strategies in reducing uncertainty and of how such plans affect the choice of suppliers. Purchasing personnel will often develop a rank-ordered list of desired supplier attributes so as to facilitate comparisons among competing vendors.

- Value analysis is a scientifically organized method for reducing the cost of manufactured items and for encouraging vendor cooperation in lowering costs of purchased items. Its ultimate purpose is to secure improved performance of components at less cost.

- Understanding business buying situations—specifically new task, modified rebuy, and straight rebuy—allows the business marketer to identify critical buying decision phases, the information needs of the buying organization, and criteria that the buyers consider when making a buying decision.

- The make-or-buy decision will determine to a large extent the profitability of the organization; and, with this factor in mind, the activity should not be taken lightly. The buyer's objective should be to render the make-or-buy decision that will maximize the utilization of production, managerial, and financial capabilities. Through the concept of relationship marketing, the sellers should be involved in this process.

- The purchasing organization varies from one firm to another, with some purchasing managers working out of corporate headquarters and others operating at the divisional or plant level. In large companies, the purchasing operation is often separated into both operational and managerial units. Further, the question of whether the buying organization decentralizes buying activities in each plant (or division) of a multiple-plant firm or centralizes the activity at headquarters (or uses a combination of both organizational methods) must be understood by the business marketer.

- People within the business buying organization who are involved in the buying process are members of what is called the buying center. The critical task for the marketer is to be able to determine the specific role and the relative buying influence of each buying center participant. The buying-center membership and relative importance of different members varies from company to company.

- The materials management concept advocates the grouping of all materials activities into a single department. Typically, materials management includes materials planning and control, production scheduling, materials and purchasing research, purchasing, incoming traffic, inventory control, receiving, incoming quality control, stores, in-plant materials movement, and scrap and surplus disposal. Alternative approaches to materials management include both the traditional approach and the just-in-time (JIT) approach.

- Purchasing plays an important role in regard to the impacts that occur from price increases or decreases for the goods and services procured. All other things being equal, a $1 savings in purchase price results in a $1 profit increase, with a cost increase by the same amount harming the firm by $1 of decreased profit.

## Key Terms

buyer
buying situation
centralized purchasing
decentralized purchasing
decider
gatekeeper
influencer

integrated supply
just-in-time (JIT) exchange
  relationship
make-or-buy analysis
materials management
modified rebuy
negotiation

new-task buy
request for quotation (RFQ)
straight rebuy
user
value analysis (VA)

## Review Questions

1. Why is business buying no longer the simple act of placing an order with a vendor or a selling organization?

2. Describe the typical purchasing professional. In what areas of the purchasing executive's job have the major changes occurred? What is relationship marketing? What role does it play in fostering purchaser-supplier relationships?

3. Identify each of the steps in the business buying process. How is a buying situation created? Create an example to show your own understanding of how a business-to-business firm goes through the business buying process.

4. How does the organization of the purchasing department differ in regard to the size of the firm?

5. Discuss the role of price in business buying and selling. Distinguish between price and total cost.

6. What business functions are usually involved in a make-or-buy analysis? Who generally participates in a company's make-or-buy analysis? Under what conditions might a company choose to make, rather than to buy a particular product?

7. What determines the size of the buying center? What is the critical task for business marketers regarding their dealings with buying centers?

8. Discuss the reasons for having either a centralized or decentralized purchasing organization. Which form of organization is more commonly used by purchasing departments?

9. Identify and discuss three types of business buying situations. How are these types of buying situations related to the various stages of the procurement process?

10. Create your own examples of business buying situations that correspond to each of the three types of buying situations.

11. Define the materials management concept. Discuss the reasons why a company would adopt a materials management approach. Identify and explain two alternative approaches to materials management.

# Superior Electronics, Inc.

Paul Jamison, a Procurement Specialist for Superior Electronics, Inc., at its San Diego plant, faced a sourcing decision. Superior's annual contracts with the three firms that performed the final operation on Part 309 was to expire at the end of the month, on December 31. Since the future demand for Part 309 was very uncertain, Paul wondered how to approach the coming year's sourcing decisions.

## Company Background

Superior Electronics, Inc., a U.S. based Fortune 500 firm, manufactured and distributed a wide range of electronic parts and components to a variety of industrial users. Superior earned revenues in excess of $4 billion the preceding year. Customers and competitors regarded Superior as an innovative company and industry leader.

Superior supplied Part 309, a semiconductor component, to aerospace firms with U.S. military contracts. There was no other market for Part 309. Part 309's specifications were established by the federal government. The government audited the quality of the product by making surprise plant visits during the various stages of its production. The specifications for Part 309 had not changed for many years.

Superior was one of three suppliers of Part 309. Since there were large capital barriers to entering the market, it was unlikely that new competitors would emerge. The three suppliers of Part 309 were very price competitive with one another (i.e., their prices were virtually identical). The aerospace firms were price conscious—they preferred better service (i.e., a shorter lead time), but they were not willing to pay more for it.

Though Part 309 did not contribute significantly to corporate profits, it was an important product because Superior's customers demanded that their suppliers provide an extensive product line. It was highly probable that stockouts of Part 309 would lead to a significant reduction in demand for some of Superior's more profitable products. As a result, corporate policy mandated that Superior's 60 percent share of the market be maintained or increased. Once market share was lost, it was costly and time consuming to regain. (It generally took three to four years to regain market share unless competitors failed to satisfy market demand.)

Superior had a 26-week backlog of orders for Part 309 or, in other words, customers encountered a 26-week lead time for the product. However, for unknown reasons, Superior had not received an order for Part 309 for two months. Paul felt that customer uncertainty about the following year's Federal defense budget may have had an impact.

Superior employed external sources for the last stage of production of Part 309. Superior supplied these sources with the semifinished components. The contracts with these manufacturers expired in two weeks.

## Contracts with External Sources

Traditionally, Superior negotiated one-year contracts for the final stage of production on Part 309 with each of three manufacturing firms. These were the only known suppliers capable of providing this service. Superior's competitors also utilized these three suppliers.

The contracts guaranteed a specific amount of capacity for the final operation on Part 309 for the period covered by the contract. Once a contract was in effect, capacity could neither be added nor reduced. Thus, Superior was contracting for a specified level of output at a guaranteed total cost. Superior did not have the capability to perform the last stage of production, nor would it devote resources for such capability. The equipment required for this operation was not adaptable to other uses and was very costly.

Superior's supplier preferred at least a one-year contract due to high start-up costs and the need for a large number of employees. The duration of the contract affected both the per-unit price and the lead time. Whereas a supplier guaranteed the price when the contract covered at least one year, prices increased when shorter term contracts were used. Obviously, customer lead time improved when shortened term contracts were in effect. Superior had no knowledge of the time frame of its competitors' contracts.

Over the long term, each of Superior's suppliers had provided comparable service, in terms of product quality and delivery time, and nearly identical prices. However, over the previous three years, each of the suppliers had upon occasion encountered operating problems that produced lengthy periods of down-time.

Superior was a major customer of each of the three suppliers. At least 33 percent of the total business of each came from Superior. With respect to Part 309, Superior gave 50 percent of its volume to one supplier and 25 percent to each of the others. Part 309 contracts amounted to approximately $750,000.

Though Superior utilized three suppliers, Paul knew the previous year's demand could have been served by two suppliers at a cost savings of $50,000. However, if one of the two suppliers had experienced a shut down of average duration, the cost to Superior would have been $300,000 in lost sales.

In the past, Superior assigned three-person teams to negotiate Part 309 with suppliers. Since superior was obligated to pay the guaranteed cost for all Part 309 units ordered regardless of whether they were produced, contracting for volume in excess of demand would result in an unnecessary cost. On the other hand, Paul felt that if demand increased between 5 percent and 10 percent and Superior did not contract for enough product, the potential loss of sales was $400,000. Superior held a large inventory of the semifinished components used by the suppliers in completing Part 309.

Superior's contract negotiation team had a meeting scheduled for December 17. Paul knew that his recommendations would carry substantial weight in the decisions and strategies pursued by the team.

## Assignment

Review the Business Marketing Action Feature in this chapter concerning both sole source relationships and contracts. Also review the case in the pricing chapter concerning sole source bidding. It is not required nor suggested that Superior utilize a sole source, only that the students involved are aware of the option.

**Team 1 (representing Superior Electronics):** Without Team 2 in the classroom, present your analysis of the above, your strategy for negotiations with the suppliers, and your preliminary contract offer. Before entering the classroom for your presentation, provide a copy of your preliminary contract offer to Team 1, (so that they can be in another room considering it while you are presenting). Be ready to answer questions from the class.

**Team 2 (representing a supplier):** You will have analyzed the situation from the prospective of the suppliers, and have prepared responses depending on what you project Superior will propose. Be ready to review their offer and be ready to negotiate and make decisions.

Following Team 1's presentation, Team 2 will join the class and the two teams will negotiate the terms of the contract to a resolution. Both teams should remember who they are. Suppliers are marketers, and the "marketing concept" has some meaning to them. The buyers in this case also have a need to satisfy their customers. Negotiations should be conducted professionally.

Reprinted with permission from the publisher, the National Association of Purchasing Management, "Superior Electronics" by Michael Crum, *Cases in Purchasing and Supply Chain Management. Strategies, Practices, and Problems,* 1995, Case 1.4, pp 7–8.

# Quality Assurance—Placido Engine Company

It was four o'clock on Friday, October 12, and Ronald Penson, Senior Buyer—Castings, for the Placido Engine Company of Detroit, Michigan, had just finished a telephone conversation with an upset supplier. It was the fourth such call Ronald had received in response to a letter he had sent to his magnesium castings suppliers concerning a severe corrosion problem. All four had told Ronald that they could not adhere to his request without a significant increase in their costs.

## The Placido Engine Company

The Placido Engine Company was a division of the General Products Corporation, a two-billion dollar company that enjoyed a world-wide reputation for quality and leadership in aviation, aerospace, and industrial products. In its nearly four decades of operations, Placido had built more than 45,000 gas engines for a wide variety of commercial, industrial, and military applications. While the most significant part of Placido's sales was in the commercial and general aviation markets, the company was attempting to move toward a balance between commercial and military sales.

## The Executive Corrosion Task Force

During the summer, Placido started receiving complaints from their customers concerning corroded gear boxes and engines. The problem was significant and serious enough to warrant the attention of Fred Thompson, Senior Vice President of the company. In order to resolve this problem and find a permanent solution, Fred created an Executive Corrosion Task Force. This task force immediately solicited inputs from purchasing, quality assurance, manufacturing, engineering, production control, materials, and the Magnesium Corrosion Task Circle for suggested solutions to the corrosion problem, as well as recommendations for implementing suggested programs. The Magnesium Corrosion Task Circle had been established three years previously to deal with the general problem of magnesium corrosion. It was part of Placido's reliability circles program. The Executive Corrosion Task Force was under extreme pressure from Fred Thompson to take immediate steps to resolve the corrosion problem.

### Corrosion-Free Magnesium Castings

Upon investigation, it was determined that a large part of the corrosion problem centered in the Turbo 110 engine and its magnesium castings. It was also found that a significant proportion of these castings were already corroded upon receipt from Placido's suppliers. However, instead of rejecting these castings, quality assurance was processing them through for rework. The basis for this action was the need for parts to meet production schedules. It was believed that the delay encountered by rejecting unacceptable castings would be more costly than the cost of reworking them internally.

The task force decided that this process of reworking unacceptable castings was no longer desirable and directed the purchasing department to take immediate steps to insure that corrosion-free magnesium castings were received by Placido. As a first step in this direction, the purchasing department was further instructed to notify its castings suppliers that strict adherence to the previously issued Mil Spec-M-3171 and the cleaning and corrosion prevention procedure prescribed by Placido would now be required. Failure to meet these specifications would result in rejection of unacceptable castings. In lieu of rejection, the supplier would be debited for the cost of the reprocessing work involved.

The responsibility for notifying the castings suppliers of this decision fell to Ronald Penson who was the senior buyer for Placido. Given the urgency of the situation and the political sensitivity of the issue, Ronald thought it best to send a letter to his current magnesium castings suppliers immediately (see Exhibit 4-13 below).

## Negative Reactions from Suppliers

Ronald was not prepared for the quick and negative responses he received from his suppliers. The general sense of the comments from the suppliers was that they were already properly treating the castings to prohibit corrosion and that they disagreed with the procedure Placido was requiring. Furthermore, they all told Ronald that if they were required to follow the procedure prescribed by Placido, it would be necessary for them to expend a considerable amount of time to retool their current processes and to purchase new equipment. These actions would result in substantially higher costs in producing the castings which would be passed on to Placido.

Ronald was now facing a serious dilemma and was not sure what to do. One thing was certain. He had to act quickly as Fred Thompson was demanding an immediate solution to the corrosion problem.

## Assignment

Review the Business Marketing Action Feature in this chapter concerning sole source relationships, value analysis, and contracts. Also review the case in the pricing chapter concerning sole source bidding. It is not required nor suggested that Placido consider sole source relationships, only that the students involved are aware of the option. Also review Chapter 1 and the marketing concept.

**Team 1 (representing Placido):** Without Team 2 in the classroom, present your analysis of the above, your strategy for negotiations with the suppliers, and your preliminary resolution. Be ready to answer questions from the class.

**Team 2 (representing a supplier):** You will have analyzed the situation from the perspective of the suppliers and have prepared responses depending on what you project Placido will propose. Be ready to negotiate and make decisions. Team 2 should give special consideration to this chapter's text material on what happens when a "straight rebuy" turns into a "modified rebuy."

**EXHIBIT 4-13   Letter Sent to Castings Suppliers Concerning Corrosion-Free Castings**

---

Dear Supplier:

An intense corrosion prevention program for magnesium castings has recently been undertaken at Placido Engine Company. An integral part of this program is the assurance that castings are corrosion free upon receipt of shipment from our suppliers. Your strict adherence to the following Cleaning and Corrosion Prevention Procedures Per MIL-M-3171 is requested:

Heat treatment, penetrative inspection, cleaning in alkali, hydrofluoric acid pickle, chrome pickle, rinsing and backing to dry at 250° F + 255° F, dipping in 7220 rust oil B, packing to insure that the castings do not come into contact with each other rubbing away protection.

The responsibility to deliver corrosion-free magnesium castings per casting drawing, engineering blueprint or M.O.T. is placed with you, the supplier. Failure to do so necessitates an immediate rework at Placido to stop the corrosion process that may ultimately scrap parts. The cost incurred for the rework will be passed on to you in the form of a debit initiated by an Inspection Transfer Report (I.T.R.). The I.T.R. will also have a negative effect on your quality rating.

Your support in this effort is imperative. Please forward the aforementioned procedure to the appropriate personnel in your company. Direct any questions regarding processing to Robert Deer, Quality Assurance Engineer, (405) 876-1241.

Thank you,

Ronald Penson
Senior Buyer
cc: Executive Corrosion Task Force members

Following Team 1's presentation, Team 2 will join the class and the two teams will negotiate and resolve the corrosion problem. Both teams should remember who they are. Suppliers are marketers, and the "marketing concept" has some meaning to them. The buyers in this case also have a need to satisfy their customers, and to do that they need good suppliers. Negotiations should be conducted professionally.

Reprinted with permission from the publisher, the National Association of Purchasing Management, "Quality Assurance—Placido Engine Company" by Michael Kolchin, *Cases in Purchasing and Supply Chain Management: Strategies, Practices, and Problems,* 1995, Case 3.3, pp. 53–54.

## Case 4-3

# Nanophase Technologies Corporation

Lawrence M. Lamont, Washington and Lee University

The 2001 business year was finished and Nanophase Technologies Corporation, the industry leader in commercializing nanotechnology, had just reported financial results to shareholders. It was a discouraging year for the Romeoville, Illinois, company, with revenues declining to $4.04 million from $4.27 million in 2000. The year was disappointing in other respects as well. Nanophase reported a loss of $5.74 million for 2001, even though management had been optimistic about achieving operating profitability. Reflecting on the Statement of Operations shown in Appendix Table 1 and the Balance Sheet in Appendix Table 2, the company's President and CEO, stated:

> "2001 was disappointing in terms of revenue growth due to the economic recession, especially in the manufacturing sector that represents our primary customer and business development market, and the events in September, which lingered through the end of the year," stated Joseph Cross, President and CEO. "However we believe that the company had several outstanding accomplishments that provide a solid basis for future revenue growth." (Nanophase Technologies Corporation, Press Release, February 20, 2002)

Later, Cross expanded on the operating results and future prospects when Nanophase hosted a quarterly conference call for investors which was broadcast over the Internet and posted on the company website (www.nanophase.com). In the transcript of his prepared remarks, Cross said:

> Entering 2002, we believe that the company is stronger and better positioned than at any time in its history. We have established the vital delivery capabilities to succeed with our enlarged platform of nanoengineering technologies and delivery capability investments, our market attack is broader and at the same time better focused, the infrastructure-people and equipment are ready to deliver, our processes have been proven demonstrably scalable and robust, and we have strengthened the company's supply chain. (Nanophase Technologies Corporation, Fourth Quarter Conference Call, February 21, 2002)

While Cross was encouraged about the future, there were reasons to be cautious. After all, the company had been in business since 1989 and had not yet earned a profit. Questions

**Nanophase Technologies Corporation** was prepared by Dr. Lawrence M. Lamont, Professor Emeritus of Management, Washington and Lee University. The case is the property of the author and may not be copied or reproduced without written permission. Case material is prepared as a basis for class discussion and not designed to present illustrations of either effective or ineffective handling of administrative problems.

The author gratefully acknowledges Nanophase Technologies Corporation for reviewing the accuracy of the case study and granting permission to reproduce certain materials used in the preparation. Copyright 2002.

**EXHIBIT 4-14**
**Revenue, Costs and Profit (Loss), 1993–2001**

Source: SEC form 10-K, 1997 and 2002.

| Year | Revenues | Net Profit (Loss) | Cost of Revenues |
|---|---|---|---|
| 2001 | $4,039,469 | $(5,740,243) | $4,890,697 |
| 2000 | 4,273,353 | (4,518,327) | 4,754,485 |
| 1999 | 1,424,847 | (5,117,067) | 2,610,667 |
| 1998 | 1,303,789 | (5,633,880) | 3,221,996 |
| 1997 | 3,723,492 | (3,072,470) | 3,935,766 |
| 1996 | 595,806 | (5,557,688) | 4,019,484 |
| 1995 | 121,586 | (1,959,874) | 532,124 |
| 1994 | 95,159 | (1,287,772) | 167,746 |
| 1993 | 25,625 | (729,669) | 61,978 |

arose about 2002, because the U.S. economy was only beginning to emerge from a significant manufacturing recession. Nanophase management remembered that in 2001, after its largest customer had expanded and extended its supply agreement, a weak economy had caused the customer to delay receipt of shipments of zinc oxide powder during the year to adjust inventory. Given the short notice provided by the customer, Cross had indicated that the company would not be able to find additional business to fill the revenue shortfall. Later in 2001, a UK company, Celox, Ltd., failed to fulfill a purchase contract for a catalytic fuel additive which resulted in a substantial loss of revenues and a nonrecurring inventory adjustment. In late November, Nanophase announced a temporary hourly manufacturing furlough until January 7, 2002 to enable the company to reduce existing inventory and lower its cost of operations during the holiday period. (Nanophase Technologies Corporation, Press Releases: October 25 and November 14, 2001 and February 20, 2002)

Transition times from start-up to commercialization exceeding 10 years were not unusual for companies developing emerging technologies. Typically new hightechnology firms struggled with product development, experienced set-backs in bringing products to market and were slow to earn profits. Nanophase experienced some of these problems, but the company had managed to achieve a solid record of revenue growth since introducing its first commercial products in 1997. Exhibit 4-14 summarizes the revenues, profit (loss) and cost of revenues for the 1993–2001 time period.

Nanophase records revenue when products are shipped, when milestones are met regarding development arrangements or when the company licenses its technology and transfers proprietary information. Cost of revenue generally includes costs associated with commercial production, customer development arrangements, the transfer of technology and licensing fees. It does not include all of the costs incurred by the company. Gross margin, a useful indicator of a business's move toward profitability, can be calculated as revenue minus cost of revenue divided by revenue.

## What Is Nanotechnology?

Nanotechnology is the science and technology of materials at the nanometer scale— the world of atoms and molecules. It is a multidisciplinary science drawing on chemistry, biology, engineering materials, mathematics and physics. Scientists use nanotechnology to create materials, devices and systems that have unusual properties and functions because of the small scale of their structures. Nanophase uses the technology in its patented manufacturing processes to produce nanocrystalline materials, like microfine zinc oxide powder, sold as a component material to producers of industrial and consumer products, such as cosmetics. See Appendix Table 3 for additional description.

Over the next 20–30 years, it is expected that nanotechnology will find applications in chemicals and engineering materials, optical networking, memory chips for electronic devices, thin film molecular structures and biotechnology. Experts predict that the technology could spawn a new industrial revolution. According to Mihail Roco, senior advisor for nanotechnology at the National Science Foundation's Directorate for Engineering: "This is a technology that promises to change the way we live, the way we combat disease, the way we manufacture products, and even the way we explore the universe. Simply put, nanoscale manufacturing allows us to work with the fundamental building blocks of matter, at the atomic and molecular levels. This enables the creation of systems that are so small that we could only dream about their application years ago." "Because of nanotechnology, we'll see more changes in the next 30 years than we saw in all of the last century." (Roco, 2001)

Because nanotechnology promises to impact so many different industries, the National Nanotechnology Initiative has received the financial support of the United States government. The annual letter sent by the Office of Science and Technology Policy and the Office of Management and Budget to all agencies put nanotechnology at the top of R&D priorities for fiscal year 2001. The expenditures have reflected the priority, and in fiscal 2001 actual federal expenditures for nanotechnology were $463.85 million. In 2002, Congress enacted a fiscal year nanotechnology appropriation of $604.4 million. The 2003 budget request was set at $710.2 million, another substantial increase reflecting the continuing interest and commitment to the commercial potential of the technology. (www.nano.gov)

## History of Nanophase Technologies Corporation

Nanophase Technologies Corporation traces its beginnings to the mid-1980s and the research of Richard Siegel, who developed the "physical-vapor synthesis" (PVS) method for producing nanocrystalline materials at the Argonne National Laboratory, southwest of Chicago. Siegel, an internationally known scientist, co-founded the company in 1989 after receiving funding from the Argonne National Laboratory–University of Chicago Development Corporation. The mission of Nanophase was to produce nanostructured materials by developing and applying the PVS process. For several years, the company was located in Burr Ridge, Illinois. In 2000, Nanophase expanded its manufacturing capabilities and moved its headquarters to a facility in Romeoville, Illinois. The original Burr Ridge manufacturing facility was also retained and is currently the main source of PVS production. The Romeoville addition enables the company to increase its manufacturing operations and expand its customer application technology to meet future demand. (Stebbins, 2000; www.nanotechinvesting.com; Nanophase Technologies Corporation, 2000 Annual Report)

### DEVELOPING THE TECHNOLOGY

From its beginning as a 1989 start-up, Nanophase emphasized the development of technology, the pursuit of patents and the design of manufacturing processes to transition the company from R&D to a commercial enterprise. Through 1995, the majority of the company's revenues resulted from government research contracts. From this research, the company developed an operating capacity to produce significant quantities of nanocrystalline materials for commercial use. At the same time, Nanophase was involved with potential customers to facilitate the development of products that would utilize the capabilities of the PVS process. During 1996, Nanophase began emerging from product development and in 1997, the first complete year of commercial operations, the company significantly increased its revenues from sales to businesses.

### PROTECTING INTELLECTUAL PROPERTY

Nanophase was also successful in protecting its technology, equipment and processes with patents. Early in 2002, the company had 38 U.S. and foreign patents, patent applications, or licenses covering core technologies and manufacturing processes. (Nanophase

Technologies Corporation, Fourth Quarter Conference Call, February 21, 2002) Intellectual property such as patents and trade secrets are valuable because they protect many of the scientific and technological aspects of the company's business and result in a competitive advantage.

## REDUCING MANUFACTURING COSTS

Nanophase placed importance on research and technology development to reduce manufacturing costs. Although the company de-emphasized the pursuit of revenue from government research contracts in 1995, research was funded by the company to improve manufacturing processes for commercial production. For example, in 2001, Nanophase made expenditures to improve PVS manufacturing technology in product quality and output quantity. Nanophase was successful in reducing variable manufacturing cost by 40 to 65 percent (including a 25 percent reduction in manufacturing staff) and increased reactor output by 100 to 200 percent depending on the material. The company was also successful in commercializing a new, lower-cost manufacturing process, trademarked NanoArc Synthesis™. The new process promises to further cut some production costs by an estimated 50 to 90 percent, increase production output rates by estimated factors of 2 to 10 times, and permit the use of less expensive raw materials. The process also will allow Nanophase to increase the variety of nanocrystalline products available for sale and address the needs of potential customers who need nanoparticles in liquid solutions and dispersions. (Nanophase Technologies Corporation, Press Release, February 20, 2002; Fourth Quarter Conference Call, February 21, 2002)

## FINANCING OPERATIONS

To date, Nanophase has financed operations from a private offering of approximately $19,558,069 of equity securities and an initial public offering in 1997 of 4,000,000 common shares at $8.00 a share to raise $28,837,936 for continued development of the company. (SEC form 10-K405, 1997) In 2000, Nanophase entered into an agreement with BASF (its largest customer) to borrow $1.3 million to finance the purchase and installation of new equipment to meet the customer's requirements during 2001–2002. (Nanophase Technologies Corporation, Press Release, December 8, 2000)

Nanophase will need additional financing to complete another year of operations. At the end of 2001, the balance sheet indicated that about $7.4 million was available from cash and investments. Nanophase has reported cumulative losses of $34,754,188 from inception through December 31, 2001. (Nanophase Technologies Corporation, 2001 Annual Report)

## Transition and Changes in Management

To speed the transition to a commercial venture, executives with experience in developing high-technology businesses were hired. According to critics, Nanophase had too many development projects under way and did not have enough products and customers to generate a dependable revenue stream. As a result, the company lost its focus and progress fell behind expectations.

Joseph E. Cross came to Nanophase in November 1998 as a Director and President and Chief Operating Officer. In December 1998, Cross was promoted to CEO and he continues to serve in that capacity. Cross brings a background of directing high-technology start-ups and managing rapid growth and turnaround operations. His biography is in Appendix Table 4.

According to Cross, Nanophase was focused more on pure research than on finding practical applications for nanoengineered materials and making money. Cross stated: "We had a bunch of scientists but didn't have any engineers or a sales distribution or

**EXHIBIT 4-15**   **Profile of Executive Officers**

| Company Officer | Title | Joined | Previous Experience |
|---|---|---|---|
| Joseph Cross | President and CEO | 1998 | Senior Management |
| Daniel Billicki | VP Sales and Marketing | 1999 | Senior Management |
| Dr. Richard Brotzman | VP R&D | 1994 | Research Director |
| Dr. Donald Freed | VP Business Development | 1995 | Senior Marketing |
| Jess Jankowski | VP and Controller | 1995 | Controller |
| Dr. Gina Kritchevsky | Chief Technology Officer | 1999 | Business Development |
| Robert Haines | VP Operations | 2000 | Manufacturing |

manufacturing system." (Stebbins, 2000) Since his appointment, Cross and his management team have been concentrating on six major areas:

1. Emphasizing new business development to expand revenues.

2. Achieving a positive gross margin on products.

3. Increasing the technology and intellectual property base by developing new manufacturing processes and establishing patents and trademarks.

4. Reducing manufacturing costs by using less expensive raw materials, increasing output rates and yields and reducing supply chain costs.

5. Increasing manufacturing skills and the capability to produce products to address current and new market opportunities.

6. And, strategically positioning the company for economic recovery.

Following his appointment to CEO, Cross moved quickly to expand and strengthen the management team in the areas of marketing, manufacturing, technology and engineering. Exhibit 4-15 shows the executive officers of the company, including their title, year of appointment and previous business experience. At the end of 2001, Nanophase had approximately 51 full-time employees.

Nanophase also attracted an impressive outside Board of Directors to provide management and technical advice to the company. In addition to Cross, the Board included Donald Perkins, retired Chairman of the Board of Jewel Companies, a Chicago retail supermarket and drug chain; James A. Henderson, former Chairman and CEO of Cummins Engine Company; Richard Siegel, co-founder and internationally known scientist; Jerry Pearlman, retired Chairman of Zenith Electronics Corporation and James McClung, a Senior Vice President and a corporate officer for FMC Corporation. Donald Perkins currently serves as Chairman of the Nanophase Board of Directors. (www.nanophase.com)

## The Science of Nanotechnology at Nanophase

Nanotechnology is used to produce nanocrystalline particles in powder form using metallic materials such as aluminum, cerium, copper, iron and zinc. The extremely small size of the particles, combined with the properties of surface atoms gives nanoparticles unusual chemical, mechanical, electrical and optical properties that often exceed those of the original raw materials.

Different technologies are used to achieve these results, but two of the most important are Physical Vapor Synthesis (PVS) and Discrete Particle Encapsulation (DPE). Exhibit 4-16 illustrates the PVS process patented and used by Nanophase.

The PVS process uses a solid metallic wire or rod which is heated in a reactor to high temperatures (about 3000 F) using jets of thermal energy. The metal atoms boil off, creating a vapor. A reactive gas is introduced to cool the vapor, which condenses into liquid molecular clusters. As the cooling process continues, the molecular clusters are frozen into

**EXHIBIT 4-16**
**Nanophase Patented PVS Process**

Source: www.nanophase.com

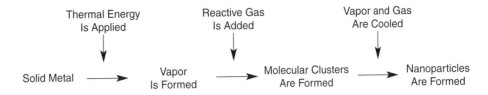

solid nanoparticles. The metal atoms in the molecular clusters mix with reactive gas (e.g., oxygen atoms), forming metal oxides such as zinc and aluminum oxide. The nanocrystalline particles are near-atomic size. For example, about nine hundred million zinc oxide crystals could be spread across the head of a pin in a single layer. (Nanophase Technologies Corporation, 2000 Annual Report)

Because of the PVS process, Nanophase is able to produce nanoparticles with properties that are highly desirable to customers. These product features include spherical, non-porous particles of uniform size and large surface area, particles virtually free of chemical residues and particles that flow freely without clustering together. The company is also able to use the PVS process and NanoArc Synthesis (TM) to custom-size the particles for a customer's application.

In some applications, the nanoparticles created by the PVS process require additional surface engineering to meet customer requirements. Nanophase has developed a variety of surface treatment technologies to stabilize, alter or enhance the performance of nanocrystalline particles. At the core of these surface treatment technologies is the patented Discrete Particle Encapsulation (DPE) process. DPE uses selected chemicals to form a thin durable coating around nanoparticles produced by the PVS process to provide a specific characteristic such as preventing the particles from sticking together or enabling them to be dispersed in a fluid or polymer to meet specific customer needs. (SEC form 10-K405, 1997)

## Product Markets and Customer Applications

Substantial commercial interest has developed in nanotechnology because of its broad application. Although most companies refuse to disclose their work with the technology, it is likely that materials science, biotechnology and electronics will see much of the initial market development. Nanotechnology has already attracted the interest of large companies like IBM (using the technology to develop magnetic sensors for hard disk heads); Hewlett-Packard (using the technology to develop more powerful semiconductors); 3M (producing nanostructured thin film technologies); Mobil Oil (synthesizing nanostructured catalysts for chemical plants) and Merck (producing nanoparticle medicines). In other applications, Toyota has fabricated nanoparticle reinforced polymeric materials for cars in Japan and Samsung Electronics is working on a flat panel display with carbon nanotubes in Korea. (Roco, 2001)

Nanophase is not active in all of the areas. Instead, the company focuses selectively on products and market opportunities in materials science that can be developed within 12–18 months. Longer range product applications in the 18–36 month time frame were also of interest, but they were pursued mainly to give the company a pipeline of new, future opportunities. Nanophase evaluated markets by using criteria such as revenue potential, time-to-market and whether or not a product developed for one application could be successfully modified for sale in other markets.

Dr. Donald Freed, Vice President of Business Development, explained the company's strategy for commercializing nanotechnology: "Opportunities for nanomaterials will mature at different rates, and there are substantial opportunities in the near term—those with a not too demanding level of technical complexity. There are truly different problems in nanotechnology, such as those falling into the realm of human genetics or biotechnology. So we are successfully pursuing a staged approach to developing products for our customers." Freed further explained that this staged approach to developing customer applications enables the company to build product-related revenues while also expanding its foundations for developing more complicated applications. Nanophase was established in six product markets and was developing one potential market that met its time-to-market criteria of 12 to 18 months. (Nanophase Technologies Corporation, Press Release, October 31, 2000; Nanophase Technologies Corporation, 2000 Annual Report; Analyst Presentation, 2000)

## HEALTHCARE AND PERSONAL PRODUCTS

The largest product market for Nanophase was zinc-oxide powder used as an inorganic ingredient in sunscreens, cosmetics and other health care products produced by the BASF cosmetic chemicals group. In early 2001, BASF signed an exclusive long-term purchase contract in which Nanophase agreed to supply a product that met technical and FDA regulatory requirements for active cosmetic ingredients. When added to a sunscreen the specially designed particles are small enough to allow harmless light to pass through the sunscreen while the ultraviolet light bounces off the particles and never makes it to the skin. Zinc-oxide formulations also eliminate the whitenose appearance on the user's skin without a loss of effectiveness. BASF Corporation is a diversified $30 billion global corporation and the third largest producer of chemicals and related products in the United States, Mexico and Canada. Sales to this company accounted for 75.5 percent of Nanophase revenues in 2001. (SEC form 10-Q , May 15, 2002)

In another healthcare application, Schering-Plough Corporation uses Nanophase zinc oxide as an ingredient in Dr. Scholl's foot spray to act as a fungicide and prevent the nozzle from clogging. (Stebbins, 2000) The unique properties of nanoparticles have also enabled their use in antifungal ointments and as odor and wetness absorbents. Both customers continue to explore opportunities for Nanophase products in other areas. The company estimated the market potential for its products in the healthcare and cosmetics market at approximately $45 million. (Nanophase Technologies Corporation, Press Release, October 31, 2000; Nanophase Technologies Corporation, 2000 Annual Report; SEC form 10-K, 2000; Stebbins, 2000)

## ENVIRONMENTAL AND CHEMICAL CATALYSTS

Nanophase was beginning to sell cerium dioxide to a manufacturing company that supplied one of the three largest automobile companies in the U.S. with catalytic converters for installation on a new car model. The product replaced expensive palladium, which was used in the converters to reduce exhaust emissions. Because a pound of nano-size particles has a surface area of 5.5 acres, less active material was needed to produce comparable emission results saving the customer money and space. Catalysts promised to be a rapidly growing market for Nanophase. Opportunities in industry for new types of nanoparticles to catalyze chemical and petroleum processes and for other environmental applications offered the potential to generate $30–$60 million in revenues. (Nanophase Technologies Corporation, Press Release, October 31, 2000; Nanophase Technologies Corporation, 2000 Annual Report)

## CERAMICS AND THERMAL SPRAY APPLICATIONS

Nanoparticles were sold for the fabrication of structural ceramic parts and components used in corrosive and thermal environments. The properties of the company's materials enabled the rapid fabrication of ceramic parts with improved hardness, strength and inertness. Fabrication costs were lower because nanoparticles reduced the need for high temperatures and pressures and costly machining during the manufacturing process. Nanophase worked with parts fabricators to design and develop ceramic parts and components using its technologies and materials. (SEC form 10-K405, 1997)

Nanophase products were also used in thermal spray materials to repair worn or eroded metal parts on naval vessels and replace conventional ceramic coatings where properties such as abrasion and corrosion resistance and tensile strength were needed for longer service life. For example, the U.S. Navy uses thermal sprays incorporating aluminum and titanium oxides to recondition worn steering mechanisms in ships and submarines. With less wear and barnacle growth on the bow planes used to steer, the Navy expects to save $100 million a year when the program is fully implemented. Nanophase sells its products to U.S. Navy approved contractors who formulate the spray with nanoparticles and then apply it to critical parts. In addition to the Navy, Nanophase has several development programs with industrial companies involving similar applications. According to Dr. Donald Freed, Vice President of Business Development, "Our materials are being evaluated in such diverse applications as improving wear resistance in the plastics molding industry and in protective coatings for industrial equipment, gas turbine and aircraft engines." The company estimates the potential market for these and similar applications to be in the range of $25 million. (Nanophase Technologies Corporation, Press Release, October 31, 2000)

## TRANSPARENT FUNCTIONAL COATINGS

Nanophase has translated the technology used to make transparent sunscreens into ingredients for coatings designed to improve the scratch resistance of high gloss floor coatings, vinyl flooring and counter tops. Apparently, nanoparticles fit so tightly together that they make vinyl flooring up to five times more scratch resistant than existing products. Additionally, Nanophase is pursuing a number of opportunities for abrasion resistant coatings. Eventually the products may end up in automobile and appliance finishes, eyeglass lense coatings, fabrics and medical products. According to management, the opportunity in transparent functional coatings is estimated at $50–$60 million. (Nanophase Technologies Corporation, Press Release, October 31, 2000; Nanophase Technologies Corporation, 2000 Annual Report)

## CONDUCTIVE AND ANTI-STATIC COATINGS

Nanophase produces indium/tin oxide and antimony/tin oxide formulations for use as conductive and anti-static coatings for electronic products. The nanoparticle coatings are stored and used at room temperatures, which is an economic advantage to manufacturers. Indium/tin oxide is used primarily as a conductive coating to shield computer monitors and television screens from electromagnetic radiation. The world market for indium/tin oxide conductive coatings is estimated at $10–$20 million.

Antimony/tin oxide materials are used for transparent anti-static coatings in electronic component packaging. Nanophase replaced coatings based on carbon black and/or evaporated metals. The key advantage of nanoparticles in this market is that the transparent coatings maintained anti-static protection while enabling end-users to see the contents inside a package. (Nanophase Technologies Corporation, 2000 Annual Report)

## ULTRAFINE POLISHING

The newest application for Nanophase was the use of nanoparticles to create ultra smooth, high quality polished surfaces on optical components. The company provided NanoTek® metal oxides engineered specifically for polishing semiconductors, memory disks, glass photo masks and optical lenses. The application was made possible because of the 2001 technology advances in the core PVS process, commercialization of the new NanoArc Synthesis™ process, and the improved technology for preparation of stable dispersions of nanocrystalline metal oxides. Nanophase received orders of $100,000 and $200,000 for the materials in early 2002 and expected the application to quickly grow to annual revenues of approximately $500,000. (Nanophase Technologies Corporation, Press Release, February 21, 2002)

## NANOFIBERS—A DEVELOPING MARKET

In a developing market called Nanofibers, engineered nanoparticles that could be incorporated directly into fibers for better wear properties and ultraviolet resistance were being developed. It was expected that the customer solution would result in a more stain- and wear-resistant fiber with a high level of permanence. The products were being co-developed with leading companies producing nylon, polyester and polypropylene fibers for industrial carpets and textiles. Nanophase estimated that the applications could be commercialized in about 18 months with a potential market opportunity of several million dollars. (Nanophase Technologies Corporation, Fourth Quarter Conference Call, February 21, 2002)

# Business Model and Marketing Strategy

## BUSINESS MODEL

For most of its revenues, the Nanophase business model used direct marketing to customers. Teams worked collaboratively with prospective customers to identify an unsatisfied need and apply the company's proprietary technology and products to solve a problem. In most cases, the nanocrystalline materials were custom engineered to the customer's application. International and some domestic sales were made through trained agents and distributors that served selected markets. Nanophase was also engaged in ongoing research, technology licensing and strategic alliances to expand revenues. The markets served were those where the technology and nanocrystalline materials promised to add the most value by improving the functional performance of a customer's product or the economic efficiency of a process.

## MARKETING STRATEGY

The marketing strategy used a business development team to work on nanotechnology applications with new customers. Business development activities included evaluation and qualification of potential markets, identification of the lead customers in each market and the development of a strategy to successfully penetrate the market. Nanophase then formed a technical/marketing team to provide an engineered solution to meet the customer's needs. Since one-third of the company staff had a masters or doctorate in materials-related fields, including chemistry, engineering, physics, ceramics and metallurgy, Nanophase had the expertise to understand the customer's problem, determine the functions needed and apply nanocrystalline technology. The team formed a partnership with the customer to create a solution that delivered exceptional value. After a satisfactory solution was achieved, application engineering and customer management staff were moved to a sales team organized along market lines. The sales team was expected to increase revenue by selling product and process solutions and broadening the customer base in the target market. Customers and applications were carefully selected so the science and materials would represent a technology breakthrough thus enabling the customer to add substantial value to its business, while at the same time making Nanophase a profitable long-term supplier. (Nanophase Technologies Corporation, 2001 Annual Report)

Although Nanophase focused its strategy in the markets previously mentioned, applications existed in related markets where the performance of products could be improved using similar technologies without extensive re-engineering. Based on market research, these included applications in fibers, footwear and apparel, plastics and polymers, paper, pigments and other specialty markets. The company strategy in these instances was to pursue only those applications which fit its primary business strategy and were strongly supported by a significant prospective customer.

Nanophase permitted prospective customers to experiment with small research samples of nanoparticles. About eight different products, branded NanoTek®, were available for sale in quantities ranging from 25 grams to 1 kilogram. The samples included aluminum oxide, antimony/tin oxide, cerium oxide, copper oxide, indium/tin oxide, iron oxide, yttrium oxide and zinc oxide. They were sold by customer inquiry and on the Nanophase website in different particle sizes and physical properties. Prices for research materials ranged from $0.80 to $10.00 per gram depending on the product and the quantity desired. (www.nanophase.com)

Customer inquiries were initiated by a variety of methods including the Nanophase web page, trade journal advertising, telephone inquiries, attendance and participation at trade shows, presentations and published papers, sponsorship of symposia and technical conferences and customer referrals. Management and staff followed up on inquiries from prospective customers to determine their needs and qualify the customer and application as appropriate for a nanotechnology solution. Cross described the process as developing a collaborative relationship with the customer. "Our particular sort of chemistry enables people to do things they can't do any other way. To make that happen, you have to have a close relationship with a customer. You have to make it work in their process or their product. So it is indeed providing a solution; not just the powder that we make, which is nanocrystalline in nature. It's formulating the powder to work in a given application." (CNBC Dow Jones Business Video, 1999)

Using management and staff to build collaborative relationships with customers was time consuming and expensive. Exhibit 4-17 provides the annual selling, general and administrative expenses for the years 1993–2001. While not all of the expenses can be attributed to personal selling, the expenditures are indicative of the substantial growth of the expense category as Nanophase built the business development and marketing capability to commercialize its business. Management expected that these expenses would decrease or stabilize as the markets for the company's products developed.

In a few instances, Nanophase leveraged its resources through partnerships with organizations and individuals focused on market-specific or geographic-specific areas. For example, licensees and agents were used to increase manufacturing, engineering and sales representation. The agents were specialized by geographic region and the types of products they were permitted to sell. Ian Roberts, Director of U.S. and International Sales stated: "The use of experienced sales agents in selected markets is a fast and cost effective way to multiply the Nanophase sales strategy. The agents bring years of industry experience and

**EXHIBIT 4-17**
**Selling, General and Administrative Expense, 1993–2001**

Source: www.nanophase.com; Nanophase 2001 Annual Report; SEC form 10-K405, 1997.

| Year | Expenditures |
|------|--------------|
| 2001 | $3,798,543 |
| 2000 | 3,388,758 |
| 1999 | 3,641,736 |
| 1998 | 3,594,946 |
| 1997 | 2,074,728 |
| 1996 | 1,661,504 |
| 1995 | 1,150,853 |
| 1994 | 799,558 |
| 1993 | 556,616 |

contacts to the task of introducing nanoparticles to potential customers. We intend to form close partnerships with selected agents for specific products to speed product introduction and horizontal applications." (Nanophase Technologies Corporation, Press Release, November 27, 2000)

In November 2000, Nanophase appointed Wise Technical Marketing, specialists in the coatings industry, to represent the line of NanoEngineered Products™ in the Midwest and the Gillen Company LLC to promote the NanoTek® metal oxides in Pennsylvania and surrounding areas. Nanophase also announced the appointment of Macro Materials Inc., specialists in thermal spray materials and technology, as its global, nonexclusive agent for marketing and sales of the company's line of NanoClad™ metal oxides for thermal spray ceramic coatings.

Nanophase retained international representation in Asia through associations with C.I. Kasei Ltd. and Kemco International of Japan. C.I. Kasei was the second largest customer, accounting for 9.4 percent of Nanophase revenues in 2001. Kasei was licensed to manufacture and distribute the Company's NanoTek® nanocrystalline products, while Kemco represented conductive coatings. Nanophase was also working with customers in Europe and intended to expand its European presence as part of its future marketing strategy. (Nanophase Technologies Corporation, Press Release, November 27, 2000; Nanophase Technologies Corporation, 2000 Annual Report; SEC form 10-Q, May 15, 2002)

## Competition

Competition in nanomaterials is not well-defined because the technology is new and several potential competitors are start-up businesses. However, the situation is temporary and eventually Nanophase could face competition from large chemical companies, new start-ups and other industry participants. Five types of industry participation seem to exist.

First, there were several large chemical companies located in the United States, Europe and Asia already involved in manufacturing and marketing of silica, carbon black and iron oxide nanoparticles sold as commodities to large volume users. The companies have a global presence and include prestigious names such as Bayer AG, Cabot Corporation, Dupont, DeGusa Corporation, Showa Denka and Sumitoma Corporation. All of these companies are larger and more diversified than Nanophase and pose a significant threat because they have substantially greater financial and technical resources, larger research and development staffs and greater manufacturing and marketing capabilities.

Second, there are OEMs making nanoparticles for use in their proprietary processes and products. For example, Eastman Kodak makes nanoparticles for use in photographic film. Similarly, the technology attracted the interest of other large OEMs like IBM, Intel, Lucent Technologies, Hitachi, Mitsubishi, Samsung, NEC, Thermo Electron, Micron Technology, Dow Chemical, Philips Electronics and Hewlett-Packard. They are pursuing applications that involve optical switching, biotechnology, petroleum and chemical processing, computing and microelectronics. These companies are potential competitors in the sense that they could sell nanoparticles not needed in their own operations to outside customers, putting them into competition with Nanophase.

Third is the group of start-up companies shown in Exhibit 4-18 that will compete directly with Nanophase. These competitors, funded by venture capital or other private sources, are located in the United States, Canada, Europe and the Middle East. Most were founded in the 1990s after nanotechnology began to gain attention. For example, Oxonica Ltd., Nanopowder Enterprises Inc. and TAL Materials are spin-off firms out of university and government research laboratories. They were founded by scientists and engineers attempting to commercialize a nanotechnology developed while they were employed in

**EXHIBIT 4-18**
**Summary of**
**Potential Nanophase**
**Competitors**

Source: Company Internet
Websites.

| Company | Location | Year Founded | Public/Private |
|---|---|---|---|
| Lightyear Technologies Inc. | Vancouver | 1996 | Private |
| Argonide Corporation | Florida | 1994 | Private |
| TAL Materials Inc. | Michigan | 1996 | Private |
| Altair Nanotechnologies Inc. | Wyoming | 1999 | Private |
| Nanomat | Ireland | 1995 | Private |
| Oxonica Ltd. | England | 1999 | Private |
| Nanopowders Industries | Israel | 1997 | Private |
| Nanopowder Enterprises, Inc. | New Jersey | 1997 | Private |
| Nanosource Technologies, Inc. | Oklahoma | Unknown | Private |

a research organization. Richard Laine, a scientist at the University of Michigan, was a driving force behind the founding of TAL Materials. TAL was incorporated to commercialize the nanotechnologies developed in the Science and Engineering Department at the university. (Spurgeon, 2001) Most of the firms listed in Exhibit 4-18 have not yet reached commercial production. Nanophase is presently the only firm capable of producing substantial quantities of nanoparticles to rigid quality standards. The company is acknowledged by industry peers as the world leader in the commercialization of nanomaterials.

Fourth, there are firms that hold process patents or supply commercial equipment to nanotechnology firms, but also have the capability to produce nanomaterials in small quantities using an alternative manufacturing process. These companies, while not competitors at present, could enter the nanocrystalline materials market and compete with Nanophase in the future. Plasma Quench Technologies is an example. This company, which holds a process patent, recently spun out two small development companies, NanoBlok and Idaho Titanium Technologies, to produce titanium powders using the company's patented plasma quench manufacturing process.

Finally, Altair Nanotechnologies is an emerging competitor that has a natural resource position in titanium mineral deposits. Altair is developing the technology to produce nanoparticles such as titanium dioxide in commercial quantities. The company is completing a manufacturing plant and offering its products for sale on an Internet website. (www.altairtechnologies.com)

## Recent Developments

As the U.S. economy dramatically slowed during 2001, companies around the world delayed the receipt of shipments and rescheduled purchase orders for future delivery. Nanophase was impacted by the slowdown, but the company continued to aggressively pursue applications of nanoparticles with selected customers in each of its product markets. Fortunately, the interest level in nanotechnology remained and some customers continued to move forward on the business development projects already initiated. Despite some setbacks, the results of Nanophase's R&D and intensified business development activities slowly began to show results.

### APRIL 24, 2002

On April 24, Joseph Cross, President and Chief Executive Officer, offered some observations about the position of the company:

Cross said that the company entered 2002 with a wider array of improved technology applications tools than it entered 2001 with, and has significantly increased momentum in business development in several markets. "The improvement in our core PVS Technology, commercialization of our new NanoArc Synthesis™ process technology, and multiple application developments during the last half of 2001 and this far into 2002, provide an integrated platform of nanotechnologies that should allow the company to engineer solutions across more markets," explained Cross. (Nanophase Technologies Corporation, Press Release, April 24, 2002)

## MAY 29, 2002

Nanophase completed a private placement of 1.37 million newly issued shares of common stock for a gross equity investment of $6.85 million. Nanophase plans to use the net proceeds to fund the continued development and capacity expansion of its NanoArc Synthesis™ process technology, expand marketing and business development activities, increase process capability and capacity in the PVS process and for general corporate purposes. (Nanophase Technologies Corporation, Press Release, May 29, 2002)

## JUNE 26, 2002

Nanophase announced a strategic alliance with Rodel, Inc., a part of the Rohm and Haas Electronic Materials Group. Rodel is a global leader in polishing technology for semiconductors, silicon wafers and electronic storage materials. The company will combine its patented technology with Nanophase's new nanoparticle technology to develop and market new polishing products for the semiconductor industry. The alliance is a five-year partnership and supply agreement with appreciable revenues targeted for 2003 and a planned ramp in volume through 2005 and beyond. Nanophase believes that the revenue opportunities approach the size of the company's personal care and sunscreen markets. Rodel, headquartered in Phoenix, Arizona, has operations throughout the United States, Asia and Europe. (Nanophase Technologies Corporation, Press Releases, June 26 and June 28, 2002)

## JULY 24, 2002

Nanophase announced financial results for the first two quarters of 2002. Revenues were $3.07 million compared with first half 2001 revenues of $2.12 million for a revenue growth of 45 percent year-over-year. Gross margin for the first half of 2002 averaged a positive 12 percent of revenues versus the annual 2001 average of a negative 21 percent. The company reported a net loss for the first half of 2002 of $2.72 million, or $0.20 per share, compared with a net loss for the first half of 2001 of $2.38 million, or $0.18 per share. Appendix Table 5 shows the comparative results for the first two quarters of operations.

Commenting on the balance of 2002, President Cross noted:

> While we are somewhat concerned with general market conditions and the normal market slowness that we expect during the summer, we remain cautiously positive about 2002. Based on information from current and prospective customers, we currently believe additional orders will be received during July through September toward our annual revenue target. Although orders are always subject to cancellation or change, and these estimates are based on various product mix, pricing, and other normal assumptions, we are maintaining our 2002 revenue target of $7.00 million or an anticipated revenue growth of approximately 75 percent compared to 2001. (Nanophase Technologies Corporation, Press Release, July 24, 2002)

## Synopsis

The 2001 business year had proven to be difficult for Nanophase. The economic recession in the manufacturing sector of the economy had impacted the company's primary customer base: the manufacturing firms using nanomaterials in their processes and products. While interest continued to remain strong in the potential of nanotechnology, it was still difficult to stimulate interest among prospective customers who were also facing economic challenges and declining business activity. Finally, as the third quarter of 2002 rolled in, a slowly improving economic environment was on the horizon. Maybe 2002 and the years that followed would be the breakout years management was planning for.

## Discussion Questions

1. Using the Internet, update the financial information on Nanophase. Construct a statement of operations for the next two unreported fiscal years. What are the assumptions and the risks in your forecast?

Answer the remaining questions using the information in the case study.

2. Review the business model of Nanophase. What are the key elements of the model?
3. Why does a technology such as nanotechnology take so long to commercialize?
4. Summarize the marketing strategy used by Nanophase. What is the role of collaboration and relationship marketing in the strategy? What problems (if any) do you see in the strategy?
5. What strategy do you think a competitor might use to compete against Nanophase? Explain.
6. Is management a strength in this company? Explain.

## References

### Nanophase Technologies Corporation—Press Releases

Nanophase Announces Second Quarter and First Half 2002 Results, July 24, 2002. PRNewswire.

Nanophase Technologies Provides Additional Information at Annual Shareholder Meeting, June 28, 2002. PRNewswire.

Rodel Partners with Nanophase Technologies to Develop and Market Nanoparticles in CMP Slurries for Semiconductor Applications, June 26, 2002. PRNewswire.

Nanophase Technologies Completes Private Equity Financing, May 29, 2002. PRNewswire.

Nanophase Technologies Announces First Quarter 2002 Results, April 24, 2002. PRNewswire.

Nanophase Receives Order for Ultrafine Optical Polishing Application, February 21, 2002. PRNewswire.

Nanophase Technologies Announces Fourth Quarter and 2001 Results, February 20, 2002. PRNewswire.

Nanophase Announces Temporary Hourly Manufacturing Furlough, November 14, 2001. PRNewswire.

Nanophase Technologies Announces Third Quarter 2001 Results, October 25, 2001. PRNewswire.

Nanophase Technologies Announces Capital Investment, December 8, 2000. PRNewswire.

Nanophase Technologies Increases Sales Representation, November 27, 2000. PRNewswire.

Experts From Nanophase Elaborate on New Technology Opportunities, October 31, 2000. PRNewswire.

### Online Magazine and Newspaper Articles

Spurgeon, Brad, "Nanotechnology Firms Start Small in Building Big Future," January 29, 2001. *International Herald Tribune.* www.iht.com.

CEO Interview with Joseph E. Cross, January 22, 2001. Reprinted from The Wall Street Transcript.

Roco, Mihail C. "A Frontier for Engineering," January, 2001. www.memagazine.org.

Stebbins, John, "Nanophase Expects to Turn Tiniest Particles into Bigger Profits," November 5, 2000. www.bloomberg.com

### Transcripts of Online Conference Calls, Analyst Presentations and Personal Interviews

Fourth Quarter Conference Call, February 21, 2002. www.nanophase.com

An Interview with Joseph Cross, President and CEO of Nanophase Technologies Corporation, January 2002. www.nanophase.com.

Analyst Presentation, 2000. www.nanophase.com.

CNBC/Dow Jones Business Video, February 9, 1999.

### SEC Documents

SEC form 10-K, 2002.

SEC form 10-Q, May 15, 2002.

SEC form 10-K, 2001.

SEC form 10-K, 2000.

SEC form 10-K405, 1997.

### Annual Reports

Nanophase Technologies Corporation, 2001 Annual Report.

Nanophase Technologies Corporation, 2000 Annual Report.

### Websites

www.altairtechnologies.com

www.argonide.com

www.ltyr.com

www.nano.gov

www.nanomat.com

www.nanophase.com

www.nanopowders.com

www.nanopowderenterprises.com

www.nanosourcetech.com

www.nanotechinvesting.com

www.oxonica.com

www.plasmachem.de

www.talmaterials.com

**APPENDIX TABLE 1**
**Statements of Operations (years ended December 31)**

Source: Nanophase Technologies Corporation, 2001 Annual Report.

| | 2000 | 2001 |
|---|---|---|
| **Revenue** | | |
| Product revenue | $ 3,824,159 | $ 3,650,914 |
| Other revenue | 449,194 | 388,555 |
| Total revenue | 4,273,353 | 4,039,469 |
| **Operating Expense** | | |
| Cost of revenue | 4,754,485 | 4,890,697 |
| R&D expense | 1,837,036 | 1,601,671 |
| Selling, general and administrative expense | 3,388,758 | 3,798,543 |
| Total operating expense | 9,980,279 | 10,290,911 |
| Loss from operations | (5,706,926) | (6,251,442) |
| Interest Income | 1,188,599 | 511,199 |
| Loss before provision for income taxes | (4,518,327) | (5,740,243) |
| Provision for income taxes | — | — |
| Net loss | $(4,518,327) | $(5,740,243) |
| Net loss per share | $(0.34) | $(0.42) |
| Common shares outstanding | 13,390,741 | 13,667,062 |

**APPENDIX TABLE 2**
**Balance Sheets (years ended December 31)**

| | 2000 | 2001 |
|---|---|---|
| **Assets** | | |
| Current Assets: | | |
| Cash and cash equivalents | $473,036 | $582,579 |
| Investments | 16,831,721 | 6,842,956 |
| Accounts receivable | 1,238,334 | 1,112,952 |
| Other receivables, net | 144,818 | 67,449 |
| Inventories, net | 892,674 | 956,268 |
| Prepaid expenses and other current assets | 770,200 | 381,696 |
| Total current assets | 20,350,783 | 9,943,900 |
| Equipment and leasehold improvements, net | 3,266,245 | 8,914,745 |
| Other assets, net | 213,135 | 325,743 |
| Total Assets | $23,830,163 | $19,184,388 |
| **Liabilities and Stockholders' Equity** | | |
| Current Liabilities | | |
| Current portion of long-term debts | $285,316 | $ 714,135 |
| Current portion of capital lease obligations | | 48,352 |
| Accounts Payable | 824,338 | 1,233,466 |
| Accrued Expenses | 884,780 | 732,427 |
| Total Current Liabilities | 1,994,434 | 2,728,380 |
| Long-term debt | 827,984 | 758,490 |
| Long-term portion of capital lease obligations | | 53,900 |
| Stockholders' equity | | |
| Preferred stock, $.01 par value; | | |
| 24,088 authorized and none issued | — | — |
| Common stock, $.01 par value; | | |
| 25,000,000 shares authorized and | | |
| 13,593,914 shares issued and outstanding | | |
| at December 31, 2000; 12,764,058 shares | | |
| issued and outstanding at December 31, 1999 | 135,939 | 137,059 |
| Additional paid-in capital | 49,885,751 | 50,260,747 |
| Accumulated deficit | (29,013,945) | (34,754,188) |
| Total stockholders' equity | 21,007,745 | 15,643,618 |
| Total liabilities and stockholders' equity | $23,830,163) | $19,184,388) |

**APPENDIX TABLE 3**
**Nanocrystalline Materials (Nanoparticles)**

Source: SEC form 10-K, 2001.

Nanocrystalline materials generally are made of particles that are less than 100 nanometers (billionths of a meter) in diameter. They contain only 1,000s or 10,000s of atoms, rather than the millions or billions of atoms found in larger size particles. The properties of nanocrystalline materials depend upon the composition, size, shape, structure, and surface of the individual particles. Nanophase's methods for engineering and manufacturing nanocrystalline materials result in particles with a controlled size and shape, and surface characteristics that behave differently from conventionally produced larger-sized materials.

**APPENDIX TABLE 4**
**Biographical Profile of Joseph E. Cross, Chief Executive Officer**

Source: The Wall Street Transcript, January 22, 2001.

Joseph E. Cross is CEO of Nanophase Technologies Corporation. Mr. Cross has been a Director since November 1998 when he joined Nanophase as President and Chief Operating Officer. He was promoted to Chief Executive Officer in December 1998. From 1993–1998, Mr. Cross served as President and CEO of APTECH, Inc., an original equipment manufacturer of metering and control devices for the utility industry and as President of Aegis Technologies, an interactive telecommunications company. He holds a BS in Chemistry and attended the MBA program at Southwest Missouri University. He brings a background of successfully directing several high-technology start-ups, rapid growth and turnaround operations.

**APPENDIX TABLE 5**
**Statements of Operations (six months ended June 30)**

Source: Nanophase Technologies Corporation, Press Release, July 24, 2002.

| | June 30, 2001 | June 30, 2002 |
|---|---|---|
| **Revenue** | | |
| Product revenue | $1,937,489 | $2,829,773 |
| Other revenue | 183,815 | 239,755 |
| Total revenue | 2,121,304 | 3,069,528 |
| **Operating Expense** | | |
| Cost of revenue | 1,857,122 | 2,696,720 |
| R&D expense | 800,189 | 1,003,726 |
| Selling, general and administrative expense | 2,226,949 | 2,091,319 |
| Total operating expense | 4,884,260 | 5,791,765 |
| Loss from operations | (2,762,956) | (2,722,237) |
| Interest Income | 416,616 | 61,177 |
| Interest Expense | (17,664) | (56,282) |
| Other, net | (12,000) | (50) |
| Loss before provision for income taxes | (2,376,004) | (2,717,392) |
| Provision for income taxes | (30,000) | (30,000) |
| Net loss | (2,406,004) | (2,747,392) |
| Net loss per share | $(0.18) | $(0.20) |
| Common shares outstanding | 13,628,562 | 13,980,694 |

## Case 4–4

# Stone & Lewis

## Introduction

Tony Grant had just been appointed the new sales manager of the San Diego district in the Health Care Products Division of Stone & Lewis. He was leaving a job as a very successful section sales manager within the Phoenix, Arizona, district of the Personal Care Division of the company. The Personal Care Division produces consumer products, as is true

This case was prepared by Neil M. Ford, University of Wisconsin at Madison. Christopher G. Gilmore and Christopher J. Pitts assisted in preparing this case. Copyright © 1996 Neil M. Ford.

for all of the other divisions of Stone & Lewis except for the new Health Care Products Division. Based on his past performance as a sales rep and section sales manager, he was among the select few who were expected to advance to upper-level management. He had interviewed for the job less than two weeks ago and was now in his second day at his new position. His predecessor, Ken Burns, had left the company suddenly, and Tony had been given very little information about the circumstances surrounding Ken's decision to leave. Tony had tried unsuccessfully to reach Ken to discuss the situation.

During the interview process, the Southern California regional sales manager of the division, Reed Taylor, had seemed reluctant to talk about the situation. He had emphasized what a great opportunity the new job would be for Tony to add to his experience by learning to deal with the problems of managing a sales force of approximately 25 people. He had seemed intent on selling Tony on the merits of the job and how it would be a necessary step in advancing his career. However, Tony had been unable to get a clear picture of exactly what types of problems he would be facing. The regional manager had seemed very eager to fill the district manager's position and had sidestepped any serious discussion of the job's negative aspects. Tony believed there were more problems than Reed Taylor was willing to discuss. However, after carefully considering what he knew of the situation, Tony decided to accept the job, thinking it would offer interesting challenges.

What little information Tony could gather in the short time before he accepted the job came from talking with the regional manager and through brief contacts with some of the other district sales managers in the Southern California region. He had found out that sales force turnover in the division was much higher than the average for the company as a whole. While the company had experienced a fairly steady annual turnover rate of 15 percent of the sales force over the past five years, the Health Care Products Division had annual turnover rates averaging 65 percent over the last three years. As if this was not bad enough, the San Diego district had experienced a nearly 225 percent turnover in the past 18 months, meaning that on the average a sales rep would be on the job only eight months before leaving. Tony learned that of all the employees in the district who had left their jobs in the past two years, only five had accepted new positions within the company. The rest had left the company.

After Tony accepted the new job, he talked with his three new section managers, each of whom supervised between six and eight sales and technical support employees. His impressions after these conversations reinforced his growing suspicions that he would be facing serious personnel problems. While it was obvious that turnover was a major problem, he sensed that his section managers were unwilling to admit to the seriousness of the situation. Each of them seemed preoccupied with presenting a picture of stability and convincing Tony they had the situation under control. They were all quick to point out that for the latest year, which had ended four months ago, they had been fairly successful in meeting the sales volume quotas for their respective areas. Only the Los Angeles area had failed to reach its objective, but it had achieved 96 percent of its targeted sales volume. For the San Diego district as a whole, the sales objective had even been exceeded by 1 percent.

Tony had told the section managers that he was impressed with these results. However, he secretly wondered if the sales force was performing as well as it could. Last year's quotas had been set at volumes that were essentially the same as for the year before, but the previous district manager's files indicated he and the division sales management had extensively debated whether to increase quotas. It appeared the district manager had won his case by keeping quota increases to a minimum. This was surprising because the business in which the Health Care Products Division was operating was widely considered to be a growth industry. Aside from the fact that his section managers seemed a little too content with such apparently insignificant sales volume progress, Tony was disturbed by their lack of concern over the high level of turnover among the sales force. He decided he would need to take a much closer look to uncover possible causes of the problems facing his district.

## Background Information

Stone & Lewis occupies a prominent position as a leading manufacturer and marketer of household consumer goods and personal care products. The majority of the company's products are sold in grocery stores and similar retail establishments. The company was founded over 75 years ago, and it has established a strong marketing tradition of advertising and promoting its products very heavily. Noted for its marketing-driven approach to sales, Stone & Lewis is also known for its conservative approach to innovation, which is usually the result of very extensive product testing and market research. The company has been criticized for being too slow to react to changing markets, with the result that it was being beaten by competitors in the introduction of new products.

Seven years ago Stone & Lewis diversified its line of products by moving into the growing and highly profitable area of health care products. The company acquired a pharmaceutical manufacturing firm that already produced some very successful nonprescription medicines. At the same time, the company began testing its own new product for adults with incontinence, or the inability to control bowel and bladder function. The new product, known as PRO-TEKS disposable briefs, is a revolutionary concept. It incorporates a patented plastic inner lining containing "mini-sorbs," which is extremely effective in drawing moisture away from the wearer's skin and trapping it in an absorbent fiber padding between the inner and outer linings.

The ability to keep skin drier for longer periods would mean healthier skin for incontinent patients in nursing homes and hospitals. Skin care is a major issue. With proper skin care, bedsores can be avoided. In some surgical cases, without proper skin care the patient may have to return for more surgery. At the same time, nursing staffs would be able to provide proper patient care with less effort and much greater convenience than afforded by other incontinence products, most of which were judged to be highly inferior to PRO-TEKS.

The basic PRO-TEKS brief is available in three sizes: small, medium, and large. The briefs have recently been improved by the addition of refastenable tapes, which allow a nurse to check a patient's condition without having to replace the brief each time. Both briefs and pads also have a pH strip that changes color when urine is present. The strips can be easily viewed by a nurse.

PRO-TEKS has now been on the market for three years and is currently the only product sold by the Health Care Products Division. Exhibit 4-19 shows the organization of the division. This organization is identical to other divisions of Stone & Lewis. Sales volume is generated primarily through nursing homes, retirement and health care centers, and rehabilitation centers. Hospitals, clinics, and medical supply stores provide a fair amount of additional sales. The product can be purchased directly from the company, but the majority of sales are made to independent wholesale distributors, which then sell to final customers. Exhibit 4-20 illustrates the distribution of PRO-TEKS.

PRO-TEKS is easily the most expensive product on the market, but the company and many health care professionals also believe it is the best product available. Exhibit 4-21 presents an evaluation of the available products prepared by an independent testing agency. PRO-TEKS currently holds a 24 percent market share. It has achieved its greatest success in Florida and the southwestern states where large numbers of relatively wealthy elderly persons reside.

The two strongest competitors are AmCo and Allied United, which are perceived by the market as having high-quality products. They have current market shares of 17 percent and

**EXHIBIT 4-19**   **Organization of Health Care Products Division: Stone & Lewis**

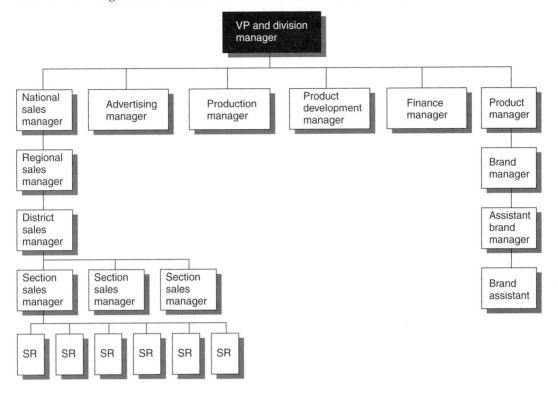

**EXHIBIT 4-20**
**Distribution of**
**PRO-TEKS**

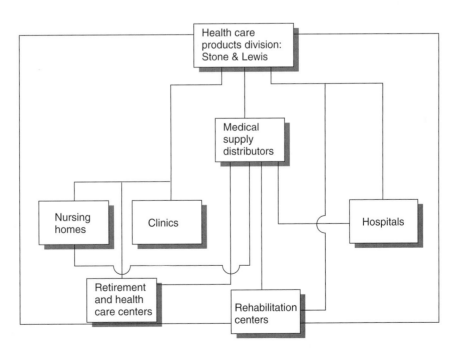

10 percent, respectively. Some 31 percent of the market have chosen reusable cloth diapers that require laundering. The remainder of the market uses lower quality disposable products of various types.

**EXHIBIT 4-21**
**Product Comparison Analysis**

Source: MED-TECH Testing Laboratory Analysis.

| Company/ Brand | Fit/ Wearability | Absorbency/ Leakage Protection | Comfort/ Breathability | Price/ Case | Quantity/ Case |
|---|---|---|---|---|---|
| Stone & Lewis | | | | $39.17 | 60 |
| PRO-TEKS | 8 | 10 | 10 | 47.64 | 60 |
| | | | | 42.32 | 40 |
| AmCo | | | | 46.24 | 96 |
| RE-LYS | 7 | 7 | 6 | 58.50 | 96 |
| | | | | 40.32 | 84 |
| Allied United | | | | 51.60 | 120 |
| COM-FORTS | 10 | 8 | 7 | 66.48 | 120 |
| | | | | 60.80 | 80 |
| AmCo | | | | 36.82 | 300 |
| Cloth diapers | 2 | 4 | 8 | 31.12 | 200 |
| | | | | 36.82 | 150 |

Note: All companies produce three sizes. Above prices are for small, medium, and large sizes. Rating scale information is based on a 10-point scale with 1 representing a weak product characteristic and 10 a strong product characteristic. According to MED-TECH, leakage protection and breathability are the most important product features.

PRO-TEKS are sold by a sales force that includes regular Stone & Lewis sales representatives of the Health Care Products Division and nurses hired under contract from the HCR Corporation to provide technical selling assistance. The standard selling procedure includes a sales rep presentation to a prospective account. The presentation emphasizes the benefits of the product in keeping patients' skin in better condition, reducing laundry costs and labor, and improving the smell and condition of the living environment within the facility to make a favorable impression on the patients' families and other visitors to the facility.

The account can be further persuaded to try PRO-TEKS by receiving free products for three weeks for all of its incontinent patients. The support nurses are on hand to administer the trial and to instruct the facility's staff on the proper use of the product. At the end of the three-week evaluation period, the sales rep returns to summarize the results, which are expected to include improved patient skin care and actual or potential cost savings due to reduced laundry and labor. Cost savings at times have been substantial owing to a reduced demand for labor. In some cases, positions have been eliminated.

Much cooperation is required from the account and its staff to use the product correctly and to accumulate the necessary information to show cost savings. This type of product and the methods by which it is sold are substantially different from the traditional consumer package goods produced by other business units within Stone & Lewis (with their heavy emphasis on advertising and promotions) in which the company has been traditionally engaged and on which it has built its great strength.

## One Week Later

Now that Tony had been on the new job for over a week, he had gathered more information from his sales reps and other district managers that would provide clues about the actions he would need to take to improve the operation of his district. The following is a summary of his findings.

1. The system of sales rep performance evaluation is based on a measure of the number of accounts that are sold, the number maintained as active customers, and the number of "theoretical" incontinent patients at each of these accounts. Theoretical users are determined by multiplying the number of beds in a facility by standard demographically based statistical percentages that indicate the expected number of incontinent patients

for different types of facilities. Sales reps are given objectives of the number of theoretical users that are to be added within a given short-run time period, typically monthly or quarterly. Sales reps are then responsible for keeping their own records of which accounts are active buyers and therefore how many theoretical users they can take credit for. The results are reported by the sales reps to their section managers each month.

There is currently no other way for these numbers to be compiled, and the managers have no easy way of assessing their accuracy. The general feeling among the sales force seems to be that there is much cheating going on about how many accounts reported are actual buyers. This has created some bitter feelings because pay raises and promotions have been based to some extent on this measure of performance and because some of the more ambitious sales reps have apparently succeeded at reporting inflated results for the number of theoretical users.

The negative effects of this situation are compounded by the fact that the standard "theoretical" percentages used in calculating performance results usually bear little resemblance to the proportion of actual users in any given facility. Therefore, a sales rep may receive too much or too little credit for the actual contribution to the company from any given account.

2. Part of the reason for the inability of managers to check the accuracy of sales reps' reported results is the method by which the product is distributed. The company has traditionally used independent distributors to make its products available to end consumers, and this method has been carried over into the PRO-TEKS business. The company has tried to make the product as widely available as possible and therefore has recruited a large number of medical supply distributors. Sales reps perform a missionary sales function by persuading end-users to buy the product, but the company generally sells only to the distributors. Because the distributors are often unwilling to disclose who their customers are and how much they are buying, the company has no way of accumulating the information on which to base actual sales results to end-user accounts. This presents a much different situation from the retail store setting in which the company has traditionally done business and for which highly organized methods and services are available for auditing end-user buying.

3. Section sales managers are evaluated on the volume of sales to distributors within their territories. However, the end-users within a given section manager's territory cannot be required to buy from distributors within that territory. Distributors compete against each other on price and order servicing, and it is not unusual for a distributor in one territory to lower its price of PRO-TEKS to lure customers in another area manager's territory. Section managers compete with each other by trying to persuade distributors in their respective territories to adjust prices or service or by "requesting" that their sales reps persuade end-users to buy only from their own distributors. Pushing end-users to buy from a particular distributor, when that distributor consistently fails to match the price or service of a competitor in another territory, may damage the total PRO-TEKS business for the company. Aside from this, sales reps may feel caught in the middle between two battling section managers, with the result that their own performance suffers from lost accounts.

4. Sales reps report that they often lose sales because the expected cost savings fail to materialize. This is often due to uncooperativeness on the part of the facility staff in providing complete and accurate costs for a before- and after-PRO-TEKS comparison. In addition, the staffs often include a majority of low-paid and unmotivated aides who actually perform the tasks associated with the use of the product. In such a situation, it would be difficult for the sales force to provide the necessary level of training and supervision for using the product and for providing for a well-controlled evaluation.

5. Essentially all prospective accounts have been contacted since PRO-TEKS was introduced. When repeat calls are made to accounts that do not use the product, sales reps report they are often confronted by decision makers who tell them not to come back until they have something new to offer. The price of the product places it beyond the budget of many potential accounts, and they often have very strong preconceived negative impressions about the product. In some cases, this results from the use of plastic in the manufacture of PRO-TEKS, whereas many of the nurses on facility staffs have been trained on the merits of traditional cloth products. When refastenable tapes were introduced to PRO-TEKS, many accounts regarded this as insignificant and were therefore unimpressed by sales reps' claims that this was something new.

   Sales reps are often told by accounts that they are simply hard-selling over and over again on the same worn-out themes, and in doing so they encounter great resistance from potential accounts. In many sales reps' opinions, the company is not responsive enough to the needs of the market and is not providing a sufficient product line to the sales reps. The reps believe the company is failing to meet the needs of customers with different financial constraints or different philosophies toward incontinent care.

6. The facilities in most accounts are headed by an administrator, who is concerned with overall management and financial considerations. However, there is also typically a director of nursing who is responsible for the facility's patient care operations. In the usual selling situation, the sales rep must persuade both persons to buy the product, although the administrator has the final authority. The two authorities often have conflicting goals: the director of nursing is interested in providing the best possible care and may be convinced of the product's merits, but the administrator sees only the short-run costs of buying an expensive product. Alternatively, the administrator may be convinced that PRO-TEKS will reduce overall costs of supplies and labor, but the nursing director and/or the rest of the staff may be opposed to using the product. The result is that the sales rep must often contend with selling to more than one decision maker, whose goals are in opposition.

   As the size of the facility increases, the sales rep typically must call on more people. In addition to those already mentioned, other people include the director of gerontology, usually a doctor, and the social worker. Social workers are important contacts (influentials) since they are in a position to recommend services and products that patients will need on discharge from the medical center. Exhibit 4-22 illustrates a daily call plan for one of Tony Grant's sales reps.

7. A final consideration is that while the product may be of the best quality available and would be chosen by the patient, the patient usually has no choice in the matter. Budget constraints in some cases render quality considerations unimportant. This is particularly true for the majority of patients in nursing homes who receive varying degrees of governmental assistance to pay for the care they receive. The current economic and fiscal climates have resulted in a reduction in government subsidies for health care of institutionalized patients.

   After reviewing the information he had gathered, Tony thought he had some clues about where to find possible causes of his district's high turnover problems. His next task would be to decide what could be done to eliminate or reduce some of these problems. He would have to plan action for his own district and make recommendations to the regional and divisional sales managers to improve performance.

   **Question:** You have been asked to work with Tony in developing a course of action. After a thorough analysis, what would you suggest?

**EXHIBIT 4-22**
**Sample Daily Call**
**Plan for Sales Reps**

| Name | Active Account | Number of Beds | Percent Occupancy | Percent Theoretically Incontinent | People to See* |
|---|---|---|---|---|---|
| Alvarado Hospital | Yes | 214 | 58.2 | 10.0 | PA<br>GER<br>DN<br>SW |
| San Diego P&S Hospital | Yes | 156 | 76.4 | 10.0 | ADM<br>DN |
| San Diego P&S Retirement Home | Yes | 78 | 64.1 | 35.0 | ADM |
| Mercy Hospital | No | 457 | 70.3 | 10.0 | PA<br>GER<br>DN<br>SW |
| Sharp Memorial Hospital & Rehabilitative Center | Yes | 415 | 76.1 | 10.0 | PA<br>DN<br>SW<br>GER<br>ADM |
| St. Paul's Health Care Center | No | 86 | 95.3 | 35.0 | ADM<br>DN |

*ADM = Administrator
GER  = Gerontologist
DN    = Direct of Nursing
PA    = Purchasing Agent
SW   = Social Worker

## References

1. *Institute for Supply Management Report,* Tempe, Arizona. *www.ism.ws.*

2. Amy L. Parsons, "What Determines Buyer-Seller Relationship Quality? An Investigation from the Buyer's Prospective" *The Journal of Supply Chain Management,* (Spring, 2002): 4–12.

3. Daniel R. Krause and Thomas V. Scannell, "Supplier Development Practices: Product- and Service-Based Industry Comparisons, *The Journal of Supply Chain Management* (Spring 2002): 13–21.

4. Richard Germain and Cornelia Droge, "Wholesale Operations and Vendor Evaluation," *Journal of Business Research* 21 (September 1990): 119–129.

5. Carolyn Pye Sostrom, "21st Century Negotiations," *Purchasing Today* (December 2000): 38–48.

6. *National Association of Purchasing Management Glossary of Key Purchasing Terms,* National Association of Purchasing Management, Tempe, Arizona.

7. *Purchasing Today* (February 1999): 60. National Association of Purchasing Management, Tempe, Arizona.

8. "Web Procurement Grows," *Information Week,* (March 1, 1999): 26.

9. "Supply Managers Report Increases in Using the Internet for Purchasing," Forrester ISM/Forrester Research Report on e-Business, reported in *Inside Supply Management,* (August 2002): 26.

# Research Analysis and Strategic Planning

## CHAPTER FIVE

# Marketing Research and Information Systems

## Learning Objectives

After reading this chapter, you should be able to:

- Differentiate between business and consumer market research.
- Discuss the steps involved in the business marketing research process.
- Recognize when it is appropriate to use either inside or outside marketing research specialists.
- Understand the differences between primary and secondary sources of research data and be aware of the disadvantages and drawbacks of each.
- Understand how business marketing research fits into a business marketing information system (MIS).
- Ascertain the major areas where marketing research is used.
- Understand how current technological and environmental factors affect the MIS and business marketing research.

## Chapter Outline

Differences Between Business and Consumer Marketing Research

The Business Marketing Research Process

Developing Information Sources

Marketing Research Versus a Marketing Information System

Major Tasks of Business Marketing Research and Information Gathering

Technology and Environmental Factors Impacting MIS and Marketing Research

# Differences Between Business and Consumer Marketing Research

**Marketing research** is the process of defining a problem or project, collecting and analyzing information, and making recommendations that are supported by the data. Just as there are many differences between business and consumer marketing, there also are differences between business and consumer marketing research. For example, compared with business to consumer (B2C) marketers, business to business (B2B) marketers are more sensitive to economic fluctuations and less remote from their markets. Further, both their current and potential customers are fewer and more easily identified than those for consumer products. Consistent with the differences between B2B and B2C organizations, in a study conducted several years ago by the American Marketing Association, more B2B than B2C firms reported that they conducted business-trends analysis and ecological-impact studies. Fewer reported that they conducted research into test markets, sales audits, promotional studies, acquisition studies, testing existing products, packaging research, ad-effectiveness studies, media research, copy research, motivation research, and consumers' right-to-know studies.[1]

Businesses have realized that buyers, influencers, and end users can be researched just as consumers can. Marketing research has become a major force in the United States, as managers seek information to reduce the uncertainty of their decisions. Most manufacturers of industrial products now have formal marketing research departments, using the same qualitative and quantitative techniques and procedures of consumer marketing research. Business marketing research focuses less on product attributes, however, than on questions regarding market potential in different areas and for different products; who makes buying decisions; who are the members of the buying center; and which trade journals will provide the biggest return per advertising dollar spent.

Since business markets are generally more sensitive to economic fluctuations than are consumer markets, product-line forecasting is correspondingly more important. Business companies use less advertising research than consumer companies because business-to-business companies rely more on the personal selling aspect of the promotional mix than do consumer firms. Business services of all kinds, from business cleaning services to freight carriers, conduct research on customer wants and needs. A mortgage banker, for example, might consider establishing a research department because it could be easier to arrange financing when the borrower's activity has been formally and objectively analyzed. Likewise, a truck-leasing agency, such as Ryder Truck, might consider conducting operating cost research to demonstrate the value of its service to a prospective customer. Another way to compare business with consumer marketing research is to examine and contrast various aspects of the survey research process. Exhibit 5-1 compares aspects of business and consumer research, pointing out some of the more important differences.

Problems encountered in conducting business marketing research often differ from those that occur in consumer research. Indeed, frequently the research processes can be very different. Depending on the particular industry, potential applications for marketing research might include customer satisfaction studies, new market analysis, segmentation research, new product concept evaluation, beta testing, packaging research, plant and warehouse location studies, and so on.[2] In Exhibit 5-1, note the differences associated with research and the relationship with the respondent and sample size. Since the population of interest to business marketers is usually much smaller than that for consumer marketers, it is more likely that the business marketing researcher's firm will have a personal relationship with the respondent's firm. Therefore, it is important for the researcher to consider using the research as a way to improve or enhance customer relations. These are important differences given the prevalence of the one-on-one interviewing process usually used to administer B2B surveys.

**EXHIBIT 5-1**   **Differences Between Business and Consumer Marketing Research**

| Activity/Topic | Business Research | Consumer Research |
|---|---|---|
| Preparing to research | Complicated: Talk with as many employees who have contact with the customer as possible, at all levels in the organization. Then summarize findings and talk to head managers to finalize identification of the problem. | Relatively simple: Talk to the senior marketing, advertising or product manager to define problem. |
| Relationship with the respondent | Close: Think about using the research as a way to improve or enhance customer relations. | Relatively distant: Treat the respondent with respect and care but it is unlikely that the organization will ever have one-to-one contact with individual respondents in the future. |
| Respondent definition and relationship | Different people in the same company may contribute to the decision to buy. So, there may be multiple respondents from each customer business that need to be surveyed. | Individuals that are aware of a category or brand, users of a category or brand, those of a particular demographic criteria. Each respondent is likely to be independent from all other respondents. |
| Sample size | Small. Fairly limited in total population and even more so if within a defined industry or North American Industry Classification System (NAICS) category. | Large. Dependent on category under investigation but usually more or less unlimited. There are about 72.5 million U.S. households and over 250 million Americans. |
| Research approach and methodology | Surveys are often administered personally (e.g., via one-on-one interviews). | Surveys are usually administered impersonally (e.g., via mail, the Internet, or phone). |

## The Business Marketing Research Process

The **marketing research process** gathers reliable marketing information to reduce uncertainty to tolerable levels and facilitate planning and control at a reasonable cost. As seen in Exhibit 5-2, it can be viewed as a process of six steps. Each step is important and therefore discussed separately in the following subsections.

### Define the Research Problem

The first step, defining the problem, is critical; if the research problem is not properly defined, the information produced by the research process is unlikely to have any value. Problem definition first involves clarifying why the information is being sought and specifying any background issues that surround it. Once researchers have clarified what information is needed to solve the defined problem, they then should determine the types of information needed to solve it and analyze **secondary data**—information that has been previously collected for some reason other than a current research question or project—to see if answers already exist. Finally, the firm needs to determine if it is possible to answer the questions. For some problems, technology simply is not yet available to solve them. To completely and accurately define a problem, then, business marketing researchers may engage in discussions with key decision makers, interview industry experts, search through secondary sources for pertinent information, and engage in **exploratory research** such as running a focus group or a small-scale pilot study, among other activities.

If information to answer a research question cannot be found in internal or external secondary data and the researcher determines that the problem can be solved, the researcher then proceeds to the next step in the research process. As an example, following discussion and appropriate interviews with top management who perceive that the firm is not selling the volume of auto parts that they have the resources and wherewithal to sell, researchers

**EXHIBIT 5-2**    **The Process of Marketing Research**

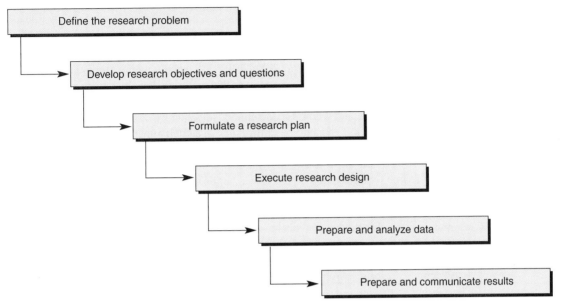

in the firm define the problem as follows: The company is an after-market supplier of auto parts to companies such as Western Auto and NAPA but that they are able, because of appropriate quality levels and resources, to be an OEM supplier. The research problem, then, would be that the firm is not an OEM supplier.

## Develop Research Objectives and Questions

The next step in the research process is to translate the research problem into research objectives and questions. In our example, researchers might translate the problem (the firm is not an OEM supplier) into the research objective "to determine how OEM suppliers are chosen for various auto parts." Once the research objective is selected then the research problem must be rephrased as a research question or questions in order to clearly guide the research. Research questions are phrased such that they ask specific information—in a who, what, where, when and how format—that is needed to address each component of a research problem. To continue our B2B auto parts example, through discussion and exploratory research, the firm's marketing researchers might develop several research questions to be answered such as:

- What aspects do buyers at companies like GM, Ford, and BMW deem to be important in selecting an OEM supplier?
- How do those buyers evaluate our firm on $x$, $y$ and $z$ attributes that are related to being an OEM supplier?
- What are the perceived strengths and weaknesses of our firm's supply operations?

Moving further into the research process necessitates collection of **primary data**—information collected for a particular research question or project. Primary data collection may be expensive and time-consuming to collect though, so the cost of obtaining primary data must be weighed against its value to market researchers.

## Formulate a Research Plan

Ideally, developing a research plan should culminate with a written plan that conveys the essence of the proposed research to management. The typical plan contains a clear explanation of the research objectives and a cost/benefit analysis. It should also include the research method to be used, what is to be measured, how data will be analyzed, and the projected cost of the research.

Depending on the research problem, objectives, and research questions, researchers may choose to engage in observational research, survey research or experimental research. **Observational studies** monitor respondents' behavior, usually without them knowing. Observations may be overt or covert, structured or unstructured, done by humans or machines, and, finally, be direct or indirect. To pick up again our B2B auto parts firm example, researchers may observe and record OEM supplier selection by target companies over time. With enough observation, the auto parts firm may eventually uncover similarities between selected OEM suppliers. This example points to the major advantage of observational studies, that is, researchers are able to note what people and/or organizations really do. Observational research requires that the behavior either be obvious and measurable or that it can easily be inferred from related behavior. A second requirement for observational research is that the behavior is repetitive, frequent, or otherwise predictable. Finally, observational research requires that the observed behavior take place over a short period of time. If these three criteria are not met, researchers would be better off choosing survey or experimental research to answer their questions.

A second type of research is **survey research**. Surveys help researchers to understand *why* particular decisions are made, *how* they are made, and/or *who* makes them. Researchers must be concerned with such things as sampling error, systematic error, and measurement error when developing and administering surveys. The interviewer must ensure that all questionnaires are completed properly and that the number of completed surveys meets the research design specifications for cost and schedule. Ensuring the validity of the research findings requires checking whether the surveys were conducted according to the specifications of the research design. If this is not done, the resultant findings may cause the firm to make a wrong decision. Using survey research, our hypothetical B2B auto parts firm may survey various target companies as to why, how, and by whom various OEM supplier decisions are made. Although surveys help researchers to collect data in an orderly and structured manner and they are an explanatory form of research, ( i.e., they help the researcher to correlate relationships between two or more variables) they cannot be used to infer causation between variables. That is left to the third type of research—experimental research.

**Experimental research** is employed when researchers want to understand cause-and-effect relationships among variables. Researchers hold constant all variables surrounding their target subjects except one (the **independent variable**), which they vary in a systematic way. They then measure the effect of that variation on some other target variable (the **dependent variable**). Continuing our auto parts firm example, say they want to know what language in a marketing communication brings more enquiries for information from potential buyers. Researchers may decide to do something as simple as prepare a new advertising message and put their old and new advertisements in alternating copies of a particular trade magazine. The independent variable, then, would be the differing messages and the dependent variable would be the numbers of enquiries following exposure to the two different ads. The researchers likely would have developed a **hypothesis**—a conjectural statement about the relationship between the independent and dependent variables—such as: *The new advertising message will result in more enquires than the old message.* The hypothesis is tested via statistics (in this case a simple $t$-test would likely suffice) in order to determine if the obtained data confirm or falsify the hypothesis.

After the researchers have determined whether to engage in observational, survey, or experimental research, they specify exactly what is to be measured, who will be observed, surveyed, or selected as subjects, how data will be analyzed, and the projected cost of the research. All of this information is then combined into a document that should be examined by the key decision makers and researchers to make sure that needed information will be collected and that the benefits of the research outweigh its costs. If the plan is approved by top management then the research process continues.

## Execute Research Design

Depending on the research method selected, research design involves engaging in observation, administering questionnaires, or manipulating variables and measuring results. Rather than being done "in-house" this step may actually be done by outside specialists. This decision is not too different from the make-or-buy analysis studied in Chapter 4.

It is not usual for business firms to have marketing research studies (or portions of studies, such as the interviewing phase) conducted by outside organizations. Many organizations perform research activities on a contract or fee basis, including most advertising agencies, marketing research firms, and management consulting firms, some universities, and trade associations. Seven factors are involved in the typical marketing research make-or-buy decision:

1. *Economy:* Can the outside firm provide the information at less cost?
2. *Expertise.* Is the necessary expertise available internally?
3. *Special equipment.* Does the study require special equipment not currently available in the firm?
4. *Political considerations.* Does the study involve deeply controversial issues within the organization? Studies designed to help resolve bitter internal disputes, or that might reflect unfavorably on some segment of the organization, should generally be conducted by an outside organization.
5. *Legal and promotional considerations.* Will the results of the study be used in a legal proceeding or as part of a promotional campaign? In either case, the presumption (which is not necessarily correct) that an outside firm is more objective suggests that one be used.
6. *Administrative facets.* Are current workloads and time pressures preventing the completion of needed research? If so, outside firms can be employed to handle temporary overloads.
7. *Confidentiality requirements.* Is it absolutely essential that the research be kept secret? As the need for confidentiality increases, the desirability of using an outside agency decreases.

If outside specialists are used, good client relations and professionalism are the top characteristics marketers want in a research firm. A survey conducted by Market Directions of Kansas City, Missouri, found the following to be the 10 most important qualities of a research firm:

1. Maintains client confidentiality
2. Is honest with client
3. Is punctual with client
4. Is flexible with client
5. Delivers against project specifications
6. Provides high-quality output
7. Is responsive to client's needs
8. Has high-quality control standards
9. Is customer-orientated in interactions with clients
10. Keeps client informed throughout project

Results of the survey also showed that marketers are willing to hire research companies that are not full-service firms, national firms, or specialty firms.[3]

## Prepare and Analyze Data

In this phase, the researcher codes and prepares the data for analysis. Data may be coded, which is the process by which numerical values or alphanumeric symbols are assigned to represent a specific response to a question. The point of data analysis is to interpret what happened in the study. Analysis attempts to turn numbers into data, and then to turn data into attainable marketing information. An important guideline is to use as simple a technique as possible for understanding, be that simple frequency analysis or complex multivariate techniques. Having analyzed the data, the researcher draws conclusions by logical inference. Data interpretation involves a clear statement of implications derived from the study's findings. These implications define the alternative courses of action consistent with the objectives and nature of the study.

## Prepare and Communicate Results

Although the technical research work ends with the interpretation of the data, the researcher's work is not yet completed. Acceptance of the research results depends on the way in which they are presented. The *reporting phase* of a research study typically involves a written report, an oral presentation, and a follow-up. Each should focus on the actionability of the results, while justifying the dollar outlay for the research study. The follow-up, which would involve questionnaire analysis and respondent analysis, among other things, should try to measure the efficiency of the research project as a whole. The aim is to improve the entire research process in order to improve decision making.

## Developing Information Sources

As noted in the previous section, information sources available to the marketing researcher can be classified broadly as either secondary or primary. Secondary data already exist; they are historical data previously gathered by people either inside or outside the firm to meet their needs. If those needs are similar to the current needs of the researcher, there is no reason to collect primary data. Secondary data are usually cheaper and quicker to collect than are primary data, but business-to-business marketing researchers must always consider their relevance, accuracy, credibility, and timeliness. On the other hand, primary data are organized and collected for a specific problem, have not been collected previously, and must be generated by original research. An important aspect of marketing research is data collection. There are different sources for gathering secondary and primary data—each with their strengths and weaknesses. These are described in the following sections.

## Secondary Data Sources

Secondary data can be found in myriad internal and external sources, each of which will be addressed below.

### Internal Sources

Internal sources include marketing plans, company reports, and marketing information system (MIS) reports. Firms produce, assemble, distribute, and store enormous amounts of internal literature and statistics. Such reports can range from a simple, informational type of memorandum to a several-hundred page report describing some future direction that the firm anticipates taking. In reality, personnel in the accounting and sales departments generally are the most prolific producers of internal secondary data.

## BUSINESS MARKETING IN ACTION

### UNDERSTANDING BUSINESS MARKETING RESEARCH RESPONSIBILITIES

In the world of consumer marketing, the term *marketing researcher* usually refers to someone who studies consumer behavior (e.g., using psychological, sociological, and anthropological research methods). Business marketing, however, is quite different. In business-to-business marketing the term refers to researchers who uncover valuable strategic information concerning customers, potential customers, products, competitors, suppliers, and even entire industries.

### Action Assignment

Contrast the role of the business market researcher with that of the consumer market researcher by preparing a report that compares job descriptions in current employment ads for consumer marketing researchers with ads for business marketing researchers. A database search on the key words *marketing research* may uncover mostly consumer-oriented jobs, whereas searching on the key words "competitive intelligence" should uncover mostly business-to-business jobs. Although the term would seem to be restricted to investigating competitors, *competitive intelligence* actually involves uncovering information that can provide a competitive advantage,

regardless of where in the supply chain the subject company resides. Obviously, competitive intelligence also can be found in consumer marketing, so read the company description carefully to be sure it is involved in business marketing.

You may want to begin your search for jobs with the Web page of your college's career (placement) center, which probably lists many Internet sites for searching through current employment ads, or you can launch from the "jobs" heading on most search engines and gateway pages. They will likely direct you to some of the popular job search sites such as: (http://employment.yahoo.com/), (www.careermosaic.com), (www.monster.com), (www.careerpath.com), (www.headhunter.net), (www.careers.org), and (www.daja.com). For a purely competitive intelligence jobs database, go to the Society of Competitive Intelligence Professionals home page at (www.scip.org) and advance to (www.scip.org/jobs/openings.html).

Present your findings in a presentation to the class and in a written report. With so many sources, and by uncovering "current" openings, your report should be quite unique from other teams' and those completed in previous semesters. Also, if you find this type of career interesting, you may want to consider the highly regarded Master of Marketing Research Program at the University of Georgia.

### External Sources

More general, more diverse, and simply "more" secondary data exist in sources outside the decision maker's firm. Sources of external secondary data include governmental, commercial, professional, and other categories. The Internet and World Wide Web have eliminated much of the drudgery associated with the collection of external secondary data. While there is an abundant amount of secondary data at our disposal, in classrooms, homes, and offices, understanding where to look and how to use the data we find is the key.

### Secondary Data on the Web

A Web connection gives a researcher access to over 75 million websites throughout the world—access to more information than any library can offer. As long as researchers have an Internet connection, they have access to all this information. If they know the **uniform resource locator (URL)**, or the site where the information is located, they simply enter it in the search window of the Web browser and go to that site. A list of some sites used by marketing researchers is provided in Exhibit 5-3.

### Governmental Sources

Federal and state governments publish so much useful literature and statistics that, collectively, they provide more secondary data than any other source. Governmental agencies publish a number of census studies and other documents that are used extensively by marketing researchers. Examples include the following: *Census of Agriculture, Statistics of U.S. Businesses, Census of Manufacturers, Census of Service Industries, Census of*

**EXHIBIT 5-3** **Some Web Sources of Secondary Data for Researchers**

| Organization | URL | Description |
|---|---|---|
| American Marketing | http://www.ama.org | Search AMA publications using key Association words |
| U. S. Census Bureau | http://www.census.gov | Source of census data |
| Strategic Mapping | http://www.stratmap.com | Geographic files with geography of all U. S. |
| Bureau of Economic Analysis | http://www.bea.doc.gov | Available government statistics |
| Bureau of Transportation Statistics | http://www.bts.gov | Source of statistics on transportation |
| Find/SVP | http://www.findsvp.com | Offers consulting and research service |
| Bureau of Labor Statistics | http://www.stats.bls.gov | Current data on various economic indicators |

*Transportation, Census of Wholesale Trade, Census of Population, Standard Industrial Classification Code (recently made obsolete),* and *North American Industrial Classification System (NAICS),* which is a result of the North American Free Trade Agreement (NAFTA).

A particularly useful source of information is the **NAICS (North American Industrial Classification System)** found at the website, *http://www.census.gov/epcd/www/naics.html.* In 1997, the NAICS was introduced, replacing SIC codes. NAICS is a valuable tool for collecting and analyzing data about our present and potential markets, knowing that the data are developed from a common base. The new system uses a common code for the United States, Canada, and Mexico.

Exhibit 5-4, provided by the U.S. Bureau of the Census, shows the NAICS sectors. NAICS groups the U.S. economy into 20 major sections, providing data that present both an opportunity and a challenge. As noted earlier, there is the opportunity to have a tremendous amount of data at your disposal, with the government, trade associations, and private research firms providing data on a national, state, and county basis. The challenge is to learn how to use the data effectively.

NAICS is based on a 6-digit number structure with the more digits shown, the more specific the classification. The hierarchical structure of NAICS allows the marketing researcher to view industry data, summarized at several levels of detail. Because of its

**EXHIBIT 5-4**
**NAICS Sectors**

The code represents the first two digits of the six-digit code that classifies industries with that sector.

| Code | Industry sector |
|---|---|
| 11 | Agriculture, Forestry, Fishing, and Hunting |
| 21 | Mining |
| 22 | Utilities |
| 23 | Construction |
| 31–33 | Manufacturing |
| 42 | Wholesale trade |
| 44–45 | Retail Trade |
| 48–49 | Transportation |
| 51 | Information |
| 52 | Finance and Insurance |
| 53 | Real Estate and Renting and Leasing |
| 54 | Professional, Scientific, and Technical Services |
| 55 | Management of Companies and Enterprises |
| 56 | Administrative and Support, Waste Management, and Remediation Services |
| 61 | Education Services |
| 62 | Health Care and Social Assistance |
| 71 | Arts, Entertainment, and Recreation |
| 72 | Accommodation and Foodservices |
| 81 | Other Services (except Public Administration) |
| 92 | Public Administration |

convenience, this source often is used as a base when researching market and sales potential by industry. The structure is as follows:

- The first two digits of the code designate a *Major Economic Sector* such as 11 (Agriculture, Forestry, and Fishing) as seen in Exhibit 5-4.
- The third digit designates the *Economic Subsector.* So, 111 refers to different types of crop farmers as opposed to animal farming (112), forestry (113), or fishing (114).
- The fourth digit designates the *Industry Group.* For example, 1111 refers to grain farming as opposed to 1112 (vegetable or potato farming) or 1113 (fruit farming). All are types of crop farming.
- The fifth digit designates the *NAICS Industry.* For example, 11111 refers to soybean farming, 11112 refers to oilseed (other than soybean) farming, and 11113 refers to dry pea and bean farming—all of these being types of grain farming.
- The sixth digit designates the *Subdivisions of NAICS Industries* for each specific country. Up until this point, the codes are standardized. The sixth digit is optional for each country—the United States, Canada, and Mexico. For example, in the United States, 111199 refers to "all *other* grain farming" while 111219 refers to "*other* vegetable (except potato) and melon farming."

Assume for a moment that a marketer is trying to find data on companies within a regional area. They can cross-reference the location with the specific code for the industry of interest, allowing easy access to similar information from all secondary sources searched. The benefits are in the code's uniformity, as it greatly reduces the amount of research to be done; the marketer would need to look at only a limited amount of reference materials, thereby eliminating information while not having to worry about overlooking a prospect. Using the NAICS code, a researcher can easily and quickly channel an area of interest down to a specific industry; without the code, one must search for the specific industry first, which can be difficult—especially when an industry has more than one product, or when its products go by more than one technical name. Additionally, without the code, a researcher may spend more time trying to find information than in collecting and analyzing it. Using the NAICS code, however, information can be gathered quickly.

Unfortunately, there is a limitation—perhaps a significant one—to using the NAICS code. This relates to the code's method of identification of an industry when a company produces many products. The code lists companies under their major product produced, with the result that many firms within that market may be omitted. Even if a firm has multiple products from a single site, it will have only one code. Despite this limitation, the use of NAICS saves the marketing researcher time and money.

Another valuable source of information can be found on the website of the Securities and Exchange Commission (*www.sec.gov*). All companies are required to file registration statements, periodic reports, and other forms electronically via EDGAR (electronic data gathering and retrieval) and anyone can access and download that information free-of-charge. For example, researchers may wish to download 10-K reports from pertinent companies and other key company information—including its name, address, telephone number, state of incorporation, Central Index Key (CIK) number, Standard Industrial Classification (SIC) code, and fiscal year end.

### Commercial Sources

Some of the publications of secondary data distributed by the private sector include the following: *Funk and Scott Index of Corporations and Industries, Annual Survey of U. S. Business Plans for New Plants and Equipment, Sales and Marketing Management, Survey of Industrial and Commercial Buying Power, Survey of Buying Power,* and *Thomas Register of American Manufacturers.* Most sources now offer database packages on CD-ROM, DVD, or immediate download for personal computers.

### *Professional Publications*

Professional associations exist in many fields of business, service, and technology, and most are interested in securing and disseminating information between and among people having common, work-related interests. *Academic publications* cut across industries and provide for the exchange of ideas between marketing people, usually with an intellectual orientation. Some, such as *Marketing News,* resemble newspapers and report current, topical marketing events and issues. Publications such as the *Journal of Marketing, Journal of Marketing Research, Journal of the Academy of Marketing Science,* and the *Journal of Business and Industrial Marketing* contain more detail and are of greater interest to marketers. Other forms of academic publications include the proceedings of professional meetings, research reports, monographs, and working papers. *Trade publications* focus on a particular industry and convey ideas and statistics to decision makers, usually with a pragmatic orientation. Most trade publications contain articles describing trends in their industry, case histories of successful firms, procedures to improve a firm's performance, and industry statistics. Most are listed in *Business Publication Rates and Data,* a publication of Standard Rate and Data Service, Inc. Each of the more than 300 trade publications listings includes the publisher's address, advertising costs, circulation, and other pertinent data.

### *Disadvantages of Secondary Data*

Secondary data were developed for purposes other than the particular study under consideration; thus, such data must be scrutinized for applicability and accuracy. Quotations or excerpts from secondary data often are misleading, and when taken out of context, secondary data may be interpreted wrongly. The very nature of secondary data makes it imperative that they be evaluated carefully before use. The researcher must also consider aspects such as the following:

*How recent are the data?* Obsolescence is often a factor to be considered when secondary data are used. Some secondary data are collected periodically; hence, the most recently available data may already be obsolete.

*Is the coverage of data adequate for present purposes?* This question relates not only to geographic coverage but also to the type of products or establishments included in the data. For example, in studying the composition of an industry as reported by a trade association, it is important to determine whether the data cover all members of an industry, or are restricted to members of a given association. The question of coverage becomes especially important in studying production data for individual products. In past *Census of Manufacturers,* plants were classified according to principal products produced. As a result, products that were produced widely, but as by-products of other goods, received little mention; a product such as nails, a by-product of some iron and steel plants, might not be included.

*In a sample survey, was an adequate sample used?* This is especially important in the case of a mail survey to which most of the sample did not reply. In this instance, bias in the data may be substantial.

*Might the data have been biased because of the nature of the sponsor or the objectives of the original study?* This danger may arise when trade associations conduct attitudinal or profit studies. Association members may be reluctant to provide confidential data. Alternatively, if the association indicated that a study had certain objectives, such as to show how poor a dealer's profit margins were, the results are likely to bear out the objectives. Here, it is advisable for the marketing researcher to obtain a copy of not only the original questionnaire but also the cover letter.

*Who gathered the data?* Federal and state agencies and most commercial marketing research firms will have conducted their research as professionally as possible. However, a chamber of commerce or trade association might advocate one position or another.

## Primary Data Sources

Although business marketing researchers must rely heavily on secondary data sources, research objectives may dictate that primary data must be collected. Primary data should be generated only after secondary data research sources have been exhausted, given the problem of respondent availability and accessibility due to travel requirements, heavy appointment schedules, and the like. The most common method of obtaining primary data for the business market is through surveys. Three survey methods commonly used with business respondents are: (1) the personal interview, (2) the telephone survey; and (3) the mail survey. Exhibit 5-5 compares these three survey methods with regard to cost, time, information quality, information quantity, the nonresponse problem, and interviewer bias.

### Personal Interviews

In the personal interview, the interviewer is in the presence of, or face-to-face with, the respondent. This allows maximum versatility of questioning methods (structured or unstructured, disguised or nondisguised) and a variety of question types. Interviews attempt to uncover content and intensity of feelings and motivations beyond the rationalized overt responses to structured questions. Because tape recordings frequently are used, interviews take a long time to complete, transcribe, and read and must be analyzed by an experienced practitioner who knows both the technique and the business product category under study.

### Telephone Surveys

A telephone survey is the most convenient means of reaching respondents, though not as flexible and versatile as the personal interview. Drawbacks of the telephone medium relate particularly to the lack of anything visual. Distance, though, is not a serious obstacle, nor is cost.

### Mail Surveys

Mail surveys are used extensively in marketing research because of the many advantages they provide to the researcher. Indeed, researchers have depended on mail questionnaires since the 1940s. They are relatively low in cost, geographically flexible, and can reach a large sample simultaneously. Further, mail questionnaires tend to be more valid because

**EXHIBIT 5-5   Comparing Business Survey Methods**

| Criteria | Personal Interview | Telephone | Mail |
|---|---|---|---|
| Cost | Highest per respondent | Second highest per respondent | Least per respondent |
| Time | Most | Least | Moderate |
| Information quality | In-depth, complex information | Complex information with prior contact | Somewhat complex information |
| Nonresponse problem | Limited due to face-to-face contact | Hard to ensure contact with proper respondent | Hard to control |
| Interviewer bias | Difficult to identify and control | Difficult to identify and control | Controllable through rigorous pretesting |

they permit leisurely and thoughtful response, and respondents may divulge confidential information if they can remain anonymous. No public opinion or marketing research technique has been used more than mail surveys. Mail surveys do have drawbacks, however. For example, there is no interviewer in a mail survey to explain the purpose of the study, to induce cooperation, to ask the questions, to record the answers, and, in general, to cope with any problems that develop. This lack of interviewer is the main difference between mail and the other two primary data collection methods, putting a great deal of importance on the construction of the questionnaire and any accompanying transmittal letters. Thus, mail cannot be used to conduct an unstructured study in which an interviewer is relied upon to improvise the questioning as the interview progresses. Once a mail survey is sent, the business researcher can only let it run its course. An additional drawback concerns time: if research results must be obtained quickly, mail is not the data collection method of choice.

### Disadvantages of Primary Data

Collecting primary data can be, and usually is, expensive. While versatility is a plus, speed and cost, along with an unwillingness (or inability) of the respondent to provide information, can be disadvantageous. Mail and telephone surveys lack flexibility, and unstructured questionnaires and questions, if answered incompletely or incorrectly, may not elicit useful data. The accuracy of information obtained can be questioned, and sequence bias—resulting when the respondent can change an answer after seeing a later question—will occasionally present a problem. In answering open-ended questions, respondents will tend to be briefer and more general in mail surveys than in personal or telephone interviews. Complex questions with rating scales or other procedures that can be confusing tend to draw more "no answers" in mail surveys. Finally, despite the improving rates of return being reported on mail surveys, many such studies still have large proportions of nonrespondents.

## Marketing Research Versus a Marketing Information System

Whereas **marketing research** is problem or project oriented, a **marketing information system (MIS)** is a much more general system. The MIS uses people, procedures, hardware, and software to scan and collect data from the environment, make use of data from transactions and operations within the firm, and then sort, integrate, analyze, evaluate and distribute that information to key marketing decision makers. It should be a planned, routine, and on-going process and it involves four subsystems; an internal reports system, a marketing intelligence system, an analytical marketing system, and a marketing research system. Hence, marketing research should be a part of a larger MIS. It is imperative today that every firm manage and disseminate marketing information as effectively as possible. If implemented well, the MIS can provide instantaneous information while, at the same time, monitoring the marketplace continuously so that management can adjust activities as conditions change. An important point to remember about the MIS is that it gathers important information from the disciplines of finance, production control, accounting, and others, and translates this information into useful information.

Exhibit 5-6 illustrates the relationship between the marketing environment, the MIS and marketing managers. Data in the form of facts, figures, and numbers, are derived from various sources in the internal and external marketing environments of the firm. They are fed into the MIS in the form of internal reports, marketing intelligence, and marketing research. **Marketing intelligence** is the collection and analysis of publicly available information about competitors and the marketing environment. It may be collected and/or submitted by employees, customers, competitors, suppliers, and/or marketing research companies. The **internal reports system** involves the collection of information from data sources within the

**EXHIBIT 5-6** **Schematic View of a Marketing Information System**

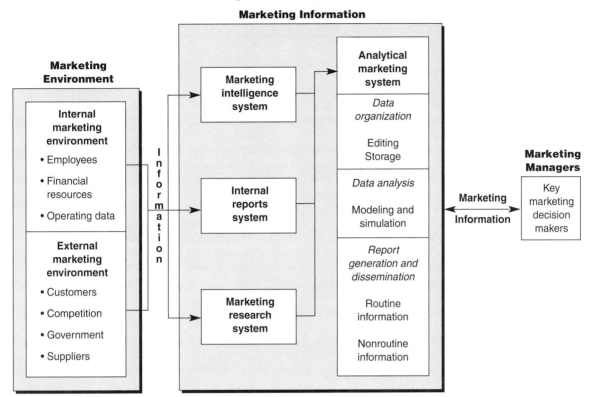

company. It may be collected, measured and/or submitted by the accounting department, the sales force, marketing, manufacturing, and/or by product sales. The **marketing research system** is charged with design, collection, analysis, and reporting of data about a specific problem or situation faced by the organization. Marketing research may be done within the organization or may be bought as needed and performed by marketing research firms. The **analytical marketing system** is charged with general data organization, data analysis, and report generation, generally for data other than that collected via marketing research. The task of data organization is especially important given the amount of information now available to business firms.[4] Once information has passed through the MIS, it is in a usable form and available to key marketing executives so that they can make decisions concerning market share, entry into new markets, product adaptations, and other important areas. This information increases the likelihood of making good decisions.

Some marketing executives think that their organizations are too small to use an MIS; they feel that their marketing research department alone will provide adequate research data for effective decision making. However, since marketing research is typically focused on a specific problem or project; its investigations have a definite beginning, middle, and end. An MIS is much wider in scope. More important, an effective MIS will enable the business marketing manager to make more effective decisions in overall marketing strategy. Making business marketing decisions without input from the marketplace is dangerous, considering the degree of competition encountered by most U.S. business firms. An MIS department is intended to provide information about customer problems and dissatisfactions, potential intermediary problems, competitive acts, and other external and internal factors before crisis situations arise. A properly formulated MIS can be preventive as well as curative for problems commonly faced by business marketing managers.

# BUSINESS MARKETING IN ACTION

## PATENT RESEARCH

Kim Lee, a recent business marketing graduate, had just received an assignment to research multinational patent information concerning a potential new product for his company's aerospace products division. Kim knew that patent files list all sorts of diagrams and technical data, some of which can be useful to R & D and marketing decision makers. The product he was working on today was a high-tech hose clamp that connected a reinforced silicone fuel line to a titanium fitting. What was unique and potentially patentable about the hose clamp was its construction. It was made of fiberglass-filled plastic with embedded (molded-in) spring wire for gripping power. The clamp was not clipped on like conventional clamps. It was wrapped around the fuel line at the fitting, and a special heated forming tool was used to permanently mold it in place. Kim's objective was to search for similar patents, to be on the lookout for potentially useful technical information, and to recommend whether a patent should be applied for on the new product.

Kim started with a list of Internet sites to perform a keyword search using the term "hose clamp" (including the quotes so that the computer would look for instances of the two words together). Beginning with the U.S. Patent & Trade Office (www.uspto.gov/patft), he searched on ttl/"hose clamp" (the ttl followed by a slash was to tell the computer to search for patent filings with the phrase "hose clamp" in the title. The Canadian site at Industry Canada (http://strategis. ic.gc.ca) was a little tricky. The last time Kim Lee was there he had made himself some notes to start at the site map, click on Research Technology and Innovation, then click on Canadian Patent Database. Under search options click on Basic, then search on the words "hose clamp." For partial coverage of Europe and Japan, he utilized the United States Patent and Trademark office website at www.uspto.gov. Additionally, he went to several general search sites such as (www.lycos.com) and (www.altavista.com), searched on the word *patent,* and uncovered several other useful patent databases through which to search.

### Action Assignment

You are Kim. Complete the patent research assignment and develop a report in written format. Make a class presentation of the process and results.

## Major Tasks of Business Marketing Research and Information Gathering

The extent to which business firms gather information is wide and varied. Below are the major areas where business marketing information is gathered and marketing research is conducted.

### Market Potential

Business marketing information may be collected in order to clarify the maximum total sales and profit potential of existing and new product markets. Such information helps in decision making concerning resources available for new product introduction and product deletion decisions.

### Market-Share Analysis

Another area where marketing information is needed is in determining the ratio of sales revenue of the firm to the total sales revenue of all firms in the industry. The competitive environment is dynamic, making **market-share analysis** a regular standard against which to compare the firm's current objectives and future performance.

### Market Characteristics

Marketing research can be used to uncover important segmentation and buying characteristics and may also identify potential barriers to buying. See Chapter 4 for a detailed discussion of various issues related to buyer and organizational behavior. The degree of success of a firm in penetrating particular markets and, more important, the reasons for the success or lack of it are crucial pieces of data for use in setting objectives and direction for the future.

# STRATEGY AT WORK

## USING RESEARCH TO DEVELOP PRODUCTS AND THEIR MARKETING STRATEGY: SANDVIK SAW AND TOOL COMPANY

Not all market research is done with surveys and computers. Many business-to-business research projects involve hands-on product design attribute work. Research is crucial to product development and development of marketing strategy. For Sandvik Saw and Tool Company, the objective is to develop ergonomic tools that can improve the comfort, safety, and productivity of its customers' production workers. Sandvik uses an 11-point design development process that requires extensive research and typically takes two to three years to complete. For this company, the product development process is customer-benefit driven, and much of the information comes from the users (the workers at customers' plants). Sandvik's marketing strategy is then based on offering the most ergonomic tools produced anywhere in the world.

Recently, Sandvik's design process resulted in the successful development of a wire cutter. Ergonomically correct wire cutters are important to electronic assembly work because such work is a repetitive precision task with a high risk of strain injuries. Since workers can be required to make up to 10,000 cuts per day (up to 120 cuts per minutes), wrist injuries such as carpal tunnel syndrome (CTS) can be a problem for individual workers and for their employers. Just one worker with CTS can cost a company $30,000 in compensation claims and lost productivity. Along with the position of the hands, the magnitude and distribution of hand loads are contributors to CTS, in that as a person squeezes a conventional pair of spring-loaded pliers, resistance increases as the tool closes. When the spring resistance of the tool is at its maximum, that resistance combines with the force needed to actually cut the wire, with a resultant possibility of injury to the wrist. To minimize the peak force for each cut, Sandvik designed an innovative spring dubbed the "Biospring" for the new cutters. The spring opens the handles automatically, but reduces the force required to close as the user squeezes. Thus, the only force required from the user is to cut the wire, not resist the spring. Also, the spring adjusts to fit different hand sizes and shapes. Sandvik researched everything from the shape of the handles to the friction material on the handles, the cutting surface angles, and the weight.

## Sandvik's 11-Point Program for Ergonomic Tool Development

1. Define the tool being developed with preliminary specifications. (What is the tool supposed to do?)

2. Conduct market analysis to determine which tools professional users prefer. (Which tools reduce risk of injury?)

3. Conduct background research on published studies. (What risks are associated with this type of tool?)

4. Build working prototypes—to focus users on product performance. Prototypes are made from the same material and in the same colors. (A user's hand and the tool handle should work in harmony.)

5. Record first prototype hand tools at work—User Test #1. (Measure each user's hand.)

6. Evaluate and modify prototypes. (Improve best prototypes based on analysis of user tests.)

7. Survey a wider selection of users—User Test #2. (Users from first test are augmented with additional users.)

8. Produce a production-representative prototype based on final design recommendations. (Use feedback from User Test #2 to determine final configuration.)

9. Generate manufacturing specifications. (A short production run validates manufacturing setup.)

10. Prepare for tool launch by production—User Test #3 (Final user test employs about 200 tools.)

11. Five-year follow-up gauges user reactions in the field. (Long-term studies validate tool design)

### Assignment

Compare Sandvik's 11-point program to the marketing research process presented in this chapter. Although Sandvik's 11-point program is a product development process (product development will be covered in more detail in Chapter 7), it is useful for you to note that many of the initial steps involved in product development actually depend on good marketing research. To demonstrate your understanding of this: (1) identify the marketing research operations in the Sandvik 11-point program; (2) identify each as primary or secondary research; and (3) explain how the wire cutters' 4P (production, price, place, and promotion) marketing mix strategy will be impacted by this marketing research.

Reprinted with permission from *Machine Design,* "Ergonomics Goes Beyond Styling," August 20, 1998, pp. 58–62. Copyright, Penton Media, Inc., Cleveland, Ohio.

## Sales Analysis

Marketing research and/or information gathering may also be useful if a firm wishes to compare actual sales records with sales goals in order to identify strengths and weaknesses. In sales analysis, also called **microsales analysis**, sales revenues can be traced to their sources, such as specific products, sales territories, or customers. Common focus areas for marketing research include the following:

- *Customer characteristics:* reason for purchase, type of firm, and user versus middleman.
- *Product characteristics:* model, size, and accessory equipment bought.
- *Geographic region:* sales territory, city, state, and region.
- *Order size:* large or small orders on average; order minimums needed?
- *Price or discount class:* check competition; changes anticipated?

This analysis is helpful to the business marketing manager in determining the direction of future efforts regarding product profitability, sales territory changes, product deletion decisions, and other important marketing areas.

## Forecasting

Marketing research and/or information gathering are also used in forecasting. Both short-range and long-range forecasting are vital inputs to the marketing planning process. The amount a firm expects to sell during a specific time period under specific conditions and to specific segments affects both the controllable and uncontrollable factors that influence future business. Forecasts form the basis of all planning activity within the organization and it is critical for cash flow estimates, plant expansions, projected employment levels, decisions regarding product-line changes, distribution channel changes, and a host of other decision areas about which the firm must act upon regularly. (See Chapter 6 for a detailed discussion on forecasting/demand projection).

## CRM and Database Development

**Customer relationship management (CRM)** is a very important part of an organization's business strategy and involves an environment in which an organization works to better manage its endeavors around identified needs of customers. It is a form of proactive customer service with the objective to increase customer loyalty. One way to think of CRM is that it is the implementation process behind relationship marketing. Exhibit 5-7 shows the flow of activities and information in the CRM process.

**EXHIBIT 5-7**
**A Simple Flow Model of the Customer Relationship Management Process**

Adapted from: Hair, Bush, and Ortinau, *Marketing Research Within a Changing Information Environment,* 2nd Ed. (New York: McGraw-Hill/Irwin, 2003): p. 128.

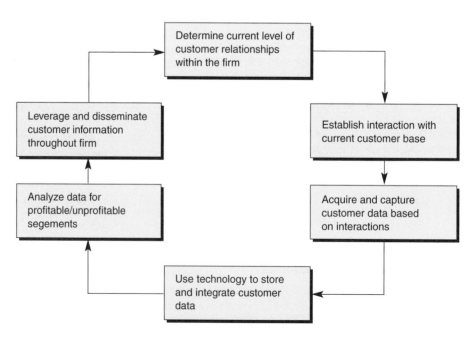

Therefore, based on the prescribed activities necessary for successful CRM shown in Exhibit 5-7, business marketing research may be charged with gathering information about customers and storing, analyzing, and integrating customer interaction information throughout the organization such that the firm achieves maximum customer satisfaction and retention. In Exhibit 5-6, we saw that those activities are part of the marketing information system (MIS) for the firm, making the MIS an important component of CRM.

In order for CRM to be successful, first and foremost the firm must know its customers. It must know who they are and who they are not; it must be able to separate profitable customers with whom the firm will want to establish deeper relationships from unprofitable customers that the firm should service at low cost. Therefore, the firm has knowledge needs that include identifying profitable and potentially profitable customers. Among questions that business marketing researchers need to investigate are the following:

- What kinds of programs and strategies will result in brand loyal customers (e.g., loyalty programs, preferred customer status)?
- What counts as "quality customer service" (e.g., direct communication to customers, information hot lines)?
- Which goods and services and which modes of delivery are considered to be most valuable to customers (e.g., Web-enabled cell phones, JIT delivery)?
- What are customers' responses to marketing and sales campaigns (e.g., trade shows, sales contests)?

In addition to marketing research, other marketing personnel within the firm would be charged with establishing and maintaining the internal reports system (often, the sales force will play a key role in gathering market data via call reports, quotes submitted, and lost-order reports), the marketing intelligence system, and the analytical marketing system. That information, however, should not remain with the marketing department but should be integrated in a timely manner into the CRM system—which is actually just an organization-wide version of the MIS. Once information that has been collected, found, or generated by others is integrated into the CRM system, it is further expected that CRM personnel will use that system to anticipate customers' needs and wants and to develop or refine business offers (marketing mixes) such that those needs and wants are met.

In order for CRM to work properly, a firm must have an effective and efficient database. A **database** is a collection of information about what customers are buying, how often they buy, and the amount they buy. As a result of the development of new software we now have electronic **data warehouses**—the intelligent storage of aggregate data (sales, production, returned merchandise, etc.), which is used by management to make better decisions. A good data warehouse allows the marketer to retrieve and analyze information quickly, promoting prompt and efficient decision making. A data warehouse saves time and energy and, when combined with networked PCs, provides marketing management with a valuable vehicle for storing and retrieving data.

Most firms develop a database from secondary sources, using existing data gathered by people inside or outside the firm, or they buy a desired database. On-line database searching is the most common method of developing a database today. This method saves an enormous amount of time, as compared to previous methods of library research or of gathering primary data. The Internet allows marketers to retrieve massive amounts of relevant secondary data, customized for particular needs. Instead of going to the library, the library comes to us via the Internet. In addition to on-line availability, most databases are also available on CD-ROM or DVD.

## Other Applications

Additional areas of focus for business marketing research and information gathering include studies on sales quotas and territories, pricing, test-marketing audits, business trends, new product acceptance, advertising research, and competitive differences. Certainly, marketing research and information gathering are widely diverse marketing functions.

## Technology and Environmental Factors Impacting MIS and Marketing Research

Information technology and other environmental factors have changed the way marketers gather and use marketing research data in decision-making activity. For example, the **Internet** has transformed methods of collecting data and information. Using the Internet to search for and locate important and valuable sources of secondary data can now be done swiftly and economically. The Internet may also be used as a way to collect primary data since Web-based surveys are becoming more and more common. Concerning primary data, at the least, firms may collect what is called **passive data**—information automatically obtained by a business when a person sends an e-mail or visits a website. Two such automatic pieces of information are the Internet protocol (IP) address and domain name of each visitor to its website, which provide geographic and specific user information. If visitors to a website interact with it, a firm can collect **active data**. With the advent of **e-commerce**—selling, trading, bartering and conducting transactions over the Web—companies can now quickly gather information from customers when they visit company websites. Firms may track visitors' progress through the website and it may induce them to provide even more information voluntarily. Finally, a firm may collect **directed data** which involves information collected about particular customers on the Internet through a comprehensive directed search for specific information. Given today's emphasis on CRM, various types of business-related behavior may be recorded and quickly integrated with technology-driven online and offline databases. Using information collected while customers are on-line may also lead to use of **data mining** (also known as *data* or *knowledge discovery*)—the process of analyzing data from different perspectives and summarizing it into useful information.

Another factor impacting business marketing research and information gathering is increased concern about privacy. Whereas the Internet and e-commerce have worked to facilitate data collection, privacy concerns have resulted in new barriers for research. For example, organizations now routinely face "do-not-call" laws at both the state and federal levels and, in June 2003, the FTC instituted a national "Do-Not-Call Registry" for consumers. Although that registry is more of a problem for B2C than B2B firms, it is likely that future legislation may affect B2B data collection and telemarketing.

Privacy concerns have resulted in a third factor—**gatekeeper technologies** (e.g., caller ID, electronic answering devices, voice messengers, traditional answering machines)—which impacts MIS and marketing research. Gatekeeper technologies serve to protect customers from unwanted contact with others and are, therefore, another barrier to gathering information.

A fourth factor that impacts information gathering today is related to increasing globalization. Businesses no longer operate within the confines of their own national borders but, because of the Internet or other reasons, have international customers. B2B firms must survey international as well as domestic customers but different cultures and languages make communication and information gathering more difficult. See Chapter 12 for a more detailed discussion of the challenges of international business marketing.

All-in-all, new methods of data acquisition have increased the quantity and quality of available information. Business marketing managers must understand the impact that new data collection methods have on information gathering, the research process, and statistical relationships and assumptions as well as the difficulties associated with them. Specifically, the marketing manager needs to know and understand the following:[5]

# WHAT WOULD YOU DO?

## IS IT PATENTED IF IT CAN'T BE ENFORCED?

Mike Racklin, newly hired director of engineering, was touring one of the plants under his responsibility with Lynn Mello, director of marketing. Lynn was explaining that the automated equipment Mike was looking at was the most productive in the world. Taking a mentor tone, Lynn said, "Mike, we researched the best equipment in the world for this process, but you know what happens if you buy the best equipment in the world?" Mike figured that he did, but let her go on. Lynn continued, "Then we are only as good as all the other companies that also purchase that equipment. The only way to develop a sustainable differential advantage is to surpass the best available equipment. That's what we are looking for from you, Mike. Make equipment do things far beyond what anyone was thinking when it was designed. This equipment, for example, runs faster, and with little waste, and provides us the lowest cost in the industry."

Mike nodded and said, "That's true, we do need to push the edge of what can possibly be done, and be better at it and more creative than our competitors." Lynn smiled. Then Mike continued, "But what I see you have done here is copy a patented process developed by my last employer, who is our competitor. It must be expensive to pay the royalties, but I can't imagine them licensing you to use this. Besides, this wouldn't produce the lowest cost in the industry—it would only match the lowest cost in the industry." Lynn frowned and brushed off Mike's comment, saying, "There are no patent police and no royalties on internal processes. Besides, if they thought the process was important, they never would have patented it and made it public."

Mike went back to his office wondering what kind of a company he had gone to work for and what kind of a stormy relationship he could expect with marketing. He asked his assistant to bring in all the engineering development files on the process he had just seen. As he looked through the material, he saw even more than he was expecting; there were copies of research information that marketing apparently had gathered. As he went through the file, he found copies of the competitor's patent showing the materials and process steps, details from the equipment manufacturer indicating the competitor's specific purchases, process rates from a competitor's bid to a customer that his company also supplied, the competitor's SEC filings, the competitor's annual report, a Freedom of Information request concerning chemicals used by the competitor in the process, and a picture from the competitor's company newspaper showing an employee being given an award. In the background the process equipment could be seen in a blowup, as magnified prints had been made.

Mike was disgusted. Although he understood Lynn saw nothing wrong in what had been done, Mike knew many professionals would not agree. Some of the research methods represented in the file were unethical, but, at least from his point of view, the main problem was that the whole file reflected a misuse of the research process. Ethical professionals do not start out with the objective to do whatever it takes to uncover and copy a competitor's patented proprietary process. To Mike, a more honorable action would have been to challenge the engineering department to come up with a whole new approach. Instead, he felt that the company was sending out a message that it is OK to act unethically. There was no telling where that kind of a company culture would lead. The word had gone out to everyone, from the office staff to the machine operators, not to talk to anyone outside the company about the process. Despite that directive, he knew that people would talk, and the process would become common knowledge anyway.

Mike wondered what he should do about it. On the one hand, he liked his new job as director of all technical departments, and his family liked their big new house. That argued pretty persuasively just to let it go. On the other hand, there are few secrets in this industry (people move from job to job, salespeople brag about a new process to a customer and it gets back to the competitor, etc.). Mike thought, "The company could be sued, and they might sue me, too. They are going to think that I did this, since I used to work for the competitor and know the process." Mike considered the following options: Option 1—Bring it up to the division general manager, but obviously he already knows about it and approved it. (Lynn, as marketing director, has a lot of influence with him.) Mike also knew that the new process had increased sales significantly and that the general manager's bonus was tied directly to sales. Option 2—Go over the general manager's head and bring the issue to corporate headquarters. That didn't sound like a very wise option, but maybe he could simply ask for some confidential advice from the corporate vice president of engineering. He would know what to do.

### Assignment

Define the ethical issues for those involved, and decide what Mike should do. Does he have other options?

- Technologies currently available
- The interface of technology and data acquisition
- How new technologies change or eliminate gaps that existed with previous marketing research methods, and
- Limitations associated with new technologies

In our get-it-done-yesterday world of business, virtually every company's survival depends on its ability to quickly locate critical information about customers, competitors, suppliers, and internal operations—no matter where those data can be found. Most business firms have always seen information technology as a way to work faster, better, and cheaper. Clearly, automating tasks has made companies more efficient. But in the hypercompetitive global economy, operational efficiency is no longer just a way to boost the bottom line. For many firms, it is central to their ability to compete.

Technology allows marketing researchers to do a better job, faster. The challenge is in understanding how new technologies can be applied to capture and collect data that are more accurate and more representative—not necessarily more abundant. As a case in point, Terry Hinge and Hardware Company, a 125-person furniture hardware manufacturer, uses new software (Market's Marketplace) to gather data; if done manually, the task would require a marketing department of dozens. "Smaller companies have one or two people to do all their marketing. If we want research, we have to get it all ourselves," says marketing manager Dena Zeller, Terry Hinge's one-person marketing department.[6]

## Summary

- A number of major differences exist between consumer research and business research. Business marketers are closer to their markets than are consumer marketers, and they can ascertain buyer preferences more easily. Business marketing research focuses on buying decisions and the buying center, whereas consumer research emphasizes product attributes and buyer motivation.

- Marketing research is undertaken to gather reliable marketing information to facilitate planning and control. Marketing research should be viewed as a process of steps including: define the research problem, develop research objectives and questions, formulate a research plan, execute research design, prepare and analyze data, and prepare and communicate results. It is not unusual for companies to contract outside firms to do either some or all of their marketing research. The decision to use either inside or outside marketing specialists is somewhat similar to the business make-or-buy decision.

- Information sources available to the business researcher are of two types: secondary or primary data. Secondary data sources include both internal and external data. Internal secondary data include marketing plans, company reports, and marketing information system (MIS) reports. External secondary data involve government documents, commercial sources, professional publications, and secondary data on the Web. There are a number of disadvantages and drawbacks to secondary data that the business researcher must consider. Primary data sources include personal interviews, telephone surveys, and mail surveys. The business researcher must be aware of the disadvantages of using primary data, as well.

- Whereas marketing research is problem oriented or project oriented, a marketing information system combines procedures, hardware, and software and then accumulates, interprets, and disseminates marketing information as effectively as possible.

- The extent to which business firms use marketing research studies is wide and varied. The major areas in which marketing research is conducted usually fall within one or more of the following: market potential, market-share analysis, market characteristics, sales analysis, forecasting, and CRM and database development.

- Information technology has changed the way marketers collect and use research data in decision making. New methods of data acquisition have increased the quantity and quality of data available, allowing business marketing researchers to do a better job, faster.

## Key Terms

active data

analytical marketing
  system

customer relationship
  management (CRM)

data mining

data warehouses

database

dependent variable

directed data

e-commerce

experimental research

exploratory research

gatekeeper technologies

hypothesis

independent variable

internal reports system

Internet

marketing information
  system (MIS)

marketing intelligence

marketing research

marketing research process

marketing research system

market-share analysis

microsales analysis

North American Industrial
  Classification System
  (NAICS)

observational studies

passive data

primary data

secondary data

survey research

uniform resource locator
  (URL)

## Review Questions

1. Define marketing research. Point out the major differences between business and consumer marketing research.

2. Explain and elaborate on the primary phases of a research project.

3. Distinguish between primary and secondary data, and between internal and external secondary data. Identify the primary types of external secondary data. How can technology assist the researcher in locating relevant external secondary data?

4. Distinguish between personal interviews, telephone surveys, and mail surveys as methods of collecting primary data. Discuss some of the major disadvantages of both primary and secondary data sources.

5. Distinguish between marketing research and a marketing information system. What are the basic components of a marketing information system, and how is a marketing information system used?

6. Identify and elaborate on the seven major tasks of business marketing research.

7. Explain the importance of information technology and marketing research. What does the marketing manager need to know and understand about the relationship between information technology and marketing research?

## Case 5-1

# T-Chem Corporation

Perry McClain, chairman of the board of T-Chem Corporation, formerly the Tuttle Corporation, was reminiscing about how far the company had come in ten years. Back in the mid-nineties the company was a manufacturer of industrial detergents and waxes with about $225 million in annual sales. Now T-Chem was a rapidly growing global producer of cleaning systems, chemicals, equipment, and franchised services with annual sales of $3.2 billion per year and growing. Perry attributed much of the growth to dynamic marketing strategy. Such a strategy can only be based on good information.

Perry recalled, "T-Chem's marketing information systems have come a long way. In the mid-nineties, many strategy reports would come in monthly or even quarterly. Everyone knew that such delayed information wasn't very useful for tactical operating and marketing decisions, but it was a different world back then. The technology that we could afford didn't allow more frequent reporting, and most domestic markets in narrow lines were not that competitive. At the time, good field sales impacted the sales of industrial detergents much more than did marketing information systems. Nowadays, we still have field sales, but we sell ten times more with a smaller sales force. Most of our customers purchase through automated 'computer-to-computer' systems, and many others purchase from our Internet website. Back then we had functional areas such as detergent sales, detergent manufacturing, detergent distribution, and detergent R & D, but today everyone is an information manager, no matter what area in the firm he or she may be assigned to. All the information that used to come in via weekly, monthly, or even quarterly reports now is available in real time (continuously updated). Lots of additional information also is just a mouse click away. Today we can routinely process hundreds of times the information available to us ten years ago."

Perry thought back to the piles and piles of hard copy reports (accordion-folded, light-green computer printouts), many copies of which went to people who didn't use them. Today little actually gets printed out. Analysis, sorting, modeling, simulations, and testing of alternatives all are constantly in process from just about every functional area.

All this reminiscing gave Perry an idea. He pulled out an old marketing information system report schedule for Tuttle Corporation as it was in the early nineties. He read it and thought, "You know, our current information systems are bench-marked against the global best—regardless of industry. I probably know more about marketing information systems at Coca-Cola and Intel than I do about the industry in this geographical area. I wonder how much other industries have advanced their marketing systems."

Of course, a chairman of the board doesn't have to wonder about things for long. That afternoon he had a team of assistant product managers (entry-level new hires) in his office. He handed each a copy of the old MIS report. Perry knew that every one of these young people thought that he was about 100 years old (even though he was actually only 50), but that was OK. Technology was changing so fast that people who didn't keep up might as well be over 100 years old. That's why this was an assignment for new hires with the latest technology skills.

Perry began, "I've asked your supervisors to send me their best and brightest for a short research project. And here you are. I've always believed that two things will determine the future of our company: (1) our ability to attract and motivate the next generation of managers, and (2) our ability to maintain a differential advantage in strategy based on better access to information. This project combines those two things. I know that you can appreciate our information system, and I know you understand our striving to match the systems at the world's most advanced companies, against which we benchmark ourselves. What I would like you to do is to personally survey other industrial companies in this geographical area and find out how their marketing systems compare to where we were ten years ago and where we are now. For instance, you see on the report I handed you that ten years ago we were getting sales figures on a monthly basis and new customer reports quarterly. Interview marketing people at local companies and find out for all those reports on the list (e.g., delinquent accounts) how frequently they are getting that information today. My 'a priori' hypothesis is that you are going to uncover many companies still back where we were ten years ago. That result would have certain implications for our acquisition plans. If you find that most all companies are about where we are now, then that has strategic implications too."

Stacy Martin raised her hand to ask a question. Perry knew that Stacy had not won any awards for high grades in college, but she was a natural leader who had worked her way through school. If she had a question it was probably a good one. "Mr. McClain," Stacy began, 'why would these companies be willing to give us any information at all?" "Well, Stacy," McClain replied, 'that is an excellent question. You probably know that most business marketers would not cooperate with strangers asking for company information. But I think you have two important things on your side. First, you have your sales training from college. In this case, the objective of your sales call is to gather information, and you will need to use your interpersonal skills just like any other salesperson or marketer. Second, you will not really be a stranger. T-Chem is well known in this area, we are clearly not competitors to any local firms, and many of these companies also use us as a source of information. Probably you will find that their executives know our executives through professional meetings, civic organizations, and as neighbors. It won't be easy, but it is doable. Of course, if it were easy, I would assign some administrative assistants and clerical staff to complete the project. This requires your communications training and your knowledge of marketing information systems. Give it your best shot, but you have only four weeks to complete the assignment."

## Assignment

You are on the project team. Contact local companies and gather the information that Perry requested. While you are not actually from T-Chem, you are from your local college or university. Using your college ID and a short note from the professor (on college letterhead), most companies will be comfortable that you are not competitors and will not publish the information with their company identified. As a last resort, you may need to have a local company representative complete an anonymous survey and return it by mail. Do that only after you have met with the representative personally, however. One of the objectives of this project is for you to practice your interpersonal skills through face-to-face interactions with real-world marketing professionals. Present the results to Mr. McClain (the class). In addition, prepare a written report of your findings. At the end of the report, identify the name, title, company, address, and phone number of each professional marketer or buyer with whom you met personally for this project.

Exhibit 5-8 shows a copy of the old MIS report schedule at the Tuttle Corporation, which Perry handed out to the research project team:

**EXHIBIT 5-8**
**1. Internal Records Components**

| Subject | Frequency of Report | Type of Data and Their Breakdown |
|---|---|---|
| Dollar sales | Monthly | (a) Current; (b) Cumulative for year; (c) As percentage of forecasted figure for (a) and (b) by:<br>• product<br>• customer<br>• type of customer<br>• geographical territory<br>• branch office making the sale<br>• salesperson |
| Gross margin on sales | Monthly | Same types and breakdowns as for dollar sales |
| Sales rep's expenses | Every two months if more than 2½% off projected | (a) Dollar amount; and (b) As percentage of sales by:<br>• salesperson<br>• geographical area |
| New customers | Quarterly | Forecasts of new customers' demand by:<br>• customer<br>• product<br>• salesperson |
| Delinquent accounts | Monthly | (Dollar amount;<br>Length of delinquency by:<br>• customer<br>• salesperson |

*(continued)*

**EXHIBIT 5-8–***cont.*
**2. Marketing
Intelligence
Component**

| Subject | Frequency of Report | Type of Data and Their Breakdown |
|---|---|---|
| Inventory of finished goods | Fifteenth and last of the month | Physical units by:<br>• product<br>• location<br>• product and location |
| Complaints from dealers, business users, and ultimate consumers | Quarterly | Twenty percent random sample of complaints by complainant |
| Monitoring of Tuttle sales force of competitors' displays, apparent personal selling tactics, prices, etc. | Quarterly | |
| Monitoring of competitors' introduction of new or redesigned products | Immediately | |
| Buying and monitoring of competitor's national and regional advertising from marketing research agencies | Monthly | |
| Monitoring of changes in policies and practices of pertinent government agencies | Quarterly; if warranted, immediately | |
| Buying research reports on consumption, brand preference, and stock levels from marketing research agencies that operate national panels of users | Quarterly or every two months | |
| Buying a forecast of the U.S. economy from a consulting business economist | Every six months | |

**3. Marketing
Research Component**

Gathering, evaluating, interpreting, and reporting information on the basis of specific research projects having to do with (a) solving particular problems; (b) general planning; (c) determining strategy; and (d) determining tactics. A detailed report is submitted to the vice president at the end each project.

**Example 1.** The current test market for Experimental Product 2.31 in Syracuse, N.Y.; Akron, Ohio; Sacramento, Calif.; and Charlotte, N.C.

**Example 2.** Study on perceived price-quality relationships of cleaning products.

**Example 3.** Image study of Tuttle Corporation's lavender-scented air freshener

## Case 5-2

# Superior Software Systems (A)

This case was written by Dr. Roger Gomes and Dr. Patricia Knowles, Clemson University, © 1999

Ron Mullins was watching his computer screen scroll by with what seemed like hundreds and hundreds of customer company names. Somehow Ron was going to have to collect competitive intelligence on all of these customers. The information on the customers would help marketing with their strategic marketing program choices. Ron thought, "Wow, this is the kind of assignment that has a lot of visibility. It's going to be obvious if I try to take any shortcuts." Ron considered listing each company's financial information, a 10K review, a section on customers served, a section on the top managers and their backgrounds, new products, number of plants and employees, the corporate structure, competitors, and, of course, products. Ron figured that he would add some additional topics that would be useful to marketing as he discovered them in his search.

## Background

Superior Software was a rapidly growing ($550 million in annual sales) Silicon Valley firm that had been started by Karen Rice and Jason Jackson, both of whom were in their late twenties. After graduation from college, Karen and Jason had joined a leading software applications group and had worked in field sales for five years before approaching venture capital firms with their proposal to start a new firm. Karen and Jason decided to start their own software company to fill a market niche the larger companies had not, and, for technical reasons, would not be addressing.

Karen and Jason succeeded with Superior because they were driven to exceed customer expectations, and they demanded excellence from their staff. Although the company was now quite large, it had a flat management structure that represented individuals on the company's organizational chart as overlapping circles, rather than the traditional hierarchical pyramid of boxes and connecting lines.

## Ron's Research Project

Ron was excited about using his marketing research skills to help the company. Ron knew that people with his skills were in short supply, and his salary reflected the company's high regard for these skills. Ron knew that the company's future was also his future. Superior invested in its employees' professional development, and in Ron's case that had included full-time advanced marketing research training at Virginia Tech. There, he had learned the latest Internet methods of researching information on companies.

As a first step in the project, Ron went to several Internet search sites, starting with (www.search.com), or the mirror site (www.search.cnet.com), and worked through searching on a few companies with (www.lycos.com) and (www.altavista.com) to see what kind of information would be uncovered. Getting more focused, Ron also gathered sample information from valuable links at the (www.corporateinformation.com) site (to search on the company name, go to the bottom of the page, choose "all," and enter the name). Ron knew that public companies were required to keep investors apprised of strategic developments, so he particularly wanted to access each company's 10K filing. From his training he also knew enough to go to the competitive intelligence site (www.fuld.com), from their home page click on "strategies and tools," and then click on "Internet index"; that should bring you to (www.fuld.com/i3/index.html). From there, Ron often went to (www.hoovers.com) and (www.freeedgar.com). One of Ron's favorite research sites included text on research theory, (www.babson.edu/library/index. html)—under "reference" click in "companies," and you should arrive at a screen titled "Researching a Company."*

Ron then turned to each company's home page and copied useful information (and cut and pasted it into Microsoft Word). He also decided to use WebWhacker or First Mate software (www.ffg.com) (www.documagix) to automatically monitor the subject's home site and notify him by e-mail about changes and additions. Ron tried to think what else would be helpful, and went back to the company's management personnel list from the company's SEC filing. He wondered where he could get a biography of each individual. As he did whenever he needed assistance, Ron called the reference librarian at the local university,

*The research process is adapted from: D.S. Janal, *Online Marketing Handbook*. (New York: John Wiley & Sons, 1998).

and he was told where to look. He was also sent a list of new databases and research sites that might prove useful.

## Assignment

Your assignment is to help Ron. While it is nice to read about marketing research (and a necessary first step), at some point in your development as a marketer you will need to start actually doing marketing research. In this case you will: (1) search through actual company websites for useful information and (2) utilize Internet sites that are set up to help you uncover company information. As a marketer, you should find it almost second nature to zip over to a site such as "free edgar" and pull up 10K information. You will find many such sites that can be used to collect marketing information.

Be proactive when you find companies that are difficult to research or that have changed their URL site address. Research is dynamic, and the professionals who do it for a living tend to feel challenged by difficult problems that require their creativity to solve. Research can also be repetitive, but the information will be valuable to the marketers faced with making strategic decisions. Be sure that your report is complete and professional. You will present it to the management group (class), including Karen and Jason, upon completion.

## Ron's List of Customer Company Names to Research

1. Automatic Switch Co (www.ascovalve.com)
2. Conbraco Industries, Inc. (www.conbraco.com)
3. Motion Industries, Inc. (www.motionindustries.com)
4. Daniel Woodhead Co. (www.danielwoodhead.com)
5. Kaeser Compressors Inc. (www.kaeser.com)
6. Woodex Bearing Co., Inc. (www.woodex-meco.com)
7. Dresser Instrument (www. dresser. com/instruments)
8. Eagle Technology, Inc. (www.eaglecmms.com)
9. Olympus America, IPG (www olympus.com)
10. A.W. Chesterton Co. (www.chesterton.com)
11. eRegs (www.eregs.com)
12. Waukesha Cherry-Burrell (www.waukesha-cb.com)
13. Federal Hose Manufacturing, Inc. (www.federalhose.com)
14. Polycoat Systems, Inc. (www.polycoat.com)
15. General Magnaplate Corp. (www.magnaplate.com)
16. Innovative Fluid Handling Systems (www.ifh-group.com)
17. Kaman Industrial Technologies (www. kaman-ind-tech.com)
18. Loctite Corp. (www.loctite.com)
19. Ludeca, Inc. (www.ludeca.com)
20. Moyno Industrial Products (www.moyno.com)
21. NewAge Industries (www.newageind.com)
22. Ogontz (www.ogontz.com)
23. Edlon-PSI (www.edlon-psi.com)
24. Penherthy (www.pcc-penberthy.com)
25. PSDI (www.maximo.com)
26. Ounce of Prevention Software (www.oops-web.com)
27. Datastrearn Systems, Inc. (www.dstm.com)

28. Trico Mfg. Corp. (www.trico.com)
29. Magnatex Pumps, Inc. (www.rnagnatexpumps.com)
30. U. S. Electrical Motors (www.usmotors.com)
31. Victaulic Co. of America (www.victaulic.com)
32. Warman International, Inc. (www.warman.com)
33. NTN Bearing Corp. of America (www.ntnamerica.com)
34. Filtomat, Inc. (www.filtomat.com)
35. Albany International (www.albint.com)
36. The Foxboro Co. (www.foxboro.com)
37. Spectronics Corp. (www.spectroline.com)
38. Magnaplan Corp. (www.visualplanning.com)
39. Hertz Equipment Rental Corp. (www.hertzequip.com)
40. Baldor (www.baldor.com)
41. EXTECH, Inc. (www.extech.com)
42. Yale's Material Handling Care (www.yale.com)
43. BEKO Systems (www.bekousa.com)
44. Cybermetrics (www.foresightweb.com)
45. U.S. Tsubaki (www.ustsubaki.com)
46. Entek IRD (ww.entek.com)
47. Rytec (www.rytecdoors.com)
48. Philips Lighting Co. (www.philipslighting.com)
49. Marcam Solutions, Inc. (www.marcam.com)

## References

1. Results taken from data reported by 798 companies to the American Marketing Association, 1999.
2. Kenneth C. Schneider and James C. Johnson, "Stimulating Response to Market Surveys of Business Professionals," *Industrial Marketing Management* 24 (August 1995): 265–276.
3. "Marketers Value Honesty in Marketing Researchers," *Marketing News* 29 (5 June 1995): H-27.
4. Ashby Jones, "What a mess! For corporations, e-mail and other electronic documents have become the modern equivalent of a toxic waste site—trouble just waiting to happen," *American Lawyer,* 24 (December 2002): S30–34.
5. Thomas C. Boyd, Timothy C. Krehbiel, and James M. Sterns, "The Impact of Technology on Marketing Research," *Journal of Marketing Management* (Summer/Spring 1998): 24–33.
6. Jeff Sweat, "Closeness Counts," *Information Week,* (March 1, 1999): 65–69.

## CHAPTER SIX

# Market Segmentation, Positioning, and Demand Projection

## Learning Objectives

After reading this chapter, you should be able to:

- Appreciate the difficulty involved in successfully segmenting business markets.
- Know the similarities and differences between business and consumer marketing segmentation.
- Distinguish among undifferentiated marketing, differentiated marketing, and concentrated marketing.
- Differentiate between the micro/macro and nested approaches to business market segmentation.
- Understand how to evaluate potential market segments.
- Discuss six approaches by which a firm can position its products.
- Recall the purpose, problems, and general methods of sales forecasting.

## Chapter Outline

General Market Segmentation Strategy

Business Marketing Segmentation Versus Consumer Marketing Segmentation

Market Strategies for Business Segmentation

Approaches to Market Segmentation

Segmenting Business Markets

Evaluating Potential Market Segments

Product Positioning Strategy

Business Demand Projection

Selecting Forecasting Methods

**EXHIBIT 6-1**
**Elements in a Typical Strategic Planning Process**

I. Situation analysis
   a. Mission and objectives
   b. Market orientation analysis
   c. Demand analysis
   d. **Market segmentation**
   e. Buyer behavior by segment
   f. Customer decision process by segment
   g. Value proposition and differential advantage by segment
   h. Marketing mix analysis
   i. **Product positioning analysis**
   j. Financial analysis
   k. Environmental analysis
   l. Competitive analysis
   m. SWOT (Strengths, Weaknesses, Opportunities, Threats) analysis
II. Best alternatives 4P marketing mix strategies
III. Evaluation of alternative strategies (including use of **demand projection**)
IV. Decision and Implementation Plan

In chapters 3 and 4, you learned how the B2B sales process is related to the purchasing process of business buyers for the mutual benefit of both organizations. Given this, you can appreciate how completely the future of a B2B firm depends on continuously uncovering customer needs, creating product offerings with distinctive value propositions, and successfully forecasting demand. This chapter covers three important tools that strategic marketers use in their analysis of markets and evaluation of alternative strategies, namely, market segmentation, product positioning, and demand projection.

**Market segmentation** is the development and pursuit of marketing programs directed at specific groups within the population that the organization could potentially serve. The segments may be different from each other in terms of demographics, buyer behavior, and/or purchase decision processes among other attributes. Following segmentation, the firm chooses one or more target segments on which to focus. Prior to developing one or more marketing mixes for the chosen target segments, the firm decides on a **product positioning** strategy for each segment. Product positioning involves emphasizing one or more attributes important to selected target segments. The position chosen is highlighted when developing one or more marketing mixes for the selected target segments. Finally, **demand projection** involves analyzing past sales in light of the customer needs that were present, the marketing mix elements used, the economic conditions and competitive reactions that were present, and then projecting that understanding forward to predict future sales by target segments under potential future conditions. To better visualize these tools and their importance, Exhibit 6-1 shows where these tools fit into the overall strategic planning process. The overall strategic planning process leads to product, price, promotion, and distribution strategies that customers value.

## General Market Segmentation Strategy

Market segmentation plays a key role in the strategic planning process because there are potentially many alternative ways to group customers and some will provide more competitive advantage than others.[1] Companies with similar capabilities often segment their markets according to different attributes and end up with different target markets and different marketing mixes. A classic mistake is to segment only around a firm's current customers. However, any customer group left out at this stage will not be a potential target segment for the company. If all potential customers of a firm's products are not included in

**EXHIBIT 6-2**
**Proposed Segmentation for Small Precision Servomotors**

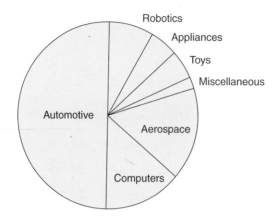

the initial segmentation analysis, the company risks missing out on potentially lucrative marketing relationships.

Exhibit 6-2 shows potential target markets for a producer of small precision servomotors. Seven potential segments exist in the exhibit—based on industry type. Following analysis of the firm's mission, resources, and capabilities, one or more of these segments may be selected as the firm's target segments. Although the company may be tempted to simply select high-volume users (e.g., the automotive industry in the exhibit), lower volume users (e.g., toys) may be more appropriate for the firm instead, based on its mission, resources, and capabilities. Further, the firm may decide to combine two or more segments if they are found (via research) to respond similarly to a particular marketing mix. The critical question is, "Which segments will perceive the most differential value in our marketing mix offering that is custom-created for that segment?" It may very well be that one competitor's approach to segmentation does not recognize another firm's most attractive segments. Effective segmentation skill, like any other art, takes serious study and considerable practice. It is a fundamental tool of marketing management that deserves detailed consideration.

Basically, to be useful to the marketing strategist, market segments must meet a number of criteria. First, the various segments that are identified through research must be *measurable;* they must be able to be identified and their needs/wants measured as they relate to one or more attributes. Second, useful target segments should be *differentiable*—homogeneous within segments and heterogeneous between segments. That is, members of one segment should respond similarly to one particular marketing mix and members of different segments should respond differently to different marketing mixes. Third, target segments should be *substantial;* they should be large enough to warrant special treatment by the firm. Fourth, target segments should be *actionable;* they should be responsive to development of unique marketing mixes. Finally, useful target segments should be *accessible;* a firm must be able to reach them via marketing communications and be able to serve their needs and wants.

Precision segmentation may be an excellent strategy, but creating customer-tailored bundles of customer benefits can be expensive. Decisions on the selection of one or more target segments must be based on the projected revenue to be gained from them. In fact, the demand-analysis planning step, which occurs prior to segmentation, should always fully explore which sales to which customers are providing the greatest rate of return. Then the option of segmenting on the basis of economic value can be considered.[2] In the case of very large groups of potential customers "data mining" software may be used to identify customer clusters based on characteristics including profit margin.[3]

# Business Marketing Segmentation Versus Consumer Marketing Segmentation

Few business marketers or academicians have written extensively on business segmentation strategy. Thus, some concepts from psychology and sociology, which consumer marketers have found useful in their segmentation strategies, have received only limited application in business segmentation strategy. In fact, business market segmentation as part of the strategic planning process can assist firms in several areas:

- *Market analysis*—developing a better understanding of the total marketplace, including how and why customers buy
- *Market selection*—making a rational choice of market segments that best fit the company's capabilities
- *Marketing management*—developing strategies, policies, and programs to meet the needs of different market segments profitably and to give the company a distinct competitive advantage

Business-to-business firms vary in needs and wants, size, economic activities, procurement structure, and location. Each year, more and more industrial firms are finding that the strategy of carefully planned market segmentation, is an efficient and productive strategy for building positions in new markets and holding positions in old markets. Exhibit 6-3 shows how the process of segmenting a market and selecting specific segments as targets is the link between identifying various organizational buyers' needs and taking strategic marketing mix actions. In practice, identifying, analyzing, and pursuing target segments is not a straightforward task. In planning, it would be common to need to try a number of segmentation and other strategic combinations before settling on the best approach to serve customer needs and meet your own company objectives. The resulting strategy implementation will often cost millions or even tens of millions of dollars and its success determines the company's (and the marketer's) future.

It is important to remember that the segmentation process is not only required for the strategic marketing of business products, but also for most consumer products. Producers of products such as snow boards, hiking boots, soft drinks, cell phones and clothing tend to use "pull" marketing (they advertise and use sales promotions) aimed at final consumers. But first, they must sell their products directly to distributors or retail chains usually through personal selling and sales promotions (push marketing). For these consumer product producers, then, the strategic planning process needs to be done twice in that they need to segment final consumers as well as business customers. The resultant business market segmentation and marketing mix will likely be quite different than the consumer market segmentation and

**EXHIBIT 6-3   Marketing Segmentation Links Market Needs to an Organization's Marketing Actions**

mix. For producers of both business and consumer products this is a time of intense pressure to improve the efficiency and cost effectiveness of serving customer needs.[4]

## Market Strategies for Business Segmentation

Early in the planning process, business marketing managers must consider alternative overall approaches to meeting customer needs (i.e., how much to segment or whether to segment at all, to target one or many segments). Three alternative market-selection strategies are an undifferentiated strategy, a differentiated strategy, and a concentrated strategy.

### Undifferentiated Marketing Strategy

An **undifferentiated marketing strategy** uses the concept of "market aggregation," wherein the total market is treated as if it were one homogeneous market segment. Marketing management creates a single marketing mix to serve potential customers within this market. This approach focuses on common needs among buyers, rather than on how buyers' needs differ. Consider, for example, the marketing mix adopted by a business cleaning or business waste removal firm. The price per hour or per pickup would be the same for all potential users of the service, and the same promotional package would be aimed at buyers in several different industries. Undifferentiated marketing is appropriate due to cost economies, with the narrow product line keeping down production, inventory, and transportation costs. This particular strategy also lowers the cost of marketing research and product management. An undifferentiated marketing strategy might be employed by firms offering a homogeneous, staple product, such as gasoline or industrial lubricants, for which product usage varies little by customer type.

### Differentiated Marketing Strategy

A **differentiated marketing strategy** attempts to distinguish a product from competitive products offered to the same aggregate market. An example of a firm using a differentiated marketing strategy is IBM, which offers many hardware and software variations to different segments in the computer market. By differentiating its product or product line, the firm identifies several potential target markets. Each of these target markets may be attractive in demand but may differ from one another substantially in other important aspects (such as size, product application, and technical expertise). With this strategy, the firm hopes to engage in nonprice competition and thus avoid, or at least minimize, the threat of severe price competition. Differentiated marketing strategy is justified when each segment is distinct, when there is very little cross-elasticity of demand (the effect that demand for one product has on the demand for another product), and when the potential size of each segment is large enough to provide a satisfactory return.

Although usually it can be shown that total sales may be increased with the marketing of a more diversified product line, such activity does increase the cost of doing business. The following costs are likely to be higher when a firm elects to pursue a differentiated marketing strategy:

1. *Product modification costs.* Modifying a product or product line to serve different segment requirements usually involves additional research and development, engineering, and/or special tooling costs.
2. *Production costs.* For each product, the longer the production setup time and the smaller the sales volume, the more expensive it becomes. For a product sold in large volume, however, the higher costs of setup time can be quite small per unit.
3. *Administrative costs.* The firm must develop separate marketing plans for different segments, usually necessitating additional effort in marketing research, forecasting, sales analysis, promotion planning, and channel management strategy.

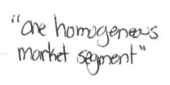

*See Pg 212 for Bus. Mktg Segmentation*

*"one homogeneous market segment"*

**EXHIBIT 6-4   Three Alternative Market Segmentation Strategies**

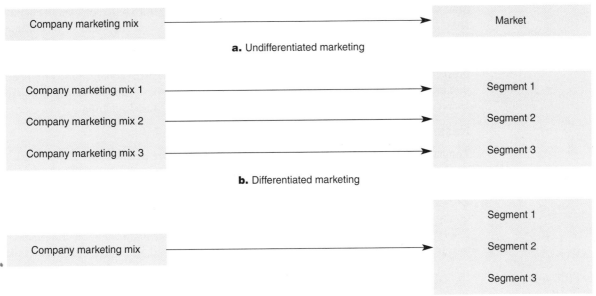

a. Undifferentiated marketing

b. Differentiated marketing

c. Concentrated marketing

*[handwritten notes in margin:]*
*Segmentation Approach*
*-differential (Different)*
*-accessible*
*-actionable*

*Not Adaptable*
*consistent*
*Consistent*

4. *Inventory costs.* Managing inventories is more costly generally than managing an inventory of only one product.

5. *Promotion costs.* In trying to reach different market segments with variations of the promotional mix, each segment may require separate creative advertising planning, sales strategy, and so forth.

## Concentrated Marketing Strategy

A firm using **concentrated marketing strategy** selects one or a relatively few segments on which to focus all its marketing effort. Through concentrated marketing, the firm achieves a strong market position in the segment because of its greater knowledge of the segment's needs. Furthermore, the firm enjoys many operating economies through specialization in its production, distribution, and promotion functions.

Concentrated marketing is, however, not without risk. A particular market segment's demand can turn downward, or a competitor may decide to enter the same segment. The defense industry offers a good example of this situation. The Electric Boat Division of General Dynamics builds submarines in Connecticut and Rhode Island for one customer, the U. S. Navy. As defense spending is being curtailed in this area, thousands of the firm's employees are feeling the effect. Also, the addition of the Newport News, Virginia, facility as a competitor has increased the competition. Risks such as these lead some business-to-business firms to operate in more than one segment.

Exhibit 6-4 summarizes the key differences between undifferentiated marketing, differentiated marketing, and concentrated marketing.

## Approaches to Market Segmentation

Fundamental means of segmenting business markets include macro/micro segmentation, the nested approach to segmentation, segmentation for maturing markets, and segmentation by purchase responsibilities of individuals within organizations. Each of these is discussed next.

## Macro/Micro Segmentation

**Macro segmentation** involves dividing the market into subgroups based on overall characteristics of the prospect organization (usage rates, NAICS category, and so on). **Micro segmentation**, on the other hand, involves dividing the market into subgroups based on specific characteristics of the decision-making process and the buying structure within the prospect organization (buying-center authority, attitudes toward vendors, and so on). In either case, the business marketer identifies subgroups that share common macro or micro characteristics and then selects target segments from among these subgroups.

## Nested Approach

Thomas Bonoma and Benson Shapiro have developed a more detailed approach to market segmentation that they refer to as a **nested approach**.[5] Their premise is that the distinction between macro segments and micro segments noted above leaves out a number of potentially valuable segmentation variables. In contrast, the nested approach stresses segmentation according to the amount of investigation required to identify and evaluate different criteria. Layers of the nest are arranged according to ease of assessment of the information, beginning with organization demographics. As diagrammed in Exhibit 6-5, then come

**EXHIBIT 6-5**
**Major Potential Bases for Segmentation (Nesting)**

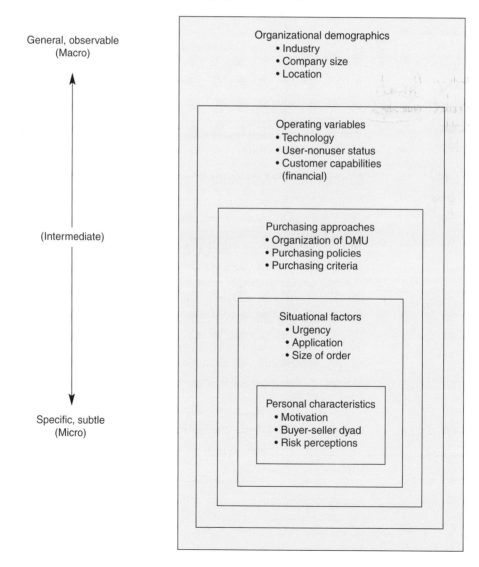

General, observable (Macro)

(Intermediate)

Specific, subtle (Micro)

Organizational demographics
- Industry
- Company size
- Location

Operating variables
- Technology
- User-nonuser status
- Customer capabilities (financial)

Purchasing approaches
- Organization of DMU
- Purchasing policies
- Purchasing criteria

Situational factors
- Urgency
- Application
- Size of order

Personal characteristics
- Motivation
- Buyer-seller dyad
- Risk perceptions

## STRATEGY AT WORK

### U.S. CAN CORPORATION TURNS TO SEGMENTED MARKETING

While others in their industry are racing toward integrated marketing campaigns, U.S. Can Corp. is confidently moving in the opposite direction. In July 1998, the company unveiled a corporate restructuring plan that focuses on the segmentation of marketing, marketing strategy, and sales. Paul Jones, the company's new chairman-CEO, stated that growing customer sophistication coupled with the ever increasing demands of the global marketplace led to the reorganization. Under the new plan, each of the company's container-producing operations—aerosol, paint, plastic, specialty, and international—will be responsible for its own marketing, sales, manufacturing, and strategy.

Under the company's previous structure, one person took charge of all sales and marketing efforts. Mr. Jones says that in today's environment an organization is better served to split the responsibility by product line and by sales versus marketing. "When you have someone over both sales and marketing, 98 percent of their time is spent on managing the sales organization. The amount of time devoted to marketing is little or none."

With much of the rest of the industry centralizing for communication, coordination, and economic benefits, U.S. Can is hoping to find significant differential advantage in a segmentation plan focused on customer needs, but with the additional benefits of a corporate marketing council and a corporate business support organization across their 35 plants. U.S. Can is a leading manufacturer of steel and plastic nonfood and nonbeverage containers in the United States and Europe. Its products house everything from paint to shaving cream to car wax. It produces nearly half of the one-gallon paint containers sold in the United States each year. In addition, it is the leading producer of aerosol cans in North America, and the number two producer in Europe. Inside- and outside-sales representatives market products to approximately 7,500 customers, including Sherwin-Williams, Gillette, and Procter & Gamble. Sales for 2001 exceeded $772 million.

### Assignment

Learn more about U.S. Can Corporation at its Web page (www.uscanco.com). From its home page, consider its mission statement and statement of guiding principles. Relate the information you discover to the decision by U.S. Can to utilize a segmented marketing strategy. Compare U.S. Can to its competitors (www.ball.com) (www.daiwa-can.co.jp/english). Present your findings to the class.

Reprinted from J. Cook, "U.S. Can Steps Back," *Business Marketing* 83 (9), pp. 1, 2. © 1998 Crain Communications, Inc.

increasingly complex criteria, including company variables (operating and purchasing), situational factors, and personal characteristics. The nested approach assumes a hierarchical structure that moves from broad, general bases for segmentation to very specific bases. As illustrated, macro layers, or characteristics, are outermost, and micro characteristics are innermost, in the exhibit. In other words, more specific customer characteristics are nested inside the broader organizational basis.

To understand this approach, assume a business-to-business firm is selling copiers and initially wishes to segment the potential market on broad organizational characteristics, such as company size, NAICS category, or general location. The firm may decide to concentrate only on companies with several hundred or more employees, on companies engaged in manufacturing, or on companies located in the northeastern United States. However, rather than stopping there and focusing on all companies that meet the desired criteria, the firm further segments the potential market on operating variables, such as whether the companies have a centralized copy center, buy or lease present equipment, or financial capability. If the firm focuses only on those prospects that have a centralized copy center, it might go one step further and target only those prospects that emphasize low price as a purchasing criterion, and so on. The marketer can move through all five phases of the nesting model if more specialization is needed, or it can stop at any point. After several attempts at working completely through the nesting process, most firms will discover which segmentation criteria are likely to yield the greatest benefits.

## Other Approaches to Market Segmentation

In mature markets, some try to segment on size, industry, or products alone. However, segmenting on these variables alone, while often done, is rarely sufficient. Customer behavior in terms of trade-offs between price and service is an important additional criterion. Often, the nested approach (and others) do not capture the underlying dynamics of a maturing market. Considerable value can often be gained by attempting to move toward buying-behavior based segmentation.

Many marketers believe that the use of purchase responsibilities among individuals within organizations as a basis for segmenting business markets is a valid approach to segmentation. Knowledge that a firm's market may be segmented by purchase responsibilities may lead to more effective deployment of marketing resources. The use of purchase responsibilities to classify organizations represents an attempt to reduce some of the complexity involved in understanding the concept of the buying center. Different kinds of organizations may give rise to different kinds of buying centers, at least insofar as purchase responsibilities within the buying center are concerned.

1. Why is it necessary to engage in business market segmentation?

2. What are the criteria for successful segments?

3. What is the fundamental difference between a macro segmentation strategy and a micro segmentation strategy?

4. What is the basic premise of the nested approach to market segmentation?

## Segmenting Business Markets

Many of the variables generally used by the marketer to segment the consumer market also can be used by the business marketer to segment the organizational market (for example, user status, degree of customer loyalty, and customer attitude toward the product). To expand upon the previous discussion of business market segmentation, some of the categories of variables for segmenting organizational markets are identified in Exhibit 6-6 and are discussed in the following sections.

### Type of Economic Activity

The North American Industrial Classification System (NAICS), discussed in Chapter 5, is a useful starting place to segment business-to-business firms according to primary economic activity. In addition to NAICS data, several other sources of secondary data, also discussed in Chapter 5, will identify prospects for the business marketer's products or services.

### Size of Organization

Segmentation on the basis of size, using variables such as volume of shipments, number of employees, market share enjoyed, and so on, may be a useful technique for business market segmentation. However, a note of caution is in order. Segmentation based on size alone is rather risky, as the prospect may or may not be a viable target. Just because an organization is large does not necessarily mean that it will be a heavy user of a product.

### Geographic Location

Segmentation on the basis of location is another criterion for segmenting organizational markets, as some industries such as textile manufacturing and furniture manufacturing are concentrated geographically.

**EXHIBIT 6-6** **Examples of Segmentation Variables for Organization Markets**

```
                                            ┌─────────────────┐
                         ┌─ Type of ────── Segmentation ── • Agriculture,
                         │   economic       variables          forestry, fisheries
                         │   activity                       • Mining
                         │                                   • Construction
                         │                                   • Manufacturing
                         │                                   • Transportation
                         │                                   • Communication
                         │                                   • Wholesale trade
                         │                                   • Retail trade

                         ├─ Size of ────── Segmentation ── • Number of
                         │   organization   variables          establishments
   Categories            │                                  • Number of employees
   of segmentation ──────┤                                  • Volume of shipments
   variable              │                                  • Annual sales volume

                         ├─ Geographic ─── Segmentation ── • Global regions
                         │   location       variables          • Nations
                         │                                   • National regions
                         │                                   • States
                         │                                   • Counties
                         │                                   • Cities
                         │                                   • Neighborhoods
                         │                                   • Climate
                         │                                   • Terrain
                         │                                   • Population density
                         │                                   • Market density

                         ├─ Product ────── Segmentation ── • How used
                         │   usage          variables          • Usage rate

                         └─ Structure of ── Segmentation ── • Centralized
                             the procurement  variables          • Decentralized
                             function                         • Buyer center
                                                              • Buyer situation
```

## Product Usage

Many products are used in a number of different ways, making it possible to segment a market on the basis of product application. For example, the manufacturer of an industrial fastener may attempt to market to industries incorporating the product into machine tools, precision instruments, office equipment, and missile systems. Additionally, segmentation is possible by product usage rate, that is, light, moderate, and heavy use.

## Structure of the Procurement Function

Market segmentation strategy can be affected by the structure of the buying organization, as well. Consider, for example, the buying behavior of the firm that centralizes the buying function. In a **centralized buying situation**, the members of the buying center will be in a stronger position to buy in larger quantities and make quicker buying decisions—and they will be attractive targets to many potential competitors. In a **decentralized buying situation**, in contrast, the potential order size will be smaller, the number of potential competitors will be limited geographically, and a final decision on the price and quality aspects of the purchase (especially in a modified-rebuy or new-task situation) may need central authorization. Also, the composition of the buying center can present considerable demographic and psychographic differences among members of the center that the business marketing manager must accommodate. Finally, buying situations (as presented in Chapter 4) will impact segmentation strategy. As noted, the effort necessary to appeal to buying center members in a new-task situation is very different from that needed to appeal to buyers in a straight-rebuy situation.

## Evaluating Potential Market Segments

Market segmentation reveals the potential market opportunity faced by firms and what would appear to be the most attractive markets the business firm can serve. Before target markets can be chosen, however, the marketing manager has to decide which segments will provide the best return, given limited resources.

By examining the relationship between business marketing strategy and financial performance in a **profitability analysis**—an analysis of the profitability of a market segment, a product line, or an individual product within a product line—the marketing manager can select those market segments that appear to be profitable and disregard those that do not appear so. Segments selected must be served at a reasonable cost to the firm, in order to provide the necessary or required return on investment. Additionally, it's important to undertake a **competitive analysis** to assess both the strengths and weaknesses of competitors within a segment and to identify other areas of opportunity. A brief examination of two useful tools in the overall evaluation of potential segments—the profitability analysis and the competitive analysis—follows.

## Market Profitability Analysis

A market segment might have desirable size and growth characteristics, yet still not be attractive from a profitability point of view. (Many marketers would cite government defense procurement as an example of this phenomenon.) Michael Porter has identified five forces that determine the intrinsic long-run attractiveness of a whole market, or any segment within it.[6] Exhibit 6-7 shows that the firm must assess the impact on long-run profitability of five groups: industry competitors, potential entrants, substitutes, buyers, and suppliers. The collective strength of these five competitive forces determines the ability of firms in an industry to earn, on average, rates of return on investment in excess of the cost of capital. The strength of these five forces varies from industry to industry and can change as an industry evolves. Further, the strength of each of the competitive forces is a function of industry structure, or the underlying economic and technical characteristics of an industry. The five-forces framework does not eliminate the need for creativity in finding new segments in which to compete within an industry. Instead, it directs managers' creative energies toward those aspects of industry structure that are most important to long-run profitability, thereby raising the odds of discovering a desirable strategic innovation and the particular segment within which to market it. Even if the segment fits the firm's objectives,

**EXHIBIT 6-7  Elements of Industry Structure**

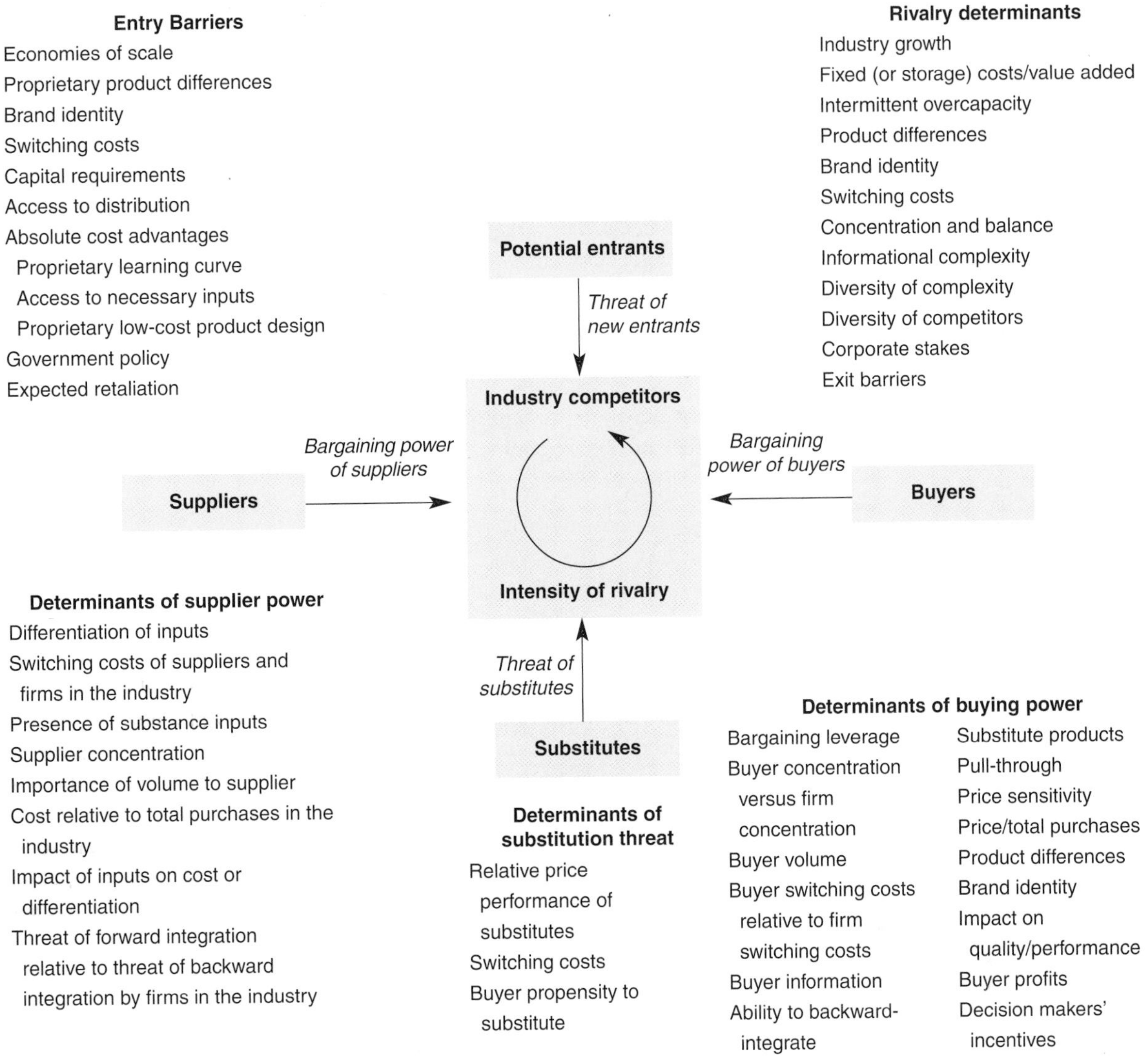

**Entry Barriers**

Economies of scale
Proprietary product differences
Brand identity
Switching costs
Capital requirements
Access to distribution
Absolute cost advantages
  Proprietary learning curve
  Access to necessary inputs
  Proprietary low-cost product design
Government policy
Expected retaliation

**Rivalry determinants**

Industry growth
Fixed (or storage) costs/value added
Intermittent overcapacity
Product differences
Brand identity
Switching costs
Concentration and balance
Informational complexity
Diversity of complexity
Diversity of competitors
Corporate stakes
Exit barriers

**Potential entrants**

*Threat of new entrants*

**Industry competitors**

*Bargaining power of suppliers*

**Suppliers**

*Bargaining power of buyers*

**Buyers**

**Intensity of rivalry**

*Threat of substitutes*

**Determinants of supplier power**

Differentiation of inputs
Switching costs of suppliers and
  firms in the industry
Presence of substance inputs
Supplier concentration
Importance of volume to supplier
Cost relative to total purchases in the
  industry
Impact of inputs on cost or
  differentiation
Threat of forward integration
  relative to threat of backward
  integration by firms in the industry

**Substitutes**

**Determinants of substitution threat**

Relative price
  performance of
  substitutes
Switching costs
Buyer propensity to
  substitute

**Determinants of buying power**

| | |
|---|---|
| Bargaining leverage | Substitute products |
| Buyer concentration versus firm concentration | Pull-through |
| | Price sensitivity |
| | Price/total purchases |
| Buyer volume | Product differences |
| Buyer switching costs relative to firm switching costs | Brand identity |
| | Impact on quality/performance |
| Buyer information | Buyer profits |
| Ability to backward-integrate | Decision makers' incentives |

however, the firm must consider whether it possesses the skills and resources to succeed in that segment. The firm should avoid market segments for which it cannot produce some form of superior value (positioning strategy), resulting in predetermined profitability objectives.

## Market Competitive Analysis

Demand and profitability are not the only key variables in a marketing plan; the number and types of competitors must also be analyzed. This is accomplished through a competitive analysis, which answers such questions as: How many competitors are there? What are their strengths and weaknesses? What is their market share?

Competition both within and between segments is stronger today than ever before, partly because of the increasing strength of both domestic and foreign markets. The strategic approach that is most likely to succeed is a comprehensive one that starts with market segment preferences, and considers competitors' capabilities and costs and the way in which competitive offerings are perceived. Foreign competitors are strong and are important factors to consider in the markets for machinery, steel, and chemicals, to name only a few. In response to market changes and unprecedented global competition, executives are revising their business and marketing strategies drastically to improve competitive advantage. Strategic actions may include downsizing, repositioning, market niching, altering the business portfolio, and forming strategic alliances. Competition cannot be avoided, and the actions of competitors cannot be controlled. Thus, profit potential depends to some degree on a careful analysis of the strengths and weaknesses of existing or potential competitors. In evaluating market segments, the marketing manager should ask: Who are the target competitors? What are the target competitors' strategic weaknesses? What are their strengths?

| | |
|---|---|
| **Concept Review** | 1. Segmentation based on size alone can be risky. Why? |
| | 2. How can the structure of the procurement function affect market segmentation strategy? |
| | 3. What is the role of a competitive analysis? |

## Product Positioning Strategy

Once potential markets have been identified, analyzed, and properly segmented (if appropriate), business marketers must carve a position or niche for their respective products in the minds of prospective customers. **Product positioning** is the way the product is defined by customers on important attributes, or the place the product occupies in customers' minds relative to competing products. Positioning is one of the central ideas of the marketing discipline.

**Product positioning** is the act of emphasizing one or more aspects of a product such that target segments have a particular perception of that product. **Product differentiation** involves meaningful differences in the product, services offered, personnel, channel, and/or image that distinguish one company's products from others. So, while differentiation is something that is done to the product and/or to the product offer, positioning is how the offer is actually perceived by potential customers. Generally speaking the product should be positioned so as to stand apart from competitive products, reflecting the firm's unique combination of marketing variables that differentiate the product from competitive offerings.

### Perceptual Mapping

A technique for examining a product's position, relative to strengths and weaknesses of the product and compared to competitors, is called **perceptual mapping**. Perceptual mapping attempts to uncover how buyers evaluate a set of competing products by identifying the relative dimensions or features of each. Perceptual mapping can be accomplished using statistical tools, with the most popular being multidimensional scaling (MDS). Business buyers rate sellers' products on specified attributes, thereby evaluating the firm's position relative to the competition.

Perceptual mapping involves a process of activities as shown in Exhibit 6-8. The process begins by investigating preferred levels of pertinent attributes of products by various potential market segments. The first step in the process is shown in part *A* of the exhibit. In the example, two attributes of copier suppliers, namely, product durability and customer service, are represented. Knowing that increased product durability and customer service are often related to increased cost and that different target segments have different requirements for durability and service, the first step is to gather data about the preferred

**EXHIBIT 6-8   Perceptual Map Process Using Two Potential Attributes of a Widget**

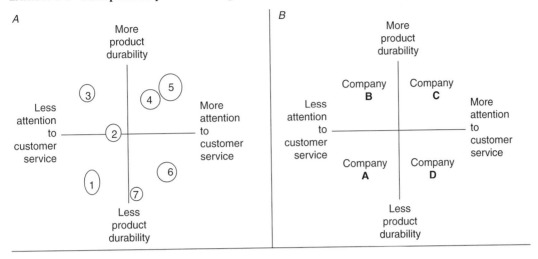

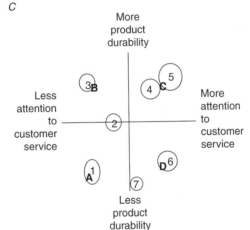

MDS= Multidimensional Scaling

levels of those two attributes by different market segments (that have been uncovered via previous research). A researcher would simply ask a sample of customers from each potential segment to rate their preference in terms of required customer service levels and then, separately, about preferred product durability levels. The resulting data would next be plotted on a two-dimensional graph. The different circle sizes indicate different sizes of the segments—thus, some segments are potentially more profitable than others. In the exhibit, Segment 1 prefers low customer service and low product durability. It may be that Segment 1 is driven by decreasing immediate costs over long-term savings. Other segments are seen to prefer higher levels of durability and customer service.

In the second part of the perceptual mapping process, those same customers would be asked to rate widgets from various companies in terms of product durability and customer service—the same attributes as in the first step. Similar to the first step, respondents would be asked to rate each product/company first on one attribute and then on the second attribute and the results would be plotted on a two-dimensional graph. This part of the process is shown in part *B* of the exhibit. To keep things simple, only four companies are shown in the graph although, in reality, all competitive widgets should be included in the research. As can be seen in the exhibit, customer perceptions of Company A's widget is that it is less durable than competitive widgets and it is accompanied by less customer service, thus, Company A is located in the lower left quadrant of the graph. Company B's widget, on the other hand, is perceived as having more durability and customer service from that company is perceived to be just slightly more attentive than Company A, thus, Company B is located in the top left quadrant.

Finally, as the last step in the mapping process parts *A* and *B* are overlapped—as seen in part *C*) of Exhibit 6-8. Doing so allows the firm to see where opportunities may lie and where repositioning may need to occur. One can see that Company A's widget is perceived by customers as meeting the needs/wants of Segment 1 while Company B's product seems to be serving Segment 3 needs/wants. Company C's product seems to be serving Segment 5's needs/wants but may be easily repositioned so that it also meets the needs of Segment 4. Finally, Company D's product seems to be meeting the needs/wants of Segment 6.

At this point, the researcher would want to analyze findings to see where opportunities may exist. For example, for purposes of discussion say that your company is Company A, your target segment in this product/market was Segment 3 and your sales were such that you believed nearly every Segment 3 customer was buying your widget. The results of this perceptual mapping exercise show you that, instead of appealing to Segment 3, you actually appeal to Segment 1. Hence, it may be that whereas you believed you were offering a moderately low level of customer service, customers actually perceive that you offer a very low level of customer service. Further, since Segment 1 is more than twice as large as Segment 3, there are actually a large number of customers in Segment 1 who are not currently buying your widget. This would be a point of opportunity for Company A—to sell to more customers who make up Segment 1. On another level, although Company A's widget is perceived by the widget-buying population as having less product durability than competitors, it may be that objective tests have shown that its product durability is very high. This points to another point of opportunity in that Company A could position itself, perhaps by emphasizing these objective tests, in marketing communications aimed at Segments 2 and 3 and significantly increase its widget sales. With such information, a seller has a chance to at least attempt to control its own destiny with regard to positioning its product favorably in relation to the competition.

Often, positioning business products is a more difficult and subtle process than positioning consumer products. While advertising is the primary tool used to position products in the consumer market, personal selling, sales promotion, advertising, and trade shows are used to position products in organizational markets. Evaluating the position of individual products or product lines relative to the competition requires not only extensive knowledge of the competitor's offerings but also access to the various members of the buying center. Few business firms recognize their product's actual position, nor do they understand how their customers perceive the position of the firm's product. A lack of support from top management combined with managerial ignorance on the concept of positioning generally are responsible for this lack of awareness. Consequently, few business organizations purposely employ positioning strategy.

## Approaches to Positioning

There are a number of positioning strategies that B2B firms may employ in differentiating its products and/or product lines from those of their competitors. As shown in Exhibit 6-9, six positioning strategies available to the marketing strategist include positioning by technology, quality, price, distribution, image, and service. An initial step in understanding the opportunity of positioning alternatives is to study some of the ways in which a product positioning strategy can be conceived and implemented. We will discuss each of these approaches in turn. Several additional positioning strategies may apply in select situations, depending upon the particular industry (or segment), the competitive structure, the marketing expertise, and so on.

**EXHIBIT 6-9**   **Approaches to Positioning Strategy**

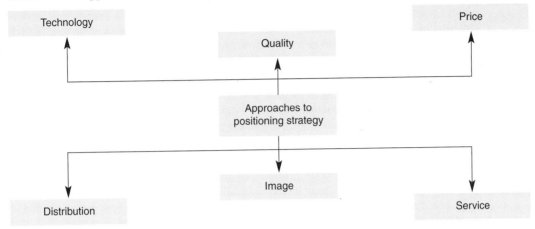

### Technology

The high-technology business marketer must target segments for the firm's products and then prioritize those segments based on sales potential; which segments would benefit most from its products or processes; and which markets, in rank order, it will choose to enter. Some target segments can be expected to value new technology more than others. Because rapid technological change is expensive, puts tremendous pressure on the marketer and is risky, a B2B firm may decide that pursuing segments that demand leading-edge technology may not be feasible.

### Quality

Although organizational buyers resist paying for unnecessary high quality, generally they will not compromise required quality for a lower price. Some B2B firms may choose to focus on a *quality position* in the target market. If at the same time they choose to also emphasize a low price they run the risk that the quality message will obscure the basic low price/value position. Quality positioning is a difficult but frequently highly lucrative positioning strategy to employ.

### Price

Astute business marketers know what their respective firms' total costs are (fixed, variable, and incremental) and will set prices accordingly. By achieving the lowest delivered-cost position relative to competition (including freight charges and installation expense), the firm can build a strong price position, in that the lowest costs generally provide the highest margins.

### Distribution

Many B2B firms think of distribution as a dilemma or, possibly, as an unpleasant problem. Too often, distribution is the neglected side of marketing. Some companies, however, have outstripped their competition using imaginative strategies for getting products to their customers. Federal Express has successfully positioned itself in the package delivery business by promising customers delivery within a specific number of hours. If it fails, the customer receives a full refund. American Hospital Supply has linked up to hospitals and clinics via a sophisticated electronic ordering system, thus gaining the edge over its competition. Clearly, business marketers can employ efficient and innovative means for *distribution positioning* and gain a competitive edge.

## Image

*Image positioning* emphasizes the importance of creating an exclusive image for a product by establishing a distinctive quality perception of the product's category that will place it in a class by itself. In some cases, however, image positioning is vulnerable to losing ground to more specific product-oriented concepts by the competition and a successful company image in one target market may be a handicap in another. For example, several years ago IBM built a blue-chip name in the world of office equipment; in the mass market, it was perceived as efficient but cold. Thus, when it launched its first mass-market product, the personal computer (PC), it had to work to humanize its image.

## Service

*Service positioning* describes an attribute provided by the business marketer to assist the ongoing activities of the business buyer. This category can include technical assistance, repair services, information, delivery, parts availability, and financing, as well as advisory services such as tax or legal counsel. In addition, it can include adding services to the current offering or providing a higher level of quality of present services overall. Again, Federal Express offers a good example of service positioning. Finding that its once unique system of overnight package delivery system had been emulated by numerous competitors, Federal Express executives redefined service as "all actions and reactions that customers perceive they have purchased." They proceeded to develop a sophisticated centralized customer service function to handle information provision, order taking, tracing, and problem solving. Federal Express executives believe they can provide a higher level of service than the competition, and they also note that it would be extremely expensive for competitors to install the equipment and systems needed to duplicate their approach. Clearly, service positioning offers the business marketer an important means of differentiation.

## Successful Positioning

When a firm establishes and maintains a distinctive place for itself and its offerings in the market, it is said to be successfully positioned. In the increasingly competitive business products sector, effective positioning is one of marketing's most critical tasks. While the concept of positioning strategy is not new, its application in the business sector has multiplied with the proliferation of products, many with similar characteristics. All this activity has given credibility to the theory of positioning. The identification of an exclusive niche in the market, or the creation of a unique perception of the product or service that satisfies an unfulfilled customer need, can serve to distinguish the product or service from competitive offerings.

How does the firm develop a positioning strategy? To help with this process, six questions (simple to ask, but difficult to answer) should be posed:

1. *What position does the firm presently own?* Determining the firm's present position in the mind of the prospect allows the marketer to tie the product service or concept to current perceptions.
2. *What position does the firm want to own?* The business marketing manager must assess the firm's best position to hold from a long-term point of view. Head-on positioning should be avoided by all but the strongest of firms.
3. *Whom must the firm outflank?* Generally, the marketing manager will attempt to avoid the competitor's strengths while exploiting its weaknesses. The marketer will try to select a position that no one else has adopted.
4. *Does the firm have enough resources?* A big obstacle to successful positioning is attempting to establish a position with only limited resources to commit to the effort. A

# BUSINESS MARKETING IN ACTION

## WEBSITES AS PART OF A PRODUCT POSITIONING STRATEGY

As in any business marketing activity requiring company money, image building and product positioning support require a discrete objective and a way of measuring accomplishment of the objective. An Internet website is an example. It is important, however, to be able to discriminate the reality of your company's Web presence from the puffery. The Internet is relatively new to many business marketers, and not all companies are investing in the type of site that enhances their image. The *Online Marketing Handbook\** offers the following as some of the reality categories of website objectives: (1) The "Hello, I'm Here Site," which includes only basic company background information, lists of products, and a feedback form; (2) The "Customer Service Substitute Site," to answer common customer questions automatically; (3) The "Computer Technowizard Site," which has wonderful computer gyrations, but none relate to relationship building or customer benefit marketing; (4) The "True Image-Enhancing Site," which supports the total marketing plan; (5) The "International Marketing Site," which truly is adapted, not just translated, for each country's business culture; and (6) "The Revenue-Producing Site," which actually processes customer orders. More sophisticated objectives usually cost more, and business marketers need to be able to evaluate their website's cost/benefit performance. (Case 6-1 at the end of this chapter includes more information on site costs and performance measures.)

### Action Assignment

Gather some local company websites, assign them to the six categories described above, and share the best examples with the class. Use overhead transparencies if your classroom does not have an Internet connection.

**STEP A.** Find complete local company names.

**Team 1.** Ask your reference librarian to point out the *Thomas Register of Manufacturers.* In the green volumes listing products produced by geographical location, look under "castings," "die castings," "machine tool manufacturers," "metal fabricators," "plating," or some similar industrial manufacturing process in your area.

**Team 2.** Ask your reference librarian to point out the *State Industrial Directory* for your state. Look up nearby geographical areas to find manufacturers similar to those listed above large enough to have websites.

**Team 3.** If you are not in a large city, consult a telephone directory for the closest large city. Look in the yellow pages' index under "Industrial," or "Manufacturing," or "Commercial" for listings similar to those cited above.

**STEP B.** Find company websites. At a basic search engine [(www.lycos.com), (www.altavista.com), (www.yahoo.com), etc.], search on company names by entering them in quotes, and look for company websites. If you uncover a subpage in the form of (www.companyname.com/something/something/), you can go to it and look for a "back to home" to click on (usually an option at the bottom of the page, or in a left sidebar list), or you can try deleting the /something/something/.

**STEP C.** Assign each of the sites you find to an *Online Marketing Handbook* category and write up your findings. Choose the best sample of each of the six categories for presentation to the class.

\*Reprinted with the permission of John Wiley & Sons from *Online Marketing Handbook* by D.S. Janal, pp. 155–156, 1998.

firm must dedicate substantial resources to establish a position and even more resources to maintain it.

5. *Can the firm stick it out?* The business marketing environment changes regularly and rapidly, so it is important for the marketer to develop a long-range point of view, determine the positioning strategy desired, and then stick to it.

6. *Does the firm match its marketing mix with its stated market position?* In determining a positioning strategy, the marketing manager must be able to match the elements of the marketing mix creatively with the stated position. Does the firm's advertising campaign, for example, match the firm's overall positioning strategy?

A business marketer must have a good understanding of the basic segments of the market that the firm's product or product line can satisfy. Some business marketing practitioners would argue that some of the positioning strategies cited above should be used but that others would serve no useful purpose. The validity of many of their arguments depends upon the firm's position within the industry. Is the firm a leader or a follower, an innovator or a laggard? Regardless of a firm's position, product positioning studies are useful for giving the marketing manager a clearer idea of customer perceptions of market offerings.

## Business Demand Projection

When business marketers have successfully carved out a position for their product lines, they are ready to begin **forecasting** potential sales volume (that is, to estimate demand) for each product or product line. Today, most large industrial companies use forecasting techniques to predict future demand for their products. The variety of forecasting methods available for this purpose has grown significantly. There are both qualitative and quantitative methods from which to choose. The nature and reliability of the data desired determine the appropriate forecasting method. Before discussing each of these methods, however, we begin by discussing the strategic importance of forecasting as well as some of the typical problems found in the forecasting function.

### Strategic Importance of Forecasting in Decision Making

With increasing complexity, competition, and change in the business environment, organizations need more reliable performance forecasts to be able to maintain a favorable marketing position. Few would deny that forecasting is one of the most important activities undertaken by the business products firm or that there are few other activities as shrouded in mystery and as misunderstood. Forecasting is used in the analysis, measurement, and improvement of current marketing strategy and in the identification and/or development of new products and new markets. Forecasting promotes and facilitates the proper functioning of the many aspects of the firm's activities (production, marketing, finance, research and development, purchasing, and so on). Accurate sales forecasting helps the marketing manager plan strategies and tactics and compile a marketing plan to achieve realistic profit targets or other objectives in the short, medium, and long run. It further assists the marketer in integrating a firm's mission, operating plans, and objectives with opportunities in existing and/or potential markets or market segments. H. O. Crafford, president of Crafford Tool and Die Corporation in Worcester, Massachusetts, insists on revising sales forecasts monthly. Crafford asks, "How can I plan, hire, train, buy materials, allocate vacation times, and/or do any number of things if I don't know what is going to happen over the next several weeks and months? Without an accurate current sales forecast, I am flying blind, and I absolutely refuse to do that."[7] In short, accurate sales forecasting is imperative in the business market sector.

### Common Forecasting Problems

Before discussing general sales forecasting techniques, we will consider some common forecasting problems encountered by business marketers.

#### *Mystique*

Many business marketers, uninitiated and untrained in forecasting techniques, are apprehensive about forecasting methods for three primary reasons: Forecasting techniques range: (1) from simple to complex, (2) from qualitative to quantitative, and (3) from traditional to very nontraditional. Keeping current with these techniques in light of daily pressures is difficult.

#### *Accuracy*

Business marketers tend to be "optimistic doers," and their forecasts often are unrealistically high and lack accuracy of detail.

### Inconsistency

The continual subjective modifications made both by forecasters and other decision makers tend to cloud forecasting data, which, in turn, impacts results. Modifications to a submitted forecast might range from adjusting or throwing out data because of unusual variations within the market or individual market segment to adjusting the forecast because of a known bias by one of the participants in the forecasting process. While these modifications usually will make the ending forecast more accurate, the motive for these changes often is difficult to understand and explain.

### Accountability

In some situations, the decision maker who develops a forecast does not have to live with a forecast decision that greatly impacts the line organization. Forecasting and the line organization become two different functions—one area being responsible for developing the forecast, the other area being responsible for achieving the forecast.

### Implementation

Forecasts are the best estimates of sales in a given period. However, the distinction between forecasts and sales quotas, targets, and goals is not always made, thereby increasing the likelihood of misunderstanding and consternation between those people responsible for making the forecast and those responsible for carrying it out.

## Selecting Forecasting Methods

Preparing a sales forecast is intrinsic to the management function. Some business marketers make forecasts on a short-term basis (from one to six months); others prepare them on an intermediate-term basis (from six months up to two years); and still others prepare them on a long-term basis (over two years) in combination with one or the other above. There is, however, a measure of commonality here: Business marketers prepare sales forecasts on a routine basis because the performance of the marketing manager is determined and measured (to a certain degree, at least) by the accuracy of the forecasts he or she makes. In this section we will review several forecasting methods, including the general top-down and bottom-up approaches. We will then examine briefly various qualitative and quantitative approaches to forecasting.

### General Approaches to Forecasting

Two very subjective, very basic categories of sales forecasting methodology based on management judgment in estimating potential are the top-down method and the bottom-up method. With the *top-down method,* management begins by developing an aggregate measure of potential. Sales potential is first estimated, sales quotas are developed, and then a sales forecast is constructed. The initial estimate includes an analysis of economic and specific industry variables that might influence the sale of the firm's products, including indicators such as GNP, capital expenditures, price indices, and others. Often, a model or mathematical equation is created to link economic and industry variables to individual company sales; it serves as a starting point in the forecasting process. An area of concern—and one that inhibits the expanded use of this general approach—is the assumed correlation of economic variables and quantity demanded, along with the assumption that this observable relationship will continue. Nonetheless, it is a macro approach, is initiated by top management decision makers, and is appropriate in many situations.

In contrast, the *bottom-up method,* also called the *build-up method* of forecasting, originates with the sales force. This process estimates the number of potential buyers by adding the individual estimates by product line, geographic area, or customer group. Potential is

## BUSINESS MARKETING IN ACTION

### FORECASTING AND DEMAND PLANNING RESPONSIBILITIES

Forecasting and demand planning skills are required across organizational areas. Although many important extensions and applications are made in accounting, distribution, and production planning, the basis for almost all forecasting rests with marketing's projections of future customer purchases. As a marketer, you will be called on to provide forecasts, and other departments will rely on your training and skill in the area (i.e., they will base their own forecasts on yours). An interesting fact concerning forecasting responsibility is that it is so central to the marketing function that it is often overlooked.

### Action Assignment

Research current professional employment ads that mention the terms "forecasting" or "demand planning." Group the jobs advertised into categories: (1) general sales and marketing, (2) distribution, logistics, and supply chain management, and (3) nonmarketing areas. Compare the ads' emphasis on forecasting and demand planning by category. Present your results to the class.

Since you will be searching for specific terms (key word search), your assignment is well suited to online databases. The webpage of your college's career (placement) center probably lists many Internet sites for searching through current employment ads, or you can launch from the "jobs" heading on most search engines and gateway pages. Often, they will direct you to some of the popular job search sites such as: (http://careers.yahoo.com/), (www.careerbuilder.com), (www.monster.com), (www.quintcareers.com), (www.jobs.com), (www.careerjournal.com), and (www.careers.org). Since this is a business marketing course, you should not include companies involved in direct retail marketing to consumers.

The sample ad below is an example of a typical 2003 ad that would be placed in the distribution, logistics, and supply chain management category—the category that includes areas many would consider part of marketing.

**Title:** Supply chain director. **Salary:** $100,000–$160,000. **Experience:** 10–15 years. **Location:** California. **Summary:** Sets the vision for and leads the supply chain process for a multisite, progressive, and globally oriented $300 million industrial products company. **Responsibilities:** Optimize supply chain effectiveness. Manage forecasting, demand planning, customer service, inventory, warehousing, transportation, purchasing, and production planning functions. Develop and implement plans to affect sourcing, production, distribution, and inventory of finished products.

---

estimated at the field level, and these estimates are then tallied to obtain total sales predicted. The logic behind this approach is that salespeople have a better feel for customer product requirements, customer inventory requirements, and conditions within specific sales districts or territories.

## Qualitative Approaches

Qualitative approaches to forecasting employ managerial judgment to determine future expectations; they often are used when data are scarce (perhaps there is no relevant history, as with a new product) or when good information is virtually nonexistent. These techniques rely primarily on qualitative or judgmental information, with the objective being to bring together in a logical, unbiased, and systematic way all information and judgments that relate to the factors being evaluated. Techniques for qualitative analyses include: (1) jury of executive opinion (sometimes called executive panels), (2) sales force composite (sometimes called sales force estimates), (3) survey of buyer intentions (sometimes called market survey of user expectations), and (4) the Delphi method. Exhibit 6-10 summarizes the qualitative forecasting techniques considered in this chapter.

### Jury of Executive Opinion

The jury of executive opinion combines and averages the opinions of top executives from internal disciplines such as finance, production, marketing, and purchasing. It can be an effective forecasting method, especially when the top executive personnel are knowledgeable about situations that might influence sales and are open-minded and realistic concerning

**EXHIBIT 6-10**   **Summary of Qualitative Forecasting Techniques**

| Technique | Approach | Major Advantages | Major Disadvantages | Potential Application |
|---|---|---|---|---|
| Jury of executive opinion | Combines and averages the opinions of top executives | Limited budget; executives usually are experienced and have a feel for customer needs | Possibility of ivory-tower thinking; use of valuable executive time; lack of the use of standard procedure | New product forecasts; medium- to long-range forecasts |
| Sales force composite | Combines salespeople's estimates of future sales | Assignment of forecasting to those who will be responsible for results; utilization of the knowledge of people in the field; good reliability and accuracy | Salespeople not usually trained in forecasting techniques; salespeople may view the function as unimportant; possibility of estimates either too optimistic or too pessimistic; lack of planning ability | Short- to intermediate-range forecast; effective when intimate knowledge of customers' plans are necessary, as in the case of probable buying plans on large proposals or bids |
| Survey of buyer intentions | Anticipates what buyers are likely to do under a given set of conditions | Provides a continual feel for the market; keeps abreast of the competition; indicates where additional advertising, promotion, and selling pressure may be needed | Buyer may not know or may be unwilling to reveal intentions; users may be too numerous, too hard, or too expensive to locate; channel intermediaries may be unwilling to participate | With a well-defined or limited market; when intermediaries play an important role in the buy-sell exchange |
| The Delphi method | Group forecasting method using feedback from others until a near-consensus is reached | Accuracy; limited budget for forecasting; used when risk and consequence of serious error are low | Length of time required; tendency toward guesswork; use of valuable executive time | Intermediate- to long-term forecasting; new product forecasts; to indicate future technological events that might affect a market |

the future. A major criticism of this approach, however, warns against ivory-tower thinking, referring to the very real possibility that executive personnel are not in tune with some of the realities faced by sales personnel in the field.

### Sales Force Composite

Among business-to-business firms, the sales force composite is the approach to sales forecasting most commonly used. This approach combines each salesperson's estimate of future sales in a particular territory with those of other salespeople, creating a total company sales forecast. This total forecast is analyzed, adjusted, perhaps compared with forecasts from other sources, and adjusted if deemed necessary by higher-level marketing management. Advantages associated with this forecasting method include making forecasting the task of those who will be held responsible for results, utilizing specialized knowledge of people in the field, and usually obtaining greater reliability and accuracy. Disadvantages include using people not trained in forecasting who may not view the function as an important part of their job; estimates that are either too optimistic or too pessimistic (as mentioned earlier in the discussion of the bottom-up approach); and the lack of potential for future planning from the salesperson's perspective, which may result in forecasts based on the present, rather than on future conditions.

### Survey of Buyer Intentions

A survey of buyer intentions anticipates what buyers are likely to do under a given set of conditions and suggests that, at the least, major organizational buyers should be surveyed. In the business products sector, various agencies carry out buyer intention surveys regarding plant, equipment, and materials purchases, with the two best-known surveys being conducted by the U.S. Department of Commerce and the McGraw-Hill Book Company. Most of the estimates, surprisingly enough, have been within 10 percent of the actual outcomes. Advantages include giving the marketer a continual feel for the market and its needs, keeping the marketer abreast of competition, and the possibility that, as a side benefit, the approach will indicate where additional advertising, promotion, and personal selling pressure may be needed. Disadvantages of this approach would include the likelihood that many buyers may not know, or may be unwilling to reveal, their buying intentions; users may be too numerous, too hard, or too expensive to locate; and, if indirect channels of distribution are used, distributors and representatives may not be willing to take on the extra work of tracing and questioning customers or potential customers on future buying intentions.

### The Delphi Method

The Delphi method is a group forecasting model that is a modified version of the *expert-opinion approach.* It is accomplished by questioning experts individually and then providing them with anonymous feedback from others in the group until there is a convergence of the estimates or opinions of the total group. This approach was developed during the late 1940s by the Rand Corporation. Any set of information available to some experts is passed on to each of the other experts, enabling all to have access to the information pertinent to the forecasting function. All questioning is handled impersonally by a coordinator, which virtually eliminates committee activity. This reduces the influence of certain psychological factors, such as specious persuasion, unwillingness to abandon publicly expressed opinions, and the "bandwagon effect" of majority opinion. A coordinator analyzes the forecasts submitted, sends an averaged forecast back to participants, and asks each expert to submit another forecast. This process continues until the group is a near consensus. Advantages of this approach include accuracy, as results will tend to be better than with other methods that neither employ the same level of detail, nor give the necessary attention to obtaining unbiased estimates. Also, it is an attractive approach when the budget for sales forecasting is limited and when the risk and consequences of serious error in forecasting are low. Disadvantages of using the Delphi method include the length of time needed to develop the consensus sales forecast, the tendency toward using guesswork, and the possibility of infringing too much on valuable executive time.

## Quantitative Approaches

Quantitative approaches to forecasting tend to be of a statistical/mathematical nature and can be divided into two broad categories: time-series techniques and causal techniques. *Time-series techniques* focus on historical data; *causal techniques* rely on the relationship among various factors, both past and present, within the marketing environment. Five different time-series techniques are introduced first: (1) trend fitting, (2) moving average, (3) exponential smoothing, (4) adaptive control, and (5) Box-Jenkins. Then six different causal techniques are introduced: (1) regression, (2) econometrics, (3) leading indicators, (4) diffusion index, (5) input-output analysis, and (6) life-cycle analysis. Exhibits 6-11 and 6-12 summarize the quantitative forecasting techniques considered in this chapter.

## Time-Series Techniques

### Trend Fitting

Trend fitting is a popular technique in which the forecaster fits a trend line to a series of deseasonalized sales data. Once the line is established, the forecaster simply extends it farther to project sales for the future. Put another way, the analyst estimates the trend from past data and adds this figure to current sales to obtain a forecast. Trend fitting is very accurate for short-term forecasting.

**EXHIBIT 6-11**  **Summary of Time-Series Forecasting Techniques**

| Technique | Approach | Major Advantages | Major Disadvantages | Potential Application |
|---|---|---|---|---|
| Trend fitting | Estimates the trend from past data and extends it to project future sales | Low cost; excellent short-term accuracy; easy to use; quick | Many observations required for accuracy; not effective in identifying turning points | Good technique for products in the maturity phase of the product life cycle |
| Moving average | Computed with the average progressing forward in time, as the earliest period is dropped and the latest is added | Low cost; short-term accuracy; easy to use; quick | Will not forecast turning point; not accurate for long-term forecasting | Often used for inventory control for standard or low-volume items |
| Exponential smoothing | A moving average technique with recent data being given more weight | Low cost; easy to use; quick | Will not forecast turning points; not accurate for long-term forecasting | Best used to forecast a highly stable sales series, similar to the application presented with the moving average technique |
| Adaptive control | Similar to smoothing with the addition of optimum weights that reduce statistical error | More sensitive to historical data than methods above; short-term accuracy | Costly; more time consuming than methods above | Excellent for forecasting sales demand on a monthly basis |
| Box-Jenkins | A mathematical technique whereby the computer selects the statistical model of the time series that gives the best fit | Short-term accuracy; easy to use | Costly; time consuming; not accurate with long-term forecasting | Best used in production and inventory control of large-volume items and forecast of cash balances |

### Moving Average

With the moving average method of forecasting, the forecaster computes the average volume achieved in several recent periods and uses it as a prediction of sales in the next period. This approach assumes that the future will be an average of past achievements, with the earliest period being dropped and the latest being added. Forecasters usually employ moving averages in conjunction with other methods, as this method is good only for short-term forecasting.

### Exponential Smoothing

*Exponential smoothing* is a moving average technique with past forecast errors being adjusted by a weighted moving average of past sales by periods. The average is modified or weighted in proportion to the error in forecasting the previous period's sales. The new forecast is basically equal to the old one, plus some proportion of the past forecasting error. The more recent the observation, the heavier the weight assigned. This method is effective when the more recent period's sales are better predictors of the next period's sales than are those of earlier periods. Exponential smoothing will normally provide a highly accurate, short-term forecast.

### Adaptive Control

*Adaptive control* is similar to exponential smoothing, the difference being that optimum weights that will reduce the statistical error are derived from historical data. These weights are then used to forecast future demand. With each forecasting period, actual sales data are used to recalculate the optimal weights. Forecasts are more sensitive to historical data than

**EXHIBIT 6-12** **Summary of Causal Forecasting Techniques**

| Technique | Approach | Major Advantages | Major Disadvantages | Potential Application |
|-----------|----------|------------------|---------------------|----------------------|
| Regression | Relates sales predictions to elements of the internal and external environment | Low cost; short-term accuracy; easy to use | Data generated are only as good as the data from which derived; lacks accuracy for long-term forecasting | Prediction of overall market demand for a generic product type |
| Econometrics | An application of regression analysis; a system of interdependent regression equations that describe an area of economic or profit activity | Good for short-, intermediate-, and long-term forecasting | Costly; time consuming | Used in the prediction of overall market for a generic product type |
| Leading indicators | A time series of an economic activity whose movement in a given direction precedes the movement of some other time series in the same direction | Will identify turning points; will forecast overall business conditions | Accuracy is questionable; limited application; costly; time consuming | Forecasting changes in overall business conditions |
| Diffusion index | The percentage of a group of economic indicators that are going up or down | Will identify turning points; fair to good short-term forecasting accuracy | Costly; time consuming; poor long-term forecasting accuracy | Used for forecasting sales of overall product classes |
| Input-Output analysis | Concerned with interindustry and interdepartmental flow of goods or services | Will identify turning points; good for intermediate- and long-range forecasting | Costly; time consuming; poor short-term forecasting accuracy | Forecasting sales of business products and services for long periods of time |
| Life-cycle analysis | Phases of product acceptance are analyzed | Good for forecasting new product sales; good for intermediate forecasting | Limited accuracy; will not identify turning point; costly; time consuming | Forecasting of new product sales |

the moving average and exponential smoothing techniques. This method is good for short- to intermediate-term forecasting.

### Box-Jenkins

*Box-Jenkins* is the most comprehensive time series analysis/projection technique used, as it enables the computer to select the statistical model of the time series that gives the best fit. The forecaster fits a time series with a mathematical model, which is optimal in the sense that it has smaller errors or variability than any other model fitted to the data. It is a very accurate computational procedure, but it is costly and time consuming.

## Causal Techniques

### Regression

*Regression models* are the most widely used causal models for forecasting. They attempt to relate sales predictions to elements of the system. The accuracy of these models is excellent for short-term forecasting; the cost of use is reasonable, and the technique is not overly complex.

## WHAT WOULD YOU DO?

### UNEXPECTED DEMAND CHANGE AT BELMONTE METAL STAMPING COMPANY

Robert Masters, president of Belmonte Metal Stamping Company, is facing a complex business decision. Belmonte's marketing manager, Sally Rodericks, has just brought him a major order revision that greatly decreases the shipping schedule from their major OEM customer, Alto Automobile Company. Sally was still irate from her conversation with the Alto buyer. She explained that the buyer had stated that since the business was split 50/50 between Belmonte and Burr Stamping, and since Belmonte had been producing at double that rate for the last six months, it was only reasonable that Burr (which had finally resolved its production problems) should be allowed to make up the business that it had lost. Sally had tried to remind the buyer that when Belmonte's competitor (Burr) failed to receive quality certification on the new assembly (AAC part #456342 Rev B), Belmonte had made significant efforts and sacrifice to keep the Alto assembly line supplied. Belmonte had made up for its competitor's shortcoming by turning down other customers' orders, adding extra employees, utilizing less-efficient production equipment, and working overtime (including every weekend and holiday for six months). Sally said, "I tried to tell those people that after all we did for them, Alto is repaying us by essentially shutting us off for the next six months. But the buyer keeps saying that while they greatly appreciate our efforts, they did cover

our extra expenses, and they do have contractual agreements with both us and Burr for each to produce half of Alto's annual usage of the assembly. I told Alto, as firmly as I could, that we never for a moment thought that they would cut us off when Burr came back on-line. I told them that any reasonable person who had been involved in the situation would have come away with the understanding that Burr's share (because of its shutdown) was lost business. When they came on-line, we assumed we would share the business, but only from that point on." Sally continued, "I've tried to explain that 600,000 assemblies per month for six months is not the same as 300,000 assemblies per month for twelve months. We were expecting that after we covered Burr's shipments plus our own (600,000 per month for six months) that we would then continue with our normal 300,000 per month for the remaining six months. What are we supposed to do with our employees, and what about the other customers' orders we turned down? At our standard selling price of $3.27 each, Alto is taking away almost $6 million from our projected sales. That's just not fair."

### Assignment

Define the ethical issues and devise a plan for Belmonte Metal Stamping Company. What is the marketing manager's role in this situation.

### Econometrics

*Econometrics* is the application of regression analysis to business and economic problems. The model is a system of interdependent regression equations that describe an area of economic or profit activity and provide good forecasting accuracy for short, intermediate, and long-term time periods.

### Leading Indicators

A *leading indicator* is a time series of an economic activity whose movement in a given direction precedes the movement of some other time series in the same direction. If the company has products with a dependent relationship on a variable whose changes precede changes in the firm's sales, profitable use can be made of this indicator. Accuracy for leading indicators is fairly good for short-term forecasting, but it is questionable for intermediate and long-term forecasting.

### Diffusion Index

A *diffusion index* is the percentage of a group of economic indicators that are going up or down. A succession of low index numbers over a number of months in an expansionary period should precede an economic downturn. Short-term forecasting accuracy is only fair at best, and costs can be high.

### Input-Output Analysis

*Input-output analysis* is concerned with the interindustry or interdepartmental flow of goods or services in the economy or in a company and its markets. This method is not appropriate for short-term forecasting, is costly, and is time consuming.

### Life-Cycle Analysis

*Life-cycle analysis* consists of an analysis and the forecast of new product growth rates based on S-shaped curves. Central to the analysis is the phase of product acceptance by various groups such as innovators, early adopters, early majority, late majority, and laggards. A growth curve is estimated and is reviewed as sales data are corrected. Forecasts are made by reading future points along the S-curve.

A company's senior management team expects marketers to forecast accurately because they know that accurate forecasts reduce costs, increase on-time delivery performance, and improve customer satisfaction. Research suggests that inaccurate forecasts can reduce profit by 10 percent or more because of inventory shortages or overages.[8] As a result, marketers are constantly evaluating new forecasting approaches. Two that are showing promise are: (1) a combination approach where several simple techniques are weighted and averaged, and (2) a collaborative approach where suppliers and their customers analyze markets and develop forecasts together.[9] Marketers will face a continuous learning process to keep up with the latest approaches to strategic business forecasting.

---

**Concept Review**

1. Why is quality positioning difficult to do?
2. What does perceptual mapping attempt to uncover?
3. What is the strategic importance of forecasting (or demand estimation)?

---

**Summary**

- Segmenting business markets is difficult. To be successful, the marketer must be able to identify, analyze, and evaluate potentially attractive business segments; target the segments to be served; and then develop and communicate a positioning strategy that will differentiate the firm's offerings from others. Business market segmentation is the practice of dividing a business market into distinct groups of buyers with similar requirements and that will respond similarly to a specific set of marketing actions.

- Business marketing managers must determine what strategy will be used for different market segments. By adopting a strategy of undifferentiated marketing, the organization treats its total market as a single entity. Differentiated marketing is the strategy by which a firm attempts to distinguish its product from competitive brands offered to the same aggregate market. Through concentrated marketing, the firm achieves a strong market position in the segment because of its greater knowledge of the segment's needs and the special reputation it builds.

- Macro segmentation involves dividing the market into subgroups based on overall characteristics of the prospect organization; micro segmentation pertains to characteristics of the decision-making process and the buying structure within the prospect organization. The nested approach stresses segmentation according to the amount of investigation required to identify and evaluate different criteria. This method integrates and builds on previous schemes for segmenting business markets. It offers an approach that enables not only the simple grouping of customers and prospects but also more complex grouping of purchase situations, events, and personalities.

- Many of the variables generally used to segment the consumer market can be used by the business marketer to segment the organizational market. Five primary ways of segmenting business markets include: type of economic activity; size of organization; geographic location; product usage; and structure of the procurement function.

- Before target markets can be chosen, the business marketing manager must decide how many segments and which segments will provide the best return, given limited resources. A competitive analysis should be undertaken to assess both the strengths and weaknesses of competitors within a segment in order to further identify the areas of opportunity for the firm. Porter's five-force model shows that the firm must appraise the impact upon the long-run profitability of five groups: industry competitors, potential entrants, substitutes, buyers, and suppliers. In formulating strategy, the existing and potential competitors' strengths in the areas of research and development, finance, technical service, sales force development, advertising, distribution, and organizational design must be studied.

- Positioning is the act of emphasizing one or more aspects of a product such that target segments have a particular perception of that product. Six approaches to positioning strategy include positioning by technology, quality, price, distribution, image, and service.

- With increasing complexity, competition, and change in the business environment, organizations need more reliable performance forecasts to be able to maintain a favorable marketing position. Forecasting, or demand estimation, is used in the analysis, measurement, and improvement of current marketing strategy and in the identification and/or development of new products and new markets. Common forecasting problems faced by business products marketing managers include forecasting mystique, accuracy, inconsistency, accountability, and implementation.

- There are two major techniques for forecasting business demand. Qualitative approaches to forecasting employ managerial judgment to determine future expectations and often are used when data are scarce or when good information is virtually nonexistent. Quantitative approaches to forecasting tend to be of a statistical/mathematical nature and can be divided into time-series and causal techniques. Time-series techniques focus on historical data, while causal methods rely on the relationship among various factors, both past and present, within the marketing environment.

## Key Terms

centralized buying situation
competitive analysis
concentrated marketing
    strategy
decentralized buying
    situation
demand projection

differentiated marketing
    strategy
forecasting
macro segmentation
market segmentation
micro segmentation
nested approach

perceptual mapping
product differentiation
product positioning
profitability analysis
undifferentiated marketing
    strategy

## Review Questions

1. In what kinds of areas can business market segmentation assist business-to-business firms? How is segmentation achieved in business marketing? What are three criteria used to be successful in selecting business market segments?

2. Distinguish among undifferentiated marketing, differentiated marketing, and concentrated marketing as business market segmentation strategies.

3. Compare macro segmentation with micro segmentation. What is the nested approach to business market segmentation? What is its major premise? Why are outer-nest criteria generally inadequate when used alone to segment markets? How can mature business markets be segmented? What is the value of using purchase responsibilities among individuals within organizations as a method of segmenting business markets?

4. Identify five ways in which business markets can be segmented. Can you think of any additional ways in which a market might be segmented?

5. What is the role of a competitive analysis in business market segmentation? Distinguish between a market profitability analysis and a market competitive analysis as preconditions to selecting market segments.

6. What is meant by product position? Why is perceptual mapping used? Identify six ways by which a company could position a business product. What six questions should a firm ask before getting started with a positioning strategy?

7. When is forecasting used? What is the value of accurate sales forecasting?

8. Discuss five common problems encountered by business marketing managers in sales forecasting.

9. Distinguish between the top-down and the bottom-up methods of sales forecasting. Discuss four qualitative methods of sales forecasting.

10. Differentiate between time-series techniques and causal methods of quantitative sales forecasting. Identify and explain five types of time-series techniques and six examples of causal methods.

## Case 6-1

# Jiang Metal Products Company

This case was written by Dr. Roger Gomes and Dr. Patricia Knowles, Clemson University © 1999

Jing Liu had just graduated from James Madison University (JMU) with a degree in marketing and a computer science minor. Immediately upon graduation, she joined Jiang Metal Products Company (JMPC) as assistant to the marketing manager. Because of her background, one of her new responsibilities was to create a useful website for the company.

Jing Liu would be relying on the business-to-business theory she had learned at JMU to develop content that would actually be useful to the company. She knew that she would have to begin with an objective. Due to the business-to-business relationship marketing nature of company sales, it was not realistic to expect that the website would generate orders. However, she knew that site visitors would typically be buyers, engineers, and other buying center members who influence the purchase decision. They would want to see useful information, and they would require quick, accurate, and personal answers to inquiries. Jing knew that her budget was limited, so she decided to start by doing some business marketing research herself.

### The Company

Tao Jiang, an engineering graduate of the University of Virginia, founded the Jiang Metal Products Company in 1992 in Roanoke, Virginia. The company produced high-precision progressive metal stampings for local high-tech industries and sales, cost and income data about the company appear in Exhibit 6-13. Tao's family had been in a similar business in China, and he had worked for his father throughout his secondary school years. Even though Tao was only in his late twenties, he had the business experience of someone much older. He had based the company's differential advantages on exceptional customer responsiveness and flexibility. Customers knew that Tao would do whatever was required to meet their schedules and requirements. Everyone, including Tao and his office staff, had occasionally worked double shifts running production machines to meet unscheduled customer orders. Everyone in the company knew that "quality" and "delivery reliability" were their number one objectives. The metal stamping industry was very competitive and JMPC's customers were constantly being approached by competitors in stamping. A second differential advantage for JMPC was a high-precision niche. If a product required standard tolerances and materials, it would be difficult for JMPC to stand out. Tao believed that when the company won large orders on standard products, it was mostly due to the great relationship-building skills of the company's manufacturers representatives, who sold the majority of the company's output.

The company's largest customer produced night vision goggles for military and commercial applications. Other low-volume–high-margin markets included the medical device

**EXHIBIT 6-13**
**Jiang Metal Products Company Financial Data—1999**

| Operations (in thousands) | |
|---|---|
| Net sales | $14,555 |
| Cost and expenses | $ 1,751 |
| Selling, Admin., and General | |
| Depreciation | $ 609 |
| Interest expense | $ 280 |
| Other [Cost of sales (direct)] | $11,085 |
| | $13,725 |
| Income before taxes | $ 830 |
| Income taxes | $ 285 |
| Net income | $ 545 |

industry and the aerospace industry. Higher-volume–lower-margin products came from a great variety of industries.

## Marketing Research

To research possible Internet site contents, Jing Liu pulled out her old business marketing textbook and reviewed several chapters. She also referred to the *Thomas Register of Manufacturers* directory and looked up the names and websites of: (1) similar-sized competitors and (2) the biggest and best competitors. Jing Liu figured that this would produce a variety of website types to look at for ideas.

In the textbook, Jing recalled a case in which students were required to create a website for a hypothetical company. To make expenditures appropriate to the size of the company's budget site, typical development costs were provided (with reference citations). She found:

Small Site—Wants to be on the Web, but needs only basic services. These companies typically want to provide easy access to information for OEM customers, distributors, and potential customers. Site will include product lists and specifications, and the ability to e-mail directly into customer service. The site developer will expect to do a lot of hand holding because the company's management doesn't understand Web capabilities and marketing. It is common for management to want a website but not to include it in their integrated marketing plan (in fact, often they are not sure why they want it). Typical site development specifications include: design about 20 simple pages with graphics, virtual server and domain registration, Web publishing forms, Internet connections for five staff members, e-mail capability, and considerable training. The average cost estimate: Low-end site—$750, High-end site—$167,500, Median = $78,000.* Exhibit 6-14 contains data which includes median costs for different sized sites.

Medium Site—Wants a more sophisticated site that can provide access to databases of password-protected proprietary data. Customers, distributors, and field salespeople will actively interact with the site on a regular basis (checking inventory, order status, etc.). The information needs to be searchable and sortable. There will be an impressive corporate section and areas devoted to making technical sales presentations (no video). Typical site development specifications: design about 100 pages with advanced graphics, virtual server and domain registration, Web publishing forms, Internet connections for 25 staff members, e-mail capability, standard search engine, password-protected directories, databases, and ongoing training. The average cost estimate: Low-end site—$4,500, High-end site—$311,570, Median = $150,000.*

There was also information about Large Mega-Sites, but Jing Liu could see that the costs (sometimes over $1 million) were way beyond her company's budget and need.

Jing Liu also noted from the text that NetMarketing surveyed leading Web developers monthly concerning prices for hypothetical sites. With more and more companies going on the Web, demand had been driving prices up. Jing thought that she might be able to get an idea about what the new website would cost by extending the price trends into the present.

**EXHIBIT 6-14**
**Changes in Typical Website Development Median Costs from October 1997 to February 1999***

|  | Oct. '97 | June '98 | Feb. '99 |
|---|---|---|---|
| Small site | $ 25,000 | $ 44,500 | $ 78,000 |
| Medium site | $ 83,000 | $ 99,750 | $150,000 |
| Large site | $275,000 | $302,975 | $440,000 |

## Assignment

You are Jing Liu. Do the research necessary to develop the website, including market segmentation and positioning. Next, project (forecast) costs to the present, and develop a rough storyboard (layout) of the contents of the website. Be sure your objective and contents are consistent with the product positioning you have planned. Include a method to measure whether the website meets your objectives. Be sure that your approach is based on good textbook marketing theory.

*Reprinted from M. Carmichael, "Web Site Development Costs Climbing," *Business Marketing*, February 1, 1999, pp. 21, 24. © 1999 Crain Communications, Inc.

---

**Case 6-2**

# Superior Software Systems (B)

This case was written by Dr. Roger Gomes and Dr. Patricia Knowles, Clemson University © 1999

Ron Mullins was watching his computer screen scroll by with what seemed like hundreds and hundreds of customer and potential customer company names. Somehow Ron was going to have to go through all these again, because when he had collected competitive intelligence information on them, he had not been thinking about potential segmentation variables. Ron's supervisor had liked the Web research information [Case 5-2 (A) Chapter 5] so much that he had thought up this new segmentation assignment.

Ron thought, "There are lots of potential ways to segment these companies, but there must be some objective to the process—something that segmentation is trying to achieve. I also seem to remember that there were some segmentation criteria—one of those lists they made us memorize in college. Let's see, the segmentation variable must be . . . ? Well, it's a good thing I have my old business marketing text right here on my bookshelf. It says:

> *Business market segmentation is the practice of dividing a business market into distinct groups of buyers with similar requirements. It is the foundation of the marketing strategy process and the driver of resource allocation. The goal of segmentation in a business setting is to divide larger markets into smaller components that are homogeneous with respect to their response to a market mix. The business marketer must be able to identify, analyze, and evaluate potentially attractive market segments; target the segments to be served; and then develop and communicate a positioning strategy that will differentiate the firm's offerings from others.*

"OK, that's helpful, but this sure sounds like a major strategic issue that could impact the entire future of the company." Ron thought, "Wow, this is the kind of assignment that has a lot of visibility. It is going to be obvious if I try to take any shortcuts. Now, where is that list to test the segments?" Ron pulled out some additional marketing textbooks he had used in college. "Here it is," he said. "Segments must be distinguishable from each other, measurable, substantial, accessible, and actionable." He would have to review what all this meant, but he could see a great presentation forming in his mind. "I'll bet they had not even invented this stuff way back when the managers were in college. I sure never thought when I was in my marketing classes that I would ever have to actually do any of this in a job."

## The Company

The company information on Superior Software can be found in Part A of this case, located at the end of Chapter 5. Be sure to review the entire Part A case.

## Ron's Segmentation Project

Ron was excited about using his marketing skills to help the company. As a first step in the project, Ron reviewed the company information he had discovered on the Web. He tried sorting the companies by industry, benefits sought, and several other ways. By then he was fairly sure that he would need a more sophisticated approach such as nesting several variables.

## Assignment

You are Ron. Consider alternative market segmentation strategies from a theory-based approach. A "steps in segmenting a market" list would be useful. If you need to, ask your reference librarian to help you locate resources. When you have developed the segmentation approach you will be recommending, put each of the companies below into their proper segments and prepare a presentation to the management group (class). The presentation should show the segments and the benefits to the company that your approach will bring. Note: It is very unlikely that your segmentation approach will be similar to other teams with the assignment. There is no one correct segmentation, but each team does need to be able to show how its approach meets theory requirements.

## Ron's List of Customer Company Names to Segment (i.e., the current and potential market for Superior Software)

1. Automatic Switch Co (www.asco.com)
2. Conbraco Industries, Inc. (www.conbraco.com)
3. Motion Industries, Inc. (www.motionindustries.com)
4. Daniel Woodhead Co. (www.danielwoodhead.com)
5. Kaeser Compressors, Inc. (www.kaeser.com)
6. Woodex Bearing Co., Inc. (www.woodex-meco.com)
7. Dresser Instrument (www. dresser.com/instruments)
8. Eagle Technology, Inc. (www.eaglecmms.com)
9. Olympus America, IPG (www olympus.com)
10. A.W. Chesterton Co (www chesterton.com)
11. RegScan (www eregs.com)
12. Waukesha Cherry-Burrell (www.waukesha-cb.com)
13. Federal Hose Manufacturing, Inc. (www.federalhose.com)
14. Polycoat Systems, Inc. (www.polycoat.com)
15. General Magnaplate Corp. (www.magnaplate.com)
16. Innovative Fluid Handling Systems (www.ifh-group.com)
17. Kaman Industrial Technologies (www.kaman-ind-tech.com)
18. Loctite Corp. (www.loctite.com)
19. Ludeca, Inc (www ludeca.com)
20. Moyno Industrial Products (www.moyno.com)
21. NewAge Industries (www.newageind.com)

22. Ogontz (www.ogontz.com)
23. Edlon-PSI (www.edlon-psi.com)
24. Penberthy (www.penberthy-online.com)
25. MRO Software (www.mro.com)
26. Oracle Corp. (www.oracle.com)
27. Datastream Systems, Inc. (www.dstm.com)
28. Trico Mfg. Corp. (www trico.com)
29. Magnatex Pumps, Inc. (www magnatexpumps.com)
30. U.S. Electrical Motors (www.usmotors.com)
31. Victaulic Co. of America (www.victaulic.com)
32. Warman International, Inc. (www.warman.com)
33. NTN Bearing Corp. of America (www.ntnamerica.com)
34. Filtomat, Inc. (www.filtomat.com)
35. Albany International (www.albint.com)
36. The Foxboro Co. (www.foxboro.com)
37. Spectronics Corp. (www.spectroline.com)
38. Visual Planning Group (www.visualplanning.com)
39. Hertz Equipment Rental Corp. (www.hertzequip.com)
40. Baldor (www.baldor.com)
41. EXTECH, Inc. (www.extech.com)
42. Yale's Material Handling Care (www.yale.com)
43. BEKO Systems (www.bekousa.com)
44. Cybermetrics (www.foresightweb.com)
45. U.S. Tsubaki (www.ustsubaki.com)
46. Entek IRD (ww.entek.com)
47. Rytec (www.rytecdoors.com)
48. Philips Lighting Co. (www.lighting.philips.com)
49. INVENSYS (www.invensysproductionsolutions.com)

## References

1. Sally Dibb and Robin Wensley, "Segmentation Analysis for Industrial Markets," *European Journal of Marketing* 36 (Jan/Feb 2002): 231–51.
2. Gerald E. Smith, "Segmenting B2B Markets with Economic Value Analysis," *Marketing Management* 11 (2002): 35–40.
3. Sean Kelly, "Using Data Mining for Market Segmentation," *Direct Response* 30 (January 2003): 35.
4. C. M. Sashi and Vaman S. Kudpi, "Market Selection and Procurement Decisions in B2B Markets, *Management Decision* 28 (2001), 190–6.
5. Thomas V. Bonoma and Benson P. Shapiro, *Segmenting the Industrial Market.* (Lexington, MA: Lexington Books, 1983).
6. Michael E. Porter, *Competitive Advantage: Creating and Sustaining Superior Performance.* (New York: The Free Press, 1985): 4–8, 234–6.
7. Based on a personal interview with H. O. Crafford, September 7, 1999, Worcester, MA.
8. John G. Wacker, "Sales Forecasting for Strategic Resource Planning," *International Journal of Operations and Production Management* 22 (2002): 1014–31.
9. Teresa M. McCarthy and Susan L. Golicic, "Implementing Collaborative Forecasting to Improve Supply Chain Performance," *International Journal of Physical Distribution and Logistics Management* 32 (2002): 431–54.

## CHAPTER SEVEN

# New Product Development, Management, and Strategy

## Learning Objectives

After reading this chapter, you should be able to:

- Recognize the importance of product strategy in business marketing.
- Classify new products into four distinct types.
- Understand the important role of marketers in new product design and development.
- Discuss new product developments, including approaches, processes, and organization.
- Understand the product life cycle and the importance of effective marketing strategies over a product's projected life cycle.
- Relate how experience and learning curves can determine what happens to a product as it matures.
- Explain the forces impacting a firm's decision to expand, contract, or maintain its product mix.
- Describe three options for product elimination.
- Understand the important characteristics of business services.
- Appreciate the challenges and opportunities found in the marketing of business services.
- Discuss the strategic importance of new service development.

## Chapter Outline

## Product Strategy in Business Marketing

Product development, management, and strategy are important components of business marketing. Measuring and predicting success and executing proper strategy over the life of the business product are of considerable importance. Indeed, a unique or superior product, knowledge of the market, and an effective marketing strategy are critical to a company's success.

Effective product management and strategy are, in fact, more important today than ever as the B2B sector positions itself to compete against an onslaught of offshore competitors that have impacted the domestic market. In business marketing, it is critical to position products, the company, its distribution channels, and, often, production technologies. Once the market is segmented and targets are chosen, the product that will give the company legitimate claims to the position it wants to occupy is developed and fine-tuned. New product development, a greater marketing orientation, more sophisticated marketing research, improved new product introduction efforts, better attention to customer service and after-sales service, a closer linkage with customers, and an increased global marketing effort are among the keys to making good in the marketplace. Compared to B2C marketers, B2B marketers tend to develop new products to meet very specific needs of other businesses. Because they are closer to their target markets than are B2C marketers, the new product failure rate tends to be lower for B2B firms—about 20 percent or less.[1] Although the actual figure for new product failure rates is widely disputed, it is estimated that when products do fail it seems to be overwhelmingly the fault of marketing and management (e.g., the product was not well designed, the product was incorrectly positioned in the market, marketing research was not done).[2] The good news is that those sorts of deficiencies can be fixed.

## Product Lines Defined

Product lines of B2B marketers may be defined in several ways. One is to classify them as durable goods, nondurable goods, and services. Another is to classify them as materials and parts, capital items, and supplies and business services. A third way to classify them is to combine the first two classification schemes and include an additional element, interaction with the target market. Doing so results in four distinct product types—proprietary and catalog products, custom-built products, custom-designed products, and industrial services—that will be discussed briefly.

### Proprietary or Catalog Products

These include standard product offerings made and usually inventoried in anticipation of sales orders. They may be available only through professional selling or may appear in a catalog. Such products may include durable or nondurable **materials and parts** that enter the manufacturer's product completely. There are two sorts of materials and parts, namely, **raw materials** (farm products and natural products) and **manufactured materials and parts** (component materials and component parts). Proprietary and catalog products may also be **capital items**—long-lasting goods that facilitate developing or managing the finished products. Capital items include **installations** such as buildings and large, fixed equipment and **equipment** such as portable factory equipment and tools. Finally, proprietary and catalog products may include **supplies**—operating supplies or maintenance and repair items—that facilitate developing or managing the finished product. As a case in point, DoAll Company (www.doall.com) keeps an abundant supply of the DoAll No. C916A

Band Saw in inventory to ensure quick delivery to customers. DoAll marketing managers must be concerned with new product development, repositioning strategy, and product deletion strategy.

## Custom-Built Products

These include durable and nondurable materials and parts, capital items, and supplies that are customized for individual business customers. Industrial Custom Products (www.industrialcustom.com) offers die-cutting, lamination and assembly solutions, custom O.E.M. components, and other customizable products. Management concern here is to know what options and accessories will be demanded by customers, and when.

## Custom-Designed Products

These products include one-of-a-kind units, customized for a particular user or small group of users. DoAll custom-designed a unique band saw for the U.S. Army, created for the sole purpose of cutting up live ammunition (Howitzer rounds). The firm designed the saw with a custom-fixtured table and remote control operation.

## Industrial Services

Industrial services include maintenance and repair services and business advisory services. Thus, with a service, the buyer is purchasing an intangible, such as maintenance, machine repair, or a warranty. Maintenance and repair services may be supplied under contract from small producers or from manufacturers of the products delivered. For example, DoAll Company warrants every machine sold for a period of two years. In addition, a saw and coolant specialist makes regular courtesy inspections at customers' plants to assist in product applications. On the other hand, specialized services may be purchased on an as-needed basis from independent companies such as Team Industrial Services (www.teamindustrial services.com) which offer mechanical inspection services and emissions control services among other offers or GE Capital (www.gecapital.com) which offers commercial finance and insurance. Special attention will be given to services marketing later in the chapter.

## Business New Product Development

For products, the old proverb, "If it works, don't fix it" is overtaken by the new proverb, "If it works, it's probably out of date."[3] Innovation is the fuel of corporate longevity. Heightened competition in both domestic and international markets often forces firms to develop new products or find new markets for their existing products.[4] Without continuous innovation, organizations sputter and die. In the opinion of many, the United States is losing its innovative prowess, yet there are some U.S. corporations still considered to be some of the world's best innovators. Among them, Caterpillar, 3M, Hewlett-Packard, Merck, and Intel have the ability to churn out new products at a dizzying pace. A recognized sign of a world-class organization has come to be its ability to get a new product to market ahead of its competition.

In many business-to-business firms, the design of new products (especially scientific and technical products) is the sole responsibility of people within the engineering discipline. However, much marketing literature argues that business marketing managers should play a major role in the design (development) of new products through the guidelines that marketing research can provide. It appears today that the important role of business marketers in the design and development of new products finally is being recognized. Marketing and sales personnel frequently are called on to work with—and sometimes to lead—specialists from other functional areas in the development of new products. Of necessity, a major concern of sales and marketing managers must be new product development.

Two important trends are facing managers as we enter this century. First, worldwide enterprises are creating new technology at an increasing rate. In some segments of industry, technology is changing both how business is conducted and the nature of competition. It also is changing product development and introduction processes by shortening the time firms have to bring new products to market (*time-to-market*). New product introduction in today's technology-driven business sector is loaded with risk, yet it is something that must occur if a firm is to remain viable.

In addition to technological change that is revolutionary rather than evolutionary, an unprecedented level of aggressive competition from across the globe resulting in unbelievably rapid market saturation is characteristic of many business markets today. As an example of this second important trend marketers face, an adhesives producer in New Jersey that traditionally has competed for orders with regional competitors now competes with producers from South Africa to East Asia—all wanting part of the market. In addition to a daunting force of competitors, twenty-first-century adhesive marketers will have to be constantly alert for substitute products in development and new approaches to adhesiveless processes (such as heat bonding, or bonding with pressure in the presence of intense sound waves). All too quickly, a product line can be obsoleted by a less expensive, or stronger, or longer-lasting, or more environmentally friendly alternative. A company must look to its marketing function to assure that its product lines are positioned optimally.

## New Product Approaches

Most new product development processes can be classified as the technology- push process or the market-pull process.

### Technology Push

When the perceived value of a particular technology is great, *technology push* usually results. Once the product or process has been developed, the marketing function becomes important. The marketing firm has some form of technology, only a vague notion of possible applications, and usually little else. Most telecom products start with a technology-push phase. A growing number of customers buy for reasons of availability, novelty, and price, even if the benefits are not fully defined. Most of the truly great inventions of the period 1830–1915 fall into this category (for example, the steam turbine, triode, and telephone). With a great invention, it is difficult to estimate the ultimate size of the market. For example, who, at the outset, could have estimated the market for computers or xerography? In fact, Sperry Univac is purported to have initially estimated that the size of the computer market by the year 2000 would be 1000 or 2000 machines. This type of product, in effect, follows *Say's Law* in economics: "Supply creates demand." Such momentous success inspires all technology-push efforts, whether warranted or not.

### Market Pull

*Market pull* is primarily the result of marketing research methodologies of interviewing potential users about their needs and then developing solutions to meet those perceived needs. This method carries the least business risk because there is less chance that the developed product cannot be sold. This approach is considered more difficult to manage than technology push, however, because it requires more input and coordination from both the internal and external environments. Exhibit 7-1 shows a comparison of these two processes. Note that the only differences between the two approaches are in the first and second steps. The market-pull approach identifies customer values and then creatively identifies solu-

**EXHIBIT 7-1**
**A Comparison of Two New Product Processes**

| Technology-Push Process | Market-Pull Process |
|---|---|
| 1. Identify technology. | 1. Identify customer values. |
| 2. Creatively identify possible customers and applications. | 2. Creatively identify solutions and approaches. |
| 3. Do homework. | 3. Do homework. |
| 4. Validate with market research. | 4. Validate with market research. |
| 5. Test. | 5. Test. |
| 6. Launch. | 6. Launch. |

tions and approaches; the technology-push approach identifies technology and then creatively identifies possible customers and applications.

Note that there are more similarities than differences between these two new product processes. The key to success with either approach lies in pursuing each step of the process thoroughly, professionally, and objectively.

## The New Product Development Process

New product success is a vital but elusive goal for many firms. In the last two decades numerous studies have been conducted to try to determine what makes a new product succeed or fail. The research has been intensive because new product success has long been valued as essential to the economic health of a business unit and as a critical means for improving business performance. Five basic attributes are found to be of exceptional importance in new product success: (1) an open-minded, supportive, and professional management, (2) good market knowledge and strategy, (3) a unique and superior product, (4) good communication and coordination, and (5) proficiency in technological activities. An effective new product development process must be firmly in place and operational within the organization if the company is going to remain viable and effective in the marketplace. The new product development process shown in Exhibit 7-2 shows the six phases management must address to offer the best chance for the product's success. The student should note that this

**EXHIBIT 7-2**
**The New Product Development Process**

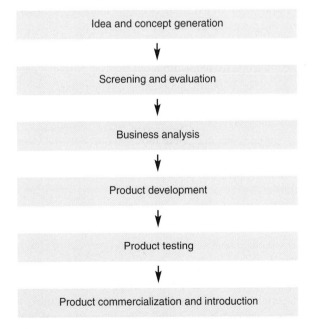

Idea and concept generation

↓

Screening and evaluation

↓

Business analysis

↓

Product development

↓

Product testing

↓

Product commercialization and introduction

new product development process is more appropriate for proprietary or catalog products than it is for custom-built or custom-designed products. The following discussion will explore each of the six phases in this process.

### Idea and Concept Generation

The **idea and concept generation** phase involves the search for product ideas or concepts that meet company objectives. These new ideas often will come from the customer, although the sales department's distributors, suppliers, other employees, and research and development play an important role in this effort.

Many marketing analysts suggest that an open perspective is essential for generating new ideas. For example, a 3M employee came up with the idea for notepaper that could be stuck to telephones, desks, paper, and walls by a small adhesive strip on the back. The employee thought of the idea because his placemark kept falling out of his hymn book during church choir practice. Today, annual sales of Post-It self-stick notes are over $40 million. Likewise, top managers at Lockheed Corporation encourage entrepreneurship among their staff members, welcoming new ideas for products and processes from all workers and giving individuals and groups seed money to nurture those ideas. These entrepreneurs (or "intrapreneurs," to use another catchphrase) are given timetables to prove their ideas have merit. They are not penalized for failure; rather, they are encouraged to learn from their mistakes and to try again.

### Screening and Evaluation

The next phase is a **screening and evaluation** to determine which ideas submitted merit a detailed study as to potential feasibility and market acceptance. A screening process can focus company energies on creating and developing products that have greater likelihood of succeeding in the marketplace. For its internal screening and evaluation phase, Medtronic, a high-technology medical firm, applies the weighted-point system shown in Exhibit 7-3. This system establishes screening criteria and assigns weights to each criterion used to evaluate new product ideas. The 17 specific factors in the exhibit are grouped into six categories commonly cited as reasons for new product failures. Medtronic believes that a total score of at least 120 points is needed on the point system to find a winning new product.

The nature of this part of the analysis can be indicated by a series of questions meant to be informative but not exhaustive:

1. Do we have or can we develop access to the necessary raw materials?
2. Is the project's scope feasible within our existing financial capability?
3. Is there some synergy within our existing product line?
4. Is it likely that our present customers represent a potential market, or must we develop entirely new markets?
5. Could the product be marketed through our existing sales force and distributor organization?
6. Does the idea appear to be within the capability of our product development organization?
7. What impact would the successful development of this product have on our existing products, markets, and marketing organization?
8. Can the new product be manufactured within our existing production facilities and with our existing skills?

Negative answers to several such questions, or the recognition that significant new financial, managerial, marketing, production, or supplier resources would be required, would reduce the attractiveness and feasibility of producing the new product.

**EXHIBIT 7-3** **Medtronic's Weighted-Point System for Evaluating New Product Ideas**

| General factor | Specific factor | Scale | Total points |
|---|---|---|---|
| Size of target market | Incidence of malady | Undefinable (0) — 10,000s (5) — 1,000,000s (10) ✓ — (15) — 100,000,000s (20) | 12 |
| | Product usage | One per many patients (0) — One per patient (5) ✓ | 5 |
| | Cost-effective for health care system | No (0) — (5) ✓ — Yes (10) | 7 |
| | Application of product | Other (0) ✓ — Spine (5) — Brain (10) — Brain-heart (15) — Heart (20) | 3 |
| Significant point of difference | Treatment evaluation | Similar to existing approaches (0) — Better than existing approaches (5) — Clearly superior to existing approaches (10) ✓ | 10 |
| | Clearness of function | Questioned or uncertain (0) — (5) ✓ — Direct cause and effect (10) | 8 |
| Product quality | Restore natural physiology | (0) — (5) ✓ — Partial (10) — (15) — Total (20) | 6 |
| | Restore viability | (0) — (5) — Partial (10) ✓ — (15) — Full (20) | 13 |
| | Characteristic of product | Capital Equipment (0) — External (5) — Permanently worn (10) — Implantable (15) ✓ — Totally implanted (20) | 20 |
| | Mode of operation | (0) — Chemical (5) ✓ — Mechanical (10) — Electrical-mechanical (15) — Electrical (20) | 7 |
| | Product development team | Physician only (0) — Engineer only — Physician and engineer (5) ✓ — Physician with engineering training (10) | 6 |
| Access to market | Physician users know Medtronic name? | No (0) — Some (50%) (5) — Yes (all) (10) ✓ | 10 |
| | Inventor's ability, willingness to be champion | Not well-known, Not willing to promote (0) — (5) ✓ — (10) — (15) — Well-known, Willing to promote (20) | 8 |
| Timing | Technologies in place | No (0) — Partially (5) ✓ — Yes (10) | 6 |
| | Entrepreneur in place | No (0) ✓ — Partially (5) — Totally (10) | 4 |
| | Social acceptance | Negative (0) — (5) — Positive (10) ✓ | 8 |
| Miscellaneous | Gut feel about success | (0) — Uncertain (5) — Good chance (10) ✓ — Positive (15) — Highly positive (20) | 12 |
| **Total** | | | **145** |

### Business Analysis

The **business analysis** phase, along with the remaining phases in the process, expands the idea or the concept through creative analysis into a "go" or "no go" recommendation. Management examines return-on-investment criteria as well as competition and the potential for profitable market entry. A more specific list of considerations during the business analysis stage includes demand projections, cost projections, competition, required investment, and profitability. Further, business marketers sometimes use break-even analysis, discounted cash flow, the Bayesian decision model, and simulation models to assess the likely profitability of promising new product ideas.

### Product Development

The **product development** phase takes the product to a state of readiness for product and market testing. Activities during this particular stage are more difficult and time consuming than many would expect. Something that looks great on paper can fail miserably when scientists, engineers, and production technicians try to create the physical product. Many new product ideas are either abandoned or sent back for more study at this point in the development process.

### Product Testing

The firm conducts commercial experiments necessary to verify earlier business judgments during the **product testing** phase. Testing takes place both in the laboratory and in the field and usually involves pilot production testing as well as market testing for acceptance or rejection. More companies now are turning to market testing to indicate the product's performance under actual operating conditions, the key buying influencers, reactions to alternative price and sales approaches, the market potential, and the best market segments to pursue. Some market test methods commonly used by business marketers in the new product development process include product use tests and trade shows, along with distributor and dealer display rooms. The market test does not come without risk, however. While product testing is necessary to some degree, there is a danger of tipping the firm's hand to the competition during field testing.

### Product Commercialization and Introduction

The final phase of development involves launching the new product through full-scale production and sales and committing the company's reputation and resources to the product's success. The **product commercialization and introduction** phase is critical in any new product development process. The success of the product is likely to depend heavily on how well marketing managers deal with the launch.[5]

Although the new product development process is complex, difficult, interdisciplinary, challenging, and expensive, it is nonetheless vital to sustain the profitable growth of the firm. A primary purpose of this process is to eliminate new product ideas that do not seem feasible before extensive resources are expended on a potential product failure. New product ideas within the development process follow a characteristic decay curve, with a progressive elimination of product ideas during each stage of the process. Exhibit 7-4 illustrates product idea elimination as new products move through the stages of the development process.

## Organization of the New Product Effort

In most B2B firms, the new product development effort involves a complex structure of line and staff relationships, with several departments involved in the development of new product ideas. The problem of fusing these individuals and groups in a manner that will

**EXHIBIT 7-4**
**Typical Mortality Rate of New Products by Stage of Development**

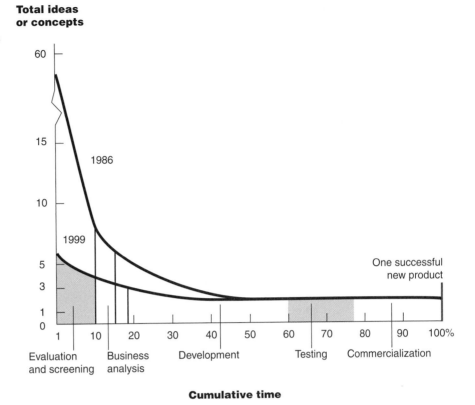

bring maximum productivity for the new product and will not jeopardize their effectiveness in producing and marketing existing products is one of the most difficult problems that management faces. U.S. companies must make a special effort to extend participation in the new product process to include all departments (including sales), as well as customers, end users, suppliers, production-equipment makers, and long-range planners. There are a number of ways that management can get these players involved in the new product effort. Some of these will now be discussed.

## Product Manager

Product management often is viewed as one of the more effective organizational forms for multiproduct firms. A **product manager** is charged with the success of a product or product line. The overall responsibility of the product manager is to integrate the various segments of a business into a strategically focused whole, maximizing the value of a product by his/her knowledge of changing market needs.[6] Product managers in the business market often are considered to play a role equivalent to that of brand managers in the consumer market. Exhibit 7-5 lists typical responsibilities of business product managers. Notice the wide variety of tasks for which product managers are responsible and the technical nature of some of those tasks. Some organizations, such as the B2C firm Procter & Gamble, also assign product managers to new product development. This activity, sometimes referred to as a functional structure option of new products development,[7] usually results in very little project focus primarily because the product manager along with representatives from various other departments are very busy with existing responsibilities to their existing product or product line. Product managers that take on new product development, thus, take on twice their normal responsibilities and must divide their activities between the new product and the old. New products that are developed with this sort of structure are often those

# BUSINESS MARKETING IN ACTION

## PRODUCT REQUIREMENTS COMMUNICATION

Continuous learning and innovation are fundamental requirements both for companies and for business professionals. In the past, marketers' involvement ended where detailed technical requirements started, but "leaving the details to the engineers" is no longer acceptable in current competitive markets. To provide value to the customer, marketers must know the company's technical capabilities and how they can be applied to meet the customer's technical requirements. As you look at the myriad products you come in contact with today, the details of virtually all of their components were designed and communicated by engineering drawings and product specifications. Engineering drawings (such as those shown here) are used to show shape, dimensions, and details; specification describes the properties of items purchased in bulk or liquid form. Business marketers should be able to understand these drawings and their role in almost every purchase process and new product innovation.

In interpreting engineering drawings, the idea is to visualize the product in three dimensions by looking at a front view, a top view, a bottom view, a left side view, and a right side view. The order of presentation of these views is not important. The intent is to visualize the whole by looking at the views from each direction. In an actual drawing, engineering views may be omitted if they do not provide additional information. For example, for the part shown below, the right side view and the bottom view of the part might be left out. Question: How many views would it take to fully define a sphere? How many to define a cube? How many to define an unwrapped stick of gum?

In an engineering drawing for an actual part, all dimensions and information required to manufacture the part have to be shown (this drawing shows only some of the necessary dimensions). Thus, when customers ask a component supplier to bid on a part (of the customer's design), they must supply drawings that are clear and complete. Indeed, supplier estimators are not happy when their salespeople bring them incomplete drawings from which to work. A missing dimension, allowable tolerance on a dimension, or incomplete material specification can invalidate the estimator's work, resulting in the need for additional operations or an entirely different process.

**Simplified Part Drawing**

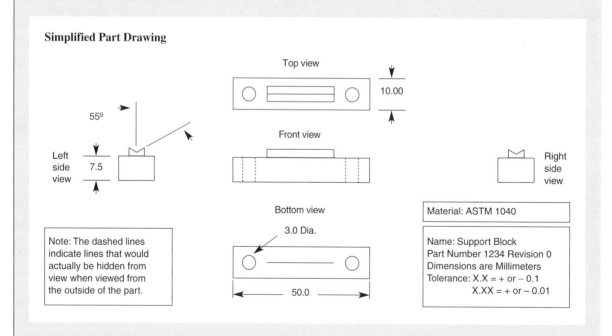

Note: The dashed lines indicate lines that would actually be hidden from view when viewed from the outside of the part.

Material: ASTM 1040

Name: Support Block
Part Number 1234 Revision 0
Dimensions are Millimeters
Tolerance: X.X = + or − 0.1
X.XX = + or − 0.01

*(continued on next page)*

*(continued from previous page)*

### Action Assignment

The customer has requested a 2mm increase in the overall height and a 4.25 mm decrease in the overall length of a given part. The customer wants to know: (1) how long it will take to manufacture, (2) the cost to make the change, and (3) whether the final product price will change. The product is a support block produced in low quantity and used to support the center of a nonrotating shaft that is 300 millimeters long.

As product manager, your group is assigned to calculate as much of this information as possible. Be prepared to present your findings to management (the class). As a student, you may be unaware of how such a product would be produced. As a future marketer, however, you will find resources all around you to draw upon (you might consider asking a local manufacturer or even an engineering student to be a resource). In this exercise, more important than the numbers themselves is your ability to clearly define the steps in the process. Be sure to do a professional job, since at least one other team will likely be making a similar report.

Another group will be assigned to utilize the value analysis process (as explained in Chapter 4) and present its recommended product improvements and innovations. Be sure to present the results as professionally as a marketer would present them to a professional buyer.

| | |
|---|---|
| **EXHIBIT 7-5**<br>**Typical Responsibilities of Product Managers in the Business Market** | Oversee progress of product(s)<br>Decide the nature of, or initiate changes in, ongoing products<br>Initiate product reengineering<br>Determine product deletion<br>Determine product phaseout<br>Determine markets to enter or depart<br>Initiate and control new product conceptualization<br>Have responsibility for product profitability<br>Develop and present product's budget requests<br>Initiate process changes | Initiate promotional strategy<br>Initiate market research analysis<br>Set pricing strategy<br>Develop sales goals and objectives<br>Attend product committee meetings<br>Develop product control criteria<br>Have chief responsibility and decide which new products are added<br>Determine product's channel of distribution<br>Chair product committee meetings<br>Decide the type of promotional mix to be used<br>Control packaging requirements and changes |

that involve very little risk and will probably be some sort of modification of an existing product of the firm.

## New Product Manager

A more innovative type of structure for new product development is the **new product manager** structure. This structure is used in many B2C firms such as Kraft and Johnson & Johnson. New product managers plan, organize, implement, and control new product development; they also manage the product as it travels through its life cycle. The new product management approach requires the new product manager to move the new product from the idea generation stage to the product introduction stage—complete with service, technical assistance, and performance feedback. Union Carbide, Bell Helicopter, Texas Instruments, Uniroyal and General Dynamics all have subscribed to the new product management concept. An advantage to this structure is that the new product function is professionalized and is no longer something that is done when busy managers are able to find the time. A problem with many new product managers is that, perhaps to reduce risk, they have a propensity to think only in terms of modifying existing products and/or line extensions targeted toward existing market segments.

## New Product Committee

The **new product committee** approach involves a top management committee, comprising representatives from marketing, production, accounting, engineering, and other areas, that reviews new product proposals. Though not necessarily involved in the actual development process, the committee is charged with evaluating new product proposals. This approach allows for a minimum of organizational disruption. Generally, new product committee participation is a part-time activity, secondary to the needs of a particular department within the firm. A disadvantage to this form of organizational structure is the possibility that demands of departmental priorities might supersede those of the committee. Nonetheless, most firms must feel that the advantages of using a new product committee outweigh the disadvantages because the new product committee is the most common form of organizational structure for managing new products.

### New Product Department

The **new product department** generates and evaluates new product ideas, directs and coordinates development work, and implements field testing and precommercialization of the new product. This arrangement allows for a maximum effort in new product development but incurs major overhead costs in the process. The department head typically has substantial authority and relatively easy access to top management.

### New Product Venture Team

The **new product venture team** represents various departments and gives responsibility for new product implementation to a full-time task force. Members of this team are charged with bringing a specific product to the market or a specific new business into being. This approach consolidates the communication between technical, marketing, and internal resource experts, resulting in sharing of information, an appreciation of other perspectives, and more rapid decision making. Marketing's role is to coordinate, integrate, and lead the process to implementation.[8] The venture team normally is dissolved once a new product is established in the market.

Signode Industries creates independent venture teams in which half the members have a technical background and half are drawn from marketing and sales. The company, which was founded in 1916 and went private in recent years in a leveraged buyout, is a $750 million producer of steel and plastic strapping systems and business products. How do its venture teams work? After two weeks of listening to outside experts talk about trends and possible opportunities, a team spends about six months searching for unmet or unperceived market needs. Its only preconceived direction is that the company's strategic strengths should be emphasized. The full-time task of the team members, performed away from the company itself, is to generate new product ideas. Team members are challenged to be creative and to encourage one another in soliciting new product ideas. They search widely for information and ideas, with sensitivity to research and development, but using a market-driven, customer-oriented approach. They narrow their list of ideas from a few hundred to two or three at a later stage, and eventually, they carry a product to market.[9]

| **Concept Review** | 1. Why is there less risk involved with market pull than with technology push?<br><br>2. What does the new product development process involve in most business-to-business companies? | 3. What are some advantages in the product manager form of new product effort? In the new product venture team form? |
|---|---|---|

## Product Life-Cycle Analysis

The *product life cycle* (PLC) is a concept that explains how products go through four distinct stages from birth to death. As you will recall, these stages are introduction, growth, maturity, and decline. All new products will go through this cycle, even industrial products,[10] so the management of new products throughout their useful lives is of paramount

## BUSINESS MARKETING IN ACTION

### JAPAN INCREASES OVERSEAS PROCUREMENT OF PARTS AND COMPONENTS

*Focus Japan,* published internationally (monthly) by the Japanese External Trade Organization (JETRO), has reported an increasing trend for Japanese manufacturers to purchase component parts from overseas suppliers. Facing tremendous price pressure from world competitors, Japanese manufacturers are searching for cost savings from foreign suppliers, but only if the suppliers can meet rigid Japanese specifications. Japanese manufacturers report that continuing quality and technological improvements in European, North American, and East Asian supplier industries will now allow their products to be considered.

Toyota Motor Corporation has set up a system to select the most beneficial and competitive suppliers from anywhere in the world and assist them through a qualification process. To ensure that the purchasing process is made even fairer and more open, Toyota provides a Supplier's Guide that clarifies procedures, selection criteria, projected product needs, and the location of all purchasing offices. If selected new suppliers have difficulty meeting all of Toyota's expectations, the automaker will dispatch specialists to help improve supplier systems. JETRO points out that Toyota's policy of nurturing suppliers is an indication of how earnestly the automaker is pursuing overseas procurement.

### Action Assignment

As product manager for XYZ Automotive Subassemblies, evaluate the JETRO website (http://www.jetro.go.jp) as a resource for your efforts to become an overseas supplier to Japanese industry. Prepare your report to company management (the class) in a professional manner because at least one other team will make a similar report.

**Source:** *Focus Japan,* March 1997.

importance. The **product life-cycle model** and new product development have been emphasized frequently in the marketing literature in showing how sales of a product vary over time and how every product eventually becomes obsolete. While life cycles once were measured in years, more often they are measured today in months. For example, the average effective life span for commercial electronics is only two years. At 3M, products fewer than five years old account for 25 percent of sales.[11] Exhibit 7-6 reflects that sales grow sharply during the growth stage but begin to flatten out during the maturity stage of the product life cycle. Sales reach their peak during the maturity stage, then dramatically fall off during the decline stage. Information from the product life-cycle analysis has been used to suggest effective marketing strategies over a product's projected life span. While the shapes of the sales-volume and profit-margin curves will vary from product to product, the relationship between the curves is illustrated in Exhibit 7-6. Note that profit peaks during the growth stage, whereas sales top out during the maturity stage.

**EXHIBIT 7-6**
**How Sales and Profits of a Business Product Vary over Time**

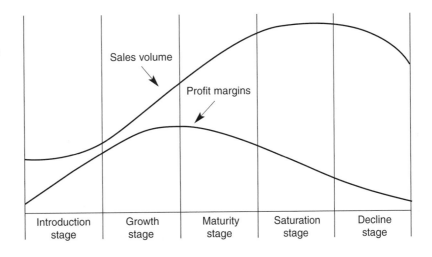

It is important that management recognize a product's stage in the life cycle at any given time because the competitive environment and the resultant marketing strategies reflect that position. As a product moves through the PLC, some strategic elements that come into play in making business marketing decisions include competitor strategy, return on investment requirements, distribution coverage decisions, and advertising strategy. The product life cycle should be looked upon as a dynamic model, as opposed to a static one.

**Learning curve analysis**, linked with the product life cycle, is another base for developing business product strategy. It has long been observed that manufacturing costs seem to fall with cumulative experience, and not just with scale of production. The relationship between cumulative production and labor cost is known as the *learning curve.*

In the 1960s, evidence began mounting that this phenomenon was broader than originally thought. The Boston Consulting Group (1970), in particular, showed that each time cumulative volume of production of a product doubled, marginal value-added costs—including sales, administration, and so on—fell by a constant percentage. This relationship between marginal costs and cumulative production became known as the *experience curve.* For example, the curve in Exhibit 7-7 is an 85 percent experience curve. With every doubling of experience, costs per unit drop to 85 percent of their original level—a 15 percent reduction in cost for every doubling of cumulative production. Studies of numerous industries support the experience curve phenomenon, including the chemical, steel, paper, and electronics industries. The learning curve concept is especially relevant in high-technology markets such as semiconductors and computer memories.

The learning curve phenomenon was discovered in the 1920s in the aircraft industry and was subsequently reported in 1936.[12] Simply stated, the rate of learning is such that as the quantity of units manufactured doubles, the number of direct labor hours it takes to produce an individual unit decreases at a uniform rate.

In a related concept, the term **economies of scale** (often confused with the experience curve) refers to the production efficiency attained as increased units are produced. It is a fixed-cost phenomenon because an increase in production seldom requires an equivalent increase in capital investment, size of the sales force, or overhead costs. In a stable environment, the firm will realize economies of scale by producing a uniform product, with perceivable demand, thereby guaranteeing efficiencies and higher profit levels. Learning, per se, helps the firm not only to increase profit levels but also to lower the break-even quantity. The result is a reduction in fixed costs because these are being spread over many additional units.

**EXHIBIT 7-7**
**An 85 Percent Learning Curve Requiring 1.0 Direct Labor Hour to Manufacture the First Unit (K = 1)**

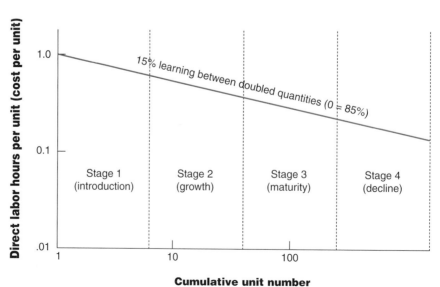

## BUSINESS MARKETING IN ACTION

### AUTOMOTIVE AIR-CONDITIONING CONTROLS

In most pre-1980 automobiles, the technology of choice for directing cool airflow was based on using vacuum from the engine. A mechanical switch provided power to the air-conditioning unit but also rotated a polymer plate faced with a complicated maze of routes for the vacuum to follow down various tubes. In those days, passengers who turned the air on or shifted the cool airflow from the back seats to the front heard a distinctive "whoosh" as the control switch turned and the vacuum opened or shut the appropriate vents. Initially, switches and tube systems tended to wear out and eventually leak, allowing cool air to be blocked or directed to the wrong areas. To improve this situation required considerable research and development, and companies specializing in these products were created.

Imagine the impact on these fairly high-tech companies when technological improvements in electronics led the automotive OEMs to shift the design to all-electronic systems. It is a typical "marketing myopia" problem, reflected in a component manufacturer's mission statement that read: We make vacuum air-conditioning switches for cars. Likewise, when plastics were developed that could outperform applications in which metal had traditionally been used, more changes ensued. The original air-conditioning switch probably had metal die cast and plated pieces (with the surfaces exposed on the dash plated with chrome). Now much of the system is plastic, is all electronic, and is even computer controlled.

Clearly, technological innovation is increasing at an increasing rate, and marketers today have to deal with it much more than those of the past. Companies that continue to thrive will employ marketers who find opportunities and solutions in environments of rapid and dramatic technological change. For instance, the manufacturers of the electronic components discussed in the example used a technology change to create a new buy situation in the buying centers at the automotive OEMs. They redefined the product, its application, and the industry sector from which it would be purchased.

### Action Assignment

Research the evolution of automotive air-conditioning and alternative future directions in automotive design. Predict the next probable evolutionary leap in air-conditioning approach and controls. As a team, take the initiative in figuring out where to look and who to interview for information.

The task at hand is to explore what happens to a product as it proceeds from one stage of the product life cycle to the next. The following discussion of model relationships examines how the learning curve can help to clarify the product life cycle.

### Introduction

**Product introduction,** the initial phase of the learning curve, represents the highest-cost stage. Initial costs are high, but they drop rapidly with additional units produced. This phenomenon is vividly demonstrated for three different learning curves in Exhibit 7-8. Given

**EXHIBIT 7-8** Cost of a Specific Unit for Three Different Learning Curves All Having a First-Unit Cost of $10

| Cumulative Number of Units Made | 90% Learning Curve | 85% Learning Curve | 80% Learning Curve |
|---|---|---|---|
| 1 | $10.00 | $10.00 | $10.00 |
| 2 | 9.00 | 8.50 | 8.00 |
| 3 | 8.46 | 7.73 | 7.02 |
| 4 | 8.10 | 7.22 | 6.40 |
| 8 | 7.29 | 6.14 | 5.12 |
| 16 | 6.56 | 5.22 | 4.10 |
| 32 | 5.90 | 4.44 | 3.28 |
| 64 | 5.31 | 3.77 | 2.62 |
| 1,000 | 3.50 | 1.98 | 1.08 |
| 10,000 | 2.47 | 1.15 | .52 |
| 100,000 | 1.74 | .67 | .24 |
| 1,000,000 | 1.22 | .39 | .12 |
| 10,000,000 | .86 | .23 | .06 |
| 20,000,000 | .78 | .19 | .04 |

an 85 percent learning curve, if the cost to make the first unit is $10.00, the cost to make the thousandth unit will be only $1.98.

This phase of the learning curve is labeled Stage 1 in order for it to coincide with the introductory stage of the product life cycle shown in Exhibit 7-7. The slope of the learning curve reflects that sales are lowest here, as the innovative firm tries to drive its costs down. As cost and price decrease, the product appeals to more users, resulting in increased sales.

## Market Growth

In the **market growth** stage of the product life cycle, rapid growth occurs, accompanied by dramatic cost decreases. During this stage, the innovative firm should be utilizing cost decreases, as described by the learning curve, to its advantage in keeping costs below those of the competition. If the firm manages to succeed in this effort, it can also expand its market share, use price as a competitive weapon, and still generate an adequate profit margin.

## Market Maturity

During the **market maturity** stage, cumulative volume reaches the point at which costs are about as low as they are going to get. (The data in Exhibit 7-8 demonstrate this point.) For example, if a firm is riding an 80 percent learning curve and has built up a cumulative volume of 10 million units, an increase in volume to 20 million units would drop its cost by only two cents (that is, for a first-unit cost of $10.00). Because further significant cost decreases are difficult to achieve, market penetration into new user segments is very slow. What the learning curve adds to the understanding of the maturity stage of the life cycle is that lower costs are associated with market penetration, which means increased sales. In Stage 3 of the learning curve (see Exhibit 7-7), cost reductions are progressively harder to achieve; thus, maturity occurs.

## Sales Decline

The **sales decline** stage is associated with Stage 4 in Exhibit 7-7. As the market becomes saturated, sales drop off. It then becomes impossible to achieve sufficient increases in cumulative production to lower costs significantly in an attempt to stimulate sales. As a result, marginal producers drop out of the market.

Other learning curve variations and their hypothesized effect on the product life cycle have been explored in depth. One theory contends that more frequent use of the learning curve will lead to enlightened marketing strategies by fostering closer cooperation between the production and marketing functions within business-to-business firms. The experience curve can create the tendency to formulate marketing policies in a vacuum because it deals with price rather than costs. Hence, the use of the learning curve in the marketing strategy selection process should help circumvent this apparent tendency.

# Determinants of the Product Mix

In planning, marketers develop a course of action that reflects a consistent pattern of decisions regarding profits, market share, sales, and cash flow. In planning, the fundamental determinants of a firm's product mix are identified, including product line depth and product mix width. The need to make such determinations continues to grow, as recent trends in market dynamics and in technology development have increased the frequency and importance of decisions concerning product mix changes. Management's role is to adjust to these forces as much as the enterprise's resources will permit, and to direct the firm along product paths that lead to future growth and profits. The determinants of the product mix discussed here are technology, computation, changes in levels of business activity, operating capacity, and market factors.

## Technology

In times of rapid technological and market change, successful firms will be the leaders not only in adopting new technology but also in introducing new technology for competitive reasons. New technology provides the means for effective product innovation. Indeed, in many industries new technology can cause a product to become obsolete virtually overnight. A prime example is the electronics industry, in which myriad inventions have led to dynamic change in products.

Technological shifts in product use and application require that firms maintain continuous contact with customers. By observing and monitoring customers, marketers can detect variations in user needs and preferences that might suggest technological shifts in product use. These are the vital signs of impending product change, signaling opportunities to introduce new products or variations or improvements to existing products.

## Competition

A second important determinant of an industrial firm's product mix is the changes in product offerings of the competition. A change in a competitor's product mix could represent a major challenge. Indeed, if that change is truly a significant improvement, such as a technological breakthrough, it may prove disastrous unless it can be matched or surpassed within a reasonable length of time.

Over the past several years, American companies have experienced dramatic changes in their domestic competitive environments. Small specialized competitors have exited or been swallowed up by larger multi-industry companies, often resulting in competition that is stronger and financially solvent, but more unpredictable. Foreign and multinational competitors have taken aim at the more profitable U.S. markets, which are easier to penetrate and pivotal to worldwide success, while building and maintaining barriers to entry by the U.S. companies themselves. This competitive change has not been limited to new configurations of traditional competitors; it has also included a considerable number of new companies and the introduction of new types of products that are complete substitutions for current offerings.

## Changes in Levels of Business Activity

Most industrial firms must deal with changes in business activity due to business cycles and seasonal variations. Many firms expand their total product offering by adding product lines having different seasonal patterns to offset their present lines. This strategy helps to smooth out production and sales volume levels throughout the year. Likewise, some firms add product lines that are less sensitive to business-cycle variations than are their existing lines.

The history of industrial output is impacted clearly by cycles of "bull or bear" stock markets and recessions followed by periods of expansion. Traditionally, production at many important industries (such as high-ticket durables) has fluctuated with business cycles, and those industries most affected are well known to business professionals and are regarded as cyclical industries. When the automotive or appliance industry is in high gear, for example, it is difficult for component parts, process material, and service suppliers to ignore the high volume and sales potential. In contrast, if a marketer lacks balance and diversification in customer industries, the company may fail when traditionally cyclical industries slow down.

## Operating Capacity

A business-to-business firm often will expand its product mix if it discovers underutilized capacity in any part of its operations. The underutilized capacity might be in any functional area, such as production, sales, or research. For example, when a firm buys new equipment, there may be a period in which the equipment is not totally utilized in satisfying existing demand and there is pressure on management to use it in alternate ways by manufacturing altogether new products. Similarly, when a marketing organization is set up to serve a particular market for a single product line, often it becomes apparent that the sales force could handle other lines as well; pressure is then generated to find new products that also can be sold profitably to that market.

## Market Factors

Several market factors impact the selling firm's product mix. A change in the business buyer's product mix, due to competitive action or technological innovation, could present an opportunity to sell additional quantities of various products or an opportunity to capitalize on additional business. Additionally, the migration of industry into an area economically served by the business producer could help to offset losses from outward migration. Such activity, along with an increase or decrease in production capabilities, can lead to changes in the business product mix.

**Concept Review**

1. What is the fundamental marketing value of product life-cycle analysis?
2. What is the value of experience curve analysis to the business marketing manager?
3. What is the role of competition in determining an industrial firm's product mix?

## The Product Adoption–Diffusion Process

Business marketers must not only estimate the duration of a new product success but also evaluate the substitution "fit" for a proposed new product. In other words, if a company decides to expand its product mix, business marketers must assess how quickly prospects will adopt a new product and to what extent it will be accepted as a replacement for the old.

The **adoption process** is the decision-making activity of the buying firm through which the new product or innovation is accepted. The **diffusion process**, in turn, is the process by which the product or service is accepted by an industry over time.

### Stages in the Adoption Process

There are many similarities between the consumer in the consumer adoption process and the members of the business buying center, as both groups go through a five-step process in deciding whether to adopt something new.

#### Awareness

At this stage, the buyer first learns of the new product or service, but he or she knows little about it. The buyer might develop awareness by being exposed to sales promotion, talking with other buyers, or by casually conversing with another member of the buying center.

#### Interest

The buyer might seek out additional information about the product or service by requesting additional data from the potential seller or, perhaps, by requesting that a member of the potential supplier's sales team make a sales call.

#### Evaluation

At this stage, the buyer (or another member of the buying center) considers whether the new product or service would be useful. This deliberation might lead to a value analysis project or, quite possibly, to a make-or-buy decision.

### Trial

In this stage, the buyer adopts the innovation on a limited basis, making a trial purchase in order to evaluate carefully the correctness of the decision to buy. If the new product or service is very expensive, radically new, or quite complex, the prospect might perceive the risk of a trial purchase to be greater than its benefits. In contrast, less expensive and less complex products might be distributed as free samples, with the goal of inducing prospects to try the new offering by reducing their perceived risk.

### Adoption

If the trial purchase works as expected, then the buyer might likely decide to use the product regularly. Likewise, if the trial falls short of buyer expectations, then the product or service probably will be rejected, at least for the time being.

### Diffusion Process

The adoption process, then, is a series of stages that a member of the buying center goes through in deciding whether to buy and make regular use of a new product or service. The diffusion process goes beyond the adoption process, representing the spread of a new product, innovation, or service throughout an industry over time. The speed with which the industrial diffusion process takes place varies among industries, being very fast in the electronics industry and possibly quite slow in the domestic steel industry. As with the adoption process, there are many similarities between the consumer group proceeding through the diffusion process and the members of the business buying center (representing a particular industry) proceeding as a group through the diffusion process over time. As shown in Exhibit 7-9, at first, a few firms (innovators) adopt, and then the number of adopters increases rapidly (early adopters and early majority) as the value of the product innovation or service becomes apparent. The rate finally diminishes as fewer potential buyers (late majority and laggards) remain in the nonadopter category. By the time laggards adopt something new, it may already have been discarded by the innovator group in favor of a newer idea or technology.

## Factors Influencing the Rate of Adoption–Diffusion

The acceptance of new products and the time a product spends in the introductory stage vary greatly among business-to-business firms. Some products diffuse very slowly into a particular market, while others may almost bypass the diffusion stage. Perceived advantage and perceived risk play a part, along with common barriers to adoption such as being tied

**EXHIBIT 7-9**
**The Product**
**Diffusion Process**

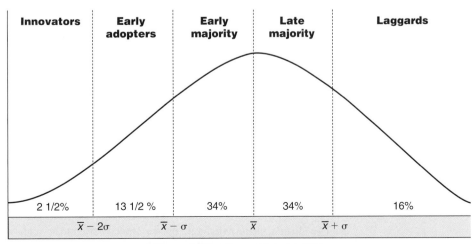

**Time of Adoption of Innovations**

to an existing facility or incompatibility with existing products. Products that require major changes in manufacturing processes, or those that require a large outlay of capital, tend to diffuse slowly.

Another factor affecting a product's acceptance is technological uncertainty. Will the technology function as expected when placed into volume production? How about the perceived likelihood of technological obsolescence? What about the unpredictable quality of a new product or innovation, or other emerging technologies that can provide similar advantages? These and other factors force some potential customers to take a wait-and-see attitude before committing to a new product adoption.

While this information may seem useful, but of little practical consequence, this material is, in fact, quite critical to your function as a marketer. The adoption process is closely attached to your strategic action plan, as all those activities move the buyer through the adoption process. The rate of adoption thus will be the foundation for your forecasts, which will be used throughout the company. Clearly, these are critical concepts that every marketer must be able to apply skillfully to real situations.

## Product Portfolio Classification, Analysis, and Strategy

Today, the underlying principle guiding new product development combines external market needs with internal functional strength. This combination allows companies to develop a product portfolio that satisfies corporate strategic objectives. **Portfolio classification models** often are used to give a visual display of the present and prospective positions of business products according to the attractiveness of the market and the ability to compete within the market. The business marketer must regularly review the product portfolio, developing strategic alternatives for each of the company's current products, businesses, and prospects for new customers. The concept of the product portfolio emphasizes viewing products not individually, but as parts of a total system. This perspective invites management's regular review of strategic alternatives and corresponding resource allocation decisions.

### What Is a Product Portfolio?

A **product portfolio** is the firm's offering of products or divisions, each of which can be identified as a **strategic business unit (SBU)**, and most of which operate as a separate profit center that may or may not have its own management, its own set of identifiable markets and competitors, and its own marketing strategies. The industrial firm's product portfolio typically consists of related businesses and/or products grouped into SBUs that are homogeneous enough to control most factors affecting their performance. Resources are allocated to SBUs in proportion to their contribution to the corporate objectives of growth and profitability. The challenge is to identify the SBUs in the firm's product portfolio that enhance the overall corporate mission, while withdrawing support for those that do not.

The concept of the product portfolio was first put forth by the founder of the Boston Consulting Group, Bruce Henderson, in a booklet published in 1970. Henderson looked at a firm's products or divisions as a mix of businesses that strategically interact and influence one another, principally in terms of their use of resources and the development of these resources against opportunities in a competitive marketplace. He described and evaluated products and divisions in terms of three dimensions:

1. The attractiveness of the market, especially in light of the SBU's stage in the product life cycle.
2. The business-to-business firm's position in the market in terms of market share.
3. The firm's acknowledged or perceived strengths and weaknesses, relative to competitors.

**EXHIBIT 7-10   Strategy Implications of Products in the Product Portfolio Quadrants**

| Quadrant | Investment Characteristics | Earning Characteristics | Cash-Flow Characteristics | Strategy Implication |
|---|---|---|---|---|
| Stars | Continual expenditures for capacity expansion<br><br>Pipeline filling with cash | Low to high | Negative cash flow (net cash user) | Continue to increase market share, if necessary, at the expense of short-term earnings |
| Cash cows | Capacity maintenance expenditures | High | Positive cash flow (net cash contributor) | Maintain share and cost leadership until further investment becomes marginal |
| Question marks | Heavy initial capacity expenditures<br><br>High R & D costs | Negative to low | Negative cash flow (net cash user) | Assess changes of dominating segment; if good, go after share; if bad, redefine business or withdraw |
| Dogs | Gradually deplete capacity | High to low | Positive cash flow (net cash contributor) | Plan an orderly withdrawal so as to maximize cash flow |

## Diagnosing the Product Portfolio

Business units can be classified into four categories. Businesses in each category exhibit different financial characteristics and offer different strategic choices. The four types of SBUs include stars, cash cows, question marks, and dogs. If market share and growth behave as expected, then this tells a compelling cash-flow story with important investment and strategy implications. However, this is only one approach to portfolio analysis, and it is rather limited.

## Product Portfolio Strategies

In a typical business-to-business company, there are products scattered in all types of SBUs of the product portfolio. An appropriate strategy for products in each category is given briefly in Exhibit 7-10. First, a primary goal of an industrial company should be to secure a position with cash cows but also to guard against the frequent temptation to reinvest in them excessively. The cash generated from cash cows can be used to support stars that are not self-sustaining. Surplus cash might be used to finance selected question marks toward a dominant market position. Question marks that cannot be funded might be divested. A dog could be restored to a position of viability by shrewdly segmenting the market, that is, by rationalizing and specializing the business into a small niche that the product can dominate. If that approach is not feasible, the firm will weigh *harvesting* the SBU by cutting off all investment in the business, giving consideration to liquidating the unit when and if the opportunity develops (see discussion on next page).

This concept provides the business marketer with a useful synthesis of the analysis and judgments necessary as an SBU moves through the product life cycle, presenting a provocative source of strategic alternatives. The business marketer must remember that a *strategy* is a decision about what must be done; likewise, a *tactic* is a decision about how to do it. Marketing planners must plot the projected positions of each SBU under both present and alternative strategies, enabling them to decide on strategies for each SBU, the tactics to use in carrying out those strategies, and the resources to assign each SBU.

## Product Deletion Strategy

Any discussion of product development, management, and strategy would not be complete without a brief review of a very difficult business marketing decision: when to drop a product, product line, or division. In identifying and analyzing product performance deviations from established norms, management often discovers that seldom is weak product performance the result of one factor only. Often, poor sales, inadequate profit, and decline in market potential, among other factors, play roles in poor performance. Generally, a variety of factors are interrelated. In addition, noncompetitive price, production problems, inferior technology, and uneconomic production batches are other reasons cited for unsatisfactory product performance.

The idea that some products entering the decline stage of the product life cycle must be eliminated reflects the strategic thinking that every SBU plays an important part in making the product portfolio viable. When the SBU becomes a drain on the financial and managerial resources of an organization, management has three alternatives in the strategy for product deletion: harvesting, line simplification, and total-line divestment.

## Harvesting

**Harvesting** is a strategy applied to a product or business with slowly declining sales volume and/or market share. It is an effort to cut the costs associated with the SBU in order to help improve the cash flow. Harvesting leads to a slow decline in sales; when the business ceases to provide positive cash flow, it is divested. The implementation of harvesting strategy requires, where appropriate, reducing maintenance of facilities, cutting advertising and research budgets, curtailing the number and scope of channel intermediaries used, eliminating small-order customers, and reducing service levels in terms of delivery time, sales assistance, and so on. DuPont followed the harvesting strategy for its rayon business; BASF Wyandotte applied harvesting to soda ash.

## Line Simplification

**Line simplification** is a product deletion strategy that trims a product line to a manageable size by pruning the number and variety of products and services offered. This can lead to a variety of benefits, such as potential cost savings from longer production runs, reduced inventories, and a more focused concentration of marketing, research and development, and other efforts on fewer products.

The decision to drop an SBU from the product line is a difficult one to make. Despite the emotional aspects of this decision, the need for objectivity in this matter cannot be overemphasized.

## Divestment

**Divestment** is a situation of reverse acquisition and is also a key dimension of marketing strategy. Divestment decisions are principally economic or psychological in nature; they may allow the firm to restore a balanced product portfolio. If the firm has too many high-growth businesses, its resources might be inadequate to fund such growth. In contrast, if the firm has too many low-growth businesses, frequently it will generate more cash than is required for investment purposes. For the firm to grow evenly over time, while showing regular earnings increments, a portfolio of both fast- and slow-growing businesses is necessary. Divestment can help to achieve this type of balance.

---

Concept Review

1. Why will some products diffuse slowly into a particular market while others may almost bypass this stage?

2. What is the primary goal of a business firm with regard to cash cows?

3. When is harvesting of an industrial product or product line appropriate? Line simplification? Divestment?

# STRATEGY AT WORK

## MARKET ENTRY TIMING

Usually, we think of business marketing as addressing product line sales to individual business customers, but it can concern strategy and operations on a much larger scale, as well. C. J. Waylan, CEO of Constellation Communications, developed a strategic plan to enter the satellite mobile phone business well after his competitors. He hopes that the competitors will have resolved international regulatory issues and incurred all the promotional expenses to develop primary demand (for the general product category), particularly among business users. His plan is simple: "Once the competitors have paved the way, Constellation will barge in two years later with much cheaper if somewhat more limited service."

While the competition is investing in the neighborhood of $5 billion each to blanket the world with low earth-orbit satellites, Constellation is taking a conservative approach, targeting only regions that do not yet have extensive copper wire or fiber optic systems (Latin America, Africa, and Southeast Asia). With a modest $840 million string of satellites covering only the area from the Tropic of Cancer to the Tropic of Capricorn, Constellation expects to be able to charge at least 40 percent less than its competition. Waylan predicts that his product positioning strategy as the low-cost service provider will be difficult for competitors to match. Both main competitors will have much more capital investment to recover and much higher marketing costs. One competitor, Globalstar, already suffered a major setback when a rocket carrying 12 of its system's satellites crashed shortly after launching.

## Assignment

Your company produces components that may be used in portable telephones. Search your college library's business periodical database and update management (the class) on the market status of each of these companies. Also report on the information available on the companies' home Web pages.

Adapted from "Let the Big Boys Go First," *Forbes,* October 19, 1998, p. 68; "Inexpensive Standardized Satellites Deploy Payloads Faster, Better, and Cheaper," by Lee Goldberg. Electronic Design 45, April 1, 1997, pp. 100–102; and Constellation Communications website, September 26, 1997, www.cciglobal.com/news/970926/html.

## Marketing of Business Services

The market for business-to-business services is large and expanding. **Services** comprise all economic activity in which the primary output is neither a product nor a construction. In terms of an industrial life cycle, most services are now in the mature stage, analogous to the position of manufacturing firms in the 1960s and 1970s. In the same way these manufacturing firms began to engage in strategic thinking in response to a new situation, service firms today must also adopt a strategic posture.

In traditional goods marketing, the physical goods (products that are the outcomes of a production process) are the key variable around which other marketing activities revolve. When there is no good, marketing becomes different: because there is no ready-made, pre-produced object of marketing and consumption; there is only a process that cannot begin until the customer or user enters the process.[13] This can make competition in the business market intense and fierce. Business customers are becoming more professional, won't hesitate to use outsourcing strategies, and often globalize their approaches. Technological changes, the globalization of competition, and deregulation are revolutionizing markets.[14] Also, as illustrated in Exhibit 7-11, the service sector accounts for approximately 70 percent of U.S. employment and still is expanding.

Marketing slowly is coming of age in the service sector, as it becomes obvious that the most basic trend of the last half of the twentieth century was the transformation of our economy from an industrial- to a services-orientation. Providers of business services (e.g., consulting, legal, payroll, benefits, maintenance, and research and design functions) are becoming convinced of the need to adopt a greater marketing orientation. The purpose of this section is to acquaint the reader with some of the special problems and opportunities of services marketing.

**EXHIBIT 7-11**
**Employment in the Service Sector**

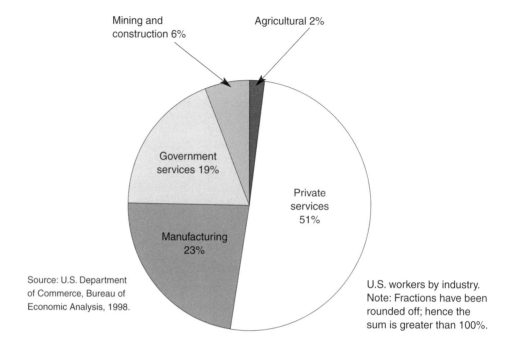

Mining and construction 6%

Agricultural 2%

Government services 19%

Private services 51%

Manufacturing 23%

Source: U.S. Department of Commerce, Bureau of Economic Analysis, 1998.

U.S. workers by industry. Note: Fractions have been rounded off; hence the sum is greater than 100%.

## Important Characteristics of Business Services

A number of characteristics not only distinguish services from goods but also impact business services marketing program development. Four characteristics are unique to services and influence the way they are marketed: intangibility, perishability and fluctuating demand, simultaneity, and heterogeneity.

### Intangibility

Services are intangible and, therefore, abstract. Most business services cannot appeal to the buyer's sense of taste, touch, sight, or hearing before buying, which places some strain on the seller's marketing organization. Proven strategies of goods marketing cannot be applied when the product being marketed cannot be seen, felt, or guaranteed to provide specific and measurable results. Because of the lack of tangibility, business service marketers find it difficult to differentiate their offerings, and as a result, services must be made tangible by visual representation and symbolism. Marketing promotion becomes critical in services marketing, since the product itself is incapable of communicating its benefits. *Intangible* products such as freight forwarding, consulting, repair, brokerage, or education seldom can be tried out or tested in advance of purchase. Buyers are forced to view advertising copy, listen to a sales presentation, or consult current users to determine how well a service will perform.

### Perishability and Fluctuating Demand

Services are perishable—they cannot be stored—and the markets for most business services fluctuate by the day, week, or season. Unused electric power, an empty airplane seat, and an idle machine in a factory all represent business that is lost forever. This combination of perishability and *fluctuating demand* has created some very special problems with regard to strategy implementation for marketers of business services. Before service levels suffer, marketers must make key decisions on the maximum amount of capacity to be available to cope with surges in demand. Further, there is a need to make decisions in times of low levels of usage on whether short-term policies (differential pricing, special promotions, and the like) will be adopted to even out fluctuations in demand. Business service marketers thus lose the valuable buffer function of inventory that allows a tangible products producer to manufacture for inventory during slow periods and to draw on inventory during periods of peak demand.

### *Simultaneity*

Production and consumption of services are inseparable: selling comes first, followed by production and consumption simultaneously. Services are used at the time they are produced, which typically puts the business marketer of services in close contact with the customer. As a result of this simultaneity, service customers tend to perceive relatively greater risk when they are shopping for a service. Word-of-mouth advertising is a significant factor in generating new business for complex, hard-to-evaluate services. In the marketing of many business services, a client relationship exists between the buyer and the seller. An example of this type of relationship would be the business consulting relationship: the buyer considers the suggestions or advice provided by the seller, and the relationship is ongoing. In addition, since many business service firms are client-serving organizations, the marketing function is very professional, as seen in financial, legal, and educational services.

### *Heterogeneity*

Heterogeneity of services is a recognition that a service is an experience and thus cannot be duplicated exactly for each customer.[15] It is difficult to standardize services, and, as a result, output can vary widely in quality. A major problem created by heterogeneity is quality control, whereby the provider of the business service can control the production but not the quality or the consumption of the service. The services marketer tries to control quality; indeed, some go to great lengths to standardize their services, in addition to investing in high-quality employees. Although standardization of some services (e.g., insurance, transportation, and utilities) has increased, it is improbable that services ever will become as standardized as most tangible goods. Further, the quality of service performance varies from one business service provider to another. Not all consulting firms, airlines, or insurance companies offer the same level of service. The quality of the service provided also will vary for the same provider from one occasion to another. For example, a group seminar presented by a psychological consulting firm, such as Nordlie Wilson, Incorporated, will achieve varying results, depending on client response and cooperation. The variability of business service output makes it difficult for the service firm to establish, maintain, and guarantee quality continuously.

## Business Services Marketing—Challenges and Opportunities

Although marketing functions are basically the same for many services and products, there is a difference in the organization and implementation for gaining a competitive advantage in business service marketing. American industry is changing. For example, General Motors, a "goods" manufacturing giant, generates 20 percent of its revenue from its financial and insurance businesses, and the car maker's biggest supplier is Blue Cross/Blue Shield, not a parts supplier or a large steel producer as you might have thought.

### *Services Marketing Versus Goods Marketing*

It is perhaps incorrect to ask whether service marketing is different or whether it requires a special marketing approach. A more appropriate focus is how to market a service successfully. Service marketers are not more marketing oriented because of their preoccupation with the unique characteristics of services. In fact, this preoccupation is somewhat myopic because it encourages service providers to ignore successful marketing techniques that have worked well for many products and could work just as well for services.

With a business product, the unit is usually well defined. This is not necessarily so in service marketing. A product can be measured objectively against specifications by checking tolerances and comparing weight, color, shape, and so on. Measuring an office-building cleaning service or a new product consulting service is not so easy. What is clean? What is efficient, feasible, and marketable? In product marketing, once the need is defined, the manufacturing process takes over. With business service marketing, however, the product is not created until the service is performed. With an office-building cleaning service, delivery of the service occurs when the vendor employees arrive to do the work. Did they do a good job? Is the office clean? Did they arrive on time?

With a business good, there is no need for a distribution channel until after a product is manufactured, packaged, priced, and ready to ship. With a business service, the channel of distribution and delivery are one and the same. That is, the employees of the office-building cleaning service are at the same time manufacturing and distributing the product. With a business product, little change can be made without substantial costs of time and money, in most cases. However, with a service provider, the product can be altered quite easily. The office-building cleaning service can provide additional services, such as window washing and carpet cleaning, on very short notice.

Finally, in tangible product development, time is required to develop, test, introduce, and provide an inventory buildup. In contrast, with a business service, the provider distributes the product—usually within a 24-hour period. Again, the office-building cleaning service offers an appropriate example.

### *Positioning Strategy*

Because a differentiated position generates superior returns only until competitive imitation takes place, business services marketers must recognize the need to formulate and implement durable strategies. The image that a business service has in the mind of the user, especially in relation to competitive offerings, follows naturally after identification of the market segment sought. When the service provider establishes and maintains a distinctive place for itself and its offerings in the market, it is said to be successfully positioned. In the increasingly competitive service sector, effective positioning is one of marketing's most critical and difficult tasks.

Competitive positioning with both services and goods is key to success in today's marketplace, as was noted in Chapter 6. Success depends on a marketer's ability to clearly differentiate the service from its competition in a way that is meaningful to the customer. Effective positioning requires marketing research—something foreign to nearly all but the best-managed business service firms. It is more complicated to research reactions to a service than to a good because potential customers find it harder to put themselves into the role of using a prospective service than of using a product that they can hold and see.

### *Bundling of Services*

Broadly defined, **bundling** is the practice of marketing two or more goods and/or services in a single "package" for a special price. Most often, a firm with a broad line of complementary products uses bundling, with its effectiveness being a function of the degree to which it stimulates demand in a way that achieves cost economies. The objective of bundling is to add value while keeping cost increments small, thus adding value without increasing price. Price bundling is, in effect, a special form of discount pricing in which two or more services are combined into a single package and sold at a special price.

Examples of bundling include the sale of a maintenance contract with computer hardware, with the lease of a truck, or with a piece of machinery. Other examples include combining software applications, optional packages for cars, menu combinations at restaurants, and season tickets for sports or art performances. The rationale for bundling is based primarily on the reality that the cost structure of most business services is characterized by a high ratio of fixed to variable costs and by a high degree of cost sharing (such that the same facilities, equipment, and personnel are used to provide multiple services).

### Service Strategy and the Marketing Mix

Since Jerome McCarthy popularized the Four Ps in 1964, marketing plans have incorporated these elements as key building blocks for marketing programs.[16] The controllable variables of *product, price, place,* and *promotion* have been the key in the development of strategy that involves identifying a target market segment and then developing a marketing program to deliver that product to members of the segment. All of these marketing mix elements must be combined into a cohesive package by the astute business service marketer.

***Product*** Improving existing services and eliminating those that are unprofitable are key strategies service providers—like marketers of products —must employ. Likewise, developing new services is as important to a business service provider as new products are to a product-marketing firm. One of the more difficult challenges managers in the service sector face is designing and introducing new service offerings. While a service orientation may not be right for all manufacturers, chief executives who ignore service opportunities risk limiting their companies' growth and losing their market position to more farsighted rivals. The growth of the service sector will not displace industry, but it will add to the economy by leveraging manufacturers' resources in a whole new way. Service businesses usually require considerably less time and money than manufacturing requires; however, it is more difficult to recruit, train, and manage employees who perform services. Clearly, the transition from a product-marketing to a service-marketing orientation is not a simple process:

> New product development is inherently more difficult, messier, and less successful in the service sector. In industry, research and development labs can usually come up with new designs that incorporate certain predictable functions and characteristics. On the other hand, when a service firm correctly, if subjectively, perceives a need, it cannot have the same confidence in its ability to deliver all the ingredients that comprise successful new service products. As a result, service organizations are more likely to be conservative about innovations. They focus most of their attention on geographical extensions of their service, or on minor modifications to the primary service package. True inventiveness is rare . . . innovation in the service sector is frequently the result of trial and error . . . original or imitative ideas exist in abundance. Yet, new ideas often ignore the deep and subtle linkages among the variables in the service package. Between imagination and execution lies a dark gulf that has swallowed up many a bright new idea.[17]

Despite the difficulties involved, every service industry has companies and managers noted for their ability to foster new product development or design and implement new internal processes. In banking, Citicorp, Basic One, and VISA are noted for their cash transfer service systems. In financial services, Merrill Lynch often is the first to produce new products that are later imitated by others. Dun and Bradstreet, too, relies on new product development for a significant share of its revenue. In communications, Dow Jones and Gannett are recognized as service innovators, as is the Marriott Corporation in the lodging industry.

***Price*** A second controllable variable of the marketing mix for services is price. The price of a service should be related to the achievement of marketing and organizational goals and should be appropriate for the service firm's overall marketing programs. In setting price objectives for services, a number of factors must be considered. The more significant of these are as follows:

- ***The Planned Market Position for the Service Product.*** How the service product is seen in relation to other like services available will clearly influence price strategy. Price is an important element in the marketing mix and, as noted earlier, influences positioning strategy. Services often are positioned on the basis of intangible attributes. Price will influence market position.

- ***The Stage of the Life Cycle of the Service Product.*** The price of a service will relate to its life cycle, much the same as the price of a tangible product will fluctuate as the product moves through the stages of its life cycle. At introduction, management may opt to use a *skimming* or a *penetration* strategy, adjusting prices as competitive pressure dictates (see Chapter 8). Identifying a company's position in the life cycle and the major objectives, decisions, problems, and organizational transitions needed for the future can be anticipated.

- ***The Elasticity of Demand.*** *Elasticity of demand* refers to the responsiveness of demand to changes in price. If the firm reduces its price and demand is inelastic, then the effect is to reduce margins with no compensating increase in demand. Thus, elasticity imposes limitations on certain price options.

- ***The Competitive Situation.*** In situations in which there is little differentiation between business service products and competition is intense, price discretion is limited. In other settings, tradition and custom may influence the prices charged (for example, advertising agencies' commission systems).

- ***The Strategic Role of Price.*** Pricing policies have a strategic role aimed at achieving organizational objectives, so the pricing decision on any particular business service should mesh with the firm's strategic objectives. Additionally, any given pricing strategy must reflect the way other elements of the marketing mix are manipulated to attain strategic ends.

In the business service sector, pricing decisions are affected by the demand for the services; production, marketing, and administrative costs; and the influence of competition. Further, price negotiation is integral to many business service transactions, such as financial and legal assistance, equipment rental, insurance, maintenance, and protection services. Quantity discounts, payment terms, cash discounts, price bidding, trade discounts, adjustments in price that reflect peak-load pricing (seasonal, yearly, or fluctuations in demand and/or supply), and bundling arrangements also influence pricing in business strategy development.

***Place*** The function of distribution channels for business services is to make the service available and convenient to the buyer. Services (unlike tangible goods) cannot be transported, so the channel is usually simpler and shorter than for business products. For example, an attorney, an accountant, and a business loan officer will work directly with a client. This short, direct channel is due, in large part, to the intangibility of services, as well as the need for continuing personal relationships between service providers and their customers. For marketers of business services, this involves providing optimum service and coverage at minimum cost. Business marketers must clearly delineate their markets and understand the buying patterns for their services—when, where, how, and by whom the service is purchased.

Historically, little attention has been paid to distribution in business service marketing. However, as competition grows, the value of distribution is being recognized. Hospitality firms such as the Hyatt chain and accounting firms such as Touche-Ross use multiple locations for distribution of their services. Using a channel intermediary is another way to broaden distribution. For example, it is now quite common for companies to deposit paychecks directly into their employees' bank accounts, thereby becoming an intermediary in distributing a bank's service. Travel agents, tourist boards, hotel representatives, and centralized reservation systems are additional examples of intermediaries serving the function of place in the service marketing mix.

***Promotion***   As noted previously, the fact that many business services cannot appeal to the buyer's sense of touch, taste, smell, sight, or hearing before purchase places a heavy burden on the business marketing organization in general and on the promotion element of the marketing mix in particular. The business-to-business firm is selling an idea, not a product, and often is unable to illustrate, demonstrate, or display the service in use. In order to tell the buyer what the service will do, service marketing uses many of the same promotional tools as product marketing: advertising, personal selling, publicity, and sales promotion all are available for developing an overall promotion plan. The inseparability of production and consumption usually necessitates face-to-face interaction between the buyer and the seller of business services. Indeed, what the customer is purchasing are the qualifications and expertise of the service provider. Thus, business marketers need to ensure that the employees who have client contact and actually administer the service convey consistently an appropriate, quality image.

### New Service Development

New services are the lifeblood of any business service organization. The best way, if not the only way, to generate new service marketing ideas is to remain close to customers. If the business service industry is properly nurtured, it will grow and generate much of America's future wealth. Strategy options for service businesses have been discussed elsewhere in this section and include market segmentation and positioning, among others. It is useful at this point in the discussion to highlight strategic choices by depicting the alternative directions that business service firms can take in their new service efforts. The firms can pursue newness in terms of markets, offerings, or a combination. Given this framework, there are, accordingly, four avenues available: share building, market extension, line extension, and new business.

***Share Building***   *Share building* (also known as market penetration) means selling more existing services to current buyers. To build share, the business marketer promotes aggressively, perhaps employing discount pricing. For example, there have been "accounting wars" among large accounting firms. Likewise, many professionals, such as business marketing consultants, aggressively promote through direct mail to attract new clients. Although share-building activities such as aggressive promotion are appropriate in growing markets, they are expensive and may be futile in mature markets in which market share has stabilized.

***Market Extension***   *Market extension* seeks new groups of buyers for the firm's current business service offering. A firm such as Blue Cross/Blue Shield may go beyond group plans offered through employers to make individual coverage available to self-employed business people. Likewise, banking institutions may decide to offer services abroad. This strategy also is known as market development.

*Line Extension* Line extension, or *product development,* is appropriate in mature business service industries in which growth is not likely to come from established services. The hospitality industry is an example, where hotels in popular vacation spots develop special packages to attract business groups during the off-season.

*New Business* A new product department, new product manager, or a business marketing research department should stimulate a steady flow of new business, or *diversified,* service ideas. Although implementation is risky, contemplating new service offerings allows the business marketer to look for unserviced gaps in the marketplace.

Without a steady flow of new service offerings, the business service firm is not likely to survive over the long run. Indeed, too many service firms are slow to invest in new market opportunities and research facilities. They stay with old concepts and concentrate on cost cutting rather than providing customers with services they want and need. In contrast, businesses that are working at diversifying or segmenting have a better understanding of how their operations must change as the marketplace changes over time.

---

**Concept Review**

1. Why is marketing coming of age in the service sector?

2. How can price bundling be an effective service sales tool?

3. What is a prerequisite to the effective positioning of a business service?

---

**Summary**

- Product development, management, and strategy are important parts of the business marketing process, with the major concerns being both to measure and predict success and to execute proper strategy over the life of the business product.

- Business marketers are now beginning to take their place along with engineers as having the most important role in the development of new product ideas. Technology push and market pull are the two major approaches to new product development. Technology push results when the driving force of a new product's development is the perceived potential of the technology itself; market pull is primarily the result of marketing research methodologies of interviewing prospective users about their needs and then developing solutions to those perceived needs. The new product development process includes six stages: idea and concept generation, screening and evaluation, business analysis, product development, product testing, and product commercialization and introduction.

- New product development, evaluation, and management must follow good management practice if effectiveness, efficiency, and a reasonable likelihood of success are to be achieved. The major options available to the business marketer in organizing the new product development process include a product manager system, a new product committee, a new product department, and a new product venture team.

- The information derived from product life-cycle analysis generally is used to suggest appropriate marketing strategies over a particular product's life span. Experience and learning curves can be used in conjunction with product life-cycle analysis to determine more specifically what is happening to a product as it moves from one stage in its life cycle to the next. Stages in the product life cycle include product introduction, market growth, market maturity, and sales decline.

- Technology, competition, changes in the level of business activity, and the utilization of plant

# WHAT WOULD YOU DO?

## MARKETING VERSUS ENGINEERING PERSPECTIVES ON NEW PRODUCT OPPORTUNITIES

Pete Santos, director of marketing, was having a problem with Carl Pace, the new technical director of engineering. Pete had analyzed the market for large assemblies used in the rail industry and determined that the competition was limited and the market would be growing dramatically. Pete and the area sales representative had called repeatedly on the major contractors, and were excited by their apparent interest. In order to present a bid to the contractors, the product part drawings and specifications had been provided to the cost and process estimators in Carl's department, who would calculate cost items such as labor, material, and overhead for the manufacturing process. It was left for Pete to set the final price.

As Pete looked at the cost estimate, he thought that he might be seeing a "fat" (exaggerated costs) estimate. Pete understood that the estimators used their own judgment in many parts of the cost estimate. For example, one estimator might envision a conservative process that will produce products at 500 units per hour and be 100 percent sure that it can be done. Another estimator may be more aggressive and be willing to specify a 750- units-per-hour process that he or she is only 85 percent certain can be done. Often, the estimator's major concern is to be able to produce the product for the cost his or her department estimated.

In competitive industries, conservative estimating of process rates, material usage, and other factors easily can produce an estimate of direct cost that exceeds aggressive competitors' bid prices (i.e., even before adding a profit margin, Pete's price is too high). It was common knowledge that Carl didn't think the company should be pursuing this product line, and it wasn't surprising that his estimators might be conservative with the cost estimate. Pete, in turn, can price the product at a point he believes is in the best interest of the company (even below the projected cost estimate).

Pete could have negotiated with Carl, or have brought the issue to top management, but instead he decided to take more decisive action. Pete had two of his new product development engineers (who report to marketing) redo the estimate. He based his bid on the new, lower cost estimates and easily received a trial order. Pete now faces a problem: Carl's process development engineers, who will actually develop the manufacturing process to be used, could: (1) work hard to create a process to match Pete's cost estimate, (2) make the process as expensive as Carl's department estimated (proving Pete wrong), or (3) make the manufacturing process fail altogether.

### Assignment

Define the ethical issues for *all* those involved and advise Pete on what he should do to resolve the situation.

---

capacity all can have a marked impact on a firm's decision to expand, contract, or maintain the current product mix. The effective business marketer must understand each of these market forces in order to make appropriate decisions with regard to possible product-mix changes.

- Business marketers have the responsibility of deciding how quickly prospects will adopt a new product and to what extent they will replace the old one. To perform such a task, marketers frequently rely on the adoption-diffusion process. The adoption process is the decision- making activity of the buying firm through which the new product or innovation is accepted. The diffusion process shows how a product is accepted by an industry over time.

- The business-to-business firm should regularly review its product portfolio, developing strategic alternatives for each of the company's current products, businesses, and new business possibilities. The Boston Consulting Group categorizes each product or business division in a company according to four types of strategic business units (SBUs): stars, cash cows, question marks, and dogs. Strategies have been formulated for use with each of these four categories.

- Determining when to drop a product, product line, or company division is a very difficult task for the business marketer. Common product-elimination options include harvesting, line simplification, and total-line divestment.

- For the most part, the entire area of service marketing remains ill defined. Marketing, however, is slowly coming of age in the service sector, as it becomes obvious that the last several years of the twentieth century represented the transformation from a product-oriented economy to a service-oriented economy.

- Four characteristics are unique to services and influence the way they are marketed: intangibility, perishability and fluctuating demand, simultaneity, and heterogeneity. Services are intangible in that they cannot appeal to the senses. Promotion, through the sales force and advertising department, must communicate the benefits of various business service offerings. Services are perishable and cannot be stored. Key decisions must be made on what maximum capacity level should be available to cope with surges in demand before service levels suffer. Production and consumption of services are inseparable; selling comes first, followed by production and consumption. It is difficult to standardize services; as a result, output can vary widely in quality.

- Although marketing functions are basically the same for many services and products, there is a difference in the organization and implementation strategies for gaining a competitive advantage in business service marketing. With business service marketing, the product is not created until the service is performed. When the service firm establishes and maintains a distinctive place for itself and its offerings in the market, it is said to be successfully positioned. The marketing mix can be applied to business services, just as it can to business products. The strategies for different services must be incorporated into the entire corporate strategy, and the development of new services is just as important as the development of new products. Business service companies can expand their service offerings through share building, market extension, line extension, and cultivation of new business.

## Key Terms

| | | |
|---|---|---|
| adoption process | market growth | product development |
| bundling | market maturity | product life-cycle model |
| business analysis | new product committee | product manager |
| diffusion process | new product department | product portfolio |
| divestment | new product manager | product testing |
| economies of scale | new product venture team | sales decline |
| harvesting | portfolio classification | screening and evaluation |
| idea and concept generation | model | services |
| learning curve analysis | product commercialization | strategic business unit |
| line simplification | and introduction | (SBU) |

## Review Questions

1. Why are effective product management and strategies so important today? What are the major concerns of product management and strategy?

2. Why was there reluctance in the past to give marketing personnel a major role in the design and development of new products? Discuss three major styles in organizing the new product development process. Identify two approaches to new product development. Describe each of the six stages in the new product development process.

3. Identify and discuss the four distinct types of product lines useful in a discussion of product development, management, and strategy.

4. Discuss the fundamental difference between technology push and market pull.

5. What are the five basic attributes found to be of importance in new product success? Would these same attributes be appropriate in new service development?

6. In business-to-business firms, several departments usually are involved in the development of new product ideas. With this in mind, what are some of the options available to management to actively involve appropriate management personnel in this important activity?

7. What is the fundamental value of product life-cycle analysis? How are learning curve analysis and experience curves used in product life-cycle analysis? Identify and describe each of the four stages involved in the product life cycle.

8. How do technology, competition, changes in the level of business activity, and the utilization of plant capacity impact possible changes in a business-to-business firm's product mix?

9. What are the adoption and diffusion processes? How can they be utilized together? Identify and describe the stages in the adoption process. What factors influence the rate of adoption? The rate of diffusion?

10. Define product portfolio analysis. According to the Boston Consulting Group approach to product management, what is a strategic business unit? Identify four categories into which each strategic business unit within a business-to-business firm can be placed and indicate appropriate strategies for use with each of the four categories.

11. What are some common reasons for product failure? Describe three strategic approaches for the elimination of weak products.

12. How does business service marketing differ from business product marketing? When is a business service properly positioned? What is meant by the bundling of services?

13. Identify and discuss four important characteristics of services. Provide an example of each.

14. How does each element of the marketing mix contribute to the overall strategy used for a particular business service? Identify and discuss four methods by which a business-to-business firm can expand its service offerings.

## Case 7-1

# New Product Resolves Customer Problems: *Ultra's 1999 Model Washing Machine*

## Part A

Kim Lee, Field Sales Representative for TTX Inc. (a high-volume manufacturer of electric pump/drive motor assemblies) was pleased. As part of planning for his next day's sales call at Ultra Corporation, he had developed a powerful PowerPoint presentation, entitled, "TTX Solutions for Customer Needs." As he clicked through his slides, he tried to visualize how each person in the customer's buying center would interpret the graphic information and how they would individually respond to what was being shown. Like any experienced salesperson, Kim spent a lot of time trying to see situations through his customer's eyes. Since this was his biggest account, Kim had spent years calling on Ultra and developing relationships across departments and levels. Each slide in the presentation was intended to present the TTX marketing and technical group as rapidly responding to a recent field failure problem at Ultra Manufacturers, Inc. The new product which would resolve the customer's problem was presented with graphic fanfare as "the New HD" TTX pump/drive motor assembly.

### Background

As soon as Ultra Corporation's "new and improved" 2002 model year washing machine reached one year in the field (and off warranty to the final consumer), some pump/drive motor assemblies in the machines started to fail. The failure rate was not high, but it represented a huge public relations problem for Ultra's marketing department. Ultra had positioned the machine as being "Ultra Reliable" and the increase in the failure rate had been picked up and reported on in consumer-oriented media. While Ultra sold directly to channel members, it had invested hundreds of millions of dollars in pull television and print advertising to position its product at the high end of the consumer market. Its ongoing ad campaign retained a theme that humorously stressed that its products needed so little service that customers who had owned them for years would have no idea who serviced them.

Because Ultra sold their products through large chain dealers who also carried competitor product lines, dealer pressure had made it necessary for Ultra to extend their warranties to cover these untypical failures.

TTX had been supplying the same pump/drive motor assembly to Ultra since 1996. Indeed Kim and TTX had been part of the "early supplier involvement group" that had originally worked with Ultra's engineering department to design the basic washing equipment pump/drive motor assemblies. The assemblies were so reliable that accelerated life tests predicted a six-sigma life projection beyond fifty years at normal usage. Accelerated life test results from random samples of assembly production and other quality control processes were strict. TTX was ISO 9000 certified and statistical process control was used throughout its manufacturing process. Three years ago when TTX was approved as Ultra's sole source just-in-time pump/drive motor assembly supplier, Ultra's quality control and engineering experts had completely evaluated and approved all of the steps in the TTX production process. This highest level quality approval meant that TTX would no longer have to share Ultra's business with competitors, and that it would be completely responsible for its own quality. TTX assemblies would be received directly into Ultra's production line without requiring incoming inspection.

As soon as the field failures started, Kim was called. He dropped what he was doing, and drove directly to the Ultra plant. He spent time in the engineering labs and air-expressed samples of failed pump/drive motor assemblies to the TTX technical labs where engineers confirmed that the problem was a pump sleeve bearing failure that had overloaded the motors. The sleeve bearings were purchased from a leading bearing supplier (a JIT ISO 9000 certified producer that also sold this standard product to hundreds of other producers including automotive OEMs). Because the problem had started with the Ultra's new model year, Kim had suspected that the new, more expensive model somehow created a higher loading on the sleeve bearing. From Kim's experience (unless the Ultra was bringing out an entirely new machine) almost all model year changes were cosmetic. But it was either that or that the sleeve bearing had somehow changed. It seemed extremely unlikely for the bearing to have suddenly changed since it was the same one that had always been used. Kim knew that the pump insides had not changed, and the pump was still working fine and without field failures in other similar applications.

The final slides in Kim's presentation covered what Kim thought would be the solution to Ultra's problems. Since other companies were also TTX customers for the same pump/drive motor assemblies and did not have the problem, Kim had looked to see how their pump systems were designed. He discovered a heavier duty roller bearing in place of the lighter duty, less expensive sleeve bearing specified by Ultra. Kim had arranged for a series of test runs to determine if a different bearing design would solve the problem and he was anxious to present his test results to Ultra showing that he and TTX had come up with a solution to their problem.

## Problem Solution

In Kim's presentation to Ultra's executives, he planned to sell Ultra on the new HD pump/drive motor assembly. His presentation would consist of slides showing:

1. the reliability history of previous model years,
2. that the problem started with the 2002 model year,
3. a graphic animation of the effect of overloading the sleeve bearing causing it to heat weld to the pump shaft,
4. even higher loads on the new HD assembly operating without a problem, and
5. the "closer" financial figures showing the expected costs of the field failures versus the expense of going to the new HD pump/drive motor.

Kim knew that Ultra had priced the new 2002 equipment higher than previous models, but he did not include the $50.00 increase in his presentation. What he did include was the cost to Ultra of a distributor's repair call $27.00, plus the cost of the pump assembly $34.66, with a 3.7% failure rate, from 1999 to the present, at a sales rate of just over 500,000 units per year. Although, the roller bearing (without a mark-up) increased the pump assembly by $1.17 each, TTX had not yet priced the new HD assembly. Kim expected that at the end of his presentation, Ultra's team would enthusiastically thank him, and if the situation were handled correctly he and TTX would come out looking very good.

Kim thought, "This would be the perfect opportunity to close on next year's contract prices with a small increase as a reward for our efforts at quickly resolving their problem." After discussing the pricing opportunity with TTX's marketing manager, an increase of $2.00/unit was set. Kim would stress that TTX manufacturing was constantly working on cost savings to improve the efficiency of the production process and to hold off the necessity for substantial price increases. He would also stress that TTX worked closely with all their suppliers to apply value analysis to improve components and control costs. Since the marketing manager was responsible for setting prices, Kim would go along with her decision. But he felt that it was a very tiny percent price increase considering how much of a hero he was going to be. Opportunities like this didn't come up very often in this highly cost conscious market.

### Assignment

**Team One:** Prepare Kim's presentation, and present it to the Ultra team (the class). See if at the end of the presentation the Ultra executives have found your presentation to be logical, convincing, and professionally presented. Have you created a customer perception of value that exceeds the increased cost of the HD pump and motor?

---

### Case 7-2

# New Product Resolves Customer Problems: *Ultra's 1999 Model Washing Machine*

## Part B

Kristen Hendricks, Senior Quality Engineer for Ultra Corporation was looking over load test results for what seemed like the hundredth time. The results showed that under any conditions that she could think to test under, the loads on the pump/drive motor assembly in the 2002 model year washing machines never exceeded design limits and were no different than the loads that Ultra equipment had always produced. Yet she had been plagued for months by field failures. Field failures of the machines were serious in that they had the potential to cost Ultra hundreds of thousand of dollars in repair and replacement costs, not to mention the cost of lost sales due to negative publicity concerning the reliability of the product. Repeated meetings with the assembly manufacturer TTX Inc., Ultra's supplier, produced little insight into the problem. Ultra had been buying the pump/drive motor assembly for many years with a minimal failure rate, when six months ago, pump sleeve bearings had suddenly started to degrade and fail at an alarming rate. TTX had firmly held that since the failures started with the new model year at Ultra, the problem had to be a higher loading on the sleeve bearing in the new model, since nothing about the pump or drive motor had changed. Kristen was stumped. Nothing about the so-called new model could change the loading on the pump sleeve bearing, as the changes in the model were cosmetic only, allowing marketing to reposition the equipment at a higher price.

From her analysis of Ultra's competitors' equipment, Kristen knew that they all used the same TTX assembly as Ultra, with the exception of a roller bearing on the pump shaft where Ultra used a sleeve bearing. Feedback from purchasing suggested that TTX was going to recommend a heavier duty pump/drive motor assembly, which seemed excessive if all that was needed was a change to a roller bearing on the pump. Purchasing had already contacted a bearing supplier and knew the additional cost involved ($1.17/each for the roller bearing). Kristen didn't think that TTX would be silly enough to just switch the bearing and try to present the assembly as something more (like a heavy-duty assembly). And, it didn't really make sense that a heavy-duty pump would be necessary. Any kind of a price increase on the assembly (at an annual production rate of 500,000 units), meant this problem was going to end up being very costly.

Later that afternoon, Kristen would meet with Ultra's buyer and the vice president of marketing for TTX to discuss the pricing of the heavy-duty pump option. In preparation for the meeting Kristen had collected the latest batch of failed assemblies returned from the field. Most of the analysis of the failed bearings had been completed by TTX, who always came back with the statement "Typical bearing failure due to overload." Still, her technicians had cut into many fused and failed bearings and found nothing to indicate why the failure had occurred. Ultra had also disassembled TTX pumps, removed the sleeve bearings, and sent them out for independent lab analysis. Always the results showed that the sleeve bearings met the specification, and were the same as they always had been.

Interrupting her thoughts, one of her quality engineers brought over a portable microscope and said, "Look at this TTX failed axle shaft, not at the bearing end, but look up here. There is a hairline crack, not running around the shaft, but running parallel to the axis along the length of the shaft." "Wow, look at that!" Kristen said, as she immediately realized that she was looking at a hollow shaft that had been fabricated by rolling a flat piece of steel around to meet itself. With the ends hidden and the final grinding to a precision tolerance (which had to be done even on a solid shaft), the manufacturers of the shaft (that rotated within the sleeve bearing) had mostly removed any evidence of the parting line. There was no question that this was an unauthorized TTX production change from a solid to a hollow shaft. Even as little as a micron mismatch at the parting line would turn the shaft into a sharp tool that would cut into the bearing. "So that is why the roller bearing worked and the sleeve bearing didn't," Kristen thought. 'The inside track that the rollers ride in is attached to the shaft (rather than rotating against it as in a sleeve bearing)."

Kristen now knew the cause of the failures. TTX had come up with a way to remove cost from the production of the shaft, but their savings would have been offset by having to switch to a roller bearing. So they must have come up with the idea to play dumb about what was causing the failures, and have Ultra pay for the new bearings (or even more for a "new HD pump/drive motor assembly"). Kristen asked for some shafts to be cut to show the hollow center, and had enlarged photographs made for the afternoon meeting with TTX. Just for good measure, she asked her assistant to arrange to have the senior management staff attend.

## Assignment

**Team Two:** Prepare your PowerPoint presentation to follow the presentation expected from TTX. Estimate the costs to Ultra that you will be charging to TTX (costs to replace failed shafts, technical staff time investigating the failures, damage to the company's reputation, etc.). Define the ethical issues, and recommend a resolution to the problem that will not disrupt production.

# References

1. Conrad Berenson and Iris Mohr-Jackson, "Product Rejuvenation: A Less Risky Alternative to Product Innovation, *Business Horizons* 37 (Nov-Dec 1994): 51–7.

2. Kotler (2000) Marketing Management, p. 329. and Chris Cleigston, "High-tech Demand Own New-Product Plans," *Electronic News* 41 (December 4, 1995): 33–6.

3. John Saunders and David Jobber, "Product Replacement: Strategies for Simultaneous Product Deletion and Launch," *Journal of Product Innovation Management* (November 1994): 433–50.

4. Sanjiv S. Dugal and Jonathan E. Schroeder, "Strategic Positioning for Market Entry in Different Technological Environments," *Journal of Marketing Theory and Practice* 3 (Summer 1995): 31–45.

5. Charles Beard and Chris Easingwood, "New Product Launch," *Industrial Marketing Management* 25 (March 1995): 87–103.

6. William H. Murphy and Linda Gorchels, "How to Improve Product Management Effectiveness," *Industrial Marketing Management* 25 (January 1996): 47–58.

7. Merle Crawford and Anthony Di Benedetto, *New Products Management,* 7th ed. (New York: McGraw-Hill/Irwin, 2003): 299.

8. Frank G. Bingham, Jr., and Charles J. Quigley, Jr., "Venture Team Application to New Product Development," *The Journal of Business and Industrial Marketing* 4 (Winter/Spring): 49–59.

9. Robert O. Null, "The Team Approach to Business Expansion," presentation to the Chicago chapter of the Product Development and Management Association, February 26, 1986.

10. William T. Robinson and Sungwook Min, "Is the First to Market the First to Fail? Empirical Evidence for Industrial Goods Businesses," *Journal of Marketing Research* 39 (Feb 2002): 120–28.

11. Stanley F. Slater, "Competing in High-Velocity Markets," *Industrial Marketing Management* (November 1993): 255–63.

12. T. P. Wright, "Factors Affecting the Cost of Airplanes," *Journal of Aeronautical Sciences* 3 (February 1936): 122–28.

13. Christian Gronroos, "Marketing Services: The Case of a Missing Product," *Journal of Business and Industrial Marketing* 13 (4/5) (1998): 332–38.

14. Paul Matthyssens and Koen Vandenbempt, "Creating Competitive Advantage in Industrial Services," *Journal of Business and Industrial Marketing* 13 (4/5) (1998): 339–55.

15. James A. Fitzsimmons, Jeonpyo Noh, and Emil Thies, "Purchasing Business Services," *Journal of Business and Industrial Marketing* 13 (4/5) (1998): 370–80.

16. E. Jerome McCarthy, *Basic Marketing: A Managerial Approach,* 2nd ed. (Homewood, Ill." Richard D. Irwin, 1964): 38–40.

17. "Service Management: The Toughest Game in Town," *Management Practice* (Fall 1984): 8.

## CHAPTER EIGHT

# Price Planning and Strategy

## Learning Objectives

After reading this chapter, you should be able to:

- Comprehend the importance of setting price in the business-to-business sector.
- Understand the major factors that influence pricing strategy.
- Distinguish between marginal pricing strategy, the economic value to the customer concept, target return-on investment pricing, target costing, and zero based pricing.
- Discuss the concept of price elasticity and demand strategy.
- Relate the changes that occur in the pricing element of the marketing mix throughout the various phases of the product life cycle.
- Distinguish between a market skimming and market penetration strategy.
- Describe conditions under which a price leadership strategy would be used.
- Comprehend the importance and operation of competitive bidding in setting business prices in appropriate markets.
- Describe how it feels to make actual price decisions.
- Communicate the value of leasing as an alternative to purchasing in a business market.
- Distinguish among the various types of price adjustments commonly given in business purchasing transactions.

## Chapter Outline

Business Pricing: An Overview
Major Factors Influencing Price Strategy
Pricing Methods
Demand Assessment and Strategy
Life-Cycle Costing
Price-Leadership Strategy
Competitive Bidding in the Business Market
Leasing in the Business Market
Pricing Discount Strategies

## Business Pricing: An Overview

*Price planning,* like most marketing decisions, is an imprecise science. As with other business skills, it depends as much on good judgment as on quantitative calculations. "But the fact that pricing depends on judgment is no justification for pricing decisions based on hunches or intuition."[1] To develop effective price strategy, it is necessary to systematically study a variety of internal and external variables, particularly the "4Cs" of customers, competition, costs, and the correlation of demand to price. Yet even with agreement on influencing variables and a systematic analysis, the process of arriving at an actual bid price tends to be highly individualistic. A marketing manager with an engineering background would likely feel comfortable with a multivariable algorithm, while one with a background in sales may develop a less technical approach. Both are ultimately responsible for the bottom-line profitability of the company, however, and must develop a procedure that approximates the actual customer's perceived value of the offering. Some writers have concluded that many managers are relatively naïve when it comes to the price variable, and that unsophisticated pricing methods prevail because of lack of knowledge and understanding. Fortunately for those wishing to learn more about pricing, a considerable amount of academic research, textbooks, and indeed college classes are dedicated to the topic of price strategy.[2,3]

As a foundation for future price decision making, all marketing students are required to study finance, accounting, and cost systems. From that background, most students and business people become generally familiar with the representation and terms shown in Exhibit 8-1, which can be thought of as a picture of the price elements a typical marketer is thinking about while setting a selling price. To derive the actual selling price, the marketer must first consider the accuracy of the estimate for *total direct cost* of materials and labor (also known as *assignable cost* or *variable cost*) associated with the product. Next, the marketer considers the impact of the share of *fixed costs* of this type of product (also known as *overhead* or *burden*). Subtracting the sum of the direct and fixed costs from the selling price indicates whether there is an opportunity for profit.

Most price decision makers would agree that understanding the customer's perceived economic value (based on total cost of use) is the most critical issue. Many buyers have cost analysts assigned to their departments who can estimate the cost to produce a product (a **cost-price analysis**) by much the same process that the potential suppliers' cost estimators will use in developing their bid. The cost analyst's projection of the suppliers' process

**EXHIBIT 8-1**
**Price and Cost Structure**

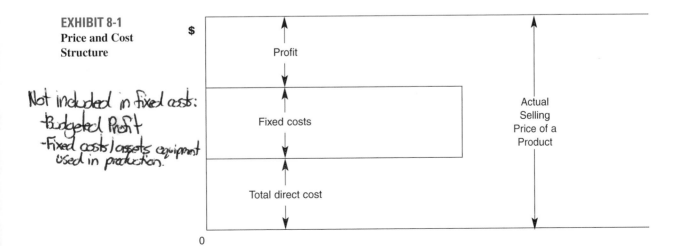

*Handwritten note:* Not included in fixed costs:
- Budgeted Profit
- Fixed costs/assets equipment used in production.

and costs becomes the basis for the buyer's perceived value and often becomes a "target price" for the supplier's bids. In addition to understanding the customer's perceived economic value, it also is important to understand the customer's perception of the other costs associated with the product's application and use (e.g., costs associated with how products are to be purchased, transported, tested, stored, assembled, maintained, and measured for performance). It is important to ensure that the buyer is aware of these areas in which products have a cost or performance advantage, so that it will be factored into the bid evaluation. Supplier marketers usually have to estimate the buyer's target price, since most buyers will divulge their target price only after the bidding process (in the negotiation stage). Understandably, if the supplier bids are less than the buyer's target price, it will not become an issue (or even be mentioned).

Because the buyer will be comparing the supplier's bid offering to competitors' bids, marketers try to predict competitor's bids. A macro approach to making the prediction starts by reviewing information on the competitor's past bidding history on similar products. This information comes from previous bid situations for which records are available, listing the companies bidding, the price of each bid (if available), and the company awarded the contract (and why). On a micro level, marketers estimate the competitor's direct cost by the same process as the buyer's cost analyst and compare that to the competitor's pricing on current products sold (or past bids). If a pattern is detected, the marketer can attempt to predict what the competitor will bid on the new product.

Before marketers can determine how to make pricing work for them, they have to know specifically what they want pricing to do for their business. For example, do they want to increase sales or market share, maximize cash flow or profit, deter competition from entering the company's niche, establish an image or position, or perhaps some combination of these objectives? Answers to these questions must be forthcoming before price planning and strategy can be done. Also, in making pricing decisions, marketing managers frequently change prices concurrently with other marketing-mix variables.[4]

Strategic price strategy objectives are typically set based on the organization's overall objectives, which in turn are developed from the mission. Then product line and other price tactics are developed to support the price objectives. Decision making for pricing is one of the oldest marketing topics, drawing significantly on the economics literature, which certainly predates most marketing pricing analyses. Other disciplines, including psychology and sociology, also have contributed to the development of strategic pricing material.

## Major Factors Influencing Price Strategy

As is shown in Exhibit 8-2, important factors that influence price strategy include customer value, competition, cost, demand, pricing objectives, the impact of price on other products, and legal considerations. Each of these is discussed below.

### Customer Value

The customer's perception of value is usually one of the most important factors influencing price decisions for suppliers who follow the "marketing concept" (i.e., uncovering customer needs and meeting them). However, it would be incorrect to view the marketers' function as just offering bids at prices customers would like to pay. The offering price needs to reflect true customer value, even when customers would prefer to pay less. An important role of the other controllable elements in the marketing mix is to raise customer's awareness of the product's true value, and their willingness to pay a price that reflects that value. Advanced sales training is also critically important. Customer price resistance is often initiated when the salesperson is not personally convinced that the offering price is justified and unconsciously signals that in their approach. A second very common sales

**EXHIBIT 8-2  Major Factors Influencing Price Strategy**

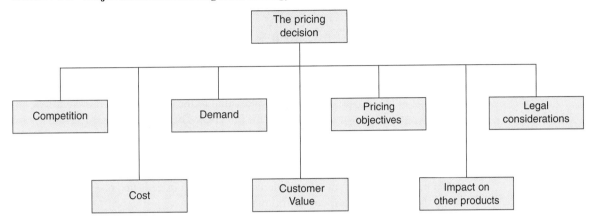

mistake is when the salesperson makes price, rather than value, the central issue.[5] What could be more natural than a salesperson delivering a bid to a buyer and asking, "How does the price look?" But doesn't that make price the main issue in the buyer's mind? What would be a better approach? More discussion of economic value to the customer appears in the next section, "Pricing Methods."

## Competition

There are two kinds of competitive factors that influence price. One factor is the competitive effect on demand for the marketer's product. This includes competition from directly comparable products—Apple Computer against IBM, Moore Business Forms against Uarco Incorporated, and UPS against Federal Express, for example. There also is competition from substitute products, such as plastic against steel and synthetic against natural substances (synthetic versus crude rubber, for example). The second competitive factor influencing price is the reaction of competitors to any price move the business marketer might make. If the marketer raises the price, will the competition hold its price level and hope to pick up customers? If the price is lowered, will the competition move in aggressively, and possibly retaliate with a lower price? In the event that the marketer is under pressure to match competitor's prices, it is important to keep in mind that BMW would not likely benefit from meeting Ford's prices, even though lower prices might indeed increase market share. Chronically low selling prices and continual pressure to match the lowest competitor prices often indicates weakness in the rest of the marketing mix.

## Cost

Fixed and variable costs are of major concern to the business marketer charged with establishing price levels. If a manufacturer is a low-cost producer relative to competition, the firm will earn additional profits by maintaining prices at competitive levels. The additional dollars generated can be used to promote the product aggressively, with the goal of increasing the overall visibility of the manufacturer's products. On the other hand, if fixed or variable costs are high in relation to the competition, the manufacturer may be in no position to reduce its prices because such action can lead to a price war that it will probably lose.

To make intelligent decisions concerning price, the marketer must totally understand the cost system used. In standard cost systems, fixed costs can be allocated across products according to factors that are not fairly related to costs. If the marketer ignores this, the allocation technique may be misleading in its indications of the types of products the company is most competitive in producing. For example, if the overhead is allocated across products based on asset utilization, an inappropriate burden may be applied to products utilizing expensive automation. Similarly, if overhead is allocated by labor usage, then labor-intensive products may be priced out of the market. Being priced out of the market on some product lines means that the fixed overhead will have to be spread over the remaining products (possibly making them less competitive). Another way to look at this issue is to ask: Can a company selling computer chips that employs 200 engineers and 300 vice presidents charge more per chip than a competitor who has much less overhead? The general rule is that if the additional overhead does not add value to the customer, then it should be removed and arguably not be considered in the bid price. These types of decisions are not for the fainthearted, and are sure to generate debate.

## Demand

Demand is based on a variety of considerations, of which price is just one. Some of these considerations are as follows.

1. Perceived quality
2. Perceived reliability
3. Perceived value
4. Ability of customers to buy
5. Willingness of customers to buy
6. Prices of substitute products
7. Potential market for the product (unfulfilled demand or saturated market)
8. Nature of nonprice competition
9. Segments in the market
10. Customer behavior in general

All these factors (and more, such as psychological aspects) are interdependent; it is not easy to estimate their relationship to each other precisely. However, they do point out that contemporary business buyers are highly sophisticated and that these buyers consider a wide variety of factors in deciding exactly what products to buy. As noted earlier, many buyers are as capable as product producers in the cost estimation process. Just as the supplier will have estimating engineers calculating process steps and costs for a new product bid, the buyer is likely to have similarly trained estimating engineers going through the same process to determine a target price to pay. Target price and price offered are both elements of customer perceived value that directly impact demand on price sensitive products.

## Pricing Objectives

An important step in *pricing strategy* is to determine goals and objectives prior to setting price points or levels. The principal pricing objectives of most business-to-business firms are to maximize general profit, achieve return on investment, and maintain or increase market share.

### Maximize General Profit

Profit probably is the company objective that is most often stated. A profit-maximization goal is likely to be far more beneficial to the firm if practiced over the long run; if short-run profit is the goal, there is the tendency to cut cost—sometimes to the detriment of product quality and customer service. A firm entering a new geographic market or introducing a new product or product line may be well advised to set low prices initially, so as to build a large customer base. In this case, the goal would be to optimize profits over the long run, focusing attention on the demand curve.

*[Handwritten margin note:]* Non-Price Elements – raise customer awareness – raise willingness to pay certain price for product

It may even be necessary for the marketer to price the product below projected cost in the hope of entering a new market, relying on internal value analysis and cost reductions from the estimated cost to restore profitability. If the attempt is successful, the marketer is applauded as a wise visionary. If unsuccessful, the marketer appears to have wasted a great deal of the company's money. Risk avoiders and unsuccessful risk takers both are likely to be assigned to the new sales territories in North Alaska! So take risks, but be reasonably certain they will pay off.

### Achieve Return on Investment

Products may be priced to achieve a certain percentage return on investment (ROI). This criterion typically is selected as a goal by firms that are leaders in their industry—firms such as General Motors or Alcoa. With this approach, an organization prices its products to achieve a specific rate of return on investment. Alcoa, DuPont, General Electric, General Motors, Johns-Manville, and U.S. Steel price many products to yield a target return. This objective makes it simpler to measure and control the performance of separate divisions, departments, and products. The trend of using a target return as a pricing objective has brought the following results:

- Increased awareness and concern for the relationships among investments, capital, and profits in planning and budgeting
- The use of simple, explicit standards in measuring the return of divisions, departments, and product groups
- The use of cost-plus pricing to ensure that target returns will be achieved

It must be noted, however, that this approach is not appropriate for all firms. Many marketers do not like *cost-plus pricing*. It ignores all the factors that typically influence a price decision (except, of course, cost), and most importantly, it ignores value to the customer. Cost-plus pricing often is done outside the marketing department (probably in accounting). This suggests a selling orientation rather than a marketing orientation, in that marketing would be given a price and expected to somehow convince the customer to purchase the product. Rather than expecting the same return from every product, many marketers prefer to achieve a target ROI utilizing a mix of margins, each strategically set as appropriate for the product, customer, and situation.

### Maintain or Increase Market Share

Maintaining or increasing market share is a popular type of pricing objective because market share is measurable and may be a better indicator of general financial corporate health than return on investment, especially when the total market is growing. Middlemen prefer to handle rapidly moving products and tend to drop those falling behind. Gaining market share because of a good reputation for quality and customer service will generally affect long-run profits favorably. However, being totally focused on building market share often involves imprudent pricing below perceived customer value and even less overall profit.

These pricing objectives—maximizing general profit, achieving return on investment, and maintaining or increasing market share—are not necessarily mutually exclusive, nor is this list complete. Other objectives such as overhead absorption, demand regulation, the establishment of market leadership, image projection, line extension differentiation, and cash generation may also work toward achievement of the firm's overall marketing objectives.

## Impact of Price on Other Products

Often, the purchase of one product increases the likelihood of the purchase, by the same customer, of another product or product line. One product may enhance the value or the effective use of the other product, in addition to the possibility that some buyers might encounter savings in time and effort by purchasing two or more products from the same source. If, for example, a business buyer is buying a particular grade of tool steel from a local distributor to do a particular job, that buyer would be inclined to buy other grades of tool steel from the same supplier as the need arose. There is strong likelihood that the buyer would also buy needed cutting tools and lubricants from that supplier. These complementary products probably would be *price inelastic,* because the supplier's inventory and delivery capabilities would more than offset a price advantage the buyer might gain by shopping around. This scenario may not hold true if the purchase involved a major new-buy situation, however, or when the quantity to be bought is large enough to make price a major buying determinant.

## Legal Considerations

Business marketers should be prepared to justify price levels, along with quantity and trade discounts. As shown in Exhibit 8-3, under the **Robinson-Patman Act** quantity discounts are legal if the resulting price differentials do not exceed the cost differentials in manufacturing, selling, and delivering the product to buyers who are in competition with each other.

Being aware of this legal requirement, some competitors will request bids from their competitor's suppliers even though they have no intention of purchasing from them. What would you do if your customer's competitor asked your company to bid on their needs? It would be tempting to try and supply both, but in the process you may be providing the cost information that results in your customer (and your company) losing the business.

Further, although the Act does not discuss trade discounts specifically, several court cases seem to uphold the legality of offering separate discounts to separate classes of buyers, as long as the discounts are offered in return for services rendered (that is, marketing functions performed). Business marketers should be aware of the possible legal problems that can arise in using certain types of discounts and allowances, taking care to avoid engaging in illegal price discrimination, price fixing, the exchange of price information among competitors, and predatory pricing.

### *Price Fixing*

**Price fixing**, the illegal practice of several competitors setting a price (also known as collusion) is a direct violation of the Sherman Antitrust Act. Such price fixing is illegal even if the fixed prices are fair. Price fixing is more likely to happen when the number of firms in a particular industry is small and the product is relatively homogeneous (as in the case of oligopolies). When there are many firms, or when heterogeneous products are involved, competitors will find it difficult to agree on what the fixed price will be.

### *Exchanging Price Information*

This activity occurs when competitors exchange information regarding prices, inventory levels, and the like. It becomes illegal when it leads to price agreements, however, as this

**EXHIBIT 8-3** Robinson-Patman Act (1936)

| | |
|---|---|
| Section 2(a) | Makes it illegal to discriminate in price among different buyers of commodities of like grade and quality when the effects result in a reduction in competition at the sellers' level, at the buyers' level, or at the buyers' customers' level. Different prices can be charged if they do not exceed differences in the costs of serving different customers. The power to establish maximum limits on quantity discounts granted to any customer or class of customers—regardless of differences in the costs of serving—is given to the FTC. |
| Section 2(b) | Continues the Clayton Act's provision of "meeting competition in good faith." |
| Section 2(c) | The granting of "dummy" brokerage allowances—given by a seller to a buyer or a brokerage firm owned by the buyer—is illegal. |
| Section 2(d) and (e) | Supplementary services or allowances such as advertising allowances must be made to all purchasers on a proportionately equal basis. |
| Section 2(f) | It is illegal for buyers knowingly to induce discriminatory prices from sellers. |

is tantamount to price fixing. Informal exchanging of price information often is done by a price leader, who, under the guise of announcing a price increase to its customers, actually is signaling its competitors to follow with their own price increases. The followers can choose to increase their prices and maintain their relative market shares, or they can decide to hold their lower prices in hopes of gaining additional customers. Holding the lower price assumes the customers will buy on price and the price leader will not respond. In application, followers know that if they gain appreciable market share, the price leader simply will lower its price. When faced with the prospect of the latter scenario, competitors are likely to follow the price leader.

### *Predatory Pricing*

**Predatory pricing** involves the cutting of prices (usually by a larger producer) to a point that is at or below cost for the purpose of eliminating competition. It is an attempt to monopolize the market and, in most cases, is illegal. Once the competition is eliminated, then the firm generally will raise its prices to monopoly levels. The capital investment and management performance systems of some countries allow their industries to routinely take long-term low or even negative returns. While in the United States this might be regarded as restraint of trade and destructive of our industrial base, other cultures often see it merely as aggressive competition. While our producers would demand protection, customers would enjoy the lower prices, and locals involved in marketing the foreign products would lobby for "free trade."

## Pricing Methods

After completing a thorough study of all the variables that can have a major impact on pricing in business markets, marketing managers can turn their attention to developing specific pricing methods likely to appeal to these markets. In business pricing, neither cost nor demand approaches can succeed without regard for the other. Generating enough revenue to cover costs is a function of having a competitive cost structure as well as sufficient demand. In the long run, all costs must be covered; yet, unless there is sufficient demand for the goods, there will not be revenues to cover the costs. Many strategic marketers prefer to set prices individually across products, markets, and customers, with margins reflecting the specific market situations, but with the goal of meeting a budgeted targeted company profitability figure. This means the marketer is using strategic pricing skills, as opposed to approaches that dictate a single pricing method regardless of market realities. Several pricing methods will be examined.

### Marginal Pricing

**Marginal pricing**, also known as *contribution pricing,* is a basic conceptual approach to setting prices, with the aim being to maximize profits by producing the number of units at which marginal cost is just less than, or equal to, marginal revenue. The product is sold at that price. If the amount of additional revenue the firm receives from selling one more unit is greater than the marginal cost of producing the unit, then a profit is made. If the marginal revenue attained by producing an additional unit is less than the marginal cost of producing it, the firm will lose money on that additional unit and should not produce it. Consider the case of Chainco, a manufacturer of tread chain for crawler tractor vehicles.

> Chainco's regular business is the manufacture of tread chain for OEMs that produce crawler tractors for construction, agricultural, and military markets. Chainco employs a full-absorption cost system, which means that sales volume, revenue, and costs of manufacture are preplanned and that variable and fixed costs are allocated over a program period, usually one year. This accounting method allows Chainco to calculate standard costs and levels of

## STRATEGY AT WORK

### CONNER TECHNOLOGY TO PRODUCE LOWEST-COST DISK DRIVES

When Conner Peripherals was sold to Seagate Technology in 1996, one of the conditions was that Finis Conner, Conner Peripherals' owner, would not compete for two years. Now Conner is back with a new entrepreneurial drivemaker, Conner Technology. Finis Conner's major strategy will be based on price—to be without a doubt the lowest-cost company in the business. On the surface that would seem a risky strategy, considering that the disk drive industry is in the throes of an ongoing, punishing price war.

Conner's plan includes bare-bones production of low-cost commodity drives. Incorporated in Ireland for a 10 percent tax rate, he assembles in China, scrimps on R & D, and minimizes overhead by outsourcing. As a result, the new company already is profitable and is selling drives for low-end computers at prices 5 percent lower than rivals'. Sales were projected to be 8 million units in 2000. Conner plans for the company to grow quickly, but it will be difficult for him to match the record growth rate of his previous company. That company hit the $1 billion mark within four years. The CEO of Seagate, whose company employs some 85,000 to Conner's 85, says, "I just feel bad for them. If you want to play with us in the cost arena, you are going to die."

### Assignment

Research Conner Technology's progress with this price strategy and report the results to the class. Explore how a technology change can impact a price strategy.

See "The New Buzzword in Disk Drives: Cheap," *Fortune*, May 10, 1999, p. 140.

---

profitability of all its products for the program period. This approach is typical of many business-to-business companies and is characterized by an annual forecasting and budgeting ritual, with updating of standard costs. Chainco limits its planned government business to 10 percent of total forecast. Government items are distinguished as such and have standard costs, including allocation of appropriate program and standby fixed costs. At midyear, Chainco received a bid invitation from the Department of the Interior for a considerable amount of crawler chain of a type similar to that manufactured for OEM customers. This was a one-time sales opportunity that would not require selling expense or the normal allocation of administrative expense and fixed costs. Chainco decided to use a marginal pricing approach and bid the proposal on the basis of out-of-pocket variable and fixed costs, plus profit. Using this approach, Chainco was awarded the contract. The bid price was less than standard cost for the items.

Was this transaction a sound business deal? Most executives would agree that it was. Marginal pricing often is used by contract bidders to gain unplanned business, or to utilize idle capacity. Exhibit 8-4 illustrates the factors involved in this approach. The overall objective of marginal pricing is to recover variable cost for marginal volume with add-on for profit and/or to recover from negative variance. The graph shows the difference between regular business-planned volume for a period and marginal business. In marginal pricing, adjusted fixed costs and marginal profit are substituted for conventional amounts.

### Economic Value to the Customer

Many customers buy on price, which is visible and measurable. Some suppliers compete on the same basis for the same reasons. However, a strategic advantage based on the total value delivered to the customer is far less easily duplicated by competitors. A value-based strategy such as economic value to the customer can be a uniquely effective way over time to gain a commanding lead over the competition. Recognizing this fact, some firms use a relatively new method of analyzing their products' **economic value to the customer (EVC)**. The economic value of a product to a business buyer is based on such factors as: (1) purchase price, (2) additional post-purchase costs such as training or retraining of employees, (3) costs associated with installation modifications; and (4) the product's ability to raise profits.

**EXHIBIT 8-4  Marginal Pricing**

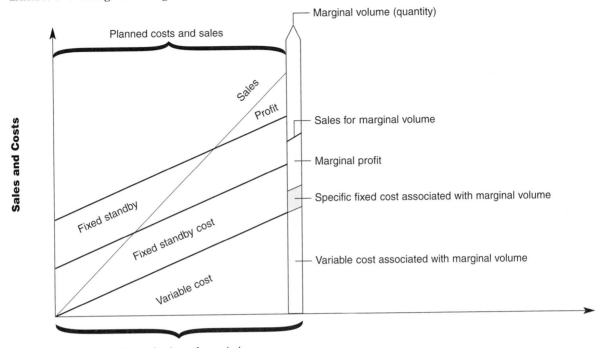

**Pricing objective:** Recover variable cost for marginal volume with add-on for profit and/or to recover from negative variance.

**Pricing Strategy:** Depending on demand and capacity situation, price to gain volume to reduce idle capacity with profit add-on depending on specific situation.

**Legend:** Sales: Gross revenue from sale or profit
Profit: Gross profit above designated costs
Variable Cost: Material, labor, variable overhead, and variable selling expense
Fixed standby cost: Planned operating cost under zero-volume condition
Fixed program cost: Planned cost for R & D, marketing, advertising, and improvement programs

This economic value is illustrated in Exhibit 8-5, when two products, X and Y, are compared. Because of favorable start-up and postpurchase costs, as well as an additional incremental value of $100 for Product X, the buyer (customer) should be willing to pay twice as much for Product X ($600) than for Product Y. From the manufacturer's viewpoint, it costs $300 to produce Product X. Therefore, any price in excess of $300 constitutes profit. Because any price under $600 gives the buyer a better deal than will be realized from buying Product Y, the supplier of Product X has a $300 competitive advantage. In addition, Supplier X could price the product to the customer at $475, which would result in $175 in profit and a $125 advantage over Product Y for the customer.

Adding value in this way also can mean making the product easier to use, making it more profitable, or giving it some other value advantage. Most professional buyers will pay a higher price when they perceive a greater value or benefit to them than they would receive from a competitive product.

## Break-Even Analysis

**Break-even analysis** defines the point (break-even point) at which a firm's revenue equals its total fixed and variable costs at a given price. Using various prices, a buyer can apply

**EXHIBIT 8-5   Economic Value to the Customer (EVC) Concept**

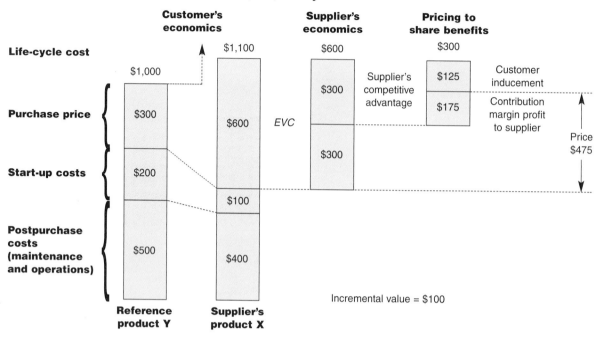

the following formula to calculate the number of units that would have to be sold at each price to break even:

$$\text{Break-even point (BEP)} = \frac{\text{Fixed cost}}{\text{Unit price} - \text{Unit variable cost}}$$

To calculate a break-even point, consider a company that manufactures a water sealer used to stop leaks in cement retainer walls. In 2003, the company sold 1,600,000 gallons of the sealer at a price of $3.00 per gallon with a variable production cost per gallon of $1.50. The fixed manufacturing costs were $1,550,000.

In 2004, more automated equipment will be used in production. This will increase the fixed manufacturing costs for the year to $1,785,000. The variable production cost per gallon has been estimated at $1.30 per gallon, and sales volume has a forecasted increase of 12.5 percent.

In 2003, the break-even point was 1,033,333 units, calculated as follows:

$$\frac{\$1,550,000}{\$1.50} = 1,033,333 \text{ units.}$$

In 2004, the break-even point will be 1,050,000 units, calculated as follows:

$$\frac{\$1,785,000}{\$1.70} = 1,050,000 \text{ units.}$$

Break-even analysis is used by the business marketer to determine the level of sales required to cover all relevant fixed and variable costs. This analysis indicates the impact that different pricing strategies will have on profit margins; it also identifies the minimum price below which losses will occur. Business managers should not set price without first determining what will happen to profits at various price levels.

## BUSINESS MARKETING IN ACTION

### BUYER PRICE SENSITIVITY

As marketing manager for a supplier of fuel injection systems, you would like to capture the contract for these systems on the next model of a German auto company's U.S. assembled sports car. Clearly, the quality and reliability requirements will be exceptionally demanding, but price will likely also be a factor. In making your pricing decision, you would like to estimate the price sensitivity of the buyer.

### Assignment

Develop a plan to estimate the price points where the buyer will perceive that the system is: (1) too expensive to purchase; (2) expensive but value justified; (3) inexpensive and accept-able, and (4) too inexpensive and implies questionable quality, service, a supplier that is not capable of accurately estimating, or a supplier that is intentionally underbidding to gain the business but has no intention of holding the price there very long. This assignment is much more challenging than it first appears. You will need to contact local companies and personally explore the issue with several product marketing managers, field sales people, and buyers. Be sure to consider the implications of setting a price without knowing these four price points, and whether real marketers are actually capable of estimating them accurately. Share your research and final plan with the class.

## Target Return-on-Investment Pricing

Some business-to-business firms set annual return-on-investment (ROI) targets, such as an ROI of 20 percent. **Target return-on-investment pricing** is a method of setting prices to achieve such an investment goal; it is one of the most widely used methods of establishing price strategy. Price is determined by adding a desired rate of return-on-investment total costs. A break-even analysis is performed for expected production and sales levels, and a rate of return is added.

Assume that a small business owner sets a target ROI of 10 percent—double that achieved the previous year. The owner considers raising the average price of a business widget to $54 or $58—*up* from last year's average of $50. To do so, the owner can improve product quality, which will increase cost but probably also will affect the decreased revenue from the lower number of units that can be sold next year.

To handle this variety of scenarios, the use of spreadsheets to project operating statements based on various assumptions clearly is in order. Exhibit 8-6 depicts such spreadsheet, with the assumptions shown at the top and the projected simulation results at the bottom. The results from a prior year's operating statement are shown in the column headed "Last Year," and the assumptions and spreadsheet results for four different sets of assumptions are shown in columns A, B, C, and D.

In choosing a price or another action using spreadsheet results, the owner must study the results of the computer simulation projections and then assess the realism of the assumptions underlying each set of projections. For example, the owner sees that the bottom row of the spreadsheet in Exhibit 8-6 shows that all four spreadsheet simulations achieve the after-tax target ROI of 10 percent. Yet, after more thought, the owner judges that it would be more realistic to set an average price of $58 per unit, allow the unit variable cost to increase by 20 percent to account for increased quality, and settle for the same unit sales as the 1,000 units sold last year. In this spreadsheet approach to target ROI pricing, the owner selects Simulation D and has a goal of 14 percent after-tax ROI.

## Target Costing

**Target costing** is an important area where marketing and the accounting function overlap. The target-costing process begins by identifying a product's desired features based on market research and its likely selling price. From this target selling price, the desired profit is

**EXHIBIT 8-6**   **Results of a Computer Spreadsheet Simulation to Select Price to Achieve a Target Return on Investment**

| Assumptions or Results | Financial Element | Last Year | Simulation | | | |
| --- | --- | --- | --- | --- | --- | --- |
| | | | A | B | C | D |
| Assumptions | Price per unit (P) | $50 | $54 | $54 | $58 | $58 |
| | Units sold (Q) | 1,000 | 1,200 | 1,100 | 1,100 | 1,000 |
| | Change in unit variable cost (UVC) | 0% | +10% | +10% | +20% | +20% |
| | Unit variable cost | $22.00 | $24.20 | $24.20 | $26.40 | $26.40 |
| | Total expenses | $8,000 | Same | Same | Same | Same |
| | Owner's salary | $18,000 | Same | Same | Same | Same |
| | Investment | $20,000 | Same | Same | Same | Same |
| | State and federal taxes | 50% | Same | Same | Same | Same |
| Spreadsheet simulation results | Net sales (P × Q) | $50,000 | $64,000 | $59,400 | $63,800 | $58,000 |
| | Less: COGS (Q × UVC) | $22,000 | $29,400 | $26,620 | $29,040 | $26,400 |
| | Gross margin | $28,000 | $35,760 | $32,700 | $34,760 | $31,600 |
| | Less: total expenses | 8,000 | 8,000 | 8,000 | 8,000 | 8,000 |
| | Less: owner's salary | 18,000 | 18,000 | 18,000 | 18,000 | 18,000 |
| | Net profit before taxes | $2,000 | $9,760 | $6,780 | $8,760 | $5,600 |
| | Less: taxes | 1,000 | 4,880 | 3,390 | 4,380 | 2,800 |
| | Net profit after taxes | $1,000 | $4,880 | $3,390 | $4,380 | $2,800 |
| | Investment | $20,000 | $20,000 | $20,000 | $20,000 | $20,000 |
| | Return on investment | 5.0% | 24.4% | 17.0% | 21.9% | 14.0% |

subtracted to determine the target cost. Teams from many departments then perform functional cost analyses in an attempt to reach the target cost. If the current cost estimate is at target, the firm must decide whether to introduce the new product. If the current cost estimate is above target, functional cost analysis is used to make changes and prepare another cost estimate.[6]

Management accountants help motivate market-driven behavior by using a market-based allowable cost that has to be realized if the company is to be profitable in a competitive market. Both the manufacturing and marketing functions are encouraged to respond to market demand and competitive trends rather than merely focus on internal performance indicators. A number of companies have begun to apply target costing with very favorable results.

## Zero-Based Pricing

**Zero-Based Pricing (ZBP)** is actually not a pricing method as much as it is the accounting of the method to the customer and the resulting requirement to maintain consistency. Zero-based pricing is the practice of business buyers demanding a cost breakdown to justify a price increase by a seller. Promoted by Polaroid for many years, ZBP was adopted by many buyers as an approach to control price increases. When a supplier requests a price increase, the customer asks to see how costs have increased, the premise being that the supplier would have to supply all of the cost elements from base zero (information that many suppliers would consider proprietary). The customer maintains that no single cost element increase justifies a price increase because: (1) other elements may have gone down, (2) the element cost increase may be something that the supplier would be expected to absorb (such as an efficiency decrease), and (3) the examination of the cost elements may uncover savings unaccounted for, such as volume efficiencies and fully recovered R&D costs. Suppliers not willing to provide all the cost element information must retract their request for a price increase. In single-source situations, common in just-in-time (JIT) relationships, the buyer often requires ZBP access to supplier cost information. Since the JIT buyer is not

## BUSINESS MARKETING IN ACTION

### PRICING EXTREME EQUIPMENT

As marketing manager for EUCLID heavy mining equipment, you notice a press release from your competitor, Caterpillar, for their new 797 mining truck. In reading the announcement over, you see that the new model, at 1.2 million pounds loaded, is the biggest mining truck ever built. For a truck that size you estimate fuel usage would run 160 gallons per hour, an oil change about $500, and a replacement tire about $30,000. You wonder what Caterpillar will set the selling price at for the 797. You certainly are hoping that it will not be priced less than your biggest EUCLUD, which sells for over $2,000,000.

### Action Assignment

Research and report on websites that may be useful in your search for additional information on the pricing of

the 797. Note that Caterpillar does not have to sell a particular customer at its announced list price. In addition to sites and information you uncover, report on the potential for pricing information contacts from the program listings for heavy equipment industry conferences such as the World Mining Equipment Conference (www.wme.com) and (www.wme.com/wme/conferences/haul_II). Also report on why information such as the "news" price releases from www.atchisoncasting.com could be useful. Your presentation to the class should include downloaded pictures comparing the 797 to your product (www.euclid-hitachi.com).

searching for competitive bids, the cost information is necessary to ensure that the price quoted by the supplier is fair.

## Demand Assessment and Strategy

Before deciding on a pricing method to use in a particular market, the marketer must have a clear understanding of the nature of the demand in that market. *Demand* refers to the amount of a good or service that a buyer or buyers are willing and able to purchase at a particular moment at each possible price. Demand is more than a desire to purchase; it is the ability to purchase, as well.

### Price Elasticity of Demand

At lower prices, one may assume that more is bought. But how much more? Similarly, at higher prices, less is bought. Yet, how much less is bought— much less or only a little less? To answer questions such as these, a business marketer should apply the concept of **price elasticity of demand**, which states simply that demand is elastic if quantity is highly responsive to price and inelastic if it is not. In other words, *elasticity* is the relative change in the dependent variable divided by the relative change in the independent variable. The dependent variable is quantity demanded; the independent variable is price. Price elasticity (E) of demand is expressed as follows:

$$E = \frac{(\text{Initial quantity demanded} - \text{New quantity demanded}) / \text{Initial quantity demanded}}{(\text{Initial price} - \text{New price}) / \text{Initial price}}$$

Price elasticity of demand assumes three forms: elastic demand, inelastic demand, and unitary demand. **Elastic demand** exists when a small-percentage decrease in price produces a larger-percentage increase in quantity demanded. Price elasticity is greater than 1 with elastic demand. **Inelastic demand** exists when a small-percentage decrease in price produces a smaller percentage increase in quantity demanded. With inelastic demand, price elasticity is less than 1. **Unitary demand elasticity** exists when the percentage change in price is identical to the percentage change in quantity demanded. In this instance, price elasticity is equal to 1.

Price elasticity of demand is determined by a number of factors. First, the more substitutes a product or service has, the more likely that product will be price elastic. Plastic and steel may be a substitute for each other in particular situations, so one or the other can be said to be price elastic. Second, products and services considered to be necessities are generally price inelastic. For example, office supplies, in general, are price inelastic, whereas new office furniture is price elastic. However, although the office supplies product category is price inelastic, the demand for a specific brand within it, such as BIC pens, may be highly elastic. Thus, individual brands within a product category may have elasticities of demand totally different from the product category itself. Price elasticity is important to the business marketing manager because of its relationship to total revenue and price-setting strategies. For instance, with elastic demand, total revenue increases when price decreases but decreases when price increases. With inelastic demand, total revenue increases when price increases and decreases when price decreases. Finally, with unitary demand, total revenue is unaffected by a slight price change.

Although price elasticity of demand is useful for understanding micro consumer markets, such as the market for ball point pens, price elasticity of demand is not a simple tool for the typical business marketer to apply. The business marketer, in fact, often has little access to elasticity information. As a case in point, suppose a supplier of brake sets knows that Ford Motor Company will buy enough brake sets to match the number of cars it produces. If the brake producer lowers the price, the result will not likely mean that more Fords will be sold. The only elasticity might be that the Ford buyer may award the brake producer a larger share of its purchases in return for the lower price. To assume that its share will increase, the supplier must assume that the buyer considers only price as a factor, and that the competition will not respond. In application, it is not uncommon for the buyer's performance to be measured by its ability to reduce purchasing costs by 10 percent per year. Under heavy price pressure, the marketer rarely turns to theoretical demand curves. Economics is theoretically correct, but difficult to apply in many business marketing situations.

## Cost-Benefit Analysis

**Cost-benefit analysis** (not to be confused with value analysis as discussed in Chapter 4) is the technique of assigning a dollar value to the costs and benefits of a product or service. When used in determining demand, cost-benefit analysis is an analysis of benefits received and costs incurred by the customer in buying and using a business product. The comparison of costs and benefits can be used to gain the customer's perspective of the business product or service, thereby allowing the business marketer to set prices more realistically. Some firms see the buyer's perception of value—not the seller's cost—as the key to pricing. They use the nonprice variables in the marking mix to build up perceived value in the buyer's mind. Price is set to capture the perceived value.

If the business marketer charges more than the buyer's perceived benefits from the product or service, company sales will suffer. Other firms may underprice their products or services. In such a situation, the product or service sells well, but less revenue is generated than if price were raised to the perceived-value level.

---

**Concept Review**

1. What is the basic purpose of the Robinson-Patman Act?

2. What is the primary purpose of using marginal pricing? Target return-on-investment pricing? Zero-based pricing?

3. What is price elasticity of demand? Why is it a difficult tool for business marketers to use?

# Life-Cycle Costing

In addition to controllable internal factors, business marketers must consider external factors in developing prices for new products. Further, changes in either of these environments may require a review of the prices of products already on the market. If a large, dominant firm in the industry raises or lowers prices, other firms in the industry will be forced to examine their prices as the product or product line moves through the stages of the product life cycle. This process is known as **life-cycle costing**. From the buyer's perspective, a product's life-cycle cost includes the initial purchase price plus future expenses such as start up, maintenance, and power. To accurately compare competitive offerings, the buyer calculates a net present value for these projected future expenses. Thus, a product's high initial cost may be economically justified by lower operating costs.

## Introduction Phase: New Product Pricing Strategies

A new product usually enjoys its greatest degree of differentiation during the introductory stage of the product life cycle (PLC), with demand being more inelastic at this stage than at any other stage. However, the substantial investment that the firm must recover forces the price setter to decide how soon the firm must recover that investment. Whether an investment will be recovered quickly or over the product life span depends on factors such as the nature of the product, the projected product life, the nature of the potential competition, and the financial strength of the firm. Two opposite pricing strategies for introducing a new product are *price skimming* and *market penetration.*

### *Price Skimming*

With **price skimming**, the introductory price is set relatively high, thereby attracting buyers at the top of the product's demand curve. This permits the recovery of research and development costs more quickly as the firm attempts to "skim" the market. DuPont often is cited as a prime user of a price-skimming practice. On new discoveries such as cellophane and nylon, the firm determined the highest price it could charge given the benefits of the new product over other products customers might buy. DuPont set prices at a level that made it just worthwhile enough for some segments of the market to adopt the new material. After the initial sales slacked off, the firm lowered the price to draw in the next more price-sensitive layer of customers. In this way, DuPont skimmed a maximum amount of revenue from the various segments of the market. As demonstrated in Exhibit 8-7, a skimming strategy assumes that layers of customers can be peeled off the demand curve.

**EXHIBIT 8-7   Price Skimming**

If the original skimming price is within Expected Price Range 1, the marketer will peel off customers along the A portion of the demand curve.

If the price is lowered within Expected Price Range 2, the marketer will peel off the second layer of customers along the B portion of the demand curve.

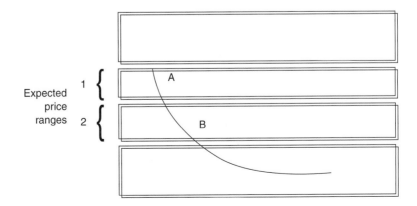

A price-skimming maneuver is not without potential problems, however. The high initial price tends to attract competition, as other firms see that the product is selling well at a relatively high price. Consequently, competitors tend to introduce rival offerings. By the time the business marketer is ready to peel off the next layer of customers, these rival offerings may already be on the market. Therefore, a skimming strategy will be more effective when the product has a strong patent position, or when there are other barriers to market entry, such as extremely complex technology or very high capital requirements.

At least one powerful polymer producer makes particularly effective use of price skimming (more tactfully referred to as *high value-added pricing*) due to custom formulations, high-volume production requirements, and the high barriers of entry in their industry. It is difficult for a competitor to fund the R&D necessary to match the material and gain enough volume orders to justify the capital equipment and efficient production runs. When a competitor does manage to enter the market with a lower price, the powerful producer responds not by lowering price, but by advising customers that if purchase volume drops, they will withdraw from the market. The customers know that if the powerful producer withdraws, the new supplier will almost certainly raise prices. The powerful producer's strategic market approach is to only use its resources to pursue markets where it has a sustainable differential advantage that can justify high profit margins. Companies that pursue low value-added generic markets would tend to have lower technical capacity, less overhead, and, often, older processing equipment.

### Market-Penetration Pricing

Despite the many advantages, a skimming-price policy is not appropriate for all new product introductions. High prices may maximize profits during the early part of the introductory phase of the PLC, but also they may prevent sales to many of the buyers upon whom the firm relies. **Market-penetration pricing** involves setting a price at or near the point it will eventually reach after competition develops. This low-price wedge allows the firm to gain a large volume of initial sales even though profit per unit may be low.

A market-penetration pricing approach is likely to be desirable under any of the following conditions: (1) when sales volume of the product is very sensitive to price, even in the early stages of introduction, (2) when it is possible to achieve substantial economies in unit cost of manufacturing and distributing the product by operating at large volume, (3) when a product faces threats of strong potential competition very soon after introduction, and (4) when there is no elite market—that is, no class of buyers willing to pay a higher price to obtain the newest and the best.

While a penetration pricing policy can be adopted at any stage in the product life cycle, this strategy should at least be examined before a new product is marketed at all. Texas Instruments is a prime user of market-penetration pricing. This firm historically sets a price as low as possible, wins a large share of the market, experiences falling costs through experience relating to the learning curve concept, and cuts its price further as costs fall. According to this theory, as the cumulative production volume of a product increases, the per-unit cost of producing that product will decline at a predictable rate due to the accumulated experience in producing the product. Costs drop, workers become more productive, and operations in general become more efficient.

In contrast to DuPont's skimming strategy, Dow Chemical has used penetration pricing for some products. Dow prices low, builds a dominant market share, emphasizes low-margin, commodity products, and focuses on the long term.

## Growth Phase

A product in the growth phase of the PLC generally is faced with severe competitive pressures, with business buyers focusing primarily on price in the buying decision. The benefits of economies of scale, and the effects of the experience curve referred to earlier, might allow the firm to lower price as a competitive strategy. Competition is aggressive, as this is a period of rapid market acceptance and increasing profits. Profits tend to peak toward the end of the market-growth phase, and the producer faces a trade-off between high market share and high current profit.

### Maturity Phase

To price appropriately in the maturity phase, the business marketer needs to know when the product is approaching maturity. The marketer may find it desirable to reduce prices as soon as symptoms of deterioration appear. Some of these symptoms are as follows:

1. *Weakening in brand preference.* This may be evidenced by a higher cross-elasticity of demand among leading products, with the leading brand being unable to continue demanding as much of a price premium as it initially did, without losing any position.
2. *Narrowing physical variation among products.* This occurs as the best designs are developed and standardized.
3. *Market saturation.* The ratio of replacement sales to new equipment sales serves as an indicator of the competitive degeneration of products.
4. *The stabilization of production methods.* This is indicated by the slow rate of technological advance and the high average age of equipment.

### Decline Phase

The decline phase of the PLC presents the business price setter with a number of opportunities. Cost control becomes increasingly important as demand drops, possibly allowing the marketer to leave the price unchanged while maintaining short-term profit objectives as the product dies a natural death. In the absence of tight cost control, the strategy may be to raise price, taking advantage of the segments with inelastic demand. A final pricing strategy could be to use the product as a **loss leader**. Pricing the product at cost, or even under cost—much the same as is done in consumer retail pricing strategy—might help sell complementary products in the line.

## Price-Leadership Strategy

In pricing a firm's products over their respective life cycles, business marketing managers in a leadership position must decide whether they will pursue their task as a market leader, and how to do so. *Price-leadership strategy* prevails in oligopolistic situations; it is the practice by which one or a very few firms initiate price changes, with most or all the other firms in the industry following suit. When price leadership prevails in an industry, price competition does not exist. The burden of making critical pricing decisions is placed on the leading firm; others simply follow the leader.

Price leadership is found most often in industries whose products are similar, even standardized, and are therefore considered by customers to be good substitutes for each other. In such industries, a firm would lose market share if it charged a higher price than its competitors. Price leadership is a way of coordinating prices without colluding. This practice is at once a sign of so much competition in an industry that all firms involved have to sell at about the same price in order to stay in business, or of so little competition that firms are able to coordinate their prices as they would under a collusive agreement. Usually, the leader is the firm with the largest market share, such as U.S. Steel or IBM, or the firm that makes the first upward move. Implicit in price leadership is a willingness to live and let live. Price wars are rare, as price deviation is quickly disciplined. Successful price leaders are characterized by the following description:

1. Large share of the industry's production capacity
2. Large market share
3. Commitment to a particular product class or grade
4. New, cost-efficient plants
5. Strong distribution system, perhaps including captive wholesale outlets
6. Good customer relations, such as technical assistance for business buyers, programs directed at end users, and special attention to important customers during shortage periods
7. An effective market-information system that provides analysis of the realities of supply and demand
8. Sensitivity to the price and profit needs of the rest of the industry
9. A sense of timing to know when price changes should be made
10. Sound management organization for pricing
11. Effective product-line financial controls, which are needed to make sound price-leadership decisions
12. Attention to legal issues

Price leadership requires certain things of the leaders. For example, the presence of a specific and consistent pricing strategy, the use of controlled power, and the recognition of the rights of followers to their respective market positions will sustain a leadership position. The threat of independent pricing action is always there, ready to break out if the leader fails to make the right decisions. The leader must be aware that if wrong decisions are made, followers will likely destroy that position of leadership.

## Competitive Bidding in the Business Market

Buyers for business market leaders and followers alike engage in competitive bidding. *Competitive bidding* is a process in which a business buyer requests bids from interested suppliers on a proposed purchase or contract. Stated another way, competitive bidding is the method by which firms efficiently and effectively compare supplier offerings and negotiate for the best combination of quality, service, and price. This process is used not only for custom-engineered products but also for standard manufactured products, components, and services. The buyer sends inquiries or requests for quotations (RFQ) to firms able to produce in conformity with requested requirements. A request for proposals (RFP) involves the same process, but here the buyer is signaling that everything is preliminary, and that a future RFQ will be sent once the specifics are determined from the best proposals.

### The Bidding Process

The marketer must decide whether to bid on a specific supply requirement or job. For the prospective supplier who receives the RFQ invitation to bid, the bidding process itself represents an investment of company resources and an estimate of the likelihood of being awarded the contract must be considered.

Whether to bid, as earlier mentioned, can present the marketer with a dilemma. A number of criteria in determining whether to bid on a job are included in the following questions:

1. Is the dollar value of the job large enough to warrant the expense involved in making the bid?

## BUSINESS MARKETING IN ACTION

### SELLING ORIENTATION AND UNDERPRICING CAN LEAD TO BANKRUPTCY

XYZ Custom Machines boasted of customers such as Néstlé and Campbell Soup and of the fact that it supplied them with unique and specialized food processing and packaging machines. Between 1989 and 1995 the company was successful and enjoyed a well-earned reputation for "machine design problem- solving wizardry." At that point the president began a bold expansion plan, tripling the company's floor space, and committing to more and more customer projects. Instead of keeping current customers satisfied, XYZ was constantly looking for bigger and bigger contracts. By the end of 1997, the large number of contracts in process resulted in problems in quality and delivery schedules. It was reported that larger contracts were gained by underpricing, and that the down-payment money from one project was being used to try to finish projects started earlier. When it filed for Chapter 11 bankruptcy in 1999, XYZ showed $57,000 in assets and about 200 creditors

with $1,000,000 in claims. Some of the claims were from customers that sent down payments but never received the machines they ordered.

### Action Assignment

Interview purchasing agents (buyers) from local companies concerning how they protect themselves from this type of problem (i.e., underbidding to get the business, even though it will be unprofitable for the supplier). Buyers know that some suppliers will try to "buy" the business (with an unrealistically low bid) and then try to raise the price later, or, as in XYZ's case, fail to perform. Present your findings to the class and discuss whether the buyers you interviewed routinely purchase from the lowest bidder (the answer may depend on the nature of the product).

Adapted from "Machine Maker Unhinged by Sales Emphasis," *INC*, March 1999, p. 251

2. Are the product or service specifications ("specs") precise enough for the cost of production to be accurately estimated?
3. Will the acceptance of the bid adversely affect production and the ability to serve other customers?
4. How much time is available to prepare the bid?
5. What is the likelihood of winning the bid, considering the presence and strength of other bidders?

Exhibit 8-8 shows a typical bid process in which marketing accepts the RFQ; a cost estimator sorts out information on necessary outside purchases and forwards them to purchasing; a materials engineer specifies what material to use; a process engineer designs a process to produce the product; the cost estimator determines the labor and cost involved in the two previous steps and brings in the component bids from the outside suppliers; and the marketing manager receives all the cost information and determines a final price, as well as any other terms and conditions of sale. One of the lesser-known functions of the marketer is to evaluate the final cost estimate for overstatement or excess conservatism. While estimators are rarely rewarded for estimating in such a way to ensure that the bid is successful, they may be punished if the bid is successful and the product cannot be produced within the cost estimated. This sometimes leads to "fat" or overly conservative estimates. From the estimators' perspectives, if they take a risk estimating a job aggressively, the field salespeople may earn big commissions from the orders and the estimators may end up with the extra work of actually having to create a process that produces the product as estimated.

Firms that bid for work must deal with the risks and uncertainties connected with such bidding. Different companies have different cost formulas, different processes, and different objectives for pricing. Competitive bids from several different firms for basically identical items will vary, even when internal cost structures might be essentially the same for all competitors. The market price level is therefore not a specific value for a given item; rather, it is a wide range of prices with fairly well-defined limits for each industry. Also

**EXHIBIT 8-8**  **Estimating Process on a New Product**

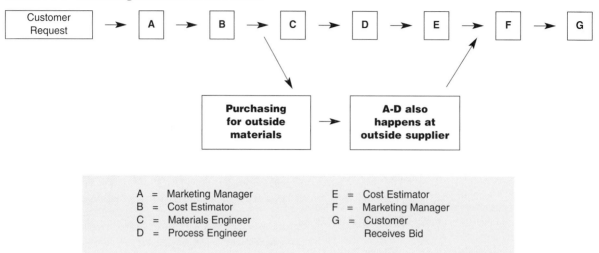

| | |
|---|---|
| A = Marketing Manager | E = Cost Estimator |
| B = Cost Estimator | F = Marketing Manager |
| C = Materials Engineer | G = Customer |
| D = Process Engineer | Receives Bid |

important in deciding whether to bid is excess capacity and alternative opportunities to utilize this capacity. Related to this is the extent to which competitive bidders have excess capacity and, therefore, would be expected to bid low.

When a potential customer creates an RFQ, it contains a date specifying when the completed formal bid must be received. Marketing must ensure that the estimating process is complete by that date. An on-time bid with all issues covered greatly increases the likelihood of success, and signals the buyer that the supplier is sensitive to customer needs, professional, responsive, and efficient.[7] It is easy to understand why engineers and estimators often want extra time to research and experiment to ensure the most accurate projections possible, but a late bid is often a lost bid.

## Closed Versus Open Bidding

Government units (federal and local) and most public institutions are required to buy products and services on the competitive bidding system. The contemplated purchase is advertised in advance, giving the potential business supplier the opportunity to consider submitting a bid. Many of these bids are made public; thus, price competition is emphasized. A price setter often is required to submit a performance bond along with the bid to assure that quality and service will not suffer due to the emphasis on price. Such a requirement may discourage some marketers from competing in this arena.

Competitive bidding can take the form of **closed bidding** which consists of sealed bids, all opened, reviewed, and evaluated at the same time. Again, price is stressed, with the lowest bid usually winning the contract. Although the lowest bidder is not guaranteed the contract, this bidder normally will win the business if the bid is for standard products or services or if the product is to be made to exact buyer specifications.

Competitive bidding also can take the form of **open bidding**, which is more informal, allows for negotiation, and often is used when there is much flexibility with regard to buyer specifications. Complex technical requirements would utilize an open bidding process, as would the purchase of products for which specific requirements are hard to define precisely.

As an example, assume the buying firm needs tooling or machinery to accomplish a production task but does not know exactly what configuration the tooling or machinery should be. The buyer can show the seller what needs to be done, giving the seller great latitude in solving the problem. The buyer is, in effect, asking the seller to solve a problem. The seller

**EXHIBIT 8-9**
**Some Reasons Why Selling Prices are Changed**

Competition-driven price adjustments may be necessary when:

- A new aggressive competitor appears
- An old aggressive competitor withdraws from the market
- Competitors introduce new offerings
- Competitors adjust their prices enough to impact your market share

Internally driven price adjustments may be necessary when:

- The cost of production changes
- Capacity changes
- Corporate profitability requirements change

Externally driven price adjustments may be necessary when:

- Levels of recession, business cycles, seasonality, and other factors change to create new demand variability
- Rates of inflation change significantly
- Government actions impact markets

Note: Although professionals in marketing and purchasing are well-trained in dealing with price change negotiations, some changes result in the buyer shifting from a "straight rebuy" to a "modified rebuy" in that they may seek a new source.

would submit an open bid or idea and possibly discuss and modify it with members of the buying center, negotiate price, delivery, terms, and so on and receive the contract. This open bidding process is quite common in high-tech industries. A downside of the process would be if the supplier provided an innovative solution to the buyer's problem, but then the business was put out for competitive bids and the helpful supplier lost (perhaps because the R & D capability that was employed to find a solution was reflected as increased overhead and made the supplier's bid higher than a competitor's that had no such capabilities).

## Price Changes

Theoretically, product managers can strategically choose to adjust selling prices for new orders or existing products either up or down. In the real world of competitive markets and aggressive purchasing, raising prices can be particularly difficult. When either raising or lowering price, wise marketers cost justify their actions to the customer. For example, production improvement and value analysis innovations can justify reducing a selling price. Facing uncontrollable increased material costs may be used to attempt to justify a price increase. Marketers are often under considerable internal pressure to increase prices, while at the same time, under customer and field sales pressure to reduce them. Typically, prices are formally reviewed at set intervals but, occasionally, as seen in Exhibit 8-9, immediate action is necessary.

**Concept Review**

1. What are the advantages and disadvantages of market skimming and market penetration?

2. Why does the price leadership strategy prevail in oligopolistic situations?

3. What is the major difference between open bidding and closed bidding?

## Leasing in the Business Market

In addition to the choice of whether to engage in competitive bidding, business buyers must also decide in appropriate situations whether to buy or to lease an asset. Many business customers choose to lease rather than to purchase; for the astute business marketer, leasing

# BUSINESS MARKETING IN ACTION

## LEARNING HOW IT FEELS TO MAKE ACTUAL PRICE DECISIONS

To: Marketing Manager (you)
From: Field Sales
Subject: New Price for XYZ Company Part # 45367 Rev. C

As you know, Therese Garcia, our buyer, is under a lot of pressure to reduce purchasing costs by 10 percent. The current price of the above-referenced product is $10.00 and the projected quantity is 1,000,000 units per year. What price can we offer her for the next year?

### Assignment A

You call up the part number on your computer and note that the price and quantity are correct and the cost system states that the direct cost is $5.00 per unit and the overhead is $2.00 per unit. The marketing information system suggests weak competitive activity with no other internal or external factors to be considered. Make a price decision and formally respond to the field salesperson.

___

To: Marketing Manager
From: Manufacturing Manager
Subject: New cost for XYZ Company Part # 45367 Rev. C

Because of strict cost controls and production improvements, the cost will be reduced from $5.00 per unit to $4.95 per unit.

### Assignment B

Calculate the annual cost saving and send manufacturing a note of congratulations and appreciation. Also decide how much of this savings to pass on to the customer (if any).

___

To: Marketing Manager
From: Field Sales
Subject: Customer need—XYZ Company Part # 45367 Rev. C

XYZ still is plating each of our parts received to protect them from rust. It is a messy job, and it costs them $1.00 per unit. XYZ is requesting that we put this issue at the head of our value analysis (see Chapter 2) projects.

### Assignment C

Compose an e-mail to R &D requesting assistance, and provide a priority and spending guidelines.

___

To: Marketing Manager
From: R & D Manager
Subject: Rust Resistance, XYZ Company Part # 45367 Rev. C

Good news! We have just invented a rust-preventative material additive that will meet XYZ's requirements. We can add it when we produce the part, and it will increase our cost by only $.01 per unit, therefore the cost will now be $4.96 per unit.

### Assignment D

Calculate that savings based on alternative prices such as $11.00 per unit, $10.01, and $10.51. Develop and justify a final price and proposal for XYZ.

___

can provide a very viable alternative to buying capital equipment. A lease involves a **lessee** and a **lessor**, with the lessee being the party that acquires the right to use the property, plant, or equipment, and the lessor being the party that relinquishes the right in return for some form of consideration.

In the business market, leasing strategy is employed by most capital goods and equipment manufacturers, including those that market production machinery, postage meters, packaging equipment, textile equipment, copiers, and the like. As an example, in its 1988 financial statements, Farmland Industries reported leased assets including "railroad cars, automobiles, . . . three fertilizer manufacturing facilities, electronic data processing equipment, and other manufacturing facilities." Indeed, almost any asset that can be acquired through purchase can be obtained through lease.

Leasing also lends itself to a *bundling pricing strategy*. **Bundling**, or *iceberg pricing*, refers to the inclusion of an extra margin (for support services) in the price over and above the price of the product as such. This type of pricing strategy has been popular with companies that lease rather than sell their products. IBM once followed a bundling strategy whereby it charged one fee for hardware, services, software, and consulting. The main rationale behind product bundling is that it increases the firm's performance in creating a competitive advantage.

## Advantages of Leasing for the Buyer

From both the buyer's and seller's points of view, there are several advantages of leasing over purchasing. The following advantages pertain to the buyer.

### No Down Payment

Lease agreements are frequently structured so that 100 percent of the value of the equipment is financed through the lease, making this an attractive alternative to a company that does not have sufficient cash for a down payment or that wishes to use available capital for other operating or investing purposes.

### No Risks of Ownership

There are many risks of ownership, including casualty loss, obsolescence, changing economic conditions, and physical deterioration. The lessee may terminate the lease (usually with a predetermined penalty) and thus avoid assuming the risk of these events. This flexibility is especially important to the buyer in a business in which innovation and technological change make the future usefulness of a piece of equipment or facility highly uncertain. A good example of this condition in recent years has been the electronics industry, with its rapid change in areas such as computer technology, robotics, and telecommunications.

## Advantages of Leasing for the Seller

### Increased Sales

By offering potential customers the option of leasing products, the marketer can significantly increase sales volume. Leasing can be a vehicle to attract customers who otherwise might find a product unaffordable. Market growth can be boosted because many more customers can afford to lease products than can afford to buy them.

### Ongoing Business Relationship with the Lessee

In leasing situations, the lessor and lessee maintain contact over a period of time, so that long-term business relationships will be promulgated through leasing.

### Residual Value Retained

In many lease arrangements, title to the asset does not pass to the lessee. The lessor benefits from economic conditions that can result in a significant residual value at the end of the lease term. The lessor may lease the asset to another lessee or sell the property and realize an immediate gain.

## Types of Lease Arrangements

There are three basic ways of leasing equipment in the business sector. First, the business firm can lease directly to the customer, financing the lease arrangements itself. In essence, the seller acts as a financial institution would, operating on the basis of monthly or quarterly payments— much like repaying a debt to a financial institution. Second, several large firms have established leasing subsidiaries to provide this service to the business customer (John Deere and General Electric, for example). Third, lease transactions are arranged for customers through a lending institution involved in leasing to the business market. Examples of companies using such a practice include General Finance Corporation, U.S. Leasing, and C.I.T. Financial. This is called a *direct-financing lease* and involves a lessor that is engaged primarily in financial activities, such as a bank or finance company.

## Types of Business Leases

The two types of leases from the lessor's standpoint are the operating lease and the direct-financing leases.

### *Operating Lease*

An *operating lease* usually is short term and cancelable. The lessor gives up the physical possession of the asset, but the transfer is considered temporary in nature. As such, the lessor continues to carry the leased asset as an owned asset on the balance sheet, and the revenue from the lease is reported as it is earned. Depreciation of the leased asset is matched against the revenue. Generally, the lessor provides maintenance and service, and the lease will not contain a purchase option. Under an operating lease, the lessor retains substantially all the risks and benefits of ownership.

### *Direct-Financing Lease*

A *direct-financing lease* is noncancelable, usually long term, and fully amortized over the period of the contract. The sum of the lease payments exceeds the price paid for the asset by the lessor. The lessee is responsible for operating expenses and is usually given the option of purchasing the asset; often, a portion of the lease payments will be applied toward the purchase of the asset.

## Pricing Discount Strategies

Another important decision faced by business-to-business firms is the marketing manager's choice of pricing policies to follow. The prices charged by the marketer are influenced by different types of customers, characteristics of the channel system, and different geographic regions served. Initially, the business price setter must be concerned with *net price,* which is the list price minus allowances for trade-ins and other cost-significant concessions made by the buyer, such as volume purchases and order pick-up versus delivery. Examination of business practice indicate that most firms offer discounts of one form or another to their business customers. Further, it appears that discounts are important components of the pricing policies of many firms. The establishment of a list price provides the base from which discounts can be subtracted. Discounts come in many forms, with trade, quantity, and cash discounts being most prevalent. In theory, discounts are simply cost savings realized by the manufacturer and passed on to intermediaries.

### Trade Discounts

A **trade discount** is a deduction from the list price that is offered to an intermediary in return for services performed. Generally, the more services performed by the intermediary, the higher the trade discount. These services include inventory holding, providing of customer credit, technical support for the manufacturer, and missionary sales. A note of caution, however, is in order here. As business price setters contemplate trade-discount strategy, they should give considerable thought to the Robinson-Patman Act. As pointed out in Exhibit 8-3, this piece of legislation takes a dim view of price discrimination practices, such as giving a different discount schedule to basically the same types of customers. Discounts must be nondiscriminatory, and while the Robinson-Patman Act is difficult to police and enforce, the price setter should at least be aware of possible ramifications if charged with a violation of this act.

### Quantity Discounts

A **quantity discount** is a deduction in the list price that a manufacturer gives either to channel intermediaries or to OEM users for buying in large amounts. Cost savings can be found in inventory storage, transportation cost per unit, sales calls, follow-up service, and order processing. The two primary types of quantity discounts available are *noncumulative discounts,* which are discounts taken on each order made, and *cumulative discounts,* which are given on a series of orders over a particular period of time. Quantity discounts are considered legal as long as business sellers can demonstrate that their costs are reduced by selling in large volume. In the case of cumulative quantity discounts, savings are harder to prove, in that the granting of such discounts does not necessarily result in reduced storage or order-processing costs. Manufacturers, with judicial support, may claim that they legally provide cumulative quantity discounts to meet similar competitive offerings.

## Cash Discounts

A **cash discount** is a price reduction strategy to encourage buyers to pay their bills promptly, with a discount of 2/10, net 30 being common. (Payment is due within 30 days, but the buyer can deduct 2 percent from the total invoice amount for payment within 10 days.) This strategy typically improves the seller's liquidity and reduces credit collection costs and bad debts. Again, as listed in Exhibit 8-3, the seller must be aware of the provisions of the Robinson-Patman Act, which stipulate that the terms must be offered to all buyers, large and small alike.

## Geographical Price Adjustments

Shipping costs heavily impact the ultimate cost of business products to the buyer, with prices being adjusted upward or downward, depending on who pays the transportation bill (the buyer or the seller). Transportation fees are an especially important factor when pricing large bulky products, such as business machinery and equipment, that must travel a long distance. This part of the ultimate cost of the business product usually is settled through a negotiated agreement between the buyer and the seller. Several alternative price strategies are available to sellers, as the rate structure of transportation in the United States is highly complex, with class and commodity rates, local and joint rates, contract and transit rates, and so on. There are separate rate tariffs (or price lists) for various geographic regions; shipments are classified into a number of groupings, called *classes,* for rate-quotation purposes. Given the complexity of the rate structure, the determination of the applicable (or lowest) rate for shipment between two points sometimes is difficult and has become an important function of traffic management. Traffic management personnel must have knowledge of transportation tariffs, classifications, and rate structures.

---

**Concept Review**

1. What are the main advantages of leasing to the seller? The buyer?

2. Why are trade discounts important to an intermediary?

---

## Summary

- Because there are so many variables to consider whose precise influence cannot be anticipated, pricing decisions often are made by intuition or reliance on methods such as traditional markup percentages. The major factors on which the success of pricing strategy is based include competition, cost, demand, pricing objectives, impact on other products, and legal considerations. An important step in pricing strategy is to determine goals and objectives prior to setting price points or levels. The principal pricing objectives of most firms include profit generation, a satisfactory return on investment, and the maintenance or increase of market share. Often, the purchase of one product increases the likelihood of the purchase of another product or product line by the same customer. Business marketers should be prepared to justify price levels, along with quantity and trade discounts.

# WHAT WOULD YOU DO?

## PRECISION COLOR FIBERS AT EFFI

Mike Walters, a sales representative for Extreme Fibers & Fabrics Inc. (EFFI), was presenting his samples of various brightly colored woven nylon fabrics to a prospective customer at ABM Industries. ABM produced a variety of final assemblies for OEMs, only a few of which called for synthetic fabric or webbing as components. Mike's company was well known for the variety and intensity of color it could impart to nylon fibers. Mike knew ABM's customers were very demanding about color matching. That could be quite a challenge, considering that ABM's assemblies would be installed right next to assemblies of other materials, produced by other manufacturers (and all would have to match perfectly). Mike also knew his company's differential advantage in color matching was reflected in the higher-than-industry-average profit margins it charged. In fact, if the customer didn't care much about having an exact color with excellent "lot to lot" match, his company would not be competitive. Low-end competitors without good color control priced their products much too low. Mike suspected they either didn't have the kind of overhead that EFFI carried, or they just price cut each other to death (probably both).

As the sales presentation proceeded and Mike probed for the benefits and issues that truly mattered to this buyer, he wasn't surprised to find that exact color match was indeed the critical factor. Mike realized that was why the buyer had contacted EFFI and invited a representative to call. Seeing the critical nature of the need, Mike decided to go for maximum markup, which would provide a very high profit margin indeed.

The buyer's reaction to Mike's trial pricing told him that the price would not be a problem. He might even have been able to get a little more. His qualifying questions to the buyer also had indicated that in the buying center (the group of people who influence the purchase decision for this product), the buyer would make the final decision.

Much to Mike's surprise, the color the buyer finally settled on did not require a custom match, nor was it one from the many color standard chips in his sales kit. The buyer went right to a chip of white that Mike had occasionally used to demonstrate the color of the raw material prior to the EFFI coloring process. The buyer's lab tested the sample and confirmed that under a particular light, it did indeed match their requirement.

Mike considered his options, but only for a split second. He could: (1) tell the buyer that all nylon started out that color and any low-cost producer could supply his needs at a lower price; (2) lower the price to reflect the true nature of the product; (3) maintain the higher price; or (4) maintain the higher price and describe how "controlling such a light color would require extra processing that would be very difficult," and in light of that he had probably offered too low a price, (but he would see that the technical and operations people did everything they could to be able to produce the product at the price quoted).

### Assignment

Define the ethical issues and develop an action plan for Mike. Consider the role of company values that would influence Mike's actions.

---

- Among the pricing methods and strategies commonly used by price setters are marginal pricing, break-even analysis, and target return-on-investment pricing. Marginal pricing often is used by contract bidders to gain unplanned business or to utilize idle capacity. A value-based strategy, such as the relatively new method of analyzing a product's economic value to a customer, can be a uniquely effective way to gain a commanding lead over the competition. Break-even analysis is used to determine the point at which a firm's revenue will equal its total fixed and variable costs at a given price. Target return-on-investment pricing is a method of setting prices to achieve a particular percentage return on capital invested in the product in question.

- Demand refers to the amount of a good or service that a buyer or buyers are willing and able to purchase at a particular moment at each possible price.

Demand is elastic if quantity is highly responsive to price and inelastic if it is not. Unitary demand elasticity exists when the percentage change in price is identical to the percentage change in quantity demanded. When attempting to determine demand, cost-benefit analysis is an analysis of benefits received and costs incurred by the customer in buying and using the business product or service.

- A new product generally enjoys its greatest degree of differentiation during the introductory stage of the product life cycle. Pricing decisions at this stage of the product's life center either on price skimming or market-penetration pricing, depending on the nature of the market and the type of customer involved. There are specific price considerations that the marketer must ponder during each phase of the product life cycle with respect to profit, demand, and marketing strategy.

- The price-leadership strategy prevails in oligopolistic situations; it is the practice by which one or a very few firms initiate price changes, with one or more of the other firms in the industry following suit. Price leadership is found most often in industries where products are similar, and even standardized; therefore, they usually are considered by customers to be good substitutes for each other.

- Competitive bidding is a process whereby a business buyer will request price bids from interested suppliers on a proposed purchase or contract. Government agencies and most public institutions are required in most cases to use the competitive bidding system in buying products and services. Competitive bidding can take the form of either closed (sealed bid) bidding or open bidding.

- Many business customers choose to lease an asset rather than purchase it; for the marketer, leasing can provide a very viable alternative to selling capital equipment. In the business market, leasing is employed by most capital goods and equipment manufacturers. There are several advantages of leasing over purchasing from both the buyer's and the seller's points of view. Two primary forms of business leases are the operating lease and the direct-financing lease.

- The business marketer must be concerned with net price, which is the list price minus allowances for trade-ins and other cost-significant concessions made by the buyer. The establishment of a list price provides the base from which discounts can be subtracted. Discounts come in many forms, with trade, quantity, and cash discounts being the most prevalent. Geographical price adjustments also are frequently made to the list price.

## Key Terms

| | | |
|---|---|---|
| break-even analysis | lessee | price skimming |
| bundling | lessor | quantity discount |
| cash discount | life-cycle costing | Robinson-Patman Act |
| closed bidding | loss leader | target costing |
| cost-benefit analysis | marginal pricing | target return-on-investment |
| cost-price analysis | market penetration pricing | pricing |
| economic value to the | open bidding | trade discount |
| customer (EVC) | predatory pricing | unitary demand elasticity |
| elastic demand | price elasticity of demand | zero-based pricing (ZBP) |
| inelastic demand | price fixing | |

## Review Questions

1. Why is price planning not a precise science? Identify and describe the six major factors influencing pricing strategy. Discuss three common pricing objectives. What is meant by a complementary relationship?

2. Explain the pricing methods of (1) marginal pricing, (2) EVC, (3) break-even analysis, and (4) target return-on-investment pricing. What is the fundamental reason for using each of these methods?

3. What is price elasticity of demand? Distinguish among elastic, inelastic, and unitary demand. How can cost-benefit analysis be utilized in determining demand for business products?

4. Differentiate between price skimming and market-penetration pricing. Under what circumstances would you use each? What are the primary price considerations in each phase of the product life cycle?

5. What is a price-leadership strategy? In what kinds of industries is such a pricing strategy commonly found? How does a business-to-business company maintain its price-leadership position?

6. What is the competitive bidding process, and what types of organizations typically use such a process? Identify five criteria that should be used by a firm considering whether to bid on a particular piece of business. What is the fundamental difference between an open bid and a closed bid?

7. What is involved in a leasing agreement? What type of organization uses leasing transactions most frequently? Identify three advantages of leasing from a buyer's perspective and three from a seller's perspective. Distinguish between an operating lease and a direct-financing lease.

8. How is net price determined? Identify and discuss the three most prevalent types of price discounts. When are transportation fees an important pricing consideration?

---

### Case 8-1

# Seneca Plastics Inc.

This case was written by Dr. Roger Gomes and Dr. Patricia Knowles, Clemson University, © 1999

Brian Pickett, director of marketing for Seneca Plastics, was facing one of the most important pricing decisions of his eight-year career. His largest customer (referred to here as "Computer OEM 1") had just announced that it would be reducing the number of suppliers of plastic products from the present six suppliers to just one. The customer intended to have only one source for each commodity type (molded plastics was considered one type). Each of the present six molded plastic suppliers would be allowed to bid on the total ($6.9 million), and one would be chosen (winner takes all). Since all of the present suppliers were reliable, certified ISO 9000, and qualified, the decision would be based heavily on the price offered. The buyer had made it clear that she intended to purchase the total at a 15–20 percent savings over what she was presently paying to Seneca and the others, meaning next year she wanted to be paying $5.5 to $5.8 million for the same quantities that she had paid $6.9 million this year. The problem for Brian was that Seneca already had the largest share of this customer's business. The other suppliers would probably be willing to cut margins in order to gain a huge increase in sales. Seneca, on the other hand, would be gaining less new sales, yet cutting margins across it all.

Brian knew that in order to make this decision, he would have to study the financial condition of Seneca Plastics both with all of this customer's business at a lower margin and without this customer's business at all. He would also look at this customer's sales trends and margins over time, compared to those of other customers. Since Seneca already was going through a bad year, Brian knew that losing this account could mean the end of the company. He also suspected that gaining additional business at too low a margin might not be much help. He suspected that the competitors' margins were in line with Seneca's, but there was no telling how they would bid on the total of this customer's business. Some might offer a few percent savings, stressing that the margins were already too low and that the customer would be saving on transaction costs by dealing with one supplier. "But," Brian thought, "what if one supplier sends in a bid even lower than the buyer is asking for and takes it all?"

Brian started by looking at direct cost (net sales minus marginal income equals direct cost) and gross profit (marginal income, also called contribution, minus fixed overhead equals gross profit). The financial information Brian worked with is presented in Exhibit 8-10.

### Assignment

Each team will independently prepare its analysis as Brian would have and then prepare a bid on the total business of this customer. The bids will be handed in to the professor prior to the beginning of class, where each team will present its analysis of the situation (pro forma with and without the additional business) and the rationale for their bid. The class will be acting as the Seneca Plastics' senior management group, which is being asked to approve Brian's decision. Knowing that Brian is in the best position to make this decision,

**EXHIBIT 8-10**

| Seneca Plastics Inc. Net Sales/Marginal Income (for top 10 customers) $ (X 1000) | | | |
|---|---|---|---|
| Year | Computer OEM 1 | Computer OEM 2 | Computer Peripheral 1 | Computer Peripheral 2 |
| 1999 | 4910/2210 | 2105/947 | 735/262 | 2940/1050 |
| 1998 | 5880/2527 | 2520/1083 | 797/275 | 3118/1100 |
| 1997 | 6678/3038 | 2862/1300 | 600/271 | 2640/1085 |
| 1996 | 6219/3421 | 2666/1460 | 777/312 | 3225/1251 |
| 1995 | 4571/2331 | 2731/1360 | 435/216 | 1856/867 |

| Net Sales/Marginal Income $ (X 1000) | | | |
|---|---|---|---|
| Year | Copier OEM | Automotive OEM 2 | Automotive Aftermarket | Misc. Industrial 1 |
| 1999 | 2107/853 | 3182/626 | 5150/1290 | 125/22 |
| 1998 | 2650/965 | 1384/357 | 3964/777 | 351/73 |
| 1997 | 3625/1102 | 1221/260 | 4287/850 | 70/12 |
| 1996 | 4108/1125 | 1101/153 | 2390/525 | 426/94 |
| 1995 | 3325/851 | 1677/251 | 2746/609 | 111/26 |

| Net Sales/Marginal Income $ (X 1000) | | |
|---|---|---|
| Year | Misc. Industrial 2 | Misc. Industrial 3 |
| 1999 | 1170/416 | 410/110 |
| 1998 | 650/228 | 385/115 |
| 1997 | 310/108 | 460/147 |
| 1996 | 110/38 | 425/175 |
| 1995 | 0/0 | 377/171 |

| Seneca Plastics FIINANCIAL RESULTS 1995–1999 $ (X 1000) | | | | | |
|---|---|---|---|---|---|
| | 1995 | 1996 | 1997 | 1998 | 1999 |
| Net Sales | 17829 | 21447 | 22753 | 21699 | 22834 |
| Marginal income | 6682 | 8554 | 8173 | 7500 | 7786 |
| Fixed expense | 1444 | 2627 | 3345 | 3590 | 4598 |
| Gross profit | 5238 | 5927 | 4828 | 3910 | 3188 |
| Selling expense | 1105 | 747 | 678 | 697 | 833 |
| Administrative expense | 1693 | 2349 | 2562 | 2870 | 3300 |
| Other expense | 25 | 165 | (70) | 14 | 113 |
| Operating profit | 2415 | 2666 | 1658 | 329 | (1058) |
| Corporate expense | 320 | 395 | 441 | 351 | 730 |
| Pretax profit | 2095 | 2271 | 1217 | (22) | (1788) |

they will not override his decision. At the end of the class the professor (buyer) can announce the lowest bidder. The other teams, it is hoped, will have presented ways to save the business just in case they lost the bid. This simulation is intended to represent a competitive bidding situation, even though each "competitor" will be using Seneca financial data (this would be representative of a situation in which competitors have similar costs and costing methods). To increase the reality, each team can replace the Seneca name with its own unique company name.

# Meta-Tronics LTD.

This case was written by Dr. Roger Gomes and Dr. Patricia Knowles, Clemson University © 1999

Hans Muller, marketing manager for Meta-Tronics Ltd, North American Division, had just received an e-mail assignment from corporate headquarters in Germany asking him to prepare a report on the potential for exporting finished electronic goods and subassemblies to countries with soft currency problems. It was rare for the corporate office to involve him directly in its consideration of global issues that involved multiple divisions. Hans suspected that the top management team needed to show a considerable amount of additional sales, and his involvement indicated that the company's Silicon Valley plants would be leading the effort. Essentially, he was to identify mechanisms and opportunities for countertrade to increase corporate sales. Hans, an optimistic person, thought, "I'll bet that if I can come up with a good analysis they will put me in charge of this entire project. Clearly the project could involve hundreds of millions of dollars in new sales."

What worried Hans was that even though he had been born overseas, his schooling had been entirely American. Thinking back to his undergraduate days (six years ago), the only mention of countertrade he could recall was Coca-Cola (or was it Pepsi Cola?). Except for excellent German language skills, Hans had little experience—and even less training—in international commerce. Fortunately, like almost all marketers, Hans loved a challenge. He started searching the Internet and marketing texts for background information, and by the end of the day he had compiled the following notes:

## Background Information

Countertrade is a barterlike method for conducting business in markets with nonconvertible "soft currencies" such as found in many third-world countries and in "hyperinflation" economies. Even though most American companies are uncomfortable with the countertrade process, it has been in use since the beginning of trade. It is estimated that well over 10 percent of world trade is based on some form of countertrade, and for lessor-developed countries the percentage increases to over 50 percent.

### Countertrade Types

- Barter—A direct exchange of goods for goods. The exporter receives title to goods in payment and is then responsible for storage, shipping, and selling costs to bring the goods to a country where they can be sold for hard currency.
- Counterpurchase—The exporter is paid in hard currency, but the exporter agrees to a reciprocal purchase that returns the foreign exchange to the customer country.
- Switch trading—Utilizing third-party trading companies who (for a substantial fee) will locate buyers for goods received in countertrade.
- Offset—The exporter is paid in local soft currency that the exporter agrees to use immediately to buy local products for use or export.

Many companies are ill-prepared to become world goods traders for products with which they have no market experience. There could be quality problems, delivery problems, standard problems, commodity value fluctuations, or any of a host of factors that could increase the risk and complexity of the transactions. Even with all the inherent risk, the incidence of countertrade seems likely to increase. Where there is potential for profitable transactions, aggressive global marketers will find ways to satisfy customer needs.*

## Examples

There are a great many examples of creative and profitable countertrade strategies. For decades, PepsiCo has been countertrading with Russian bottling plants. Originally, payment was made in Stolichnaya vodka and, more recently, Russian-built ships. PepsiCo similarly accepts Permiat Romanian wine. Estee Lauder, another American company successfully doing business in Russia, uses revenue from Russian sales (e.g., sales of perfume) to buy Russian chemicals that it sells in western markets for hard currency. China paid for the construction of a seaport with coal. GE accepted a contract to supply Sweden $300 million worth of jet aircraft engines, but GE had to agree to purchase an equivalent amount of Swedish industrial products. A Japanese company sold sewing machines to China and received payment in the form of an equal value of pairs of pajamas (produced on the machines). The examples go on and on.

Not all countertrade has been without problems, however. The former McDonnell-Douglas company signed a contract to sell 250 aircraft to the former Yugoslavia by agreeing to accept part of the payment in foods, textiles, leather goods, wine, beer, mineral water, and tourist tours. Some of the items proved very difficult to convert to cash.**

Even with the possibility of problems, countertrade is growing in importance. It is a pricing tool every international marketer must be ready to employ.*** While many U.S. firms are reluctant to countertrade, they have little choice if they want to do business with Eastern European and Third-World countries. Some countries even require countertrade for all imports.

## Internet Resources

U.S. Department of Commerce, International Trade Administration (www.ita.doc.gov). Click on site map.

U.S. Department of Commerce, Economics and Statistics Administration (www.stat-usa.gov).

Multi-Lateral Investment Guarantee Agency (www.miga.org).

Business Information Service—Newly Independent States (www.bisnis.doc.gov).

Argent Trading (www.argenttrading.com).

*World Trade Magazine* (www.worldtrademag.com).

Google.com (click "Directory," click "Business," click "International business and trade")

*Commerce Business Daily* (http://cbdnet.access.gpo.gov/) search on "electronics."

American Countertrade Association (www.countertrade.org).

Los Angeles Area Chamber of Commerce's Tradeport site (www.tradeport.org).

Ernst & Young International (www.eyi.com). Click on a country.

Internet Public Library (www.ipl.org/ref). Click on "Business & Economics." Then click on "International Business."

# Company Background

Meta-Tronics Ltd, U.S.A. Division, is a multiplant electronics company that manufactures high-quality products to be sold under their customer's brand names. Meta-Tronics has the capability to produce finished products or major subassemblies. It is similar in size and capabilities to Solectron Corporation (www.solectron.com), its biggest competitor. Globally, Meta-Tronics operates 21 plants, including operating divisions in Asia, South America, North America, Western Europe, and Eastern Europe.

## Assignment

Help Hans evaluate the mechanisms (procedures) and potential for Meta-Tronics to increase its sales of electronic goods by means of countertrade. Start with Hans's reference websites listed above and find additional useful sites. Also identify target countries and justify your decisions. Your presentation to the class should be similar to the presentation Hans will make at corporate headquarters.

*B. Toyne and P. G. P. Walters, *Global Marketing Management* (Boston: Allyn and Bacon, 1993).

**S. Onkvisit and J. J. Shaw, *International Marketing* (Englewood Cliffs, NJ: Prentice-Hall, 1996).

***P. R. Cateora and J. L. Graham, *International Marketing*. 11th ed. (New York: McGraw-Hill/Irwin, 2002).

---

## Case 8-3

# Pfizer, Inc. Animal Health Products[1]—Industry Downturns and Marketing Strategy

Jakki Mohr, University of Montana; Sara Streeter, MBA, University of Montana

Gail Oss, Territory Manager of Pfizer, Inc., Animal Health Group in western Montana and southeastern Idaho, was driving back to her home office after a day of visiting cattle ranchers in her territory. The combination of the spring sunshine warming the air and the snow-capped peaks of the Bitterroot Mountains provided a stunningly beautiful backdrop for her drive. But the majestic beauty provided little relief to her troubled thoughts.

The NAFTA agreement with Canada and Mexico had hit local ranchers particularly hard. The influx of beef cattle into the U.S. market from these countries, as well as beef from other countries (e.g., Australia) that entered the U.S. via more lenient import restrictions in Mexico, had wreaked havoc over the past year. Prices of beef had declined precipitously from the prior year. Ranchers in the past had retained sufficient reserves to come back from a bad year, but this year, things were particularly bad. The prices being offered for the calves by the feedlot operators were, in many cases, less than the costs of raising those calves. Ranchers' objectives had changed from making some modest income off their cattle operations to minimizing their losses.

In this environment, ranchers were actively seeking ways to cut costs. Gail sold high-quality animal health products, oftentimes at a premium price. One way in which ranchers could cut costs was either to scrimp on animal healthcare products, such as vaccines and antibiotics, or to switch to a lower-cost alternative. The current environment posed a particularly severe threat, not only to Gail's company, but also to her very livelihood. Gail had spent a substantial amount of time and effort cultivating long-term relationships with many of these ranchers—many of whom she had had to convince of her credibility, given her gender. Given the time and effort she had spent cultivating these relationships, as well as the camaraderie she felt with her customers, she did not want to see the ranchers in her territory go under. Ranching was an important part of the history of Montana; many ranchers had ties to the land going back generations. They took pride in producing the food for many tables in the U.S. and other areas of the world. Gail felt that Pfizer could use its fairly significant resources in a very influential manner to help these ranchers. Merely lowering the price on her products (if that was even possible) was merely a band-aid solution to the problem.

---

[1]Some of the information in this case has been modified to protect the proprietary nature of firms' marketing strategies. The case is intended to be used as a basis for class discussion rather than to illustrate either effective or ineffective marketing strategies.

As part of Gail's weekly responsibilities, she communicated via an automated computer system to her sales manager, Tom Brooks, (also in Montana) and to the marketing managers at headquarters (in Exton, Pennsylvania). She knew she needed to report the severity of the situation, but more importantly, she wanted to encourage headquarters to take the bull by the horns, so to speak. So, she was pondering the message she would write that evening from her kitchen table.

## Industry Background

The supply chain (Exhibit 8-11) for beef begins with the cow/calf producer (the commercial rancher). Commercial ranchers are in the business of breeding and raising cattle for the purpose of selling them to feedlots. Ranchers keep a herd of cows that are bred yearly. The calves are generally born in the early spring, weaned in October, and shipped to feedlots generally in late October/early November. The ranchers' objectives are to minimize death loss in their herd and to breed cows that give birth to low birth-weight calves (for calving ease), produce beef that will grade low choice by having a good amount of marbling, and produce calves that gain weight quickly. Success measures include conception rate of cows exposed to bulls, live birth rates, birth weights, weaning weights, death loss, and profitability. By the time a rancher sells his calves to the feedlot, the name of the game is pounds. The rancher generally wants the biggest calves possible by that time.

Within a commodity market, basic laws of supply and demand are influenced by those in a position to control access to the markets. Four meatpackers controlled roughly 80% of the industry. Meatpackers have acted as an intermediary between the meat consumer and the meat producer. This situation has not facilitated a free flow of information throughout the supply chain, and therefore, the industry has not been strongly consumer focused.

Exhibit 8-12 traces the market share for beef, pork, and poultry from 1970–1997 and projects changes in the market through 2003. The market share for beef has fallen from 44 percent in 1970 to 32 percent in 1997, a 27 percent drop.

**EXHIBIT 8-11**
**Supply Chain for Beef**

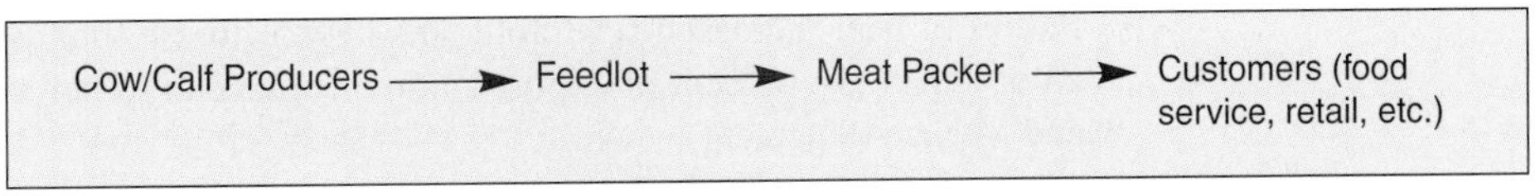

Cow/Calf Producers ⟶ Feedlot ⟶ Meat Packer ⟶ Customers (food service, retail, etc.)

**EXHIBIT 8-12**
**Per Capita Meat Consumption % Market Share (Retail Weight)**

Source: USDA & NCBA.

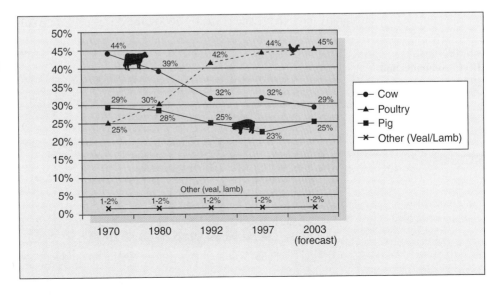

Some of the reasons for the decline included

- Changes in consumer lifestyles (less time spent in preparing home-cooked meals); an interesting statistic is that two-thirds of all dinner decisions are made on the same day and of those, three-quarters don't know what they're going to make at 4:30 PM.
- Health/nutritional issues (dietary considerations involving cholesterol, fat content, food-borne diseases, etc.).
- Switching to alternative meat products.

In addition, the pork and poultry industries had done a better job of marketing their products. During 1997, the number of new poultry products (for example, stuffed chicken entrees, gourmet home meal replacements) introduced to the market increased 13 percent from the prior year, compared to an increase of only 3.5 percent for new beef products. And, retail pricing for beef remained stubbornly high (although this high price did not translate into higher prices of the calves on a per-weight basis to the ranchers, as discussed subsequently).

Based upon historical data, shown in Exhibit 8-13, the beef production cycle spans a twelve-year period in which production levels expand and contract. As Exhibit 8-13 shows, the amount of beef produced (bars in the chart, millions of pounds on the left-hand scale) increased through the mid-90s—despite the declining beef consumption in the U.S. shown in the prior figure. This relationship between production and consumption is consistent with other commodity markets, where there exists an inverse relationship between supply and demand.

Some of the reasons for increased beef production in the mid-90s included

- Herd liquidation: low cattle prices, coupled with the high cost of feed, drove some producers out of business.
- Improved genetics and animal health/nutrition increased production yields; indeed, although cow numbers had decreased by 10 percent since 1985 (as noted by Exhibit 8-14), productivity per cow increased by 29 percent.
- Export of beef increased sevenfold since 1985 (to 2 billion pounds); key markets include Japan (54 percent of export volume); Canada (16 percent); Korea (11 percent), and Mexico (9 percent).

Exhibit 8-13 also shows that the price the ranchers received for their beef cattle varied inversely with production (right-hand scale). Although calf prices were expected to rise slightly through the late 90s/early 2000s, the prices paid were still far below the relatively

**EXHIBIT 8-13**
**Beef Production and**
**Price**

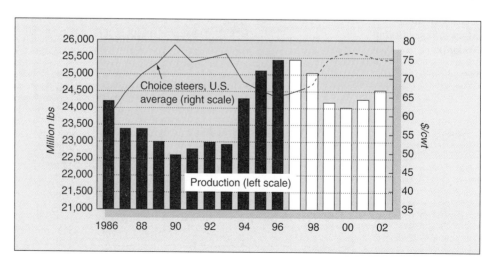

high prices consumers paid at retail. One of the reasons given for the relatively low prices paid to ranchers on a per-pound basis for their calves was the high degree of concentration at the meat packer level of the supply chain. As noted previously, four packing houses controlled access to the market. Some ranchers believed this gave the packing houses near-monopoly power in setting prices (both for what they would pay feedlot operators for the calves, and in charging prices to their downstream customers (e.g., the grocery store chains). Although the U.S. government had investigated the possibility of collusion among packers, the evidence was not sufficient to draw any firm conclusions.

To further complicate matters, the NAFTA agreement passed in 1989 had given open access to the U.S. markets from Mexican and Canadian ranchers. The lowering of trade barriers, coupled with weakness in the Canadian dollar and the Mexican peso, made imported livestock cheap, compared to U.S.-grown animals. As a result, thousands of head of cattle came streaming across the borders. The flow was heaviest from Canada.

During the summer of 1998, ranchers had been quite vocal in drawing attention to the influx of cattle from Canada. Local governments were somewhat responsive to their concerns. Indeed, trucks carrying Canadian cattle had been turned back at the U.S./Canadian border for minor infractions, such as licensing. In addition, the trucks were consistently pulled over for inspections. A private coalition of ranchers, calling itself the Ranchers-Cattlemen Action Legal Foundation (R-CALF) filed three separate petitions with the U.S. International Trade Commission (ITC) on October 1, 1998, two against Canada and one against Mexico, asking for U.S. government trade investigations. The group requested that anti-dumping duties be levied on meat or livestock imports from the two countries. The Montana Stockgrowers Association had been an early and steadfast supporter of R-CALF.

The ITC determined that there was evidence to support the charge that Canadian cattle imports are causing material injury to U.S. domestic cattle producers. The Department of Commerce began to collect information on Canadian subsidies and prices at which Canadian cattle are sold in Canada and in the United States. In the case against Mexico, the ITC determined that there was no indication that imports of live cattle from Mexico were causing "material injury" to the domestic industry in the U.S. Dissatisfied with the response, R-CALF decided to appeal the case to the Court of International Trade.

Ranchers were doing what they could to minimize the impact of the NAFTA agreement on their livelihoods; however, some could not sustain their operations in light of the lower cattle prices. The number of cattle operations was declining. In many cases, smaller ranchers were selling out to their larger neighbors. This reality was reflected in the cattle inventory statistics, shown in Exhibit 8-14. The number of cattle kept by U.S. ranchers had declined from a high of approximately 132 million head in 1975, to just under 100 million head in 1998. As noted previously, improvements in genetics and animal health and nutrition allowed ranchers to increase production yields, even with fewer head.

## Additional Industry Changes

Some of the changes that had occurred in the poultry and pork industries, including more ready-to-eat products and branded products, were expected to diffuse into the cattle industry. Industry analysts believed that the beef industry would need to develop products that could be more easily prepared, and to develop branded products that consumers could recognize and rely upon for quality and convenience. In addition, industry analysts believed that the beef industry would need to improve the quality of its products (in terms of more consistent taste and tenderness), as currently only 25 percent of the beef produced met quality targets.

The development of branded beef would require a tracking system from "birth-to-beef" in the supply chain. Such tracking would allow standardized health, quality, and management protocols, as well as improved feedback through the entire production model.

**EXHIBIT 8-14**
**Total U.S. Inventory**

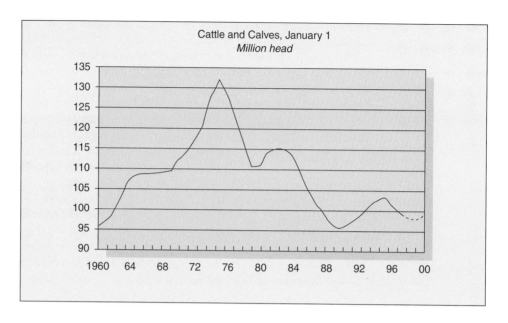

This change would also necessitate the producers being more closely linked to the feedlots to improve the quality of the beef. Branded beef production would move the industry from a cost-based (production) model to a value-added model. Better coordination along the supply chain would insure an increased flow of information from the consumer to the producer. Alliances between the cow/calf producer and the feedlots would allow ranchers to better track the success of their calves (based on health and weight gain). Such data could allow the ranchers to further improve the genetics of their herd by tracking which cow/bull combinations had delivered the higher-yield calves. As part of these trends, some degree of integration or vertical coordination will occur in the beef industry. Ranchers will need to participate in order to ensure market access for their product. Ranchers will have to think beyond the boundaries of their own ranches.

## Pfizer Animal Health Group

Pfizer Inc. is a research-based, diversified health care company with global operations. Pfizer Animal Health is one of the corporation's three major business groups (the other two being the Consumer Health Care Group and U.S. Pharmaceuticals). The Animal Health Products Group accounted for roughly 12 percent of the company's revenues in 1998 (Pfizer Annual Report).

Pfizer Animal Health products are sold to veterinarians and animal health distributors in more than 140 countries around the world for use by livestock producers and horse and pet owners; the products are used in more than 30 animal species. Pfizer Animal Health is committed to providing high-quality, research-based health products for livestock and companion animals. The company continues to invest significant dollars for research and development. As a result, Pfizer has many new animal health products in its research pipeline, a number of which have already been introduced in some international markets and will become available in the United States in the next several years.

As Exhibit 8-15 shows, the Animal Health Group is divided into a North America Region with a U.S. Livestock Division, a U.S. Companion Animal Division (cats, dogs, etc.), and Canada. The Cow/Calf Division falls under the Cattle Business Unit within the Livestock Division. That Division is organized further by product type (Wood Mackenzie Report).

**EXHIBIT 8-15**   **Pfizer Animal Health Organization**

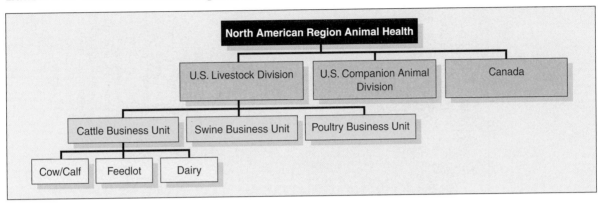

The marketing managers for each cattle market segment work closely with product managers and sales managers to ensure timely, accurate information back from the field. Territory managers responsible for all sales activities report to an Area Sales Manager, who in turn reports to the national sales and marketing manager. Territory managers are typically compensated on a roughly 80 percent salary/20 percent commission basis. This percentage would vary by salesperson by year: in a good year the commission might be a much higher percentage of overall earnings, while in a bad year, the salary component might be a greater percentage of the salesperson's overall earnings.

## Marketing Strategy

Pfizer's Cow/Calf Division offers a full range of products to cattle ranchers, including vaccines for both newborn calves and their mothers, medications (for example, de-wormers, anti-diarrheals), and antibiotics (for pneumonia and other diseases). Pfizer's sophisticated research-and-development system resulted in a number of new and useful products for the market. For example, Pfizer developed a long-lasting de-wormer that was simply poured along the cow's back. This technology was a significant time-saver to the rancher, eliminating the need to administer either an oral medication or an injection. Moreover, Pfizer had been the first company to come up with a modified-live and killed virus vaccine, a significant technological breakthrough which provided safety in pregnant animals and the efficacy of a modified-live virus.

Pfizer offered a diverse product line to cow/calf ranchers. Some of Pfizer's key product lines are compared to those of competitors in Exhibit 8-16.

Pfizer segmented ranchers in the cow/calf business on the basis of herd size, as shown in Exhibit 8-17.

"Hobbyists" are so called because in many cases, these ranchers run their cattle as a sideline to some other job held. "Traditionalists'" main livelihood is their cattle operation. The "Business" segment operations are large ranches, owned either by a family or a corporation.

Pfizer's extensive network of field sales representatives visits the ranchers to inform them about new and existing products. Time spent with accounts was typically allocated on the basis of volume of product purchased.

Pfizer positioned its products on the combination of superior science (resulting from its significant R&D efforts) and high-quality production/quality control techniques. For example, although other companies in the market (particularly generics) used similar formulations in their products, on occasion they did not have good quality control in the

**EXHIBIT 8-16  Comparison of Product Lines***

| Company | Pfizer | American Home Products (Fort Dodge) | Bayer | Merial |
|---|---|---|---|---|
| **Sales and Profitability** | 10-year average annual sales growth increase of 3.8%; average for global veterinary market is 6.9%. Profit rate in 1997 was 8.4%. Market share in 1997 was 15.3% | 10-year average annual sales growth increase of 7.8%; average for global veterinary market is 6.9%. Profit rate in 1997 was 11.0%; market share was 9.0% | 10-year average annual sales growth increase of 10.2%; average for global veterinary market is 6.9%. Profit rate in 1997 was 16.8%; market share was 10.9%. | 10-year average annual sales growth increase of 11.9%; average for global veterinary market is 6.9%. Profit rate in 1997 was 22.8%; market share was 16.4%. |
| **Bovine Diseases Covered by Product Range** | IBR; P1–3; BVD; BRSV; leptospira; rotavirus; coronavirus; campylobacter; clostridia; E.Coli; pasteurellosis; haemophilus. | Pasteurellosis; enterotoxaemia; chlamydia; salmonella; IBR; P1–3; brucellosis; rabies; E.Coli; anaplasmosis; tetanus; BVD; BRSV; leptospirosis; trichomonas; campylobacter; papilloma; haemophilus | IBR; FMD; IPV; P1–3; balanoposthitis; clostridia; haemophilus; BRSV; BVD; leptospira; E.Coli; rhinotracheitis; campylobacter. | Foot and mouth; rabies; brucellosis; paratuberculosis; rhinotracheitis; rotavirus; coronavirus; colibaccillosis; parainfluenza; BVD; aglactia; foot rot; black leg; IBR; leptospira; clostridia; pasteurella; BRSV; E.Coli. |
| **Significant Products for Cattle** | Comprehensive product line; anti-infectives have formed basis of product line for many years; vaccine businesses also very important; also sells a performance enhancer, virginiamycin; parasiticides, led by Dectomax, starting to make significant impact on sales; Valbazen anthelmintic; broad range of general pharmaceuticals. | Predominantly a vaccine company; antibiotics centered on anti-mastitis products; anti-infectives based on penicillins, tetracyclines, sulphonamides and quinolones; parasiticides led by Cydectin; main products in general pharmaceuticals are anabolic implants for muscle growth. | Product range biased towards parasiticides, particularly ectoparasiticides, and antibiotics; overall product range is diverse; some mastitis anti-microbials; wide range of pharmaceuticals, but sales value of each product is limited; focus is more towards companion animal market. | Most important product sector is parasiticides, with product range dominated by Ivermectin, which was the first endectocide to reach the market; success of Ivermectin has drawn strong competition; remainder of product range made up primarily of anthelmintics and a range of general pharmaceuticals and vaccines. |

*(continued)*

*This information is taken from the Wood MacKenzie Animal Health Market Review and its Veterinary Company Profiles, both done on a worldwide basis.

**EXHIBIT 8-16** *(concluded)*

| Company | Pfizer | American Home Products (Fort Dodge) | Bayer | Merial |
|---|---|---|---|---|
| Strengths | Strong manufacturing capabilities based on fermentation expertise and capacity; global marketing coverage supported by strategic local manufacture; strong range of new products in early commercialization; broad product range with strength in companion animals. | Leading global vaccine business; good international exposure; comprehensive vaccine product range; potential for growth through Cydectin. | Growing market in expanding companion animal sector; solid in-house manufacturing supported by global distribution capability; business focused on key market areas. | Leading veterinary vaccine company with broad product portfolio; strong line of new product introductions; good companion animal business; global distribution network; strength in parasiticides and vaccines sectors. |
| Weaknesses | North America still dominates turnover; high proportion of sales due to off-patent products; heavily dependent on performance of livestock markets. | Business with disparate parts requiring strong central focus; except for vaccines, product range is dominated by commodity products; R&D likely to be reduced. | Underweight in USA; lack of critical mass in biologicals; no blockbuster product in North American market; narrow anti-infectives product portfolio; current R&D emphasis away from new product discovery. | Specialist pharmaceutical product line, not significantly involved in livestock sectors; aging anti-infectives portfolio; Ivermectin subject to intense competition. |
| % of R&D to Sales* | 5 | 3 | 3 | 2 |
| Position on Quality vs. Price** | 5 | 3.5 | 3 | 3 |
| Price Support of Distribution Channel*** | 2 | 4 | 3 | 3 |

* Specific ratios are considered proprietary. Hence, a general rating scale is used where 5 means a higher percentage of R&D/Sales and 1 is a lower percentage.

** 5 = Focus on Quality only; 1 = Focus on Low Price only

*** 5 = Strong emphasis on SPIFs (Special Promotional Incentive Funds) and price-related trade promotions; 1 = low emphasis

**EXHIBIT 8-17**
**Pfizer Market**
**Segments, 1998**

| Segment | # of Cattle | # of Operations | % of National Cattle Inventory |
|---|---|---|---|
| Hobbyist | < 100 | 808,000 | 50% |
| Traditionalist | 100–499 | 69,000 | 36% |
| Business | 500 + | 5,900 | 14% |

production line, resulting in batches of ineffective vaccines and recalls. Pfizer backed its products completely with a Technical Services Department. If ranchers had any kind of health or nutritional problem with their herds, they could call on a team of Pfizer technical specialists who would work with the local veterinarian, utilizing blood and other diagnostics to identify the problem and suggest a solution.

Pfizer also was very involved in the cattle industry itself. Each territory manager was given an annual budget that included discretionary funds to be spent in his/her territory to sponsor industry activities such as seminars on herd health, stock shows, 4-H, and so forth. Gail Oss, for example, chose to spend a significant portion of her discretionary funds sponsoring meetings and conferences for the Montana Stock-grower's Association, which might include a veterinarian or a professor from the Extension Office of a state university speaking on issues pertinent to ranchers.

The majority of Pfizer's trade advertising was focused on specific products and appeared in cattle industry publications, such as *Beef Magazine* and *Bovine Veterinarian.* One ad read, "More veterinarians are satisfied with [Pfizer's] Dectomax Pour-On," and went on to describe veterinarians' superior satisfaction and greater likelihood of recommending Dectomax compared to a key competitor, Ivomec:

> Eighty-four percent of veterinarians who recommended Dectomax Pour-On said they were satisfied or very satisfied with its performance—compared to only 51 percent who were satisfied or very satisfied with Ivomec Eprinex Pour-On. . . . If choosing only between Dectomax and Ivomec, over three out of four veterinarians would choose to recommend Dectomax Pour-On.

Another ad read, "Calf Health Program Boosts Prices by Up to $21 More per Head." The data in the copy-intensive ad highlighted that "cow-calf producers enrolled in value-added programs like Pfizer Select Vaccine programs are being rewarded for their efforts with top-of-the-market prices." Such programs are based on a consistent program of vaccinating animals with specific products, and they provide optimal disease protection. The programs result in cattle that perform more consistently and predictably in terms of weight gain and beef quality—resulting in higher prices at sale time.

Although the territory managers called on ranchers (as well as the veterinarians, distributors, and dealers) in their territories, they sold no product directly to ranchers. Ranchers could buy their animal health products from either a local veterinarian or a distributor or dealer (such as a feed-and-seed store). The percentage of product flowing through vets or distributors and dealers varied significantly by region. In areas where feedlots (versus cow/calf ranchers) were the predominant customers, 95 percent of the product might flow through distributors. In areas where ranchers are the predominant customers, vets might sell 50 percent of the product, depending upon customer preferences.

Vets were particularly important given that the overwhelming majority of ranchers said that the person they trusted the most when it came to managing the health of their herd was their veterinarian. Pfizer capitalizes on this trust in the vet in its marketing program. When the vet consults and recommends a Pfizer product to a rancher, the vet gives the rancher a coded coupon which may be redeemed at either a vet clinic or supply house. When the coupon is sent back to Pfizer for reimbursement, the vet is credited for servicing that product, regardless of where the product is purchased.

Pfizer offers some trade promotions to vets and distributors, including volume rebate programs, price promotions on certain products during busy seasonal periods, and so forth. However, Pfizer's competitors oftentimes gave much more significant discounts and SPIFs to distributors. As a result, when a rancher went to a distributor to buy a product the vet had recommended, the distributor might switch the rancher to a similar product for which the distributor was making more profit. If it was a Pfizer product the vet had recommended, the distributor might switch the rancher to a competitor's product. Pfizer had historically avoided competing on the basis of such promotional tactics, feeling instead that redirecting such funds back into R&D resulted in better long-term benefits for its customers.

So, as Gail pondered these various facets of the company's market position and strategies, she decided to take a strong stance in her weekly memo. It was time to cut the bull.

## Discussion Questions

1. Evaluate the trends affecting the cattle ranching industry.

2. To what degree is a high quality/premium price position a strength or a liability during an industry downturn? What are the various ways Pfizer could handle this situation?

3. Evaluate the various dimensions of Pfizer's marketing strategy: Market segmentation and positioning; product/price; distribution; trade advertising and trade promotion; personal selling; public relations and sponsorships. What makes sense and what doesn't? Why or why not?

4. Would Pfizer benefit from a relationship marketing focus? How would its marketing strategy need to be modified to take such a focus?

5. When an industry is in decline, to what extent should a supplier be involved in ensuring its customers' livelihoods?

---

### Case 8-4

# 3DV-LS[1]: Assessing Market Opportunity in the Computer Visualization Market

Robin Habeger, Iowa State University; Kay M. Palan, Iowa State University

As Pat Patterson, director of the 3DV Litigation Services business unit, was reviewing the second quarter sales numbers, he sighed heavily and rubbed his temples in an attempt to avert an impending migraine blooming behind his eyes. The sales numbers were disappointing, to say the least. In fact, sales had been low over the last four quarters. Sales had dried up on the east and west coasts because of increased competition, resulting in an alarming 16 percent average sales decline each of the last four quarters. 3DV had recently reorganized several of its business units, closing some and combining others. To avoid a similar fate, it was imperative that Litigation Services post increasing sales and profits. The decline in sales, Pat knew, put the business unit in jeopardy.

Pat sighed again as his mind ran through the available options. He could give the marketing and sales efforts more time to increase sales. A new Web page, giving the unit improved Internet presence, would soon be implemented, which might spark some sales activity. But, as he pondered the situation, Pat believed that it would take more than this to

[1]The name of the company and the principal players in this case were disguised to protect the competitive interests of 3DV-LS.

reverse the declining sales trend. When he joined the company in the mid-1990s as a salesman, he shared a cubicle with three other people. He remembered the lean days when it was touch and go as to whether or not he would even get a paycheck. Now, in December 2000, he had his own corner office. He had helped build the Litigation Services unit into the nationwide competitor it now was. Pat was determined to overcome the recent sales decline. He had invested too much of his own time and energy into the business unit to let it fail now.

Just then, Pat heard a knock on his door. Glancing up, he saw Lance Wolffe, one of 3DV-LS's project managers. Lance had an air of excitement about him. "Pat, I've got to show you this magazine article I came across last night!" He tossed the magazine into Pat's hands and continued, "The article discusses how some construction and transportation projects are beginning to use computer-generated models to help clients visualize finished projects—that's something we could be doing, only better!"

Pat briefly looked at the civil engineering trade magazine turned to the article Lance had marked. Pat, too, could see that the kind of computer visualization process used by 3DV might be transferable to other industries such as the construction and transportation industries illustrated in the article. But any enthusiasm Pat shared with Lance was tempered by the realization that entering a new market would take time and resources, and, in the end, might not be any more fruitful than improving the unit's marketing efforts.

To Lance, he said, "It certainly does look like there's some potential for us to expand our efforts into other markets, but there's a lot of information we need to know before we make such a decision. Let's make a list of questions we need to answer."

Pat and Lance created a list of questions to answer regarding this new market opportunity. The list addressed issues such as quantifying market potential, determining 3DV-LS's competitive advantage, and identifying threats and weaknesses to market entry.

As the list grew longer, Lance observed, "What we essentially need to do is a cost/benefit analysis."

Pat agreed, but added, "We need to focus our analysis just on the construction and transportation industries, but we also need to compare the results of the cost/benefit analysis to maintaining the status quo. If we can't demonstrate that entry into this new market will be profitable in a reasonable period of time, then we just won't be able to do it."

Lance felt his bubble burst. He really felt in his gut that expanding 3DV-LS's technological capabilities to the construction and transportation industries was the right thing to do. He grew quiet for a few minutes, trying to settle his desire for immediate market entry.

Finally he said, "We do need to go into this with our eyes open and that means finding as much information as we can. Where do you want me to start?"

"At the beginning," Pat replied. "Find out everything you can about the customers and competitors in the construction and transportation industries, the costs and profits, the attractiveness of the market. You should probably ask Sandy to help you. Since she is in charge of marketing she will have some idea where to find the information you need. Let's plan to meet again in a couple of weeks to review the situation."

As Lance turned to leave, Pat allowed himself a momentary glimmer of hope—could this be the break 3DV-LS needed to improve sales and profitability?

## 3DV: History of the Company

3DV, founded in 1988 for the purpose of accurately creating 3-D accident reconstructions, used a revolutionary programming code developed by the founders. Attorneys, representing automobile manufacturers, hired 3DV to construct visual animations of automobile accidents. These visualizations were used in court cases to demonstrate how an automobile accident had most likely occurred.

Although the company's primary focus in the early years was accident reconstruction for automobile manufacturers, by 1999 3DV had several distinct products and services, each targeting a select market. For example, using the basis of the original programming code, 3DV developed several different types of software packages that allowed manufacturing companies to use the Internet for project collaboration and visualization. That is, the software enabled employees in different locations to view, modify, and work with the same 3-D model simultaneously, while at the same time maintaining secure online access. Another product helped companies in various industries improve the ergonomics of product designs and workplace tasks. Companies could use still other 3DV software to cost-effectively model and view an entire 2-D/3-D manufacturing facility by designing optimal factory floor plans and testing efficiency through virtual simulation. 3DV provided software support and training and implementation services for all of its software products.

3DV's software had revolutionized the visualization industry. Relative to other companies that provided computer visualization, 3DV produced animation and 3-D models that were the highest quality visualizations available. Consequently, although 3DV had once been fairly unknown, it now enjoyed an international reputation, having served such customers as General Motors, Ford, Toyota, Honda, Eastman Kodak, Lockheed Martin, Johnson & Johnson, Dow Chemical Company, and Motorola. Moreover, 3DV had benefited from the public trading frenzy accorded to high-tech companies in the mid-90s.

But 3DV's fortunes in the last few years had not been good. The stock price had reached a high of $72, but it was currently trading under $20, and the company as a whole had reported a net operating loss of over $40 million in 1999. As a result, 3DV had gone through two major restructurings within the last two years. It closed several business units that fell outside of its core competencies. A second reduction in support staff (human resources, technical support, etc.) followed the first by approximately six to eight months. Although 3DV still employed approximately 600 people worldwide, managers were aware that additional staff reductions were possible in unprofitable business units.

## 3DV: The Litigation Services Business Unit

From the outset, 3DV had created a specialized business unit, known as 3DV Litigation Services, to focus specifically on litigation visualization services. 3DV Litigation Services (3DV-LS) specialized in animation and 3-D models for attorneys to use as displays or demonstrative evidence in court cases. 3DV-LS offered some additional visualization services, including secure on-line project management workspace, DVD presentation systems, digitally altered photographs for use as before versus after displays, videotape production, and visuals needed for presentation materials. 3DV-LS differentiated itself from other visualization providers by using computers to hardware render the frames (individual pictures) used to make an animation (see Exhibit 8-18). This method, relative to the more commonly used software rendering, created customized animations faster and with more precision and greater detail. For clients, the primary advantage of hardware rendered animations was the ability to make changes to animations within days, whereas software rendering processes required weeks to make similar changes. In particular, in the litigation industry, attorneys sometimes requested changes right up to the day before the animations were used in a trial. Hardware rendering, unlike software rendering, accommodated these last-minute changes.

However, the process, and, consequently, the advantage of hardware rendering was not well understood by potential clients. Simply put, hardware rendered visualizations were created directly by computer hardware, while software rendered visualizations were created from software packages. Pat liked to explain the difference between hardware and software rendering to clients as analogous to how the brain functioned in humans. The

**EXHIBIT 8-18** Definitions for Computer Visualization Terms

| Term | Definition |
| --- | --- |
| Animation | A group of computer-rendered frames shown in a sequential manner to portray movement or show a specific angle. It takes 1,800 frames to make one minute of animation. |
| 3-D model | A computer-generated picture of a virtual 3-D object usually created in a CAD package that contains all the spatial information (x, y, z, and scale) of a real object. |
| Rendered frame | A 3-dimensional photograph of the subject material created by a computer, i.e., a picture of a building from a specific angle. |
| Software render | A computer image rendered using a software program. The speed is restricted by the central processing unit (CPU) processing speed and available RAM. The rendering of one frame is completed in several minutes to several days depending on image complexity. Ongoing programming throughout the development of a visualization is required. |
| Hardware render | A computer image rendered directly by computer hardware with preprogrammed construction sets. The rendering of an average frame can be completed in approximately 5 to 10 seconds using this process. Some highly complex images may take up to 30 seconds to render. Visualizations take less time to develop because ongoing programming with software is not required. |

brain (the "hardware") was programmed to tell the lungs when to breathe, the eyes to blink, or the heart to beat. It did not require any conscious thought to do these functions and, therefore, no conscious thought ("processing power") was required to complete the tasks. In contrast, Pat would continue, a human activity such as playing chess required a great deal of concentration and conscious thought, thereby slowing down or replacing all brain functions except the preprogrammed tasks like breathing. Software rendering was, therefore, similar to playing chess in that it required the computer to perform higher level processing that required more time and effort than did hardware coded functions. Software rendering required ongoing programming throughout the development of a visualization, but hardware rendering was preprogrammed.

Despite the advantages of hardware rendering, more and more firms were using software rendering to create computer visualizations. As one salesperson had reported to Pat, "We've been losing lots of cases to small mom and pop shops that are located in the same cities as the law firms. The law firms seem to think that it's important for the visualization firm to be geographically close, so they use local firms that do software rendering. They don't seem to 'get it' that our animation and modeling process is more precise and faster." This was directly impacting 3DV-LS's sales.

## Financial Position

By 1999, 3DV-LS had created visualizations and reconstructions for thousands of cases involving patent infringement, product liability, medical malpractice, insurance defense, and aviation and automobile accident reconstruction. In 1998 alone, it produced more than 10,000 minutes of litigation animation. 3DV-LS was the giant in the litigation visualization services market. Despite this success, however, the litigation services unit had slowly lost its place of importance within the company as 3DV developed other areas of specialization. The unit's financial position was also worrisome. While sales were decreasing, operating expenses remained the same, including the annual $10,000 marketing budget. At the current level of operations, Pat calculated that 3DV-LS needed to generate at least $2.4 million in yearly sales for the unit to break even. If 3DV-LS entered a new market, there was the possibility of additional costs, such as the training and hiring of salespeople. The cost of hiring just one salesperson was $50,000. Revenues in FY2000 (January 1–December 31) were expected to be $2.7 million.

Contracts for litigation visualizations varied greatly based on the depth and breadth of the case. For example, the animations created for biomedical cases tended to be longer than those created for ground/vehicle accident projects because the information was less common and harder to understand. On average, though, the typical project required approximately 6 to 12 minutes of animation at an average cost of $26,000 to $60,000. For smaller projects, such as still models or storyboards that did not require animation, the cost of the project averaged $5,000 to $15,000. Prices were set at rates that covered variable costs plus a 25–30 percent profit margin.

## Organization Structure and Culture

3DV-LS had 33 employees, most of whom worked on-site. Nearly all of the employees on-site had engineering or technical backgrounds. Pat Patterson, who reported directly to a 3DV vice-president, had a Ph.D. in construction engineering and a law degree. Five project managers reported directly to Pat. Two managers had Ph.D.'s in mechanical engineering, one had a Ph.D. in biological medicine, one had a master's degree in engineering mechanics, and one had a degree in architecture. The qualifications of the project managers gave 3DV-LS an advantage in the litigation market because attorneys preferred dealing with doctorate-prepared managers.

Underneath the project managers were production crews. These employees were either engineers with bachelor's degrees or "technical animators" who had either a two- or four-year degree in graphics art design. Rounding out the on-site group was an administrative assistant who did secretarial tasks and a marketing coordinator who performed a variety of marketing functions. However, most of the marketing efforts required by the unit were performed or controlled by 3DV, which also handled 3DV-LS's accounting and human resource management needs.

3DV-LS employed five field salespeople. These people were dispersed across the country in large metropolitan centers (two in Chicago and one each in New York, Texas, and California). None of the salespeople had backgrounds in the computer or technology industries, but they all had extensive experience in working with and selling to attorneys. The salespeople reported directly to Pat.

The litigation services unit was different from the rest of the company. Whereas 3DV's culture was formal, 3DV-LS's was markedly informal. There were frequent informal meetings among the production staff and project managers to exchange ideas on individual projects. The project managers also talked informally with Pat on a daily basis and kept him apprised of progress on the various projects. Project managers met weekly to allocate the production staff. Every two weeks, the entire business unit met informally over lunch. Nicknamed 'Lit Lunch' (for 'Litigation Lunch'), it was a time to catch up on personal news as well as to informally discuss projects.

In sharp contrast, however, to this free-flowing exchange of technical and creative ideas was the lack of communication between the production section of the business and the marketing coordinator. The marketing coordinator, Sandy Clarke, had been relocated to headquarters from a remote office during one of the reorganizations about two years earlier. The 3DV-LS director tightly controlled and supervised her activities and did not promote interaction with the other employees. About a year later, when Pat Patterson became the 3DV-LS director, his attempts to integrate marketing activities with production failed. Neither the project managers nor the sales staff knew what Sandy did and rarely talked to her about projects. Salespeople independently made decisions about what kind of marketing efforts to use in their region—only rarely would they ask Sandy for help or ideas. Even Sandy, who had extensive experience marketing in the legal industry, was confused about her job responsibilities. Any efforts she made to influence the unit's marketing decisions were ignored.

## Marketing Communications

Salespeople generally used either e-mail or direct mail campaigns to generate sales leads. Qualified sales leads then received personal sales calls at which the salesperson showed product demos. The marketing coordinator also maintained a customer database and identified sales leads by staying current with various industry publications.

3DV-LS was dependent on 3DV for publicity, advertising, and marketing support. Publication of marketing materials, which had been designed by Sandy Clarke, had to be approved by and contracted by 3DV. News releases were submitted to 3DV's publicity department for release. Unfortunately, as 3DV-LS's favored status within the company declined, so did the marketing support it received.

A recent addition to 3DV-LS's communications package was development of a Web site, which potential clients could access to view all its products. In addition, the site included a feature that allowed viewers to contact a project manager via the Web site. Other than including information about the Web site in all client contacts, 3DV-LS did not develop any specific strategy detailing how to use the site to develop new business.

## Assessing the Market Opportunity

Lance hurried to his desk to start compiling the information he would need to complete the analysis. He had worked at 3DV-LS as a project manager for two years, but had yet to complete a task such as this. His usual duties included discussing project-specific concepts and issues with the attorneys that hired 3DV-LS, monitoring the progress of the modeling and animations, and dealing with the production crew. Completing an analysis of the construction and transportation industries in a two-week period would be difficult considering that some of his projects were reaching drop-dead dates.[2]

Lance decided that this was definitely a situation that required more help. He grabbed his list and went to see Sandy Clarke, the marketing coordinator. Lance knew Sandy, but had never worked with her on a project. Because the market and this type of technology were so new, finding accurate and relevant information would be difficult; he was hopeful that Sandy would be able to help. After Lance shared his list with her, Sandy took a deep breath.

"Whew," Sandy said, when Lance finished, "that's a lot of information to find and make sense of in two weeks."

"But is it possible?" Lance queried. "If it helps," he continued, "I've been doing some research on my own, so I already know a little about what's happening in the construction and transportation industries."

"Well, that's a start," Sandy replied, "tell me what you know."

### The Construction and Transportation Industries

The transportation and construction industries utilized hand-drawn renderings (pictures) of buildings and landscapes in the development of projects. These hand-drawn renderings provided general concept ideas in a washed-out, two-dimensional picture, but they did not allow stakeholders and the public to grasp how the finished project would look in the surrounding environment. Several companies released computer applications that created computer-generated two-dimensional pictures conveying aesthetics and design concepts. However, because many of these computer software programs relied on software rendering, they were not capable of creating complicated or highly detailed pictures in a short period of time. Using the software required high-end computer equipment and an experienced user who was familiar with Computer Aided Drafting (CAD).

Lance learned that certain aspects of construction and transportation projects differed depending on whether or not they were publicly or privately funded. Both types of funded projects used a bidding process, starting with RFPs (Requests for Proposals), to select

---

[2] A drop-dead date was the date that visualizations and materials were due to attorneys. Material that did not arrive by the drop-dead date could not legally be admitted into evidence.

project consultants. In turn, consultants were responsible for hiring subcontractors, such as 3DV-LS. Any firm could submit bids in response to an RFP, but for public agencies, contracts would only be awarded to firms that had been preapproved by the governing agency. Moreover, the pre-approval process extended to subcontractors. In contrast, privately funded large-scale construction projects did not require a pre-approval process.

Publicly funded and privately funded projects also differed in the project design phase. Publicly funded designs had to go through a public participation process, while privately funded designs used a marketing process. The public participation process, required by all government agencies for any type of construction project, consisted of several meetings at which the public asked questions and provided input to the governing agency. Frequently, the public had very strong opinions concerning these projects, especially those dealing with land acquisition or condemnation. The government agency's role was often to educate the public about the necessity and value of the project.

In contrast, private large-scale development projects were promoted to governing agencies, the public, and investors. This process was mainly concerned with convincing officials and the public that the project was beneficial to the community and would not have any negative impact. For investors, the promotion process centered on the project design issues and associated costs. For either process, accurate visualization of the finished project enhanced the participants' ability to understand the proposed project, and, consequently, could be very important to securing project approval.

In addition to needing computer visualizations of construction and transportation projects, the construction and transportation industries also needed to study human factors in the design of construction and transportation projects. For example, human reaction time to construction zone signing was a concern, as were potential weather effects. The merging of 3-D visualization with Geographical Information Systems (GIS) was a hot topic in many trade publications. GIS was a mapping technology that was the norm in the transportation industry. Light Detection and Ranging (LIDAR) technology, a revolutionary laser scanning system, could also revolutionize the industry. In fact, Lance had been looking into purchasing LIDAR technology for 3DV-LS, but with a price tag of $250,000 he thought it was cost prohibitive. However, purchase of the technology might be justified if 3DV-LS expanded into the transportation industry.

After Lance briefed Sandy on what he knew, they decided to spend the next several days contacting and questioning firms that had won construction and transportation consulting contracts. As Sandy put it, "We need to know more about the size of the market, whether or not it's growing, and more specific information on the use of computer visualization."

## Use of Computer Visualization in Construction and Transportation Projects

Firms reported that computer-generated pictures were beginning to replace the hand-rendered sketches that had been the industry standard. However, after talking with several consultants, Lance and Sandy found that only large consultants were heavy users (there was a reluctance to use animations for anything but large-scale projects, i.e., those involving hundreds of millions of dollars) because acquiring the hardware, software, and personnel capable of creating quality models or pictures was extremely expensive. Even those consultants who subcontracted for visualization services were concerned about the cost of computer-generated pictures. "Unless computer visualizations are required, I avoid using them because they add unnecessary expense to an already expensive project," one consultant observed.

Nonetheless, some of the consultants Lance and Sandy talked to mentioned that the benefit of computer visualizations, though not immediately obvious, was still significant. As one consultant put it, "I can show a group of investors a hand-drawn sketch of how a building will look like when it's done, or I can show them a computer-generated picture of the finished building that's about as close to a real picture of the finished building as possible without actually erecting the building. They're always much more impressed with the computer-generated pictures. It saves a lot of time in securing final project approval. I figure the time I save by using computer-generated pictures more than outweighs the expense of creating the pictures." Another consultant stated that computer visualizations made it easier to respond to "what if" scenarios frequently requested by customers.

## Growth in Construction and Transportation Industries

As Sandy delved deeper into the market trends she found a report released by the American Institute of Architects (AIA). In this report, she found several pieces of interesting information. The AIA projected:

- 1 percent increase in building activity paralleling population growth, as compared to levels in the first half of the 1990s.
- A 13.91 percent increase in the average annual volume of contract awards (see Exhibit 8-19).
- An emphasis on growth in construction spending in the commercial and industrial categories, especially for office buildings.
- A growing share of construction spending for building renovations over the next fifteen years. By 2010, building renovations would exceed new building construction.

The AIA report also reported preliminary results indicating that approximately $24 billion was billed for architectural services in 1999. Roughly one-third of that amount related to the commercial/industrial sector, whereas institutional billings accounted for almost one-half of the billed services.

From a contact in the Department of Transportation, Lance learned that transportation projects would also continue to become available due to the federal government's commitment to rehabilitating the nation's road infrastructure. Billions of dollars were allocated annually for road enhancement projects and large-scale interstate construction.

## Perceptions of Computer Visualization

Next, Sandy put together a list of questions and spent several hours on the phone talking to potential clients. Sandy found that consultants networked through a variety of conferences, most held in conjunction with trade organizations. Consultants usually worked on projects in teams, with the same three or four consultants completing several different types of projects for the same government agency or private developer. Often, the consultants who designed projects for government-initiated projects were the same consultants who designed large-scale commercial projects. The designated primary consultant changed depending on the project but had the same subcontractors. Most consultants decided who to work with based on experience, quality, past working relationship, availability, and price.

The consultants Sandy talked to also shared with her some of their perceptions of 3DV-LS. For example, one consultant told her that 3DV-LS had a reputation of charging high

**EXHIBIT 8-19**
**Average Volume of Contract Awards (in billions of 2000 dollars)**

Source: Ammerican Institute of Architects 2000 Firm Survey. Originally given in 1987 dollars, converted to 2000 dollars.

| | 1991 to 1995 | 1996 to 2010 | % Change |
|---|---|---|---|
| Educational Facilities | $ 24.3 | $ 24.1 | −1% |
| Health Care Facilities | 13.3 | 13.3 | 0 |
| Public Buildings | 7.1 | 7.9 | 10% |
| Retail Facilities | 23.2 | 22.7 | −2% |
| Office Buildings | 16.4 | 28.1 | 42% |
| Industrial Facilities | 19.1 | 21.7 | 12% |
| Total | $103.5 | $117.9 | |

fees for standard services. Another reported a concern that 3DV-LS's prices were too high, since it did not provide any expertise concerning design issues. Sandy was surprised by this, because her research showed 3DV-LS's prices, even with a 25–30 percent profit margin, to be competitive in the litigation market. She was afraid that the perception of high prices derived from the early years in computer visualization when any type of computer-generated models or animation had been extremely expensive.

Sandy also queried the consultants on whether or not the visualizations they contracted for were software or hardware rendered. Most were uncertain. "I didn't know that there was more than one way to get pictures," was a typical response.

## Pricing

The consultants were reluctant to share what they were paying for visualization services in the construction and transportation industries. However, after some digging, Lance was able to identify the going rates for animation and photo simulations in the transportation industry. The rates did not specify what kind of process was used (i.e., hardware or software rendering) to create the visualizations. But, because Lance knew of no other companies who did hardware rendering besides 3DV-LS, he assumed the prices reflected software rendered visualizations.

- Animation—$3,000 to $6,000 per minute
- Digitally altered photographs—$5,000 to $7,000 per image
- Photo-images or 3D models—$800 to $1,500 per image

In the transportation industry, most of the projects were large-scale transportation projects funded by government agencies. The government agency often specified the amount of money to be spent on visualizations. For example, the allowable costs for visualization on a recently approved $500 million transportation project ranged from $70,000 to $150,000.

Neither Sandy nor Lance was able to find a range of prices in the construction industry, but assumed that the rates were most likely comparable to those in the transportation industry. Moreover, because many construction projects were also funded by the government, Lance and Sandy surmised that the government would specify the computer visualization budgets for those projects, also.

## Competition

After talking to several consultants, Sandy looked into how competitive the market was. She identified two types of competitors and profiled each of these.

The first competitor was typically a large firm that provided a full complement of services desired by the construction and transportation industries. These firms had the ability to design a project, conduct marketing campaigns and public participation workshops, and manage the implementation or construction of the project. Competitors in this group, such as Howard, Needles, Tammen, and Bergendoff (HNTB), the 8th largest architecture firm nationwide and 4th largest in transportation design, had national brand recognition and many years of extensive and varied experience. Not surprisingly, these firms rarely hired subcontractors, relying, instead, on in-house technology departments for their visualization needs. For example, HNTB's Technology Group employed content planners, media designers, 3-D animators, and networking and programming professionals to provide high-tech communication and information solutions to the architecture, transportation, environmental engineering, and construction services industries. However, HNTB relied on software rendering for its visualization projects.

Another firm that fit this competitor profile was Parsons Brinckerhoff, Inc., a global engineering giant. This firm provided planning, engineering, construction management, and operations and maintenance services to a wide variety of clients around the world. Similar to HNTB, Parsons Brinckerhoff had started Parsons and Brinckerhoff 4D Imaging (PB4D) in 1988 as an advanced computer visual simulation business unit. While PB4D was the industry leader for the visualization of transportation projects, it was also a large-scale multimedia and Internet business unit. Like HNTB, PB4D also relied on software rendering.

The second type of competitor was characterized as firms specializing in design visualization services. Typically, these firms were smaller than 3DV and had regional brand recognition. Although these firms' staffs were small, they also had specific experience with architects, landscape architects, planners, and civil engineers. Consequently, these competitors knew how to communicate with these professionals using industry jargon. Interestingly, most of these firms also relied on software rendering and did not provide extensive product or service lines. One firm typical of this type of competitor was Newlands & Co., a consulting firm located in Portland, Oregon that specialized in design visualization, 3D animation and Web development services. Newlands & Company, Inc. produced high-quality visual simulations, animations, Web and multimedia presentations for transportation, urban design and architecture. Its mission was to employ the best in art and technology to facilitate communication between designers and their clients. Its services included photography, 3-D modeling, photo simulation, animation, multimedia presentation creation, Web development, and training.

## The Future

Lance met with Pat two weeks later to present the information he and Sandy had uncovered about the construction and transportation industries. When Lance finished the brief overview, he handed over a complete written report of the findings to Pat. "So," Pat said, "based on what you've learned, what do you think we should do?"

Lance, expecting this question, carefully formulated his response. "I think there's an excellent opportunity for 3DV-LS in this new market. The construction and transportation industries are growing, and there's increasing use of computer visualizations on projects. Plus, I think the advantage of hardware rendering—that is, being able to quickly create and change visualizations—will be just as important to the construction and transportation industries as it has proven to be in the litigation industry. But we'll have to convince consultants of this fact and at the same time compete against companies that are already firmly established in this market. It won't be easy."

Pat thanked Lance for all his hard work. Left alone with his thoughts, Pat pondered his options. One option was to hire and train one to two new salespeople to focus on developing business in the construction and transportation industries. This would require some investment, but would allow the current salesforce to stay focused on the litigation industry. Another option was to allocate the time and efforts of one or two current salespeople to developing small scale bids for regional projects in the construction and transportation industries. This option was less risky financially, but might further affect sales in the litigation industry.

Pat couldn't help but speculate. What if the sales decline in the last year was just temporary? What if the Web site proved to be an effective tool in cultivating sales? Several times over the last few months, Pat had wondered whether the declining sales were a direct effect of poorly communicating the advantages of hardware rendering relative to software rendering. At especially low moments, he worried that, to the average client, the advantages of hardware rendering were not tangible enough to clearly differentiate it from software rendering.

With respect to the new market opportunity, Pat had other nagging questions. Did 3DV-LS have the necessary skills and resources to enter the construction and transportation market while at the same time maintaining its litigation business? In particular, could the current five salespeople adapt their skills, honed in the litigation market, to the construction and transportation market? Could 3DV-LS successfully differentiate its hardware rendering visualization method from the more commonly used software rendering in the new market? Would entry into the new market pull necessary attention from the litigation industry? While Pat appreciated Lance's opinion, he knew that whether or not 3DV-LS should enter the construction and transportation market depended on the answers to these questions.

## References

1. T. Nagle and Reed K. Holden, *The Strategy and Tactics of Pricing* (Englewood Cliffs, NJ: Prentice Hall, 1991).
2. Heather Bergstein and Hooman Estaelami, "A Survey of Emerging Technologies for Pricing New-to-the-World Products," *Journal of Product and Brand Management* 11 (May 2002): 303–19
3. Thomas Dudick, *Handbook of Product Cost Estimating and Pricing* (Englewood Cliffs, NJ: Prentice Hall, 1995).
4. Francis J. Mulhern and Robert P. Leone, "Measuring Market Response to Price Changes: A Classification Approach," *Journal J Business Research* 33 (July 1995): 197–205.
5. Joel E. Urbany, "Justifying Profitable Pricing," *The Journal of Product and Brand Management* 10 (March 2001): 141–59.
6. Margret L. Gagne and Richard Discenza, "Target Costing," *The Journal of Business and Industrial Marketing* 10 (1995).
7. Conan M. Buzby, Arthur Gerstenfeld, Lindsay E. Voss and Amy Z. Zeng, "Using Lean Principles to Streamline the Quotation Process: A Case Study," *Industrial Management and Data Systems* 102 (Sept. 2002): 513–20.

# Communication and Delivery

## CHAPTER NINE

# Promotional Strategy

**Learning Objectives**

After reading this chapter, you should be able to:

- Appreciate the role of promotion in business marketing and how it differs from the role of consumer promotion.
- Identify the steps involved in creating a business promotion plan.
- Explain how objectives are set for a business promotion campaign.
- Understand how promotional budgets are developed.
- Understand how business marketers develop and implement the promotional mix.
- Differentiate among the various promotional tools available to the business marketer.
- Recall two primary methods by which the effectiveness of business promotion campaigns can be measured.

**Chapter Outline**

The Role of Promotion in Business Marketing
Setting Objectives for a Promotional Plan
Developing the Promotional Budget
Developing and Implementing the Promotional Mix
Measuring the Effectiveness of the Business Promotion Campaign
Following Up and Making Necessary Changes

## The Role of Promotion in Business Marketing

*Advertising, publicity,* and *sales promotion* are communication methods used by marketers to remind or persuade current and potential customers that a particular product exists. In the business market, advertising, publicity, and sales promotion pave the way for the sales call. As Exhibit 9-1 shows, **business promotion** refers to the use of the seller-generated promotional tools to deliver messages to business markets. Most basically, there are three purposes of marketing communication—to inform, to persuade, and to remind customers and potential customers about a product or a company. The promotional tools used in marketing communication—*professional selling, advertising, public relations, sales promotion,* and *direct marketing*—are often referred to as the **promotional mix.**

Since professional selling was examined in detail in Chapter 3, we will only address advertising, publicity, sales promotion, and direct marketing here. Compared with professional selling, the cost of using advertising, publicity, sales promotion, and direct marketing is relatively inexpensive. Further, the promotional tools discussed in this chapter tend to be used to support the professional selling function. This is because business markets tend to be geographically concentrated, with relatively few companies purchasing large amounts. Due to the geographic concentration of these markets and the substantial purchasing volume of such firms, personal selling dominates the promotional mix.

Despite the fact that our discussion of professional selling appears in a separate chapter, today, successful organizations use what is called **integrated marketing communications (IMC).** IMC is defined as the coordination of the promotional mix elements along with other marketing activities (e.g., packaging) such that all communication with the firm's customers is consistent. The idea is that all communications that come from an organization about a product, be they professional selling, advertising, public relations, sales promotion, or direct marketing, should present a consistent message about that product. By doing so, the firm can have more impact on its target market than if each promotional tool is presented singularly and with no effort to integrate messages.

Organizational buyers tend to be part of a larger buying center or decision-making unit, tend to purchase in large quantities, and tend to base their purchases on relatively exact specifications. Therefore, some consider purchasing managers to be less susceptible to

**EXHIBIT 9-1   Business Promotional Tools and the Flows of Information, Persuasion, and Reminder Messages**

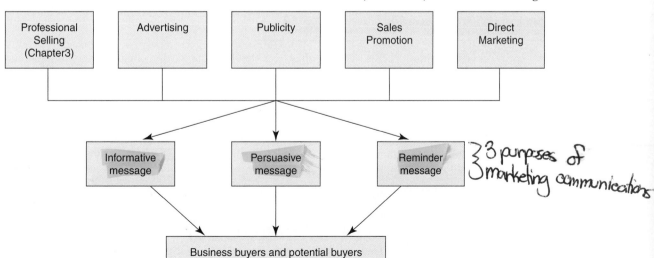

*3 purposes of marketing communications*

**EXHIBIT 9-2** **Steps in a Business Promotion Campaign**

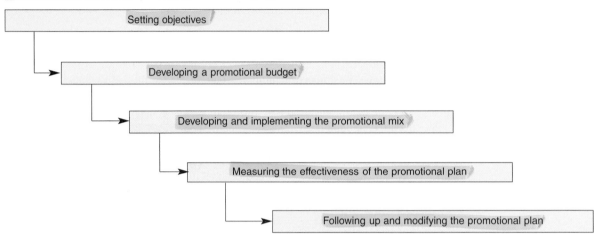

promotional appeals that emphasize brand names. Nonetheless, business buyers are human and are subject to the same appeals found to be effective in consumer advertising. Likewise, not all business markets are concentrated geographically, nor do all purchase in large volume. Thus, at times, other aspects of the promotional mix may carry a larger burden in communicating with buyers when it comes to small orders or low-margin products.

Of course, if promotion is going to stimulate sales, it must be carefully tailored to the product or product line and convey an appropriate message. Effective promotion can increase sales, but ineffective promotion can waste millions of dollars and even damage company image.

Exhibit 9-2 demonstrates that creating a promotional campaign for business markets involves the following five steps: (1) setting objectives, (2) developing a promotional budget, (3) developing and implementing the promotional mix, (4) measuring the effectiveness of the promotional plan, and (5) following up and modifying the promotional plan, if necessary. This process results in a **promotional campaign**—a sequence of promotions reflecting a common theme and geared to specific objectives. Developing such a campaign is the focus of this chapter.

## Setting Objectives for a Promotional Plan

Establishing specific, realistic objectives should be the starting point for every promotional campaign. It is difficult—and probably even imprudent—to plan a promotional program unless marketers have first established the objectives they are trying to attain. When setting promotion objectives, depending on the promotional mix element selected, the promotion manager may want to set communication and/or sales objectives. Communications objectives include increasing awareness and informing and reminding buyers and potential buyers about a product, product line and/or company. Specific communications objectives include: (1) building product awareness, (2) inducing trial and/or retrial of new products, (3) countering competitors' offerings, (4) building product-line acceptance, (5) obtaining space with distributors, (6) intensifying usage, (7) aiding the sales staff by introducing buyers to product offerings, (8) reviving a brand that is in the decline stage of its product life cycle, and (9) confirming buyers' purchase decisions.

On the other hand, sales objectives are tied to sales. Specific sales objectives include: (1) increasing market share, (2) stimulating short-term sales, and (3) sustaining product preference. Some promotional elements, such as public relations, are more consistent with communications objectives whereas others, such as direct marketing, are more consistent with sales objectives. Like all objectives, promotion objectives, whether they may be communications or sales objectives, should be quantifiable, specify the target market, be realistic, be attainable, and specify a time frame. Assume that a promotional manager chooses "sustaining product preference" as an objective. A B2B firm might choose such an objective in response to introduction of a new product by a competitor. In order to be useful, that objective should be worded such that it meets the requirement of a good objective (e.g., "A result of this advertising campaign will be to sustain Product A preference during the subsequent 3 month period as measured by continued purchase among our current Product A customers at levels that at least equal purchase figures for the last 3 months"). The objective is quantified—sustained product preference is clearly defined—and it specifies a target market (e.g., "among our current Product A customers"). We assume that the objective is realistic and attainable and it specifies a time frame (e.g., "the levels of sales for the next 3 months will be compared to those of the previous 3 months").

There are differences of opinion about whether advertising objectives should be sales-oriented or communications-oriented. For example, while some marketers believe that sales objectives will keep the advertising effort focused on how it will influence sales, others believe that asking advertising (and even promotion) to take on the whole burden of the marketing mix is inappropriate. If an advertising campaign does not result in an increase in sales, there are many possible explanations for that. It could be that the price of the product is too high or that the product is inferior to the competition. Indeed, there are many factors that influence sales of any particular product, only one of which is advertising. Total sales volume and market share are widely utilized sales indices offered by A. C. Nielsen, Market Research Corporation of America, and Audits and Surveys, Incorporated. Market-share and sales-volume data such as these assist a business marketing manager in determining whether a firm's sales are meeting its objectives. Other examples of precise, realistic objectives might include improving sales volume in a particular territory, improving overall corporate image, or zeroing in on a specific segment not presently being served.

## Developing the Promotional Budget

After the marketing manager has established promotional goals for appropriate market segments, a sound, cost-effective promotional budget must be developed. This is neither a simple nor an enviable task, as there are no concrete budgeting guidelines or techniques to ensure maximum success. Ideally, the budget needs to be set at a point where the last dollar spent on promotion equals the profit from the sales that that promotional dollar produced. However, in the real world, this *marginal utility* concept is all but impossible to apply. More realistic methods commonly used for setting budgets include *percentage of anticipated sales, affordable/arbitrary, competitive parity/market share,* and *objective-and-task* methods. As illustrated in Exhibit 9-3, business-to-business organizations typically employ the objective-and-task and affordable methods to set a promotional budget.

Traditionally, business promotion budgets have been spartan for reasons too numerous, diverse, and illogical to explore here. It is the marketer's job, however, to set the budget and to ensure the most return for every dollar spent. Economists advise that the first dollar spent on promotion yields the greatest return, with a diminishing rate of return from additional expenditures. However, this rule applies only if the money is spent in an "optimal" fashion. Operationally, this requires a marketer to prioritize all promotional efforts in terms of their potential contribution to the firm. Indeed, *how* to spend the promotional budget is perhaps a tougher and more crucial question to answer than *how much* to spend. Exhibit 9-4 shows a curve representing advertising expenditures. Note that the greatest contribution to the firm is made with the initial advertising dollars spent. As advertising expenditures increase, the

**EXHIBIT 9-3** **Common Techniques for Setting the Business Promotion Budget**

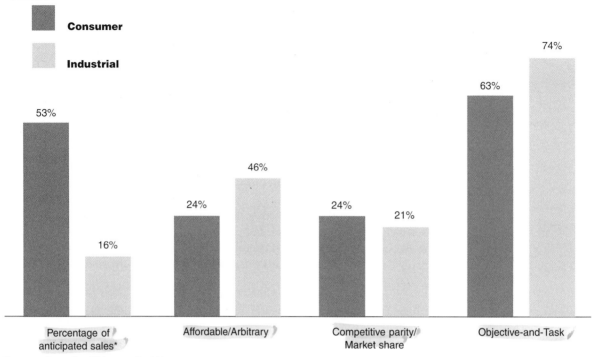

Percents total more than 100 because of multiple responses.
*Also, 20 percent of the consumer goods firms and 23 percent of the industrial goods organizations use current or past years' sales.

curve eventually begins to flatten, illustrating that, after some point, a larger budget will contribute little profit.

This lesson in economics serves to highlight the importance of a firm's determining and prioritizing target audiences before making advertising expenditures. The first step in setting promotional priorities is to identify and rank target audiences, and then to ascertain the

**EXHIBIT 9-4**
**Contribution of Advertising Expenditures to Profit**

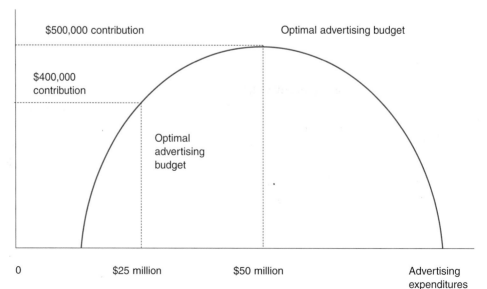

**EXHIBIT 9-5**
**Identifying Target Audiences and the Most Effective Ways to Reach Them**

| Audience | Typical Marketing Communications Tasks |
| --- | --- |
| Sales force | Sales literature |
| Editors of magazines serving target audiences | Marketing public relations programs |
| Key government officials, employees, suppliers, plant-community leaders | Special events |
| Customers and identified prospects | Direct mail, trade shows, seminars |
| Customers, known prospects, unknown prospects, and hidden buying influences | Advertisements |

*How to read:* moving downward, size of audience increases. The cost of communicating becomes more expensive, and the ability to isolate influentials becomes more difficult.

most effective means for reaching each audience. Exhibit 9-5 illustrates this concept. The astute marketing manager spends budgeted dollars by starting at the top of the pyramid and working down.

**Concept Review**

1. What is business promotion?
2. Why should appropriate objectives be the starting point for any business promotion campaign?
3. What is the ideal point at which business promotion campaign expenditures should be set?

## Developing and Implementing the Promotional Mix

### Business Advertising

As Exhibit 9-6 indicates, *business advertising* is considerably different from consumer advertising. First, as noted earlier in this chapter, business advertising comprises a smaller role in communicating with target markets as well as a smaller percentage of the sales dollar relative to consumer advertising. Further, business advertising emphasizes informational/rational appeals, which focus on the product and the reasons for buying it (e.g.,

**EXHIBIT 9-6**
**Differences Between Business and Consumer Advertising**

| Business Advertising | Consumer Advertising |
| --- | --- |
| Comprises a smaller role in the promotional mix | Comprises a larger role in the promotional mix |
| Utilizes a smaller percentage of the sales dollar | Utilizes a larger percentage of the sales dollar |
| Emphasizes informational/rational appeals | Emphasizes emotional appeals |
| Targeted toward a somewhat limited market | Targeted toward a mass market |

## STRATEGY AT WORK

### INTEGRATED BUSINESS-TO-BUSINESS PROMOTION CAMPAIGN

Needing a fresh, innovative, attention-getting promotion to ensure the success of its new family of industrial floor-coating polymers, Rohm & Haas (http://www.rohmhaas.com/) created a "New-Tech" theme suggesting a completely new way of thinking. The promotion's unconventional graphics literally turned the world on its side: the ads featured two businessmen viewing an industrial floor while standing upright on a vertical side wall. To integrate the promotion, the image was featured in print ads, direct mail pieces, and in the firm's trade show booth.

The firm sent a direct mail package that included a uniquely constructed 12-page information brochure (with business reply card) to a list of potential clients. For a select group of 50 high-potential clients, the package included a kaleidoscope with desk stand (allowing the recipients to experience a new perspective, both literally and figuratively). Ruth Cyrus, marketing area manager for Rohm & Haas, targeted multiple decision influencers at the clients (typically purchasing agents, research heads, technology directors, and department managers).

Cliff Keevan, advertising manager for Rohm & Haas, reported that the response was "tremendous." "We came up with a promotion package that wasn't just cosmetically attractive but illustrated our leadership role in developing innovative products to solve customer problems."

The package was mailed in mid-April, two weeks prior to the major industry trade show. Rohm & Haas decided to use a 20-foot booth exhibit with ten feet devoted to the new Rhoplex NT polymers ("New Tech"). At the show, small key-chain kaleidoscopes were distributed to reinforce the promotional message. As an additional reminder, 250 copies of the 12-page brochure were sent out as a follow-up after the show.

Besides serving as a centerpiece in the trade show booth, the photograph of the two businessmen standing upright on the vertical wall was used in a two-page, full-color ad that appeared in two industry trade journals for June/July. An article written about the scientists who developed the polymer ran in one issue of one of the journals. For the issue cover, Rohm & Haas supplied graphics reminiscent of their advertisement, with the scientists shown standing in the foreground. Response (qualified sales leads) to the integrated promotion far exceeded the company's expectations.

### Action Assignment

As the newly appointed product manager for Rhoplex Polymers, evaluate the website of Rohm & Haas and present to management (the class) your proposal for featuring your product line on the firm's website. Be specific, and present mockups of what you want added and where it will attach. Also explain your reasons for suggesting the changes.

**Source:** *Potentials in Marketing,* April 1998: p. 27, "Business-to-Business Promotion Gives Target Audience a Unique Perspective." © 1998 Lakewood Publications.

---

feature appeals, competitive advantage appeals, favorable price appeals, news appeals, and product popularity appeals) whereas consumer advertising emphasizes emotional appeals that relate to consumers' social and/or psychological needs. In addition, the target markets in business advertising are much smaller than the mass markets targeted by consumer advertising.

### *Goals of Business Advertising*

Specific goals and objectives should be set for business advertising. They should follow from the objectives set for the promotional plan and should be consistent with the role advertising is intended to play in the IMC plan.

Business advertising generally has one or more of four specific goals.

1. *To make current or potential customers aware of the marketer's firm.*

Business advertising can have a significant beneficial effect in making potential customers aware of potential suppliers and in reinforcing satisfaction among existing customers. An enormous challenge to business executives is to select an image that will attract the eyes of readers.[1] Theodore Levitt makes the following point:

A company's [good] reputation improves the chances of getting a favorable first hearing and an early adoption of the product. Thus, corporate advertising that can build upon the company's reputation (other factors also shape its reputation) will help the company's sales representatives.[2]

**2. *To convey information about the characteristics of a particular product or products manufactured by the marketer's firm.***

Advertising should provide specific information about a firm's goods and/or services to members of a buying center so they can appraise that advertiser's offerings properly. There are two important assumptions being made here: first, that organizational buyers are looking for detailed information about the goods and/or services they buy; second, that advertisers know what information is relevant to their customers. It appears that knowledge of buying motives is no less important among business purchasers than among the consuming public. If business advertisers do not know how business customers perceive their firms or their products, they should find out, in order to avoid sending advertising messages that could be irrelevant and possibly ignored.

**3. *To ease the salesperson's job.***

Over time, one fundamental justification for advertising has been the belief that it paves the salesperson's entry into both established and prospective customers' firms, making his or her selling efforts more productive. Although it might be difficult to prove in specific situations, there is growing support that real and substantial positive interaction exists between advertising and sales efforts, justifying advertising investments.

**4. *To reduce overall selling costs.***

It is one thing to conclude that advertising helps a salesperson's performance and yet another to quantify just how much savings advertising helps to generate. No one seems to know quite how the advertising-salesperson relationship operates, or the exact economics of the relationship. Indeed, both academics and practitioners perceive much uncertainty in advertising effectiveness.[3] In short, business advertisers must figure out for themselves the proper budget levels for their advertising and personal selling programs. However, they should expect their decisions on budget to be closely scrutinized: solid evidence of productivity is necessary for business advertising operations to avoid budget cuts.

## Media Selection

Media choices for business advertising are similar to those for consumer advertising. Indeed, a business advertisement may run on prime-time specials, on business cable television networks, in consumer magazines, and via electronic media. When advertising is used, management must select the media mix to be used. The *media mix* is some combination of the following types of advertising media: print media, broadcast media, direct marketing, and electronic media.

## Print Media

*Print media* includes business publications, professional publications, general business publications, trade directories, and general consumer publications such as *Time, Newsweek, Scientific American,* and *Golf Digest.* Business publications are of two basic types: *horizontal* and *vertical.*

**Horizontal publications** are intended for buyers who have similar functions in their companies, regardless of their specific industry, such as *Industrial Maintenance and Plant Operation,* published for those maintaining and operating industrial plants of over 50 employees, and *Purchasing,* a news magazine for purchasing executives. **Vertical publications** are those discussing current issues and problems of a single industry, such as *Frozen Food Field,* edited for management personnel in the frozen food industry, and *Mechanical Contractor,* designed for the large heating, plumbing, piping, and air-conditioning contractor.

*Professional publications* include research journals and trade and professional association journals, edited for physicians, dentists, architects, and other professionals (for example, *Architectural Digest*). Their editorial range varies from reporting new technical developments to discussing how to run offices more efficiently and profitably. Much advertising is directed at professionals, as these experts are an important influence in recommending or specifying the products their clients will need.

*Industrial trade directories* have long been used as an important promotion medium in business advertising. Most industries have their own directories and buyer's guide, with descriptions of products and product lines and lists of various firms marketing and selling them. Trade directories are a highly effective way to get particular advertisers' names before their respective target audiences. Although there are numerous statewide and private trade directories, the best known and most comprehensive is the *Thomas Register of American Manufacturers,* comprising 19 volumes and over 60,000 pages, with 50,000 product headings and listings from 123,000 business-to-business companies. Regional directories also are available on CD-ROM. The greatest advantages of industrial trade directories are their high credibility and acceptance rate by both large and small advertisers and buyers.

*General business publications* such as *Fortune, Business Week,* and *The Wall Street Journal* address interests and issues across a wide variety of industries. With their business and editorial content, these publications treat a broad range of topics and concerns pertinent to executives in all aspects of business and industry. Advertising comprises about 60 percent of general business publications.

### Broadcast Media

*Broadcast media,* that is, radio and television, once thought to be only for consumer advertising, are receiving increasing attention from advertisers who serve highly geographically concentrated markets and who want to get around the intense business advertising competition in older, more traditional business media. Both large and small firms have used radio advertising through the years. Standard Oil of New Jersey attempts to speak to a select audience of managerial decision makers, financial executives, and government officials through appropriate radio stations and time periods. Another veteran radio user is Timken Roller Bearing Company of Canton, Ohio, which runs 15 radio spots a week during morning and evening drive times in the upper Midwest, to reach select audiences in cities in which there is great involvement with the automotive industry. Likewise, television advertising by business-to-business firms has become increasingly popular, making business advertisers such as IBM, Hewlett-Packard, Xerox, and Federal Express more highly visible. However, this medium is not appropriate for all business marketers.

### Business Advertising Content

The effective business advertisement starts with a short headline presenting an interesting or intriguing idea of enough significance to readers that they will wish to see or hear more. The copy describes the distinctive features of the product, offering evidence of its desirability and proof of claims made for it. The reader is urged to take some action; where feasible, specific courses of action are suggested.

Excellent photography and clear illustrations increase readership while strengthening or elaborating on headlines. Art, however, should not be used for its own sake. Generic images do not convey messages. It is better to use testimonials, case histories, and other copy-heavy advertisements than to be burdened with weak pictures. Lebhar-Friedman Research and Information Services of New York City conducted a study of 481 corporate decision makers and found that frequently run, colorful advertisements are best for business advertising. Eight out of 10 respondents said they are more favorably impressed and influenced by four-color than by black-and-white advertisements.[4]

# BUSINESS MARKETING IN ACTION

## PROMOTING LEG AIRBAG SYSTEMS

In May of 1997, Autoliv Inc. (http://www.autoliv.com), a Swedish-based autoparts maker, merged with U.S.-based Morton ASP, and in April of 1998 acquired the Japanese company Sensor Technology Corporation (STC). This combination created the world's leading producer of automotive safety equipment, including air bags, inflators, seat belts, and sensors. Autoliv now employs 21,000, with 60 plants in 28 countries, and they continue to expand with additional plants in Japan and Russia. Their customers include virtually all of the world's major OEM car manufacturers.

Autoliv began exporting to Japan in 1989, and net annual sales to that market have now grown to over U.S. $600 million (20 percent of Autoliv total sales). Prior to the acquisition of STC, Autoliv imported products into Japan from its Utah plant. As long as demand was relatively steady, minor modifications would extend delivery by two weeks. With the new STC Japanese production plant, that time lag has now been reduced to one day. Parts manufacturers can no longer just supply air bags or inflators, but are asked to supply entire systems ready for installation. The addition of STC's technology allows that. The breadth of Autoliv's capabilities are now unique in total system applications.

The late 1990s have brought difficult economic times for Japanese automakers, with unit production down 8.4 percent in 1998 from 1997. Current levels are down 25 percent from their peak in 1990. Still, Gunnar Bark, Autoliv's chairman, points out that globally, half a million people are killed in motor traffic every year and ten times as many severely injured. Even in difficult times there will continue to be a compelling need for improved automotive safety.

As part of Autoliv's ongoing development of new safety products, they are making a considerable R & D investment on the next generation of side and head air bags. Also included in future plans are inflatable carpets that will essentially function as air bags for passenger's legs and feet. Details can be found at their website (http://www.autoliv.com/appl_alv/Autoliv.nsf/pages/leg_protection).

### Action Assignment A

**Team 1**—Prepare a brand name and promotional campaign for Autoliv's inflatable carpet, with separate components directed to the Japanese automotive OEM manufacturers and consumer pull. **Team 2**—Do the same, only direct your efforts toward European OEMs and consumers. **Team 3**—Do the same, only direct your efforts toward U.S. OEMs and consumers.

### Action Assignment B

Explore Skyline Display's website at (http://www.skyline displays.com/). Be creative and design a trade show booth for Autoliv's inflatable carpet. Prepare a budget for Autoliv's trade show participation. Be sure to coordinate with the teams working on Action Assignment A.

**Source:** *Focus Japan,* "Position Reinforced by Acquisition," March 1999.

## *Use of Advertising Agencies*

*Advertising agencies* work on advertising strategy and campaigns, prepare copy and layouts, study markets, select media, and carry out the actual physical production of the advertisement, including its placement in selected media. During the past decade, the advertising management responsibility among small- to moderate-sized corporations has gradually been turned over to the well-integrated, IMC type of agency.

Among the notable concepts in today's advertising business are IMC, accountability, and strategic thinking. These concepts are business as usual for B2B agencies such as Anderson & Lembke. When Dow hired Anderson & Lembke, the company had just realigned its dozen or so widely varied plastics businesses into a single unit called Dow Plastics. The agency's tack was not only to publicize the new entity but to help Dow position it competitively. The result was a positioning strategy that went beyond the standard guarantee of customer satisfaction to a promise of customer success. In the campaign, targeted communications promoted the various individual virtues of Dow Plastics' disparate products, and all carried the tag line "We don't succeed unless you do."[5]

Contrary to these advantages, advertising agencies are not as universally used by B2B concerns as they are by consumer goods firms. Some firms believe that they can save money by avoiding hiring an agency; some may believe that they can do a better job themselves because of their greater understanding of their own business and customer base. Advertising agencies, on the other hand, counter that such companies do not know advertising, save less money than they think, and sacrifice creative independence. There is little question that the advertising agency has an important place in the marketing of business products. Although there are some types of activities it cannot perform as well as in-house departments, there are others it can do more efficiently or more economically. If an advertising agency is used, the challenge for marketers is to achieve an effective partnership between the company and the agency.

## Business Publicity

*Business publicity* can be a powerful mass-promotion tool for the business advertiser. **Publicity**, a communication in news story form about an organization, its products, or both, that is transmitted through a mass medium at no charge, can serve to help build or add to a firm's prestige; to introduce a new product, a product improvement, or a product application; to provide the salesperson with easier entry into the offices of current and prospective customers; and to increase the company's visibility and the desirability of its product mix.

The public relations or advertising department usually is charged with the responsibility for developing favorable publicity that comes to the attention of not only customers but also the company's suppliers, distributors, employees, creditors, stockholders and investors, and the general public. As Exhibit 9-7 shows, four techniques for getting in the news are the press release, the exclusive feature, the press conference, and the press kit. Management activities that are good sources for publicity include personnel changes and promotions; speeches and special appearances at banquets, graduations, and professional meetings; and stories about the company's history and future. The private lives and interesting activities—hobbies and charitable and volunteer activities—of managerial personnel show a different side to those who work for what are frequently perceived as "insensitive corporate giants."

One of the real advantages of publicity is that the media time or space used is free of charge for the company, but it must be remembered that publicity can be negative, too. For example, a two-year investigation ended in April 2003 with a $1.4 billion settlement from ten investment firms including Merrill Lynch, Salomon Smith Barney, Credit Suisse First Boston, and Citigroup. Initially, an investor sued Merrill Lynch for continually advising him to keep his stock in InfoSpace after he told them he wanted to sell. Upon investigation by New York's Attorney General, e-mails were discovered wherein the advisor described his own share tips as "junk" and "dog." Merrill Lynch agreed to pay a $400,000 settlement to the investor. The Attorney General did not stop there and went on to investigate many other firms on Wall Street, leading to the substantial settlement. Other recent business scandals have included the telecommunications company WorldCom (which has since

---

**EXHIBIT 9-7    Four Techniques for Getting in the News**

*Press Release.* An announcement to the news media of significant changes in a firm or product or to introduce a new product. It is the most popular technique for obtaining publicity.

*Exclusive Feature.* An in-depth article or broadcast message about something of interest to a particular public. An exclusive feature could highlight a new concept, an industry trend, a special technique, and so on. The feature usually does not focus solely on a company's products but will use them as examples to illustrate points. An exclusive feature usually requires extensive coordination between public relations personnel and editors or broadcast managers.

*Press Conference.* A meeting for the media sponsored by the firm. Press conferences can be overdone and used too often. They should be used to announce major news items such as the introduction of a product or the appointment of a new president.

*Press Kits.* Sometimes used in connection with a press conference, a press kit may include press releases, pictures, tapes and films, product samples, and complimentary passes.

rebranded as MCI), the energy company Enron, Enron's auditor Arthur Andersen, the photocopy company Xerox, and the development group Millennium Partners.

When faced with negative publicity, there are three guidelines that the B2B marketer should keep in mind. First, do not make the situation worse than it is. When companies look for a scapegoat, stall, deny wrong behavior, or make light of a serious situation, they make things worse. Second, get the negative situation behind you as quickly as possible. The faster a company discloses inappropriate behavior, apologizes and makes amends, the better. Finally, remember that the news media that may seem to be your enemy today is likely to be the same media that you will want to carry your positive news tomorrow. News media that seem to be scavenging for negative information from your company are, in fact, simply looking for news to report. Whether that news is good or bad for you is irrelevant to them—they are looking for stories to write—it is their job. These guidelines are summed up in the advice that Lanny Davis, a senior partner at Patton Boggs law firm, offers companies when he says, "tell it early, tell it all, tell it yourself."[6] Although publicity can work against a firm at a given point in time, its effects are usually short term; through time and positive promotional efforts, most damage can generally be reversed.

## Business Sales Promotion

Business sales promotion was formerly considered by marketers as only a set of short-term inducements to create interest among salespeople, intermediaries, and customers. In many firms today, **sales promotion** ventures well beyond creating short-term value for various prospects. It has become the driving force that links personal selling, advertising, and publicity into a meaningful, integrated promotional program. Although there are many forms of sales promotion activities available, business marketers very commonly use trade shows and exhibits; incentives, contests, sweepstakes and games; and advertising specialties.

### *Trade Shows and Exhibits*

Trade shows, trade fairs, expositions, scientific/technical conferences, conventions—the names may vary, but the basic function of the activity represents a major industry marketing event. They have emerged as a significant component in companies' total marketing and selling strategies and budgets, as well as being places where information is exchanged and major buying demands are made within a given industry. Under carefully controlled conditions, the returns from trade show investments can indeed be measured and quantified.

The gathering of an entire industry at one time in one place at a trade show is a most effective way to do business. The larger crowds of attendees often result in salespeople making more sales presentations per day at a typical show then they would normally make during an entire month in the field. Additionally, it takes companies, on average, 3.7 sales calls to close a sale if the prospect is found by the salesperson, but less than one call (.8) to close a sale if the prospect is found at a trade show.[7] As shown in Exhibit 9-8, a well-prepared trade show exhibit can provide access to key decision makers, contact with prospects, and an opportunity to further service present customers. It also offers an opportunity to introduce new products, generate sales leads, find new distributors, and recruit sales representatives, among other things.

Trade show attendance is a continuing part of the job of many managers. Trade show attendance is increasingly seen as a vehicle for visitors (and their firms) to acquire knowledge and prepare for the future. Further, over 1.5 million firms displayed their merchandise (8 percent increase over 1998) and spent in excess of $18.48 billion on trade shows in 1999. These firms utilized over 514 million square feet of floor space in 1999, which was a 17 percent increase in space rented over that in 1998. Over 102 million prospects attended a trade show in 1999.

**EXHIBIT 9-8**
**Power of Trade Shows**

Reprinted by permission of the Center for Exhibition Industry Research.

| Job Function | First-Time Attendees, % | Previous Show Attendees, % |
|---|---|---|
| Top management | 15 | 25 |
| Middle management | 11 | 9 |
| Engineer, R & D | 21 | 20 |
| Production | 4 | 2 |
| Sales and marketing | 11 | 11 |
| Purchasing | 3 | 2 |
| Data processing | 7 | 7 |
| Professional | 9 | 10 |
| Consultant | 1 | 3 |
| Educator | 1 | 1 |
| All others | 12 | 8 |
| Undefined | 5 | 2 |
| | 100% | 100% |

### Types of Trade Shows

Trade show managers classify shows as either *horizontal* or *vertical*. Similar to the distinction made in advertising earlier, vertical shows promote goods and services to a single industry or specific profession. An example of such a show would be the National Operating Room Nurses' Association Meeting and Exposition, which exhibits products designed for operating-room nurses. A horizontal show, on the other hand, promotes a good or service to a variety of industries; for example, COMDEX, the annual computer industry trade show in the United States, features computers, peripherals, and software for any and all industries.

### Deciding Whether to Participate

Why participate? Trade shows and exhibitions have been reported as the second-largest component of the promotional mix budget allocation in firms marketing business products (see Exhibit 9-9). For example, over 825,000 people attended a total of 20 computer and electronics trade shows, and over 633,700 attended a total of 29 manufacturing and engineering shows in 1998.[8] Trade shows have become a key means for big business to do even bigger business and a cost-effective way for smaller businesses to make their mark. Today,

**EXHIBIT 9-9**
**The Role of Exhibitions in the Marketing Mix**

Reprinted by permission of the Center for Exhibition Industry Research.

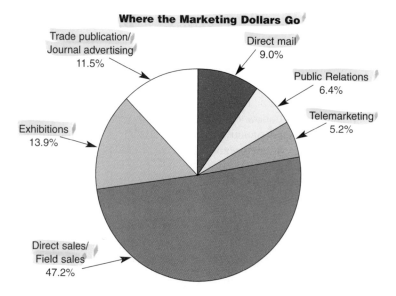

**Where the Marketing Dollars Go**

- Trade publication/Journal advertising 11.5%
- Direct mail 9.0%
- Public Relations 6.4%
- Telemarketing 5.2%
- Exhibitions 13.9%
- Direct sales/Field sales 47.2%

the trade show industry (along with the financial impact of shows) continues to grow, with no end in sight. According to the Center for Exhibition Industry Research (CEIR), an average of 10,385 people attend a business trade show. There are about 401 exhibiting companies at a typical show, with an average size of 119,849 net square feet being utilized.[9]

Research indicates that 26 percent of attendees at a typical business trade show actually signed a purchase order, and 51 percent requested a visit from a sales rep. In addition, 95 percent asked for literature to be sent, and 76 percent asked for a price quotation.[10] Further, according to the CEIR, companies save, on average, $492 per trade show lead, more than half the $1,117 cost of non-trade-show leads. In addition, salespeople close trade show leads in about 1.3 sales calls versus the 3.4 sales calls it takes, on average, to close non-trade-show leads.[11] Therefore, although trade shows may be costly, the question a company must answer in considering trade show participation is whether such an endeavor will be profitable.

Ken Schwartz, marketing manager for the hand tool division of the New Britain, Connecticut-based Stanley Works Company claims that trade shows such as the National Home Builders Association Show and the National Hardware Show are important venues because they allow for on-floor discussions with key trade customers such as the operators of home center and hardware stores. "It's important for us to be there because trade shows are a major communication device," says Schwartz. In addition to trade show marketing, merchandising program and new product development are key elements of Stanley's push strategy, which is complimented on the pull side by advertising and sales promotions, according to Schwartz. Trade shows also allow Stanley's sales representatives and brand managers to stay abreast of the latest developments in the industry.[12]

Research also indicates that 85 percent of decision makers/attendees at a business show feel that time and money are saved because there are so many vendors together at the same time, while 83 percent report that a show brings them up-to-date on the latest trends and developments in their industry. Eighty-two percent report that a show allows them to be very productive in a concentrated amount of time, while 80 percent feel that a show provides an invaluable opportunity to discuss problems and ideas with professionals in the industry.[13]

Finally, a firm should consider several factors in choosing shows in which to participate. These include:

- Expected attendance
- Total cost to participate
- Industry expectations
- Measurable results
- Staffing capability

### Trade Show Budgeting

Ideally, trade show budgeting should begin with a review of strategic objectives and realistic expectations for what can be achieved by show participation. Marketers should review the performance details of previous trade shows (number of inquiries, leads, etc.). If records are available of the numbers and quality of sales leads gathered from past shows, they should be used to estimate the number that produced actual sales, and thus a calculated approximate return on investment. Exhibit 9-10 is a worksheet that marketers can use to compare budgeted cost with actual cost when they review individual trade show effectiveness. Exhibit 9-11 shows some of the expenses marketers often overlook as they plan for trade exhibit expense allocation.

In a typical business-to-business trade show event, it would not be uncommon for the space show dollar to be divided up as follows: rental 25 percent, show services 22 percent, design and construction 15 percent, transportation 11 percent, booth refurbishing and

**EXHIBIT 9-10**  **Trade Show Budget Worksheet**

Reprinted courtesy of Skyline Displays, Inc.

| Item | Budget Cost | Actual Cost |
|---|---|---|
| Booth design and construction | | |
| Preshow mailing | | |
| Space rental costs | | |
| Freight transportation | | |
| Drayage, warehouse storage and delivery | | |
| | | |
| Booth set-up/dismantle | | |
| Electrician | | |
| Janitor | | |
| Guard | | |
| Florist | | |
| Furniture rental | | |
| Carpet rental | | |
| Audiovisual rental | | |
| Photography service | | |
| Telephone (cell phone roaming) | | |
| Utilities | | |
| Presenters, models | | |
| Handouts | | |
| | | |
| Hotel accommodations, meals | | |
| Client entertainment | | |
| Air travel | | |
| Freight transportation (return) | | |

maintenance 10 percent, miscellaneous expense 6 percent, preshow promotion 4 percent, special personnel 4 percent, and specialty advertising 3 percent.

### Incentives, Contests, Sweepstakes, and Games

*Incentives, contests, sweepstakes* and *games* are used by many business marketers to stimulate buyer frequency and interest. *Incentives* include rewards or discounts given to customers who buy often and/or buy large amounts of a firm's product. Some suggestions for getting the most from B2B frequency programs include: (1) being sure that you give rewards or discounts only to those customers who buy enough to make the incentive profitable, (2) track buying habits and customer information to help create effective and

**EXHIBIT 9-11**

**Hidden Trade Show Budget Busters**

After creating a complete budget, including the preshow and follow-up expenses, marketers often check for the possibility of the following unbudgeted costs:

- Holiday or other special occasion installation or dismantle dates, which will result in overtime labor rates
- Local fire codes that may have special requirements (particularly for large exhibits)
- Union jurisdictions (these may vary from site to site, such as scheduling carpenters for work that will have to be done by another union group)
- "Drayage" or storage of your crated booth if it arrives before the installation date, or storage of the crates themselves while the show is running
- Having the show management make all the payments to service providers and then billing for the total (may add 10–40 percent to the total)
- Booth area cleaning fees to vacuum floor area and empty wastebaskets
- Advance deposit for next year's exhibit space
- Transportation for booth personnel between airport and hotel, and daily between hotel and show
- Food and drink for a hospitality suite, if planned (obtain a firm quote from the hotel)

## BUSINESS MARKETING IN ACTION

### COST PER LASTING IMPRESSION

The Delahaye Group (http://www.delahaye.com/) is a leading provider of public relations and marketing communications research (such as evaluating corporate reputations, presence, and brand image). Their research has developed the following ranges of cost per impression for typical business-to-business promotional items.

Mug—A $5 coffee mug lasts between 1 and 2 years and will be read by 3 to 10 office colleagues per day. Roughly, this equates to 750 to 5,000 impressions at a cost of between $0.001 to $0.006 each.

Trade journal story—The average cost per impression for a story placed through press relations efforts is $0.01.

Trade journal ad—The average cost per impression for an ad is between $0.04 and $0.06.

The research notes that many advertising specialties (sometimes referred to as "adcentives") produce lower costs per impression when compared to traditional public relations and advertising. Still, a valid concern for marketers developing promotion mix strategies is this question: Do advertising specialties create the same quality and strength of impressions as public relations and advertisements?

### Action Assignment

Develop an experimental design to compare the quality and strength of the impressions created by a business marketing message on a mug versus the same message in an ad.

"Do Adcentives Work?" in *Pre-Show and At-Show Promotion.*
Reprinted courtesy of Skyline Displays, Inc.

---

attractive incentive programs, and (3) recognize your best customers with special rewards to show them that you recognize their value to your company.[14] A *contest* calls for customers to submit an entry—a jingle, an estimate, or a suggestion—to be examined by a panel of judges who select the best entries. A *sales contest* induces dealers or distributors to redouble their sales efforts over a specific time period, with prizes going to the top performers. A *sweepstakes* calls for customers to submit their names for a drawing. A *game* presents customers with something every time they buy, which may or may not help them win a prize.

### Advertising Specialties

An *advertising specialty* is a useful item with a message on it, such as a pen, a calendar, or the ever-popular back scratcher. Advertising specialties bear the company name, logo, or advertising message and are given away to present and potential customers. Marketers find advertising specialties to be one of the most effective means for reaching a target audience and holding its attention.

Advertising specialties offer great versatility when used in a planned campaign. Trade show exhibitors can specifically target their audience with an item the visitors will remember. For example, Harris Calorific, a valve manufacturer, had an objective of generating traffic to its exhibit from a select group of 240 dealers attending the American Welding Society's Trade Show. Harris was convinced that if its salespeople could spend just a few minutes with each dealer, its dealer network could be greatly increased. Prior to the trade show, Harris Calorific mailed a vinyl executive desk folder to selected dealers. Each folder included an invitation for the dealers to stop at the Harris booth. However, the front of the folder was intentionally hot stamped with gold to indicate the place for a personalized nameplate that could be picked up at the booth. This was a tactic instrumental in ensuring exhibit traffic, because recipients wanted to pick up their personalized nameplates, which could be affixed to enhance the appearance of the folder. As a result, 63 percent of the targeted dealers visited the booth to pick up their nameplates, and Harris quadrupled the number of leads normally generated at the show. The 37 percent who didn't visit were contacted later by Harris representatives. Harris signed up 25 distributors.[15]

The use of prizes, coupled with advertising-specialty items, can also be effective. The United States Surgical Corporation (USSC) increased its turnout 36 percent in one year by offering nurses a chance to win a fur coat. A customized folder was mailed to 7,000 members of the Association of Operating Room Nurses. Over 3,000 of these prospects registered for the trade show, and 2,200 visited the USSC booth. The inside cover of the folder contained a scratch-off circle. Nurses had to remove the circle at the booth to be eligible for 10 different prizes, including a color television set and a fur coat. Everyone who visited the display received a coffee mug imprinted with the company's logo.[16]

As these examples show, it is possible to gain an advantage over the competition by using specialty advertising creatively.

---

**Concept Review**

1. What is the greatest advantage of advertising in industrial trade directories?

2. Why is direct marketing expected to continue to grow so rapidly?

3. Why is a trade show such an effective way to do business?

---

## Business Direct and Interactive Marketing

B2B **direct marketing** involves a system of marketing whereby B2B firms communicate directly with customers for the purpose of generating a response and/or transaction. **Interactive marketing** involves the further step of allowing customers to, in some way, interact with the source of the message. Customers may work to actively receive information such as through a website, modify information, and/or ask or answer questions. B2B expenditures for direct and interactive marketing reached $107.4 billion in 2003 while B2B direct and interactive marketing sales reached $913.4 billion in 2003 and are forecasted to reach 1.41 trillion by 2008.[17] Direct marketing's effectiveness rests in its ability to precisely target communications and personalize messages to build lasting relationships with customers.

Direct and interactive marketing media include telemarketing, direct mail, print media, direct-response broadcast advertising, infomercials, TV advertorials, websites, catalogs, interactive CD-ROMs and DVDs, kiosks, and interactive phones. The use of direct marketing is widely integrated throughout all advertising media. Telephone marketing represents the largest category of direct marketing sales, followed by direct mail, newspaper and other media.[18] *Telemarketing* is a cost-efficient, productive medium. While it is more expensive than direct mail on a cost-per-contact basis, the response rate is greater. While American firms spend more on telemarketing than they do on any other medium, telemarketing revenues currently account for more than 50 percent of all direct marketing sales.[19] Companies use telephone systems for promotion, order processing, sales support, and customer service. Telemarketing is not a substitute or replacement for a regular sales force, however. It should supplement other elements of the promotional mix so that overall promotional efficiency can be improved.

*Direct mail* is also very important in that B2B sales attributed to direct mail are expected to reach over $430 billion by 2004.[20] Effective direct mail pieces are targeted specifically to key individuals and focus on their unique buying motives. Direct mail does not attempt to do the entire selling job; instead, it usually suggests some sort of action—perhaps only passively—as in urging willingness to listen to a salesperson when he or she calls. Direct mail also is a great promotional tool for the business marketer because it is simple to compile lists of prospects from responses to trade and professional advertisements and intracompany telemarketing operations (*house lists*). Marketing lists also can be acquired through industrial directories and mailing list firms, such as Dun and Bradstreet's Marketing Services Division and National Business Lists.

Their handicap of a comparatively short life notwithstanding, *newspapers* offer many opportunities for successful direct marketing. Newspapers also offer the impact of illustration where size can make a difference. For example, a full newspaper page has tremendous attention-getting impact that is hard to match with direct mail.

*Magazine* copy is "tell-all" copy. This means that the marketer imagines all the ways the product can answer the prospect's wants and includes as many as possible in the message. However, tell-all copy sometimes requires considerable space; it relies on a willingness on the part of the reader to read a long copy message. The writing typically is factual and no-nonsense writing that avoids the gimmicks, cute phrases, and personal writing style that characterize consumer advertising.

Any steady *television* viewer is aware that he or she is seeing an increasing number of B2B commercials with direct response offers. Television is the almost-perfect medium because viewers can see the product, watch it demonstrated, and be influenced by the enthusiasm conveyed by the announcer or spokesperson. Also, a vast audience may be exposed to the appeal. On the negative side is the cost, which is so high that disaster may loom if the product and the direct response ad aren't interesting enough to draw heavy responses. Also, in contrast to print media, the message, once given, is gone; there is no page to reread and no coupon to fill out. In addition to direct response TV ads are 30–60 minute infomercials.

*Radio* has produced good—sometimes outstanding—direct response success stories. Radio has other pleasing qualities as well, such as low cost and the fact that it can be produced far more quickly and simply than almost any other medium. However, it takes little perception to see that radio has serious handicaps when used in a marketing campaign. One of the most significant weaknesses of radio is that prospects cannot see the product. Except for cost, radio suffers from the same shortcomings as television and adds some of its own.

The *Internet,* as noted in previous chapters, has become a major sales channel and will continue to grow. The emergence of electronic commerce will continue to significantly impact advertising and sales promotion strategy in business markets. On-line sales catalogs will transform themselves from product listings to global sourcing tools. Buyers will be able to buy anything needed anywhere in the world at competitive prices. The impact of the Internet on business has barely begun. A website is open 24 hours a day accepting sales orders. By 2006, it is predicted that expenditures for interactive/Internet marketing will reach $8.4 billion with sales forecasted to reach $81.1 billion. In 2002, there were 227,148 workers employed in interactive/Internet marketing. This number is estimated to grow by 17.6 percent annually to reach over 474,000 workers in 2006.[21]

*Other media* include catalogs, interactive CD-ROMs and DVDs, kiosks, and interactive phones. These media allow customers to interact with company and product at their leisure and, like company websites, are sometimes referred to as "permission marketing" in that the customer is, in a sense, giving permission to provide him/her with information. Just like any other promotional mix element, specific and measurable objectives should be set for each of these tools.

## Measuring the Effectiveness of the Business Promotion Campaign

Two of the most commonly used methods of measuring the effectiveness of a promotion campaign are pre- and posttesting and responses to promotional or other communication messages.

### Pretesting and Posttesting

**Pretesting** of promotional messages measures subjects' awareness of or reaction to a product. Respondents answer a series of questions or indicate their reactions to a number of situations, thereby conveying their degree of understanding of the product. In **posttesting,**

# WHAT WOULD YOU DO?

## PUFFERY OR MISREPRESENTATION?

Brian and Steve Ott had done a good job with the facade of their upstart entrepreneurial company BSO Industries. Brian and Steve were production general contractors who obtained business and arranged to have the work done by subcontractors. Initially, they had had some success, but for the past few months their business had all but disappeared. As a last resort, they had used their remaining funds to participate in a key industry trade show. They borrowed a booth to use at the show and adapted it to represent their company as a successful major producer. Although they showed products and business that they would like to have, they knew that most people looking at the display would assume that Brian and Steve had produced the products.

A major OEM buyer was attending the trade show to search out suppliers for high-tech products. She listened to Brian and Steve explain their capabilities and picked up some literature on the company. The literature, like the trade show booth, presented the company as being successful, and although not directly stating misleading information, made the company look substantial.

A week after the show, both owners were ecstatic when the buyer called to arrange a visit to evaluate their company as a potential supplier. If the visitor was impressed by what she saw, Brian and Steve could receive the production orders that would solve all their business problems. They knew that they would have to do something to impress the buyer, and they knew that the office in Brian's garage wasn't going to work. Fortunately, Steve had a friend whose company was moving from a plush office suite. Steve arranged the changes to the office to make it seem as if it was the main office of their company.

Steve picked up the buyer at the airport and brought her directly to the office suite. As she entered, she noted bustling activity. Several people were on the phone clearly discussing important matters. Copying and fax machines were active, and analysts were busy at computer stations. Impressive production charts were displayed on the wall, and it appeared that sophisticated PERT project management techniques were being applied to a considerable amount of production output at many different subcontractor locations. Before the meeting began, an excited employee brought in an urgent e-mail for Brian, increasing scheduled shipments and demanding that additional commitments be scheduled. The visitor was very pleased to note that every employee she encountered, from the office receptionist to the driver Steve asked to take her back to the airport, had exhibited a uniform enthusiasm for the company. She decided to give BSO a trial production order.

After the visitor left, Brian and Steve thanked their friends who had posed as employees and helped them carry out the equipment they had borrowed from their respective companies. In fact, very little of what the visitor had seen was what it seemed. Brian and Steve had only one computer between them, almost no business, and certainly no employees. Still, neither Brian nor Steve had directly lied to the visitor. She had never asked if the people she saw were employees, nor had she asked if BSO actually had substantial current business. As planned, all of her discussion explored BSO's capability to handle her additional business. Brian had assured her that they could make room.

### Assignment

Define the ethical issues for all involved.

See also *Harvard Business Review,* September–October 1990, "Why Be Honest if Honesty Doesn't Pay?" pp. 121–29.

---

those who have been exposed to advertisements, publicity pieces, or sales promotion devices are questioned to determine the extent of their aided recall, unaided recall, recognition, comprehension, acceptance, and brand awareness (where applicable) in regard to the promotion. If respondents purchased a product as a result of the promotional piece or activity under study, usually they will be asked also to indicate their satisfaction and frequency of usage.

## Responses to Business Advertising

Traditionally, one of the most popular models of measuring the effectiveness of business advertising or other promotional messages has been through response to print and broadcast messages and direct marketing efforts. For print media, coupons or tear-away sheets often are included in advertisements placed in various forms of business publications and direct marketing pieces. Advertisers generally assume that if a particular advertisement or direct marketing effort receives a large mail or phone response, it is an effective promotional piece. Likewise, if an advertisement using a broadcast medium receives a considerable number of inquiries, it is felt to be successful.

Business marketers seeking to determine the value of advertising can use scaled-down versions of the ad-weight study developed for the Advertising Research Foundation (ARF). Marketers can learn the following:

- Whether they should advertise
- How much of the advertising they do will be profitable
- Whether advertising cuts will hurt or help profit[22]

A $390,000 research project developed by the ARF and its research project partner, the Association of Business Publishers (ABP), offers a practical model for testing business print advertising. The ARF/ABP weight test measures how different amounts of advertising affect sales for several business products. By carefully segmenting markets, matching different levels of media coverage to each segment, and accurately tracking sales, researchers can devise a marginal cost model for their advertising. They can estimate how much profit an additional dollar of advertising will generate. The overall goal of this activity is to know when advertising levels reach the point of maximum profit.

## Following up and Making Necessary Changes

Historically, most business promotional strategy programs concentrate on "what and how we are going to say what we want customers and prospects to know." Most focus on measuring "outputs," or what the organization sent out—not on "outcomes," or what the firm got back. The ability to measure results or returns allows the business firm to know when it is improperly allocating the finite resources that it has available. Knowing that awareness of a promotional campaign has improved or grown or diffused quickly has little real value to the marketer, unless he or she can relate that awareness in some way to what the organization has invested, and tie that back to greater returns than would have been achieved without the investment. Marketers invest dollars to develop, implement, and deliver messages; therefore, they must find some way to connect results to dollar returns back to the organization.

Marketers must set promotional objectives to provide a benchmark or standard against which the success or failure of a promotional campaign can be measured. If specific objectives have not been set, it becomes extremely difficult to determine what was accomplished by the firm's advertising and promotion efforts. Objectives should be measurable; there should be a method and criteria for determining how well a promotional program worked. By setting specific and meaningful objectives, the marketer is essentially providing a measure(s) that can be used to evaluate the effectiveness of the campaign. As covered earlier in this chapter, business marketers must set promotional objectives to provide a benchmark or standard against which the success or failure of a promotional campaign and/or IMC can be measured. If specific objectives have not been set, it becomes extremely difficult to determine what was accomplished by the firm's promotion efforts. By setting specific and meaningful objectives, the marketer is essentially providing measures that can be used to evaluate the effectiveness of the campaign. Therefore, given that quantified, realistic, attainable objectives have been set for specific target markets within specified time periods, the task to be completed for this step of the promotional campaign is simply to compare goals and objectives with outcomes.

Previously, in the section covering setting objectives, an objective was offered that we suggested met the criteria of a good objective, namely, "A result of this advertising campaign will be to sustain product A preference during the subsequent 3 month period as measured by continued purchase among our current Product A customers at levels that at least equal purchase figures for the last 3 months." During the follow-up step of the promotional campaign process, the marketer would compare expectations with reality, and then be in a position to alter objectives for the next campaign. Attempts should be made to change what must be changed and to fix what must be fixed in order to improve on future promotional campaigns.

## Summary

- Promotion in business marketing refers to the use of the promotional tools of advertising, publicity, and sales promotion. Business promotional tools generally serve to strengthen the personal selling effort and can be very effective in paving the way for sales representatives, in introducing new products and product lines to both established and prospective customers, and in creating good will between the selling and purchasing firms.

- Creating a promotional campaign involves five steps: setting objectives, developing the promotional budget, determining the promotional mix, measuring the effectiveness of the promotional plan, and making any necessary changes in the campaign.

- There is a great need for specific, realistic objectives for any promotional campaign. The establishment of appropriate objectives should be the starting point for every promotional campaign. Whenever possible, it is preferable to state objectives in quantitative terms so they can be more easily measured.

- Ideally, the promotional budget should be set at a point where the last dollar spent on promotion equals profits from the sales produced by that dollar. This is possible, however, only if the money is spent in an optimal fashion. Therefore, there must be a prioritization of all promotional efforts in terms of their potential contribution to the firm.

- In addition to professional selling, a firm can use advertising, publicity, sales promotion, and direct and interactive marketing in its promotional mix. Business advertising has very specific goals and generally employs printed media, broadcast media, and direct marketing to deliver its message to selected target markets. The advertising agency pro-

vides the client with a wide breadth and depth of experience that can seldom be duplicated by a single firm; yet, a number of firms prefer to use their own in-house advertising departments. Business publicity can be generated from the five major areas of management activities, product promotions, sales activities, manufacturing and engineering, and personnel activities. Business sales promotion has become the driving force that links personal selling, advertising, and publicity into a meaningful, integrated promotional program; it includes trade shows and exhibits, contests, sweepstakes, games, and advertising specialties. Business direct and interactive marketing include telemarketing, direct mail, print media, direct-response broadcast advertising, infomercials, TV advertorials, websites, catalogs, interactive CD-ROMs and DVDs, kiosks, and interactive phones.

- Two of the most commonly used methods of measuring the effectiveness of promotional campaigns are pretesting and posttesting, and determining responses to print media advertisements. Pretesting and posttesting methods reveal how much respondents knew about the product or service before the advertisement and how much they learned about the product from the advertisement. If a business advertisement is successful, usually there will be strong mail or telephone response.

- In order for marketing managers to determine the degree of success of promotional campaigns, they must first determine whether the campaign has met its initial objectives. If the objectives were not met, each stage of the campaign should be analyzed and modified as needed.

## Key Terms

business promotion
direct marketing
horizontal publication
integrated marketing
  communications (IMC)

interactive marketing
posttesting
pretesting
promotional campaign
promotional mix

publicity
sales promotion
vertical publication

## Review Questions

1. What three promotional tools are commonly used in business promotion campaigns? When does promotion play a primary role in selling business products and services? Why is promotion usually only a support effort for personal selling activities in business marketing?

2. What are the five stages in the development of a business promotion plan? What is a promotional campaign?

3. Why is it preferable to express the objectives of promotion in dollar amounts? How are market-share and sales-volume data useful to the business marketer?

4. Ideally, at what point should the promotional budget be set? Identify the four major methods by which business promotion budgets are determined.

5. Discuss four major goals of business advertising. How is business advertising different from consumer advertising?

6. Identify the primary media mix elements in business advertising. Discuss four types of print media, two types of broadcast media, and several types of direct marketing efforts.

7. What should the typical effective business advertisement contain? How can advertising agencies be of great value to the firm? Why are many firms reluctant to use advertising agencies? How do advertising agencies counter this reluctance?

8. What role does publicity play in the business-to-business firm? From what five major areas does the firm generally derive its publicity? How can business publicity be negative? Provide a recent example of this phenomenon.

9. How has the perception of sales promotion changed for the business-to-business firm from a decade ago to the present? Discuss three types of business sales promotion tools.

10. Discuss two of the most commonly used methods to evaluate the effectiveness of a promotional campaign. What is involved in following up and modifying (when necessary) a business promotion campaign? What advertising research questions does the ARF/ABP weight study model answer for the business marketer?

---

**Case 9-1**

# Kaptonic Industries Inc.

This case was written by Dr. Roger Gomes and Dr. Patricia Knowles, Clemson University © 1999

Lee Camden, vice president of Kaptonic Industries Inc. (KI), was deep in thought as he unconsciously tapped the corner of his desk with the bound edge of the most recent copy of the *Harvard Business Review*. He thought: "advertising objective" (tap), "message" (tap), "media" (tap), "buyer need level" (tap), "buyer interest" (tap), "buyer preference" (tap), "buyer loyalty" (tap); and then, as he had for perhaps twenty times, he repeated the list again. Sometimes he changed the order of the list, and sometimes he left out some parts. It was just like Lee to meditate on a problem by repeating related concepts and letting free associations form in the back of his mind. Lee really didn't use it as a creativity exercise, but just his own private way of thinking things through.

## Company Background

Kaptonic Industries Inc. is one of the largest global manufacturers of solid tantalum and multilayer ceramic capacitors in the world. According to industry sources, tantalum and ceramic capacitors are the two fastest growing segments of the capacitor industry. During fiscal year 1999, KI shipped approximately 20 billion capacitors and approximately 25,000 different types of capacitors, with "types" being distinguished by dielectric material, configuration, encapsulation, capacitance level and tolerance, performance characteristics, marking and packaging. Capacitors store, filter, and regulate electrical energy and current flow and are found in virtually all electronic applications and products. The Company's capacitors are used in a wide variety of electronic applications, including communication systems, data processing equipment, personal computers, automotive electronic systems, and military and aerospace systems. KI markets its capacitors to a diverse and growing number of original equipment manufacturers (OEMs) as well as a worldwide network of distributors. Its largest customers include Alcatel, Arrow, Compaq Computer, Ford Motor Company, General Motors Corporation, Hewlett-Packard Company, IBM Corporation, Intel, Lucent Technologies, Motorola Inc., SCI Systems, Inc., Siemens, Solectron, and TTI.

## The Meeting

Later in the day, after dealing with several other matters, Lee returned to his thoughts on advertising. As often happened, now he could see his problem more clearly. What had been bothering him was "buyer need level" and "message." "Our product advertising may be typical of what is done in the industry," he thought, "but it seems to me that it must be wrong. Even though our advertising approach is benefit-based, it probably addresses a level of need that is too basic. The business world is changing and our advertising is not; we must be sending the wrong message!"

Feeling that the issue required fresh perspectives, Lee asked Danny Anker, Jill Alderson, and Doug Oakley to grab something from the juice bar and join him in the New Ways of Thinking room (a meeting space where brainstorming was facilitated and nurtured). In a traditional company, Doug would probably have been director or group product manager and Danny and Jill (as recent college graduates) would have been assistant product managers. But at Kaptonic, almost no one had special titles, and team leadership varied by whomever was best at what was needed for that portion of the project.

Vice presidents, of course, did have titles, so Lee began to share what had been on his mind. "I need some of your group creativity on the subject of advertising. Ten years ago we were a manufacturer of micro-miniature electronic components, and our customer's buying center members valued product and service issues of quality, delivery, and price. So our ads in trade journals were product-oriented and were based on those issues, plus features as benefits. Back then, we hired the best graduates from the top universities. We gave them goals, rewarded their successes, and punished their failures. We were successful to an extent, but what we found was that our top graduates had been trained to follow other people's thinking, and we reinforced that tendency with a management-by-objectives philosophy. Good performance required doing as you were told and avoiding risk taking."

All that has changed. Now, ten years later, we begin the 21st century as much more to our customers than just a supplier that manufactures components. We are a learning organization and an extension of our customers' learning capacity. Now we hire only individuals who can think in new ways, adapt, continuously improve, and see change as a strategic necessity. The company culture is such that you know that you have to take risks to approach new challenges in new ways. As the business world becomes more dynamic, interconnected, and complex, the only successful companies will be those who are quickest to learn how to evolve to meet new market realities. A true learning organization is driven by continuous learning, knowledge sharing, and creativity by all its people at all its levels, focused not just on customer satisfaction but on the continuing success of the entire channel cooperative.*

Doug smiled and said, "I think that I see what's bothering you, Lee. The company has changed in a direction that the market values, yet our advertising continues to be focused at the product level." A period of silence followed. (Although traditional Western business meetings rarely have periods of "thinking silence," it is quite common in Asian business cultures. Although Kaptonic was headquartered in the United States, its management style and organizational culture was influenced by its many Far Eastern operations and joint ventures. The Company always tried to benchmark from the best in the world.)

Jill broke the silence with the observation, "It's possible that while our customer's top management want supplier alliances with companies that can match their speed of learning (or exceed it and teach them), purchasing departments could still be operating at the product level." Danny added, "But, it could be that buyers just haven't kept up, and we need to be directing promotional efforts at the organizational function or level that will assume dominance in channel alliance and supply chain integration." Doug was excited by the possibility of new, more effective promotion approaches, but cautioned, "We are about at the end of our 15-minute time limit on New Thinking Room meetings. What is the next step?" Jill replied, "Doug, you know the market best, so you could contemplate the best ways to promote our being a learning organization." Danny added, "And look for indications in the market and with our field sales force that customers have indeed refined their thinking as to indicators of learning quality, or speed, or something. We may need to be addressing a higher-level organizational need or individual. And, I suppose that could mean new promotion mix elements." Doug said, "OK. Why don't you two scan the trade journals and search for indications of that type of ad approach or appeal in any industry, but particularly concentrate on high-tech. Since you will already be searching, it would be good to take a random sample of fifty ads and sort them according to approach." Jill said, "No problem. We could probably sort them into groups like: (1) focuses on product features, (2) focuses on benefit(s) to customer(s), (3) focuses on new types of customer/supplier relationships, and (4) has no focus or just uses some dumb pun." Standing up, Doug said, "Sounds good. As always, continuous electronic communication will make it obvious if, when, and how, we should meet again. Thanks Lee, I think the group will be quick to incorporate this into our other 'changing strategic path' initiatives."

Back in his office Lee was thinking, "What a team. I pondered this for hours and couldn't come up with a direction. But with the right group and company culture, only 15 minutes and they are off and running. Management sure is different than it used to be."

## Assignment

Complete Jill, Danny, and Doug's assignments, recognizing that in this company your judgment and creativity are valued. In the process of working toward the objective, the realities of what you are uncovering may open up new paths and approaches. Present your results to the class.

Start by reviewing or researching:

- Business-to-business trade journal ads. Your school's reference librarian should be able to help you find industry (vertical) and industrial discipline (horizontal) trade journals (e.g., *Plastics World, Design Engineering, Aviation Week, Oil & Gas Journal*, etc.). Also look under (www.penton.com/corp/markets/de/de_pub.html) and (www.penton.com/corp/markets/manu/manu_pub.html) for lists of trade journals.

- Search your school's library database for articles and information on "learning organizations" and "management by objectives."

- Look up *Business Marketing*'s criteria for their annual Sawyer Awards for the best in business-to-business ads and campaigns. These may be useful in identifying effective ad approaches.

Then, report on the number of ads that you find within the four categories listed by Jill, explaining how/why the ads fit within those categories. Develop a set of recommendations for Lee to consider in making his decision.

*P. Senge, *The Fifth Discipline* (New York: Doubleday, 1990).

## Case 9-2

# Cincinnati Milacron—Winning Against Foreign Competition

Bruce Kozak, a regional sales manager for Cincinnati Milacron (CM), bumped into Harold Faig, a product manager also for CM, one Sunday in 1990. What started as a simple conversation over a cup of coffee resulted in their company's best selling plastics molding machine. Kozak complained to Faig that the Japanese were overwhelming the market for plastics molding machinery. Up to that point, Milacron had been relatively blind to the Japanese invasion.

Although CM's plastics machinery sales had been increasing each year, a closer inspection revealed that the market was growing even faster. Thus, CM was losing market share even though its sales were increasing. Faig and Kozak began listing specifications that a machine would need to compete in global markets. Within a month, Faig called Kozak and invited him to join a company venture team to create a new machine. Crossing functional boundaries they selected the most talented individuals from marketing, engineering, and manufacturing to join them. The development schedule for the new machine was under nine months—several months less than any previous machine development schedule in CM's history.

The group began by researching the market and found that most buyers wanted two things: (1) quick delivery of the machines once ordered, and (2) a low total cost of purchase and use of the machines. These were not the factors the group had expected. Being a technical-driven company, CM had always assumed that its customers bought equipment based mostly on its technical features and flexibility. The group's objective became to produce the company's first totally metric machine, standardize wherever possible, and meet a cost target that was 40 percent under previous machines. The new machine was named "Vista" and was introduced on time in December 1991. First year sales exceeded previous machines by 2.5 times, and CM locked in its reputation as "the world's broadest-line supplier of equipment to the plastics processing industry."

But that was then. Now it's years later and a new product manager has been appointed to rejuvenate sluggish sales of the "Vista" plastic injection molding machines. Japanese machines are still fierce competitors, but now Taiwan and other countries are even more of a problem. The new product manager is definitely going to need to develop an integrated marketing strategy fundamentally built around relationship marketing. Still, there will be room in the strategy for image building trade advertising, and advertising that captures qualified leads for the field sales force. An example of an ad that generates qualified leads would be one that is in a trade journal that is read by buying center members who are then motivated to respond via the reader service card or by directly contacting the company for additional information on the product. Trade ads that are not noticed, that are dismissed as silly, or that do not motivate action, are considered ineffective and a waste of company funds. The budget for advertising will be set as needed for the task of increasing sales by 25 percent (objective and task method). Initial estimates set the ad budget at $500,000.

## Assignment

Congratulations on your appointment as product manager for "Vista" machines. Begin by familiarizing yourself with Cincinnati Milacron and the Vista product line at (www. milacron.com). If you have trouble finding the Vista product line, try (www.milacron .com/PL/Pldefault.htm) where you can click on "injection molding" on the left bar, which shows a list including Vista V Series, Vista Toggle, and Vista Large. Also analyze the competition and their advertising approaches. A small sampling of competitors would include Husky Injection Molding Systems Ltd. (www.husky.on.ca/home.htm); VAN DORN Demag Corporation (www.vandorn.com); Sanjo Seiki Co. Ltd. (www.sanjo.co.jp); Fu Chun Shin Machinery Co. Ltd. (www.Fcs.com.tw/fcs-6.html) or (www.Fcs.com.tw/ index.html); and Hsou Yie Enterprise Co. Ltd. (www.yellowpage.com.tw/~hsouyie/ main.htm). There are also directories of equipment manufacturers and trade journals directed at the plastics industry which your library's reference desk can help you locate.

Develop and provide example ads, placement, and frequency for your campaign to rejuvenate the Vista product line. To help decide on media expenditures refer to Machine Design magazine for typical rates and circulations. Look under (www.penton.com/corp/ markets/de/de_pub.html) and (www.penton.com/corp/markets/manu/manu_pub.html) for lists of trade journals and circulation data. For rates for various sizes, location, and color ads refer to (www.penton.com/md/) or (www.machinedesign.com/mediakits/magrates/). For the cost of ad exposure on the Machine Design website see (www.machinedesign.com/ mediakits/internetrates/sponsor.html).

Present your campaign objective, sample ads, explanations about where you will be placing them, their frequency, your expenditures, your justifications, and the methods you would use to measure accomplishment of the campaign objective to the class.

The first half of this case is adapted from an earlier case, "Cincinnati Milacron," which appeared in the previous edition of this text and was originally published by C. Lamb, J. Hair, and C. McDaniel, in *Principles of Marketing,* 1st ed., Cincinnati, Ohio: South-Western 1992, pp. 277–78.

**References**

1. "Making It Pretty When Your Product Is Nitty Gritty," *Business Marketing* 76 (April 1991): 55–57.
2. Theodore Levitt, *Industrial Purchasing Behavior: A Study in Communication Effects* (Boston: Division of Research, Harvard Graduate School of Business, 1965).
3. Don Y. Lee, "The Impact of Firms' Risk-Taking Attitudes on Advertising Budgets," *Journal of Business Research* 31 (October-November 1994): 247–56.
4. "Study Shows That Frequent Four-Color Ads Attract More Attention in Trade Press," *Marketing News* 22 (March 14, 1988): 13.
5. Nancy Arnott, "Getting the Picture," *Sales & Marketing Management* 138 (June 1987): 109.
6. Thor Valdmanis, "Crisis Lawyer Tackles New Target: Hedge Funds," *USA Today* (5/7/2003): p. 1
7. John F. Tanner, *Faculty Curriculum Guide to Trade Shows* (Center for Exhibition Industry Research, 1997).
8. Geoffrey Brewer, "Shout It Out," *Sales & Marketing Management* (February 1996): 30–42.
9. Tanner, 1997.
10. Ibid.
11. Rick Kelly, "Do Trade Shows Pay Off?" *Trade Show Times* (July 2001): 1.

12. Edmund O. Lawler, "Trade Shows Drove 'Push-Pull' Marketing," *Advertising Age's Business Marketing* 79 (November 1994): A3–A4.

13. Tanner, 1997.

14. Chad Kaydo, "How to Build a B-to-B Frequency Program," *Sales & Marketing Management* (April 1999): 80.

15. H. Ted Olson, "Trade Show Techniques," *Direct Marketing* (March 1989): 82–86.

16. Ibid., 1989, p. 82.

17. The Direct Marketing Association, *Statistical Fact Book,* 24th ed., (Washington, D.C.: The Direct Marketing Association).

18. Ibid.

19. Ibid.

20. Ibid.

21. Ibid.

22. Bob Donath, "How Should You Advertise?" *Business Marketing* 78 (April 1988): 82–86.

## CHAPTER TEN

# Business Marketing Channel Participants

## Learning Objectives

*After reading this chapter, you should be able to:*

- Recognize the functions of marketing channel members.
- Understand the nature of channel decisions.
- Appreciate the role and importance of direct channels.
- Comprehend the role and importance of various types of indirect channels.
- Discuss the nature of, and the contributing factors to, channel cooperation.
- Relate the reasons for channel conflict and the available remedies.
- Determine when to use intensive, selective, and exclusive distribution policies.

## Chapter Outline

Functions of the Channel Intermediary
The Nature of Channel Decisions
Direct Channels
Indirect Channels
Combining Direct and Indirect Channels
Channel Cooperation
Channel Conflict
Channel Width

## Functions of the Channel Intermediary

Business channel strategy must be an integral part of the firm's total operating system, meshing with production, finance, research, purchasing, and other functions of the business to make the maximum contribution to company objectives. Business marketing managers are learning that channels can create differential advantages that can be especially important in instances in which competitors' products, prices, and promotional efforts are almost homogeneous. The types of outlets available and the functions these outlets perform represent structural elements of channel strategy.

**Channel management** is a cooperative marketing strategy in which manufacturers augment their direct sales channels with indirect channels of distribution to reach different segments more efficiently and effectively. Also, manufacturers must occasionally modify their channels of distribution to keep their products available in broadening and maturing markets. As business managers seek to increase their efficiency and effectiveness, they must also find better means of exchanging information. While the need to form close ties can be applied to any exchange situation, it is particularly acute for interactions between channel participants.

For the majority of business products and services, a number of channel functions must be performed. Exhibit 10-1 illustrates the marketing functions of buying, selling, storage, transportation, sorting, financing, risk taking, and market information that must be carried out within the channel system. The types of organizations that perform these functions and tasks are an important channel management consideration. A brief explanation of these functions will create a framework from which the various channel alternatives available to the business marketer can be studied.

### Buying

Some channel members buy products for resale to other intermediaries, to a final business user, or for their own use. Most, however, act as purchasing managers or buyers, trying to determine how much of a particular product their customers will need over the next week, month, quarter, or other time period for which they must plan and buy. Buying in advance usually is a risky undertaking, as channel members are betting that their customers will indeed buy the material or parts on hand. Since intermediaries purchase and take title to the goods, they are clearly customers of the producer (in addition to being fellow channel members). Keep in mind the fact that intermediaries are customers for a later discussion of channel conflict.

**EXHIBIT 10–1**
**Basic Channel**
**Functions**

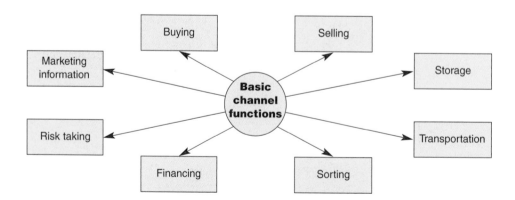

## Selling

Intermediaries must be innovative in their application of persuasion and problem-solving skills as they close sales and develop strong business relationships. In most cases, the channel intermediary is chosen because of its experience, knowledge, and expertise. A potential intermediary with a capable salesforce supported by established warehouse distribution centers, and which already is serving other product needs of a wide customer base, would likely be considered a valuable channel addition.

## Storage

Effective inventory management requires a proper balance among buying, selling, and production. An inventory commitment is composed of products to satisfy average or typical customer purchase requirements and to provide for a safety buffer to cover unexpected variations in demand and other types of customer buying emergencies. Inventory must be in convenient locations to ensure timely delivery, and it must also be protected to prevent deterioration and loss. Distribution intermediaries such as W. W. Grainger Corporation provide distinctive customer value by offering next-day delivery from its 335 branches nationwide.

## Transportation

The business marketing manager is broadly concerned with managing the physical flow of the product through the intermediary and into the hands of the business user. (When title passes, the marketing manager of the business-to-business firm is no longer responsible for transport to the user; this function is assumed by the channel intermediary.) A vast array of transportation alternatives is available to intermediaries for use within their respective physical distribution systems, with the most common modes being rail, motor carrier, water, pipeline, and air. Each of these modes will be examined in detail in Chapter 11.

## Sorting

Most intermediaries buy in large quantities and then break these shipments into smaller lots for resale to business users. The term **breaking of bulk** is commonly used to describe this function performed by intermediaries who take physical possession of the goods. This procedure allows the intermediaries to buy large quantities at reduced prices and to resell the goods at prices that allow the intermediaries to make a profit.

## Financing

If the intermediaries invest in inventory, sell and deliver the merchandise to the business user, and provide acceptable credit terms, then the intermediary is financing the exchange process. Most intermediaries who take title to and then resell merchandise allow the business user quite liberal terms in paying for the purchase. (Thirty days to pay is standard, with periods of 60, 90, and even 120 days not uncommon.) Most of these intermediaries operate small businesses and know their customers well. They are, in a sense, financing the purchase for their customers, much like a local department store or specialty shop would finance a consumer's purchase of a new suit, with payment (or at least partial payment) due in 30 days.

## Risk Taking

Because of obsolescence and deterioration, risk is inherent in the ownership of inventory; this phenomenon is especially true today because of rapid advances in technology. Those intermediaries who buy in bulk and take title are betting that the merchandise will not become obsolete and will not deteriorate prior to its resale to the business user. The intermediaries in this situation must buy in large enough quantities to make the resale at a profit; at the same time, they must be careful not to buy in such large quantities that either obsolescence or deterioration could occur before resale to the business customer.

## Market Information

Channel communication is necessary and should be continuous as products are transferred and stored in anticipation of future transaction requirements. Information on assortment, quantity, location, and time is important and must be communicated between channel members to maximize market opportunity. The degree of accuracy of information concerning merchandise availability, pricing conditions, product quality, and competitive conditions is so important it can determine the type of channel intermediary that will be used by the business marketer.

## The Nature of Channel Decisions

The business marketing manager must regularly perform a critical reappraisal of the channels of distribution in use, with a careful eye on how well each channel member is carrying out its assigned functions. Business product users and intermediaries need a systematic framework for adjusting channel strategies in changing environments. This framework should recognize and balance the service needs both of producers and end users. If the marketing manager changes the channel structure, a whole complex of marketing decisions is affected. Channel decisions are, by necessity, long-term arrangements, and the channel intermediary is a valued customer. To change or disrupt a long-term working relationship, while perhaps necessary, can become somewhat difficult and expensive. As with all customer relationships, it is a business marketing responsibility to strategically decide which customer relationships to nurture and which to divest.

A "nurture versus divest" decision (and, indeed, any strategic channel decision) requires a great deal of understanding of business fundamentals. The logistical science of efficient material flow, inventory control, and cost systems are all critically important. But efficiency is often not enough. Each channel member and each of their functions can only be justified if it creates more value for the end user than it consumes in cost. Additionally, the resulting total channel (i.e., value chain) must create more "end user perceived value" than competing channels. This puts "end user value creation" at the center of all channel decisions.[1,2]

**Concept Review**

1. Why is "breaking of bulk" an important intermediary function?

2. Why do channel decisions tend to create long-term commitments?

## Direct Channels

One alternative channel decision that the business marketing manager can make is the selection of a direct channel of distribution. **Direct channels** involve "direct" selling (that is, no external intermediary is involved) to the producer, with or without the use of sales branches. A direct sale would include both generalists and specialists. (Generalists sell the entire product line to all customers, whereas specialists concentrate on particular products, customers, or industries.) A **sales branch** is broadly defined as an off-site manufacturer's sales office, operating within a major market area, staffed with some technical personnel,

# STRATEGY AT WORK

### CHANNEL ALLIANCE EXPECTATIONS: A STRATEGY TO BE ONE OF THE BEST

Each year *IndustryWeek* announces finalists for the America's Best Manufacturing Organizations Award. Tracking the performance of the award finalists tells us a lot about increasing channel alliance expectations. If a company wants to be among the top-performing channel members, it should be able to compare and benchmark its performance against that of its peers in the industry.

Among these top-performing operations, tightly knit channel relationships are the norm. For example, Lockheed Martin emphasizes long-term agreements using a preferred supplier base and the incorporation of a Supplier Product & Process Improvement Program. This partnership program looks for ways to reduce waste in suppliers' processes. Ultimately, Lockheed Martin says it benefits with improved supplier quality, reduced lead times, and lower costs. Twenty-three of the 25 finalists utilize similar long-term purchase agreements with their suppliers. And, 100 percent say they work with their suppliers to improve supplier cost, quality, and delivery performance. In return, all expect their major suppliers to contribute to cost reduction and quality improvement efforts. All 25 finalists report that they evaluate suppliers on a total cost basis, rather than by unit price. Twenty-four of the 25 report that their key suppliers provide JIT delivery. They also report that a median figure of 95 percent of the incoming material does not receive incoming inspection; it goes right to the production line. All 25 emphasize early supplier involvement in product and process development. Information technology also binds suppliers, producers, and their customers, with 84 percent reporting use of enterprise integration and other EDI computer links.

When evaluating companies for channel alliances, it would be useful to compare them to the performance improvement figures of the 25 finalists, reported as follows:

| | |
|---|---:|
| Reduction in mfg. cycle time* | 51% |
| Reduction in order-to-shipment lead time* | 45 |
| On-time delivery rate | 98 |
| Reduction in total inventory* | 36 |
| Reduction in WIP turns* | 41 |
| Increase in value-added/employee* | 58 |
| Increase in annual sales/employee* | 60 |
| Mfg. cost reductions/unit (w/o purchased materials)* | 35 |
| Mfg. cost reductions/unit (with purchased materials)* | 22 |
| Plant level return on assets | 238 |
| Increase in return on assets* | 154 |

*For a 5-year period.

Reprinted with permission from *IndustryWeek*, February 15, 1999, pp. 23–30. Copyright, Penton Media, Inc., Cleveland, Ohio.

and having the ability to ship most orders immediately from stock. The Internet also is a direct channel and will be discussed here.

## Sales-Volume Base

Whether the sales-volume base is sufficient to support a direct-selling program is a matter of judgment. The variables that will affect this judgment are absolute sales volume, the breadth and depth of the product line, the relative concentration or dispersion of potential customers, the size of the customers, and the amount of business that can be expected from each. If, at one extreme, the line of products that the manufacturer sells to any one market segment is narrow, if the products are not expensive or technically complex, and if potential customers are small and geographically dispersed, it is likely to be uneconomical to engage in a direct-selling program. At the other extreme, if the manufacturer's product line is broad, if customers are geographically concentrated, if products are expensive, high margin or complex, and if many buyers have the potential for purchasing in large quantities, it would be difficult to make a case for selling any other way.

In sharp contrast to consumer goods, most manufactured business goods (as much as 60 to 70 percent) are sold directly to users. This trend will continue. Rockwell International's Municipal and Utility Division markets water, gas, and parking meters to local municipalities and gas utilities through a direct sales organization. The direct sales approach is viable because the customers are large and well defined; the customers often insist upon direct sales; sales involve extensive negotiations with high-level utility management; and control of the selling and service process is necessary to ensure proper technical implementation of the total product package and to guarantee a quick response to market conditions.

## The Internet

Electronic Commerce on the Internet is also a direct channel of distribution. Intel Corporation, which is booking $1 billion a month in orders over the Internet, highlights on-line results as contributing to overall, improved efficiencies. Since instituting a system to take orders over the Internet, on-line sales have been brisk. Intel officials note that the sales are coming from existing customers, not new accounts. "If we tried to turn this system off, the customer would not let that happen," says Sandra Morres, Director of Internet Marketing and Electronic Commerce for Intel. "It won't be replacing the channel anytime soon, but if I were a distributor, I would be worried," says Stephen Murray, an analyst at International Data Corporation, a market research firm in Framingham, Massachusetts.[3]

An example of how the Internet is used as a direct channel of distribution would be the use of on-line sales catalogs. Many suppliers will offer their on-line catalogs with access given through their websites. This scenario is advantageous to the buyers because the burden of maintenance and accuracy is placed upon the seller. For smaller buying companies, buying on the Internet, especially for low-value items, this may be the easiest, most cost-efficient route to take.

W.W. Grainger was one of the first nationwide distributors to recognize that the market for maintenance, repair, and operating (MRO) supplies could benefit from low transaction cost, centralized Internet purchasing.

> MRO Market Overview (Approximate)
> Customers . . . . . . . . . . .8 million
> Suppliers . . . . . . . . . . .150,000
> Total sales . . . . . . . . . .$100 billion/year
> Grainger . . . . . . . . . . . .5% market share

Start-up Internet entrepreneurs seek out such fragmented markets to create Internet portal marketplaces (e.g., Amazon.com with books). However, a market leader such as Grainger—with $5 billion in sales—already has brand awareness and a great deal more in Internet resources than any start-up. With Grainger's Internet sales growing in double digits (Grainger.com), dot.com entrepreneurs will have to look elsewhere for market opportunities. The combination of Grainger's state-of-the-art Internet catalog, inventory availability, and regional distribution centers and branches provide unprecedented customer value.

> Example of One Nationwide Industrial Producer[4]
> MRO buy  →  66.6% purchased from Grainger.com with a
>                 total annual transaction cost of $300,000.
>            →  33.3% purchased from 1300 other distributors
>                 with a total annual transaction cost of
>                 $2.4 million.

With such a difference in transaction cost, it is easy to see why this customer company is working to buy more and more online. (Note: The transaction cost involves only the costs of ordering and does not include the price of the product ordered. Given its buying power with suppliers and manufacturers, Grainger is known for price-value plus low transaction costs.)

## Indirect Channels

The business marketing manager can elect to use indirect channels. An **indirect channel** is a distribution method that involves selling to the industrial user through an external intermediary. Indirect channels are warranted when the market is widely scattered, when many firms must be contacted, when small orders are common, and when goods are made for inventory rather than to fill specific orders. Once the manufacturer has determined that indirect channels are appropriate, the paramount question becomes, Which type of indirect channel should be chosen? As shown in Exhibit 10-2, business products distributors and sales agents and brokers are possible choices, depending on the nature of the industry involved and the distribution structure required.

### The Business Products (Industrial) Distributor

**Business products distributors**, also known as industrial distributors, are intermediaries who buy and take title to business products, who usually keep inventories of their products, and who sell and service these products. Typically, industrial distributors are fairly small businesses and have been traditionally owner managed and well endowed with product expertise, market knowledge, and customer contacts. They are the most important single force in indirect business distribution channels, numbering approximately 12,000. (See Exhibit 10-3 for a more comprehensive profile of the business products distributor.) The compensation business products distributors receive for their services is the difference between what they pay to the manufacturer and what they charge their customer. In addition to the traditional channel functions previously identified and explained, many distributors offer an interesting portfolio of services. Those most frequently offered are stockless purchasing, literature updating, systems engineering, and guidance on such issues as pollution control.

The distributor is, first of all, a *merchant intermediary,* taking title to the goods for the purpose of resale. Operating generally as full-service wholesalers, distributors perform the

**EXHIBIT 10-2**
**Alternative Channel Options**

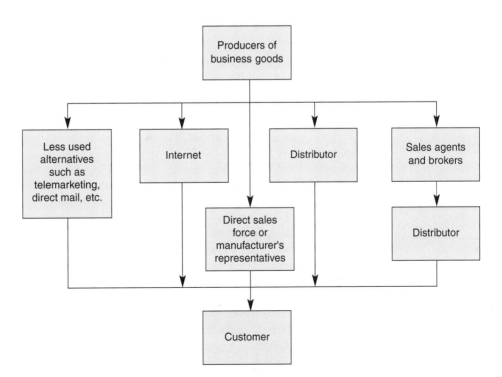

**EXHIBIT 10-3**
**Profile of the**
**Business Products**
**Distributor**

| Characteristics | General Line | Specialist |
|---|---|---|
| Median sales | $2,430,000 | $2,239,750 |
| Sales from stock | 65.5% | 60.0% |
| Number of invoices per year | 13,000 | 7,500 |
| Average invoice | $187 | $299 |
| Collections—median number of days outstanding | 42 | 45 |
| Year-end receivables value | $239,600 | $268,000 |
| Average monthly inventory values | $397,000 | $309,000 |
| Median inventory turnover on stock sales | 3.5 | 4.0 |
| Total number of employees | 18.0 | 15.5 |
| Number of outside salespersons | 4 | 4 |
| Number of inside salespersons | 3 | 2 |
| Square feet of warehouse space | 15,000 | 10,000 |
| Percent with 1 stocking location—no branches | 67% | 63% |
| Percent with 2 stocking locations—1 branch | 13% | 16% |
| Percent with 3 stocking locations—2 branches | 8% | 9% |
| Percent with 4 to 6 stocking locations—3 to 5 branches | 8% | 10% |
| Percent with 7 or more stocking locations—6 or more branches | 4% | 2% |
| Computerized operations | 59.2% | 55.1% |
| Percent of computerized users with own equipment | 39% | 93% |
| Percent of computerized users using outside services | 11% | 7% |
| Computer applications | | |
| Accounts receivables | 92.4% | 90.1% |
| Sales analysis | 89.4% | 87.6% |
| Billing | 88.6% | 84.5% |
| Accounts payables | 85.6% | 73.9% |
| Customer analysis | 73.8% | 75.8% |
| Inventory records | 78.8% | 78.9% |
| Unit sales pricing | 68.9% | 57.8% |
| Purchasing | 67.4% | 54.7% |
| Sales order processing | 65.2% | 60.2% |
| Payroll | 54.5% | 45.3% |
| All others | 61.4% | 60.2% |

same tasks that a manufacturer would have to provide in selling directly to the business user, very often at a lower final cost to customers. This cost efficiency is often due to the fact that distributors are set up to sell in smaller quantities and their customers are typically purchasing other products as well (one-stop shopping). The distributor undertakes the performance of buying, selling, storing, transporting, sorting, financing, risk taking, and market information; a full-service channel member such as this becomes an expert in the provision of the above-mentioned functions.

There are two major types of business products distributors: *general-line distributors,* handling a wide variety of business supplies and minor equipment, and selling to a broad spectrum of customers; and *limited-line distributors,* handling fewer, high-volume items such as steel, paper, or chemicals. Such limited-line distributors often are called *jobbers;* although they take title, they do not necessarily carry the goods in inventory. In this situation, jobbers would have the manufacturers "drop-ship" the goods directly to their (the jobbers') customers. Limited-line distributors also include specialists who carry a line of particular goods, such as electrical wiring supplies, or who serve a particular industry, such as shoe manufacturers.

**EXHIBIT 10-4**
**Problems with the Use of Business Products Distributors**

1. While the manufacturer might desire to retain larger customers as house accounts, the distributor wants access to these accounts.
2. The sophistication and managerial practices of many smaller distributors, operating "mom-and-pop" type of businesses, often are questioned.
3. Manufacturers desire to keep somewhat high inventory levels in distributors' warehouses, whereas distributors wish to minimize inventory levels.
4. Distributors like to carry second lines in an effort to provide a greater selection of competitive offerings for their customers; manufacturers want distributors to feature their products, and not those of competitors.
5. Distributors' networks often contain overlapping territories.
6. Distributors frequently demand many small and/or rush orders.
7. Distributors often do not seem sensitive to the operational policies, procedures, and problems of manufacturers.
8. Many distributors do not see manufacturers' promotional advice as relevant and ignore manufacturers' sales representatives' guidelines.

### *Limitations to Using Business Products Distributors*

After reading and thinking about the previous section, one could get the idea that signing on a distributor is a relatively easy task, and that once such a distributor has been obtained, the marketer has no additional distribution problems. Unfortunately, such is not the case. Markets are constantly changing and for many manufacturers, the continued use of a distributor might not make sense. Exhibit 10-4 examines problems involved in using business distributors, ranging from overlapping territories to distributors' lack of appreciation for manufacturers' operational policies, procedures, and problems.

On many occasions, distributors will not emphasize the business marketing manager's products in particular. Additionally, the average distributor often does not possess the technical or service know-how to handle high-tech products.

Business products distributors also seek products that will ensure high inventory turnover and profit margins. Naturally, they will tend to emphasize sales of lines that meet these criteria.

### *Trends for Business Products Distribution*

After discussions with a number of executives in distribution, it appears that some major changes are taking place within their ranks, including the following:

- Consolidation forced by the weakening economy.
- Manufacturers outsourcing or moving offshore.
- Globalization of purchasing.
- Steadily increasing customer emphasis on total value.
- More heavy (capital) equipment (machine tools, etc.) is being marketed through distributors.
- Manufacturers are increasing their support of distributors to include sales aids, sales training, and other full-support services.
- Distributors' operations are becoming more sophisticated as more college graduates and quality engineers join their ranks.
- A trend toward specialization among distributors is evident.
- Manufacturers that use distributors are tending to depend more on them for a wide variety of marketing activities, including research, new product development, and additional market coverage.

## BUSINESS MARKETING IN ACTION

### NEW RELATIONSHIPS BETWEEN OEMS AND ELECTRONICS COMPONENTS DISTRIBUTORS

Over the past few years, transactions between OEMs and distributors have progressed from the Dark Ages to the age of computer integration. Companies found that they were spending far too much money buying, storing, handling, using, and managing inventories of maintenance, repair, and operating (MRO) equipment and supplies. In many cases the cost of the transactions to acquire products exceeded the cost of the products themselves. As in subassembly and component purchases, OEMs are reducing their distributor supply bases, using standardized automated order-processing systems to buy more items from fewer distributor channel partners.

Two increasing trends are changing OEM-distributor roles: (1) distributor personnel on-site at the OEM to handle ordering and inventory for the OEM and (2) total outsourcing of MRO products by on-site distributor-owned inventory at the OEM. With essentially a branch of the distributor within the plant, the OEM's inventory carrying costs are reduced to zero, as are lead times. Both sides benefit from this type of channel alliance. For the distributor, it is a differential advantage almost impossible for an outsider to overcome; for the OEM, it represents cost efficiency that can help in increasingly competitive markets.

Escalating customer expectations are driving a major consolidation trend in distributors. Those who can make the transition to the new market realities are acquiring those whose revenues have dropped because they were slower to react.

Even the view of what a distributor sells is changing. Value-added services such as putting together "kits" of parts to improve the efficiency of OEM assembly, cable and harness assemblies, IC programming, and integrated logistics increasingly are becoming a key part of distributor sales.

### Action Assignment

Using the Internet as well as traditional library resources, research the products, services, sales, and growth of the leading electronics component distributors listed below. Present your results to the class in an interesting and informative way.

Avnet, Inc. (www.avnet.com)

Arrow Electronics, Inc. (www.arrow.com)

Allied Electronics (www.alliedelec.com)

Ewing Electronics (www.ewinginc.com)

Future Electronics (www.future-active.com)

Marsh Electronics (www.marshelectronics.com)

Richardson Electronics, Ltd. (www.rell.com)

As you know, URL addresses can change as Web home pages are updated and industry consolidation occurs; sometimes you will need to go to a site such as (www.yahoo.com) or (www.lycos.com) and search on the company name to find its home page.

Source: *Purchasing,* Adapted from "Cost Is King in MRO Buying" by K. Fitzgerald, June 3, 1999, p. 21; "Electronics Distributors Look for Rebound in 1999" by G. Roos, May 20, 1999, pp. 43–50. © 1999 Cahners Business Information Group.

## The Manufacturers' Representative

A **manufacturers' representative** is a firm selling part of the output of one or more manufacturers whose products are related but noncompetitive. (See Exhibit 10-5 for a brief profile of a manufacturers' representative.) A manufacturers' representative assigned to a territory would provide the same functions as a field salesperson, but part of the rep's time would also be spent selling the products of the other companies the firm represents. Since typical manufacturers' representatives do not take title or carry inventory, they are considered channel transaction facilitators, rather than true channel members. They operate strictly on commission and usually limit their sales efforts to a defined geographic area.

The shift to manufacturers' representatives by larger companies reflects the growing strength of the agency method of selling, the increased professionalism of the reps themselves, and the fact that using manufacturers' representatives often is more economical than any other way of selling. Manufacturers' representatives frequently are used where a territory cannot support a full-time direct salesperson, or when the rep has unique skills or established customer relationships.

Manufacturers' representatives enter into a formal written agreement with each manufacturer, covering price policy, territories, order-handling procedures, delivery service, warranties, and commission rates. The reps know each manufacturer's product line and use

**EXHIBIT 10-5    A Brief Profile of a Manufacturers' Representative**

| | |
|---|---|
| **Company** | Central Southwest Bottling Company |
| **Location** | Claremore, Oklahoma |
| **End-user market** | Bottling industry |
| **Estimated average commission** | 8 to 12 percent |
| **Geographic market coverage** | Oklahoma, Texas, Arkansas, Kansas, Louisiana, New Mexico, Colorado |
| **Products handled** | Plastic cases, decappers, empty-bottle inspectors, bottle filler replacement parts, conveyors, and case packers |
| **Companies represented** | Medium-sized and small bottle and bottling-parts manufacturers throughout the eight-state service area |

their wide contacts to sell the manufacturer's products. Fred Holloway, manager of Yarway Corporation's Metering Pump Division of Blue Bell, Pennsylvania, values the 20 manufacturers' representatives that represent his firm. Says Holloway, "Manufacturers' representatives tend to be more knowledgeable about markets. They have a closer relationship with the key buying influences in the processing industry markets we want to penetrate. Sales costs are not the prime factors for us." Holloway admits that if he had a sales force selling directly to the customer, probably he would have stricter control over field selling; further, he wishes that he did not have to compete for selling time with the other manufacturers whose products his reps also carry. "But our representatives give us the market coverage we believe we could not win otherwise," he acknowledges.[5]

Not all firms using manufacturers' representatives are small. Manufacturers such as National Semiconductor, ITT, Corning, Monsanto, Teledyne, and Mobil Oil also use manufacturers' reps. National Semiconductor, for example, began using manufacturers' representatives in the early 1960s when the firm's sales were less than $50 million; the company continues this practice today, even though it has become a billion-dollar manufacturer.

Advantages of using a manufacturers' representative include predictable selling expense; little or no selling cost until sales are forthcoming; cost savings because manufacturers do not have to utilize their own sales forces; and more intense coverage of a given territory in that the representative is able to make a profit in a smaller territory by selling multiple lines there.

### *Limitations to Using Manufacturers' Representatives*

Again, one might think it is an easy task for a manufacturer to acquire a representative and have selling problems eliminated entirely. Yet, for many manufacturers, the use of manufacturers' representatives is not appropriate.

The problem may be that representatives often are difficult for the manufacturer to control. For instance, if the manufacturer's product line requires special care, representatives may be unwilling to offer the extra attention the manufacturer expects. Additionally, only partial representation is secured at best because the representative carries other manufacturers' lines. Also, the representative generally prefers to concentrate on large customers and large orders. Thus, if the manufacturer has several small business customers in an area, these accounts may be visited infrequently and the customers slighted.

Of great concern to reps is the nature of the relationship between manufacturer and customer. If the two become close, one or the other may conclude that the value created by the rep has passed. Either the manufacturer or the customer may then decide to save the rep's commission for themselves. For example, on the manufacturer's side, a major foreign computer chip manufacturer utilized an American rep to court the business of a major computer manufacturer. After the firms agreed to a sole source strategic alliance, the rep's contract was not renewed. The rep's best defense against such an outcome is to be clearly adding continuous value through services. Indeed, a manufacturers' representative who suffers the fate of being dismissed as in the scenario described may have little recourse. Manufacturers' representative firms tend to be small, and rarely have the legal resources of a large manufacturer.

### Trends for Manufacturers' Representatives

Discussions with several manufacturers' representatives highlighted the following changes as we enter the twenty-first century:

- Many entering the business today have engineering backgrounds and technical sales expertise.
- Firms are representing fewer manufacturers, but for those they do represent, they have expanded authority, making some of the marketing decisions usually made by the manufacturer.
- The majority of manufacturers' representatives are male, but more females are beginning to enter the field.
- Commission rates are rising, with the current rate averaging between 10 and 12 percent of gross sales dollars.
- The use of manufacturers' representatives will continue to grow, providing inexpensive coverage to remote areas and areas where demand is insufficient to require a full-time salesperson.

## Sales Agents and Brokers

**Sales agents** and **brokers,** like manufacturers' representatives, are channel transaction facilitators, provide a sales effort, seldom carry inventory (unless on consignment), generally do not take title to goods, and operate on commission. The major difference between manufacturers' representatives and sales agents and brokers is that sales agents and brokers may assume responsibility for more marketing functions, including promotional and pricing responsibilities. Additionally, sales agents and brokers tend to handle the entire output of several directly competitive manufacturers. Generally, they have no geographic restrictions on their territories and will provide market data and product development guidance. Further, this type of intermediary often takes over the entire marketing and selling function of the manufacturer. Such a situation is especially appropriate where seasonal representation is desired, where marketing and sales skills are needed recurrently, where the major interests and skills of the manufacturer are focused on production, where a limited product line is offered, and where the market is widespread.

Brokers are most prevalent in the food industry. Their operation is typified by a seafood broker handling the pack from a salmon cannery. The cannery is in operation for possibly three months of the year. The canner employs a broker each year (the same one, if the relationship is mutually satisfactory) to find buyers for the salmon pack. The broker provides information concerning market prices and conditions, and the canner then informs the broker of the desired price. The broker seeks potential buyers among chain stores, wholesalers, and others. Then, when the entire pack has been sold, the agent-principal relationship is discontinued until the following year.

## Facilitating Agencies

**Facilitating agencies** facilitate the flow of goods from the manufacturer to either the channel intermediary or the final user. Facilitators include manufacturers' representatives, brokers, advertising agencies, public relations firms, transportation and warehouse facilities, banks, and others that, although not actually in the channel, help the "flow" between buyers and sellers. Advertising agencies and public relations firms provide the necessary business marketing communications, including catalogs and product literature, advertising, direct mail, trade shows, publicity, and public relations. Transportation and warehouse facilities, when viewed as part of the logistics function, maximize customer service and minimize distribution cost. Banks and other financial institutions serve as facilitating agencies when they provide the capital to purchase or lease business products.

## Combining Direct and Indirect Channels

At this point in the discussion of business distribution strategy, we must raise the question again of whether the business marketing manager should use direct channels, indirect channels, or a combination. If indirect channels are selected, should the manufacturers' representative or agent be used, or should sales agents and brokers be employed? A wrong decision could impair market penetration and lead to serious erosion in market share.

Planning and managing a mixed distribution system requires business marketers to give thoughtful consideration to the following four questions:

1. What specific functions must the distribution system perform?
2. Where in the system might these functions be carried out most economically?
3. How do different customers buy, and which elements in the system can be most effective in meeting their needs?
4. What legal constraints must be observed in relationships with independent resellers?

Direct selling to user-customers is preferred in more concentrated market areas having the sales potential to support fixed selling expenses. Likewise, in thinner market areas where their broader product lines provide the base for operating profitability, independent distributors carrying multiple lines might be appropriate.

When a company's independent distributors and its own sales force operate in the same geographic area, their roles can differ in several ways. Each seeks to serve somewhat different kinds of customers, with the company sales representatives targeting accounts that want or need significant technical assistance and a direct relationship with the factory source. Distributors, on the other hand, serve the customers for whom local sources of supply, credit, and highly personalized attention are important.

The roles of the direct sales force and independent distributors are complementary in other ways as well. Often, the direct sales force performs missionary selling in an area to develop sales volume that will ultimately go through distributors. Further, the company might assume certain distribution functions that it can perform more economically than individual distributors. For example, many companies maintain inventory on which distributors may draw, thereby reducing the inventory levels that distributors must keep in their warehouses. Some manufacturers, such as Ford, General Motors, and International Harvester, keep computerized records of dealer inventories to enable dealers to draw on each other's stock to meet customers' orders quickly.

In fact, many marketers need to learn to market to multiple channels of distribution. Marketers of a simple product such as motor oil serve as an example. Motor oil must be marketed in quick-lube shops, farm stores, auto parts outlets, supermarkets, hardware stores, warehouse clubs, and even in some drugstore chains.

**Concept Review**

1. How does Internet purchasing create value for customers? For producers?
2. What is the difference between a general line and a limited-line distributor?
3. What are some advantages of using a manufacturers' representative?
4. What are examples of channel transaction facilitators (facilitating agencies), and how do they differ from true channel members?

## Channel Cooperation

Despite its status as a significant factor in business relationships, the nature and scope of cooperation within marketing channels remains a difficult issue. The essence of channel management is to bring order and coordination to elements influencing channel relationships. In marketing channel settings, relationship marketing focuses attention on how to develop and maintain long-term, highly integrated relationships between customers and their suppliers (or other infrastructure partners).[6] Channel management researchers and practitioners have long recognized the importance of managing relationships between the people and firms performing distribution functions—functions that create value by making products and services available to customers in an appropriate form at the right place and time.

Whether direct, indirect, or both types of channels are used, business marketing managers must address the issue of how to design and operate the firm's distribution channels in order to foster enthusiastic channel cooperation. The essence of the marketing concept is customer orientation at all levels of distribution, with a particular emphasis on the idea of partnership to foster that orientation. The nature of today's highly competitive markets has put a premium on the operation of harmonious manufacturer-dealer relationships. Merck and Company, for example, is purposefully entering a series of highly committed relationships with channel partners who perform research, sales, and other distribution functions.

How do suppliers project their organizations into their respective distribution channels? How do suppliers make the organization and the channel into one? One means of achieving such a goal is, again, for the supplier to foster a sense of partnership with intermediaries. Upon choosing a distribution network and determining the type and numbers of intermediaries needed, the business marketer must next consider what is expected from channel members and what they expect in return. Five methods for promoting channel cooperation are presented here.

### Relationship Marketing

In place of traditional "arms length" (sometimes adversarial) producer-intermediary relationships, relationship marketing fosters highly interdependent, cooperative alliances, joint ventures, and networks.[7]

### Use of Missionary Salespeople

**Missionary salespeople** aid the sales of channel members and bolster the overall level of activity and selling effort in the channel. Training of resellers' salespeople and executives is an effective weapon of cooperation. The channels operate more efficiently when all are educated in the promotional techniques and uses of the products involved.

### Involvement in the Planning Function of Channel Members

Involvement in planning is another powerful weapon of the supplier. Helping resellers to set quotas for their customers; studying the market potential for them; and forecasting a member's sales volume, inventory planning and protection, and so on all are aspects of planning assistance.

### Promotional Aid

Aid in promotion through the provision of advertising materials (mats, displays, commercials, literature, direct-mail pieces), ideas, funds (cooperative advertising), and sales contests is another form of cooperation.

### AGILE AND VIRTUAL COMPANIES REDEFINE CHANNEL RELATIONSHIPS

The strong push by manufacturing companies to retain core competencies and outsource other activities is changing the nature of organizations and their channel relationships. Two important business terms are involved: "agile organizations" and "virtual organizations." An agile organization is structured to operate profitably in a competitive environment of continually and unpredictably changing customer opportunities. Such companies must be able to develop short-life cycle, easily customizable, information-rich products and services targeted at niche markets, and to do so much more quickly and less expensively than in the past. Already, the agile model is displacing the mass production model as the global norm. The virtual organization helps in accomplishing the agile objective by creating a custom mix of companies (a custom channel) to create a unique customer solution; later, it changes the mix of companies involved to create a new mix, as the market situation changes.

An example of a mass production model would be a vertically integrated automotive company. Since it is invested in every part of the present approach to the product and its components, any market shift can create problems. An agile automotive company would have outsourced everything but its core competency of final assembly. For example, if car technology switches to electric motors, the agile OEM realigns its strategic alliances accordingly. If technology makes the OEM's outsourced accounting people and systems obsolete, it simply realigns with a different strategic partner who handles that service.

**Action Assignment**

The e-Sonic Industries case at the end of this chapter involves a company's possible outsourcing of manufacturing to several "contract" manufacturers; i.e., (www.solectron.com), (www.celestica.com), (www.flextronics.com), (www.jabil.com), and (www.sanmina.com). Your assignment is to research the growth in outsourcing and to compare the profitability and growth rates of these companies to the growth rates of companies in other industries. Present your findings to the class. As part of your presentation, you might want to survey the class to learn how many students are aware of each of these companies and have considered employment with them after graduation. It would be interesting to compare their size, profitability, and growth rate with those of the companies at which students are interviewing. New graduates tend to want to join companies that advertise on TV or recruit on campus. Experienced business-to-business professionals tend to look for growth and profitability and would find these companies, with billion dollar sales and annual growth of over 50 percent, to be quite impressive.

Source: *Agile Competitors and Virtual Organizations—Strategies for Enriching the Customer* by S. L. Goldman, R. N. Nagel, and K. Preiss, © 1995 by Von Nostrand. Reprinted by permission of John Wiley & Sons, Inc.

### Acting as a Management Consultant

The large supplier can serve as a management consultant to channel members, dispensing advice in all areas of business, including accounting, personnel, planning, control, finance, buying, Internet systems or office procedures, and site selection. Aid in financing would include offering extended credit terms, consignment selling, and loans.

## Channel Conflict

When a business-to-business firm is not able to achieve cooperation among its various channel members, channel conflict arises. **Channel conflict** can be described as a situation in which one channel member perceives another channel member to be engaged in behavior that is preventing or impeding the other from achieving a set goal. It is, in essence, a state of frustration brought about by a restriction of role performance.[8] Exhibit 10-6 lists examples of typical channel conflict problems.

Most business marketing managers agree on the importance of channel control. Conflict exists when a channel member senses that the behavior of another channel member (usually a dyadic counterpart) is impeding the attainment of the channel member's goals or effective performance. Conflict may result when channel members have mutually exclusive

**EXHIBIT 10-6** Examples of Channel Conflict Issues

| Issues Embodied in Conflict Incidents Occurring in the Manufacturer-Distributor Dyad | |
|---|---|
| **Manufacturer Complaints** | **Distributor Complaints** |
| 1. Lack of service by distributor's personnel | 1. Product unavailability |
| 2. Ineffective communication | 2. Lag time in new product development |
| 3. Warranty administration | 3. Ineffective communication for problem solving |
| 4. Distributor cash-flow tightness | 4. Product quality and defects |
| 5. Documenting rebates and payments | 5. Faulty sales forecasting |
| 6. Loss and damages in delivery | 6. Damages due to packing |
| 7. Documenting advertising expenditures | 7. Off-season financing burden |
| 8. Weak market penetration by distributor | |
| 9. Violation of sales policy | |
| 10. Gaps in product line | |

or inconsistent values, interests, or goals. Manufacturers want control of distribution channels for better execution of their marketing strategies. Likewise, intermediaries have been assumed also to want control of the channel to avoid being bound by manufacturer-determined strategies. The stage is set for conflict!

## Conflict Management and Resolution

For the business marketer, the problem of how to manage conflict must be resolved. The firm faced with a conflict situation with another channel member has several strategies available to it to manage the conflict. Some of these strategies would include waiting to see whether the conflict issue and cause subside. This offers the firm the opportunity to monitor the conflict situation and to develop a well-thought-out plan to resolve the conflict. Using of various bargaining techniques that require compromise to solve the conflict often is helpful. Frequently, organizational changes are necessary not only to reduce conflict but also to serve as a warning system to identify stress in an early stage before it becomes a conflict. Possible organizational changes may include the appointment of a distributor ombudsman, the appointment of an advisory board, and/or the short-term exchange of people between firms to develop more empathy in channel relationships.

## Typical Problem Areas in the Manufacturer-Intermediary Relationship

To avoid conflict while promoting effective channel strategy is difficult—and sometimes it seems impossible. The business marketing manager must make and enforce a number of basic policy rules. These rules involve potential problem areas such as service and technical assistance, house accounts, inventory levels, marketing information and feedback, training and support services, and second product lines carried. A brief review of each of these potential problem areas follows.

### *Service and Technical Assistance*

Service and technical assistance are big factors in the business market; out of necessity, they must extend into the channel of distribution. As an example, a business marketing manager can be forced to use a direct-channel strategy because of an inability to find intermediaries who want to provide service and technical assistance or because of difficulty in finding an intermediary capable of providing such service. Or, the marketing manager could choose a particular intermediary, especially a business products distributor, on the basis of proven service facilities or personnel. If the product line requires significant service and/or technical assistance, the business marketing manager must be sure that the desired service is available and that it is equal to, or better than, the service offered by other manufacturers and middlemen competing for the same market.

### House Accounts

A *house account* can be loosely defined as a customer with whom the manufacturer would rather deal directly (usually because of volume and/or service requirements), while turning the balance of the territory over to an intermediary. House accounts can be a touchy area, especially if the account is a very large or profitable one the intermediary would desire to have as a customer. Here, in essence, the manufacturer tells the intermediary that all present and potential accounts within a defined geographical territory belong to the intermediary, except the house account. Obviously, a loose, inconsistent policy regarding house accounts presents, in all likelihood, a potential legal problem area in the manufacturer-intermediary relationship.

### Inventory Levels

What should the policy be regarding how much inventory a stocking distributor will carry? Too little might result in lost sales due to stockouts, while too much might jeopardize an intermediary's cash flow. Should the business marketing manager allow an intermediary to return obsolete or excess inventory? The basic objective of the inventory function is to have products available to end users when they need them; thus, the crucial problem is to determine the level of customer service desired or needed and then to pinpoint the optimal balance between inventory availability and the cost of carrying the inventory. The higher the field inventory level, the higher the cost of invested dollars, potential obsolescence, and storage costs. This area is ripe for spawning manufacturer-intermediary conflict.

### Marketing Information and Feedback

Will the marketing manager expect market feedback to assess trends in distribution patterns, to discern customer needs, to assess the effect of promotional campaigns, to obtain feedback regarding company image, and to gauge competitive pressures? Some marketing managers expect market feedback from their channels of distribution and make this expectation a very specific channel objective. This operating procedure could lead to channel members' selection being based on their willingness to provide such feedback. One might view such a managerial expectation of feedback as rather unrealistic. Is an intermediary likely to take time from the selling effort to search out market information, trends, and the competitive posture in a particular territory, region, or industry? If a certain level of cooperation and mutually beneficial communication is not forthcoming, might there be channel conflict brewing?

### Training and Support Services

Most intermediaries expect and, frequently, even demand merchandising assistance from the manufacturer. Business marketing managers who want to stimulate and hold intermediary interest must consider developing advertising and sales-promotion programs. Also, effective sales meetings and training programs must be implemented as incentives for both sales and technical training. Factory training of intermediary sales personnel is indispensable. A substantial amount of knowledge can be acquired through programmed learning techniques at a relatively low cost.

What training and support service policies should the business marketing manager adopt? What is affordable? Should the policies call for joint training programs, with both the manufacturer and the intermediary sharing the cost equally? Will cooperative advertising be utilized, and will missionary sales work be required? Reasonable and carefully considered answers to these questions should enable the marketing manager to develop policies that will be attractive to intermediaries.

## WHAT WOULD YOU DO?

### CHANNEL CONFLICT: CUSTOMER POWER VERSUS FAIRNESS TO THE SUPPLIER

Gil Young, Gorin Plastic Products Division Marketing Manager, figured that someone in purchasing at his biggest customer, Automated Office Machines Inc. (AOM), must be getting chewed out. AOM apparently had discovered a warehouse location housing a couple of hundred thousand dollars worth of an obsolete and overage part number. Rumor had it that the buyer (who had since retired) kept purchasing the part, even though it was not being used. At the time of production, Gil had no idea that the products were not being used. Gil had been receiving standard production requirement schedules. Now AOM would have to charge the loss directly to its bottom line, or find some other resolution. From the letter in front of him, Gil feared that AOM wanted him to accept the parts back or refund the purchase price.

Gil decided to fly to the customer's headquarters for a meeting. Although they didn't state it in the letter, Gil quickly discovered that the message from the buyer was that either he make good their loss, or AOM would eliminate Gorin Plastic Products (along with the other divisions of his parent company) as suppliers. Gil quickly calculated that being eliminated as a supplier would cost his firm several million dollars in lost sales, and much more for the other divisions.

Gil reminded the buyer that the purchase terms stated that AOM could return the goods only "for cause" and only within sixty days of receipt. Today's date was more than two years past the sixty days! Gil also reiterated that the parts were custom-made to AOM's design, and would have no value as returned goods. If Gil approved the parts return, he would have to explain to his top management the two hundred thousand dollar reduction to the bottom line, just as the AOM's buyer would have to explain it to AOM top management if Gil refused their request.

Gil knew that people get fired for this type of oversight. At AOM, probably it would be the buyer's supervisor, or someone even higher who should have been monitoring purchasing activities. At his company, Gil figured that he would be fired if he accepted the parts for return. It was a marketing decision and his responsibility to decide: Gil could try to keep his own job safe by not allowing the return, but, in doing so, could lose AOM as a customer.

### Assignment
Define the ethical issues for all concerned. What should Gil do?

---

### Second Product Lines Carried

The stocking of competing lines of merchandise also can constitute a problem area in the manufacturer-intermediary relationship. Manufacturers tend to favor intermediaries who can afford them some measure of protection from competition. One way to gain this fragile security is to choose intermediaries who will limit the number of competing lines they carry.

Business marketing managers whose marketing and sales programs increase channel member profits, who regard intermediaries as customers when negotiating transactions, and who regard intermediaries as partners when pursuing specific customers usually will find that such intermediaries accept direction willingly. Some firms recognize the relationship concept between manufacturer and intermediary by preparing formal contracts to be signed by both parties.

## Channel Width

Market coverage should be analyzed by market segment. While a products' overall market coverage may be satisfactory, it could be poor when market coverage is analyzed for a specific target market. **Channel width** refers to the number of independent members at any stage of distribution. A business marketing manager can choose from one of three degrees of channel width: Intensive distribution, selective distribution, and exclusive distribution. A brief examination of each follows.[9]

### Intensive Distribution

With **intensive distribution**, the marketing manager attempts to gain access to as many resellers as possible within a particular geographic area. The more intensive a product's distribution, the higher its sales potential. If a business user cannot purchase the product immediately from a nearby source, a substitute will be used. On a standard type of product with typically low unit cost and immediate delivery, this is important (nuts and bolts, for example).

On the negative side, the sales efforts of competing dealers may overlap within a given territory. The reseller's loyalty to the manufacturer may be reduced, price competition increased, and the reseller's willingness to service an account diminished.

### Selective Distribution

With **selective distribution**, the business marketing manager distributes the product to a limited number of resellers in a particular geographic region, expecting a better-than-average selling effort. Materials-handling equipment, electric motors, power transmissions equipment, and tools typically fall into the category of straight- or modified-rebuy situations. The time spent in evaluating sources for these products is not great, yet the purchase is not always simple and repetitive. The buyer needs advice about applications, maintenance, and repairs, and the buyer usually demands rapid product delivery, repair, and service. The manufacturer wants to be represented by a distributor who can satisfy these customer requirements.

### Exclusive Distribution

With **exclusive distribution**, only one channel member can sell a manufacturer's products in a given geographic area. Exclusive distribution is characterized by low competition and a low degree of market coverage. Manufacturers use exclusive distribution with the expectation that this form of channel width will induce strong selling support by the reseller. The marketing manager also can exercise more control over pricing, promotion, credit, and other marketing functions by limiting the number of intermediaries handling products in a particular geographic area.

---

**Concept Review**

1. What are four common methods for securing cooperation in a business marketing channel?

2. What are some of the most common reasons for channel conflict?

3. What are some potential problem areas a manufacturer using intensive distribution might encounter?

---

## Summary

- From earliest times, geographically separated buyers and sellers have required a capability to move or to transfer goods and commodities physically. The marketing functions of buying, selling, storage, transportation, sorting, financing, risk taking, and market information must be carried on within the channel system. Each channel function must be performed at least once in every channel, and some functions might be performed by several channel members.

- Business marketers must decide whether to use direct or indirect channels. By their nature, channel decisions are long term, so a careful consideration

of channel needs and requirements is essential for the business marketing manager.

- Direct channels involve direct selling to the business user, with or without the use of sales branches. In sharp contrast to consumer goods, most manufactured business goods are sold directly to users.

- The use of indirect channels is warranted when the market is widely scattered, when many firms must be contacted, when small orders are common, and when goods are made for inventory rather than to fill specific orders. If the business marketer decides to use an indirect channel, there is a variety of options, including business products distributors, manufacturers' representatives, sales agents or brokers, and other facilitating agencies. There are, of course, both advantages and limitations to each of these options, and the business marketing manager must carefully weigh requirements in light of what each of these intermediaries can offer.

- The question of whether to use direct or indirect channels continues to be of the utmost importance to the business marketer. Direct selling to user-customers might be preferred in more concentrated market areas, whereas independent distributors carrying multiple lines might be the choice in thinner market areas.

- Channel cooperation, in essence, is the application of the marketing concept to the channel area in marketing. Business marketers must be aware of methods by which channel cooperation can be achieved.

- Business marketing managers must constantly be vigilant in looking for evidence of present and potential conflict situations within the channel. They must be alert to ways in which such conflict can be reduced and/or avoided through greater efforts toward channel cooperation. In attempting to reduce channel conflict, the business marketer must be ever mindful of the legal issues involved in catering to the needs and desires of channel members.

- Business marketers must decide the degree of market exposure that they desire for their products or product lines. The three primary choices include intensive, selective, and exclusive distribution. The marketing manager must determine exactly which type of exposure offers the most appropriate benefits.

## Key Terms

breaking of bulk
broker
business products
  distributor
channel conflict
channel management

channel width
direct channel
exclusive distribution
facilitating agency
indirect channel
intensive distribution

manufacturers'
  representative
missionary salesperson
sales agent
sales branch
selective distribution

## Review Questions

1. Identify and briefly discuss each of the eight functions of distribution channels.

2. What is a direct channel? Under what general conditions would direct channels be used?

3. What is an indirect channel? Under what general conditions would indirect channels be used?

4. What is a business products distributor? What are the major limitations involved with the use of business products distributors? What major trends are currently associated with business products distributors?

5. Identify manufacturers' representatives. What are the major limitations involved with the use of manufacturers' representatives? Discuss the major trends currently related to the work of manufacturers' representatives.

6. How are sales agents and brokers used as intermediaries in indirect channels of distribution?

7. In general, what is the role of facilitating agencies in business marketing channels? What are some examples of business facilitating agencies?

8. How can business-to-business firms apply the marketing concept to their respective channel activities? What are some possible reasons for channel conflict? When can channel conflict benefit overall channel performance? Discuss several methods for reducing channel conflict and promoting greater channel cooperation.

9. Discuss six typical problem areas in the manufacturer-intermediary relationship.

10. Identify three levels of market exposure commonly used in business distribution. When would a physical distribution manager use each?

## Case 10-1

# E-Sonic Industries

This case was written by Dr. Roger Gomes and Dr. Patricia Knowles, Clemson University, ©1999

At e-Sonic Industries, team decision making was part of the company culture that had kept the company on top in the highly competitive Silicon Valley electronics industry. In a relatively short time, the company had grown to be a household name, as well regarded as the largest Japanese consumer electronics firms. Today, at their weekly meeting, the strategic directors were considering the potential outsourcing of their entire manufacturing process. It was a decision with huge ramifications, involving gaining a significant differential cost advantage over competitors but impacting the careers of thousands of employees. It was a topic that the directors had been struggling with for some time.

As the meeting was called to order at 10:00 A.M., the secretary noted those in attendance: Brian Cortez, director of manufacturing; Sasha Johnson, director of engineering; Kyle Mendonca, director of purchasing; and Beth Michaels, director of marketing. Brian began by stating that he still was opposed to outsourcing manufacturing as it was e-Sonic's main "core competency." Like a good marketer, Beth was ready with a PowerPoint presentation that started by showing the criteria for a "core competency" as being: (a) the function must provide access to a variety of profitable markets; (b) the function must provide significant customer-perceived benefits; and (c) the function must be difficult for competitors to imitate. Beth proceeded to go over the history of e-Sonic and their customers around the globe. With colorful diagrams showing many connections throughout the supply chain, Beth drove home the point that, at least from her perspective, e-Sonic's core competency was its relationships with its customers. High-quality manufacturing was critical, but it was available in many countries, and the industry was constantly shifting to the lowest-cost location. Kyle, as usual, supported marketing's position, but with the caveat that once the decision was made to outsource manufacturing, the process became a purchasing department responsibility. Supplier selection, coordination, and supply chain–channel management was the most basic of purchasing functions. As the conversation went back and forth, Sasha followed her usual strategy of listening closely, not getting into political debates, and when least expected, casually mentioning some huge factor that all would have to agree that they were overlooking. Today her only comment was that outsourcing manufacturing would go against the company's mission statement. Beth happened to have another overhead titled "Marketing Myopia," and launched into a discussion of the necessity for continuous change to address continuously changing markets. By that time everyone was ready for lunch.

Kyle, as director of purchasing, knew he needed to be better prepared for next week's meeting. Skipping lunch, he began by calling up PowerPoint on his computer and entered his department's standard operating procedure (SOP) for selecting suppliers. He knew that he would have to adjust and improve the content for this level of decision, but he thought that it was a good place to start. He typed: (1) Identify all potential suppliers. (2) Develop a detailed analysis of each potential supplier. (3) Prepare a list of the five best supplier candidates. (4) Evaluate RFQs from each candidate. (5) Conduct negotiations with suppliers offering the most value. (6) Coordinate and manage the project of bringing the new channel member on line. (7) Manage the relationship, including additional products and changes. (8) Negotiate the extension of the contract with the objective of increasing value to e-Sonic.

Next, Kyle called up a new blank slide and typed in the title: Criteria for Comparing Supplier Candidates: (1) level of technology (rate 1–50, with 50 being the leader in the world), (2) annual sales, (3) annual sales growth, (4) annual profit, (5) current ratio, (6) quick ratio, (7) debt-to-equity ratio, (8) capacity remaining, and (9) rate management team (1–50); rate quality reputation (1–50). As Kyle looked over what he had done, he couldn't help but sigh and say to himself, "I'll have to make this all much more useful before I show it to anyone." Kyle began by switching from PowerPoint to the Internet and called up the websites of the candidate suppliers. Kyle thought, "Soon one of these companies will be doing all of our manufacturing, and of course the importance of purchasing will increase considerably. Thank goodness for our company's team orientation. I need some help with this."

## Assignment

Kyle has discussed the situation with Beth in marketing, and she has assigned you to help Kyle (with both the analysis and the presentation). You have access to his PowerPoint information (above) and also his list of supplier candidate websites, i.e., (www. solectron.com), (www.celestica.com), (www.flextronics.com), (www.jabil.com), (www. sanmina.com). As you understand the assignment, you need to optimize the supplier selection process, evaluate the suppliers, and recommend the best candidate to take over manufacturing. It hasn't been said, hut you also suspect that you should come up with some analysis that supports outsourcing. You will be making your report to Kyle and Beth (and also to the class), so be sure to make it professional and convincing.

Adapted from: E. Baatz, "Rapid Growth Changes Rules for Purchasing," *Purchasing*, June 17, 1999, pp. 33–39: and F. A. Kuglin, *Customer-Centered Supply Chain Management*. (New York: AMACOM, 1998).

---

### Case 10-2

# Northern New England Manufacturing Company: Influencing Manufacturers' Representatives Sales Efforts

Northern New England Manufacturing Company was a producer of several kinds of industrial equipment, which are listed in Exhibit 10-7. It developed from the efforts in the late 1970s of a gifted engineer and inventor, Sidney Harvey, who patented several of his ideas for variations on standard products. He founded and was active in the firm for over 26 years until his death.

Harvey had been very interested in all aspects of his company including its selling activities and had a strong sense of professionalism that he used in personally selecting people for his sales force. He himself had managed the sales force until it grew to a size of three people, at which time he secured the services of Herbert Staley as sales manager.

**EXHIBIT 10-7**
**Northern New England Manufacturing Company Sales by Product, Selected Months**

| Product | September | July | September Last Year | September Two Years Before |
|---|---|---|---|---|
| Dryers | $21,000 | $34,500 | $35,000 | $32,200 |
| Sprayers | 7,700 | 7,500 | 8,000 | 7,800 |
| Planers | 4,100 | 4,300 | 4,000 | 3,900 |
| Power saws | 3,200 | 3,000 | 3,000 | 3,100 |
| Drills | 4,200 | 4,100 | 4,000 | 3,900 |
| Sanders | 9,500 | 7,300 | 7,200 | 7,000 |
| Metal buffers | 7,500 | 4,900 | 5,000 | 4,800 |

Before Staley's arrival and for several years thereafter, Harvey told the field salespeople expressly the names of firms on which he wanted them to call. The founder was acutely interested in the reputation of his company, and with the salespeople on straight salary, he knew that his wishes would be followed. His concern with reputation included product characteristics as promised, delivery on time (critical to customers for these goods), and ethical, highly reserved business conduct by the field salespeople. However, this concern for reputation was not restricted to these factors. Harvey also wanted to have as his customers those who enjoyed the finest reputations themselves. For example, he told his field salespeople never to solicit the orders of a small firm then known by the name of Reihnan and Loyks, because he considered the owners to be social climbers without proper backgrounds. In addition, he did not like an advertisement of theirs he once saw in a weekly business newspaper. He also instructed his salespeople not to call on Heather Glow, Inc., because it had once been turned down for a loan at the bank that Harvey used. This was despite the fact that Heather Flow found credit at another bank.

Not all the instructions to the sales force were negative, however. Harvey had the salespeople, all of whom were engineers, visit Camden Mills, Stone and Kruger, and South Coast Metals time after time, even though all three were committed to only purchasing from Harvey's competitors. He wanted Northern New England Manufacturing Company to be a name that such firms knew and respected. He also cultivated several large national companies, such as Combustion Engineering, American Machine and Foundry, Kaiser Industries, Westinghouse, and Melpar.

After Harvey's death, Staley continued these policies for the better part of a year. At that point, James Watts, the new president hired in from the outside, had a long talk with the sales manager and explained that some changes were desirable. The firm should try to minimize costs and abandon all these "notions and pretensions," as he termed them. To do so, he felt it would he better to move from maintaining a direct sales force on salary, to selling exclusively through "manufacturer's representatives" paid on a 7 percent straight commission basis. Watts said, "This is the first company I have seen that sells through conservative engineering types. Real salespeople aggressively pursue selling. Besides being true professional sales types, 'manufactures representatives' cover all their own benefits, transportation, and selling costs. They have to aggressively sell our products because their only income is from commissions on sales." Watts finished with, "I think that they are the future of our company. Oh, and don't worry, Herb, your job will remain essentially the same. You will be responsible for setting up and managing the reps."

Herb did not at all like this turn of events but knew that the heads of accounting and production would support the idea. The accounting head would love it because selling costs would go from fixed overhead to varying as sales fluctuated (at a fixed percent of sales). The production head would love it because he had always thought that Herb's salespeople were not aggressive enough. Also, from the production manager's perspective, the change would decrease the internal power and influence of marketing and sales (which by default would increase the power and influence of production).

Herb did express his reservations to Watts, reminding him that there were sometimes problems with manufacturers' representatives. Herb said, "I know that a lot of equipment producers use 'manufacturers' representatives,' but remember, with them our fate will not be in our own hands but in the hands of independent companies who sell for us. Each territory will have its own rep company, and each of those companies will have their own objectives and policies." Even as he said it Herb knew what Watts' reply would be. As expected Watts said, "Well Herb, in the tens of thousands of companies who are quite successful using manufacturers' representatives, it is the sales manager's job to coordinate their efforts and assure proper and consistent representation."

Herb was wise enough to recognize something that was already decided and not open to discussion. Instead he switched topics and expressed concern for his current field salespeople. After some negotiation, it was agreed that those who were nearing retirement would be offered generous early retirement packages; the younger ones would be offered reassignment back into engineering; and if any were young and entrepreneurial spirited they could be considered for the "manufacturers' representative" contract in their territory.

On August 1st, Herb announced the new plans to the four sales reps and indicated that all changes would occur in 30 days. Two of the four sales reps opted to retire, one opted to take a position back in engineering, and one opted to become a manufacturers' representative for the firm. Three other manufacturers' representatives were contracted with, and all the changes took place on September 1st. Sales in August slumped about 17 percent from the same month one year earlier and about 14 percent from the same month two years earlier.

After one month with the manufacturers' representatives in place, Herb conducted a preliminary inquiry into the results of the new policy of selling through channel facilitators. The results appeared to be that the easier to sell items were moving adequately, and the one item that was rather difficult to sell (the dryer) was moving very poorly. Exhibit 10-7 gives the comparison of September to the last month under the old policy (July) and to September one year before. Staley presented his analysis to Watts but cautioned him about premature inferences from those data. He said that he would repeat his comparisons after another month. In the meantime, the president told Staley to urge the manufacturers' representatives to solicit orders for dryers.

At the beginning of November, Staley anxiously studied the results for October, as presented in Exhibit 10-8. He had taken a preliminary look at some fragmentary data about October 16th, but he knew that those data were undependable. In addition, the company has usually experienced a mild upswing in the fall season.

Herb was in his office reflecting on the figures in Exhibits 10-7 and 10-8 when Douglas Guglielmi, the production manager, and Richard Acker, the finance and accounting manager, walked in. After several minutes of friendly conversation about sports and the weather, Guglielmi said, "We seem to have a problem. To be specific, the mix of sales is changing radically, and it is upsetting our production schedules, our performance to budget, and even deliveries." Richard Acker added, "You are selling more than we can make of low-margin products like sanders and buffers and decreasing quantities of high-margin products like dryers. Total profits are way down." Guglielmi said, "I can't take the people and equipment on the dryer assembly lines and use them to make more sanders and buffers. Well, I guess I could, but it would dramatically change the organization. At a minimum, it would mean big capital expenditures, plus drastically cutting overhead." Acker said, "Do you really want to change us into a high-volume, low-margin, producer of power hand tools? That would put us head to head with the likes of Black & Decker and Skil, not to mention Makita and Hitachi. I worry that if sales decline much more, the board of directors may find us another president, one with much less patience."

**EXHIBIT 10-8**

**Northern New England Manufacturing Company Sales by Product, Selected Months**

| Product | October | October Last Year | October Two Years Before |
|---|---|---|---|
| Dryers | $23,000 | $36,000 | $35,400 |
| Sprayers | 7,900 | 8,400 | 8,200 |
| Planers | 4,300 | 4,200 | 4,000 |
| Power saws | 3,300 | 3,200 | 3,000 |
| Drills | 4,200 | 4,300 | 4,100 |
| Sanders | 11,500 | 7,500 | 7,200 |
| Metal buffers | 9,700 | 5,300 | 5,100 |

Herb was too much of a politician to fall into the feeble trap they had set for him. He paused and thought, "These two want me to get upset and say that this situation is all their fault for supporting the change to selling to reps rather than retaining our own field sales force. With our direct field sales force we could control what products they spent their time on, while the manufacture's representatives are independent companies who have other companies' products to sell also. They are going to sell the mix that is easiest to sell and maximizes their income." Herb thought, "But these two know all this; they just want to be able to campaign to Watts that they tried to talk to me and I became overly defensive and unreasonably tried to blame sales' problem on them." But Herb knew that somewhere within each problem lies a bit of opportunity.

Suddenly, Herb was calm. He smiled at Guglielmi and Acker, and said, "You both have to appreciate that sales is something of an art. Also like an art you have to judge the intention and finished product rather than the work in process. Our new president has a vision to rejuvenate and modernize this company, and that is going to mean a lot of uncomfortable change for all of us. Rest assured that decisions about what products to sell to which customers, at what price, promotion, distribution, and even what type of channel facilitators, are all strategic decisions that sales and marketing is responsible for, and has under control."

"Doug, I respect your ability to make production decisions, and Richard, I respect your ability to make accounting policy decisions. I would probably be on pretty weak ground if I went around questioning your decisions. You probably could make me look pretty foolish, without half trying. Now, I know you guys were not questioning my operation of the sales department, you just wanted to show your interest in helping us through some challenging times."

Herb continued, "Tell you what; let's have a meeting of the management team next week, and I will lay out how our entire sales strategy supports the objectives and vision of our president. Then everyone can better understand and appreciate the president's challenge to us all." Guglielmi and Acker assured Herb that they only wanted to assist in any way they could, and went back to their own offices. On the way Guglielmi said, "Interesting turn of events." Acker replied, "Yeah, I thought we had him on the ropes, but the presentation thing puts this right into what sales types are best at." Guglielmi replied, "Well I wish him luck; if he pulls the company through this maybe he does deserve to he our next president." Acker replied, "Not likely; besides if the job doesn't go to someone from production, then accounting is next in line. Clearly it is a time for strict financial controls."

Herb was still in his office, planning his next move. Clearly something would have to he done with the sales problem, and he only had a week to create a logical, marketing-theory based, strategic presentation that revolved around a unifying vision. Something that would make the president and the top management team enthusiastic about the sales department. Herb though, "Well I wonder where I should start?"

## Assignment

With your knowledge of sales, channels, and management, develop a workable plan to resolve the sales problem, set measurable objectives, and prepare an impressive professional looking presentation for the management meeting next week (next class).

Source: "Northern New Jersey Manufacturing Company" by T. V. Greer in *Cases in Marketing: Analysis and Problems,* 2nd ed. p. 475. © 1979. Reprinted by permission of Prentice-Hall, Inc., Upper Saddle River, N.J.

# References

1. D. Walters and G. Lancaster, "Implementing Value Strategy through the Value Chain," *Management Decision* 38 (March 2000):160–178.

2. B. S. Sahay, "Supply Chain Collaborations: The Key to Value Creation," *Work Study* 52 (February 2003): 76–83.

3. Jim Carlton, "Intel's Online Orders Reach $1 Billion," *The Wall Street Journal* (November 15, 1998): 81, 84, Column 3.

4. Comments by Richard L. Keyser, CEO Grainger, Annual Meeting of Shareholders, April 25, 2001, www.investor.Grainger.com/annual/2001chairmanspeech.

5. Thomas C. Reinhart and Donald R. Coleman, "Heyday for the Independent Rep," *Sales and Marketing Management* (November 1978): 51–54. Reprinted with permission from *Sales and Marketing Management* magazine, copyright © 1978.

6. David Rylander, David Strutton, and Lou E. Pelton, "Toward a Synthesized Framework of Relational Commitment: Implications for Marketing Channel Theory and Practice," *Journal of Marketing Theory and Practice* 5 (Spring 1997): 58–71.

7. M. Soonhong and J. T. Mentzer, "The Role of Marketing in Supply Chain Management," *International Journal of Physical Distribution and Logistics Management* 30 (Sept. 2000): 765–87.

8. M. L. Emiliami, "The Inevitability of Conflict Between Buyers and Sellers," *Supply Chain Management* 8 (February 2003): 107–15.

9. This section is largely from Barry Berman, *Marketing Channels.* (New York: John Wiley & Sons, Inc., 1996): 483–85.

## CHAPTER ELEVEN

# Supply Chain Management and Logistics

**Learning Objectives**

After reading this chapter, you should be able to:

- Comprehend the concepts of value proposition, value chain, and supply chain management (SCM).
- Discuss the forces driving SCM and the barriers to effective SCM.
- Comprehend the concept of supply chain logistics.
- Understand the concept of materials management flow.
- Appreciate the importance of physical distribution.
- Understand and appreciate the functions of traffic management.
- Appreciate the strategic role and importance of customer service.
- Differentiate between public and private warehouses.
- Understand the significance of inventory control in the distribution function.

**Chapter Outline**

Supply Chain Management
Supply Chain Logistics

In the last chapter we examined the importance of basic channel decisions. In the new millennium, increasingly aggressive and competitive global competition is driving the need for more innovative and advanced approaches to improving channel efficiency. Driven by competitive pressure and enabled by dramatic increases in information technology (IT) computing power, manufacturers, suppliers, and distributors are reassessing how and where they create product value, and how they share information with other members in the channel.[1] In dynamic markets, customer needs and market realities are constantly changing. Leading edge companies anticipate these changes and reconfigure their "value added," and channel partner relationships to sustain their differential advantage.

Traditionally the focus was on individual firms, but increasingly a wider view is required. Powerful international brands are not just products, but are actually the results of the well-planned, integrated, and coordinated channel systems that produced them. To compete against the best in the world, firms need to manage much more than just their interactions with their immediate channel neighbors. Increasingly, firms must consider their strategic contribution to the channel and the specific value it creates for the channel's ultimate end user. To assist in this effort, new approaches to management have been introduced including the ideas of *value proposition*, *value chain*, and *supply chain management*.

## Value Proposition

Many companies view their value proposition as their single most important organizing principle. A **value proposition** is a clear, concise set of factual statements describing the real value (benefits) customers can expect to receive from a firm's products. A good value proposition should not speak in vague generalities. Clear, measurable benefits should be specified instead (e.g., 25–50 percent increased revenue, 90 percent faster time to market, 25–55 percent decreased costs, 85 percent improvement in operational efficiency, and 200 percent increased market share). Further, a good value proposition should differentiate the firm's offerings from those of competitors. To thoroughly understand the concept of value proposition it may be useful at this point to visit an Internet search engine, search on the term "value proposition," and compare the value propositions of various companies. Prior to engaging in any job interview, it is also important to view the value proposition for the company you plan to interview with and learn it backwards and forwards.

## Value Chain

To help firms better understand their contribution to systemwide enhancement of value (value-added), the concept of **value chain** has been introduced into strategic analysis. While traditional channel analysis visualizes a set of companies with each firm interacting with its immediate neighbors, a value chain approach takes a systemwide view and delves deeply into the value of each activity at each firm. The analysis of a value chain disaggregates the channel system into each channel member's activities and specifically considers how each activity creates value for the channel's ultimate customers.[2] In refining and re-engineering the value chain to maximize efficiency and end user benefits, each firm activity can only be justified if it creates more value than it costs. Because value and differential advantage perception is end-user-segment-specific, value chain analysis is a strategic process completed at the product manager or marketing manager level.

## Value Added

While the value chain concept is a relatively recent strategic tool, the idea of a firm seeking *value-added* products to offer to their immediate customers has been around for decades. While lacking the systemwide view of value, this older concept recognized that some firms and some processes add a great deal of value when one compares their costs and benefits. Higher-value-added products produce higher margins and, thus, more profit than lower-value-added alternatives. Given a fixed amount of production capacity, a firm's marketers would seek to build relations with those customers who represent the potential for good volumes of high-value-added products. While there is nothing basically wrong with this approach, it was usually applied when a firm's worldview reached only out to its immediate suppliers and immediate customers. It misses the point that derived demand from the end user (ultimate consumer) drives all channel activity. When firms in an interdependent channel system act in their own best interests, rather than the best interests of the total channel system, the result often creates opportunities for competing channels to provide better value to the end user. A better approach would be for each firm to seek to produce value-added products, where the value added is in terms of total channel value added to the end user.

The concepts of value added, value chain, and value proposition can be brought together under a new philosophy of integrated and synchronized *supply chain management*. While it was previously adequate to simply understand basic definitions of channels, in the current competitive environment, it is important to learn about the new view of channels as supply chains. The supply chain management philosophy is a dramatic departure from previous approaches, and it is creating whole new sets of job descriptions for this generation's business graduates.

## Supply Chain Management

Many senior executives suggest that supply chain management (SCM) will come to be regarded as an advancement similar in importance to the industrial revolution and the introduction of mass production. A **supply chain** refers to a set of value-adding companies that are sequentially linked by upstream and downstream flows of goods, services, finances, and information from initial raw material source to the ultimate end user. **Supply chain management** is defined as the multidisciplinary integration and coordination of value-adding business processes from raw material supplier through ultimate end user. Designing a supply chain that can provide differential value is an important step, but it is futile without the ability to actually manage the system and make it work for the mutual benefit of the firms in the channel. This involves extending the type of relationship management marketers have traditionally reserved for direct customers, up and down the chain.

For students who want to become their generation's business leaders, SCM is much more than a dull distribution concept. It is the foundation for global competitiveness. Importantly, it is so different from what came before and so dependent on information technology, that a generation that is not held back by past traditions and that grew up with computers, should have a significant advantage over employees that still focus simply on value-added products.

Modern SCM impacts all the strategic activities and functional areas within firms. Because each functional area defines SCM in its own terms, we will need to explore the concept from several different perspectives. For example, purchasing executives look mainly to their suppliers as the supply chain to be managed. Logistics executives look to their outbound physical distribution as supply chain management. As marketers with a value chain systemwide perspective, we will need to look at the SCM philosophy in its complete form; coordinating the end user value-creating activities of all the firms in the entire supply chain, ranging from the first raw material producer, through the various sequential tiers of component and subassembly producers, final product assemblers, intermediaries, retailers, and finally to the end user (ultimate consumer).

Traditionally, marketers mostly concerned themselves with flows over which they had direct control. Marketers obtained needs and demand information from their immediate customers, made strategic decisions, and communicated their company's needs to their direct suppliers. Thus, the needs of the ultimate user and quantities to be produced were transmitted through the supply chain impacting activity all the way back to the first raw material supplier. The problem was that each company was in a position (for a wide variety of reasons) to add their own twist to the requirements. There was no overall coordination, and the decisions were almost always less and less system-optimal as they flowed back through the chain. This phenomenon became widely known as the "acceleration principle" or "bullwhip effect" as even small changes in end user demand would be reflected back through the chain in ever increasing magnitudes resulting in significant distortion from what would actually be optimal for efficient systemwide operations.[3]

SCM allows every one of the supply chain decision makers to operate from the same set of systemwide data. Ideally, the operations of each firm are transparent to others up and down the chain. Finally, firms can coordinate their operations and interact for mutual chainwide benefit. A truly integrated synchronized supply chain would be one where the checkout scanning of a purchased bag of potato chips initiates all the upchain activities to replace it, all the way back to the earliest raw material supplier where a farmer in Idaho plants two additional potatoes.[4] Although that example is a bit of an exaggeration, it is a good expression of the general idea of an integrated and synchronized supply chain. Another way to think of such a supply chain is the coordinated movement of a flock of birds, which illustrates synchronized movement by independent but coordinated partners.

At each firm, executives with SCM responsibilities interact with their SCM counterparts up and down the chain. They utilize the latest in information technology systems to understand actual current systemwide status, and cooperatively plan future actions and operational strategies. The overall objectives of SCM include: (1) optimizing coordination in operations and requirements, (2) minimizing duplication and non-value-adding activities, (3) reducing costs while maintaining superior quality and customer service, (4) reducing inventory, and (5) reducing cycle times.

The strategic objectives of SCM must be consistent with the product's lifecycle stage and other market realities. For example, SCM for products in dynamic growth lifecycle stages would need to quickly adapt to changing requirements and competitive challenges, whereas SCM for mature products would seek to reliably meet steady, flat demand at low cost. This means that the new value-added issues of speed and flexibility are becoming as important as the traditional measures of price, quality, and reliability.

### Forces Driving SCM toward Ever More Integration and Coordination

It is important for all marketers to remember that today's differential advantage will likely be tomorrow's standard competitor capability. The quest for constant improvement is a strategic necessity. Globalization means new markets, but also requires constant innovation since any product feature can, and likely will be, copied by low-cost imitators around the world. The fastest growing international markets are typically the ones that provide the least trademark, patent, and intellectual property protection. Increasingly, market leaders are looking for sustainable (and hard to copy) differential advantage from their integrated supply chains that can adapt quickly to changing market conditions and provide a steady flow of innovative customer value. After decades of working on internal incremental process improvements, firms are looking at systemwide coordination to provide major future efficiencies.

A process of continuously measuring supply chain performance and comparing one's performance to the best (called benchmarking) is a requirement for competition in challenging global markets. The measures would involve both the performance of the supply chain as a whole and the individual companies participating in the supply chain. The most important criteria to track would depend on the nature of the product and its markets but they would usually include: profitability, gross sales, strategic and tactical decision response time, return on investment, return on assets, state-of-the-art technology measures, transparency (availability of everyone's operational information) of data up and down the chain, product development time from concept to delivery, market share, customer satisfaction, reductions in waste and pollution, time to market, inventory levels and turns, lead times, forecast accuracy, logistics cost, warranty costs, asset management, etc.

## Barriers to SCM

SCM is a complex interdisciplinary boundary-spanning effort that involves many functions within the company and how those functional areas interact with the functional areas of other companies. Supply chain issues involve people and systems up and down the channel in accounting, marketing, production, transportation, engineering, and quality control, to name just a few. Under SCM they need to adjust their thinking dramatically. For example, a marketer who directs pull promotion toward the ultimate consumer could actually be creating short term (surge) peaks in demand, unknowingly creating additional costs and inefficiencies up the supply chain.

According to Bud LaLonde (one of the founders of modern academic logistics), several major barriers to effective supply chain management still remain.[5] These include:

- The firm's comfort level and bias toward the old system. Many senior managers' formal education predates wide incorporation of computer data, and they may fear loss of control over what they may not fully understand.

- Making matters worse, computerized SCM systems quickly become obsolete, with generation after generation offering additional efficiency and cost benefits. Even for those who are most computer proficient, it is increasingly hard to keep up with the explosion of SCM technology options.

- Executive's resistance to change is often resistance to sharing knowledge and power. For many traditional managers, the last thing they would seek out is an integrated information system that dissipates their power inside and outside the organization.

- Most worrisome is the continued lack of SCM and leadership training for today's and tomorrow's supply chain leaders. As a new area, few universities have a formal program in SCM and few companies have a career path that will lead promising managers to the supply chain function. There are a few educational bright spots. IBM and Michigan State University's Eli Broad College of Business have established the Center for On-Demand Supply Chain Research. Students will be able to study, simulate, and test relationships in an end-to-end supply chain. SCM education is also strongly supported by industry at Ohio State, Penn State, MIT, and University of Tennessee and a small handful of others.

## SCM Success Stories

### Unilever

With annual sales over $45 billion, Unilever HPC (www.unilever.com) the global leader in foods and home and personal care products employs 265,000 and has brands such as Pond's, Ragu, Dove, Bird's Eye, Ben & Jerry's, Hellmann's mayonnaise, Lipton Tea, and Best Foods. Operating globally (40 percent of sales in Europe, 26 percent North America, 7 percent Africa, Middle East and Turkey, 16 percent Asia and Pacific, and 11 percent Latin America) their supply chains cross many products, cultures, and business practices.

With the recent merger of Lever Brothers, Cheeseborough-Ponds, and Helene Curtis three distinct U.S. distribution network and supply chains needed to be integrated. Working with a third-party provider of distribution facilities and services, Prologis (www.prologis.com), the integration was completed with a 15 percent improvement in efficiency and an expected 7 percent savings in transportation, administrative, and facility costs.[6]

### *Hewlett-Packard*

Hewlett-Packard (HP) was one of the pioneers of the CD-RW drive industry. As is the case for all consumer electronics, the CD-RW industry experienced accelerated technology revolutions and product life cycles. The bad news was that the average selling price continued to drop rapidly (50 percent per year) and competition continued to grow from 3 in 1997 to over 50 in 2002. In 1998, HP was the share leader but was under serious attack. Their old supply chain was slow, expensive, and unresponsive. Basically the inventory was staying in the pipeline too long, increasing inventory-driven costs. Cycle times were too long: 128 days from the time orders were placed with suppliers to the time the units were delivered to retail customers (including up to 30 days of ocean transportation from Asia or Europe). By analyzing, simulation modeling, and re-engineering their supply chain, HP saved $50 million dollars per year in supply chain related costs. SCM helped to return a product line, with constantly decreasing selling prices, to profitability while increasing market share from 27 percent to 60 percent, and reducing supply chain cycle time from 128 days to 8 days.[7]

### *Food Industry*

Companies participating in MIT's Integrated Supply Chain Management Program report inventory buffers reduced by half, increased on-time deliveries by 40 percent, doubling inventory turns, and reducing stock-outs significantly. In the notoriously low-margin grocery supply chain, producers have been collaborating with their up- and down-channel supply chain partners to develop practices that will allow them all to operate more efficiently. The most successful supply chains have reduced costs by 3 to 7 percent. That may not sound like much, but it represents more margin than most grocery retailers operate on. So even if only half of the savings were passed on to retailers, it would represent a dramatic increase in value.[8]

## Supply Chain Logistics

As marketers cooperatively create value-producing supply chains, the issues of efficient materials flow and transportation cannot be overlooked. The inbound materials flow (materials management) of one supply chain member derives from the outbound materials flow of its direct suppliers, and that is repeated up and down the chain. All purchasers of inbound materials seek value and service, and all providers of outbound materials strive to provide their customers with the correct customer-satisfaction–producing shipments (the right product, at the right time, at the right location, in the right quantity, in the right packaging, which meets all the customer's quality requirements). To accomplish this, marketers must understand the central role of supply chain logistics in SCM and must be able to provide consistent value to direct customers and end users of the supply chain system (all while still reaching the firm's profit objectives).

The word **logistics** refers to the design and management of all activities (basically transportation, inventory, and warehousing) necessary to make materials available for manufacturing and to make finished products available to customers as needed and in the condition required. As Exhibit 11-1 shows, logistics embodies two primary product flows: (1) materials management (previously called physical supply), which represents those flows that provide raw materials, components, and supplies to the production process; and (2) physical distribution management, or those flows that deliver the completed product to customers and channel intermediaries. At the firm level, logistics management also can be defined as adding value through the management of materials, inventory, warehousing, transportation, and customer service. Supply chain logistics does the same across all the firms in the chain.

**EXHIBIT 11-1**
**Logistics Materials Flow Repeated Up and Down the Chain (information flow in reverse direction not shown)**

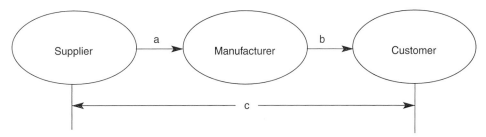

a = materials management (previously called physical supply)
b = physical distribution management
c = logistics (at the firm level)–here, the manufacturer is the focus and frame of reference

An additional way of thinking about logistics is to consider a companywide and chain-wide objective to optimize material flow "in-through-and-out" of organizations. In an effective logistics operation, the organization strives to meet target customer satisfaction goals while minimizing costs for competitive advantage.

## Materials Management and Material Flow

Chapter 3 presented many of the issues involving lean just-in-time production, purchasing processes, inventory, and other inbound considerations. In that chapter, the intent was to understand the buyer's needs and the process they use to manage the activities, goods, and services of their suppliers. A logistics point-of-view integrates the management of inbound materials flow with outbound materials flow, and an SCM view integrates all the chain's material flows. Since inbound flow has previously been covered, we can go right on to a firm's outbound materials flow commonly referred to as "physical distribution."

## Physical Distribution

**Physical distribution** can be defined as the process of planning, implementing, and controlling the efficient, effective flow and storage of goods, services, and related information from point of origin to point of consumption for the purpose of conforming to the customer's requirements.

Physical distribution has the potential to enhance the production, marketing, and profit performance of any company that produces a tangible product. Over the past several years, business marketers have recognized that logistics can provide a strong competitive advantage in the marketplace. The major roadblock to realizing this potential lies in the outdated perception that physical distribution is nothing more than a "semantic upgrading" of the industrial traffic function. As a result, physical distribution too often has been viewed in its narrow, historical context as the cost function that moves business raw materials and finished goods to meet manufacturing schedules. What far too few realize is that often up to 20 percent of the cost of a product is in the cost to move it!

## Traffic Management

Transportation is such a pervasive force that often it is taken for granted. Transportation costs have been a concern of business marketers for many years, but there has been more talk and theory development than action. However, the electronic age, marketing information systems, and integrated channel networks have led to a greater appreciation of the potential profit contribution of **traffic management**. This position is responsible for coordinating and integrating all movement of materials, including transportation, internal movement (materials handling), and warehousing; the process of implementing a "total systems" approach. Transportation management, traffic management, logistics management, or physical distribution management (whichever title fits a particular situation) is not only a dominant aspect of the economy, it offers outstanding career opportunities. Today's transportation manager enjoys a sharply elevated status from that of previous decades.

## Functions of Traffic Management

The functions of traffic management are broad and vary in intensity with the type of industry, the type of product being shipped, and the size and number of shipments being transported. A brief discussion of *mode* selection, routing, claims processing, and the operation of private transportation follows.

### Mode and Carrier Selection

The five basic transportation **modes** are motor, rail, water, pipeline, and air. Each plays an important role in the movement of business freight, specializes in certain commodities or geographical freight movement, and competes for a segment of the freight transportation industry. Exhibit 11-2 explains how each mode also has some major advantages associated with it, related to criteria such as cost, speed, flexibility, distance traveled, and dependability. A brief profile of each of the major transportation modes available to business manufacturers follows.

**EXHIBIT 11-2**
**Major Advantages by Transportation Mode**

| Mode | Major Advantages |
|---|---|
| Motor | Speed of delivery<br>Diversity of equipment<br>Great flexibility<br>Frequency of movement<br>Transfer of goods to other carriers<br>Convenient both to shipper and receiver |
| Rail | Mass movement of goods<br>Low unit cost of movement<br>Dependability<br>Long-haul moving<br>Wide coverage to major markets and suppliers<br>Many auxiliary services, such as switching and in-transit privileges<br>Transfer of goods to other carriers<br>Specialized equipment |
| Water | Very low unit cost of movement<br>Movement of low-unit-value commodities<br>Long-haul movement<br>Mass movement of bulk commodities |
| Pipeline | Lowest unit cost of movement<br>Mass movement of liquid or gas products<br>Long-haul moving<br>Large capacity<br>Most dependable mode |
| Air | Frequent service to major markets<br>Large capability<br>Overnight service<br>Most rapid speed of any carrier |
| Intermodal (combining the major advantages of two or more modes) | Cost savings<br>Lower loss and damage claims due to containerization<br>Extends service to more shippers and receivers<br>Reduced handling and storage costs |

*Motor*  The motor carrier (truck transport) is the primary mover of shipments up to about 30 tons. There are approximately 35,000 motor carriers in the United States, in addition to independent trucking and private carriage operations owned by firms that transport their own products in company-owned vehicles. Truckers handle everything from heavy machinery to liquid petroleum, refrigerated products, agricultural commodities, building materials, and motor vehicles.

The strategic advantage of motor carriage is the complete door-to-door service provided. Trucks carry only about one-quarter of all ton-mile traffic, but they carry about three-quarters of the total dollar value of merchandise transported. Trucks are faster than rail but are more expensive to use. The greatest disadvantage of motor carrier use is the carrier's susceptibility to interruptions by bad weather.

*Rail*  Rail transport competes for large-size shipments, particularly bulk commodities, as distances increase over 500 miles. A financially healthy rail system is essential to some agricultural and business producers if they are to remain competitive in markets across the country. Rail dominates the other modes of transportation in terms of ton-miles carried but has lost higher-value traffic to other modes. Approximately 37 percent of the freight hauled in the United States goes by rail. Among the advantages to rail shippers are more flexible rates and improved service due to the availability of more sophisticated equipment than was used a decade ago.

*Water*  With 8,500 miles of navigable inland waterways available, the United States inland river system functions as a major cost-efficient and practical method of transporting many business products for firms seeking reduced transportation costs.

Reduced transportation cost is the biggest advantage to the inland river system. One gallon of diesel fuel will move one ton of commodity 59 miles by truck, 202 miles by rail, or 514 miles by barge. The fact that river barge service exists as a competitive transportation system influences the rail and truck industry to keep rates down. The trade-off in moving goods by water transport, naturally, is speed. While talk of air, rail, and truck transportation is in terms of hours or days, barge delivery time is discussed in terms of weeks. The percentage of freight handled by water has remained fairly stable over the years (approximately 15 percent), and water transport is indispensable for overseas freight movement of all shipment sizes.

*Pipeline*  Pipeline transport provides low-cost movement primarily for oil-related and chemical-related liquids such as natural gas. However, a variety of products from liquids to solids can be transported via this mode, including coal in the form of slurry—ground-up coal mixed with water to form sludge. Probably the greatest advantage of pipelines, other than cost savings, is dependability. Routes are fixed, tend to be concentrated regionally, and are seldom affected by weather conditions. Speed is slow, but pipelines are second only to railroads in ton-miles carried domestically.

*Air*  Air transport offers rapid freight movement, with the air-freight buzzword being "time-sensitive." Although air freight is costly, its speed may create savings in lower inventory levels to offset the increased cost. A wide variety of business products—such as electronic parts, small but specialized machinery, and replacement parts—are shipped using this mode.

*Intermodal*  The use of two or more transportation modes to move a product is called *intermodal transport*. A shipment of subassemblies destined for Japan, for example, might move through a combination of air, rail, water, and truck before reaching its final destination. "Birdyback" (air and truck), "piggyback" (rail and truck), and "fishyback" (water and truck) are popular and economical intermodal forms of transport.

### Routing

If the traffic manager has title to the goods (either inbound or outbound), then decisions concerning specific routes over which shipments are to move become his or her responsibility. A practice related to specifying routing instructions is the use of F.O.B. ("free on board") terms, which specify which party—the shipper or the receiver—controls carrier selection and routing of a given shipment. The term *F.O.B. origin* specifies that the receiver is responsible for all transportation charges; *F.O.B. destination* indicates that the shipper is liable. Under F.O.B. origin, the freight receiver selects carriers and specifies routing. If management considers traffic control important, it will negotiate F.O.B. origin terms for inbound traffic and F.O.B. destination terms for outbound traffic.

### Claims Processing

Freight claims are made against carriers for loss or damage to freight in transit, for unreasonable delay in the movement of freight, and for freight charges that have been improperly assessed. Because of the complexity of rate structures, many companies hire outside *freight auditors* to examine their freight bills at a commission rate of 50 percent of the amount of claims recovered. The physical distribution function within the business-to-business firm must present loss or damage claims to carriers as soon as possible after receipt of a shipment, as there is a time limit for filing a claim, in addition to the very real possibility of cases of shared responsibility between the shipper and the carrier for damage or shortage.

### Operation of Private Transportation

Many firms have instituted private carriage operations rather than using "for-hire" transportation. *Private transportation* (that is, the user and the carrier are one and the same) frequently offers potential savings in transportation costs, possibly better service because of the flexibility of routes and schedules, greater speed, a reduction of loss and damages, and accessibility to transportation equipment when needed. Indeed, inadequate transportation service and uncertain delivery times may force a firm to buy or lease private transportation. While this investment can be significant, it may be necessary for service improvement.

---

**Concept Review**

1. How can physical distribution enhance the profit performance of a company?

2. What are the major advantages of pipeline transport?

3. What is intermodal transport?

## Deregulation

One of the most controversial areas in the history of American business has been the regulation of business. By the late 1970s, regulation had created so many absurd inefficiencies that lawmakers were driven to change. Then *deregulation* put transportation near the center of the controversy.

Before deregulation of the transportation industry, trucking, rail, and air freight carriers were not permitted to compete on price, to guarantee delivery time, to vary routing, or to grant long-term, confidential rate contracts. Without delivery date guarantees, however, inventory management techniques such as JIT were impossible! Benefits from deregulation have been widespread, as costs for all transportation modes have fallen. Indeed, a significant gain from deregulation has been a substantial decline in the overall logistical costs of business. It is interesting to note that, at the time of deregulation, one of the biggest problems transportation companies faced was a lack of understanding of basic business marketing fundamentals. Ironically, these fundamentals would eventually determine the new form and future of the transportation industry itself.

## BUSINESS MARKETING IN ACTION

### OCEAN LOGISTICS

Maersk Line is the world's largest provider of containerized transport solutions. Its service network spans six continents, with more than 320 offices in over 95 countries. Maersk handles over 7 million container moves per year, and its ships make more than 16,500 port calls annually.

As a business marketing professional, you should be familiar with all forms of logistics, particularly those involving intermodal containers that can be transported by ship, truck, rail, and barge. You would be amazed to discover how many of the materials, components, and finished goods that you encounter every day have been transported in containers at some point. In the business world, you will face worldwide competition from goods shipped in containers. Learning about the capabilities of a shipping giant such as Maersk will help you to develop a sense of the magnitude of the container shipping industry.

### Action Assignments

Prepare all of the following for presentation to the class (as you collect information, be sure to download photographs of containers and container ships for your class presentation):

Search the Web and discover the size of standard land/sea steel shipping containers. If you cannot find the information there, find it in a logistics text.

Also, surf through the Maersk website and learn more about the company (www.maersksealand.com). From its home page, click on "Fleet List" and then click on "container vessels." Note the ten ships with the largest freight capacities.

Again at the Maersk home page, click on "schedules" in the lower LEFT of the screen, where you can check the shipping schedules for North America to Europe. The information will vary, depending on the city you choose at the destination country. Note the information on the next available ship for a container to be shipped from Atlanta, Georgia, to Egypt; from Atlanta, Georgia, to Morocco; from Baltimore, Maryland, to Turkey; and from Baltimore, Maryland, to Greece.

## Customer Service in Physical Distribution

Customer service as it relates to the physical distribution function entails providing products at the time and location corresponding to the customer's needs. Customer service is a process of providing *value-added benefits* to the supply chain, meaning providing extra service that makes the product and/or service stand out as better than its competition's. It is an excellent competitive weapon and an important means of differentiating a firm's products and services both in transactional and relationship marketing. Further, value-added benefits can have a major influence on customer loyalty and relationship marketing.

When establishing customer service strategies, marketers need to identify the impact on corporate profitability of decisions affecting business segments such as products, channels, or customers. The customer service levels that might be provided range from very good to very poor. A 100 percent level of satisfaction would indicate that all customers are completely satisfied with product availability. In designing a physical distribution system, the ideal is to develop minimum-cost systems for a range of acceptable levels of customer service; then select the service level that makes the greatest contribution of sales less physical distribution costs. Customers would be 100 percent satisfied if a wide range of products was available at the right time and place in sufficient quantities to meet the needs and wants of all who were willing and able to buy. Of course, this condition rarely occurs because the costs would be prohibitive. Yet, it is possible to achieve high levels of customer satisfaction with properly designed distribution systems.

### Customer Service Standards

A key to success in industrial or business-to-business marketing is the ability of the marketer to satisfy buyers when they place orders. It is extremely important that buyers be able to obtain the products they order, at the right time, at the right place, and at the right price.

## STRATEGY AT WORK

### LB MANUFACTURING OUTSOURCES TRANSPORTATION TO RYDER

For close to 40 years LB Manufacturing has manufactured and provided ductwork for the heating, ventilating, and air conditioning (HVAC) industry. Huge rolls of sheet metal are trucked into LB Manufacturing's plants in Mt. Vernon, Ohio, and Byseville, Ohio. This sheet metal is then cut, formed, manufactured into ductwork, and shipped to customers all along the East Coast.

LB Manufacturing formerly used common carriers for shipments, but problems such as overages, shortages, and damaged goods caused company personnel to rethink this option. They turned to Ryder Integrated Logistics (RIL) to provide vehicles and complete transportation services under a lease agreement that includes RIL maintaining an in-plant transportation office that takes full responsibility for the perfor-

mance of a fleet of nine tractors and twenty-four trailers. The office provides and coordinates all drivers, routing, vehicle maintenance, roadside service, shipping paperwork, and regulatory compliance and also arranges for efficient backhauls (so that trucks do not return empty). Ryder has assumed all the typical traffic management responsibilities, and, in addition, works with LB Manufacturing customers to increase their satisfaction and value perception.

Using RIL as a strategic partner brings LB Manufacturing the services of transportation experts and allows the firm to focus its own resources on the business of sheet metal fabrication. Ryder has helped LB increase its revenue per load by $2,000 to $3,000.

Adapted from: www.ryder.com. July 1999 by permission of Ryder Corporation.

---

Inevitably, the marketer sometimes will fail to meet the expectations of the buyer and will deliver a product late or supply a product that does not meet buyer specifications.

Customer service has traditionally been a frustrating area of physical distribution management and strategy because of the problems involved in establishing a specific, all-inclusive statement of objectives. We can distinguish goals from objectives when establishing customer service standards. Recall that *goals* are broad, generalized statements regarding the overall results that the business firm is attempting to achieve, while *objectives* are the means by which the goals are achieved. Business-to-business firms operating effective logistics systems should develop a set of written customer service standards. These serve as objectives and provide a benchmark against which results can be measured for control purposes. In developing these standards, the place to start is with the customers. What are their service needs? What do competitors offer them? Are the customers willing to pay a bit more for better service? After these questions are answered, realistic standards can be set and an ongoing measurement program can be established to monitor results. Typical standards relate to time, reliability, and loss or damage. The standards must be quantifiable and measurable because deviations from standards must be noted and investigated.

One effective means of service improvement is to identify the causes of customer service complaints and then institute changes to eliminate or minimize customer service breakdowns. Exhibit 11-3 offers major categories of primary service complaints, including traffic and transportation, inventory control, warehousing and packaging, and sales order service.

### Examination of Cost Trade-Offs

**Trade-off analysis** can be defined as the examination of the costs associated with each component of the physical distribution system to ascertain the combination of components that will yield the lowest possible cost for a particular level of customer service. Trade-off analysis recognizes important cost trade-offs between traffic and transportation, inventory control, warehousing and packaging, and sales order service. The interrelationships of these logistical system components are illustrated in Exhibit 11-4. The arrows indicate the

**EXHIBIT 11-3**
**Major Categories of Primary Service Complaints**

*Traffic and transportation*
   Damaged merchandise
   Carrier does not meet standard transit time
   Merchandise delivered prior to date promised
   Carrier fails to follow customer routing
   Carrier does not comply with specific instructions
   Errors present on the bill of lading
   Condition or type of transport equipment not satisfactory

*Inventory control*
   Stockouts
   Contaminated products received
   Product identification errors
   Poor merchandise shipped

*Warehousing and packaging*
   Merchandise delivered late
   Problem with containers in packaging plants
   Special promotion merchandise not specified in delivery
   Warehouse release form errors
   Incorrect types and quantities of merchandise shipped
   Papers not mailed promptly to headquarters
   Field warehouse deliveries of damaged merchandise

*Sales order service*
   Delayed shipments
   Invoice errors
   Sales coding errors
   Brokerage errors
   Special instructions ignored
   No notification of late shipments

trade-offs between activities that must be evaluated in (1) estimating customer-service levels; (2) developing purchasing policies; (3) selecting transportation policies; (4) making warehousing decisions; and (5) setting inventory levels.[9]

Analyzing the costs of alternative combinations of the components for a physical distribution system is essential to guiding the design of the system:

> Storing all finished goods inventory in a small number of distribution centers helps minimize warehousing costs but leads to an increase in freight expense. Similarly, savings resulting from large-order purchases may be entirely offset by greater inventory carrying costs. In a nutshell, reductions in one set of costs invariably increase the costs of other logistical components. Effective management and real cost savings can be accomplished only by viewing distribution as an integrated system and minimizing its total cost.[10]

Because some components of the physical distribution function are more important than others in a given firm, trade-off analysis must be directed to those components that make up the major portion of distribution costs.

### *The Impact of Logistical Service on Business Channel Members*

Logistical service levels affect the relationship between the manufacturer and the customer, as well as the operations of channel members. Inefficient service to middlemen either increases their costs by forcing them to carry higher inventory levels, or results in stockouts, leading to a loss of business. In fact, poor logistical support in the channel negates the marketing effort of the firm by constricting potential sales and antagonizing middlemen (see Channel Conflict in Chapter 10). Both the length and the consistency of the order-cycle

**EXHIBIT 11-4**
**Cost Trade-Offs Required in Logistics**

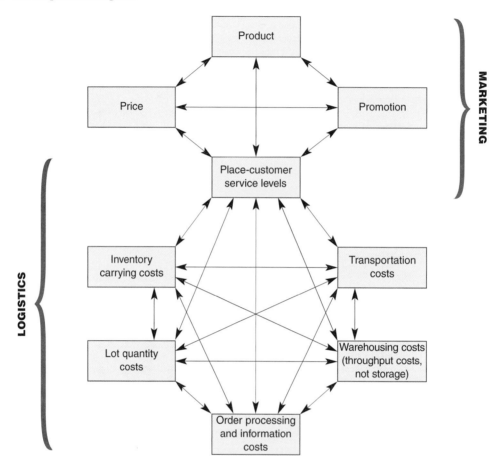

**Marketing objective:** Allocate resources to the marketing mix in such a manner as to maximize the long-run profitability of the firm.

**Logistics objective:** Minimize total costs given the customer service objective.

**Where total costs equal:** transportation costs + warehousing costs + order processing and information costs + lot quantity costs + inventory carrying costs

Reprinted from *Strategic Logistics Management,* Third Edition, by James R. Stock and Douglas M. Lambert, p. 42, © 1992 The McGraw-Hill Companies, Inc. Reprinted by permission of the publisher.

period (time from placement of orders to receipt of products) affect the level of distributors' inventories, which generally represent their highest asset investment and one of the largest distribution expenses. Rarely will distributors remain loyal if poor logistical service is harmful to end users. Inventory control systems should be linked to manufacturers' information systems, and if intermediaries are to receive a sufficient level of logistical service, information systems must provide accurate sales forecasts. Alert business marketing managers must learn and be ever vigilant for telltale symptoms of a poor physical distribution system.

## Warehousing

Decisions regarding the location of warehouse facilities offer tremendous opportunities for acquiring increased market share while generating cost savings. Decisions on warehouse

## BUSINESS MARKETING IN ACTION

### MOTOR TRANSPORT LOGISTICS

Unless your customer happens to have a rail connection or dock facilities for water transport, probably you will be making the deliveries that satisfy their needs via motor transport (trucking). Even the few companies lucky enough to have direct rail, river, or sea connections still receive many shipments by motor transport. Motor transport has such great potential to impact customer satisfaction that all business marketers must have a thorough understanding of its operations.

### Action Assignment

**Team 1:** You are the traffic manager for a major corporation with a need to ship 20,000 pounds of automotive components per week to a customer assembly plant 1,000 miles away. With your university as the origin, choose the locations accordingly, selecting a city about 1,000 miles away as the destination. Explore the websites of major U.S. motor carriers and evaluate their information in deciding which carriers to contact. Additional research will yield the rate class and prices offered by various carriers on this hypothetical shipment. Also, your university purchasing office may have information that is useful. Present your findings to the class, making a specific carrier recommendation based upon your research.

**Team 2:** Repeat the assignment for Team 1. The destination for this shipment of automotive components is Mexico City. Resources:

| | |
|---|---|
| (www.roadway.com) | (www.abfs.com) |
| (www.yellowfreight.com) | (www.overnite.com) |
| (www.schneider.com) | (www.fedexfreight.fedex.com) |
| (www.con-way.com) | (www.swiftfreight.com) |
| (www.jbhunt.com) | (www.vikingfreight.com) |
| (www.ryder.com) | |

Reprinted with permission from *IndustryWeek,* January 18, 1999, p. 69. Copyright, Penton Media, Inc., Cleveland, Ohio.

---

location affect delivery time to customers and the ability to meet customer service expectations. As part of distribution strategy, marketing decisions on the number and location of warehouses are important in improving customer service and in supporting the inventory decisions of the firm. Warehousing is an important facilitating activity. Indeed, good warehouse location eliminates (or reduces) the need for costly airfreight by keeping business products readily available in local markets.

When a supplier or reseller owns or leases storage space, it is classified as a private warehouse. Private warehouses are used primarily when an organization's sales volume is relatively stable, justifying investment in a fixed facility. In addition, private warehouses might offer property appreciation or tax advantages through depreciation of the facility, as well as allowing the marketing manager total control over the warehouse operation.

The alternative to owning or leasing storage space is using a public warehouse. Professional managers operate these firms, providing warehouse services for a fee. These for-hire facilities are available to a business requiring storage or handling of goods. Public warehousing has been growing steadily over the past several years and is a major player in today's logistics sector. Most public operators are willing to supply virtually any type of service the customer wishes.

Manufacturers offering a narrow product line to many market areas often find it economical to ship products to public warehouses instead of maintaining privately owned or leased warehouse facilities near production facilities. A public warehouse often is the most economical way to serve a marginal market—a market that the firm is beginning to develop but that does not yet justify investment in a private warehouse facility. Additionally, many public warehouses have begun to offer a variety of logistical services to their business clients beyond the physical handling and storage of materials and merchandise. Some will repackage products to meet the orders of end users, label the orders, and arrange local delivery for them. Also, many link their computer with that of the manufacturer to facilitate order processing and inventory updating. More than 15,000 public warehouses operate in the United States today.

1. Why is the establishment of customer service standards so important?

2. What is the function of trade-off analysis?

3. What effect do decisions on warehouse locations have on customer service?

## Inventory Control

Business firms recognize that too high an inventory level causes high carrying costs and potential obsolescence. (**Carrying costs** occur when stocks of goods for sale are held; they consist of the opportunity cost of the investment tied up in inventory and the costs associated with storage, such as space rental and insurance fees.) Conversely, too low an inventory can result in high restocking and production costs, as well as the risk of lost sales and damage to customer goodwill. The level of inventories maintained relates to the movement and storage of materials. The amount of inventory in storage, in transit, and in process can be substantially altered through coordinated management of the production, physical distribution, and sales functions. Capital costs in inventory, transportation, and storage, and the costs of inventory obsolescence, are traded off in order to control total costs and maintain minimal inventory levels consistent with production needs. It does not seem reasonable to expect a firm to be able to fill and ship every order from inventory.

Because of this inventory-cost trade-off, most business marketing managers seem to accept the *80/20 axiom:* 80 percent of the sales are generated by 20 percent of the product line. The major implication of the 80/20 axiom is that marketers must manage their inventory selectively, treating fast- and slow-moving items differently. If a company has half its inventory committed to products that provide only 20 percent of the unit-sales volume, it can gain significantly by reducing inventories of the slow sellers to the point at which their turnover rate approximates that of the fast sellers. Inventory represents a sizable investment for most companies. The goal of inventory management is to minimize both the investment and the fluctuation, while at the same time filling customers' orders promptly and accurately.

### Just-in-Time Inventory Concept

The *just-in-time (JIT)* approach, as introduced in Chapter 4, is a concept affecting inventory control, purchasing, and production scheduling. JIT principles are applied to multipoint distribution of product to customers. Every aspect of the process is analyzed to determine where there might be opportunities to minimize inventory levels and maximize flexibility. The basic idea of JIT is that carrying any inventory is wrong because it eats up capital and masks problems of inefficiency, poor quality, erratic delivery, poor communications, and so on. (See Exhibit 11-5 for a brief discussion of how Chrysler has improved efficiency at one of its assembly plants, thereby trimming inventory levels on the production floor by nearly $2 million.)

JIT inventory management makes sure that those involved in the manufacturing process get what is needed "just in time." For instance, a Bendix plant adopted a JIT system and was able to convert 10,000 square feet of floor space from storage to manufacturing usage. Black and Decker, IBM, Firestone, General Motors, Harley-Davidson, and many

**EXHIBIT 11-5**
**Chrysler Puts JIT into High Gear**

Compared to conventional automobile plants, there is very little inventory on the 1.3-million-square-foot production floor at Chrysler's Jefferson North assembly plant in Detroit, Michigan. High-value parts, which account for 87 percent of the value of parts that go into a Grand Cherokee, arrive at the plant less than 6 hours before they are needed. These critical parts come into the plant in sequence. The effects of in-sequence, just-in-time delivery are remarkable. Efficiency at Jefferson North has improved, and inventory levels on the production floor have been trimmed by nearly $2 million.

**EXHIBIT 11-6**
ABC Inventory
Analysis Example

| Product Grouping | Percent of Company's Total Sales | Percent of Company's Total Products | Customer Service Level |
|---|---|---|---|
| A | 80 | 20 | 95 |
| B | 15 | 30 | 90 |
| C | 5 | 50 | 85 |

other firms are experiencing decreasing costs and higher quality with the JIT inventory system.

To be effective in a firm's inventory-control function, just-in-time purchasing and production scheduling require very careful managerial monitoring. The system necessitates a high level of cooperation and coordination between business suppliers and producers, and between production and marketing personnel in the manufacturing firm. JIT demands a willingness to meet specific customer requirements, including: (1) small lot sizes, (2) frequent deliveries, (3) exact quantities, (4) precise arrival time, and (5) "six sigma" (near perfect) quality. Because production schedules require timely supplies, shipments must arrive on time or plants may have to be shut down. Because transportation modes vary in reliability, the choice of mode used is very important.

### ABC Inventory Analysis

**ABC inventory analysis** reduces inventory needs by assigning different customer service labels to goods based on sales and profits. ABC analysis resembles the 80/20 axiom discussed previously in the chapter. For example, A inventory items would represent the 20 percent of inventory that contributed 80 percent of sales. Similarly, B inventory items might represent 30 percent of inventory that contributes 15 percent of sales. So-called C inventory items might represent 50 percent of all inventory items that constitute only 5 percent in dollar sales (See Exhibit 11-6).

ABC inventory analysis assigns levels of priorities to A, B, and C inventory items. Generally, A items would have the highest level of safety stock, with B and C items having proportionately lower levels. Another way to employ the ABC inventory analysis would be to require a 95 percent customer service level for A items, a 90 percent level for B items, and an 85 percent level for C items.

Of course, a JIT relationship with a supplier would remove the issues EOQ addresses. The cost of placing an automated JIT order (computer to computer) would approach zero, inventory would be minimal, and there would be a fixed price without additional supplier set-up costs and without small quantity price penalties. Even where companies purchase key materials by JIT, there are usually other products (e.g., MRO) that are still purchased based on EOQ concepts.

### The EOQ Model

Inventory-control analysts have developed a number of techniques to help logistics managers effectively control inventory. The most basic of these techniques is the **economic order quantity (EOQ)** model. This particular technique emphasizes a cost trade-off between two costs involved with inventory: inventory handling costs, which increase with the addition of more inventory, and order costs, which decrease as the quantity ordered increases. As Exhibit 11-7 indicates, these two cost items trade off to determine the optimal order quantity of each product. The EOQ point in Exhibit 11-7 is the point at which total cost is minimized. By placing an order for this amount as needed, a firm can minimize its inventory costs. The EOQ model still is widely used in industry today, although often hidden within MRP (Materials Requirement Planning) or other purchasing software.

**EXHIBIT 11-7** **Balancing Order Costs and Holding Costs for Inventory**

**Calculating the EOQ:** The following formula is utilized to determine the EOQ.

$$EOQ = \sqrt{\frac{2DP}{CV}} \text{, where}$$

*EOQ* = the economic order quantity (in units),
*D* = the annual demand or usage of the product (in units),
*P* = the cost of placing an order (dollars per order),
*C* = the annual, inventory-carrying cost (expressed as a percentage of product cost),
*V* = the value or cost per unit of the item. The unit might consist of a single item or a prepackaged box, containing a dozen items, a gross, or even more.

In the formula, *D* is an estimate based upon the demand forecast for the item. *P* is calculated from the firm's cost records. *C*, also an estimate, is based upon the costs of handling, insurance, interest, storage, depreciation, and taxes. Since the cost of these may vary over time, *V* also is likely to be an estimate. By inserting specific data into the formula, the EOQ can be determined. Consider, for example, the following data:

*D* = 5,500 units
*P* = 7.50
*C* = 10 percent = 0.10
*V* = $12.90

$$EOQ = \sqrt{\frac{(2)(5,500)(7.50)}{(12.90)(0.10)}}$$

= 252.9 units

Because the EOQ model involves a mathematical formula, the calculation often results in a fractional answer that must be rounded to the next whole number to determine the economic order quantity. Thus, the EOQ in the example above would be rounded to 253 units.

**Concept Review**

1. What is the relationship between the 80/20 axiom and an ABC inventory analysis?

2. What is the function of the EOQ model of inventory control?

**Summary**

- To compete against the best in the world, firms must consider their strategic contribution to the channel and the specific value it creates for the channel's ultimate end user. To assist in this effort, new approaches to management have been introduced including the ideas of *value proposition, value chain,* and *supply chain management.*

- The concepts of value-added services, value chain, and value proposition can be brought together under a new philosophy of integrated and synchronized *supply chain management.* The supply chain management philosophy is a dramatic departure from previous approaches and is much more than a dull distribution concept. It is the foundation for global competitiveness. The quest for constant improvement is a strategic necessity but there are barriers to achievement of effective SCM.

- As marketers cooperatively create value-producing supply chains, the issues of efficient materials flow and transportation—supply chain logistics—cannot be overlooked. Marketers must understand the central role of supply chain logistics in SCM and must be able to provide consistent value to direct customers and end users of the supply chain system.

- Physical distribution has the potential to enhance the production, marketing, and profit performance of any company that produces a tangible product. Logistics embodies two primary product flows: physical supply and physical distribution management.

- The functions of business traffic management are broad and vary in intensity with the type of industry, the type of product being shipped, and the size and number of shipments being transported. Primary

# WHAT WOULD YOU DO?

## SHIPMENT RELIABILITY

Helen Markey, sales representative for Plastics Products Unlimited (PPU), was meeting with a very important customer's buyer. She was a little worried because she was new to the job (having just graduated from college the previous year), and this was her first experience with a late delivery and parts rejection. Helen didn't expect too much grief on the late delivery issue, because the parts had been delivered only two days late. Also, there had been a good reason: a major snowstorm had shut down most of the region.

Because the problem dimensions in question were only a few thousandths of an inch over the dimension allowed on the part print (blueprint), Helen was hopeful that the customer could be talked into using the parts. PPU certainly didn't want several hundred thousand of these parts rejected and returned, and surely there wasn't any way to rework the dimension to correct the size. Besides, a decision not to accept the parts would mean that the customer would have to stop production, since PPU was its sole source for plastic molded products.

Helen's boss had directed her to: (a) solve the problem by persuading the customer to use the parts, and (b) if possible, get a permanent revision making the tolerance allowable (so this doesn't happen again). If necessary, Helen could offer the customer a slight price reduction on the shipments in question. As a last resort, Helen should refuse the company's request to produce more parts and shut down the customer's production line. Helen was sure that it would never come to that. She felt ready for the meeting.

Across the table from Helen were buying center members, including the customer's buyer, quality manager, and design engineer. Helen started talking, but almost immediately the buyer held up the palm of her hand in a signal to stop. She looked Helen in the eye with a serious expression and said, "Helen, you are new to this and probably don't understand what is going on here. We depend totally on your company's commitment to on-time delivery and total quality. When you let us down, you harm our company, our employees, and our customers. I can't allow that. The name for suppliers who let us down is ELIMINATED."

Helen sputtered, "But there was a snowstorm!" The buyer went on, "There are acts of God that are unpredictable, but snow happens every winter in this region! If your company doesn't have backup plans for things that you know could happen, how can you call yourselves dependable? If, on the other hand, a volcanic eruption happened in Chicago, then that would be an unpredictable act of God. Problems like snow, truck breakdowns, strikes, and production delays are problems that you can anticipate. So, they are not excuses! They are nothing! Can you see that I don't need excuses—I need parts on time that are ready for production? It's my right as a customer, to have the right parts, at the right time, in the right condition!"

The buyer continued, "Regarding the unacceptable quality problem, there are only two possibilities that explain your company's shipment. First, your company did not know that the parts it shipped did not meet the part print requirements. That means that your quality system is not capable, and you should be eliminated as a supplier. The second possibility is that your company knew that the parts were bad and shipped them anyway. That would mean you *would* be eliminated as a supplier. That's where we stand, so why don't you pick it up from there?"

Helen thought to herself, "I am way over my head on this one. I could dream up a story that proves this is not my company's fault. Maybe I could blame it all on the shipper and quality control. I could beg off and say that I need to talk this over with my boss, but that would make me look ineffective. Besides, I need to show my boss that I can be firm, or he will think that I let customers walk all over me." Helen looked the buyer in the eye just as seriously and said quietly, "OK, if you want to be unreasonable, PPU will not be able to produce any of these products for you. Where would you like your injection molds and trimming dies to be sent?"

### Assignment

Define the ethical issues for all involved. Develop an action plan for Helen.

---

functions of business traffic management include mode selection, routing, claims processing, and the operation of private transportation.

- Deregulation of the transportation industry has brought about a tremendous change in the competitive environment of that industry and has forced carriers to become more customer oriented. Major benefits from deregulation have included reduced logistics costs and greater efficiency.

- Customer service standards serve as objectives and provide a benchmark against which results can be measured for control purposes. The establishment of a customer service policy is extremely important because so many facets of customer service interface with other functions of the firm, such as credit rules, complaint procedures, minimum orders, order cycles, inventory returns, stockouts, and proposed deliveries.

- Decisions regarding the location of warehouse facilities offer tremendous opportunities for acquiring increased market share and generating cost savings. Either private warehouses or public warehouses may be used, depending on the objectives of the firm involved.

- Business-to-business firms realize that too high an inventory level causes high carrying costs and potential obsolescence; likewise, too low a level can result in high restocking and production costs, as well as the loss of both sales and customer goodwill. Just-in-time inventory, ABC inventory analysis, and EOQ control models are commonly used today in maintaining efficient inventory levels.

## Key Terms

ABC inventory analysis
carrying cost
economic order quantity (EOQ)
logistics

mode
physical distribution
supply chain
supply chain management

trade-off analysis
traffic management
value chain
value proposition

## Review Questions

1. Discuss three different viewpoints of physical distribution.

2. Identify the basic functions of business traffic management. Briefly discuss six methods of transportation available to business marketers. What are the basic advantages of using private transportation?

3. Explain what is meant by customer service in physical distribution management. How does a firm decide what level of customer service it should provide for its customers? Why is a company's establishment of a customer service policy so important? How does cost trade-off analysis help to provide a minimum-cost physical distribution system?

4. What is the difference between a private and a public warehouse? How does the business marketing manager decide which to use?

5. How is the 80/20 axiom related to inventory management? Describe how JIT inventory, the EOQ model, and ABC analysis operate in business marketing.

## Case 11-1

# JIT at Portland Industries

This case was written by Dr. Roger Gomes and Dr. Patricia Knowles, Clemson University, ©1999

Clayton Jefferson, distribution manager for Portland Industries, was considering proposing that his biggest customer consolidate all its purchases with Portland and begin purchasing under a JIT system. Clayton assumed that the customer was currently purchasing on an EOQ formula based on trade-offs involving volume price breaks, cost to process an order, delivery premiums on smaller shipments, and requirements for safety stock versus usage rates. Clayton suspected that JIT would require a price discount, even though shipping costs would go up. Still, JIT could be such a differential advantage that it could be used as a preemptive strategy to gain all of the customer's business. Clayton knew that a distribution differential advantage often is very difficult for a competitor to match. (In comparison, a competitor can very quickly nullify a pricing differential advantage, which is one reason marketers do not like to compete on price.)*

*If Clayton sounds like he is thinking like a marketer (customer value driven), that is because he is. Most major universities recognize logistics as the place (P) utility of the 4Ps that define marketing responsibility. Although distribution and logistics are very interdisciplinary, their connection to marketing is strong. Marketing majors often are hired into logistics positions. Logistics managers often spend time in sales positions, and it is not unusual for distribution to manage customer service.

**EXHIBIT 11-8**

| SKU item | Current average usage per week | Current lot size | Current selling $/each | Current shipping $/unit | JIT lot size | JIT selling $/each | JIT shipping $/unit |
|---|---|---|---|---|---|---|---|
| A | 110 | 2500 | 78.77 | 5.88 | 10 | 67.58 | 9.67 |
| B | 100 | 2500 | 65.89 | 7.75 | 10 | 61.33 | 11.45 |
| C | 612 | 5000 | 11.77 | 1.55 | 25 | 10.44 | 2.35 |
| D | 30 | 1000 | 113.67 | 7.89 | 5 | 103.04 | 10.99 |
| E | 45 | 1000 | 67.66 | 9.35 | 5 | 61.45 | 13.67 |
| F | 1100 | 10000 | 5.89 | 0.75 | 40 | 5.30 | 1.23 |
| G | 23 | 1000 | 235.07 | 16.88 | 5 | 210.56 | 24.78 |
| H | 2200 | 25000 | 6.89 | 1.39 | 100 | 6.22 | 2.12 |
| I | 579 | 5000 | 16.38 | 4.67 | 25 | 14.89 | 7.11 |
| J | 390 | 5000 | 9.37 | 3.33 | 25 | 8.99 | 5.02 |

To understand the situation from the customer's perspective, Clayton wanted to analyze the potential value added from the customer's perspective. He gathered the information shown in Exhibit 11-8.

Clayton based his numbers on the customer's usage remaining the same, his estimate of the lowest probable JIT selling price, and his estimate of the minimum added cost for smaller shipments. Luckily, there was a lot of competition for "express" shipping of small lots, and Portland already was a major shipper of small quantities to many geographically diverse customers. Portland received special volume pricing discounts from UPS. Based on the above JIT numbers, Clayton would be attempting to gain an additional $1,000,000 in similar new business (i.e., new stock-keeping units, or SKUs). The average profit margin at the current selling price is 61.3 percent. Clayton found some information in industry trade journals that suggested that manufacturing direct cost might be reduced 10 percent to 35 percent if Portland utilized JIT in its own processes.

## Assignment

After working through the numbers, Clayton may or may not approach marketing with this suggestion. Put together a presentation supporting or rejecting Clayton's proposal to supply this customer using discounted JIT prices and small lot delivery. Consider both situations (if the additional business is gained, and if it is not) in your calculations. Calculate the costs from both the customer's perspective and from Portland's perspective. Where necessary, use managerial judgment or research to fill in necessary data and assumptions (just be sure to state them clearly).

### Case 11-2

## Global Motors Ltd.—Fuji Division Understanding the "Kanban" Pull Process Theory That Drives JIT Distribution

This case was written by Dr. Roger Gomes and Dr. Patricia Knowles, Clemson University, © 1999.

Mr. Shigeo Tatsuno, supply chain integrator for Global Motors Ltd.—Fuji Division, was one of a series of speakers at the company's worldwide supplier's meeting held in Hong Kong. In attendance were technical, marketing, and top management representatives from each of GML's suppliers (often called supply chain alliance partners). Each supplier company was responsible for a particular commodity group. For example, there was a company that produced all the wiring bundles that GML used, another that produced all their brake systems, another that produced their tire assemblies, etc.

Besides the usual meeting agenda of new product introduction and networking, the company had set up a presentation of the "Kanban" Pull Process Theory, a tour of GML's Hong Kong JIT automated assembly operations, and additional training sessions to further develop the theme. Mr. Tatsuno had presented the theory in a morning session and arranged for a tour of a subcompact automobile assembly operation in the afternoon. Even before the tour was complete, Mr. Tatsuno could tell that many in the group did not fully understand what they were seeing. He thought, "Western eyes are so used to seeing complex computer-based 'push' systems like Material Requirements Planning (MRP) that they miss the beauty inherent in the simplicity of Kanban." The objective of Mr. Tatsuno's second training session, to be held the next morning, was to increase the group's understanding of the Kanban process, how it reacts to demand changes, and how it drives distribution material flow along the supply chain.

The next morning, Mr. Tatsuno began with a review using PowerPoint:

*Slide 1.*   "Kanban—a simple manual pull process for driving an assembly process. It is based on the principle that in-process inventory must be minimized and that demand will pull material through each step in the process."

*Slide 2.*   "No step in the process will be completed until the next step in the process has used the lot last made by the previous step. Lot sizes will be minimal—with a lot size of one being common."

*Slide 3.*   "Example—The lot size for this example is one unit. If you are stamping an automobile door from a sheet of steel, only when the last door (lot) *you* stamped is taken by the next operation are you authorized to stamp out another door to replace the one taken. For the operation *before* yours, only when you take the sheet of steel they processed is that operation authorized to cut another sheet to replace the one you took."

*Slide 4.*   "Every step is connected by the same philosophy. When a finished car is driven off the assembly line, the operator of the previous step is authorized to complete another, and so forth back through the process all the way back to the raw materials. If the lot has not been taken by the next operation, the operator will need to work on something else (e.g., the next set-up, maintenance, etc). This is very different than the western management "push" philosophy of using "production control and scheduling" departments assisted by powerful computer programs to assign people and machines to maximize machine utilization. With Kanban we do not consider machine utilization; our mission is to minimize in-process inventory."

*Slide 5.*   "As an operation is finished, the worker places a card indicating completion on the lot. When the next operation takes the lot, the card is returned to the worker to indicate that he/she is authorized to perform the operation again. It is the card that gives the "Kanban" process its name (even though today a light or terminal indicator may perform the card's function electronically)."

Mr. Tatsuno was a wise man and a skilled interpreter of international body language. It was clear to him that many in his audience still did not understand (particularly the non-technical individuals from marketing and top management). In his younger days, he would have become frustrated, but as a senior executive he just felt even more challenged. During lunch he sketched out a classroom simulation to demonstrate a pull demand driven process.

Returning to the classroom after lunch the group was presented the following instructions:

## Kanban Exercise

1. The classroom is our assembly line and the material flow goes up the rows and across the front, to the door (see the drawing in Exhibit 11-9). The front seat closest to the door (shaded in the drawing) is the last step in the process. Fill in any empty row seats so all the empty seats (if any) are in the back of your row. The rear filled seat in each row is the beginning of the process for that row and there should be a pile of papers behind those seats (representing materials coming in from suppliers—represented by triangles in the drawing).

2. To start the simulation, each person (represented by stars in the drawing) will be handed a piece of paper. Each person is a machine assembly operator and your operation is to put your name on the paper. When you are done with your operation put the paper on the floor in the aisle between your chair and the person in front of you (so they can reach it).

3. When the simulation starts, at some point you will see the person in front of you take the paper you put down. Then (and only then), you are to reach down behind you, pick up the paper (or papers) that the person behind you put down, mark the top page with your name, and put it down on the floor between you and the next person (as you did before). That is all there is to it. Wait for the one you just put down to be taken, then reach back and pick up the last one(s) the person behind you put down, mark it, and put it down to replace the one(s) that the next operation took. By waiting to do your operation until the last one you processed has been used, you are being "pull-demand driven." (As a machine operator in a traditional American "push" driven plant, you would be assigned a

**EXHIBIT 11-9**

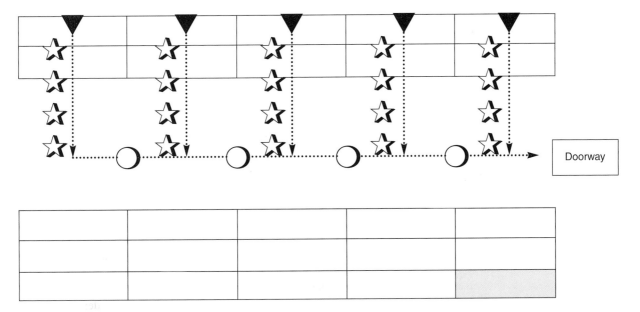

Front of Room

Front of Room

rate of perhaps 1000 pieces per hour to complete, regardless of what was needed at the next steps.)

4. Specific instructions for people in special seats.

*Last seat in a row:* Since there is no operation before yours, when necessary take a paper from the stack behind you (which is on the floor as if there was an operation behind you). The stack represents the capacity of JIT suppliers to replace each lot you take.

*First seat in the row farthest from the door:* Pick up the paper(s) from the person behind you, mark the paper, and put it on the floor toward the next seat across the front in the direction of the door (so the first person in the row second farthest from the door can reach it). Place it between you and the next front seat in the area shown as a circle in Exhibit 11-11.

*All the remaining front seats in a row:* You have the hardest job in the plant. You have to take material from behind you and from the side, combine them, and place them toward the other side (so that the person in the next front seat toward the door can reach it). Perhaps it will help if you visualize that your row is creating the car's hood. The rear-most person took the steel as it comes from the supplier and cut off a piece, the next person stamped it into the shape of a hood, the next person painted it, etc. The person right behind you put a finished hood on the floor near you. The person in the front row seat on your side away from the door just put a car body down between you. You do nothing until the person next to you (toward the doorway) takes the last "finished body plus hood assembly" you put down. When you see that one taken, reach to the side (the

**EXHIBIT 11-10**

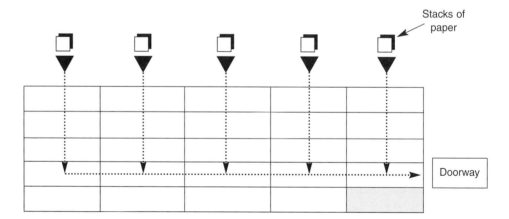

**EXHIBIT 11-11**

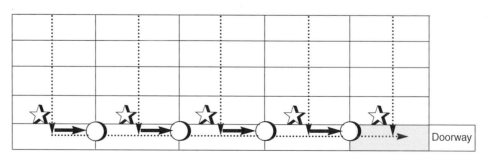

Here

circle space beside you in the diagram) and take a car body (represented by papers), then reach behind you for a hood (represented by papers) combine them, and place them so that the next person across the front can reach them (the circle space on your side toward the door). Then wait until that one is taken before you do it again. (This may sound complicated, but after one cycle it will be easy.)

5. Remember, do nothing until the next person in the process takes the "product" you just assembled. In a real plant you probably couldn't see that the one that you just assembled had been taken. Therefore, a ticket circulates between you and that location. When the next operation uses up the unit you just assembled, they take the ticket off it, and the ticket is sent back to you. When you get the ticket, you know that they used up the product you just assembled, so you assemble another, put the ticket on it, and send it forward. The name of the ticket … a *Kanban*.

6. As you would expect, as the assemblies move up the rows they will have had more and more operations done, so the stack of paper that moves on to the next operation gets bigger. Don't try to sign every sheet, just the top one.

After everyone read the instructions they were again totally confused but were reminded to simply follow the directions. At this point, people were grumbling and complaining about this task being "the dumbest most complicated thing they had ever seen." Mr. Tatsuno was not discouraged and with dignity walked to the door and with a great flourish reached down and took the "product" from the floor by the front seat closest to the door. "Observe," he said, "I drive the finished car from the assembly line."

Nothing happened for several long moments, but soon like a wave with a mind of its own, papers moved forward one position. "Again!" Mr. Tatsuno said and drove off another car (removed the paper). "Again!" "Again!" Every time he took a finished product the pull effect pulsed through the plant. After only a few repetitions everyone smiled and said, "Ahh!" Mr. Tatsuno smiled—at last learning was taking place.

Mr. Butler, who had been one of the most confused people in the room, raised his hand. "Mr. Tatsuno," he said, "I sense a certain beauty in the simplicity of this demand-driven pull process. There are no computers or people scheduling our operations, yet we all know what to do. We respond with just the right production for whatever demand that is present." Mr. Tatsuno thought, "Perhaps there is hope for us all."

Next, Mr. Tatsuno moved to the back of one of the rows for the final point of the exercise. "Now," he said, "observe what happens to our process when we do not have the product available on time." He removed one stack of papers representing a supplier and brought it with him to the door. As he passed the front seat closest to the door he reached down and snatched the papers representing a finished car. The classroom process moved to replace it, but as Mr. Tatsuno "drove off more cars" everyone could see the parts shortage progressively shutting down more and more operations. "Ahh!" the class collectively thought, "we understand!'

Mr. Tatsuno finished by saying, "This is why you need to understand what terms like *pull process* and *Kanban* mean because it is what drives our operation. All operations are interdependent. If your products are not 100 percent quality and 100 percent on time, our entire operation suffers. We cannot have suppliers who allow that to happen.

## Assignment

Make whatever adjustments are necessary for your classroom type, and conduct the above production process simulation. You will need at least a ream of paper from your instructor. Begin with Mr. Tatsuno's presentation to the class. The objective is for learning to take place.

Keep in mind that marketers do not leave things to chance. Practice with your team before you try to do the simulation with the whole class. In an empty classroom, place your team in one row, give each a sheet of paper, have them mark it and place it at their feet. Place a stack of paper behind the last person in the row. Every time you remove the front seat person's paper the process should replace it.

Once you have that working, try doing the same with the team in the front seats across the front (they will each need a stack of paper behind them and one sheet between them). Let's say you have persons "A," "B," "C," "D," and "E" in the first seat in each row across the front. "A" is toward the windows, and "E" is by the door. From their perspective the door is on their left. "A" has put a car body down between him and "B." If "A" sees "B" take that car body, he needs to reach behind him, do his operation (mark the paper), and put the next finished car body where the last one was taken from. Then he waits until that one is taken. Now when "B" sees the last unit she finished taken by "C," she reaches over for the car body "A" put down and combines it with a hood taken from behind her. She places her finished subassembly between her and "C" where the last one was taken from. Then "B" does nothing until "C" takes what she just put down.

It is very important that each operator only respond to the next person in line removing material. That is, "A" responds to an action by "B" and "B" responds to an action by "C" and so forth. It is not at all correct if everyone sees the professors drive off the car, and in response everyone does one more of his or her operation. Only "E" should respond to the car being driven off. "E" then takes the last unit "D" processed and does his operation. Then "D" responds by taking the last unit "C" finished and does her operation. It should be like a wave starting with "E" and working back toward "A." When the whole class is in place, every time a completed car is driven off from "E" a wave of activity should progressively work back across the front toward "A" and down the rows from front to back. If you drive off one car and watch, the activity should end with the last person in "A's" row.

Be sure that your team understands how the material flows up the rows and across the front. In the total class simulation, have your team members watch and help the front row. Sometimes someone in a front seat will forget that he or she has to take the papers from behind him or her and combine them with that coming from across the front. You will probably have to remind them several times that they only do their operation when the last one they completed is taken. Good luck. Actually, it is great fun when you get it set up right.

---

**CASE 11-3**

# Giles Laboratories

Paul McNaughton, director of distribution services for Giles Laboratories, a wholly owned subsidiary of the worldwide Thurber Pharmaceutical group of companies, was under strong pressure from top management to reduce the number of field warehouses that the company maintained throughout the United States. Top management believed that the company could manage on fewer distribution facilities without hurting sales operations. They were concerned about Giles having more warehouses than the parent company even though the parent carried more products at a higher unit-sales volume. They were also disturbed by the fact that Giles' main competitor had fewer warehouses giving the same national market coverage.

At the beginning of 1996, Giles Laboratories had 37 field warehouses, of which 33 were public. Four warehouses were owned by the parent company, but contractual arrangements

This case was made possible by the cooperation of a business firm that remains anonymous. It was written by Albert M. Ladores under the direction of Bernard J. La Londe of the faculty of Marketing and Logistics. The Ohio State University. Revised by Douglas M. Lambert.

with them paralleled those with public warehouses. In addition to the 37 field warehouses, Giles owned four plant warehouses that served the field warehouses and customers located in areas where these plant warehouses were situated.

By March 1996, McNaughton was faced with the decision to phase out the public warehouse at Columbus, Ohio, and serve the customers in the area directly from the main plant warehouse at Indianapolis, Indiana. This meant extending the service area of the Indianapolis facility beyond Dayton, Ohio. The contract with the Columbus warehouse was up for renewal in mid-April.

## Thurber Pharmaceuticals

Giles was part of a group of companies that was controlled by Thurber Pharmaceuticals. Although the parent corporation specialized in a variety of prescription drugs, the products of the subsidiary companies ranged from food items to consumer sundries.

Each subsidiary operated as an autonomous corporate entity with its own set of executive officers and was relatively free to set its own policies in marketing, research, and manufacturing activities. Control by Thurber took the form of broad intercorporate policies and close monitoring of significant investment decisions. With the exception of the products of one or the subsidiary companies, an international division supervised the manufacture and marketing of all products in foreign countries.

## Background on Giles Laboratories

Giles and its major competitor enjoyed about 75 percent of the nutrient and dietary-food market, with Giles' share of the total market approximately 40 percent.

### Product Lines

The company manufactured 35 variations of one basic mixture of raw materials, and product differences were determined primarily by additives and calorie content. Finished products came in both a liquid concentrate and a powder packed in cans of various sizes. The Indianapolis plant, which was the largest and oldest of the company's four plants, produced 25 items of the product line. Each of the other plants manufactured as many of 12 of the products.

### Sales Operations

Approximately 90 percent of the company's sales were derived from consumer outlets, the most significant of which were department stores, wholesale drug houses, drug chains, and supermarket chains. The balance was sold directly to hospitals for patient use while recovering from illness. Demand for the company's products was not subject to seasonal variations.

Salespeople concentrated their selling efforts on medical practitioners, hospitals, and the major retail outlets. Their function was to promote product awareness by improving the sales distribution of the product lines and to assist retailers in merchandising. With minor exceptions, they did not act as order takers.

### Distribution Organization

Mr. McNaughton, as the company's director of distribution services, reported to the vice president of operations and shared the same rank and status as the comptroller and the director of manufacturing. He had responsibility for four major areas: distribution, operations planning, purchasing, and production planning, each headed by a manager reporting directly to him. The director had control over most of the logistics functions with the exceptions of plant shipping and receiving, which were the responsibility of each plant manager, who reported to the director of manufacturing.

All of the distribution personnel were located at the company's central headquarters in Indianapolis. The coordination of receiving and shipping activities at the plants was accomplished by the plant manager.

## Distribution Policies and Practices

Giles Laboratories followed their traditional practice of distributing all products through public warehouses, which was in direct contrast to the parent company's system of ownership and control of warehouses. However, efforts had been initiated by Giles to determine the utility of continuing with its system of dealing exclusively with public warehouses.

Giles currently owned four plant warehouses, dealt with four warehouses owned by the parent company, and, as mentioned, maintained 33 public warehouses specializing in grocery products and servicing other companies in the grocery trade. In no instance did Giles totally occupy the leased space of a specific field warehouse, and individual field warehouse allocation ranged from 3,000 to 100,000 hundredweight. Giles did not share a public warehouse with any of its sister companies.

Most public warehouse rates were negotiated at least every 12 months, and rarely did a contract extend beyond two years. In all cases, a one-shot billing system applied whereby a composite rate for storage and handling was set for every 100 pounds delivered to a warehouse. Accessorial charges for such things as damaged products and telephone expenses were billed separately. The public warehouses would assess a small penalty charge for every hundredweight in excess of the stipulated storage level per month. In plant warehouses, the rule of thumb was to assess storage and handling costs at 1.5 percent per month of the manufactured cost of average monthly inventory that was valued at the full cost of production. Full cost included allocations of overhead and other fixed charges in addition to the direct variable cost of manufacturing, which at Giles represented 80 percent of the full cost.

Top management felt that it was necessary to maintain a 100 percent service level with respect to hospitals. This was a reflection of their belief that hospitals in general had poor inventory management. In actual experience, the achieved customer service level was about 98 percent. Consumer products enjoyed a 96 percent service level, which compared favorably to the target of 98 percent. The distribution manager said that studies were being conducted to determine the optimum service levels considering distribution costs (including the inventory holding costs) and actual service requirements. He explained that prior to 1996, the company did not have a documented inventory carrying cost figure and although a number had been used in plant expansion proposals he was not sure how it had been arrived at. ("Perhaps it was the cost of money at that time applied to the full manufactured cost of the inventory.") However, a study has just been completed by a distribution analyst who recently completed his MBA degree in the evenings while working at Giles. A memo outlining the results of this study is given as Exhibit 11-12.

Shipments from field warehouses to customers were carried by motor carriers at prevailing cartage rates or negotiated contract carrier rates with the exception of a few of the field warehouses that operated their own truck fleets. These customer deliveries were FOB destination. No orders below 15 cases were accepted, and truckload orders (40,000 pounds) were referred to the head office by field warehouse personnel for possible direct service from the nearest plant warehouse. Unit-sales prices for the company's products were quoted at two price break ranges: at 15 to 49 cases, and at 50 cases and over.

Shipping schedules from plant warehouses to field warehouses were initiated from central headquarters. Supervisors who reported to the distribution manager analyzed warehouse delivery receipts, in-transit stock levels, and bill-of-lading figures that indicated deliveries to customers, in order to initiate corrective action if required. Stocking

**EXHIBIT 11-12**
**Giles Laboratories**
**Interoffice Memo**

---

*GILES LABORATORIES*
*INTEROFFICE MEMO*

*Date:*     *January 30, 1996*
*To:*       *Mr. Paul McNaughton, Director of Distribution Services*
*From:*     *Wesley Scott, Distribution Analyst*
*Subject:*  *A Documented Inventory Carrying Cost*

The following four basic cost categories must be considered when calculating inventory carrying costs: (1) capital costs, (2) inventory service costs, (3) storage space costs, and (4) inventory risk costs.

    The money invested in inventory has a very real cost attached to it. Holding inventory ties up money that could be used for other types of investments. This reasoning holds for internally generated funds as well as those obtained from outside sources. Consequently, the company's opportunity cost of capital should be used in order to accurately reflect the true cost involved.

    In order to establish the opportunity cost of capital for Giles Laboratories, the comptroller, Mr. John Munroe, was interviewed. Giles' cost of capital was the charge paid to the parent company, Thurber Pharmaceuticals. Currently, this rate is 10 percent before taxes for working capital. However, due to capital rationing, the current hurdle rate on new investments is 30 percent before taxes (15 percent after taxes). The company conducts a postaudit of most projects in order to substantiate the rate of return. This is required by corporate policy, and in the majority of cases the desired return is achieved. Occasionally a 40 percent hurdle rate is employed by Giles' management to ensure that the required corporate rate of 30 percent is realized.

    Although it would seem that the 30 percent hurdle rate also should be applied to inventory since Thurber Pharmaceuticals is not cash rich and in times of capital rationing an investment in inventory precludes other investments at the 30 percent rate. Thurber Pharmaceuticals only requires a 10 percent return on inventory investments. Consequently, 10 percent before taxes is used as the cost of money in this study. However, this is an issue that must be resolved at the top management level.

    The opportunity cost of capital should be applied to only the out-of-pocket investment in inventory. This is the direct variable expense incurred up to the point at which the inventory is stored. In other words, it was necessary to obtain the average variable cost of products, FOB the distribution center. The individual cost component and the final carrying cost percentages are shown below.

**Inventory Carrying Costs**

| Cost Component | Percentage of Inventory Value |
|---|---|
| Capital costs | 10.00 |
| Inventory services costs | |
|   Taxes | 1.80 |
|   Insurance | 0.26 |
| Warehousing costs | |
|   Public warehouses (recurring storage only) | 2.94 |
|   Plant warehouses | nil |
| Inventory risk costs | |
|   Obsolescence | 0.80 |
|   Shrinkage | 0.58 |
|   Damage | 0.63 |
|   Relocation (transshipment) costs | N.A. |
|   Total | 17.01* |

*Inventory is valued at variable cost FOB the distribution center

---

requirements were determined according to normal usage levels (versus inventory levels) for each field warehouse and were reviewed periodically and changed if required.

    Although most communication with public warehouses was by telephone or fax, the company had begun to install direct data-transmission connections with warehouses located in major market areas. The lead time for processing and consolidating orders was targeted at three days for consumer outlets, but an actual average of five days was experienced. For hospital deliveries, the usual experience was two days compared to a target of one day.

## Columbus Warehouse Facts and Data

The Columbus field warehouse was serving the metropolitan area and neighboring municipalities within a 40-mile radius. The outlying areas were being serviced by wholesalers that drew stock from Columbus. The distribution manager estimated that shipments to Columbus would average in excess of 15,000 cases per month for the next year. One-third of the present shipments came from the Michigan plant and were consolidated at 40,000 pounds for shipment at a freight rate of 70 cents per hundredweight. The rest of the shipments were sent out of the Indianapolis plant warehouse in truckload quantities (40,000 pounds) by public motor carrier at a rate of 60 cents per hundredweight. The 60 cents per hundredweight was based on a contract mileage rate of $1.40 per mile for truckload shipments from Indianapolis to Columbus. In this case, motor carrier rates were more favorable than railroad rates. Shipments from Michigan represented products that were not manufactured in Indianapolis.

Mr. McNaughton was reviewing a plan that would phase out the Columbus public warehouse. Michigan shipments would be diverted to Indianapolis and could be expected to be transported at the same freight rate. Indianapolis would then serve Columbus customers by motor carrier under new rates. The new rates and mix of shipment sizes are set forth in the following schedule:

| Percent of Total Weight Shipped | Cost per Hundredweight |
|---|---|
| 40% @ | $0.60 (TL) |
| 35 | 1.50 (LTL) |
| 25 | 2.40 (LTL) |

Under the new plan another trucking firm would be contracted to provide local delivery to Columbus customers. This company was willing to offer better rates for LTL shipments and cartage (intracity) rates. Moreover, it had suggested allocating 100 square feet of space at its Columbus terminal for transit storage at no additional expense to Giles Laboratories. The lower cartage rates would result in a small saving to the company. If the contract with the Columbus warehouse was renegotiated, it was estimated that the throughput rate could be fixed at 25 cents per case plus a storage penalty when inventory turns fell below 12 times per annum.

A case of Giles products averaged 25 pounds and had a full manufactured cost of about $18. The selling price to wholesalers and chain retail accounts averaged $24.90 per case. The variable cost of marketing, such as sales commissions, promotional allowances, and local delivery costs, averaged $1.66 per case.

While reviewing the proposal, Mr. McNaughton became aware that there would be a one-time reduction in total system inventory of $135,000 valued at full manufactured cost as a result of elimination of the Columbus facility. Although this figure represented an estimate, he felt somewhat encouraged by the fact that it was the consensus among members of his department. The reduction would be comprised primarily of Indianapolis-produced products.

The phase-out possibility was not without its uncertainties. It was not clear whether additional personnel would be needed to process the orders emanating from the Columbus area. It appeared that the existing system was operating at capacity. There was also the matter of convincing the sales department to lengthen the service time from one day to two or three days. The main competitor was serving Columbus out of Pittsburgh, which is 190 miles northeast of Columbus, while the distance from Indianapolis is 171 miles. Mr. McNaughton has been advised by the president to attempt to phase out at least five field facilities within the year, and the Columbus warehouse was the first to come up for lease renewal.

## Questions

1. What are the financial implications associated with closing the Columbus warehouse?
2. How would your analysis differ if:

   - freight rates changed?
   - warehousing rates changed?
   - additional personnel were required at Indianapolis?

3. Which option would you prefer if you were responsible for transportation? For inventory?
4. How would you incorporate customer service considerations into your analysis? How much would sales volume have to change in order to change your answer to question 1?
5. Is there a better way to service the Columbus customers?
6. Should the carrier plan at Giles be changed? If so, what recommendations would you suggest?
7. What other issues need to be addressed?

---

**Case 11.4**

# SAP/Microsoft: Dancing with the Bear

*To provide enterprise business solutions for sustained competitive advantage.*

—Mission Statement

On an American Airline flight from Pittsburgh to Atlanta, in seat 4B, Stephen Rietzke (alliance director for Systems, Applications and Products in Data Processing, Inc. [SAP]) looked over the slides of a PowerPoint presentation. Stephen must present an hour-long overview at SAP's meeting in Atlanta. The presentation consists of the highlights of the recent performance and forecasts of SAP's alliance with software leader Microsoft. As Stephen sat planning his presentation, he thought back to the start of the alliance and how it all began.

In 1992, Stephen received a phone call from SAP corporate headquarters in Waldorf, Germany. The phone call instructed Stephen to analyze an expansive list of prospective alliance partners in order to instigate a change in direction for one of the largest business software application vendors in the world, SAP. Stephen hung up the phone and proceeded to compile a brief list of prospective alliance partners.

This call initiated a defining moment in the business software industry. The software market consists of numerous large and small business software companies. Many of these software vendors focused on niche markets or limited their markets to either mainframe or microcomputer formats. The crossover from mainframe to microcomputer had yet to be conquered. The phone call from Waldorf, Germany, was to change this.

Source: This case was prepared by Rick Rasor, Robert Taylor, and Amy Ward under the direction of Lou Pelton (University of North Texas) for the purpose of class discussion and is not intended to illustrate effective or ineffective management practices.

# Background

In Mannheim, Germany, in 1972, three engineers had an idea: to create a company that produces and markets standard software for integrated business solutions. The company they started, Systemanalyse and Programmentwicklung @, is now called Systems, Applications, and Products in Data Processing Inc. or SAP AG for short.

From the beginning, SAP approached application software from a business viewpoint. By collaborating with business and information technology (IT) executives and partners worldwide, SAP developed a unique understanding of the challenges faced in implementing technology solutions for business users. SAP developed software that could help companies link their business processes, tying together disparate functions and helping their whole enterprise run more smoothly. The versatile, modular software could be quickly and easily adapted to new business processes, too, so as business grew, so did its capabilities.

SAP's innovative thinking soon made it the top software vendor in Germany. Today, SAP is the largest supplier of business application software in the world and the world's fourth largest independent software supplier, overall. Led by the continued technological leadership of SAP's flagship R/3 System, sales in the last three months of 1996 were the best in the company's history.

The company's headquarters are located in Waldorf, Germany, with regional offices located in more than 40 countries worldwide. SAP currently employs 1,250 employees around the globe. And, so far, SAP has helped more than 7,500 companies in 85 countries receive better returns on information. A better return on information means meeting customers' needs faster. It means making the most of changes in the marketplace.

To make sure that customers get a better return on information, SAP has created the SAP Partner Program. The Partner Program helps SAP provide an end-to-end service for customers. The Partner Program combines leading resources, products, and services from companies worldwide. Partners provide expertise in hardware, complementary software, industry and business practices, information technology and implementation support. The Partner Program allows SAP to focus on what it does best by developing leading-edge business application software solutions.

# Microsoft

## Background

Microsoft was founded as a partnership on April 4, 1975, by William "Bill" H. Gates III and Paul G. Allen and was incorporated on June 25, 1981. Since its creation, Microsoft's mission has been "to create software for the personal computer that empowers and enriches people in the workplace, at school, and at home." Over the years, Microsoft, best known for the development of the Windows platform, has grown to become an international company with offices in more than 50 countries and with products in over 30 languages. As a global company, Microsoft strives to develop products that meet the needs of consumers worldwide. Microsoft pursues this challenge through its partnering strategy.

## Partnering Programs

Microsoft currently has 12 partnering programs in which prospective partners may become involved. Each partnering program aims to utilize the unique strengths of each channel member. By analyzing a prospective business partner's business focus, primary business, customer base, and technology focus, Microsoft determines which program best suits the prospective partner. For example, a business that resells software and whose information and resources include Microsoft Intercom and Microsoft Direct Access would qualify for the Microsoft Certified Solution Provider partnering program. By categorizing prospective business partners, Microsoft can optimize the results of the partnership and ensure that its customers' needs continue to be met.

Microsoft's partnering mission statement is as follows: "Microsoft's core business model fosters growth and opportunity for the firms that partner with us to deliver compelling customer solutions based on Microsoft platform products and tools. To respond to the diverse needs of all of our channel partners, we offer many different partnering programs and resource offerings to you to help you succeed with Microsoft products."

Microsoft chooses to pursue a *keiretsu* partnering strategy. Microsoft organizes its enterprise *keiretsus,* such as the SAP project, around value-added products and service chains.

Microsoft enterprise *keiretsus* provide customers with:

- Better enterprise operating systems, optimized for multiple hardware platforms.
- Integrated enterprise management solutions for improved centralized administration of disparate systems, as well as reduced computing costs.
- Integrated line-of-business and packaged client–server applications, optimized for Microsoft's operating systems and server applications.
- Comprehensive partner services complement Microsoft's direct services and focusing on global, multivendor services and support.
- The opportunity to leverage the core competencies of providers at every level of the supply chain to receive the best services.

According to Deborah Willingham, vice president of Microsoft's Enterprise Customer Unit, "Collaborating with industry partners is not just practical; it is critical to meeting Microsoft's goals. By partnering, we can get closer to achieving [our] goals while maintaining our focus on core products and technology."

## How Partners Benefit

Microsoft's investment in partners allows them to focus on their core competencies. Also, as demand for Microsoft products such as Windows NT and BackOffice expands worldwide, so too does the market for complementary services, solutions, and systems. As the market continues to grow, Microsoft's partners will be able to increase their business substantially. In addition to increased business, Microsoft's partners will also be able to collaborate with Microsoft on new technology, which will maintain their integration with Microsoft products. This integration of products and services will ensure the continued growth of the partnership and will ensure that the products remain compatible through upgrades.

## R/3 Technology Overview

SAP's R/3 System presents a standard business software application for client–server computing. R/3 optimally supports all business activities by allowing easy adjustment and high flexibility to change and progress. At the core (see Exhibit 11-13) R/3 contains powerful programs for accounting and controlling, production and materials management, quality management and plant maintenance, sales and distribution, human resources management, and project management. R/3 also allows integration of banks and other business partners into intercompany communications.

## Alliance Overview

With the R/3 System, SAP possesses a product with multi-tier management capability. SAP wants to obtain worldwide acceptance for R/3 by interfacing the product with current

**EXHIBIT 11-13**

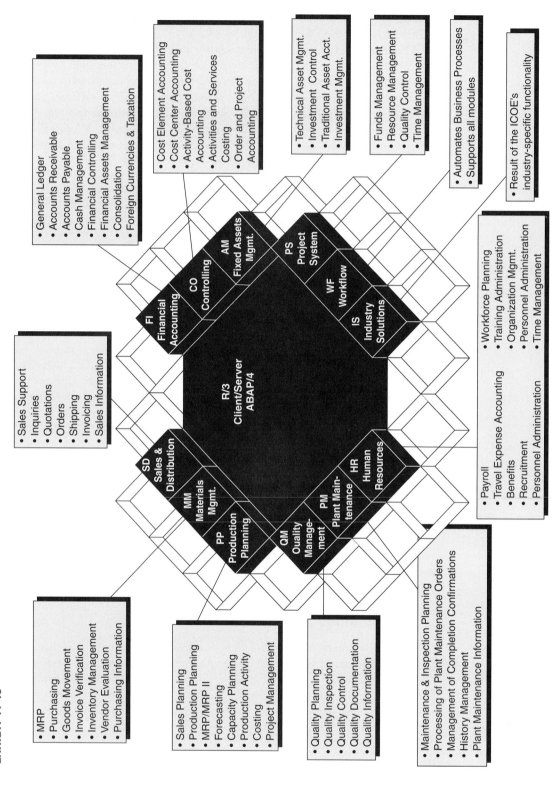

- General Ledger
- Accounts Receivable
- Accounts Payable
- Cash Management
- Financial Controlling
- Financial Assets Management
- Consolidation
- Foreign Currencies & Taxation

- Cost Element Accounting
- Cost Center Accounting
- Activity-Based Cost Accounting
- Activities and Services
- Costing
- Order and Project Accounting

- Technical Asset Mgmt.
- Investment Control
- Traditional Asset Acct.
- Investment Mgmt.

- Funds Management
- Resource Management
- Quality Control
- Time Management

- Automates Business Processes
- Supports all modules

- Result of the ICOE's industry-specific functionality

- Sales Support
- Inquiries
- Quotations
- Orders
- Shipping
- Invoicing
- Sales Information

- Workforce Planning
- Training Administration
- Organization Mgmt.
- Personnel Administration
- Time Management

- Payroll
- Travel Expense Accounting
- Benefits
- Recruitment
- Personnel Administration

**FI** Financial Accounting
**CO** Controlling
**AM** Fixed Assets Mgmt.
**PS** Project System
**WF** Workflow
**IS** Industry Solutions

R/3 Client/Server ABAP/4

**SD** Sales & Distribution
**MM** Materials Mgmt.
**PP** Production Planning
**QM** Quality Management
**PM** Plant Maintenance
**HR** Human Resources

- MRP
- Purchasing
- Goods Movement
- Invoice Verification
- Inventory Management
- Vendor Evaluation
- Purchasing Information

- Sales Planning
- Production Planning
- MRP/MRP II
- Forecasting
- Capacity Planning
- Production Activity
- Costing
- Project Management

- Quality Planning
- Quality Inspection
- Quality Control
- Quality Documentation
- Quality Information

- Maintenance & Inspection Planning
- Processing of Plant Maintenance Orders
- Management of Completion Confirmations
- History Management
- Plant Maintenance Information

management information technology systems. Integrating R/3 with existing IT systems would not only create a competitive advantage for SAP; it would also reduce costs to the customer in both time and money.

In 1993 SAP entered into a technology-based alliance with the Microsoft Corporation which allowed SAP access to Microsoft's vast technology infrastructure. SAP and Microsoft jointly integrated R/3 with a variety of Microsoft's existing software and hardware applications. In return SAP offered Microsoft access to its industry-leading advances in the client-server arena. Together SAP and Microsoft now offer fully integrated R/3 System solutions. R/3 easily integrates with Windows NT, Windows 3.1, Windows 95, and Windows for Workgroups, Microsoft Excel, Access, Word, and Microsoft SQL Server platforms.

Another major factor of consideration for the alliance is the increasing business reliance on electronic commerce and the Internet. By integrating R/3 with the Microsoft Internet Information Server companies now have the capability of sending faxes, e-mail, and Internet e-mail directly from the Microsoft Exchange while working within the R/3 System.

Microsoft (as well as other alliance partners) allows SAP simplified system consultation and provision of installations and ongoing support worldwide. To assure this, both SAP and Microsoft have opened competency centers. Competency centers provide training and customer support for the R/3–Microsoft system. Alliances such as this allow SAP access to new technologies. This gives SAP the ability to keep R/3 compatible with the latest developments in the industry.

Several factors make the SAP–Microsoft alliance a good marriage. Both SAP and Microsoft have one common goal, the co-development of the R/3 business application system and Microsoft platforms into a worldwide industry standard. Microsoft sells platforms, personal productivity software products and tools for Windows- and Intel-based systems. SAP sells enterprise business solutions (R/3 system and other products). Microsoft can provide customers with the network operating system, database, Internet and programming development products and tools, while SAP can provide the business application software that sits on top of it.

Traditionally Microsoft focused mainly on distributing its products through channels, and SAP marketed its products through a direct sales force. Recently both companies have broken these traditions. SAP now focuses on "down market" initiatives and Microsoft is trying to sell "up enterprise." In other words, both companies want to meet in the middle.

Both SAP and Microsoft now focus their attention in all business software markets, regardless of customer size, with focus on both horizontal cross-industry solutions and vertical industry solutions. This brings a common goal of "enabling the total supply chain through business software automation." Both companies possess the products and the desire necessary, making this "extended supply chain" a reality.

Another interesting factor is that SAP practices an open door policy with its competitors. SAP works with numerous horizontal and vertical information technology companies, forming marketing partnerships. On the other hand, Microsoft does not traditionally work well with others, especially companies such as IBM, Oracle, and Computer Associates. By partnering with SAP, Microsoft maintains a "back door" to the other companies in the industry.

"When you dance with the bear, you let the bear lead," is a common phrase used among SAP employees. In this case the bear represents Microsoft. Microsoft is definitely the leader in this partnership (see Exhibit 11-14). More and more organizations turn to the Microsoft NT Server Platform today because of its strong, integrated security, scalable performance, and broad choice of hardware platforms. This makes Microsoft the perfect alliance partner for SAP, but Microsoft also needs SAP. Microsoft wants to provide mission critical platforms that rival mainframe and beyond computing requirements; therefore Microsoft desires access to SAP's marketplace. At this point Microsoft and SAP do not

**EXHIBIT 3.1.2**
**SAP/Microsoft**
**relationship history**

| | |
|---|---|
| Apr. 1993 | Joint development agreement between SAP and Microsoft. |
| Apr. 1994 | First release of R/3 on Windows NT server. |
| Oct. 1995 | SAP availability of R/3 on Microsoft SQL Server. |
| Oct. 1995 | First customer goes online. |
| Sept. 1996 | More than 3,200 R/3 installations on Windows NT Server. |
| Mar. 1997 | R/3 gains Microsoft BackOffice Logo certification. |
| Sept. 1997 | More than 45% of all new R/3 installations are currently installed on Windows NT Server. |

compete with one another; this gives them a truly symbiotic alliance. Since R/3's integration into the Windows NT Server platform, more than 45 percent of all new R/3 installations have been on the Windows NT Server. Microsoft and SAP continue to expand their horizons and enjoy a successful business relationship.

## Partner Contributions

### SAP Contributions

For this alliance, SAP will contribute the business software applications (mainly the R/3 technology) for the technology infrastructure that Microsoft provides. The business software applications allow mid-market and small-enterprise customers to increase the productivity of their current systems while reducing the cost of maintaining their core systems. SAP also contributes name recognition to the alliance. In Germany, SAP's name recognition rivals Microsoft's name recognition in the United States. SAP currently ranks fourth worldwide in software providers and controls 30 percent of the business software applications market while its closest competitor controls only 10 percent of the business software applications market. Capital contributions from SAP will consist of capital for the introduction of current technology, user assistance programs, and future product development. SAP will also jointly fund and support competency centers. One of these centers will be located at SAP headquarters in Waldorf, Germany. At the competency centers, extensive joint product testing will take place to improve integration between R/3 and BackOffice and to ensure that the products remain symbiotic through future upgrades.

### Microsoft Contributions

Microsoft, although the larger partner, does not contribute a disproportionate amount of resources. Each of the partners in this alliance contributes equally, ensuring that the foundation for a true alliance exists. For this alliance Microsoft will contribute the technological infrastructure, the operating system in which R/3 works. Microsoft's tremendous name recognition around the world will also be a significant contribution to the alliance. Microsoft's name recognition provides SAP the opportunity to increase its own name recognition and provides for immense growth opportunities for SAP. Capital contributions from Microsoft will consist of capital for the introduction of current technology, user assistance programs, and future product development. A jointly funded competency center will be located at Microsoft headquarters in Redmond, Washington, where joint product testing will take place to improve integration between R/3 and BackOffice and to ensure that the products remain symbiotic through upgrades.

## Decision Environment

Alliance teams signify one hallmark of a true alliance. The SAP–Microsoft alliance has such a hallmark. Part of the formation of the alliance included the formation of an alliance team. Each partner contributes an alliance director and additional staff to make decisions regarding the alliance. With the health and survival of the alliance as their primary goals and concerns, the alliance team can ensure that the alliance remains on course. Problems that arise can be jointly resolved, which protects the interests of the alliance and of the partners. Given Microsoft's keiretsu philosophy of partnerships, the alliance team enables this to be a long-term alliance with no impending end. Without the alliance, team people would handle conflicts that arose at the corporate level of each company with their own company's agenda as their primary concern. This type of decision environment would impede the success of an alliance. The fact that SAP and Microsoft support an alliance team bodes well for the success of this alliance.

## Future Concerns

Alliances are like marriages—for success, each partner must have an enormous amount of trust for the other. Currently SAP and Microsoft seem to possess this critical trust; perhaps this stems from the lack of direct competition with one another. The "traveling companion" relationship shared by SAP and Microsoft bodes well for the continued success of the alliance. History shows us, though, that many more alliances fail than succeed.

Recently, Microsoft has been under investigation by the U.S. Department of Justice. Charged with unfair practices such as bundling (making buyers purchase unnecessary products in order to receive the desired product by bundling the products together), the company has responded by fighting back with advertising and in court. Microsoft also agreed to unbundle its web browser in an effort to reduce Department of Justice concerns. This brings up a few questions:

- What threats exist to the relationship between SAP and Microsoft?
- Will the litigation against Microsoft affect the future of the relationship? If so, in what way?
- What would stop either partner from forming alliances with the other partner's competitor? And if this happened, how would it affect the current relationship?
- How should Rietzke evaluate the quality and success of the relationship? Be specific. What measures should be used?
- Finally, what possible problems could arise from the partners' exchange of technology? How should the alliance influence product development processes? Why?

Sources of information:

http://www.sap.com/partner

http://www.microsoft.com/germany/partner/sap/us

http://www.microsoft.com

## References

1. Samuel H. Huang, Mohit Uppal, and J. Shi, "A Product-Driven Approach to Manufacturing Supply Chain Selection," *Supply Chain Management* 7 (April 2002): 189–99.
2. David Walters and Geoff Lancaster, "Implementing Value Strategy through the Value Chain," *Management Decision* 38 (March 2000): pp. 160–78.
3. B. S. Sahay, "Supply Chain Collaboration: The Key to Value Creation," *Work Study* 52 (February 2003): 76–83.
4. Joseph Bonney, "Missing Link in Supply Chain," *The Journal of Commerce* 4 (February 10, 2003): 6.
5. Bernard J. La Londe, "Three Problems That Linger," *Supply Chain Management Review* 7 (2, March–April 2003): 7–8.
6. "Consolidate your Distribution (Supply Chain)," *Modern Material Handling* 58 (February 2003): 13.

7. Todd Hammel, Tom Phelps, and Dorothea Kuettner, "The Re-engineering of Hewlett-Packard's CD-RW Supply Chain, *Supply Chain Management* 7 (March 2002): 113–18.

8. William E. Hoover, *Managing the Demand Supply Chain: Value Innovations for Customer Satisfaction* (New York: John Wiley & Sons, 2001): 26.

9. Douglas M. Lambert and Howard M. Armitage, "Managing Distribution Costs for Better Profit Performance," *Business* (September/October 1980):46.

10. Ibid, 47.

## PART FOUR

# International Applications

12 INTERNATIONAL BUSINESS MARKETING

## CHAPTER TWELVE

# International Business Marketing

## Learning Objectives

After reading this chapter, you should be able to:

- Understand the international business environment.
- Discuss the opportunities and challenges involved in international marketing.
- Recognize the complexities and significance of international law.
- Describe the impact of domestic laws in foreign markets.
- Differentiate among various methods of entry into international business markets.
- Discuss the development of global marketing mixes for international business markets.

## Chapter Outline

## The Scope and Challenge of International Business Marketing

There are basically three types of interactions that U.S. firms may have with foreign firms. First, U.S. firms may be supplied by them. Second, U.S. firms may compete against them in this country. Third, U.S. firms may export goods and/or services to a foreign country and compete with them there. Smaller, locally concentrated firms may only be supplied by foreign firms while large, multinational firms may engage in all three types of interactions. What determines how well a company does in global markets? How should performance in global markets be measured? With the globalization of markets and industries, discovering the answers to these questions has become imperative. The objective of this chapter is to identify some of the most common problems encountered and the competitive factors involved when firms begin to market business goods and services internationally.

The United States *exports* about $1 trillion worth of goods and services each year. (In March 2003, for example, the United States exported $82.8 billion worth of goods and services.) At the same time, each year the United States *imports* almost $1.4 trillion worth of goods and services. Therefore, at present, the United States is running approximately a $43 billion trade deficit—caused when the value of imports exceeds that of exports. Recently, however, the Bush administration called for the United States to strive to increase exports by attacking foreign trade barriers. Coupled with the fact that the U.S. dollar has become weaker, thus making American-made products more attractive to foreign markets, there are signs that the trade deficit may decline somewhat in coming years. The more favorable world business environment for U.S. products plus the fast-growing markets of Southeast Asia along with the growing perception of the world as one marketplace paint a promising international business picture and should encourage more U.S. business-to-business firms to adopt an increasingly global orientation.

While the potential for exporting is there, the challenges of international trade still are daunting for many U.S. businesses. Most are small- to medium-sized firms and many do not possess a sophisticated in-house capability to research, develop, and implement an international business plan. However, a company that views itself in a global context, rather than as a U.S. company doing business abroad, can indeed capture new markets with good potential for growth by identifying a need, developing a good or introducing a service that meets worldwide requirements, and positioning that product to capitalize on local needs. International expansions make sense in the long-run, even in tough economic times when brokerage analysts and venture capitalists are likely to insist on seeing short-term profits. This is because long-term gain in the larger world market is likely to be higher than that that would have been obtained in the smaller U.S. market. Furthermore, such behavior tends to be appreciated by Asian and European markets where patience and attention to relationships and loyalty are seen as virtues.[1]

## Export Opportunities and Challenges

Export training initiative studies indicate that companies in the United States have a great potential for powerful return on investment when exporting to new markets. Although it was traditionally the case that global business was an option for only the largest corporations (500 or more employees), through an increase in assistance programs from the U.S. government, the increasingly global marketplace is now open to even small- and medium-sized enterprises (SMEs) that develop a long-term export strategy. Exporting allows companies to do the following:[2]

* Increase growth potential beyond domestic capacity

- Expand into new markets with existing or new products
- Add product lines
- Extend product life cycles
- Improve profitability and competitiveness
- Save existing jobs and generate new ones
- Gain favorable publicity and recognition

Businesses must position themselves by targeting their international niche markets, developing global relationships, and acquiring the specific "export competencies" needed to transform themselves into global businesses. These include evaluating competitive factors, selecting customers from targeted foreign markets, financing export development, and receiving payments for exported products.

Small- and medium-sized enterprises encounter such challenges when developing their export strategies. SMEs need to be able to do the following:

- Analyze the capabilities of their small businesses accurately
- Recognize the export potential of their products and services
- Identify foreign markets
- Understand export logistics and distribution channels
- Develop international business relationships and market entry strategies

For these reasons, many businesses never enter the global marketplace. The task seems too ambitious. Generally, businesses need an infusion of technical assistance to develop new markets around the world. This technical assistance includes in-depth international market research; electronic tools to communicate efficiently with customers, vendors, and agents in the global community; and one-on-one consultation with trade experts who can assist SMEs in navigating the dynamic "global commerce waters."

## Stages of Economic Development

Perhaps the most significant factor affecting the business marketer seeking to do business abroad is the differing degrees of industrialization among countries. Although generalizing about particular countries and specific parts of the world can be foolhardy, the stage of economic development can serve as a rough gauge in ascertaining demand, relative risk involved, and quality of goods sought. It is logical to assume that there is a relationship between the degree of economic development and the projected demand for business goods or services found within a country or particular part of the world. For example, there are obvious financial risks associated with investing in countries that have had only brief exposure to the free enterprise system or that are struggling to overcome widespread poverty.

Every country goes through five stages of economic development, as detailed in Exhibit 12-1, and each stage relates to the extent of production capability. A production orientation allows broad generalizations to be made about the level of development and projected demand within a particular country or part of the world. However, the marketer must be cognizant of the fact that many countries are in a state of change and can overlap two economic development stages at one time. For example, a Third World country in the first stage of economic development may purchase advanced technology such as telecommunication satellites, computer systems, or nuclear power to speed up its industrialization. In general, the firm seeking to enter the international market should match its product or service to the particular stage of economic development in the country or part of the world in which it seeks to establish itself.

**EXHIBIT 12-1**
**Stages of Economic Development**

**Stage 1**
**The Traditional Society**
One with limited production functions, primarily agricultural. The level of productivity in manufacturing as in agriculture is limited by the inaccessibility of modern science, its applications, and its frame of mind.

**Stage 2**
**The Pre-Conditions for Take-Off**
Societies in transition toward modernization. Some investment in infrastructure occurs, and there is a widening scope of internal and external commerce. Some modern manufacturing appears, but the society still is mainly characterized by the old social structure and values.

**Stage 3**
**The Take-Off**
Resistance to change lessens, and the forces for economic growth come to dominate the society. Industries expand rapidly, requiring new investment. New techniques spread in agriculture as well as in industry.

**Stage 4**
**The Drive to Maturity**
Continuing growth extends modern technology over the whole range of economic activity. The makeup of the economy changes unceasingly as technique improves, new industries grow, and older ones level off. The economy extends its range into more complex technologies.

**Stage 5**
**The Age of High Mass Consumption**
The leading sectors shift toward durable consumers' goods and services. The structure of the working force changes with more employed in offices or in skilled factory jobs. The extension of modern technology as an objective is joined with a desire to improve social welfare and security.

## The International Business Environment

Many U.S. firms are unfamiliar with the potential market that lies abroad. Without knowledge of market needs and an understanding of how to negotiate business deals, the international marketer is seriously disadvantaged. Different cultural systems can produce divergent negotiating styles—styles shaped by each nation's culture, geography, history, and political system.[3] Various factors can influence international marketing strategy: the complex buying process, sociocultural dynamics, the political-legal environment, and the economic environment are to be considered in foreign markets just as they are in domestic markets.

### The Buying Process

As discussed in Chapter 4, participants in the buying process are members of what is referred to as the "buying center." The size of an international buying center can vary from one or a few people to groups of 15 to 20 (or more) individuals. The number of people involved increases as the complexity and importance of a purchase decision increases. Likewise, the composition of the buying group usually will change from one purchase to another, or even during various stages of the buying process. The initial major task of the marketer is to determine who is involved in the buying process so that communications (mail, media, electronic, or salesperson) can be aimed at the appropriate people. Although the objectives of purchasing personnel may be universal, the makeup of the buying center and the interactions between members of the buying center are in constant fluctuation.

In international marketing, it is often more difficult to identify the members of the buying center, determine their role in the buying process, and communicate the appropriate information to them. Less-developed countries may not have clear-cut staff functions, such as engineering and purchasing; buying decisions may be made by a line supervisor, such as

# STRATEGY AT WORK

## CORPORATE PARTICIPATION IN AN INTERNATIONAL HIGH-TECH TRADE MISSION

Recently, Ambassador David L. Aaron, undersecretary for international trade, led a high-tech trade mission to Malaysia, Singapore, Thailand, and the Philippines. The trade mission was intended to lend high-profile U.S. government advocacy to American companies, particularly small- and medium-sized companies, seeking business opportunities in Southeast Asia.

**Specifically, the goals of the trade mission were to accomplish the following:**

- Boost U.S. high-tech exports and market share in Southeast Asia
- Establish and expand business relationships between U.S. executives and host country government and industry leaders
- Highlight U.S. leadership and competitiveness in high-tech sectors
- Identify new and upcoming commercial high-tech opportunities in the region
- Achieve greater transparency and fairness in host country procurement and purchasing decisions
- Demonstrate high-visibility U.S. support for the Southeastern Asian economies recovering from the recent economic turndown

**Highlights of the trade mission included the following:**

- Country briefings given by embassy officials on the current state of the economy and commercial opportunities
- Prearranged one-on-one business meetings with Southeast Asian companies interested in purchasing products and services in one's field of specialty
- Meetings with ministers and other government officials responsible for high-tech portfolios
- Visits to companies and sites focused on information technology, telecommunications, and environmental technology
- Participation in roundtable discussions and presentations with local company and government leaders to assess export and partnership opportunities
- Receptions hosted by the ambassador at residence with members of the American Chamber of Commerce and local company and government leaders

Although this particular trade mission involved Southeast Asia and high technology, many other trade missions are conducted for other sectors and to other target regions.

### Assignment

At some point many of you will have company marketing responsibility that will include consideration of participation in trade missions. However, many marketers are not even aware such opportunities exist. Go to the International Trade Administration website at (www.ita.doc.gov) and click on "trade events and missions." Then click on "trade mission calendar." Ref: (www.ita.doc.gov/doctm/doctm). Your assignment is to review the upcoming trade missions and match them with local companies through your state industrial directory (or other directory). Prepare a presentation to the class concerning the opportunities and your recommendations. Advanced students will want to review the senior marketers at the local companies, assessing their awareness and interest in the trade mission.

Adapted from: "High-Technology Trade Mission . . . Recruitment Begins for U.S. Companies," *Business America,* U.S. Department of Commerce, July 1998, pp. 17–21.

---

the plant manager. In Japan, the decision maker may appear to be a senior-level, older person, but the real decision may be made by a younger, lower-level manager. The international marketer must recognize and understand these differences in the decision process from country to country. In addition, it is important to note that the level of purchasing expertise and efficiency varies among countries and will change over time.

Although frequently it is assumed that business buyers make only rational purchasing decisions in which emotion has no part, research has shown that professional purchasers also are influenced by the country of origin—even when all other variables are held constant. Fear of losing domestic market control, increasing nationalism around the world, and a rising sense of cultural identity may inhibit free market access.[4] Also, highly nationalistic countries tend to encourage economic self-sufficiency, even at the expense of economic efficiency, which could have a negative effect on the international firm. The international marketer should thus pay close attention to the level of nationalism in a country.

## Cultural Dynamics

The global environment is characterized by diverse and deep-rooted cultural norms and value systems. Considering the increasing economic interrelationships worldwide, today's marketers need to be aware of the importance of sociocultural differences in the process of adjusting and adapting a marketing strategy to foreign markets. Companies that plan to do business in overseas markets, including those in the European community, must address each as an individual market, understand its inherent characteristics, and make allowances for its uniqueness in marketing strategies. Consider the following:

- South American business people stand and talk within inches of their colleagues. An American who finds this difficult or reacts negatively can offend the potential customers or clients and ruin a business relationship.

- In Japan, it is highly unlikely that a business deal will be completed after only one sales call. To be overly aggressive may be viewed as impolite, unappreciative, or even rude. Japanese business people want to get to know their counterparts on a personal level before business can be transacted.

- Crossing one's legs to expose the sole of a shoe is unacceptable in Muslim countries.

- In an Oriental culture, touching another person can be considered an invasion of privacy, while in Southern Europe and Arabic countries, it is a sign of warmth and friendship.

- Being on time is a sign of respect in Japan. In Sweden, guests are expected to show up before the appointed time.

- Gifts in business dealings may be viewed as bribes in Hong Kong, but in Japan they are very acceptable and even expected in some business situations.

- In China it is important to avoid causing another person to lose face, so raising one's voice, correcting someone in front of their peers, or shouting at someone in public should be avoided.

Because culture deals with a group's design for living, it is pertinent to the study of international marketing.[5] When a promotional message is written (business advertisement, catalog, and the like), symbols that are recognizable and meaningful to the market (the culture) must be used. In fact, culture is pervasive in all marketing activities: pricing, promotion, channels of distribution, product, and packaging. The marketer's efforts often are judged in a cultural context for acceptance, resistance, or rejection.

As global businesses interact, executives are exposed to differences in business practices that, in turn, change business behavior, just as cultures change when exposed to the ways of others. Some suggest a world business culture is evolving and, indeed, that may be the case. However, to assume that the trend toward similarities means that differences in business behavior do not still exist is to court disaster. A lack of understanding of the differences in business customs can create insurmountable barriers that prevent an otherwise acceptable product from ever reaching the final business user. A knowledge of the business culture, management attitudes, and business methods existing in a country, and a willingness to accommodate the differences are important to success in an international market.

### *Required Adaptations*

**Adaptation**—the process of adjusting to an environment or situation—is a key concept in international marketing, and a willingness to adapt is crucial. Adaptation, or at least accommodation, is required on small matters as well as large ones. As a guide to adaptation, Phillip Cateora tells us that there are 10 basic criteria that all who wish to deal with individuals, firms, or authorities in foreign countries should be able to meet. They are (1) open tolerance, (2) flexibility, (3) humility, (4) justice and fairness, (5) adjustability to varying tempos, (6) curiosity and interest, (7) knowledge of the country, (8) liking for others, (9) ability to command respect, and (10) ability to integrate oneself into the environment. Add the quality of adaptability to the other qualities of a good executive for a composite of the ideal international marketer as Exhibit 12-2 illustrates.

The key to adaptation is to remain American while developing an understanding of and willingness to accommodate differences that exist. Foreign business people do not necessarily expect you to act as they do. However, when different cultures meet, open tolerance and acceptance are necessary. Among the many obvious differences in customs that exist between cultures, some business customs must be recognized and accommodated *(cultural imperatives)*, some are optional *(cultural adiaphora)*, and still others are ones in which an outsider must not participate *(cultural exclusives)*. Marketers need to be perceptive enough to know when they are faced with each and respond accordingly. Each type is discussed below.

### Cultural Imperatives

Business customs and expectations that must be met and conformed to or avoided if relationships are to be successful are called **cultural imperatives.** For example, in some cultures, (e.g., China, Japan, and Latin America) establishing trust and taking time to develop a relationship must be done prior to engaging in effective business negotiations.

### Cultural Adiaphora

Business customs and expectations that foreigners may wish to conform to or participate in but that are not required are called **cultural adiaphora.** These sorts of business customs comprise the largest category. For example, business people are not expected to bow during introductions in Japan, don local dress in Muslim countries, or engage in customs where one man kisses another in greeting as in Russia. Nor are they necessarily expected to partake of local foods. On the other hand, making an effort to engage in the custom, such

**EXHIBIT 12-2**
**Profile of the Ideal International Marketer**

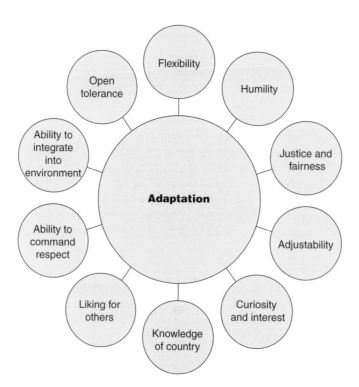

as tasting local food or drink or symbolically bowing in Japan, if done gracefully, may help in relationship building between cultures. This is especially true when it comes to deference to less obvious imperatives. At the least it demonstrates interest and sensitivity to the culture and to the relationship.

### *Cultural Exclusives*

**Cultural exclusives** are customs or behavior from which a foreigner is excluded. For example, only Catholics can take communion in a Catholic church and Muslims would be perturbed if a non-Muslim attempted to practice Islam. Also offensive is a foreigner criticizing a country's politics, customs, and peculiarities even though local residents may criticize these issues themselves.

## The Political and Legal Environment

As much as most managers would like to ignore them, political and legal factors often play a critical role in international marketing activities. Unfortunately (or fortunately), business and government need each other; business can prosper only when there are stable economic and political environments. These are prerequisites for business planning and risk taking. Even the best marketing plans can go bad as a result of unexpected political or legal influences. Political tumult—the war in Iraq, the unstable situations in North Korea, Iran, Syria, and the Middle East as well as in Brazil—has prompted growing ranks of international marketers to weigh political risk, whether they operate manufacturing plants, participate in joint ventures, or simply export to foreign countries. **Political risk** is the chance that a company will lose money and property. Specifically, political risks of global business include *confiscation* (the seizing of a company's assets without payment) *expropriation* (the seizing of a company's assets with reimbursement) and *domestication* (when host countries gradually transfer foreign companies to national control). In addition, companies may face the endangerment of their employees lives. Reasons for such risk arise from events beyond the company's control, such as revolution, political changes in regime or ideology, policy changes such as currency devaluations, or altered profit repatriation rules, to name just a few.

### *The Political Environment*

Besides the business marketer, the principal players in the political arena are the host country governments, the home country governments, and the transnational bodies or agencies involved. The respective interactions of these groups result in a given political climate that may positively or negatively affect the operations of a business marketer to do business in the international arena. The task of the marketing manager is to assess the political forces that comprise the firm's political environment and to analyze their impact on marketing strategy. Exhibit 12-3 presents a checklist of questions that can guide this process.[6]

The climate for international investment varies greatly from country to country. An investment climate depends on both the type of investment involved and the political mood at the time. In general, local manufacturing is preferred over imports and over exports of natural resources for manufacturing elsewhere. Business investment in economic sectors with high unemployment rates usually are welcomed, as is the introduction of sophisticated technologies, provided that those technologies do not displace existing jobs.

One problem often encountered with foreign politics is the conflicting signals sent by the host country to foreign firms. On one hand, the host country actively woos investment. To win foreign capital and new technology, the country pledges cooperation and various tax and financial incentives. On the other hand, the host country is often quick to accuse foreign firms of not providing the latest technology and expertise in local operations. It may also criticize these companies for making excessive profits and draining the nation of

## BUSINESS MARKETING IN ACTION

### INTERNATIONAL BUSINESS IS METRIC. ARE YOU?

Although English is an accepted language for international business communication, English measurement systems are not. The metric system has long been the established standard set by the International Standards Organization (ISO). The United States has been working on conversion to the metric system for over twenty years and is perhaps only 20 percent converted. The only country further behind is Belize, which has a total population of 127,000. Continental Europe is nearly 100 percent metric, whereas the United Kingdom, Canada, India, and Australia apply metric measurement about 50 percent of the time.

From an export-marketing standpoint, the issue involves cost savings for customers through standardization and is not negotiable. For example, when Airbus purchases standard-sized airframe bolts internationally, it requires that they have the same nominal dimensions, threads, tolerance, and metal quality. Nominal English sizes, tolerances, and material standards do not have exact matches in the metric system (as standard sizes). Very soon the market will force U.S. exporters to supply totally metric products and to have their quality system ISO9000 certified to assure process control. What would have been a differential advantage a few years ago will soon be a market requirement.

For those firms in the European Union who had not gone metric, January 1, 2000, was the cutoff date. All products had to be in metrics and labeled as such. As of that date, all measures in user instructions, technical manuals, catalogues, and advertising had to be metric. If marketers were not already thinking in metrics, it would hamper their growth as international business marketers.

### Action Assignment

While many students are familiar with grams and kilograms (liquid measure is somewhat familiar, thanks to two-liter soft drink bottles), still it is common for Americans to embarrass themselves on simple linear measures (which are learned in elementary school in the rest of the world). With most major American companies pursuing at least some international markets, professional business marketers have no alternative but to completely master the metric system.

Survey five friends, asking each about his or her familiarity with the metric system. Bring the survey results to class, where your instructor will combine them to determine the number of respondents who chose each of the possible answers.

Note: closed book; closed notes; no calculators.

This is a short test—only one multiple-choice question.

1. Which of the following would measure closest to 100 millimeters?
   A. The width of your car
   B. The width of your dining room chair
   C. The width of the short side length of your lunch tray
   D. The width of the short side length of your business marketing textbook
   E. The width across your hand
   F. The diameter of your pencil
   G. The diameter of one strand of your hair

See: "How ISO Cuts Manufacturing Costs," *Machine Design,* November 5, 1998; "Speak Metric," *Manufacturing Engineering,* February 1998; and "Sell Metric," *Manufacturing Engineering,* March 1998.

---

its wealth. To indicate displeasure, the host government may restrict the repatriation of profits to corporate headquarters abroad.

Another problem is **trade barriers**, which escape fixed definitions, but can be defined as government laws, regulations, policies, or practices that either protect domestic products from foreign competition or artificially stimulate exports of particular domestic products. Foreign trade barriers include the following:[7]

- Import policies (e.g., tariffs and other import charges, restrictions, licensing, or barriers)
- Standards, testing, labeling and certification (including restrictive measures and self-certification of conformance to foreign products standards)
- Government procurement (e.g., "buy national" policies and closed bidding)
- Export subsidies (e.g., export financing on preferential terms)
- Lack of intellectual property protection (e.g., inadequate patent/trademark protection)
- Services barriers (e.g., regulation of international data flows and restrictions on the use of foreign data processing)

**EXHIBIT 12-3**
**Checklist for**
**Analyzing the**
**Political**
**Environment**

1. What is the country's political structure?
2. How do citizens, political parties, and special-interest groups participate in political decision making?
3. What is the current government's political philosophy? How is it implemented?
4. What are the philosophies of opposing political forces?
5. What role does the current government see for foreign business?
6. Is foreign business treated differently from local firms in public policy? If so, how?
7. What is the country's history in dealing with foreign businesses?
8. What is the process whereby changes in public policy are made?
9. What are the current and foreseeable trends in the relationship between the government in this country and in my home country?
10. What general role does government see for private business in this country's economic life?
11. What restrictions on international transfers of resources will affect my firm's operations in this country?
12. What are the major trends in the regulatory environment?
13. What incentives does the government give to private business and foreign investors?
14. What are the trigger points for increased nationalistic feelings in the host country?
15. How does the government assert its economic sovereignty?
16. What are the specific risks of loss of ownership or control of assets?
17. What are the chances of political harassment, and what forms is it likely to take?
18. What tools can be used to build a mutually beneficial relationship with this country's government? Will they survive a possible change of government?
19. What are the possibilities of a change in government or other expressions of political instability?
20. Are my firm, my industry, and/or my products likely to be politically vulnerable?

- Investment barriers (e.g., limitations on access to foreign government-funded research, and restrictions on transferring earnings and capital)
- Trade restrictions affecting electronic commerce (e.g., burdensome and discriminatory regulations and standards, and discriminatory taxation)
- Other barriers (e.g., bribery and corruption)

When discussing the international political environment, domestic politics must also be considered. Domestic criticism of a business product firm's international activity comes largely from labor and political organizations, which may accuse the company of exporting capital and jobs (as happened during the debates prior to the implementation of the *NAFTA* agreements). These organizations charge that imports and direct investment abroad create unemployment. So, instead of providing support for international trade, the government of the home country can turn out to be a significant hindrance.

### The Legal Environment

From the political environment is generated the legal environment for business, that is, the nation's laws and regulations pertaining to business. A firm must know the legal environment in each market that it does business in because these laws constitute the "rules of the game." The legal principles governing today's international arena result from centuries of commercial transactions between different nations. For the most part, the framework for the international trading system is based upon straightforward concepts of contract law. There are, however, important nuances. The international marketing manager must be aware of the laws that will govern all foreign business decisions and contracts. The best preparation for understanding the legal requirements governing international commerce begins at home, with a solid understanding of U.S. export enforcement and foreign corrupt practices policies.

### Local Legal Systems

Legal systems and the laws they create differ dramatically in countries around the world.[8] Most legal systems do not adhere to the common law system followed in the United States.

For most business issues, international law is primarily a question of which national laws apply and how to apply them to cases involving contracts, shipping, or parties. Laws and legal systems vary significantly across countries.

Three principal legal "systems" are used in the majority of countries: common law systems, code law systems, and Islamic law systems. *Common law systems* base the interpretation of law on prior court rulings (legal precedents and customs). The majority of the codes in the United States follow common law systems. *Code (written) law systems* rely on statutes and codes for the interpretation of the law. There is very little "interpretation," so the law must be detailed enough to prescribe appropriate and inappropriate actions. The majority of the world's governments rely on a code law system. *Islamic law systems* rely on the legal interpretation of the Koran and the words of Mohammed. Unlike common and code law systems, which hold that law should be man-made and can be improved over time, Islamic legal systems hold that God established a "natural law" that embodies all justice.

### Antitrust Laws

It might seem strange that U.S. *antitrust laws* affect the foreign business activities of American companies. However, that is a fact of life for international business marketers. The opinion of the U.S. Justice Department is that even if an act is committed abroad, it falls within the jurisdiction of American courts if the act produces consequences for the United States. When an American firm expands abroad by acquiring a foreign company, the Justice Department will be concerned about the possible impact on competition in the United States. For example, Remington Arms Company tried to acquire Sweden's AB Norma Projektilfabrik in an effort to get a foothold in the European community, where high tariffs on third-country ammunition were nearly pricing Remington out of the market. The Justice Department said that acquiring Norma would allow Remington to increase its U.S. market share, as Norma was selling 10 percent of its output in the United States already. Remington gave up its efforts in the face of the challenge by the Justice Department.

### Foreign Corrupt Practices Act of 1977

Bribery is considered the most endemic aspect of conducting business abroad. Payoffs to high government officials had often been the most effective promotional tool in international business. The most sensational cases involved United Brands and the president of Honduras, and Lockheed and the prime minister of Japan. As a result, the U.S. government passed this act to prohibit U.S. firms from engaging in payoffs abroad.

---

**Concept Review**

1. Why is a country's stage of economic development a key consideration for the international business marketer?

2. Why should the international business marketer carefully study cultural dynamics in overseas markets?

3. How do antitrust laws affect foreign business activities of American companies?

## International Law

**International law** can be defined as the collection of treaties, conventions, and agreements between nations that more or less have the force of law. International law involves some mutuality, with two or more countries participating in the drafting and execution of laws.

### Treaties of Friendship, Commerce, and Navigation

The United States has signed *treaties of friendship, commerce, and navigation (FCNs)* with many countries. FCN treaties cover commercial relations between the two signing nations. They commonly identify the nature of the right of American companies to do business in those nations with which the United States has such a treaty and vice versa. FCN treaties usually guarantee "national treatment" to the foreign subsidiary; that is, it will not be discriminated against by the nation's laws and judiciary.

### IMF and GATT

The *International Monetary Fund (IMF)* and the *General Agreement on Tariffs and Trade (GATT)* are part of the limited body of effective international law. Both agreements identify acceptable and nonacceptable behavior for the member nations. The international business marketer is interested in both IMF and GATT because of a shared concern in the maintenance of a stable environment conducive to international trade.

### UNCITRAL

The United Nations established a Commission on International Trade Law, *UNCITRAL,* with a goal to promote a uniform commercial code for the world. It bridges the communications gap between countries having different legal systems. It minimizes contract disputes and facilitates the task of selling goods between countries.

### ISO

The International Standards Organization (ISO) is working toward the development of uniform international standards. Differing national standards are a major hindrance to international trade and ISO standards make trade between countries easier and fairer. *ISO 9001:2000* is concerned with "quality management" which refers to what the organization does to enhance customer satisfaction by meeting customer and applicable regulatory requirements and to continually improve its performance in this regard. While the standards do not guarantee product quality, they do assure that a firm has a quality control system in place. *ISO 14001:2000* is concerned with "environmental management" which refers to what the organization does to minimize harmful effects on the environment. You can learn more about the ISO standards by visiting its website at http://www.iso.ch/iso/en/ISOOnline.openerpage.

### NAFTA

The *North American Free Trade Agreement* is the result of the United States, Canada, and Mexico seeking free and open markets (trading areas) for their products. There are no tariffs and/or quotas imposed on products exchanged between these countries. In theory it should be just as easy to do business between countries in this trading block as it would be to do business within a partner's home country. The purpose of this agreement is to increase trade and business between the trading partners. NAFTA was preceded by the free trade agreement between Canada and the United States.

## Domestic Laws in Foreign Markets

The importance of foreign laws to the business marketer lies primarily in domestic marketing in each foreign market. The problem arises from the fact that the laws in each market tend to be somewhat different from those in other markets.

## BUSINESS MARKETING IN ACTION

### GETTING ASSISTANCE WITH INTERNATIONAL PAYMENT PROBLEMS

In the United States, where business transactions are covered by the Uniform Commercial Code and the U.S. legal system, it is common to sell on open account. With a new customer, the accounting department will routinely run a credit check and review the company's bill-paying history. After approval, the customer orders, the firm ships the product, and the accounting department sends an invoice, typically seeking payment in 30 days (net 30). If payment is not received, a court could put a lien on the customer's assets. There are no similar courts with jurisdiction over international business.

In the following recent trade cases, the U.S. Department of Commerce was able to help with past due invoices, but most international marketers would consider that those handling the transactions were naive in the way they structured the sale.

- An American manufacturer of expensive high-tech "clean room" industrial ovens shipped its product to an international company's operation in India. Payment was due on receipt, but with a 10 percent holdback until such time as the equipment was installed and operating. After 12 months of correspondence and broken promises, the invoice still had not been paid.

- An American company stated that it had to ship on open account to a customer in Abu Dhabi because the customer had an emergency and a letter of credit or wire funds transfer would have resulted in an unacceptable delay. The American marketer said, "There was absolutely no reason to doubt that the customer, an international aircraft manufacturer, would not pay us promptly." Eight months later payment still had not been received.

Obviously, it would be best if marketers avoided these types of problems, but if they do find themselves in similar situations, they should consider filing a trade complaint with the U.S. Department of Commerce–Export Assistance Center. They have no enforcement authority, but when they contact the problem customer and suggest that the customer pay its outstanding invoices, the department often gets results. In the cases of the two companies discussed above, the results were immediate.

### Action Assignment

Most large banks have an international department that can give you information concerning how it could set up a letter of credit to assure that a company would get paid for international shipments. Go to a local bank and ask someone in the international department to walk you through the process. This should be a fun exercise, as banks are generally very supportive of local higher education (and they want your company's business after you graduate). Report to the class on what you learn at the bank and through your other research on avoiding past due international payments.

See: "Payment Received in Full: A Trade Complaint Success Story," *Business America*, July 1997, p. 23.

## Differing Legal Systems

Before considering national peculiarities in marketing law, the business marketer should look at the basic legal systems that underlie individual national law. The differences among national legal systems are important to the international business marketer. Because the legal systems of no two countries are exactly the same, each foreign market must be studied and appropriate local legal talent hired when and where necessary.

The international business marketer will find many regulations affecting the product. Local laws often constrain the marketer's freedom as to product features, too, such as package, label, and warranty. In fact, a product's label is subject to more legal requirements than its package. Brand names and trademarks are product attributes that also face differing national requirements.

In addition, foreign government policies often impact U.S. firms' pricing decisions. Value-added taxes, tariffs, and price controls often are encountered. As an example, the Chinese government fixes passenger car prices between $15,600 and $26,000.[9] An increase in the value-added tax usually will curtail demand, while tariffs typically raise the price of imports. Price controls can also play havoc with a firm's foreign pricing policies. Because health care costs are borne by some governments, drug prices in many of these countries are negotiated with the host government. Many pharmaceutical companies must face the dilemma of accepting lower prices for their drugs.[10] Further, some governments heavily encourage the prescription of generics or even stimulate parallel imports from low-price countries to put pressure on drug companies. Another variable is the fact that some countries allow price agreements among competitors.

Finally, marketers face a bewildering set of advertising and promotion regulations in foreign markets. For example, while comparative advertising is legal in the United Kingdom, Ireland, Spain, Portugal and the Philippines, it is illegal to use comparative terminology in Germany and comparative advertising in Belgium, Luxembourg, and India. Even when comparative advertising is legal there are differing regulations regarding whether it can be direct or not. In addition, there are restrictions on what types of products, such as pharmaceuticals, toys, tobacco and liquor, may be advertised.[11] What it comes down to is that most nations have some laws regulating advertising and advertising groups in many nations have self-regulatory codes. New Zealand has no fewer than 33 laws relating to advertising! Some countries allow advertising only in the local language or commercials that are produced with local talent. In general, sales promotion techniques encounter greater restrictions in most markets than in America. In the United States, often there is no constraint on contests, deals, premiums, and other sales promotion techniques. The situation is quite different elsewhere.

## International Entry Strategies

Many business marketers have learned that it is not a practical strategy to enter all markets with a single-entry method. Even large multinational corporations such as IBM have to formulate multiple-entry strategies. IBM, once known for following a policy of doing business only through its subsidiaries, now uses a portfolio of entry strategies. For example, in Europe it uses joint ventures, cooperative projects with governments and competitors, and long-term supply relationships.[12]

The general tendency for most business firms is to enter the international market slowly, cautiously, and through exporting (either directly or indirectly through a third party). As they adopt long-term perspectives, they tend to move away from exporting and toward other entry strategies that provide more permanence, more competitive power, more control, and greater long-run profits. There are many entry strategies for foreign markets, from those with little risk and minimum control to those with maximum risk and maximum control. A firm's stage of internationalization is based on the strategic choice of management with a good understanding of market opportunities and a firm's capabilities and resources. Companies have four different modes of market entry into foreign markets, namely, exporting, the Internet, contractual agreements, and direct foreign investment. Each will be discussed in turn.

### Exporting

**Exporting** is a strategy in which a company, without any marketing or production organization overseas, exports a product from its home base. The product is the same as the one marketed in the home market. Leading U.S. exporters such as General Motors, Boeing, and Lucent derive a significant part of their revenue and earnings from foreign trade. Indeed, Lucent Technologies' Microelectronics Group exports half of what it makes to Europe and Asia. It is not uncommon for some domestic exporters to derive over one-third of their revenues from foreign operations, but it is not easy to find exact figures for exports made by many large firms because many no longer carefully discriminate between domestic and overseas sales.[13] Exporting is a strategy used by mature international companies and involves relatively minimal risk and marketing effort.

## The Internet

Originally, the Internet was used to reach domestic markets. However, using the Internet as a foreign market entry strategy has become so popular that we now have the concept of **international Internet marketing (IIM)**.[14] This method of market entry allows smaller business firms to enter foreign markets with Internet catalogs and virtual storefronts, and engage in international e-tailing. Former catalog companies have led the way into IIM but older "brick-and-mortar" manufacturers are enthusiastically jumping in.

## Contractual Agreements

*Contractual agreements* are long-term associations between two or more companies and involve the transfer of technology, processes, trademarks, and/or human resources. There are several forms of contractual agreements including licensing, franchising, and joint ventures.

### Licensing

**Licensing** is an agreement that permits a foreign company to use industrial property (that is, patents, trademarks, and copyrights), technical know-how and skills (for example, feasibility studies, manuals, technical advice, and the like), architectural and engineering designs, or any combination of these, in a foreign market. A *licensor* allows a foreign company to manufacture a product for sale in the *licensee's* country. Licensing is the fastest way to enter a market that is difficult for outsiders to enter. It requires a minimum investment, as the licensee already has a sales and distribution organization and has experience in dealing with the local government. Finally, there is no danger of being expropriated or nationalized.

### Franchising

**Franchising** provides exporters with a close and tight relationship to international markets. Franchising grants to the franchisee the right to carry on a certain manufacturing process and to use the brand name of the franchisor. The franchisee generally has a small but exclusive territory and is bound by the terms of the franchise contract. The contract provides for close supervision by the U.S. franchisor to assure adherence to standards and specified marketing practices. Service companies such as Holiday Inn, Hertz, and Manpower have successfully used franchising to enter foreign markets.

### Joint Ventures

A **joint venture** is simply a partnership. An international joint venture is one in which the partners are from more than one country. Each partner agrees to a joint venture to gain access to the other partner's skills and resources. Caterpillar has a joint venture with a South Korean company to produce Caterpillar's forklift trucks for Asian markets. Caterpillar also has a joint venture in Japan with Mitsubishi, enabling it to compete with Komatsu, a major competitor, in the Japanese home market. John Deere and Hitachi have a joint venture that assembles small- and medium-sized hydraulic excavators in Great Britain.

## Direct Foreign Investment

*Direct foreign investment* is just what it sounds like—investment within a foreign country. There are several forms of such investment including investment in manufacturing, assembly operations, and turnkey operations.

### Manufacturing

The manufacturing process can be employed as a strategy involving all or some manufacturing in a foreign country. IBM, for example, has 16 plants in the United States and 18 more in other countries. As starting from scratch can be a slow process, some business firms acquire a local company. However, historically, one U.S. foreign acquisition in three has failed. Others will use local personnel in management positions. However, as Union Carbide learned in its operations in Bhopal, India, problems can occur. Local Indian personnel were inadequately trained in safety procedures, leading to one of the worst industrial accidents in modern times.

### Assembly Operations

An **assembly operation** is a variation on a manufacturing strategy. In this strategy, parts or components are produced in various countries in order to gain each country's comparative advantage. Capital-intensive parts may be produced in advanced nations, and labor-intensive assemblies may be produced where labor is abundant and labor costs are low. This strategy is common among manufacturers of electronics.

### Turnkey Operations

A **turnkey operation** is an agreement by the seller to supply a buyer with a facility fully equipped and ready to be operated by the buyer's personnel, who will be trained by the seller. In international business marketing, the term usually is associated with giant projects that are sold to governments or government-run companies. Large-scale plants requiring technology and large-scale construction processes unavailable in local markets commonly use this strategy. Such large-scale projects include building steel mills; cement, fertilizer, and chemical plants; and facilities related to such advanced technologies as telecommunications.

## Product Strategy

Just because a product is successful in one country is no guarantee that it will be successful in other markets. In a narrow sense, a product is considered as something tangible that can be described in terms of physical attributes, such as shape, dimension, components, form, color, and so on. A student of marketing, however, should realize that this definition of product is misleading because many products are intangible (services, for example). Actually, intangible products are a significant part of the American export market.[15]

In many situations, both tangible and intangible products must be combined to create a single, total product. This is clearly illustrated by the Klockner Group of Germany, which packages turnkey projects in the United States and exports them to Latin America and Third World countries. The tangible aspect of this product is the heavy input of U.S. equipment, which is well regarded and thus utilized on projects in Latin America. The intangible aspect of the package is the management expertise provided by Klockner.

The question of what products to sell in foreign markets is the essence of product policy in international marketing. Should we sell the same products we sell domestically, or should they be adapted to local conditions? Will our product line be the same abroad as at home, or should we sell a different mix of products in foreign markets? For each company and industry, the answers may be somewhat different. When firms first enter foreign markets, usually they market their domestic products with minimal adaptation to foreign conditions. As noted earlier, another approach is to acquire a foreign firm that has products designed for its own market. In its planning process, the business firm must decide what businesses and what markets it wants to pursue.

### Product Positioning

Recall from Chapter 6 that *product positioning* is a marketing strategy that attempts to occupy an appealing space in customers' minds in relation to the space occupied by other competitive products. It has been said that the ability to successfully position products in domestic markets is the mark of a good marketer, and the ability to successfully position products in the international market is the mark of a great marketer. Successfully positioning a product internationally is a sophisticated process that requires awareness and sensitivity to the needs of many markets. While input from marketing research is one of the important ingredients in establishing a positioning strategy, intuition, timing, and a marketing sense also play important parts in developing this strategy.

When we discuss positioning a product in the marketplace, we are referring to filling a void in a demand environment. The position a product fills might be based on unique functional benefits that satisfy the need of a market segment of demand. Much like market segmentation, product positioning frequently is ignored by American marketers in selling abroad.

When American products occupy attractive positions at all, usually it is by chance and not by design. How a product is positioned could be determined by local regulations. This was the problem experienced by Pfizer in Europe in marketing Mecadox, a feed supplement-plus-antibiotic for hogs. The product was approved as a feed supplement in certain countries, as an antibiotic in others, and as both in yet others.

The fastest growing U.S. export over the past several years has been business services. Accounting services, advertising, consulting, construction, insurance, auto rentals, hotel services, financial services, and others are included in the category of business services. Looking at Asia alone, the service sector now accounts for more than half of the GNP in Hong Kong, Singapore, Taiwan, and Thailand.[16] Worldwide, the service sector accounts for more than 60 percent of the world output.[17]

The primary competition for American service firms comes from Western Europe, with Latin American and East Asian companies getting in on the act. India views the service business as an infant industry that must be nurtured and protected. As a result, direct and indirect trade barriers have been imposed to restrict foreign companies from domestic markets. Every reason, from the protection of infant industries to national security, has been used to justify some of the restrictive practices.

## Adaptation Versus Standardization

A controversial issue in international marketing is the issue of product adaptation (localization) versus product standardization. Frequently debated in the international marketing literature, this issue centers on whether a business should pursue a strategy that is standardized across national markets or adapted to individual national markets. **Product adaptation** means simply changing the product to meet local needs, while **product standardization** means that a product originally designed for a particular market is exported to other countries with virtually no change, except perhaps for the translation of words and other cosmetic touches. The goals of reducing costs and complexity lead companies to consider standardization, while a customer orientation sways them toward product adaptation.

International marketing managers periodically face the decision as to how much of their marketing strategy in one market applies to another.[18] The attractions of standardization are obvious. Usually, it will result in lower costs and economies of scale in manufacturing, product development, and marketing. Managerial complexity is reduced, and export marketing is facilitated when the same product is exported to several countries. In addition, standardization offers the marketer an opportunity to present a unified brand image, worldwide.

However, there are many obstacles to the application of uniform marketing policies. Variations across markets in attitudes, competitive environments, and marketing management-related variables, as well as differences in languages, culture, and lifestyle, must be adequately assessed to ensure the success of the product in a particular market.

**Concept Review**

1. How do foreign government policies often impact U.S. firm's pricing decisions?

2. What are some of the entry strategies used by U.S. firms in their attempt to penetrate foreign markets?

3. What are some of the things U.S. firms must consider when contemplating a product adaptation versus a product standardization strategy?

## Managing the International Promotion Effort

Integrated marketing communication (IMC) is an important part of the international marketing program of firms competing in the global marketplace. More and more companies are recognizing that an effective promotional program is important for B2B firms competing in foreign markets, and many of these organizations are utilizing advertising agencies for their global advertising efforts.

An unfamiliar marketing environment coupled with customers who have different sets of values and customers, as well as different purchase motives and abilities, add to the challenge of communicating marketing messages. In addition to different languages encountered from country to country, many different languages may be spoken within a particular country, such as in India, Switzerland, or China. Many U.S. business marketers also find that media options are very different from one country to the next because of differing regulations and restrictions. As a result of all these factors, different creative and media strategies, as well as changes in other elements of the IMC program, frequently are required for foreign markets. In Chapter 9, you learned that the promotional tools used in marketing communication (also called the promotional mix) are professional selling, advertising, public relations, sales promotion, and direct marketing. Effective B2B firms consider international implications for each tool. The process of international IMC is similar to a firm's domestic communications program. The firm begins by setting objectives and ends by following up and modifying the promotional plan, if necessary (see Exhibit 9-2 in Chapter 9). There are, however, several special considerations when focusing on global markets. Some of these are discussed below.

### International Advertising

The issue of standardization is a factor that must be considered when determining the type of advertising that will be used in global markets. A 1983 article by Theodore Levitt reignited the argument about standardized products and marketing programs in international business marketing. Levitt argued that companies should globalize their marketing strategies, marketing the same product the same way in all markets, foreign and domestic.[19] The desirability of global marketing has been widely debated, and an important part of the argument concerns the desirability of standardizing advertising worldwide.[20]

A policy of *global advertising* attempts to standardize advertising programs across international markets. Global advertising can be contrasted to *localized advertising,* in which different advertising programs are used in each international market. In practice, completely global advertising and completely localized advertising represent the extreme ends of a continuum. In practice, most advertising programs fall somewhere between the two extremes. Within business markets, the opportunities for global appeals are more easily identifiable because the buying motives and purchase decisions are often similar across markets and are made explicit by established industry purchasing procedures. Many business products, including raw materials and technologically sophisticated products, are being marketed to an increasingly concentrated set of business buyers. Within these markets, standardized advertising in carefully selected trade media is more likely to play an information role, supplementing the efforts of a company's personal sales force.

A third alternative for some marketers is to "think global, act local." This means a company may develop a global theme or strategy, then adapt it as necessary for different countries. Thus, Levis uses a rugged, hip theme for all its advertisements, but conveys the brand image from country to country.[21]

## International Sales Promotion

The basic purposes of gaining attention and interest and motivating a behavioral response within a target market remain the same for sales promotion whether a business firm is operating domestically or globally. Business-to-business firms increasingly rely on trade-oriented sales promotion to help sell their products in foreign markets. The challenge for global business marketing managers is to assess the effectiveness of sales promotion efforts across different cultures and markets. This assessment of effectiveness needs to take into account the varying cultural, economic, social, and legal aspects of different markets.

Unlike advertising, which often can be done on a global basis, sales must often be adapted to local markets. There are several important differences among countries that must be considered in developing a sales promotion program. These include the stage of economic development (as noted earlier in the chapter), market maturity, customer perceptions of promotional tools, trade structure, and legal restrictions and regulations.

A discussion (however brief) of global sales promotion would not be complete without touching on business (industrial) trade shows abroad. Almost all managers acknowledge that trade shows represent a major marketing opportunity for firms operating in international business. International trade shows offer companies an excellent source of market-specific and firm-specific information.[22] As American firms seek business markets abroad, a stumbling block confronting many new entrants is that of quickly gaining access to market information and decision-makers. The business trade show is one vehicle that can serve the business marketer well in this regard. It is estimated that there are over 600 trade shows annually in 70 different countries.

European trade shows offer an excellent opportunity for business marketers to develop contacts for the emerging Eastern European market. Participation in a trade show is one of the best ways to test the potential of Europe and may be the most important step in a U.S. exporter's European marketing plan. These shows also are a fertile ground for cultivating new customers for small- and medium-sized businesses. The entry time for exporting can be cut from years to months by regularly attending foreign trade shows.

## International Publicity

Incidents such as the International Olympic Committee debacle of 1999, Exxon's *Valdez* oil spill, Union Carbide's tragic accident at its plant in Bhopal, India, and the tainted water supplied to Coca-Cola in France create situations that impact a company's image worldwide. Usually, companies have less control over global publicity relative to a domestic situation, and no firms are powerful enough to control a host country's media. At best, attempts are made to provide positive information about the company that is directed at influential targets, such as members of the broadcast media, editors, or journalists. For example, to reduce the trend of "Japan bashing" in the early- to mid–1990s in the United States, Japanese corporations made use of public relations firms that assisted in developing positive publicity regarding the companies' philanthropic activities in the United States. Some companies choose to hire outside PR firms such as the London-based Shandwick PLC and Edelman Public Relations Worldwide, or Canada's Hill & Knowlton. Several PR firms in the United Kingdom, Germany, Italy, Spain, Austria, and the Netherlands have joined together in a network known as Globalink. This global network of PR firms provides business marketers with event planning and literature design and will even tailor a promotional campaign for a particular country or region of the world.

## Trends in International Direct, Interactive, and Internet Marketing

The United States has a market environment and the skills for direct marketing that are unmatched by any other country in the world. Indeed, the United States has the world's largest number of hosts (Internet customers). International direct marketing is used in virtually every B2B category, from banks and distributors to airlines and nonprofit organizations, and uses direct mail, along with broadcast and print media. As for interactive and Internet marketing, businesses doing business with each other over the Internet comprise the largest segment of e-commerce. It is expected to grow to $4.3 trillion worldwide by 2005.[23] The Internet allows business marketers to offer products to customers around the world simultaneously. Any company that establishes a website automatically becomes a multinational company. Market researchers and students can search databases on CD-ROMs and DVDs, and marketers can find information about their competitors and their buyers (or potential buyers) by visiting a firm's website.

## Managing the International Distribution System

Factors such as political-economic environments and market structures affect international marketing decisions. Consequently, the process of locating international customers can be different from domestic marketing. One country's distribution system might be more conducive to developing its own local distributor network, while another might best be penetrated with an American-based or foreign-based intermediary.

When the B2B firm first considers entering the international market, it has to make two important decisions. First, will the new market for the product provide greater returns than would other options? Second, what is the most suitable market entry mode or type of channel structure to use? The development and maintenance of a global distribution system requires a tremendous commitment of time, money, and managerial energy that typifies the development of a global channel system. Firms may be using international channels that are not the most preferred, but they may not be able to change. Firms are not always able to obtain the best channel structure for their purposes. Foreign government restrictions, the dictates of corporate parents, resource scarcity, and contractual commitments all play a part in constraining decisions.

Many channel alternatives are available to the business marketer, including distribution through American-based export intermediaries, through foreign-based intermediaries, and through direct marketing (company-managed, direct-sales forces).[24] Business products firms can use any combination of the three distribution systems, as illustrated in Exhibits 12-4, 12-5, and 12-6, or only one, depending on the extent of their involvement in global marketing. The type of distribution system used depends on company size, level of market commitment, and market conditions (financial considerations, intermediaries available, political climate, and so forth). A brief overview of channel alternatives follows.

### *American-based Export Intermediaries*

Indirect sales methods minimize cash outlays and require limited staff efforts. Rather than setting up an international marketing effort, the firm hires one of several types of export service firms to market the product or service abroad. Each performs a slightly different role; from individual brokers, which simply set up specific deals, to export management companies (EMCs), which do more than brokers, to export trading companies (ETCs), which actually take title to the goods. The differences between the different forms of facilitators often is subtle, with most having an established network of international contacts and experience in exporting.

**EXHIBIT 12-4**   **American-Based Export Intermediaries**

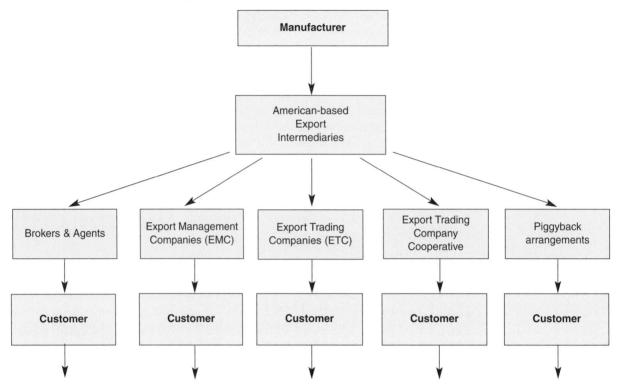

- *Brokers and Agents.* This type of intermediary sets up deals with international buyers, has specific market expertise, and has a network of contacts in the countries served. Some provide consulting services, dispensing advice on packaging, documentation, labeling, etc.
- *Export Management Companies (EMCs).* EMCs facilitate export sales but do not take title to the products. They typically have larger staffs than brokers and will arrange the details of financing and shipping. Usually, they specialize in a particular product group or country.
- *Export Trading Companies (ETCs).* ETCs offer the same services as do EMCs but take title to the goods and also pay the exporter directly. They frequently are tied in with a bank and port authority. ETCs often offer economies of scale and may provide a competitive edge over the other types of export intermediaries.
- *Export Trading Company Cooperative.* An ETC cooperative is a co-op of exporters with similar products. Partners in a co-op gain economy-of-scale advantages by working with an export organization. This type of an organization is very popular with business-to-business product exporters.
- *Piggyback Arrangements.* Some large U.S. corporations have their own trading divisions that will sell a smaller company's product. These "parent companies" take title to and sell another company's products (which do not compete with their own) to customers overseas. This is an easy way to export because a marketing and sales structure already exists. A firm using this arrangement also can gain immediate access to the global market.

**EXHIBIT 12-5**
**Foreign-Based**
**Export**
**Intermediaries**

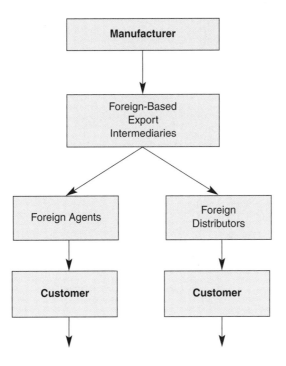

### *Foreign-based Export Intermediaries*

With this method of indirect sales, a firm sells its product to the intermediary, which then finds a way to market it. Local marketing representatives act on an exporter's behalf and also serve as cultural liaisons and advisors. They enjoy considerable independence—it takes time and commitment to establish a strong relationship with this type of intermediary. The exporting firm also needs to provide the intermediary with technical and promotional materials (which may have to be translated).

- *Foreign Agents.* A foreign agent is analogous to a manufacturer's representative in the United States. He or she becomes an exporter's sales representative for a given country or geographic area, working on a commission basis, selling products to distributors and manufacturers. A foreign agent develops marketing strategies for markets, makes contacts, and sells.

- *Foreign Distributors.* A foreign distributor is a merchant who either sells a product on a commission basis or actually buys the product for resale. The distributor does the marketing and often handles product service and after-sale support. Distributors also extend credit to the buyers, as well as handling advertising and promotion. A foreign distributor is analogous to an industrial distributor in the United States.

### *Direct Marketing*

Direct marketing means selling directly to the customer/end user of a product. Often, it is the most appropriate method, as when a foreign manufacturing firm uses a U.S. product as a component in its product line. However, direct marketing can be the most expensive approach in terms of cash outlays and time, as well as being the riskiest strategy. Likewise, it can be the most lucrative, and often is the method of choice for the long term. Business products and services frequently are sold directly through professional sales staffs throughout the world, since specialized knowledge and service may be requirements that remain constant across markets.

**EXHIBIT 12-6**
**Direct Marketing**

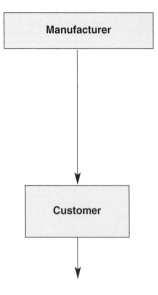

## International Pricing Strategy

Pricing considerations in international business operations are not only more numerous than those in strictly domestic ones but also are more ambiguous and risky. A selling firm must consider at least two different sets of laws, two competitive markets, the reactions of two sets of competitors, and two governments. It is not surprising that determining prices for international sales is such a difficult problem, even for the occasional exporter. Successful pricing is a key element in the profitability of any business operation, domestic or international.

Pricing is one area of international business marketing that has been largely overlooked. Of the Four Ps of marketing, pricing probably is the one that receives the least attention, especially in the international business context. As competition for the world's markets becomes more intense, price will be increasingly important as a competitive tool. The international business marketer is responsible for establishing price policies for a company's international operations.

Pricing for the international business products market can be influenced by a wide variety of factors, with only a few under the firm's direct control. Exhibit 12-7 identifies the most common variables that can influence international pricing strategy. While company factors, market factors, and environmental factors are separated for discussion, keep in mind that they are, in fact, interrelated. In addition, the more uncontrollable market and environmental forces are usually the most disruptive elements that affect international pricing. Taken together, these three sets of factors often are the best explanation as to why an otherwise well-conceived marketing strategy ends up unprofitable.

### Company Factors

#### *Global Corporate Objectives*

The increased emphasis by firms on global marketing, the deregulation of the European market in the early 1990s, and the shift to overseas production have all contributed to the development of pricing policy within globally oriented firms. By understanding the strategic emphasis on price in the marketing mix of the firm, and by appreciating other marketing mix

**EXHIBIT 12-7**
**Common Variables that Influence International Pricing Strategies**

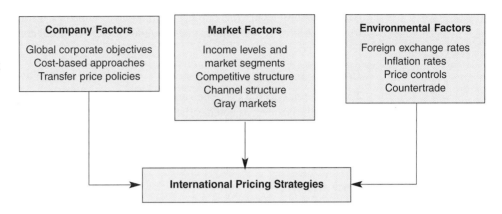

| Company Factors | Market Factors | Environmental Factors |
|---|---|---|
| Global corporate objectives<br>Cost-based approaches<br>Transfer price policies | Income levels and market segments<br>Competitive structure<br>Channel structure<br>Gray markets | Foreign exchange rates<br>Inflation rates<br>Price controls<br>Countertrade |

**International Pricing Strategies**

influences in global markets (such as advertising, personal selling, and promotion differentiation), a business products marketer can, hopefully, make decisions based on company global objectives.

### Cost-Based Approaches

The basis for any effective pricing policy is a clear understanding of the cost and profit variables involved. A clear definition of relevant costs and profits is often difficult to achieve. Understanding the various cost elements is a prerequisite for a successful international pricing strategy.

### Transfer Price Policies

A substantial amount of international business takes place between subsidiaries of the same company. The price charged to all these subsidiaries is known as transfer pricing. Transfer pricing policies tend to be strictly under the control of the parent company. To pursue a strategy of profit maximization, a company may lower transfer prices for products shipped from some subsidiaries while increasing prices for products shipped to others. The company will then try to accumulate profits in subsidiaries where it is advantageous and keep profits low in others.

## Market Factors

Several market factors affect the way a marketer establishes pricing structures in the international market. Some of the factors that affect pricing include the following:

### Income Levels and Market Segments

Prices need to reflect the conditions of each market in which the business firm competes. The firm must take into account local market variables and the realities of the marketplace. The challenge is to meet successfully the large number of local economic situations and market segments to be considered.

### Competitive Structure

As national economies become increasingly interdependent, the competitive pressures felt by companies all over the world are intensifying. Companies facing this onslaught of competitive pressures from firms scattered around the globe must design and implement strategies that differ considerably from those faced in their domestic markets.[25] The unique competitive structure in each market must be considered. If the company is a sole supplier of a particular business product or service, it will enjoy great pricing flexibility. If it has to compete against local firms or other international companies, however, the opposite will be true. In addition, cost structures may be quite different for local competitors, which may affect their pricing.

### Channel Structure

The final price to the customer may be influenced by channel structure, including the length of the channel, as noted earlier in this chapter. Generally, most foreign countries tend to operate with longer channels than those used in the United States. This can significantly increase end-user prices—a fact that an astute business products marketer will quickly perceive.

### Gray Markets

A major problem that international firms face is the phenomenon of different prices between countries. If price differences are large enough, entrepreneurs step in and buy products in low-price countries and re-export the products to high-price countries. Experts call this the gray market because these transactions occur outside regular trade channels. Fluctuations foster gray markets, and combating them is an endless battle for many companies.

## Environmental Factors

Several environmental factors also affect the way a marketer establishes pricing structures in the international market. Some of the factors that affect pricing include these:

### Foreign Exchange Rates

Currency swings are considered to be a major trade barrier. Movements in exchange rates, which can be 50 percent or more over a period of time, directly influence a firm's ability to compete on price. Exchange rate fluctuations are extremely critical with long-term contracts. The longer the time between the signing of an order and the actual delivery, the greater the exposure to foreign exchange risk. Firms can try to manage foreign exchange fluctuations, but they have no control over them.

### Inflation Rates

A company selling its products in a country with a high rate of inflation risks that, once the constantly devaluing local currency is converted to the seller's currency, the resulting amount will not even cover product costs. In countries with extremely high inflation rates, companies may price their products in a stable currency, such as the U.S. dollar, and translate prices into the local currency on a daily basis, or, if possible, insist on payment in another currency.

### Price Controls

A company's pricing strategy in a particular market can be influenced by the government. Price control, in one form or another, can be found in every market in the world. In the effort to control prices, governments have a number of options open to them, including dictating the market price, dictating the margins allowed to intermediaries, establishing upper and lower limits of markups (creating price floors and ceilings), and using government subsidy. Clearly, global pricing is one of the most complex decisions that business products marketing strategists must make.

### Countertrade

Global trade does not always involve cash. With countertrade (CT), or reciprocal trade, all or part of the payment for goods or services is in the form of barter (the direct, one-time exchange of goods or services for other goods and/or services). According to the New

# WHAT WOULD YOU DO?

### "BUT IN MY COUNTRY, WHITE LIES ARE A BUSINESS NECESSITY"

Jack Leader, a buyer for XXX Office Automation Products located in a foreign country, was working on a value analysis project for a key part purchased from a sole-source supplier. Value analysis (VA) usually starts with the highest-cost products, and this was no exception (see Chapter 4 for a review of VA). The heat was on from marketing to get the total cost of the machine down, so that XXX could be more competitive in the international marketplace. That meant that all the component and subassembly buyers would be working closely with their suppliers. Jack knew from his analyst's calculations (which backed into the supplier's cost), that the American supplier had a very high margin. In order to be able to show a satisfactory performance on this value analysis project, Jack would have to persuade the supplier either to lower the selling price or improve the value of the product. He knew one thing was certain: he had to show his superiors that he had made some progress.

Jack had explored sourcing the part at several of the American supplier's global competitors, and all of them could offer a much lower price. Unfortunately, none of their samples would function in application, however. Something in the formulation of the American supplier's material gave it special properties. Material specialists at all of these potential suppliers invested in ongoing programs to duplicate the material. Even at XXX Office Automation Products, the material specialists were working on uncovering the secret to the supplier's material. The leader of this effort was Dr. Frans Panner, director of materials and R&D and an internationally known expert on the material in question.

One day, Jack was inspired to visit the American supplier's operation and to bring Dr. Panner along (but identify him as another buyer). Jack figured that with Dr. Panner's knowledge of the technology, he might very well see exactly what the American supplier was doing that was unique. All was going fine until, during the plant tour, one of the supplier's materials specialists recognized Dr. Panner. He casually asked the marketing director, who was hosting the tour, if he wasn't worried that Dr. Panner was there to gather confidential information. The marketing director was horrified that the buyer, Jack Leader, would pull such a stunt, and he banned any further visits. He also was considering making a strong complaint to the buyer's boss. As Jack was flying back to his country, he turned to Dr. Panner and said, "I am surprised they got so upset. Obviously, it was just a cultural misunderstanding."

### Assignment

Define the ethical issues for all concerned. As the American supplier's marketing director, what action would you take?

---

York based Corporate Barter Council, North American companies traded $8.2 billion in goods and services in 1998, up from $3.2 billion in 1985.[26] Recent deals such as those by Xerox and General Dynamics point out the significance of countertrade activity.

Xerox sells copiers and printers in Brazil for Brazilian steel and venetian blinds to the tune of $100 million annually. General Dynamics engaged in a multimillion-dollar deal to sell F-16s to Turkey. To clinch the deal, General Dynamics agreed to purchase scores of Turkish products; invest in Hilton hotels; set up a joint venture to co-produce the F-16s; and build housing, a school, and a mosque for 400 local workers. Scenarios such as these illustrate the need for international business marketing managers to give serious consideration to including a countertrade plan in their overall international marketing plan.

Countertrade is an expansion of traditional barter practice and involves reciprocal arrangements that link sales to purchases or purchases to sales. The transfer of products, services, and technology replaces or supplements a cash transaction. CT does not require the exchange of currency, so it offers an alternative method for nations with exchange or convertibility problems to finance their international purchases. Ponder the following facts:

- Half of the Fortune 500 companies have used barter in some way.
- Approximately 300,000 companies trade through corporate barter every year, accounting for over $7.6 billion worth of goods and services.
- Barter is estimated to be growing at a rate of 8 percent per year.

- More than 80 nations currently use CT.
- Over 30 percent of world trade involves the use of CT.

Firms may have little choice in the future but to join in the increasing countertrade activity or be cut off from some of the world markets. Developing experience with CT and providing an atmosphere that encourages and provides management support for CT is a strategy that makes good sense for the international business marketer.

---

## Concept Review

1. What is the purpose of global sales promotion?

2. What are some of the forms of distribution facilitators available to the international business marketer?

3. Why should the international business marketer be concerned with environmental factors affecting pricing?

---

## Summary

- To be successful in today's foreign markets requires a reevaluation of marketing programs in light of current trends. The firm must effectively compete with competitors (foreign and domestic) actively selling to demanding customers. The complications created by cultural, legal, political, and other environmental differences among countries notwithstanding, there is a rapidly growing demand for business goods and services throughout the world; global competition is coming from western Europe, Japan, and a host of developing countries from Asia to Latin America. The U.S. firm desiring to market internationally must match its products and/or services to the stages of economic development in the countries in which they wish to do business.

- Many U.S. firms are not aware of the potential market that lies abroad. Exporting yields a powerful return on investment for not only large firms but also for small- and medium-sized enterprises (SMEs) that develop a long-term export strategy. International business marketers should be as cognizant of the complex buying process, sociocultural dynamics, the political-legal environment, and the economic environment in foreign markets as they are in domestic markets.

- International law is the collection of treaties, conventions, and agreements between nations that more or less have the force of law. International law involves some mutuality, with two or more countries participating in the drafting and execution. International law includes treaties of friendship, commerce, and navigation (FCNs), tax treaties, the International Monetary Fund, the General Agreement on Tariffs and Trade, the International Standards Organization, and NAFTA.

- The importance of foreign laws to the business marketer lies primarily in domestic marketing in each foreign market. The problem arises from the fact that the laws in each market tend to be somewhat different from those in every other market. International business marketers must become familiar with laws in each country because these individually affect the components of the company's marketing mix abroad.

- The general tendency for most business firms is to enter the international market slowly and cautiously through exporting and/or the Internet. As companies adopt long-term perspectives, they tend to turn to other entry modes, such as contractual agreements (e.g., licensing, joint ventures, or franchising) or direct foreign investments (e.g., manufacturing, assembly, or turnkey operations).

- An international business marketer must always determine the local needs of a particular country in developing product strategies. Product positioning is a sophisticated process that requires awareness and sensitivity to the needs of many markets. Some firms may have to adapt some of their products to meet a particular country's needs, while other products in their mix can be sold exactly as they are being sold in the firm's domestic market.

- Integrated marketing communications (IMC) is an important part of the international marketing program of firms competing in the global marketplace. Often, U.S. marketers desiring to promote products abroad must contend with different languages, customs, and values as well as various media options as they focus their efforts in a global market. Global trends in direct, database, and Internet marketing are all effective promotional tools available for use by the astute international business marketer.

- The international marketing manager must make distribution choices from among American-based export intermediaries, foreign-based intermediaries, or direct marketers (company-managed, direct-sales force). The development and maintenance of a global distribution system requires a tremendous commitment of time, money, and managerial energy. Firms may be using channels that are not the most preferred, but may not be able to change them.

Marketing managers must also be aware of foreign government restrictions in their international marketing efforts.

- Pricing considerations in international business markets are numerous and ambiguous. Pricing is risky because it can be influenced by a wide variety of factors. Company factors affecting pricing include global corporate objectives, and transfer price policies. Market factors affecting pricing are income levels among market segments, competitive structure, channel structure, and gray markets. Environmental factors include foreign exchange rates, inflation rates, price controls, and countertrade.

## Key Terms

adaptation
assembly operation
cultural adiaphora
cultural exclusive
cultural imperative
exporting

franchising
international Internet marketing
international law
joint venture
licensing

political risk
product adaptation
product standardization
trade barrier
turnkey operation

## Review Questions

1. Identify and briefly describe five stages of economic development through which virtually every country goes.

2. Why is it more difficult to identify the members of the buying center in international business marketing than in domestic marketing? Why is a thorough understanding of cultural dynamics among countries important to the international business marketer? Why is adaptation such a key concept in international business marketing? Distinguish between the political and the legal environments involved in international business marketing.

3. What is meant by the term *international law?* What are treaties of friendship, commerce, and navigation? What are the respective roles of the International Monetary Fund, the General Agreement on Tariffs and Trade, the ISO, and NAFTA in international law?

4. Identify and briefly explain the three "legal" systems used in the majority of countries.

5. Identify and discuss the use of major modes of entry into international business markets. What is the most common way companies first enter international business markets?

6. What should be the essence of product policy in international business marketing? What is the role of product positioning in international business marketing efforts? When would an international business company utilize product adaptation, and when would it be better to employ product standardization?

7. Distinguish between global and local advertising. Briefly discuss the importance of advertising, sales promotion, publicity, direct, interactive, and Internet marketing in global promotion.

8. Identify and explain the three basic ways in which most American companies distribute their products on an international basis.

9. Briefly describe three company factors, four market factors and three environmental factors that affect pricing in international business markets. Why do you think that pricing has historically been given so little attention by international business marketers? What is the role of countertrade in global marketing?

**Case 12-1**

# Olin International Consultants Inc.

This case was written by Dr. Roger Gomes and Dr. Patricia Knowles, Clemson University © 1999

Patricia Olin, president of Olin International Consulting (OIC), was watching an Indian culture seminar being conducted by her company's senior consultant for that country. The room was almost entirely filled with this year's newly hired associates. As Patricia looked out at the room of new college graduates, she wondered which ones would succeed. She thought, "Perhaps four or five will make it to partner level, and one may make it to my job." Although the company selected only top graduates, she thought she could pick out the "special ones" already, even after watching them for only two weeks. They were those who, when given a seminar assignment, would far exceed the company's expectations and provide exceptional value for the clients. They were greatly valued by their clients, and their relationships often meant hundreds of thousands of dollars in "billed hours" for the associate's time. They were quickly promoted (associate $50K, consultant $75K, senior consultant $125K, partner $200K, and up). The management group at OIC had no problem in approving high salaries because these individuals brought in at least five times their salary in billings to clients across the globe. Patricia had seen a few make it to partner in as little as six years. Average performers would progress much more slowly, however, and it would be unlikely that they would ever get past the consultant level.

In OIC's business, all the clients were profitable, but some countries and some clients were more important than others. Patricia had developed a procedure to determine which new associates to assign to top clients. She felt that an associate's work ethic, pride in their work, teamwork, maturity, organizational ability, and communication skills would be obvious, even in their initial assignments. She would put the new associates into teams, provide each team with an international trade assignment, and have the team present its work to the executive board. Few would do a poor job, but any that did would be reassigned to clerical work. Most would do professional- quality work, and they would be assigned to the less important clients. A few associates would make such a grand effort in research preparation (beyond what was expected) and such a clearly exceptional presentation that everyone in the room would smile and want to congratulate them personally. The future of OIC would be determined by these exceptional new associates, who would be assigned to the important clients in the most profitable countries and who would progress on the fast track. For those associates who were not there yet but were really trying, Patricia was willing to invest her time and expertise.

After the team presentations, it was not uncommon for a team that had done an average job to complain, "Well, if I had known that it was important and it would affect my career, I would have worked harder on it." These people, like those who did a poor job, were also demoted to clerical positions. Rather than work hard to create value for the client, they would often procrastinate until it was too late to do a professional job and would then come up with a plethora of excuses. They didn't seem to have any comprehension that problems always come up, but a professional sees them as challenges and overcomes them through extra effort. One thing that Patricia would never stand for was unethical conduct. Associates who copied something that someone else had created were fired immediately. The business world is smaller than most people think, and a black mark like that on a young person's record would follow him or her for a long time. Most people want to be able to trust their executive employees. Just thinking about all the effort these young people had made to get this far, Patricia winced at the thought of their tossing it away to get out of doing a proper job for the client. Problem people were difficult to screen for, but give them an assignment and they would almost always give themselves away.

Patricia didn't even try to explain to the new associates why she didn't want them exposed to OIC's customers. She knew that even if she tried to discuss the importance of taking pride in one's work, professionalism, and maturity, they were not ready to understand. On the other hand, the special associates she knew had exceeded expectations on assignments in college, would exceed expectations on these training assignments, and would exceed expectations when working with clients. That is what professionals do. She considered asking the problem associates how they would like to be operated on by a doctor who just did enough to get by. "No," she thought, "they just would not get it. Somehow they haven't figured out that OIC's providing international business-to-business services is something done by professionals. We deal across many cultures, but one constant is that our reputation is critical. When we don't do our best, our client suffers, and that can result in the client's losing business in a particular country and having to shut down operations. Yes, it is bad for the client's bottom line, but the personal impact on individuals who lose their jobs is much more tragic. Professionals always do their best because they have a responsibility to those who are depending on them."

One part of the job of an international consultant is to read everything available on topics and put it into a concise form that will be valuable and useful to clients. Some of OIC's clients were interested in general trade information, and others were interested in expanding into various countries. Patricia would assign one topic per team and would give each team one or more Internet URL addresses to get them started. The team would then relate and evaluate each of the given sites (and include that in its report as an appendix), expand to other information sources, prepare a useful format, and create a professional report (presentation with written copy). The objective is that, on seeing the team's presentation, the client would believe that it had received value for its money and would want to contract with the team for additional, more specific strategic projects. OIC would charge the client $50K–$100K for the initial project (such as this assignment) and would expect that the more intensive follow-up project would cost in the millions of dollars (over several years).

## Assignment

You are new associates at OIC. Each team will be assigned a topic from the list of nine below. A client (class) meeting will be scheduled by the instructor for your team to present its report developed for the client.

## OIC Topic List for New Associate Projects

### Trade Compliance

www.customs.ustreas.gov/imp-exp/rulings/comply/icpframe.htm

www.customs.ustreas.gov/imp-exp/auto-sys/ace/newsltr8.htm

www.customs.ustreas.gov/about/comply/index.htm

www.usia.gov/tropical-econ/wto/wto.htm

www.legal.gsa.gov/legal27q.htm

www.usitc.gov/

www.ustr.gov/

www.fplc.edu/ipmall/pointbox.htm

http://uls.tradecompass.com/ecs/

### India

www.ita.doc.gov/uscs/india/india.html

www.wtcs.org/wtc/calcutta.htm

www.trade-india.com

www.trade-india.com/tradeindia/iid/index.html

www.trade-india.com/tradeindia/tflash/content/bo.htm

www.state.gov/www/about_state/business/com_guides/1998/southeast_asia/india98.html

www.gcc.net/commerce/asia/india.htm

www.ita.doc.gov/industry/otea/usfth/india.e-iu.s.

www.indiaintl.com/news.htm

www.indiaintl.com/shows.html

## Egypt

www.ita.doc.gov/uscs/egypt/egypt.html

www.wtcs.org/wtc/cairo.html

www.ita.doc.gov/uscs/ccgoegyp.html

www.gcc.net/commerce/mideast/egypt.htm

http://mena-peacenet.nist.gov

www.planetbus.com/country/115.htm

## General International Trade

http://170.110.214.002/faqs.nsf

www.ita.doc.gov/industry/otea/state/state&re.html

http://govinfo.kerr.orst.edu/impexp.html

www.tradeport.org/cgi-bim/banner.pl/ts/buyers/index.html

http://207.137.86.24:7003/tradeport/owa/search.search_form

http://infoserv2.ita.doc.gov/ftohomep.nsf

http://infoserv2.ita.doc.gov/nedhomep.nsf

http://infoserve2.ita.doc.gov/epc.nsf

## Smaller Markets

www.itaiep.doc.gov/search/iatoc.exe

www.mac.doc.gov/ccg/search/htm

www.ita.doc.gov/how_to_export/exprog00.html

http://infoserv2.ita.doc.gov/nedhomep.nsf

www.ita.doc.gov/mena/econof.html

http://infoserv2.ita.doc.gov/apweb.nsf

www.iep.doc.gov/eebic/upevents/esttrade.htm

www.ita.doc.gov/usfes/usf/dec/

## Eritrea

www.cyberstars.com/country/eritrea/index.html

www.wtgonline.com/country/er/bus.html

www.cgtd.com/global/africa/eritrea.htm

www.aaas.org/international/africa-guide/eritrea.htm

## Estonia

www.ciesin.ee/etc/

www.hotline.ee/atlas/eng/

www.hotline.ee/atlas/eng/tegevus.htm

www.eia.ee

www.eea.ee/indexe.html

### Portugal

www.portugal.org/

www.tradecompass.com/library/books/com_guide/portugal.toc.html

www.portugal.org/doingbusiness/buyingfrom/tradeshows/tradeshows.html

### European Community

www.sce.doc.gov

www.tradeassistance.com

---

**Case 12-2**

# Global Farm Equipment Ltd.*

On January 15, 1999, Robert Hardy, international sourcing manager for Global Farm Equipment Ltd., London, UK Plant, was interrupted. Bill Jones, quality assurance manager, burst into Hardy's office, exclaiming, "The report is back from the outside lab. RSS's** shipment of drive shafts has been rejected due to inferior material! Their previous shipment, which we have already assembled into equipment, will probably turn out to be bad also. It looks like they purposely tried to cut costs, or they never knew how to make the shafts right in the first place!"

Robert was surprised. While this was only RSS's second shipment of the machined steel drive shafts from their Murmansk, Russia, manufacturing operation, GFE had been receiving castings from RSS for over two years and all had been going well. The castings alone represented £4.2 million of GFE purchases, and Robert had been looking forward to buying more from the company. There were times when RSS suffered through problems with raw materials availability and the weather, but GFE had been willing to deal with those problems since the Russian castings represented a cost savings over European Union (E.U.) suppliers (even including the extra rail transportation). Robert thought, "Apparently, RSS is an acceptable source for castings, but does not have equivalent capabilities in precision steel drive shaft production."

## Company Background

Global Farm Equipment Company, a major international manufacturer of industrial and farm equipment, had 16 plants worldwide with annual sales of £11.2 billion. Purchasing at GFE was highly decentralized. Each plant had its own purchasing staff that reported to the general manager through the materials manager. The purchasing dollars of the London plant accounted for approximately 57 percent of cost of goods sold.

---

*Adapted from Lisa Ellram, "Drive Shaft Decision: Case A, in *Cases in Purchasing and Supply Chain Management: Strategies, Practices, and Problems,* S. G. Joag ed., 1995, pp. 62–63. Reprinted by permission of the publisher, the National Association of Purchasing Management.

**RSS is a fictitious name used here to set the scene for a student negotiation.

# International Purchasing

Ten years ago, the world farming economy entered a major slump. To help offset declining sales and profitability, GFE sought to reduce costs. Thus, overseas sourcing, particularly in the Pacific Rim, became an attractive option. Five years ago, GFE was purchasing about £5.7 million worth of parts from Asian suppliers, and the volume has been increasing by about 15 percent per year. Three years ago, GFE extended its international sourcing to include suppliers in Russia and India.

# Relationship with RSS

RSS was by far the largest Russian source for GFE, accounting for about 75 percent of its Russian purchases. GFE valued RSS as a supplier because it provided GFE with good quality and service on a number of raw and machined castings, at a price 40 to 60 percent below comparable E.U. sources. Delivery time averaged 30 days. In February of last year, GFE requested that RSS provide a quotation on a machined drum drive shaft number M5555 Rev. A used in harvesting equipment. These drive shafts required a special 1045 stress-relieved cold drawn steel rod, a material that was produced by only a few steel manufacturers. A UK supplier had satisfactorily supplied the part, but GFE desired a lower price.

# Current Quality Problem

In mid-December of last year, GFE received its first shipment of part M5555 Rev. A. Receiving inspection at the GFE plant showed that the dimensions and surface hardness of the part were acceptable. Thus, the parts were used in production.

On January 12, 1999, about 30 days after the initial shipment, the second shipment of shafts arrived from RSS. Standard Quality Assurance testing at the GFE revealed that this shipment did not meet specifications; there were dimensional deficiencies. This failure concerned QA managers, who immediately sent samples to an outside lab for further testing.

On January 15, the results from the outside lab were received by QA manager Bill Jones. The tests revealed that the wrong kind of steel had been used. The steel was 1045 but not "1045-stress relieved." The shafts had apparently been heat treated after machining to provide a superficial outside hardness that made the shafts appear to be the correct material. If these parts were used in production, the product would be subject to early failure. Premature failure of a product was totally unacceptable to a quality company like Global Farm Equipment.

The implications were staggering. The sales of harvesting equipment are highly seasonal, and GFE had no backup shafts. Harvesting equipment production would be unable to proceed. GFE was no longer using its UK supplier for this particular item, although it was buying other parts from that supplier. Further, the shaft generally had a lead time of about three months. RSS also had another shipment of shafts in transit to GFE.

# New RSS Pricing on the Shaft

On January 20, GFE received a revised harvester drive shaft price bid from RSS. Robert Hardy looked through the document and saw no mention of the fact that RSS had been using the wrong material, nor what the resolution would be concerning the costs involved in shutting down GFE production, rush purchasing from the original supplier with overtime costs, and reworking the equipment already assembled. What he did see was that RSS was raising its price to produce the shaft beyond what GFE paid its domestic supplier. To say the least he wasn't pleased. Cost savings from the Russian supplier had already been included in the plant's budget. Robert had no choice but to cancel the order at RSS and order the shaft from the domestic supplier. Each unit would carry a negative price variance from standard of £8.01.

GFE Drive Shaft Bids
| | |
|---|---|
| Original price from domestic source | £16.91/unit |
| Original price from RSS | £ 8.90/unit |
| New revised price from RSS | £22.57/unit |

## Defective Policy

It was GFE's policy to bill its suppliers for all costs associated with defective material, including labor to repair and replace the part. The policy was clearly stated in the purchase order.

This correspondence had taken place requesting reimbursement:

| GFE's ACTION | | RSS's RESPONSE |
|---|---|---|
| February 15: | Fax reimbursement request (with all costs identified) | None |
| March 2: | Repeat fax reimbursement request | March 15: are investigating |
| April 1: | Fax inquiry as to outcome of investigation | April 18: still investigating |

| Costs Associated with RSS Shipment of Defective Materials | |
|---|---|
| Purchased materials | £ 8,122 |
| Assembly labor, cost of materials welded with shaft that were destroyed | £16,400 |
| Disassembly labor only | £12,600 |
| Total | £37,122 |

## GFE Management Meeting

On April 25, 1999, Rodger Whitley, general manager for GFE's London plant, called for a meeting to go over the RSS problem. He started by expressing his satisfaction with the international sourcing that had reduced costs and increased profitability. Speaking directly to Robert he said, "We have made significant progress in achieving our cost reduction goals, and I do not want to see those gains lost. Your assignment is to learn how to deal with RSS so that we do not repeat this defective materials error, and also recover our costs (£37,122) from them. We do a lot of business with them on castings, so you should have plenty of leverage. Somehow you need to also get them back supplying that shaft and at somewhere near the original price. We just can't go on indefinitely with an £8/unit negative variance."

Robert got the message but didn't know why RSS was ignoring repeated GFE requests for reimbursement for costs incurred due to RSS's shipment of defective drive shafts. On the one hand, he understood that they had little understanding of the western view that "the customer is always right" and that "you never win an argument with a customer," or that "even if you do win a battle with a customer, you will lose the war." In fact, when problems developed with RSS, they seemed quite determined to deal with a "winner take all" approach. Robert wasn't used to being treated this way, but if he could get RSS producing acceptable shafts at their original price, the price difference of £8.01 × 100,000 units meant it was certainly worth his trouble.

Robert decided to start by researching Russian culture and business practices. As part of that effort, Robert contacted his old international marketing professor at Bradford University to discuss the situation. Professor Kingsford noted that the Russian business culture was in a state of transition from many years in a centralized controlled economy. Sounding professorial, Kingsford said, "Things are done much differently there, and you can be sure they would like the problem to just go away. In the old days whoever was responsible for such a problem would have been more than fired. And you can bet it is going to be a big mess for them to pin down the responsibility. From what I understand of your materials specification, you probably were specifying a steel material that was common in your culture, but too specialized for them to be familiar with. If you had worked backward through their costs, wouldn't you have noticed that they had vastly understated the cost of the steel? Since Russia is a sovereign country, the defective material clause in your purchase is unenforceable in the legal sense. If it was an honest misunderstanding and you apply threats concerning your other business with them, they will most likely respond very poorly. It would be like an American arriving unannounced in your London office, ignoring all the implications of what he was demanding, ignoring how things are properly clone, and demanding that you take actions that would probably cost the jobs of some of your people (who really hadn't done anything wrong). You would probably think him a barbarian, and get quite huffy with him."

Kingsford continued, "Still, in their culture these matters can be dealt with only in person, and with some delicacy. Rather than one meeting with everyone there who must be involved in the decision, there will undoubtedly be a series of meetings, each lacking someone with necessary responsibility (necessitating another meeting). As you would like to return home sometime soon, you will be at an immediate disadvantage. As you recall from class, none of this is done with an evil heart. It is just standard business practice, and an attempt to get to know you, and through common business interactions learn how much you respect them. Another disadvantage you have is that you are not a top executive. This decision will have to come from their top executive, and from their perspective, GFE is sending an underling. Still, I would think that you are probably much more sensitive to cross-cultural negotiations than are your bosses. I'll fax you some notes that Professor Black developed on business negotiations with Russians. Be sure to keep in mind that they are a capable and proud people. They were the first in space and still hold many records for engineering accomplishments. They have been conducting international trade for thousands of years, and were quite good at it while our ancestors were still painting themselves blue and living in sod huts."

Robert thanked Professor Kingsford, and both agreed that they would continue the conversation before Robert left for Russia. Later that afternoon, Robert's assistant brought him the following fax from Professor Kingsford.

# Appendix: Russian Negotiating Style[***]
*(As developed by Professor Black)*

## Negotiation Primer

Negotiation approaches can be broken down into two basic categories: distributive and collaborative. Distributive describes the idea most people carry in their minds when they think of negotiating—there is a fixed amount of a good that should be "distributed" among the negotiators. A good example of this is slicing a pie into pieces between two or more separate parties. Unless the pie is cut exactly equally, the more one party gets, the less the others get. In a distributive agreement, how the pie is actually cut depends mainly upon the real and perceived power each party has and the effectiveness of the negotiating tactics

---

[***]Source: J. S. Black and M. Shinkarev, "Technogrid Group and A/O Navicon," in *Cases in International Organizational Behavior,* C. Oddou and M. Mendenhall eds., Oxford, UK: Blackwell Publishers Ltd., 1998, pp. 224–27. Reprinted by permission of Blackwell Publishers, Ltd.

each employs. This is the classic "zero-sum" game in which one side's gain can come only at the other side's loss.

The collaborative approach to bargaining, on the other hand, looks beyond the basic negotiating transaction. It focuses on what is driving the negotiators to come together in the first place, and tries to develop a range of options to mutually satisfy the needs of both parties.

## Russian Primer

The Russian people have never lived under a democratic, individual-oriented political system. Until the Bolshevik Revolution in 1917, Russia was an absolute monarchy, ruled by tsars. There were three classes of people: the aristocracy, with its court nobles and military commanders; a tiny middle class of shopkeepers and artisans; and a vast population of agricultural serfs. The 1917 Revolution brought a small amount of freedom to the serfs, but Stalin quickly turned Russia into a ruthless, autocratic state where decisions were taken out of the hands of individuals and put into the hands of the *nomenklatura,* the elite circle of Communist Party officials. The state determined an individual's future. There was no resistance. Thus, the decision-making system of the tsars was replaced by the Soviet system.

## Russian Negotiation

Negotiation with Russians is a long and arduous process. Russians are master chessmen and strategists; they begin negotiations from power positions and give up space only when they are ready. Many American firms become frustrated by the complexity of, and the rituals involved in, Russian negotiations. Less than half of started negotiations end up in completed contracts or agreements.

Russians employ a classic distributive approach. Some of the typical comments used to describe negotiating with the former Soviets are: lengthy, difficult, manipulative, uncompromising, risk-averse, and secretive. Russians have always had a high power distance. It is more difficult for them to accept authority to make decisions in negotiations than it is with their Western counterparts.

## Negotiation Structure

The structure of the negotiations is fairly complex: the old Soviet system placed layers of bureaucracy between the producer and the end user. The following are characteristic patterns in Russian negotiations:

### Protocol/Setting

Perhaps due to a long history of isolation, Russians view relations with foreigners as important and deserving of special treatment. They prefer to deal directly with the principals involved rather than through intermediaries, and the level of the principal within the foreign company is an important indicator to the Russians about the sincerity of the negotiations. Foreign companies that send over senior-level executives and/or open a representative office in Russia invariably wind up making a better impression. The settings for negotiations usually are chosen by the Russians, who try to keep a home court advantage.

### Process

Russian negotiations are two-phased. The first phase involves contacting many vendors and estimating the technical competency of their products. This often requires repeated explanations of the product merits to different parties. During this stage most companies feel compelled to disclose more information about the product than is usual. Once the top candidates are chosen, the second phase—the bidding process—begins. Bidding typically is the most frustrating phase for Western businesspeople because even minute details are debated.

### Preparation

Russian negotiators come to the table very well briefed about the strengths and weaknesses of their counterparts. Whatever information they lack is requested formally. Ironically, requests by the counterparty to get similar information from the Russians is typically met with opposition and delays. Russians usually will lay out an overall structure for the negotiations. Detailed agendas are laid out for each meeting, and changes to the proposed agendas tend to disrupt the flow of negotiations.

### Length

Though the Russian negotiation process has historically been a lengthy one, as the Soviet bureaucracy is replaced by enterprise managers eager to do deals, the time-span will shorten. From the Russian perspective, doing business with a foreign company is a serious matter and needs to be considered carefully. Relationships need to he cultivated to determine the best fit for the long term.

### Contracts and Penalty Clauses

Contracts are carefully worded, usually to benefit the Russian party. Product specifications and working conditions must he precisely laid out. Contracts must spell out every possible detail and foresee every possible eventuality. Penalty clauses are usually installed as insurance against failure and delays.

### Countertrade

Russians often bring up countertrade. Their reasoning is simple—they don't have much hard currency available for foreign trade. Countertrade is a useful alternative for getting their products into export markets. It can also be used as part of the negotiations on price. Suppliers who refuse the request for countertrade will be asked to lower their price in return for wanting an all-cash settlement.

## Negotiation Style

Russians are true bargainers. There is little attempt to create a joint solution that increases the negotiation value for both parties. They will start off with maximum positions and attempt to place the burden for compromise on the other side. Russians will accept only the parts of proposals that benefit them and will try to ignore the rest, Concessions are yielded only when necessary; they usually are treated as points on a scoreboard, and Russians focus on keeping the total numbers in balance rather than on the relative importance of each concession.

The Russians view negotiation as a competition, and so most tactics are justified in their zeal to "win." Russians have learned to use their counterparts' time constraints and contract loopholes to their own advantage. They also will use information collected during negotiations with rival companies to better their own positions. Lastly, most observers have mentioned peculiar twists, such as last-minute venue, agenda, or negotiator changes, outrageous demands that are later denied, and abrupt cancellations of meetings.

## Conclusions

Russians are extremely reliable in honoring their commitments and making payments on time. Their negotiation tactics are used to weed out all but truly committed parties. In this way personal relationships based on mutual respect and trust can be developed and nurtured. Russian business relations thrive on deep personal relations. As the legal structure continues to undergo reform, the emphasis on the interpersonal aspect of business may decrease, but only over the long term.

## Assignment

**Team One:** You will be accompanying Robert on his trip to Russia. Learn all you can about British and Russian culture and business practices. It would be very helpful if you could identify some business people from the UK and Russia and explore their views on business negotiations. The meeting will be held at the RSS offices (actually it will be held in your classroom). Your objectives are: (1) collect the £37,122 charges for the defective products, (2) establish a procedure that will ensure better communication of technical requirements and prevent a reccurrence of this type of problem, (3) persuade RSS to agree to produce the shaft with the correct material at as close to its original bid as possible, and (4) continue to build GFE's relationship with this important supplier. After all, compared to our previous domestic prices for the castings it supplies, RSS is saving us hundreds of thousands of £, (i.e., Do not let the problem with the defective shafts damage the relationship).

**Team Two:** You will be the Russians in this negotiation simulation. Learn all you can about British and Russian culture and business practices. It would be very helpful if you could identify some business people from the UK and Russia and explore their views on business negotiations. As far as the defective shafts are concerned, you made them according to your country's interpretations of the technical requirement specified. In your engineers' technical experience the heat-treating process you used is referred to by several expressions, one of which translates into English as "relieving stress." Also from your engineers' technical experience, it would be logical to apply that treatment to a shaft in this type of application. How were you to know that the English used the term to describe a special product from the steel mill? Your steel mills make no such products. As you now understand the requirement, you would have had to import the steel and process it differently than parts in similar applications are treated in your country. Even at the increased price, you are not sure that your costs will be covered. You think, "Instead of kissing our feet for saving them so much on the casting parts, they treat us with disrespect because of an honest mistake on the shafts. They insult us further by sending an underling as a bill collector, where we have done nothing wrong, and the amount is small compared to what we are saving them." Still you are culturally sensitive enough to understand that this Englishman must take back something or he will look weak to his supervisor. Perhaps you can discuss his charges for the defective products, but also have printed up on the table a price increase on the castings of an equal amount. Then perhaps this man can say that he collected from you, and cover up that he will be paying you an equal amount for the other products. In fact, perhaps the message will be better understood if the price increase on the castings is many times the charges for the defective shafts. You think, "Yes, this Robert Hardy will have an interesting learning experience at this negotiating." Of course you cannot be so rough with him that you lose the casting business, but that seems unlikely.

## Case 12-3

# Starnes-Brenner Machine Tool Company: To Bribe or Not to Bribe?

The Starnes-Brenner Machine Tool Company of Iowa City, Iowa, has a small one-man sales office headed by Frank Rothe in Latino, a major Latin American country. Frank has been in Latino for about 10 years and is retiring this year; his replacement is Bill Hunsaker, one of Starnes-Brenner's top salespeople. Both will be in Latino for about eight months, during which time Frank will show Bill the ropes, introduce him to their principal customers, and, in general, prepare him to take over.

Frank has been very successful as a foreign representative in spite of his unique style and, at times, complete refusal to follow company policy when it doesn't suit him. The company hasn't really done much about his method of operation, although from time to time he has angered some top company people. As President Jack McCaughey, who retired a couple of years ago, once remarked to a vice president who was complaining about Frank, "If he's making money—and he is (more than any of the other foreign offices)—then leave the guy alone." When McCaughey retired, the new chief immediately instituted organizational changes that gave more emphasis to the overseas operations, moving the company toward a truly worldwide operation into which a loner like Frank would probably not fit. In fact, one of the key reasons for selecting Bill as Frank's replacement, besides Bill's record as a top salesperson, is Bill's capacity to be an organization man. He understands the need for coordination among operations and will cooperate with the home office so that the Latino office can be expanded and brought into the mainstream.

The company knows there is much to be learned from Frank, and Bill's job is to learn everything possible. The company certainly doesn't want to continue some of Frank's practices, but much of his knowledge is vital for continued, smooth operation. Today, Starnes-Brenner's foreign sales account for about 25 percent of the company's total profits, compared with about 5 percent only 10 years ago.

The company is actually changing character, from being principally an exporter, without any real concern for continuous foreign market representation, to having worldwide operations, where the foreign divisions are part of the total effort rather than a stepchild operation. In fact, Latino is one of the last operational divisions to be assimilated into the new organization. Rather than try to change Frank, the company has been waiting for him to retire before making any significant adjustments in their Latino operations.

Bill Hunsaker is 36 years old, with a wife and three children; he is a very good salesperson and administrator, although he has had no foreign experience. He has the reputation of being fair, honest, and a straight shooter. Some back at the home office see his assignment as part of a grooming job for a top position, perhaps eventually the presidency. The Hunsakers are now settled in their new home after having been in Latino for about two weeks. Today is Bill's first day on the job.

When Bill arrived at the office, Frank was on his way to a local factory to inspect some Starnes-Brenner machines that had to have some adjustments made before being acceptable to the Latino government agency buying them. Bill joined Frank for the plant visit. Later, after the visit, we join the two at lunch.

Bill, tasting some chili, remarks, "Boy! This certainly isn't like the chili we have in America."

"No, it isn't, and there's another difference, too. The Latinos are Americans and nothing angers a Latino more than to have a 'Gringo' refer to the United States as America as if to say that Latino isn't part of America also. The Latinos rightly consider their country as part of America (take a look at the map), and people from the United States are North Americans at best. So, for future reference, refer to home either as the United States, States, or North America, but, for gosh sakes, not just America. Not to change the subject, Bill, but could you see that any change had been made in those S-27s from the standard model?"

"No, they looked like the standard. Was there something out of whack when they arrived?"

"No, I couldn't see any problem—I suspect this is the best piece of sophisticated bribe taking I've come across yet. Most of the time the Latinos are more 'honest' about their *mordidas* than this."

"What's a *mordida*?" Bill asks.

"You know, *kumshaw, dash, bustarella, mordida;* they are all the same: a little grease to expedite the action. *Mordida* is the local word for a slight offering or, if you prefer, bribe," says Frank.

Bill quizzically responds, "Do we pay bribes to get sales?"

"Oh, it depends on the situation, but it's certainly something you have to be prepared to deal with." Boy, what a greenhorn, Frank thinks to himself, as he continues, "Here's the story. When the S-27s arrived last January, we began uncrating them and right away the *jefe* engineer (a government official)—*jefe,* that's the head man in charge—began extra-careful examination and declared there was a vital defect in the machines; he claimed the machinery would be dangerous and thus unacceptable if it wasn't corrected. I looked it over but couldn't see anything wrong, so I agreed to have our staff engineer check all the machines and correct any flaws that might exist. Well, the *jefe* said there wasn't enough time to wait for an engineer to come from the States, that the machines could be adjusted locally, and we could pay him and he would make all the necessary arrangements. So, what do you do? No adjustment his way and there would be an order cancelled; and, maybe there was something out of line, those things have been known to happen. But for the life of me, I can't see that anything had been done since the machines were supposedly fixed. So, let's face it, we just paid a bribe, and a pretty darn big bribe at that—about $1,200 per machine. What makes it so aggravating is that that's the second one I've had to pay on this shipment."

"The second?" asks Bill.

"Yeah, at the border, when we were transferring the machines to Latino trucks, it was hot and they were moving slow as molasses. It took them over an hour to transfer one machine to a Latino truck and we had ten others to go. It seemed that every time I spoke to the dock boss about speeding things up, they just got slower. Finally, out of desperation, I slipped him a fistful of pesos and, sure enough, in the next three hours they had the whole thing loaded. Just one of the local customs of doing business. Generally, though, it comes at the lower level where wages don't cover living expenses too well."

There is a pause and Bill asks, "What does that do to our profits?"

"Runs them down, of course, but I look at it as just one of the many costs of doing business—I do my best not to pay, but when I have to, I do."

Hesitantly, Bill replies, "I don't like it, Frank. We've got good products, they're priced right, we give good service, and keep plenty of spare parts in the country, so why should we have to pay bribes? It's just no way to do business. You've already had to pay two bribes on one shipment; if you keep it up, the word's going to get around and you'll be paying at every level. Then all the profit goes out the window—you know, once you start, where do you stop? Besides that, where do we stand legally? The Foreign Bribery Act makes paying bribes like you've just paid illegal. I'd say the best policy is to never start: You might lose a few sales, but let it be known that there are no bribes; we sell the best, service the best at fair prices, and that's all."

"You mean the Foreign Corrupt Practices Act, don't you?" Frank asks, and continues, in an I'm-not-really-so-out-of-touch tone of voice, "Haven't some of the provisions of the Foreign Corrupt Practices Act been softened somewhat?"

"Yes, you're right, the provisions on paying a *mordida* or grease have been softened, but paying the government official is still illegal, softening or not," replies Bill.

Oh boy! Frank thinks to himself as he replies, "Look, what I did was just peanuts as far as the Foreign Corrupt Practices Act goes. The people we pay off are small, and, granted we give good service, but we've only been doing it for the last year or so. Before that I never knew when I was going to have equipment to sell. In fact, we only had products when there were surpluses stateside. I had to pay the right people to get sales, and besides, you're not back in the States any longer. Things are just done different here. You follow that policy and I guarantee that you'll have fewer sales because our competitors from Germany, Italy, and Japan will pay. Look, Bill, everybody does it here; it's a way of life, and the costs are generally reflected in the markup and overhead. There is even a code of behavior involved. We're not actually encouraging it to spread, just perpetuating an accepted way of doing business."

Patiently and slightly condescendingly, Bill replies, "I know, Frank, but wrong is wrong and we want to operate differently now. We hope to set up an operation here on a continuous basis; we plan to operate in Latino just like we do in the United States. Really expand our operation and make a long-range market commitment, grow with the country! And one of the first things we must avoid is unethical . . ."

Frank interrupts, "But really, is it unethical? Everybody does it, the Latinos even pay *mordidas* to other Latinos; it's a fact of life—is it really unethical? I think that the circumstances that exist in a country justify and dictate the behavior. Remember, man, 'When in Rome, do as the Romans do.'"

Almost shouting, Bill blurts out, "I can't buy that. We know that our management practices and relationships are our strongest point. Really, all we have to differentiate us from the rest of our competition, Latino and others, is that we are better managed and, as far as I'm concerned, graft and other unethical behavior have got to be cut out to create a healthy industry. In the long run, it should strengthen our position. We can't build our futures on illegal and unethical practices."

Frank angrily replies, "Look, it's done in the States all the time. What about the big dinners, drinks, and all the other hanky-panky that goes on? Not to mention PACs' [Political Action Committee] payments to congressmen, and all those high speaking fees certain congressmen get from special interests. How many congressmen have gone to jail or lost reelection on those kinds of things? What is that, if it isn't *mordida* the North American way? The only difference is that instead of cash only, in the United States we pay in merchandise and cash."

"That's really not the same and you know it. Besides, we certainly get a lot of business transacted during those dinners even if we are paying the bill."

"Bull, the only difference is that here bribes go on in the open; they don't hide it or dress it in foolish ritual that fools no one. It goes on in the United States and everyone denies the existence of it. That's all the difference—in the United States we're just more hypocritical about it all."

"Look," Frank continues, almost shouting, "we are getting off on the wrong foot and we've got eight months to work together. Just keep your eyes and mind open and let's talk about it again in a couple of months when you've seen how the whole country operates; perhaps then you won't be so quick to judge it absolutely wrong."

Frank, lowering his voice, says thoughtfully, "I know it's hard to take; probably the most disturbing problem in underdeveloped countries is the matter of graft. And, frankly, we don't do much advance preparation so we can deal firmly with it. It bothered me at first; but then I figured it makes its economic contribution, too, since the payoff is as much a part of the economic process as a payroll. What's our real economic role, anyway, besides making a profit, of course? Are we developers of wealth, helping to push the country to greater economic growth, or are we missionaries? Or should we be both? I really don't know, but I don't think we can be both simultaneously, and my feeling is that, as the company prospers, as higher salaries are paid, and better standards of living are reached, we'll see better ethics. Until then, we've got to operate or leave, and if you are going to win the opposition over, you'd better join them and change them from within, not fight them."

Before Bill could reply, a Latino friend of Frank's joined them and they changed the topic of conversation.

## Questions

1. Is what Frank did ethical? By whose ethics—those of Latino or the United States?
2. Are Frank's two different payments legal under the Foreign Corrupt Practices Act as amended by the Omnibus Trade and Competitiveness Act of 1988?
3. Identify the types of payments made in the case; that is, are they lubrication, extortion, or subornation?
4. Frank seemed to imply that there is a similarity between what he was doing and what happens in the United States. Is there any difference? Explain.
5. Are there any legal differences between the money paid to the dockworkers and the money paid the *jefe* (government official)? Any ethical differences?
6. Frank's attitude seems to imply that a foreigner must comply with all local customs, but some would say that one of the contributions made by U.S. firms is to change local ways of doing business. Who is right?
7. Should Frank's behavior have been any different had this not been a government contract?
8. If Frank shouldn't have paid the bribe, what should he have done, and what might have been the consequences?
9. What are the company interests in this problem?
10. Explain how this may be a good example of the SRC (self-reference criterion) at work.
11. Do you think Bill will make the grade in Latino? Why? What will it take?
12. How can an overseas manager be prepared to face this problem?

---

**Case 12-4**

# National Office Machines—Motivating Japanese Salespeople: Straight Salary or Commission?

National Office Machines of Dayton, Ohio, manufacturers of cash registers, electronic data processing equipment, adding machines, and other small office equipment, has recently entered into a joint venture with Nippon Cash Machines of Tokyo, Japan. Last year, National Office Machines (NOM) had domestic sales of over $1.4 billion and foreign sales of nearly $700 million. Besides in the United States, it operates in most of Western Europe, the Mideast, and some parts of the Far East. In the past, it has had no significant sales or sales force in Japan, although the company was represented there by a small trading company until a few years ago. In the United States, NOM is one of the leaders in the field and is considered to have one of the most successful and aggressive sales forces found in this highly competitive industry.

Nippon Cash Machines (NCM) is an old-line cash register manufacturing company organized in 1882. At one time, Nippon was the major manufacturer of cash register equipment in Japan, but it has been losing ground since 1970 even though it produces perhaps the best cash register in Japan. Last year's sales were 9 billion yen, a 15 percent decrease from sales the prior year. The fact that it produces only cash registers is one of the major problems; the merger with NOM will give them much-needed breadth in product offerings. Another hoped-for strength to be gained from the joint venture is managerial leadership, which is sorely needed.

Fourteen Japanese companies have products that compete with Nippon; other competitors include several foreign giants such as IBM, National Cash Register, and Unisys of the

United States, and Sweda Machines of Sweden. Nippon has a small sales force of 21 men, most of whom have been with the company their entire adult careers. These salespeople have been responsible for selling to Japanese trading companies and to a few larger purchasers of equipment.

Part of the joint venture agreement included doubling the sales force within a year, with NOM responsible for hiring and training the new salespeople, who must all be young, college-trained Japanese nationals. The agreement also allowed for U.S. personnel in supervisory positions for an indeterminate period of time and for retaining the current Nippon sales force.

One of the many sales management problems facing the Nippon/American Business Machines Corporation (NABMC, the name of the new joint venture) was which sales compensation plan to use. That is, should it follow the Japanese tradition of straight salary and guaranteed employment until death with no individual incentive program, or the U.S. method (very successful for NOM in the United States) of commissions and various incentives based on sales performance, with the ultimate threat of being fired if sales quotas go continuously unfilled?

The immediate response to the problem might well be one of using the tried-and-true U.S. compensation methods, since they have worked so well in the United States and are perhaps the kind of changes needed and expected from U.S. management. NOM management is convinced that salespeople selling its kinds of products in a competitive market must have strong incentives to produce. In fact, NOM had experimented on a limited basis in the United States with straight salary about ten years ago and it was a bomb. Unfortunately, the problem is considerably more complex than it appears on the surface.

One of the facts to be faced by NOM management is the traditional labor-management relations and employment systems in Japan. The roots of the system go back to Japan's feudal era, when a serf promised a lifetime of service to his lord in exchange for a lifetime of protection. By the start of Japan's industrial revolution in the 1880s, an unskilled worker pledged to remain with a company all his useful life if the employer would teach him the new mechanical arts. The tradition of spending a lifetime with a single employer survives today mainly because most workers like it that way. The very foundations of Japan's management system are based on lifetime employment, promotion through seniority, and single-company unions. There is little chance of being fired, pay raises are regular, and there is a strict order of job-protecting seniority.

Japanese workers at larger companies still are protected from outright dismissal by union contracts and an industrial tradition that some personnel specialists believe has the force of law. Under this tradition, a worker can be dismissed after an initial trial period only for gross cause, such as theft or some other major infraction. As long as the company remains in business, the worker isn't discharged, or even furloughed, simply because there isn't enough work to be done.

Besides the guarantee of employment for life, the typical Japanese worker receives many fringe benefits from the company. Bank loans and mortgages are granted to lifetime employees on the assumption that they will never lose their jobs and therefore the ability to repay. Just how paternalistic the typical Japanese firm can be is illustrated by a statement from the Japanese Ministry of Foreign Affairs that gives the example of A, a male worker who is employed in a fairly representative company in Tokyo.

> To begin with, A lives in a house provided by his company. and the rent he pays is amazingly low when compared with average city rents. The company pays his daily trips between home and factory. A's working hours are from 9 A.M. to 5 P.M. with a break for lunch which he usually takes in the company restaurant at a very cheap price. He often brings home food, clothing, and other miscellaneous articles he has bought at the company store at a discount ranging from 10 percent to 30 percent below city prices. The company store even supplies

furniture, refrigerators, and television sets on an installment basis, for which, if necessary, A can obtain a loan from the company almost free of interest.

In case of illness, A is given free medical treatment in the company hospital, and if his indisposition extends over a number of years, the company will continue paying almost his full salary. The company maintains lodges at seaside or mountain resorts where A can spend the holidays or an occasional weekend with the family at moderate prices. . . . It must also be remembered that when A reaches retirement age (usually 55) he will receive a lump-sum retirement allowance or a pension, either of which will assure him a relatively stable living for the rest of his life.

Even though A is only an example of a typical employee, a salesperson can expect the same treatment. Job security is such an expected part of everyday life that no attempt is made to motivate the Japanese salesperson in the same manner as in the United States; as a consequence, selling traditionally has been primarily an order-taking job. Except for the fact that sales work offers some travel, entry to outside executive offices, the opportunity to entertain, and similar side benefits, it provides a young person with little other incentive to surpass basic quotas and drum up new business. The traditional Japanese bonuses are given twice yearly, can be up to 40 percent of base pay, and are no larger for salespeople than any other functional job in the company.

As a key executive in a Mitsui-affiliated engineering firm put it recently, "The typical salesman in Japan isn't required to have any particular talent." In return for meeting sales quotas, most Japanese salespeople draw a modest monthly salary, sweetened about twice a year by bonuses. Manufacturers of industrial products generally pay no commission or other incentives to boost their businesses.

Besides the problem of motivation, a foreign company faces other different customs when trying to put together and manage a sales force. Class systems and the Japanese distribution system with its penchant for reciprocity put a strain on the creative talents of the best sales managers, as Simmons, the U.S. bedding manufacturer, was quick to learn.

In the field, Simmons found itself stymied by the bewildering realities of Japanese marketing, especially the traditional distribution system that operates on a philosophy of reciprocity that goes beyond mere business to the core of the Japanese character. It's involved with *on,* the notion that regards a favor of any kind as a debt that must be repaid. To wear another's *on* in business and then turn against that person is to lose face, abhorrent to most Japanese. Thus, the owner of large Western-style apartments, hotels, or developments buys his beds from the supplier to whom he owes a favor, no matter what the competition offers.

In small department and other retail stores, where most items are handled on consignment, the bond with the supplier is even stronger. Consequently, all sales outlets are connected in a complicated web that runs from the largest supplier, with a huge national sales force, to the smallest local distributor, with a handful of door-to-door salespeople. The system is self-perpetuating and all but impossible to crack from the outside.

However, there is some change in attitude taking place as both workers and companies start discarding traditions for the job mobility common in the United States. Skilled workers are willing to bargain on the strength of their experience in an open labor market in an effort to get higher wages or better job opportunities; in the United States, it's called shopping around. And a few companies are showing a willingness to lure workers away from other concerns. A number of companies are also plotting how to rid themselves of deadwood workers accumulated as a result of promotions by strict seniority.

Toyo Rayon company, Japan's largest producer of synthetic fibers, started reevaluating all its senior employees every five years with the implied threat that those who don't measure up to the company's expectations have to accept reassignment and possibly demotion; some may even be asked to resign. A chemical engineering and construction firm asked all its employees over 42 to negotiate a new contract with the company every two years. Pay raises and promotions go to those the company wants to keep. For those who think they are worth more than the company is willing to pay, the company offers retirement with something less than the $30,000 lump-sum payment the average Japanese worker receives at age 55.

More Japanese are seeking jobs with foreign firms as the lifetime-employment ethic slowly changes. The head of student placement at Aoyama Gakuin University reports that each year the number of students seeking jobs with foreign companies increases. Bank of America, Japan Motorola, Imperial Chemical Industries, and American Hospital Supply are just a few of the companies that have been successful in attracting Japanese students. Just a few years ago, all Western companies were places to avoid.

Even those companies that are successful work with a multitude of handicaps. American companies often lack the intricate web of personal connections that their Japanese counterparts rely on when recruiting. Further, American companies have the reputation for being quick to hire and even quicker to fire, whereas Japanese companies still preach the virtues of lifelong job security. Those U.S. companies that are successful are offering big salaries and promises of Western-style autonomy. According to a recent study, 20- to 29-year-old Japanese prefer an employer-changing environment to a single lifetime employer. They complain that the Japanese system is unfair because promotions are based on age and seniority. A young recruit, no matter how able, has to wait for those above him to be promoted before he too can move up. Some feel that if you are really capable, you are better off working with an American company.

Some foreign firms entering Japan have found that their merit-based promotion systems have helped them attract bright young recruits. In fact, a survey done by *Nihon Keizai Shimbun,* Japan's leading business newspaper, found that 80 percent of top managers at 450 major Japanese corporations wanted the seniority promotion system abolished. But, as one Japanese manager commented, "We see more people changing their jobs now, and we read many articles about companies restructuring, but despite this, we won't see major changes coming quickly."

A few U.S. companies operating in Japan are experimenting with incentive plans. Marco and Company, a belting manufacturer and Japanese distributor for Power Packing and Seal Company, was persuaded by Power to set up a travel plan incentive for salespeople who topped their regular sales quotas. Unorthodox as the idea was for Japan, Marco went along. The first year, special one-week trips to Far East holiday spots like Hong Kong, Taiwan, Manila, and Macao were inaugurated. Marco's sales of products jumped 212 percent, and the next year sales were up an additional 60 percent.

IBM also has made a move toward chucking the traditional Japanese sales system (salary plus a bonus but no incentives). For about a year, it has been working with a combination that retains the semiannual bonus while adding commission payments on sales over preset quotas. "It's difficult to apply a straight commission system in selling computers because of the complexities of the product." an IBM Japan official said. "Our salesmen don't get big commissions because other employees would be jealous." To head off possible ill feeling, therefore, some nonselling IBM employees receive monetary incentives.

Most Japanese companies seem reluctant to follow IBM's example because they have doubts about directing older salesmen to go beyond their usual order-taking role. High-pressure tactics are not well accepted here, and sales channels are often pretty well set by custom and long practice (e.g., a manufacturer normally deals with one trading company, which in turn sells only to customers A, B, C, and D). A salesman or trading company, for that matter, is not often encouraged to go after customer Z and get him away from a rival supplier.

The Japanese market is becoming more competitive and there is real fear on the part of NOM executives that the traditional system just won't work in a competitive market. On the other hand, the proponents of the incentive system agree that the system really has not been tested over long periods or even adequately in the short term because it has been applied only in a growing market. In other words, was it the incentive system that caused the successes achieved by the companies or was it market growth? Especially there is doubt because other companies following the traditional method of compensation and employee relations also have had sales increases during the same period.

The problem is further complicated for NABMC because it will have both new and old salespeople. The young Japanese seem eager to accept the incentive method, but older ones are hesitant. How do you satisfy both since you must, by agreement, retain all the sales staff?

A study done by the Japanese government on attitudes of youth around the world suggests that younger Japanese may be more receptive to U.S. incentive methods than one would anticipate. In a study done by the Japanese prime minister's office, there were some surprising results when Japanese responses were compared with responses of similar-aged youths from other countries. Exhibit 12-8 summarizes some of the information gathered on life goals. One point that may be of importance in shedding light on the decision NOM has to make is a comparison of Japanese attitudes with young people in 11 other countries—the Japanese young people are less satisfied with their home life, school, and working situations, and are more passive in their attitudes toward social and political problems. Further, almost a third of those employed said they were dissatisfied with their present jobs primarily because of low income and short vacations. Asked if they had to choose between

**EXHIBIT 12-8**
**Life Goals**

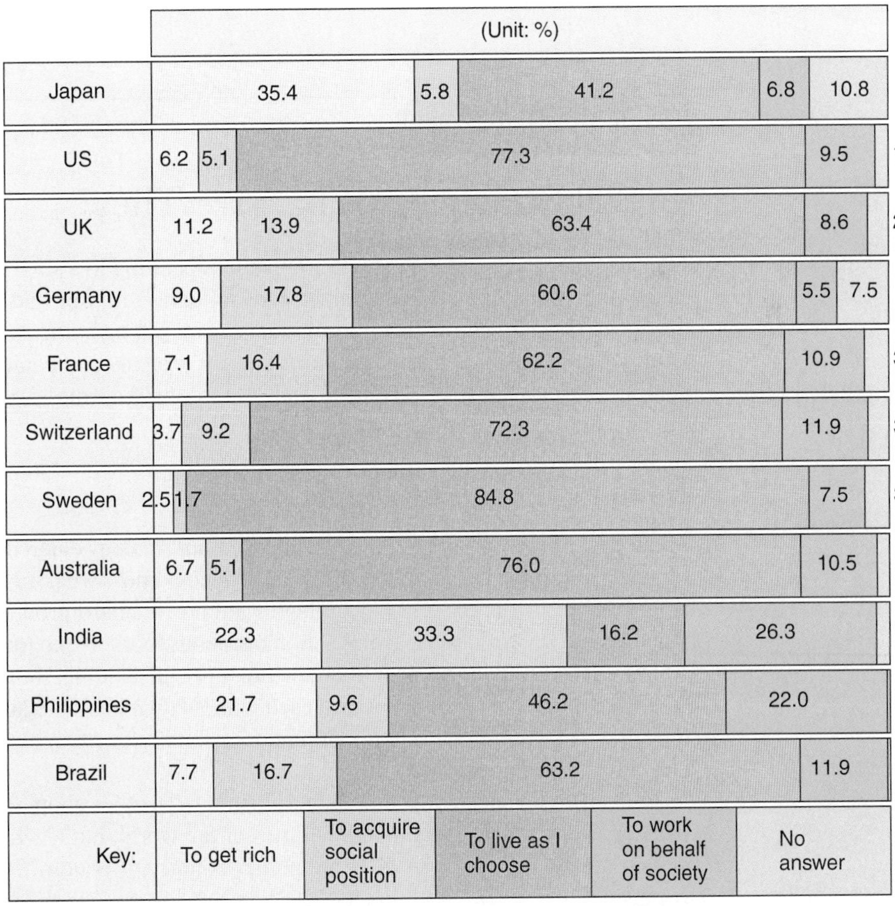

| Country | To get rich | To acquire social position | To live as I choose | To work on behalf of society | No answer |
|---|---|---|---|---|---|
| | (Unit: %) | | | | |
| Japan | 35.4 | 5.8 | 41.2 | 6.8 | 10.8 |
| US | 6.2 | 5.1 | 77.3 | 9.5 | 1.8 |
| UK | 11.2 | 13.9 | 63.4 | 8.6 | 2.9 |
| Germany | 9.0 | 17.8 | 60.6 | 5.5 | 7.5 |
| France | 7.1 | 16.4 | 62.2 | 10.9 | 3.4 |
| Switzerland | 3.7 | 9.2 | 72.3 | 11.9 | 3.0 |
| Sweden | 2.5 | 1.7 | 84.8 | 7.5 | 3.4 |
| Australia | 6.7 | 5.1 | 76.0 | 10.5 | 1.6 |
| India | 22.3 | 33.3 | 16.2 | 26.3 | 1.8 |
| Philippines | 21.7 | 9.6 | 46.2 | 22.0 | 0.5 |
| Brazil | 7.7 | 16.7 | 63.2 | 11.9 | 0.5 |

a difficult job with responsibility and authority or an easy job without responsibility and authority, 64 percent of the Japanese picked the former, somewhat less than the 70 to 80 percent average in other countries.

Another critical problem lies with the nonsales employees; traditionally, all employees on the same level are treated equally, whether sales, production, or staff. How do you encourage competitive, aggressive salesmanship in a market unfamiliar with such tactics, and how do you compensate salespeople to promote more aggressive selling in the face of tradition-bound practices of paternalistic company behavior?

## Questions

1. What should NABMC offer—incentives or straight salary? Support your answer.
2. If incentives are out, how do you motivate salespeople and get them to compete aggressively?
3. Design a U.S.-type program for motivation and compensation of salespeople. Point out where difficulties may be encountered with your plan and how the problems are to be overcome.
4. Design a pay system you think would work, satisfying old salespeople, new salespeople, and other employees.
5. Discuss the idea that perhaps the kind of motivation and aggressiveness found in the United States is not necessary in the Japanese market.
6. Develop some principles of motivation that could be applied by an international marketer in other countries.

---

### Case 12-5

# Global Strategies: What Are They?

Global strategies do not mean huge companies operating in a single world market. They are much more complex. Global competitive strategies are a bit like supernatural creatures: They can be imagined by each individual to suit his or her own reality while evoking a common concern. The best illustrations are the slogans companies use to describe themselves. These range from "Think Local, Act Global" all the way to its opposite, "Think Global, Act Local," with everything in between.

## Defining Global Strategies

Some 15 years have gone by since the term *global strategy* entered our vocabulary, enough time to bring some clarity to its definition. We now know what it is and what it is not. Consider first what it is not. Global strategies are not standard product and market strategies that assume the world to be a single, homogeneous, border-free marketplace. The Uruguay Round of trade and investment liberalization notwithstanding, the world is still a collection of different independent economies, each with its own market characteristics. Each, moreover, has its own societal aspirations that occasionally find expression in protectionist policies of one form or another.

Global strategies are also not about global presence or about large companies. A company can very well operate in all countries of the world, but if what it does in one country has no meaning for what it does in another country, it is no different from the domestic companies it competes with in each location.

To qualify as pursuing a global strategy, a company needs to be able to demonstrate two things: that it can contest any market it chooses to compete in, and that it can bring its entire worldwide resources to bear on any competitive situation it finds itself in, regardless of where that might be.

## Selective Contestability

Just as companies possessing a certain set of technologies and business competencies choose particular market segments to concentrate on, so a global company can be selective about the countries in which it operates. Many small high-technology companies and luxury good manufacturers do just that. They compete where there is adequate demand to justify the investments needed to access the market; they focus their investments to achieve critical mass only in those markets they are interested in.

The important thing is that they can and are prepared to contest any and all markets should circumstances warrant. They constantly scour the world for market openings, they process information on a global basis, and they constitute a potential threat even in places they have not yet entered.

Markets where such contestability exists, as a corollary, start to behave almost as if the company had already entered—provided, of course, the threat of entry is a credible one. This explains why telecom markets the world over are so fiercely competitive from the day they are no longer government or private monopolies. The handfuls of international players in the equipment business not only are waiting in the wings but have products that conform to international standards and resources they can deploy for market access as soon as opportunity arises.

## Global Resources for Each Main Street

The corner shop that carries products by IBM, Philips, Coca-Cola, or DuPont knows from experience that there is something special about these products compared with those supplied by a small local company. In comparison, products from companies such as Nestlé, Unilever, or even Procter & Gamble did not seem so special—in the past, at least. Their names, formulations, and the way they were produced and marketed were not too different from domestic products. Just being present in several countries, in other words, does not constitute a global strategy. Globalism is an earned notion rather than being entitlement created by the fact of operating in several countries.

A basic characteristic of a global company is its ability to bring its entire worldwide capabilities to bear on any transaction anywhere regardless of the products it makes. This underlies the importance of organizational integration in global strategies. Transporting capabilities across borders on an as-needed basis requires all local units to be connected and permeable, not isolated from one another.

This is also what allows global strategies to be "within-border" strategies while, at the same time, being "cross-border" ones. They are manifest on each Main Street, with local companies sensing they are dealing with a worldwide organization even while the latter employs a local competitive formula.

## Main Attributes of Global Strategy

This dual notion of market contestability and bringing global resources to bear on competition wherever a company is present is really what global strategies are about. Industries where such strategies are prevalent assume a character of their own in which strategies that are geared to one country alone cannot be adopted. What companies do in one country has an inevitable consequence for what they do in others.

There is, of course, nothing absolute about global strategies. Being near-cousins of multidomestic strategies, the best way to judge them is in terms of "degrees of globalness." At the risk of oversimplification, the more a company scores in each of the following five attributes, the more it can be considered a global competitor based on the definition just given. These include possessing a standard product (or core) that is marketed uniformly across the world; sourcing all assets, not just production, on an optimal basis; and achieving market access in line with the break-even volume of the needed infrastructure.

1. **Standard products and marketing mix.** Although the advantages of having a standard product and marketing mix are obvious, this attribute involves several trade-offs in practice. Economies of scale in design, production, and promotion need to be compared with the greater market acceptance that local adaptation often provides.

   If a general conclusion can be drawn, it would be the need at least to aim for a standard "core" in the product and to limit marketing adaptations to those absolutely necessary. The more integrated countries become economically, the less latitude there is anyway for things such as price discrimination and channel selection. The same applies to situations where buyers themselves are global and expect similar products and terms on a worldwide basis.

2. **Sourcing assets, not just products.** Sourcing products and components internationally based on comparative advantage and availability has long been a feature of international business. What is new is the possibility to source assets or capabilities related to any part of the company's value chain. Whether it is capital from Switzerland or national credit agencies, software skills from Silicon Valley or Bangalore, or electronic components from Taiwan, global companies now have wider latitude in accessing resources from wherever they are available or cost-competitive.

   The implication of this is that global strategies are as much about asset deployment for market access purposes as they are about asset accumulation abroad. The latter include local capital, technical skills, managerial talent, and new product ideas, as well as the host competencies that local partners and institutions can provide. Also, whereas previously assets accumulated locally were mainly to support a local business, it is increasingly possible—and desirable—to separate those needed for local market access from those intended to support the company's business elsewhere.

   It is here that we associate partnerships and alliances with global strategy. They can supplement what a company already possesses by way of assets or complement what is missing, thereby speeding up the creation of the needed infrastructure as well as reducing costs and risks.

3. **Market access in line with break-even.** For a company to be a credible global competitor it does not need to be among the biggest in its industry. But it has to be big enough to generate the volume of sales the required infrastructure demands and to amortize up-front investments in R&D and promotion.

   Today, it is the latter investments that count most. In the pharmaceutical industry, for example, it now costs around $400 million to come up with a successful new drug. This puts a natural floor on the amount of sales to be generated over the life of the drug. The greater the presence of a company in all of the large markets, and the greater its ability to launch the drug simultaneously in them, the higher the likelihood of profiting from the investment made.

   The same argument applies to other investments in intangibles such as brands. If we associate global competitiveness with size, it is chiefly on account of these types of investments. Unlike investments in plants and physical infrastructure, which can result in diminishing returns to scale, intangibles almost always translate into "bigger is better."

4. **Contesting assets.** Another distinguishing feature of a global company is its ability to neutralize the assets and competencies of its competitors. If a competitor switches its supply from a high-cost to a low-cost factory, it too can do so; if a competitor gains

access to a critical technology, it can do the same. Similarly, if a competitor is using one market to generate excess cash flow in order to "invest" in another, it is able to neutralize this advantage by going to the relatively more profitable market itself.

Purely domestic companies and even those that are run on a multidomestic basis lack such arbitrage possibilities. Just as in sourcing, to exploit these possibilities requires a global view of the business and the capacity to manage it in an integrated fashion.

5. **Functions have a global orientation.** As much of the foregoing suggests, global competition today is a lot more than simple cross-border competition at the product or service level. It is equally about building and managing a multinational infrastructure. Frequently, the latter means internationalizing all of the competencies and functions of a company: its R&D, procurement, production, logistics, and marketing, as well as human resources and finance.

These functions are all geared to providing customers with superior products and services on a worldwide basis. The more they have a global orientation of their own, the greater their contribution to the overall effort. Hence, even if their focus may be primarily national in scope—supporting a local business with no trade, for example—any contribution they can make to other units of the company helps.

These five attributes, taken together, operationalize a global strategy. The degrees of globalness in a strategy are the extent to which each is fulfilled in practice. The fact of not having a standard global product, for example, diminishes the scope of a global strategy but does not entirely destroy it, provided the company scores high on the other attributes. If anything, stressing one attribute to the exclusion of others can even be counterproductive and unfeasible. A good balance between all of them is needed.

## Local Adaptation

Another important point to make about these attributes is that they do not assume a single, open global marketplace. Trade and investment liberalization coupled with improvements in transportation and communications are what have made global strategies possible. Trade protection, labor policies, investment incentives, and a host of regulations continue to force a country-by-country adaptation of strategies.

It is also these realities, along with the sociocultural differences between countries, that have caused many companies to stress the "local" dimension in their business—and rightly so. If all companies confront the same set of market conditions, advantage goes to those that adapt their strategies best.

The best way to reconcile these local differences with the attributes required of a global strategy is to see them as constraints to global optimization. Localness, in other words, is another variable to incorporate in decision making. Considering it as the basis for the strategy itself, however, is to deny all of the advantages a global company possesses. This is perhaps the biggest conundrum companies face today.

While adapting strategies to local conditions offers greater opportunities for revenue generation, it has two main impacts: It causes overinvestment in the infrastructure needed to serve markets, and brings about a lack of consistency in whatever strategy is being pursued. Neither is intrinsically bad. They can even contribute positively to the end result if approached correctly. All that is needed is to factor them in as variables to be considered, without losing sight of the overall objective of competing effectively both within and across borders.

Consider the issue of overinvestment, especially in capital-intensive businesses such as semiconductors. Companies such as Texas Instruments, NEC, and Mitsubishi Electric have consciously located abroad. This not only permits them to benefit from generous investment incentives provided by local governments that want such facilities, but also allows them to mobilize local companies as co-investors to share the capital burden and help with market access.

More contentious is the issue of strategic focus. Should local subsidiaries be allowed to modify products and diversify into businesses that make sense for them only? Or should they be consistent with what the parent company focuses on? The answer to this depends on several things: a company's definition of its business scope and growth vectors; the subsidiary's domain within the overall organization; and the locus of its strategy-making process.

Business scope and growth vectors pertain to a company's attitude to diversification generally. If its products and technologies provide adequate growth opportunities on a worldwide basis, it is probably better off restricting each subsidiary to just those. If, on the other hand, growth is primarily driven through exploring and creating new market opportunities, then local initiatives are usually welcome.

Logitech, a world leader in pointing devices for the personal computer industry, for example, permitted and even encouraged its Taiwanese company to develop special software products for the Chinese market because that would be an additional product to fuel its growth, reduce its dependence on the mouse, and, incidentally, facilitate access to a new market. A company that comes up with a new cancer treatment, on the other hand, is likely to want to invest all its resources in commercializing that worldwide as quickly as possible.

The more a company's infrastructure and skills become dispersed and the more global responsibilities individual subsidiaries take on, the greater the need to see the initiation of strategies as a global process. What the parent knows and sees may not be the same as subsidiary management. Giving subsidiaries too narrow a mission based on a centralized notion of between-country competition not only constrains their potential for accumulating local resources but also diminishes their potential for competing within their country.

## Organizational Implications

How companies ought to structure and manage their international operations has been debated as long as the debate on strategy itself. Because organizations need to reflect a wide range of company-specific characteristics (such as size, diversity, age, culture, and technology) in addition to their global posture, it has proven hard to be normative. There are, however, certain key design considerations related to global posture that have dominated thinking and practice in recent years.

The most important consideration has to do with the greater need for organizational integration that global strategies require. When companies first tried to adapt their structures in the 1970s and early 1980s, most of them created elaborate matrix organizations giving equal status to products, geography, and functions. Although such organizations worked well for some companies, ABB being the leading example, they did not for others. ABB succeeded because of the nature of its business, its superior information system (called Abacus), its investment in developing a number of globally minded managers, and a small but highly effective top management team. What ABB was able to do was to balance finely the need for local autonomy in decision making with the strategic and organizational integration that managing the business on a global basis demanded.

Others that were not able to achieve this balance opted for tilting their matrix in favor of one or the other dimension. Most often, the dominant dimension became product groups or strategic business units, the assumption being that integrating each product's business system on a worldwide basis was the best way to optimize strategy and achieve coherence among different local units.

Where these "product headquarters" were located mattered less, and many companies consciously spread them around as a better way to integrate country organizations, give particular local managers a broader domain to look after, and exploit country-specific assets or competencies. Such dispersal had the attendant benefit of also reducing the role (and size) of corporate headquarters.

This fine-tuning of structures continues today. To the extent one can discern a trend for the 1990s it would consist of three things: reverting to a single locus of direction and control, giving greater emphasis to functional strategies instead of business-by-business ones, and creating simple line organizations based on a more decentralized "network" of local companies.

The move to a single locus is partly on account of the difficulty companies have experienced in managing dispersed product headquarters. The complex interactions between units they gave rise to, the lack of global reach on the part of some country organizations, and the potential for confusion between corporate roles and business unit functions were apparently not compensated by whatever advantage they offered. But it is equally on account of the recognition of the importance of a coherent set of values, goals, and identity, as well as the need to avoid duplication of functions across the world.

Having functions as the primary dimension to coordinate global strategies also reflects the dual nature of the latter, combining asset deployment for market-access reasons and asset accumulation for sourcing purposes. Another virtue of a functional orientation is that it is usually at this level that global alliances and asset accumulation take place—the R&D function cooperating with other companies' R&D departments, procurement with suppliers, finance with local finance companies, and so on.

While marketing can and should be managed nationally or regionally, R&D, finance, and manufacturing lend themselves better to global coordination. Texas Instruments, for example, used to manage its business, including manufacturing, on a regional basis. In 1993, it introduced the notion of the "virtual fab," linking all its 17 manufacturing sites around the world into a single organization. In addition to standardizing equipment and procedures across plants, this allows the company to transfer expertise across units efficiently, allocate production optimally, and interact with development on a global basis. Whereas previously the company had country-by-country sales forces, it now has market-based teams with global responsibility for a product's success. The latter has proved particularly effective in serving the needs of global customers who expect similar conditions worldwide.

Whether to have a single set of global functions or to have them specialized by business unit depends on how diverse the latter are. The lesson companies have learned, however, is to avoid overly complex matrix structures and to allow local units sufficient autonomy at the business level.

The last point refers to the way individual units in a global company need to be treated. Based on the arguments made earlier, what one is seeing is an upgrading of their role, both as a locus for independent entrepreneurial effort and as contributors to the business worldwide.

To perform this expanded role coherently they need greater empowerment coupled with all of the things that a network organization possesses: a commonly shared knowledge base, common values and goals, a common understanding of priorities and precommitments others have made, and a common set of measures to judge performance. Shared values are known to replace the need for elaborate direction and control. Rather than planning for the synergies and interdependencies that are at the heart of a global strategy, effective networks create them voluntarily and in real time. Global strategies in their present form have proved far too complex and demanding to be implemented in a centralized manner.

## Questions

1. Write a critique of each of the major points presented in this case. Based on this critique, write your own definition of a global strategy.

2. What does the author mean by selective contestability? How practical is this idea for a small international company?

3. The case discusses five attributes that, taken together, operationalize a global strategy. How would you use these attributes to define a global company? A global strategy?

4. Evaluate one of the following companies as to its degree of globalness: Nestlé, Procter & Gamble, Unilever, or a company of your choice. Be sure to discuss both why you believe and why you do not believe the company is a global company, has a global product, or has a global strategy. You may find some information that is helpful at the websites for Nestlé (www. nestle.com), Procter & Gamble (www.pg.com), and Unilever (www.unilever.com).

**Source:** Vijay Jolly, "Global Strategies in the 1990s," *Financial Post,* February 15, 1997, p. S6.

# References

1. Philip B. Clark, "Smart firms take long view," *B to B 85* (November 2000): 9.

2. Department of Commerce, "Highlights from a Profile of U.S. Exporting Companies, 2000–2001," *U.S. Department of Commerce News* (Feb 20, 2003).

3. Robert Gulbro and Paul Herbig, "Negotiating Successfully in Cross-Cultural Situations," *Industrial Marketing Management* 25 (May 9, 1996): 235–41.

4. Bruce D. Keillor, Gregory W. Boiler, and Robert H. Luke, "Firm-Level Political Behavior and Level of Foreign Market Involvement: Implications for International Marketing Strategy," *The Journal of Marketing Management* (Spring/Summer 1998): 1–11.

5. Philip R. Cateora and John L. Graham, *International Marketing,* 11th ed. (New York: McGraw-Hill, 2002): 125–40.

6. From Sak Onkvisit and John J. Shaw, *International Marketing: Analysis and Strategy,* 2nd ed. (New York: Macmillan, 1993), Chapters 4 and 5. See also Michael R. Czinkota and Iikka A. Ronkainen, *International Marketing* (New York: Dryden Press, 1993), Chapter 4.

7. 2002 National Trade Estimate Report on *Foreign Trade Barriers,* U.S. Government Printing Office, Washington, D.C. Accessed through the website: http://www.ustr.gov/reports/nte/2002/

8. From Masaaki Kotabe and Kristiaan Helson, *Global Marketing Management* (New York: John Wiley & Sons, Inc., 1998): Chapter 5.

9. "Where's the Pot of Gold?" *Business Week,* Asian Edition (February 3, 1997): 14–15.

10. "Health Policy: Advocate-General Says Drug Price Fixing May Be Justified," *European Report* (May 24, 2003): 481.

11. Cateora and Graham, *International Marketing,* 488–89.

12. From Onkvisit and Shaw, *International Marketing,* Chapter 9.

13. Philip Siekman, "Industrial Management & Technology/Export Winners," *Fortune,* (January 10, 2000): pp. 154–63.

14. Cateora and Graham, 332.

15. From Onkvisit and Shaw, *International Marketing,* Chapter 10; M. Czinkota and I. Ronkainen, *International Marketing,* Chapter 17; and P. R. Cateora, *International Marketing,* Chapter 13.

16. "Asia at Your Service," *The Economist* (February 11, 1995): 53.

17. Joseph A. McKinney, "Changes in the World Trading System," *Baylor Business Review* (Fall 1995): 13.

18. Imad B. Baalbaki and Naresh K. Maihotra, "Standardization versus Customization in International Marketing: An Investigation Using Bridging Coprint Analysis," *Journal of the Academy of Marketing Science* 23 (Summer 1995): 182–94.

19. Theodore Levitt, "The Globalization of Markets," *Harvard Business Review* (May–June 1983): 92–102.

20. From David W. Nylen, *Advertising,* 4th ed. (Cincinnati, Ohio: South-Western Publishing, 1993): Chapter 20.

21. B. G. VandenBergh and H. Katz, *Advertising Principles* (Chicago, IL: NTC/Contemporary Publishers, 1999).

22. Alex Sharland and Peter Balogh, "The Value of Nonselling Activities at International Trade Shows," *Industrial Marketing Management* 25 (January 1996): 59–66.

23. *Cyberatlas,* "B2B E-Commerce Will Survive Growing Pains," (November 28, 2001), cited in Diane Zabel, Stephanie Jakle Movahedi-Lankarani, "E-commerce: Resources for Doing Business on the Internet," *Reference & User Services Quarterly* 41 (Summer 2002): 316–25.

24. Cateora and Graham, Chapter 14

25. Carl R. Freer, Mary S. Alguire, and Lynn E. Metcalf, "Country Segmentation on the Basis of International Purchasing Patterns," *Journal of Business and Industrial Marketing* 10 (1995): 59–68.

26. Laura B. Forker and Gerard S. Doyle, Jr., "The Current on Countertrade," *Purchasing Today* (July 1998): 46–47.

(The number in parentheses following each entry refers to the chapter number in which more information about the topic can be found.)

# A

**ABC inventory analysis**   Reduces inventory needs by assigning different customer service labels to goods based on sales and profits; assigns levels of priorities to A, B, and C inventory items. (chapter 11)

**acceleration principle**   Demand volatility caused when consumer demand leads to a much larger percentage increase in the demand for plant and equipment necessary to produce the additional output (also called multiplier effect) (1).

**adaptation**   The process of adjusting to an environment or situation. (12)

**adoption process**   The decision-making activity of the buying firm through which a new product or innovation is accepted; stages include awareness, interest, evaluation, trial, and adoption. (7)

**analysis**   Attempts to turn numbers into data, and then to turn data into useful marketing information. (5)

**assembly operation**   An international entry strategy in which parts or components are produced in various countries in order to gain each country's comparative advantage; a variation on a manufacturing strategy. (12)

# B

**benefit segmentation**   Divides the total business target market into individual groups according to the particular utilities or benefits expected from a specific product or service. (3)

**benefit selling**   A selling approach that appeals to the customer's professional and personal motives by answering the questions, What's in it for my company? and What's in it for me? (3)

**bid rigging**   An agreement among potential bidders about which companies will bid for certain contracts. (2)

**break-even analysis**   An approach to price setting that defines a product's break-even point, at which a firm's revenue is equal to its total fixed and variable costs at a given price. (8)

**breaking of bulk**   Breaking large-quantity shipments into smaller lots for resale to business users; a function performed by channel intermediaries. (10)

**broker**   A channel intermediary who sells the output of one or more potentially competitive manufacturers and may assume responsibility for some marketing functions, including promotion and pricing; also known as a *sales agent.* (10)

**bundling**   The practice of marketing two or more products and/or services in a single "package" for a special price (7); also, the inclusion of an extra margin for support services in the price over and above the price of the product as such (sometimes called *iceberg pricing*). (8)

**business analysis**   The third stage in the new product development process; the expansion of the idea or concept through creative analysis into a "go" or "no go" recommendation. (7)

**business market segmentation**   The practice of dividing a business market into distinct groups of buyers with similar requirements and that will respond similarly to a specific set of marketing actions. (6)

**business marketing**   Those activities that facilitate exchanges involving products and customers in business markets; also known as *industrial marketing.* (1)

**business marketing transaction**   A transaction in which a good or service is sold for any use other than personal consumption. (1)

**business products distributor**   A channel intermediary who buys and takes title to business products, who usually keeps inventories of the products, and who sells and services the products; also known as an *industrial distributor.* (10)

**business promotion**   The use of the seller-generated promotional tools of advertising, publicity, and sales promotion in delivering both information and persuasive messages to business markets. (9)

**buyer**   The person in the business purchasing process who is assigned the formal authority to select vendors and complete the purchasing transaction. (4)

**buying center**   The people who participate in the business buying process, often including technical experts and senior management. (1)

**buying-decisions model**   A sales presentation model in which the salesperson tailors the presentation to achieve a number of smaller decisions aimed at an ultimate decision to purchase the product or service in question. (3)

**buying situation**   A situation created when some member of the organization perceives a problem that can be solved through the purchase of a product or service; essential steps include recognizing need, developing specifications, soliciting bids, making the purchasing decision, issuing the contract, inspecting delivered goods for quality, and evaluating vendor performance. (4)

# C

**carrying cost**  The opportunity cost of the investment tied up in inventory and the costs associated with storage, such as space rental and insurance fees; occur when stocks of goods for sale are held. (11)

**cash discount**  A price reduction strategy to encourage buyers to pay their bills promptly; typically improves the seller's liquidity and reduces credit collection costs and bad debts. (8)

**centralized buying situation**  A buying situation in which the members of the buying center are in a position to buy in larger quantities and to make quicker buying decisions; as such, they are attractive targets to many potential customers. (6)

**centralized purchasing**  A purchasing approach in which an individual or department is given authority to make all purchases. (4)

**centralized sales organization**  An organization that is structured so that major decisions such as recruitment, training, forecasting, and short- and long-term planning are carried out by upper management personnel at a centralized headquarters location. (3)

**Certified Purchasing Manager (CPM)**  A designation earned by an individual who has obtained a degree from a recognized college or university, completed three years of purchasing training, and passed a series of examinations; a professional buyer. (1)

**channel conflict**  A situation in which one channel member perceives another channel member to be engaged in behavior that is preventing or impeding the other from achieving a set goal. (10)

**channel management**  A cooperative marketing strategy in which manufacturers augment their direct sales channels with indirect channels of distribution to reach different segments more efficiently and effectively. (10)

**channel width**  Refers to the number of independent members at any stage of distribution.(10)

**closed bidding**  A form of competitive bidding that consists of sealed bids, all opened, reviewed, and evaluated at the same time. (8)

**compensation plan**  Financial and nonfinancial methods of rewards. (3)

**competitive analysis**  An analysis to help a firm determine whether it can compete effectively in relevant market segments; firms must determine answers to questions regarding number, strength, and market share of competitors. (6)

**concentrated marketing strategy**  A market selection strategy in which a firm selects one or a relatively few segments on which to focus all its marketing effort. (6)

**cost-benefit analysis**  The technique of assigning a dollar value to the costs and benefits of a product or service. (8)

**cost-price analysis**  An estimation of the cost to produce a product. (8)

**cultural adiaphora**  The areas of behavior or customs that cultural outsiders may wish to conform to or participate in but that are not required. (12)

**cultural exclusive**  Custom or behavior from which a foreigner is excluded. (12)

**cultural imperative**  The business customs and expectations that must be met and conformed to if relationships are to be successful. (12)

# D

**database**  A collection of information about what customers are buying, how often they buy, and the amount they buy. (5)

**data warehouse**  The storage of bulk data (sales, production, returned merchandise, etc.), for use by management to make better decisions. (5)

**decentralized buying situation**  A buying situation in which the potential order size is small, the number of potential competitors is limited geographically, and a final decision on the price and quality aspects of the purchase may need central authorization. (6)

**decentralized purchasing**  A purchasing method in which the buying function is done at the local or regional level, with division buyers buying all products and services needed to support a production operation. (4)

**decentralized sales organization**  An organization that is structured so that major decisions such as recruitment, training, forecasting, and short- and long-term planning are made at the local or regional level by branch sales managers. (3)

**decider**  The person in the business purchasing process who, in reality, makes the buying decision, regardless of whether he or she holds the formal authority; often difficult to identify. (4)

**demand projection**  Involves analyzing past sales in light of the customer needs that were present, the marketing mix elements used, the economic conditions, and competitive reactions that were present, and then projecting that understanding forward to predict future sales by target segments under potential future conditions. (6)

**derived demand**  The demand for a business product that is linked to demand for a consumer good. (1)

**differentiated marketing strategy**  A market selection strategy in which one firm attempts to distinguish a product from competitive products offered to the same aggregate market. (6)

**differentiation**  Involves meaningful differences in the product, services offered, personnel, channel, and/or image that distinguish one company's products from others. (6)

**diffusion process** The process by which a product or service is accepted by an industry over time; phases include innovators, early adopters, early majority, late majority, and laggards. (7)

**direct channel** A channel of distribution that involves direct selling (i.e., no external intermediary is involved) to the industrial user, with or without the use of sales branches. (10)

**direct marketing** Involves a system of marketing whereby B2B firms communicate directly with customers for the purpose of generating a response and/or transaction. (9)

**divestment** A product elimination strategy that is a situation of reverse acquisition; used to allow a firm to restore a balanced product portfolio. (7)

# E

**economic order quantity (EOQ) model** Emphasizes a cost trade-off between inventory handling costs and order costs; the EOQ is the point at which total cost is minimized. (11)

**economic value to the customer (EVC) pricing** An approach to price setting. (8)

**economies of scale** The production efficiency attained as increased units are produced; a fixed-cost phenomenon. (7)

**elastic demand** Exists when a small-percentage decrease in price produces a larger-percentage increase in quantity demanded. (8)

**ethics** A standard of behavior by which conduct is judged. (2)

**exclusive distribution** A degree of channel width in which only one channel member can sell a manufacturer's products in a given geographic area. (10)

**exporting** An international entry strategy in which a company, without any marketing or production organization overseas, exports a product from its home base. (12)

# F

**facilitating agency** Any agency that facilitates the flow of goods from the manufacturer to either the channel intermediary or the final user, including manufacturers' representatives, brokers, transportation and warehouse facilities, advertising agencies, banks, and others that help the "flow" between buyers and sellers. (10)

**fluctuating demand** Exists when a given percentage increase in consumer demand leads to a much larger percentage increase in the demand for plant and equipment necessary to produce the additional output; also known as the *acceleration principle*. (1)

**forecasting** Used in the analysis, measurement, and improvement of current marketing strategy and in the

identification and/or development of new products and new markets; a business activity used to predict demand. (5)

**formularized model (AIDA)** A sales presentation model in which the salespeople takes the prospect through the first three stages in order to evoke purchase (action) from the buyer; AIDA is an acronym for **a**ttention, **i**nterest, **d**esire, and **a**ction. (3)

**franchising** An international entry strategy that grants the franchisee the right to carry on a certain manufacturing process and to use the brand name of the franchisor. (12)

**functional organization** A sales organization structure in which a staff specialist is given line authority to control a function. (3)

# G

**gatekeeper** The person in the business purchasing process who keeps tight control on the flow of information to other buying center members; this person can open the gate to members for some salespeople, yet close it for others. (4)

# H

**harvesting** A product elimination strategy that is applied to a product or business whose sales volume and/or market share are slowly declining; a means of cutting the costs associated with the strategic business unit to help improve cash flow. When sales cease to provide positive cash flow, the business is divested. (7)

**horizontal publication** A print publication intended for buyers who have similar functions in their companies, regardless of their specific industry. (9)

# I

**idea and concept generation** The first stage in the new product development process; involves the search for product ideas or concepts that meet company objectives. (7)

**indirect channel** A channel of distribution that involves selling to the industrial user through an external intermediary. (10)

**inelastic demand** Exists when a small-percentage decrease in price produces a smaller-percentage increase in quantity demanded. (1, 8)

**influencer** The person in the business purchasing process who provides information to other members for evaluating alternative products or who sets purchasing specifications; can operate within or outside the buying center. (4)

**Institute for Supply Management (ISM)** An association of purchasing and supply chain management people which exists to educate, develop, and advance the purchasing and supply management profession. (4)

**integrated marketing communications (IMC)**   The coordination of the promotional mix elements along with other marketing activities (e.g., packaging) such that all communication with the firm's customers is consistent. (9)

**integrated supply**   A special type of partnering arrangement usually developed between a purchaser and distributor on an intermediate to long-term basis; the objective is to minimize, for both buyer and seller, the labor and expense involved in the acquisition and possession of items that are repetitive, generic, high transaction, and have a low unit cost. (4)

**intensive distribution**   A degree of channel width in which the marketing manager attempts to gain access to as many resellers as possible within a particular geographic area. (10)

**interactive marketing**   Involves the further step of allowing customers to, in some way, interact with the source of the message. (9)

**international internet marketing**   Using the Internet as a foreign market entry strategy. (12)

**international law**   The collection of treaties, conventions, and agreements between nations that more or less have the force of law; involves mutuality, with two or more countries participating in the drafting and execution of laws. (12)

**interpretation**   Involves a clear statement of implications derived from the study's findings. (5)

# J

**joint demand**   Occurs when two or more items are used in combination to produce a product. (1)

**joint venture**   An international entry strategy that is simply a partnership between companies from more than one country that allows each partner to gain access to the other's skills and resources. (12)

**just-in-time (JIT) exchange relationship**   An operational philosophy thought to epitomize the relationship marketing model, it involves low inventory for original equipment manufacturers and fast delivery from suppliers of component parts and materials. (4)

# L

**leadership**   A qualification for the sales manager; the ability to establish values, share visions, create enthusiasm, maintain focus on a few clear objectives, and build a sales force that works as a team. (3)

**learning curve analysis**   Linked with the product life cycle; a base for developing business product strategy; based on the discovery that costs decline by a predictable and constant percentage each time "accumulated" product experience doubles. (7)

**lessee**   The party that acquires the right to use the property, plant, or equipment in a lease agreement. (8)

**lessor**   The party that relinquishes the right to use the property, plant, or equipment in a lease agreement, in return for some form of consideration. (8)

**licensing**   An international entry strategy agreement that permits a foreign company to use industrial property, technical know-how and skills, architectural and engineering designs, or any combination of these, in a foreign market. (12)

**life-cycle costing**   The process of examining industry prices as the product or product line moves through the stages of the product life cycle; required when a large, dominant firm in the industry raises or lowers prices. (8)

**line and staff organization**   A sales organization structure that, in addition to salespeople, involves staff people with highly specialized skills reporting to the sales manager. (3)

**line organization**   The simplest sales organization structure, it prescribes that the sales manager recruits, hires, trains, and supervises the salespeople, in addition to designing sales territories, forecasting sales levels, and carrying out other functions or special projects as assigned by top management. (3)

**line simplification**   A product elimination strategy in which a product line is trimmed to a manageable size by pruning the number and variety of products and services offered. (7)

**logistics**   The design and management of all activities (transportation, inventory, and warehousing) necessary to make materials available for manufacturing and to make finished products available to customers as needed and in the condition required; can also be defined as adding value through the management of materials, inventory, warehousing, transportation, and customer service. (11)

**loss leader**   A pricing strategy used in the decline phase of the product life cycle in which the product's price is set at or under cost in order to help sell complementary products in the line. (8)

# M

**macro segmentation**   Involves dividing the market into subgroups based on overall characteristics of the prospect organization, such as usage rates and NAICS category. (6)

**make-or-buy analysis**   The task of deciding whether to manufacture a product in-house or to purchase it from an outside source. (4)

**manufacturers' representative**   A channel intermediary who sells part of the output of one or more manufacturers whose products are related but noncompetitive. (10)

**marginal pricing**   A basic approach to setting prices, with the aim being to maximize profits by producing the number of units at which marginal cost is just less than, or equal to, marginal revenue. (8)

**market allocations**   Agreements among competitors that they will not compete with respect to specified customers, geographical territories, or products. (2)

**market growth**   The second phase of the product life cycle, in which rapid growth and dramatic cost decreases occur. (7)

**market maturity**   A phase of the product life cycle in which cumulative volume has reached the point at which costs are about as low as they are going to get. (7)

**market penetration pricing**   A new product pricing strategy used in the introduction phase; involves setting a price at or near the point it will eventually reach after competition develops. This low-price wedge allows the firm to gain a large volume of initial sales even though profit per unit may be low. (8)

**market segmentation**   The development and pursuit of marketing programs directed at specific groups within the population that the organization could potentially serve. (6)

**market-share analysis**   The task of determining the ratio of sales revenue of the firm to the total sales revenue of all firms in the industry; a marketing research task. (5)

**marketing ethics**   Moral judgments, standards, and rules of conduct relating to marketing decisions and marketing situations. (2)

**marketing information system (MIS)**   A system that scans and collects data from the environment, makes use of data from transactions and operations within the firm, and then filters, organizes, and selects data before presenting them as information to management. (5)

**marketing research**   The process of defining a problem or project, collecting and analyzing information, and making recommendations that are supported by the data. (5)

**materials management**   The grouping of functions involved in obtaining and bringing materials into a production operation; also known as *logistics,* which incorporates materials management and physical distribution. (4)

**micro segmentation**   Involves dividing the market into subgroups based on specific characteristics of the decision-making process and the buying structure within the prospect organization, such as buying-center authority and attitudes toward vendors. (6)

**missionary salesperson**   A manufacturers' salesperson who aids the sales of channel members and bolsters the overall level of activity and selling effort in the channel. (10)

**mode**   One of the five ways (motor, rail, water, pipeline, air) in which goods and/or services are transported. (11)

**modified rebuy**   A type of business buying situation in which the distinctive element is a reevaluation of alternatives that are necessary because the buying

requirements have changed such that the relatively routine buy or purchase *(straight rebuy)* no longer is routine. (4)

# N

**NAICS (North American Industrial Classification System)**   A tool for collecting and analyzing data about present and potential markets using a common hierarchal structure as its base. (5)

**negotiation**   A technique for communicating ideas in which both buyers and sellers attempt to convince the other party to yield to their demands, with the ultimate objective being a mutually beneficial agreement. (4)

**nested approach to market segmentation**   Stresses segmentation according to the amount of investigation required to identify and evaluate different criteria. These criteria are arranged in layers according to ease of assessment, with organizational demographics first, then more complex criteria such as company variables, situational factors, and personal characteristics. (6)

**new product committee**   A top management committee, consisting of representatives from marketing, production, accounting, engineering, and other areas, that reviews and evaluates new product proposals; an approach to new product development. (7)

**new product department**   A specific department that generates and evaluates new product ideas, directs and coordinates development work, and implements field testing and precommercialization of the new product; an approach to new product development. (7)

**new product venture team**   A full-time task force representing various departments and given responsibility for new-product implementation; an approach to new product development. (7)

**new-task buy**   A business buying situation that is new and very different from anything that the buyer has faced previously. (4)

# O

**open bidding**   A form of competitive bidding that is more informal than closed bidding and allows for negotiation; often used when there is much flexibility with regard to buyer specifications. (8)

**organization by specialization**   A sales organization structure that involves attaining additional efficiencies and economies through organizing by specialization, such as geography, sales activities, product line, customer, or a combination. (3)

**original equipment manufacturer (OEM)**   A firm that typically buys business goods to incorporate into the products the firm produces for eventual sale to either the business or consumer market. (1)

# P

**perceptual mapping**   A technique for examining a product's position, relative to strengths and weaknesses of the product and compared to competitors; attempts to uncover how buyers evaluate a set of competing products by identifying the relative dimensions or features of each. (6)

**personal selling**   Involves persuasive, deliberate contact between a buyer and a seller for the specific purpose of creating an exchange between them. (3)

**physical distribution**   The process of planning, implementing, and controlling the efficient, effective flow and storage of goods, services, and related information from point of origin to point of consumption for the purpose of conforming to the customer's requirements. (11)

**political risk**   The chance that a company will lose money and property and even endanger employees' lives because of events beyond its control, such as revolution, political changes in regime or ideology, policy changes such as current devaluations, or altered profit repatriation rules. (12)

**portfolio classification model**   A model used to give a visual display of the present and prospective positions of business products according to the business attractiveness of the market and the ability to compete within the market. (7)

**positioning**   Placing a product in that part of the market at which it will have a favorable reception compared to competing products. (6)

**posttesting**   In promotion, measures those who have been exposed to a promotional item for aided recall, unaided recall, recognition, comprehension, acceptance, and brand awareness (where applicable) in regard to the promotion. (9)

**predatory pricing**   The cutting of prices (usually by a larger producer) to a point that is at or below cost for the purpose of eliminating competition. (8)

**pretesting**   In promotion, measures subjects' awareness of or reaction to a product or service through a series of questions about it, or indicates subjects' reactions to situations, conveying their degree of understanding of the product or service. (9)

**price elasticity of demand**   A concept stating that demand is elastic if quantity demanded is highly responsive to price and inelastic if it is not. (8)

**price fixing**   The illegal practice of several competitors setting a price; also known as *collusion.* (8)

**price skimming**   A new product pricing strategy used in the introduction phase in which the price is set relatively high, thereby attracting buyers at the top of the product's demand curve. This permits the recovery of research and development costs more quickly. (8)

**primary data**   Marketing research data that must be organized and collected for a specific project and may be obtained only after expending much money, time, and effort. (5)

**problem-solving model**   A sales presentation model that centers on the specific needs, motives, and objectives of the prospect. (3)

**product adaptation**   In international marketing, changing a product to meet the needs of individual countries. (12)

**product commercialization and introduction**   The final stage in new product development; involves launching the product through full-scale production and sales and committing the company's reputation and resources to the product's success. (7)

**product development**   The fourth stage in new product development; involves taking the product to a state of readiness for product and market testing. (7)

**product introduction**   The initial, highest-cost, lowest-sales phase of the product life cycle. (7)

**product life-cycle model**   Shows how sales of a product vary over time and how every product eventually becomes obsolete. (7)

**product manager**   The person charged with the success of a product or product line; this person's overall responsibility is to integrate the various segments of a business into a strategically focused whole, maximizing the value of a product through knowledge of changing market needs and championing the processes involved in bringing the product to the market. (7)

**product portfolio**   A firm's offering of products or divisions, each of which can be identified as a strategic business unit, and most of which operate as a separate profit center that may or may not have its own management, its own set of identifiable markets and competitors, and its own marketing strategies. (7)

**product position**   The way the product is defined by customers on important attributes, or the place the product occupies in customers' minds relative to competing products; one of the central ideas of the marketing discipline. (6)

**product positioning**   Emphasizing one or more attributes important to selected target segments such that target segments have a particular perception of that product. (6)

**product standardization**   In international marketing, exporting to other countries a product originally designed for a particular market. Virtually no changes are made to the product. (12)

**product testing**   The fifth stage in the new product development process; involves conducting commercial experiments to verify earlier business judgments. (7)

**professional selling**   Long-term, relationship-based personal selling done in business marketing. (3)

**profitability analysis**   The profitability of a market segment, product line, or an individual product within a product line. (6)

**promotional campaign**   A sequence of promotions reflecting a common theme and geared to specific objectives. (9)

**promotional mix**   The promotional tools used in marketing communication—*professional selling, advertising, public relations, sales promotion,* and *direct marketing.* (9)

**publicity**   A communication in news story form about an organization, its products, or both, that is transmitted through a mass medium at no charge. (9)

# Q

**qualitative research**   Market research that generally involves subjective, open-ended responses from a small sample. (5)

**quantitative research**   Market research that generally involves objective, data-driven responses from a large sample. (5)

**quantity discount**   A deduction in the list price that a manufacturer gives either to channel intermediaries or OEM users for buying in large amounts. (8)

# R

**reciprocity**   A process whereby buyers choose suppliers who also purchase from them. (1)

**relationship marketing**   The process whereby a firm builds long-term alliances with both prospective and current customers so that both seller and buyer work toward a common set of specified goals; also known as *alliance* or *strategic partnership.* (4)

**reporting phase of research**   Typically involves a written report, an oral presentation, and a follow-up. (5)

**request for quotation (RFQ)**   A form that describes the quantity needed, the delivery date requested, and the product specifications. (4)

**Robinson-Patman Act (1936)**   A regulation that makes it illegal to discriminate in price among different buyers of the same product when the effect is a reduction in competition. (8)

# S

**sales agent**   A channel intermediary who sells the output of one or more potentially competitive manufacturers and may assume responsibility for some marketing functions, including promotion and pricing; also known as a *broker.* (10)

**sales analysis**   The task of tracing sales revenues to their sources, such as specific products, sales territories, or customers; a marketing research task. (5)

**sales branch**   An off-site manufacturer's sales office, operating within a major market area, staffed with some technical personnel, and having the ability to ship most orders immediately from stock. (10)

**sales decline**   The final phase of the product lifecycle, at which the market becomes saturated and sales drop off such that it becomes impossible to achieve large enough increases in cumulative production to lower costs significantly in an attempt to stimulate sales. (7)

**sales promotion**   The driving force that links personal selling, advertising, and publicity into a meaningful, integrated, promotional program; includes trade shows and exhibits, contests, sweepstakes and games, and advertising specialties. (9)

**sales quota**   A goal; set for a particular product line, division, or sales representative to stimulate the sales effort. (3)

**screening and evaluation**   The second stage in the new product development process; involves an analysis to determine which ideas submitted merit a detailed study as to potential feasibility and market acceptance. (7)

**secondary data**   Marketing data—facts and figures—available in previously published sources; historical data previously gathered by people either inside or outside the firm to meet their needs. (5)

**selective distribution**   A degree of channel width in which the marketing manager distributes the product to a limited number of resellers in a particular geographic region. (10)

**services**   All economic activity in which the primary output is neither a product nor a construction. (7)

**straight rebuy**   The most common type of business buying situation, in which the buyer purchases a part, material, or service routinely, with little thought going into the buying process. (4)

**strategic business unit (SBU)**   A product or division in a firm's product portfolio. (7)

**supply chain**   Refers to a set of value-adding companies that are sequentially linked by upstream and downstream flows of goods, services, finances, and information from initial raw material source to the ultimate end user. (11)

**supply chain management**   The multidisciplinary integration and coordination of value-adding business processes from raw material supplier through ultimate end user. (11)

# T

**target costing**   A method of price setting in which a target profit and cost are established, a functional cost analysis is performed to determine if the actual cost is on target, and then a decision is made whether to introduce the product at the target cost. (8)

**target return-on-investment pricing**    A method of setting prices to achieve an annual return-on-investment goal; one of the most widely used methods of establishing price strategy. (8)

**trade barrier**    A government law, regulation, policy, or practice that either protects domestic products from foreign competition or artificially stimulates exports of particular domestic products. (12)

**trade discount**    A deduction from the list price offered to an intermediary in return for services performed; generally, the more services performed by the intermediary, the higher the trade discount. (8)

**trade-off analysis**    The examination of the costs associated with each component of the physical distribution system for the purpose of ascertaining the combination of components that will yield the lowest possible cost for a particular level of customer service. (11)

**traffic management**    The coordination and integration of all movement of materials, including transportation, internal movement (materials handling), and warehousing. (11)

**turnkey operation**    An international entry strategy that is an agreement by the seller to supply a buyer with a facility fully equipped and ready to be operated by the buyer's personnel, who will be trained by the seller; usually associated with giant projects that are sold to governments or government-run companies. (12)

**tying**    An agreement to sell one product but only on condition that the buyer also purchase a different (or tied) product. (2)

# U

**undifferentiated marketing strategy**    A market selection strategy that uses the concept of "market aggregation," wherein the total market is treated as if it were one homogeneous market segment; focuses on common needs among buyers, rather than on how buyers' needs differ. (6)

**uniform resource locator (URL)**    An Internet address. (5)

**unitary demand elasticity**    Exists when the percentage change in price is identical to the percentage change in quantity demanded. (8)

**user**    The person in the business purchasing process who will use the product in question; this person's influence on purchasing decisions can range from minimal to major. (4)

# V

**value analysis (VA)**    The task of studying a product and all of its components in order to determine ways to produce it at a lower cost, to improve its quality, or to make it with a material in greater or more stable supply. (4)

**value chain**    Takes a systemwide view and delves deeply into the value of each activity at each firm. (11)

**value proposition**    A clear, concise set of factual statements describing the real value (benefits) customers can expect to receive from a firm's products. (11)

**vertical publication**    A print publication that discusses current issues and problems of a single industry. (9)

# Z

**zero-based pricing (ZBP)**    The practice of business buyers demanding a cost breakdown to justify a price increase by a seller. (8)

**Exhibit 1-2**  U.S. Department of Commerce, *Statistical Abstract of the United States,* 1997, 11th ed. (Washington, D.C.: U.S. Government Printing Office, 1997), 747.

**Exhibit 1-3**  Adapted from John T. Mentzer, *Marketing Today,* 4th ed. Copyright 1985 by Harcourt Brace & Company.

**Exhibit 2-1**  Reprinted by permission of the American Marketing Association, Chicago, IL.

**Exhibit 3-2**  H. Robert Dodge, "The Role of the Industrial Salesman," *Mid-South Quarterly Review,* January 1972, 13. Used with permission.

**Exhibit 3-3**  Alan J. Dubinsky and Thomas N. Ingram, "A Classification of Industrial Buyers: Implications for Sales Training," *Journal of Personal Selling and Sales Management* 1 (Fall-Winter 1981-1982): 46–51. Used with permission.

**Exhibit 3-15**  Reprinted with the permission of John Wiley & Sons from *Marketing Management: Strategy and Cases,* 4th ed., by Douglas J. Dalrymple and Leonard J. Parsons, p. 695, 1990.

**Exhibit 3-16**  *Sales Manager's Handbook* by C. Robert Patty, pp. 118–120, © 1982. Reprinted by permission of Prentice-Hall, Inc., Upper Saddle River, NJ.

**Exhibit 3-17**  Reprinted with the permission of the American Marketing Association for *Marketing News,* April 1984, "To Become an Effective Executive, Develop Leadership and other Skills," p. 1.

**Exhibit 4-1**  *Basic Steps in Value Analysis,* a pamphlet prepared under the chairmanship of Martin S. Erb by the Value-Analysis-Standardization Committee Reading Association, National Association of Purchasing Management, New York, 4–18.

**Exhibit 4-7**  Adapted from P. J. Robinson, C. W. Faris, and Y. Wind, *Industrial Buying and Creative Marketing* (Boston: Allyn & Bacon, 1967), 28.

**Exhibit 4-8**  Adapted from P. J. Robinson, C. W. Faris, and Y. Wind, *Industrial Buying and Creative Marketing* (Boston Allyn & Bacon, 1967) 183–210.

**Exhibit 4-10**  Adapted from "Finding the Real Buying Influence," *Industrial Distribution* 67 (June 1977): 36, 37, 39.

**Exhibit 4-11**  Adapted from Wesley Johnston and Thomas Bonoma, "The Buying Center: Structure and Interaction Patterns," *Journal of Marketing,* Summer 1981, 150–151.

**Exhibit 4-12**  Reprinted by permission from Joseph L. Cavinato, *Purchasing and Materials Management,* Copyright 1984 by West Publishing Company. All rights reserved.

**Exhibit 5-4**  Copyright © 1998, Manufacturers' Agents National Association, 23016 Mill Creek Road, P. O. Box 3467, Laguna Hills, CA 92654-3467, phone (949) 859-4040; toll-free (877) 626-2776; fax (949) 855-2973. All rights reserved. Reproduction without permission is strictly prohibited.

**Exhibit 5-8**  Copyright © 1998, Manufacturers' Agents National Association, 23016 Mill Creek Road, P. O. Box 3467, Laguna Hills, CA 92654-3467, phone (949) 859-4040; toll-free (877) 626-2776; fax (949) 855-2973. All rights reserved. Reproduction without permission is strictly prohibited.

**Exhibit 5-5**  Thomas V. Bonoma and Benson P. Shapiro, *Segmenting the Industrial Market* (Lexington, Mass: Lexington Books, D. C. Heath and Company, 1983). Used with permission.

**Exhibit 6-5**     Michael E. Porter, *Competitive Advantage: Creating And Sustaining Superior Performance* (New York: Free Press, 1998), 4–8, 234–236. Used with permission.

**Exhibit 6-6**     Thomas V. Bonoma and Benson P. Shapiro, *Segmenting the Industrial Market* (Lexington, Mass: Lexington Books, D. C. Heath and Company, 1983). Used with permission.

**Exhibit 7-3**     Ed Bakken and Medtronics, Inc. Used with permission.

**Exhibit 7-4**     Booz, Allen & Hamilton, Inc., 1982. Used with permission.

**Exhibit 7-5**     Reprinted by permission of the publisher from Robert W. Eckels and Timothy J. Novotney," Industrial Product Managers' Authority and Responsibility," *Industrial Marketing Management* 13 (1984), 73. Copyright © 1984 by Elsevier Science, Inc.

**Exhibit 7-7**     Reprinted with the permission of the American Marketing Association from the *Journal of Marketing* 47, "Diagnosing the Experience Curve," by George S. Day and David B. Montgomery, Spring 1983, pp. 44–58.

**Exhibit 7-8**     Reprinted with the permission of the American Marketing Association from the *Journal of Marketing* 47, "Diagnosing the Experience Curve," by George S. Day and David B. Montgomery, Spring 1983, pp. 44–58.

**Exhibit 7-9**     Source: "The Experience Curve—Reviewed IV: The Growth Share Matrix or the Product Portfolio," The Boston Consulting Group, 1973.

**Exhibit 7-10**    From *Market Planning and Strategy,* 3rd edition, by Subhash C. Jain. © 1990. Reprinted with permission of South-Western College Publishing, a division of Thompson Learning. Fax: 800-730-2215.

**Exhibit 9-3**     Reprinted with the permission of the American Marketing Association from the *Journal of Marketing,* Fall 1984, "The Advertising Budget Practices of Industrial Marketers," by Vincent Blasko and Charles Patti, pp. 104–110.

**Exhibit 10-3**    Source: *Purchasing,* July 1984, "Profile of the Business Products Distributor," pp. 43–51. © 1984 Cahners Business Group.

**Exhibit 10-4**    Reprinted from *Industrial Distribution,* July 1984, 30. Copyright © 1984 by Cahners Publishing Company.

**Exhibit 11-3**    Charles A. Taff, *Management of Physical Distribution and Transportation,* 7th ed. (Homewood, IL: Richard D. Irwin, 1984), 252. Used with permission.

**Exhibit 11-4**    Reprinted from *Strategic Logistics Management,* Third Edition, by James R. Stock and Douglas M. Lambert, p. 42, © 1992 The McGraw-Hill Companies, Inc. Reprinted by permission of the publisher.

**Exhibit 11-5**    Gary Forger, "Jeep Puts JIT in High Gear," *Modern Materials Handling* 48 (January 1993): 42–45. Used with permission.

**Exhibit 11-7**    "Balancing Order Costs and Holding Costs for Inventory," from David L. Kurtz and Louis E. Boone, *Marketing,* 3rd ed. Copyright © 1987 by The Dryden Press, a division of Holt, Rinehart and Winston, Inc. Reprinted by permission of the publisher.

**Exhibit 12-1**    Source: *The Stages of Economic Growth,* Second Edition, by Walt Rostow, 1971. Reprinted by permission of Cambridge University Press.

**Exhibit 12-7**    Richard J. Semenik and Gary J. Bamossy, *Principles of Marketing: A Global Perspective* (Cincinnati, Ohio: South-Western Publishing Co., 1993). Used with permission.

# NAME INDEX

## A

Aaron, David L., 398
Alguire, Mary S., 447
Ansberry, Clare, 46
Armitage, Howard M., 392
Arnott, Nancy, 327

## B

Baalbaki, Imad B., 446
Baatz, E., 350
Balogh, Peter, 447
Bark, Gunnar, 311
Barnes, James H., 46
Beard, Charles, 247
Beckett, Paul, 45
Berenson, Conrad, 247
Bergstein, Heather, 299
Berman, Barry, 354
Bingham, Frank G., Jr., 92, 247
Black, Ron, 38
Boiler, Gregory W., 446
Bolman, L. G., 28
Bonney, Joseph, 391
Bonoma, Thomas V., 184, 210
Boyd, Thomas C., 177
Braham, J., 28
Brewer, Geoffrey, 46, 327
Bush, Robert, 166
Buzby, Conan M., 299

## C

Campbell, Kenneth D., 46
Campbell, Scott, 77
Cannon, Joseph P., 21
Carlton, Jim, 354
Carmichael, M., 208
Carter, Joseph R., 21
Cateora, Philip R., 280, 399, 446, 447
Chen, F., 21
Chowdhury, Jhinuk, 93
Clapp, Donna, 20
Clark, Philip B., 446
Cleigston, Chris, 247
Cochran, P. L., 45
Cohen, Andy, 92
Coleman, Donald R., 354
Conner, Finis, 256
Cook, J., 185
Corey, E. Raymond, 20
Crafford, H. O., 210

Crawford, Merle, 247
Cross, Joseph E., 124–125, 127–128, 133, 135–136, 140
Crum, Michael, 121
Cummings, Betsy, 46
Cundiff, Edward W., 71, 92
Cyrus, Ruth, 308
Czinkota, Michael R., 446

## D

Dabholkar, Pratibha A., 21
Davis, Lanny, 313
Deal, T. E., 28
Di Benedetto, Anthony, 247
Dibb, Sally, 210
Discenza, Richard, 299
Dodge, H. Robert, 49, 92
Donath, Bob, 328
Doyle, Gerard S., Jr., 447
Droge, Cornelia, 147
Dudick, Thomas, 299
Dugal, Sanjiv S., 247

## E

Easingwood, Chris, 247
Ebbers, Bernard J., 23
Eichenwald, Kurt, 45
Ellram, Lisa, 425
Emiliami, M. L., 354
Erickson, Karyn, 48
Estaelami, Hooman, 299

## F

Farber, Barry J., 92
Fastow, Andrew, 23
Feurerstein, Aaron, 27
Fiorina, Carly, 31
Fitzgerald, K., 338
Fitzsimmons, James A., 247
Ford, M., 140
Forker, Laura B., 447
Freed, Donald, 129, 131
Freer, Carl R., 447

## G

Gagne, Margret L., 299
Germain, Richard, 147
Gerstenfeld, Arthur, 299

# SUBJECT INDEX

## A

A. C. Nielsen, 305
Abbott Laboratories, 28
ABC analysis, 371
Acceleration principle, 9, 358
Acme Foods, 13
Active data, 168
Activity quotas, 80
Adaptation, 399–400, 410
Adaptive control, 201–202
Adaptive selling, 54, 55
Adcentives, 317
Adelphia, 23
Administrative costs, 182
Adoption process, for new products, 228–230
Advent Management International Ltd., 39
Advertising; *see also* Business advertising; Promotion
    broadcast media, 310
    comparative, 40–41
    consumer versus business, 307–308
    ethics and, 39–41
    expenditures, 305–306
    international, 411–412
    media selection, 309
    print media, 309–310
    as a promotion tool, 303
    sales promotion activities, 313–318
    truth in, 39
    use of agencies, 311–312
Advertising Research Foundation (ARF), 321
Advertising specialties, 317–318
Affordable/arbitrary budget method, 305–306
Agencies, advertising, 311–312
Agency method of selling, 338
Agile organizations, 343
AIDA, 55–56
Air transport, 363
Alberto Culver, 97
Alcatel, 324
Alcoa, 253
Alliances, 35, 96–97, 385–391
Altair Nanotechnologies, 135
American Excelsior, 87–89
American Express, 115
American Hospital Supply, 193
American Marketing Association, 25–26, 151
American Megatrends, 291
American-based export intermediaries, 413–414
America's Best Manufacturing Organizations Award, 333
AMP Inc., 28
Analytical marketing system, 163
Anderson & Lembke, 311
Andover Plastics, 52
Antitrust, 33–36, 254, 404
Apple Computer, 251

Archer Daniels Midland (ADM) Company, 33
Argonne National Laboratory, 126
Armstrong World Industries, Inc., 77
Arrow, 324
Arthur Andersen, 23, 313
Assembly operation, 409
Asset turnover, 117
Assignable costs, 249
Association of Business Publishers, 321
AT&T, 31
Attention, interest, desire, and action, 55–56
Audits and Surveys, Incorporated, 305
Aurora Foods, 23
Autoliv Inc., 311

## B

Baker Hughes, Inc., 112
Bank One Corp., 23
Bankruptcy, 23
Barter, 278, 418–420
BASF Corporation, 130
BASF Wyandotte, 232
Basic One, 237
Bayer AG, 62, 134
Bayerische Motoren Werke AG, 28
Bayesian decision model, 218
Bell Helicopter, 221
Belmonte Metal Stamping Company, 203
Benchmarking, 321, 358
Benefit segmentation, 53
Benefit selling, 53
Bidding
    closed, 268
    collusive, 29
    competitive, 35, 103, 266–269
    lowest, 12
    open, 268–269
    process, 266–268, 276–277
    rigging of, 34
    sealed, 268
BioGenex Laboratories, 28
Birdyback, 363
Black and Decker, 370
BlackBerry, 62
Blue Cross/Blue Shield, 235, 239
BMW, 153, 251
Boeing, 3, 12, 25, 407
Borg Warner, 7
Bose, 105
Boston Consulting Group, 224, 230
Bottom-up forecasting method, 197
Boundary spanners, 64
Box-Jenkins, 201, 202
Brand managers, 219